Praise for *The iPhone Developer's Cookbook*

"This book would be a bargain at ten times its price! If you are writing iPhone software, it will save you weeks of development time. Erica has included dozens of crisp and clear examples illustrating essential iPhone development techniques and many others that show special effects going way beyond Apple's official documentation."

—**Tim Burks**, iPhone Software Developer, TootSweet Software

"Erica Sadun's technical expertise lives up to the Addison-Wesley name. *The iPhone Developer's Cookbook* is a comprehensive walkthrough of iPhone development that will help anyone out, from beginners to more experienced developers. Code samples and screenshots help punctuate the numerous tips and tricks in this book."

—**Jacqui Cheng**, Associate Editor, Ars Technica

"We make our living writing this stuff and yet I am humbled by Erica's command of her subject matter and the way she presents the material: pleasantly informal, then very appropriately detailed technically. This is a going to be the Petzold book for iPhone developers."

—**Daniel Pasco**, Lead Developer and CEO, Black Pixel Luminance

"*The iPhone Developer's Cookbook* should be the first resource for the beginning iPhone programmer, and is the best supplemental material to Apple's own documentation."

—**Alex C. Schaefer**, Lead Programmer, ApolloIM, iPhone Application Development Specialist, MeLLmo, Inc.

"Erica's book is a truly great resource for Cocoa Touch developers. This book goes far beyond the documentation on Apple's Web site, and she includes methods that give the developer a deeper understanding of the iPhone OS, by letting them glimpse at what's going on behind the scenes on this incredible mobile platform."

—**John Zorko**, Sr. Software Engineer, Mobile Devices

"I've found this book to be an invaluable resource for those times when I need to quickly grasp a new concept and walk away with a working block of code. Erica has an impressive knowledge of the iPhone platform, is a master at describing technical information, and provides a compendium of excellent code examples."

—**John Muchow**, 3 Sixty Software, LLC; founder, iPhoneDeveloperTips.com

"This book is the most complete guide if you want coding for the iPhone, covering from the basics to the newest and coolest technologies. I built several applications in the past, but I still learned a huge amount from this book. It is a must-have for every iPhone developer."

—**Roberto Gamboni**, Software Engineer, AT&T Interactive

"It's rare that developer cookbooks can both provide good recipes and solid discussion of fundamental techniques, but Erica Sadun's book manages to do both very well."

—**Jeremy McNally**, Developer, entp

The iPhone™ Developer's Cookbook

Building Applications with the iPhone 3.0 SDK

Second Edition

Erica Sadun

Addison-Wesley

Upper Saddle River, NJ • Boston • Indianapolis • San Francisco
New York • Toronto • Montreal • London • Munich • Paris • Madrid
Cape Town • Sydney • Tokyo • Singapore • Mexico City

The publisher offers excellent discounts on this book when ordered in quantity for bulk purchases or special sales, which may include electronic versions and/or custom covers and content particular to your business, training goals, marketing focus, and branding interests. For more information, please contact:

U.S. Corporate and Government Sales
(800) 382-3419
corpsales@pearsontechgroup.com

For sales outside the United States, please contact:

International Sales
international@pearson.com

Visit us on the Web: informit.com/aw

Library of Congress Cataloging-in-Publication Data:

Sadun, Erica.

The iPhone developer's cookbook : building applications with the iPhone 3.0 SDK / Erica Sadun. — 2nd ed.

p. cm.

Includes index.

ISBN 978-0-321-65957-6 (pbk. : alk. paper) 1. iPhone (Smartphone)—Programming. 2. Computer software—Development. 3. Mobile computing. I. Title.

QA76.8.I64S33 2010

004.167—dc22

2009042382

Pearson Education, Inc
Rights and Contracts Department
501 Boylston Street, Suite 900
Boston, MA 02116
Fax (617) 671 3447

ISBN-13: 978-0-321-65957-6
ISBN-10: 0-321-65957-0

Text printed in the United States on recycled paper at Edwards Brothers in Ann Arbor, Michigan.

First printing December 2009

Editor-in-Chief
Karen Gettman

Senior Acquisitions Editor
Chuck Toporek

Senior Development Editor
Chris Zahn

Managing Editor
Kristy Hart

Project Editor
Anne Goebel

Copy Editor
Geneil Breeze

Senior Indexer
Cheryl Lenser

Proofreader
Sheri Cain

Technical Reviewers
Joachim Bean,
Aaron Basil,
Tim Isted,
Mr. X,
Tim Burks,
Daniel Pasco,
Alex C. Schaefer,
John Muchow
(3 Sixty Software, LLC Founder, iPhoneDeveloperTips.com),
Roberto Gamboni

Editorial Assistant
Romny French

Cover Designer
Gary Adair

Composition
Jake McFarland

❖

I dedicate this book with love to my husband, Alberto, who has put up with too many gadgets and too many SDKs over the years while remaining both kind and patient at the end of the day.

❖

Contents at a Glance

Table of Contents

Acknowledgments

This book would not exist without the efforts of Chuck Toporek (my editor and whip-cracker), Chris Zahn (the awesomely talented development editor), Romny French (the faithful and rocking editorial assistant who kept things rolling behind the scenes), and to Karen Gettman (Chuck's Editor-in-Chief) for her continued support of this ever-growing (and I do mean growing—just check out the page count) book. Also, a big thank you to the entire Addison-Wesley/Pearson production team, specifically Kristy Hart, Anne Goebel, Gary Adair, Keith Cline, Geneil Breeze, Cheryl Lenser, Chelsey Marti, and Jake McFarland. Thanks also to the crew at Safari for getting my book up in Rough Cuts and for quickly fixing things when technical glitches occurred.

Thanks go as well to Neil Salkind, my agent of many years, to the tech reviewers who helped keep this book in the realm of sanity rather than wishful thinking, and to all my colleagues, both present and former, at TUAW, Ars Technica, and the Digital Media/Inside iPhone blog.

Special thanks go to Joachim Bean and Aaron Basil. In addition to tech reviewing this book, these two men provided early feedback as I was developing each chapter, offering critical insight and advice. More than anyone else, they helped shape the book you now hold in your hands. They delivered a level of feedback that was both astonishing, and deeply, deeply appreciated, even when queried at inhuman hours of the day. Thanks also to Tim Isted (author of *Core Data for iPhone*, coming soon from Addison-Wesley), for his valuable input on the Core Data chapter in this book. I'd also like to thank someone for placing some keen eyes on the GameKit chapter, but I can't, so I'll just have to say, "Thanks, Mr. X." I couldn't have done this without the help of my technical review team, so thank you all very much. Special thanks to the rest of my technical review team including Roberto Gamboni, John Muchow, and Scott Mikolaitis.

I am deeply indebted to the wide community of iPhone developers, including Alex Schaefer, Nick Penree, James Cuff, Jay Freeman, Mark Montecalvo, August Joki, Max Weisel, Optimo, Kevin Brosius, Planetbeing, Pytey, Roxfan, MuscleNerd, np101137, UnterPerro, Youssef Francis, Bryan Henry, Daniel Peebles, ChronicProductions, Greg Hartstein, Emanuele Vulcano, Sean Heber, Steven Troughton-Smith, Dick Applebaum, Kevin Ballard, Jay Abbott, Tim Grant Davies, Landon Fuller, Stefan Hafeneger, Scott Elich, chrallelinder, J. Roman, jtbandes, Artissimo, Aaron Alexander, Scott Lawrence, Kenny Chan Ching-Kin, Sjoerd van Geffen, Absentia, Nownot, Matt Brown, Chris Foresman, Aron Trimble, Paul Griffin, Nicolas Haunold, Anatol Ulrich (hypnocode GmbH), Kristian Glass, Yanik Magnan, ashikase, Eric Mock, and everyone at the iPhone developer channels at irc.saurik.com and irc.freenode.net, among many others too numerous to name individually. Their techniques, suggestions, and feedback helped make this book possible. If I have overlooked anyone who helped contribute, please accept my apologies for the oversight.

Special thanks go out to my family and friends, who supported me through month after month of new beta releases and who patiently put up with my unexplained absences and frequent howls of despair. I appreciate you all hanging in there with me. And thanks to my children for their steadfastness, even as they learned that a hunched back and the sound of clicking keys is a pale substitute for a proper mother. My kids provided invaluable assistance over the last few months by testing applications, offering suggestions, and just being awesome people. I am such an insanely lucky mom that these kids are part of my life.

About the Author

Erica Sadun has written, coauthored, and contributed to about three dozen books on technology, particularly in the areas of programming, digital video, and digital photography. An unrepentant geek, Sadun has never met a gadget she didn't need. Her checkered past includes run-ins with NeXT, Newton, iPhone, and myriad successful and unsuccessful technologies. When not writing, she and her geek husband parent three adorable geeks-in-training, who regard their parents with restrained bemusement.

Preface

Few platforms match the iPhone's unique developer technologies. The iPhone combines OS X-based mobile computing with an innovative multitouch screen, location awareness, an onboard accelerometer, and more. When Apple first introduced the iPhone SDK beta in March 2008, developers responded in droves, bringing Apple's servers to its knees. In less than a week, developers downloaded the iPhone SDK more than 100,000 times.

Since then, more than 50,000 applications have been delivered to the App Store for an audience that now exceeds 30 million iPhones and more than 20 million iPod touches. As the iPhone ecosystem continues to grow, *The iPhone Developer's Cookbook* will continue to evolve as an accessible resource for those new to iPhone programming.

What's New in This Edition?

If you purchased the first edition of this book, you might ask yourself, *Why do I need to buy the new edition, too?* The answer is pretty simple: Just compare the size of the two books. This new edition is more than 200% larger than the original edition. That's right, we've packed on almost 500 pages of new material so we could cover everything that's new to the iPhone 3.0 SDK, as well as expand on some of the topics covered in the first edition.

Some things you'll find new to this edition include chapters or coverage on

- How to use Xcode and Interface Builder
- An Objective-C jump-start tutorial
- Core Data for the iPhone
- MapKit and Core Location
- Using GameKit beyond games to add chat and Bonjour networking
- Advanced motion detection including shake-to-undo support
- The new search display controller class, along with custom table headers and footers
- Apple's new device capabilities specifications
- In-App purchasing with StoreKit
- Push notification, both from the client and server side
- Searching for and playing media from the onboard iPod library

- Video capture and editing, plus the new AV audio player and recorder classes
- How to leverage the Accessibility framework, including VoiceOver, in your app
- And much, much more!

You'll also notice that we've taken your feedback to heart. When the first edition came out, there was some confusion about who the target audience was for this book. Was it for new developers or experienced developers? Well, we've taken care of that, too. While this book is for experienced iPhone and Mac developers already familiar with Objective-C, Xcode, and the Cocoa frameworks, this new edition includes an "Objective-C Boot Camp" (see Chapter 3), and coverage of Xcode and Interface Builder, to help developers who have experience working in other languages (or on other platforms) quickly get oriented into the Mac/iPhone world.

While it is true that one book can't be everything to everyone, we're certainly giving it a shot in this new edition. We hope you like the changes you see throughout this bigger book, and if you do, be sure to post a review on Amazon or send me a note (erica@ericasadun.com).

Audience for This Book

This book is written for experienced developers who want to build apps for the iPhone and iPod touch. You should already be familiar with Objective-C, the Cocoa frameworks, and the Xcode Tools. That said, if you're new to the platform, this new edition of *The iPhone Developer's Cookbook* includes a quick-and-dirty introduction to Objective-C, along with an intro to the Xcode Tools, to help you quickly get up to speed.

> **New to the Mac or iPhone?**
>
> If you have some C experience, or have spent some time with another object-oriented language such as C++ or Java, we included a section in this Preface to help guide you down the road to being a Mac developer. Be sure to read the section "Your Roadmap to Mac/iPhone Development," later in this Preface.

Although each programmer brings different goals and experiences to the table, most iPhone developers end up solving similar tasks in their development work:

- "How do I build a table?"
- "How do I create a secure Keychain entry?"
- "How do I search the Address Book?"
- "How do I move between views?"
- "How do I use Core Location and the iPhone 3GS's magnetometer?"

And so on. If you've asked yourself these questions, then this book is for you. Complete with clear, fully documented examples, *The iPhone Developer's Cookbook* will get you up to speed and working with the iPhone SDK in no time. Best of all, all of the code recipes in the book have been tested—and put to the test in real-world applications—offering you ready-to-use solutions for the apps you're building today.

What You'll Need

It goes without saying that, if you're planning to build apps for the iPhone or iPod touch, you're going to need at least one of those devices to test out your application. The following list covers the basics of what you need to begin programming for the iPhone or iPod touch:

- **Apple's iPhone SDK**—The latest version of the iPhone SDK can be downloaded from Apple's iPhone Dev Center (http://developer.apple.com/iphone). You must join Apple's (free) developer program before you download; however, if you plan to sell apps through the App Store, you will need to become a paid iPhone developer, which costs $99/year for individuals and $299/year for enterprise (i.e., corporate) developers. Registered developers receive certificates that allow them to "sign" and download their applications to their iPhone/iPod touch for testing and debugging.

University/Student Discounts

Apple also offers a University program for students and educators. If you are a CS student taking classes at the university level, check with your professor to see if your school is part of the University Program. For more information about the iPhone Developer University Program, see http://developer.apple.com/support/iphone/university.

- **An Intel-based Mac running Mac OS X Leopard or Snow Leopard**—Snow Leopard is recommended, as it offers access to Xcode 3.2 with its many new features like "Build and Analyze." You need plenty of disk space for development, and your Mac should have at least 1GB RAM, preferably 2GB or 4GB to help speed up compile time.
- **An iPhone or iPod touch**—Although the iPhone SDK and Xcode include a simulator for you to test your applications in, you really do need to have an actual iPhone and/or iPod touch if you're going to develop for the platform. You can use the USB cable to tether your unit to the computer and install the software you've built. For real-life App Store deployment, it helps to have several units on-hand, representing the various hardware generations, so you can test on the same platforms your target audience will use.
- **At least one available USB 2.0 port**—This enables you to tether a development iPhone or iPod touch to your computer for file transfer and testing.
- **An Internet connection**—This connection enables you to test your programs with a live Wi-Fi connection as well as with an EDGE or 3G service.

- **Familiarity with Objective-C**—To program for the iPhone, you need to know Objective-C 2.0. The language is based on ANSI C with object-oriented extensions, which means you also need to know a bit of C, too. If you have programmed with Java or C++ and are familiar with C, making the move to Objective-C is pretty easy. Chapter 3, "Objective-C Boot Camp," helps you get up to speed.

> **Note**
>
> Although the SDK supports development for the iPhone and iPod touch, as well as possible yet-to-be-announced platforms, this book refers to the target platform as iPhone for the sake of simplicity. When developing for the iPod touch, most of the examples in this book are applicable; however, certain features such as telephony and onboard speakers are not applicable to the iPod touch.

Your Roadmap to Mac/iPhone Development

As mentioned earlier, one book can't be everything to everyone. And try as I might, if we were to pack everything you'd need to know into this book, you wouldn't be able to pick it up. There is, indeed, a lot you need to know to develop for the Mac and iPhone platforms. If you are just starting out and don't have any programming experience, your first course of action should be to take a college-level course in the C programming language. While the alphabet might start with the letter A, the root of most programming languages, and certainly your path as a developer, is C.

Once you know C and how to work with a compiler (something you'll learn in that basic C course), the rest should be easy. From there, you'll hop right on to Objective-C and learn how to program with that alongside the Cocoa frameworks. To help you along the way, I've put together the flowchart shown in Figure P-1 to point you at some books of interest.

Once you know C, you've got a few options for learning how to program with Objective-C. For a quick-and-dirty overview of Objective-C, you can turn to Chapter 3 of this book and read the Objective-C Boot Camp. However, if you want a more in-depth view of the language, you can either read Apple's own documentation, *Object-Oriented Programming with Objective-C 2.0*,[1] or you can opt to buy a book such as Stephen Kochan's *Programming in Objective-C 2.0* (Addison-Wesley, 2009).

[1] See http://developer.apple.com/mac/library/documentation/Cocoa/Conceptual/OOP_ObjC/OOP_ObjC.pdf.

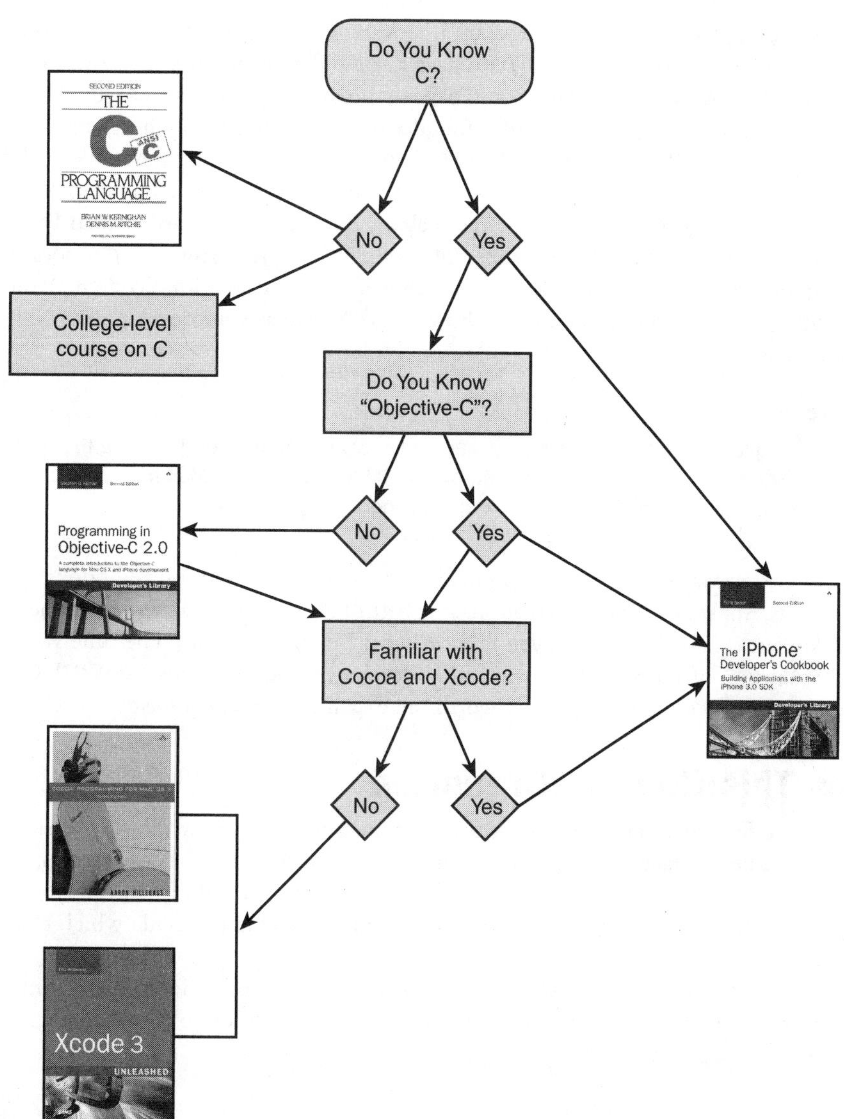

Figure P-1 What it takes to be an iPhone programmer.

With the language behind you, next up is tackling Cocoa and the developer tools, otherwise known as Xcode. For that, you have a few different options. Again, you can refer to Apple's own documentation on Cocoa and Xcode,[2] or if you prefer books, you can learn from the best. Aaron Hillegass, founder of the Big Nerd Ranch in Atlanta,[3] is the author of *Cocoa Programming for Mac OS X,* now in its third edition. Aaron's book is highly regarded in Mac developer circles and is the most-recommended book you'll see on the cocoa-dev mailing list. To learn more about Xcode, look no further than Fritz Anderson's *Xcode 3 Unleashed* from Sams Publishing. While the current edition doesn't cover iPhone-specific features of Xcode (which were introduced with Xcode 3.1), the book will give you a solid grounding in how to use Xcode as your development environment.

Note

There are plenty of other books from other publishers on the market, including the best-selling *Beginning iPhone 3 Development*, by Dave Marks and Jeff LaMarche (Apress, 2009), so don't just limit yourself to one book or publisher.

To truly master Mac development, you need to look at a variety of sources: books, blogs, mailing lists, Apple's own documentation, and, best of all, conferences. If you get the chance to attend WWDC or C4, you'll know what I'm talking about. The time you spend at those conferences talking with other developers and in the case of WWDC, talking with Apple's engineers, is well worth the expense if you are a serious developer.

How This Book Is Organized

This book offers single-task recipes for the most common issues new iPhone developers face: laying out interface elements, responding to users, accessing local data sources, and connecting to the Internet. Each chapter groups related tasks together, allowing you to jump directly to the solution you're looking for without having to decide which class or framework best matches that problem.

The iPhone Developer's Cookbook offers you "cut-and-paste convenience," which means you can freely reuse the source code from recipes in this book for your own applications and then tweak the code to suit your app's needs.

2 See the *Cocoa Fundamentals Guide* (http://developer.apple.com/mac/library/documentation/Cocoa/Conceptual/CocoaFundamentals/CocoaFundamentals.pdf) for a head start on Cocoa, and for Xcode, see *A Tour of Xcode* (http://developer.apple.com/mac/library/documentation/DeveloperTools/Conceptual/A_Tour_of_Xcode/A_Tour_of_Xcode.pdf).

3 Big Nerd Ranch: http://www.bignerdranch.com.

Here's a rundown of what you find in this book's chapters:

- **Chapter 1, "Introducing the iPhone SDK"**—Chapter 1 introduces the iPhone SDK and explores the iPhone as a delivery platform, limitations and all. It explains the breakdown of the standard iPhone application and helps you get started with the iPhone Developer Portal.
- **Chapter 2, "Building Your First Project"**—Chapter 2 covers the basics for building your first Hello World-style applications. It introduces Xcode and Interface Builder, showing how you can use these tools in your projects. You read about basic debugging tools, walk through using them, and pick up some tips about handy compiler directives. You'll also discover how to create provisioning profiles and use them to deploy your application to your device, to beta testers, and to App Store.
- **Chapter 3, "Objective-C Boot Camp"**—If you're new to Objective-C as well as to the iPhone, you'll appreciate this basic skills chapter. Objective-C is the standard programming language for both the iPhone and for Mac OS X. It offers a powerful object-oriented language that lets you build applications that leverage Apple's Cocoa and Cocoa Touch frameworks. Chapter 3 introduces the language, provides an overview of its object-oriented features, discusses memory management skills, and adds a common class overview to get you started with Objective-C programming.
- **Chapter 4, "Designing Interfaces"**—Chapter 4 introduces the iPhone's library of visual classes. It surveys these classes and their geometry. In this chapter, you learn how to work with these visual classes and discover how to handle tasks like device reorientation. You'll read about solutions for laying out and customizing interfaces and learn about hybrid solutions that rely both on Interface Builder-created interfaces and Objective-C-centered ones.
- **Chapter 5, "Working with View Controllers"**—The iPhone paradigm in a nutshell is this: small screen, big virtual worlds. In Chapter 5, you discover the various view controller classes that enable you to enlarge and order the virtual spaces your users interact with. You learn how to let these powerful objects perform all the heavy lifting when navigating between iPhone application screens.
- **Chapter 6, "Assembling Views and Animations"**—Chapter 6 introduces iPhone views, objects that live on your screen. You see how to lay out, create, and order your views to create backbones for your iPhone applications. You read about view hierarchies, geometries, and animations, features that bring your iPhone applications to life.
- **Chapter 7, "Working with Images"**—Chapter 7 introduces images, specifically the `UIImage` class, and teaches you all the basic know-how you need for working with iPhone images. You learn how to load, store, and modify image data in your applications. You see how to add images to views and how to convert views into images. And you discover how to process image data to create special effects, how

to access images on a byte-by-byte basis, and how to take photos with your iPhone's built-in camera.

- **Chapter 8, "Gestures and Touches"**—On the iPhone, the touch provides the most important way that users communicate their intent to an application. Touches are not limited to button presses and keyboard interaction. Chapter 8 introduces direct manipulation interfaces, multitouch, and more. You see how to create views that users can drag around the screen and read about distinguishing and interpreting gestures.
- **Chapter 9, "Building and Using Controls"**—Control classes provide the basis for many of the iPhone's interactive elements, including buttons, text fields, sliders, and switches. This chapter introduces controls and their use. You read about standard control interactions and how to customize these objects for your application's specific needs. You even learn how to build your own controls from the ground up, as Chapter 9 creates a custom touch wheel.
- **Chapter 10, "Alerting Users"**—The iPhone offers many ways to provide users with a heads-up, from pop-up dialogs and progress bars to audio pings and status bar updates. Chapter 10 shows how to build these indications into your applications and expand your user-alert vocabulary. It introduces standard ways of working with these pop-up classes and offers solutions that allow you to craft more linear programs without explicit callbacks.
- **Chapter 11, "Creating and Managing Table Views"**—Tables provide a scrolling interaction class that works particularly well on a small, cramped device. Many, if not most, apps that ship with the iPhone and iPod touch center on tables, including Settings, YouTube, Stocks, and Weather. Chapter 11 shows how iPhone tables work, what kinds of tables are available to you as a developer, and how you can use table features in your own programs.
- **Chapter 12, "Making Connections with GameKit and Bonjour"**—GameKit is Apple's new ad hoc networking solution for peer-to-peer connectivity. It's built on a technology called Bonjour that offers simple, no-configuration communications between devices. Chapter 12 introduces GameKit, allowing you to build games and utilities that move information back and forth between iPhones or between an iPhone and a desktop system. This chapter covers standard GameKit, introduces GameKit Voice for walkie-talkie-style voice chats, and offers some basic Bonjour programming that extends beyond GameKit limitations, allowing you to expand your iPhone communications to the desktop.
- **Chapter 13, "Networking"**—As an Internet-connected device, the iPhone is particularly suited to subscribing to Web-based services. Apple has lavished the platform with a solid grounding in all kinds of network computing services and their supporting technologies. Chapter 13 surveys common techniques for network computing and offering recipes that simplify day-to-day tasks. You read about

network reachability, synchronous and asynchronous downloads, working with the iPhone's secure keychain to meet authentication challenges, and more.

- **Chapter 14, "Device Capabilities"**—Each iPhone device represents a meld of unique, shared, momentary, and persistent properties. These properties include the device's current physical orientation, its model name, battery state, and access to onboard hardware. Chapter 14 looks at the device from its build configuration to its active onboard sensors. It provides recipes that return a variety of information items about the unit in use. You read about testing for hardware prerequisites at runtime and specifying those prerequisites in the application's Info.plist file. You discover how to solicit sensor feedback and subscribe to notifications to create callbacks when those sensor states change. This chapter covers the hardware, file system, and sensors available on the iPhone device and helps you programmatically take advantage of those features.
- **Chapter 15, "Audio, Video, and MediaKit"**—The iPhone is a media master; its built-in iPod features expertly handle both audio and video. The iPhone SDK exposes that functionality to developers. A rich suite of classes simplifies media handling via playback, search, and recording. Chapter 15 introduces recipes that use these classes, presenting media to your users and letting your users interact with that media. You see how to build audio and video players as well as audio and video recorders. You discover how to browse the iPod library and how to choose what items to play.
- **Chapter 16, "Push Notifications"**—When developers need to communicate directly with users, push notifications provide the solution. They deliver messages directly to the iPhone screen via a special Apple service. Push notifications let the iPhone display an alert, play a custom sound, or update an application badge. In this way, off-phone services connect with an iPhone-based client, letting them know about new data or updates. Chapter 16 introduces push notifications. In this chapter, you learn how push notifications work and dive into the details needed to create your own push-based system.
- **Chapter 17, "Using Core Location and MapKit"**—Core Location infuses the iPhone with on-demand geopositioning based on a variety of technologies and sources. MapKit adds interactive in-application mapping allowing users to view and manipulate annotated maps. With Core Location and MapKit, you can develop applications that help users meet up with friends, search for local resources, or provide location-based streams of personal information. Chapter 17 introduces these location-aware frameworks and shows you how you can integrate them into your iPhone applications.
- **Chapter 18, "Connecting to the Address Book"**—The iPhone's Address Book frameworks allow you to programmatically access and manage the contacts database. Chapter 18 introduces the Address Book and demonstrates how to use its frameworks in your applications. You read about accessing information on a contact-by-contact basis, how to modify and update contact information, and how to

use predicates to find just the contact you're interested in. This chapter also covers the GUI classes that provide interactive solutions for picking, viewing, and modifying contacts.

- **Chapter 19, "A Taste of Core Data"**—Core Data offers managed data stores that can be queried and updated from your application. It provides a Cocoa Touch-based object interface that brings relational data management out from SQL queries and into the Objective-C world of iPhone development. Chapter 19 introduces Core Data. It provides just enough recipes to give you a taste of the technology, offering a jumping off point for further Core Data learning. You learn how to design managed database stores, add and delete data, and query that data from your code.
- **Chapter 20, "StoreKit: In-App Purchasing"**—New to the 3.0 SDK, StoreKit offers in-app purchasing that integrates into your software. This chapter introduces StoreKit and shows you how to use the StoreKit API to create purchasing options for users. In this chapter, you read about getting started with StoreKit. You learn how set up products at iTunes Connect and localize their descriptions. And you see what it takes to create test users and how to work your way through various development/deployment hurdles. This chapter teaches you how to solicit purchase requests from users and how to hand over those requests to the store for payment. This chapter covers the entire StoreKit picture, from product creation to sales.
- **Chapter 21, "Accessibility and Other iPhone OS Services"**—Applications interact with standard iPhone services in a variety of ways. This chapter explores some of these approaches. Applications can define their interfaces to the iPhone's VoiceOver accessibility handler, creating descriptions of their GUI elements. They can create bundles to work with the built-in Settings applications so that users can access applications defaults using that interface. Applications can also declare public URL schemes allowing other iPhone applications to contact them and request services that they themselves offer. This chapter explores application service interaction. It shows you how you implement these features in your applications. You see how to build these service bridges through code, through Interface Builder, and through supporting files.
- **Appendix A, "Info.plist Keys"**—This appendix gathers together many of the keys available for the iPhone's Info.plist file, the file that describes an application to the iPhone operating system.

About the Sample Code

For the sake of pedagogy, this book's sample code usually presents itself in a single main.m file. This is not how people normally develop iPhone or Cocoa applications, or should be developing them, but it provides a great way of presenting a single big idea. It's hard to tell a story when readers must look through 5 or 7 or 9 individual files at once.

Offering a single file concentrates that story, allowing access to that idea in a single chunk.

These samples are not intended as stand-alone applications. They are there to demonstrate a single recipe and a single idea. One main.m file with a central presentation reveals the implementation story in one place. Readers can study these concentrated ideas and transfer them into normal application structures, using the standard file structure and layout. The presentation in this book does not produce code in a standard day-to-day best practices approach. Instead, it reflects a pedagogical approach that offers concise solutions that you can incorporate back into your work as needed.

Contrast that to Apple's standard sample code, where you must comb through many files to build up a mental model of the concepts that are on offer. Those samples are built as full applications, often doing tasks that are related to but not essential to what you need to solve. Finding just those relevant portions is a lot of work. The effort may outweigh any gains. In this book, there are two exceptions to this one-file rule:

- First, application-creation walkthroughs use the full file structure created by Xcode to mirror the reality of what you'd expect to build on your own. The walkthrough folders may therefore contain a dozen or more files at once.
- Second, standard class and header files are provided when the class itself *is* the recipe or provides a precooked utility class. Instead of highlighting a technique, some recipes offer these precooked class implementations and categories (that is, extensions to a preexisting class rather than a new class). For those recipes, look for separate .m and .h files in addition to the skeletal main.m that encapsulates the rest of the story.

For the most part, the samples for this book use a single application identifier, com.sadun.helloworld. You need to replace this identifier with one that matches your provision profile. This book uses one identifier to avoid clogging up your iPhone with dozens of samples at once. Each sample replaces the previous one, ensuring that SpringBoard remains relatively uncluttered. If you want to install several samples at once, simply edit the identifier, adding a unique suffix, such as com.sadun.helloworld.tableedits.

Getting the Sample Code

The source code for this book can be found at the open source GitHub hosting site at http://github.com/erica/iphone-3.0-cookbook-/tree. There, you find a chapter-by-chapter collection of source code that provides working examples of the material covered in this book.

Sample code is never a fixed target. It continues to evolve as Apple updates its SDK and the Cocoa Touch libraries. Get involved. You can pitch in by suggesting bug fixes and corrections as well as by expanding the code that's on offer. GitHub allows you to fork repositories and grow them with your own tweaks and features, and share those back to the main repository. If you come up with a new idea or approach, let us know.

We'd be happy to include great suggestions both at the repository and in the next edition of this Cookbook.

Getting Git

You can download this Cookbook's source code using the git version control system. A Mac OS X implementation of git is available at http://code.google.com/p/git-osx-installer. Mac OS X git implementations include both command line and GUI solutions, so hunt around for the version that best suits your development needs.

Getting GitHub

GitHub (http://github.com) is the largest git hosting site, with more than 150,000 public repositories. It provides both free hosting for public projects and paid options for private projects. With a custom Web interface that includes wiki hosting, issue tracking, and an emphasis on social networking of project developers, it's a great place to find new code or collaborate on existing libraries. You can sign up for a free account at their Web site, allowing you to copy and modify the Cookbook repository or create your own open source iPhone projects to share with others.

Contacting the Author

If you have any comments or questions about this book, please drop me an e-mail message at erica@ericasadun.com, or stop by www.ericasadun.com for updates about the book and news for iPhone developers. Please feel free to visit, download software, read documentation, and leave your comments.

1

Introducing the iPhone SDK

The iPhone and iPod touch offer innovative mobile platforms that are a joy to program. They are the first members of Apple's new family of pocket-based computing devices. Despite their diminutive proportions, they run a first-class version of OS X with a rich and varied SDK that enables you to design, implement, and realize a wide range of applications. For your projects, you can take advantage of the iPhone's multitouch interface and powerful onboard features using Xcode, Apple's integrated design environment. In this chapter, you discover the components of the SDK and explore the product it creates: the iPhone application. You learn about Apple's various iPhone developer programs and how you can join. You explore the iPhone application design philosophy and see how applications are put together. Finally, you read about setting up your program credentials so you can put that philosophy to use and start programming.

iPhone Developer Programs

Are you ready to start programming for the iPhone? Ready to see what all the fuss is about? Apple's iPhone Software Development Kit (SDK) is readily available to members of Apple's iPhone developer programs. There are four. These programs include the free online program, the paid enterprise program for in-house development, the paid standard program that allows developers to submit their products to the App Store, and a special University program (see Table 1-1).

Table 1-1 **iPhone Developer Programs**

Program	Cost	Audience
Online Developer Program	Free	Anyone interested in exploring the iPhone SDK without commitment
Standard iPhone Developer Program	$99/ Year	Developers who want to distribute through App Store

Table 1-1 **Continued**

Program	Cost	Audience
0Enterprise iPhone Developer Program	$299/ Year	Large companies building proprietary software for employees
University iPhone Developer Program	Free	Free program for higher education institutions that provide an iPhone development curriculum

Each program offers access to the iPhone SDK, which provides ways to build and deploy your applications. The audience for each program is specific.

Online Developer Program

The free program is meant for anyone who wants to explore the iPhone SDK programming environment but who isn't ready to pay for further privileges. The free program limits you to Mac-only programming. While you can run your applications in the simulator, you cannot deploy those applications to the device or sell them in App Store.

Although each version of the simulator moves closer to representing actual device performance, you should not rely on it for evaluating your application. An app that runs rock solid on the simulator may be unresponsive or even cause crashes on the actual device. The simulator does not, for example, support vibration or accelerometer readings. These and other features present on the device are not always available in the simulator. A discussion about simulator limits follows later in this chapter in the section "Simulator Limitations."

Standard Developer Program

To receive device and distribution privileges, you must pay the $99/year program fee for the standard iPhone developer program. Once paid, you gain access to App Store distribution and can test your software on actual iPhone hardware. This program adds ad hoc distribution as well, allowing you to distribute prerelease versions of your application to up to 100 registered devices. The standard program provides the most general solution for the majority of iPhone programmers who want to be in App Store. If you intend to conduct business through selling applications, this is the program to sign up for.

Enterprise Developer Program

The $299/year Enterprise program is meant for in-house application distribution. It's targeted at companies with 500 employees or more. Enterprise memberships do not offer access to the iPhone App Store. Instead, you can build your own proprietary applications and distribute them to your employees' hardware through a private storefront. The Enterprise program is aimed at large companies that want to deploy custom applications to their employees such as ordering systems.

University Developer Program

Available only to higher education institutions, the University Developer Program is a free program aimed at encouraging universities and colleges to develop an iPhone development curriculum. The program allows professors and instructors to create teams with up to 200 students, offering them access to the full iPhone SDK. Students can share their applications with each other and their teachers, and the institution itself can submit applications to App Store.

Registering

Register for the free program at the main iPhone developer site at http://developer.apple.com/iphone. You can sign up for the paid programs, Standard or Enterprise, at http://developer.apple.com/iphone/program.

Getting Started

Regardless of which program you sign up for, you must have access to an Intel-based Mac running a current version of Mac OS X. It also helps to have at least one, and preferably several, iPhone and iPod touch units to test on to ensure that your applications work properly on each platform, including legacy units like the first generation iPhone and iPod touch.

There are often delays associated with signing up for paid programs. After registering, it can take weeks for account approval and invoicing. Once you actually hand over your money, it may take another 24 to 72 hours for your access to advanced portal features to go live.

Registering for iTunes Connect, so you can sell your application through App Store, offers a separate hurdle. Fortunately, this is a process you can delay until after you've finished signing up for a paid program. With iTunes Connect, you must collect banking information and incorporation paperwork prior to setting up your App Store account. You must also review and agree to Apple's distribution contracts. Apple offers full details at itunesconnect.apple.com.

Downloading the SDK

Download your copy of the iPhone SDK from the main iPhone developer site at http://developer.apple.com/iphone. Use your program credentials to access the download page. So be sure you've signed up for one of the three programs before attempting to download. The free program offers access only to fully released SDKs. The paid program adds early looks at SDK betas letting you develop to prerelease firmware.

The kit, which typically runs a few gigabytes in size, installs a complete suite of interactive design tools onto your Macintosh. This suite consists of components that form the basis of the iPhone development environment. iPhone-specific components include the following software:

- **Xcode**—Xcode is the most important tool in the iPhone development arsenal. It provides a comprehensive project development and management environment, complete with source editing, comprehensive documentation, and a graphical debugger. Xcode is built around several open source GNU tools, namely gcc (compiler) and gdb (debugger).
- **Interface Builder**—Interface Builder (IB) provides a rapid prototyping tool for laying out user interfaces graphically and linking to those prebuilt interfaces from your Xcode source code. With IB, you place out your interface using visual design tools and then connect those onscreen elements to objects and method calls in your application.
- **Simulator**—The iPhone Simulator runs on the Macintosh and enables you to create and test applications on your desktop. You can test programs without connecting to an actual iPhone or iPod touch. The simulator offers the same API used on the iPhone and provides a preview of how your concept designs will look. When working with the simulator, Xcode compiles Intel x86 code that runs natively on the Macintosh rather than ARM-based code used on the iPhone.
- **Instruments**—Instruments profiles how iPhone applications work under the hood. It samples memory usage and monitors performance. This lets you identify and target problem areas in your applications and work on their efficiency. Instruments offers graphical time-based performance plots that show where your applications are using the most resources. Instruments is built around the open source DTrace package developed by Sun Microsystems. Instruments plays a critical role in tracking down memory leaks and making sure your applications run efficiently on the iPhone platform.
- **Shark**—Shark provides performance optimization by analyzing where an application spends most of it its time. It locates and identifies bottlenecks, enabling you to speed your application performance.

Together, the components of this iPhone SDK suite enable you to develop your applications. From a native application developer's point of view, the most important components are Xcode, Interface Builder, and the simulator, with Instruments providing an essential tuning tool. In addition to these tools, there's an important piece not on this list. This piece ships with the SDK but is easy to overlook. I refer to Cocoa Touch.

Cocoa Touch is the library of classes provided by Apple for rapid iPhone application development. Cocoa Touch, which takes the form of a number of API frameworks, enables you to build graphical event-driven applications using user interface elements such as windows, text, and tables. Cocoa Touch on the iPhone is analogous to Cocoa and AppKit on Mac OS X and supports creating rich, reusable interfaces on the iPhone.

Many developers are surprised by the size of iPhone applications; they're tiny. Cocoa Touch's library support is the big reason for this. By letting Cocoa Touch handle all the heavy UI lifting, your applications can focus on getting their individual tasks done. The result is compact, focused code that does a single job at a time.

Using Cocoa Touch lets you build applications with a polished look and feel, consistent with those developed by Apple. Remember that Apple must approve your software. Apple judges applications on the basis of appearance, operation, and even content. Using Cocoa Touch helps you better approximate the high design standards set by Apple's native applications.

Development Devices

A physical iPhone or iPod touch provides a key component of the software development kit. Testing on the iPhone is vital. As simple and convenient as the SDK Simulator is, it falls far short of the mark when it comes to a complete iPhone testing experience. Given that the iPhone is the target platform, it's important that your software runs its best on its native system rather than on the simulator. The iPhone itself offers the fully leaded, unwatered-down testing platform you need.

Apple regularly suggests that the development unit needs to be devoted exclusively to development. Reality has proven more hit and miss on that point. When you first tether your iPhone to your computer using a standard USB cable, Xcode detects your unit. If you want to use your device for development, confirm that; otherwise, click Ignore.

Using a device as a development unit means that it is subject to onboard data changes and might no longer work reliably as a field unit, but experience shows that once you're past early betas of new SDKs that the devices seem to hold up fine for regular day-to-day use. It's still best to have extra units on hand devoted solely to development, but if you're short on available units, you can probably use your main iPhone for development; just be aware of the risks.

When developing, it's important to test on as many iPhone platforms as possible. Be aware that there are real platform differences between each model of iPhone and iPod touch. For example, the second generation iPod has a built-in speaker; the first generation does not. It also uses a faster processor than the first-generation iPod touch. iPhones have cameras, which none of the current iPod touches offer. A discussion of model-specific differences follows later in this chapter.

Simulator Limitations

Each release of the Macintosh-based iPhone Simulator continues to improve on previous technology. That having been said, there are real limitations that you must take into account. From software compatibility to hardware, the simulator approximates but does not equal actual device performance.

The simulator uses many Macintosh frameworks and libraries, offering features that are not actually present on the iPhone. Applications that appear to be completely operational and fully debugged on the simulator may flake out or crash on the device itself. You simply cannot fully debug any program solely by using the simulator and be assured that the software will run bug-free on the iPhone.

The simulator is also missing many hardware features. You cannot use the simulator to test the onboard camera or accelerometer feedback. Although the simulator can read acceleration data from your Macintosh using its sudden motion sensor if there's one onboard (usually for laptops), the readings will differ from iPhone readings and are not practical for development or testing. The simulator does not vibrate or offer multitouch input (at least not beyond a standard "pinch" gesture). Core location is fixed to the coordinates of 1 Infinite Loop in California, that is, the Apple Headquarters building.

From a software point of view, the basic keychain security system is not available on the simulator. You cannot register an application to receive push notification either. These missing elements mean that there are certain kinds of programs that can only be properly used when deployed to an iPhone.

Another difference between the simulator and the device is the audio system. The audio session structure is not implemented on the simulator, hiding the complexity of making things work properly on the device. Even in areas where the simulator does emulate the iPhone APIs, you may find behavioral differences as the simulator is based on the Mac OS X Cocoa frameworks.

That's not to say that the simulator does not play an important testing role. It's quick and easy to try out a program on the simulator, typically much faster than transferring a compiled application to an iPhone unit. The simulator lets you rotate your virtual device to test reorientation, produce simulated memory warnings, and try out your UI as if your user were receiving a phone call. It's much easier to test out text processing on the simulator because you can use your keyboard; this simplifies repeated text entry tasks such as entering account names and passwords for applications that connect to the net.

In the end, the simulator offers compromise. You gain a lot of testing convenience but not so much that you can bypass actual device testing.

Tethering

All interactive testing must be done using a USB cable. At this time, Apple provides no way to transfer, debug, or monitor applications wirelessly. That means you do nearly all your work tethered over a standard iPhone USB cable. The physical reality of tethered debugging can be problematic. Reasons for this include the following points:

- When you unplug the cable, you unplug all the interactive debugging, console, and screenshot features. So you need to keep that cable plugged in all the time.
- You cannot reasonably use the iPhone with a dock. Sure, the dock is stable, but touching the screen while testing interfaces is extremely awkward when the iPhone is seated at a 75-degree angle.
- The tether comes to the bottom, not the top of the unit, meaning it's easy to catch that cable and knock your iPhone to the floor.

Obviously, untethered testing would vastly improve many of these issues. Unfortunately, Apple has not yet introduced that option. If you like, you can Rube Goldberg-ize your iPhone to get around these problems. One solution is to attach Velcro to the back of an iPhone case—a case that leaves the bottom port connector open—and use that to stabilize your iPhone on your desk. It's ugly, but it keeps your iPhone from getting knocked to the floor all the time. You can also now purchase third-party cradles for the iPhone that help with development work. These stands hold the iPhone a few inches off the desk and keep the cable directed toward the back.

Always try to tether your unit to a port directly on your Mac for best results. If you must use a hub, connect to a powered system that supports USB 2.0. Most older keyboards and displays only provide unpowered USB 1.1 connections. When testing, it helps to choose a reliable, powered 2.0 port you can count on.

Understanding Model Differences

When it comes to application development, many iPhone apps never have to consider the platform on which they're being run. Most programs rely only on the display and touch input. They can be safely deployed to all the current iPhone-family devices; they require no special programming or concern about which platform they are running on.

There are, however, real platform differences. These differences are both significant and notable. They play a role in deciding how you tell App Store to sell your software and how you design the software in the first place. Should you deploy your software only to the iPhone? To the iPhone and the second generation and later iPod touch? Or should your application be targeted to every platform? Here are some issues to consider:

Camera

Each iPhone ships with a camera; iPod touches do not. These cameras are useful. You can task the camera to take shots and then send them to Flickr or Twitter. You can use the camera to grab images for direct manipulation, and so forth. The iPhone SDK provides a built-in image picker controller that offers camera access to your users, but only on camera-ready platforms. Video services are limited to the 3G S model and later.

When building camera-ready applications, know that you cannot deploy them to iPods. Camera services are limited to the iPhone family. The first and second generation iPhone's built-in 2 megapixel camera will never win awards. The third generation camera is much improved, offering autofocus, macro photography, video recording, and better low-light sensitivity.

Speakers and Microphones

First generation iPod touches lack the built-in speaker found on the iPhone and the second generation iPod touch. Although the 1G touch is perfectly capable of powering third-party speakers through its bottom connector port, Apple considers those to be unauthorized accessories and their use is rare.

Don't assume that end users will wear headphones when using applications. When designing for the first generation iPod, carefully consider the role of audio cues. If they are critical to the program, you may want to either recommend headphone use or consider skipping the 1G iPod as a distribution platform.

The second generation iPod touch supports external headset microphones. The first generation does not. If you do plan to deploy a recording application, make sure you specify clearly that the iPod will require extra equipment to use those features.

The third generation iPhone 3G S provides a number of accessibility features including voice control. It's unclear at the time of writing whether voice control APIs will be opened to iPhone developers.

Telephony

It may seem an overly obvious point to make, but the iPhone's telephony system, which handles both phone calls and SMS messaging, can and will interrupt applications when the unit receives an incoming telephone call. Sure, users can quit out of apps whenever they want on both iPhone and iPod platforms, but only the iPhone has to deal with the kind of exit that's forced by the system and not a choice by the user.

Consider how the different kinds of interruptions might affect your application. It's important to keep all kinds of possible exits in mind when designing software. Be aware that the choice to leave your app may not always come from the user, especially on the iPhone.

Another fall-out of telephony operations is that more stuff ends up running in the background on iPhones than on iPod touches. This means that as a rule, the amount of free memory is likely to be reduced on the iPhone compared to the touch. This is one reason that making the iPhone your primary development device over the iPod touch may be a smart move. Working within the iPhone's greater limitations may produce software that operates robustly on both the iPhone and touch platforms.

Core Location Differences

Core location depends on three different approaches, each of which may or not be available on a given platform. These approaches are limited by each device's onboard capabilities. Wi-Fi location, which scans for local routers and uses their MAC addresses to search a central position database, is freely available on all iPhone and iPod touch platforms.

Cell location, however, depends on an antenna that is available only on the iPhone. This technology triangulates from local cell towers, whose positions are well defined from their installations by telephone companies. The final and most accurate strategy, GPS location, is available only to second generation iPhones and newer. GPS was not built into the first generation iPhone and is not currently available to any iPod touch units.

The third generation iPhone 3G S introduces a built-in compass (via a magnetometer) along with the Core Location APIs to support it.

Vibration Support and Proximity

Vibration, which adds tactile feedback to many games, is limited to iPhones. iPod touches do not offer vibration support. Nor do they include the proximity sensor that blanks the screen when holding the iPhone against your ear during calls. Until SDK 3.0, using the proximity sensor in your applications has been theoretically off limits although it was used in a number of App Store products, most notably in the mobile Google application (http://itunes.com/apps/googlemobileapp). Starting with version 3.0, the `UIDevice` class offers direct access to the current state of the proximity sensor.

Processor Speeds

The second generation iPod touch features a 532MHz processor. The touch offered the highest power processing in the iPhone line until supplanted by the iPhone 3G S, running at a reported 600MHz. Make sure to test your software on older, slower units as well as on the newer ones. Application response time can and will be affected by the device on which it's being run.

If your application isn't responsive enough on the older platforms, consider working up your efficiency. There is no option in App Store at this time that lets you omit the first generation iPhone from your distribution base.

OpenGL ES

OpenGL ES offers a royalty-free cross-platform API for 2D and 3D graphics development. It is provided as part of the iPhone SDK. Not all iPhone models provide the same OpenGL ES support. The iPhone 3G S and newer models support both OpenGL ES 2.0 and 1.1. Earlier models including the 2G and 3G iPhone, and the first and second generation iPod touch, run only OpenGL ES 1.1. The 2.0 API provides better shading and text support, providing higher quality graphics.

To target all iPhones, develop your graphics using only 1.1. Applications leveraging the 2.0 API are limited to the iPhone 3G S and other future models.

Platform Limitations

When talking about mobile platforms like the iPhone, several concerns always arise, such as storage, interaction limits, and battery life. Mobile platforms can't offer the same disk space their desktop counterparts do. Along with storage limits, constrained interfaces and energy consumption place very real restrictions on what you as a developer can accomplish.

With the iPhone, you can't design for a big screen, for a mouse, for a physical keyboard (yet), or even for a physical always-on A/C power supply. Instead, platform realities must shape and guide your development. Fortunately, Apple has done an incredible job designing a new platform that somehow leverages flexibility from its set of limited storage, limited interaction controls, and limited battery life.

Storage Limits

The iPhone hosts a powerful yet compact OS X installation. Although the entire iPhone OS fills no more than a few hundred megabytes of space—almost nothing in today's culture of large operating system installations—it provides an extensive framework library. These frameworks of precompiled routines enable iPhone users to run a diverse range of compact applications, from telephony to audio playback, from e-mail to Web browsing. The iPhone provides just enough programming support to create flexible interfaces while keeping system files trimmed down to fit neatly within tight storage limits.

> **Note**
>
> Each application is limited to a maximum size of 2GB. To the best of my knowledge, no application has ever come close to this size, and many users complain when applications exceed about 10MB.

Data Access Limits

Every iPhone application is sandboxed. That is, it lives in a strictly regulated portion of the file system. Your program cannot directly access other applications, certain data, and certain folders. Among other things, these limitations minimize or prevent your interaction with the iTunes library and the calendar. Your program can, however, access any data that is freely available over the Internet when the iPhone is connected to a network, and, new to 3.0, you can access a shared systemwide pasteboard.

Memory Limits

On the iPhone, memory management is critical. The iPhone does not support disk-swap-based virtual memory. When you run out of memory, the iPhone shuts down your application—as Apple puts it, random crashes are probably not the user experience you were hoping for. With no swap file, you must carefully manage your memory demands and be prepared for the iPhone OS to terminate your application if it starts swallowing too much memory at once. You must also take care concerning what resources your applications use. Too many high-resolution images or audio files can bring your application into the autoterminate zone.

Apple system engineers suggest that applications need to stay within 20MB of RAM. Here is the rough rule of thumb that circulates in developer circles. At about 20MB of use, the iPhone begins to issue memory warnings. At around 30MB, the iPhone OS shuts the application down.

> **Note**
>
> Xcode automatically optimizes your PNG images using the pngcrush utility shipped with the SDK. (You find the program in the iPhoneOS platform folders in /Developer.) Run it from the command line with the `-iphone` switch to convert standard PNG files to iPhone-formatted ones. For this reason, use PNG images in your iPhone apps where possible as your

preferred image format. The open source fixpng utility, which is hosted at http://www.cyberhq.nl, goes the opposite way. It restores compressed images back to Mac-friendly formats and is a valuable tool to have on hand for iPhone development. The venerable Graphics Convert application (http://lemkesoft.com, $35) also offers iPhone PNG support.

Interaction Limits

Losing physical input devices and working with a tiny screen doesn't mean you lose interaction flexibility. With multitouch, you can build user interfaces that defy the rules. The iPhone's touch technology means you can design applications complete with text input and pointer control using a virtual screen that's much larger than the actual physical reality held in your palm.

A smart autocorrecting onscreen keyboard, built-in microphone (for all units except on the iPod touch), and an accelerometer that detects orientation provide just a few of the key technologies that separate the iPhone from the rest of the mobile computing pack. What this means, however, is that you need to cut back on things such as text input and scrolling windows.

Focus your design efforts on easy-to-tap interfaces rather than on desktop-like mimicry. Remember, you can use just one window at a time—unlike desktop applications that are free to use multiwindow displays.

Note

The iPhone screen supports up to five touches at a time, although it's rare to find any application that uses more than two at once.

Energy Limits

For mobile platforms, you cannot ignore energy limitations. That being said, Apple's SDK features help to design your applications to limit CPU use and avoid running down the battery. A smart use of technology (for example, properly suspending themselves between uses) lets your applications play nicely on the iPhone and keeps your software from burning holes in users' pockets (sometimes almost literally). Some programs, when left running, produce such high levels of waste heat that the phone becomes hot to the touch and the battery quickly runs down. The Camera application is one notable example.

Application Limits

Apple has instituted a strong "one-application-at-a-time" policy. That means as a third-party developer you cannot develop applications that run in the background like Apple's Mail and Phone utilities. Each time your program runs, it must clean up and metaphorically get out of Dodge before passing control on to the next application selected by the user. You can't leave a daemon running that checks for new messages or that sends out periodic updates.

On the other hand, Apple does support push data from Web services as of firmware 3.0. Registered services can push badge numbers and messages to users, letting them know that data is waiting on those servers. Chapter 16, "Push Notifications," introduces push notifications and shows you how to transmit these messages to users.

> **Note**
>
> According to the iPhone Terms of Service, you may not use Cocoa Touch's plug-in architecture for applications submitted to the App Store. You can build static libraries that are included at compile time, but you may not use any programming solution that links to arbitrary code at runtime.

User Behavior Limits

Although it's not a physical device-based limitation, get used to the fact that iPhone users approach phone-based applications sporadically. They enter a program, use it quickly, and then leave just as quickly. The handheld nature of the device means you must design your applications around short interaction periods and prepare for your application to be cut off as a user receives a phone call or sticks the phone back into a pocket. Save your application state between sessions and relaunch quickly to approximate the same task your user was performing the last time the program was run. This can demand diligence on the part of the programmer but is worth the time investment due to the payoff in user satisfaction.

SDK Limitations

As you might expect, building applications for the iPhone is similar to building applications for the Macintosh. Both platforms run a version of OS X. You use Objective-C 2.0 to develop your code. You compile by linking to an assortment of frameworks. In other ways, the iPhone SDK is limited. Here are some key points to keep in mind:

- Garbage Collection is MIA and probably always will be. On the iPhone, you are responsible for retaining and releasing objects in memory. The missing Garbage Collection can be explained in two ways. First, a constrained mobile platform like the iPhone demands precise performance characteristics, especially for processor-intense applications like games. Garbage Collection adds an unpredictable element to performance; it must freeze threads when it cleans up memory. Second, limited memory does not allow garbage collection to be implemented in any sane and useful manner. Garbage collected applications use a higher watermark for memory usage. This subjects applications to more OS shutdowns.
- Many libraries are still only partly implemented. Core Animation is partially available through the Quartz Core framework, but some classes and methods remain missing in action. The lesson here is that you're working in early-release software even though it has been quite some time since the first SDK debuted. Work around the

missing pieces and make sure to submit your bug reports to Apple so that it (we hope) fixes the parts that need to be used. Be aware that Apple has deliberately cut access to some proprietary classes and methods. For example, you read EXIF orientation from images, but you cannot add that data; the method to do so is unpublished.

Note

Xcode's compiler lets you mix C++ and Objective-C code in the same project. The resulting Objective-C++ hybrid projects let you reuse existing C++ libraries in Objective-C applications. Consult Apple's documentation for details.

Using the Developer Portal

The iPhone developer program portal hosts all the tools needed to set up your system for iPhone development. It is found at http://developer.apple.com/iphone/manage/overview/index.action, and you will not have access to it unless you have signed up for one of the two paid iPhone developer programs. Here is where you can set up your development team, obtain your certificates, register development devices and application identifiers, and build your provisioning profiles so you can properly sign your applications.

Because the details are subject to change, this overview focuses on the big picture. Should Apple alter any of the particulars, you'll still know what the major milestones are, so you can adjust accordingly. Figure 1-1 shows the key points of the process.

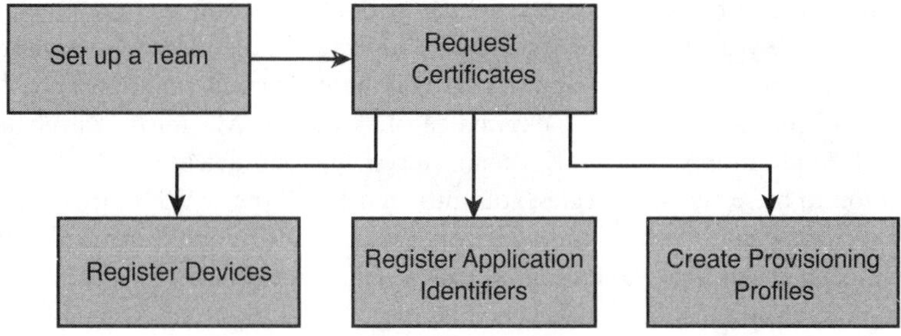

Figure 1-1 Basic functions of the iPhone developer portal.

Setting Up Your Team

An iPhone development team consists of one or more members. The primary member of the team, called the "agent," is the original person who enrolled into the iPhone developer program. The agent has basic administrative powers over the account: He or she can add other members to the team if this is not an individual account, approve certificate requests, and so forth. In addition, the agent can grant administrative privileges to other members, who are called, unsurprisingly, "admins." Members without administrative privileges can request new provisions and download them, but that's pretty much the limit.

Admins can invite new members at the portal using the Team screen. This is also where you can update e-mail, check on certificates, and add and remove members. Additional tabs in this screen let you check your technical support incidents and review your developer agreements with Apple.

Requesting Certificates

Certificates play a major role in iPhone development. You cannot deploy applications to iPhones, even for testing, without a valid development certificate. You also need a distribution certificate for selling applications through the App Store. You can request and download these certificates from the portal.

Start by generating a certificate request from your Macintosh's Keychain Access utility.

1. Launch the program from the /Applications/Utilities folder.
2. Choose Keychain Access > Certificate Assistant > Request a Certificate from a Certificate Authority. Check your e-mail address, choose Saved to Disk, and click Continue.
3. Select where to save the certificate (the Desktop is a good choice) and click Save. Wait for the certificate to generate and click Done.

You then upload the request at the portal to create either your development or distribution certificate. The portal walks you through the process. Each certificate must be approved by the team agent before it is issued. Once approved, you can download it from the Certificates window on the portal site.

Install the new certificate into your keychain by double-clicking it. Certificates are currently good for one year. Make sure you remove any expired certificates from your keychain as Xcode cannot readily distinguish between them. You will encounter problems compiling until you do so. Select the expired certificate in the Macintosh Keychain Access application (/Applications/Utilities/Keychain Access.app) and delete it.

In addition to these two certificates, you must also install the WWDR intermediate certificate issued by Apple's worldwide developer relations. It can be downloaded from the portal or directly at http://developer.apple.com/certificationauthority/AppleWWDRCA.cer. Make sure you add this to your keychain as well.

Should you need to develop on more than one machine at a time, you can export your developer and distribution certificates from the Keychain Access Utility. Right-click a certificate and choose the Export option. Choose the .p12 Personal Information Exchange option and click Save. Enter a password that you will remember and verify that password. Click OK to continue. OS X prompts you to enter your admin password for your Macintosh. Enter it and click Allow. Keychain Access generates the encrypted p12 file. You can transfer this to another Macintosh system and double-click to install. The local keychain will prompt you for the password.

Registering Devices

You must register all development iPhones at the program portal. You do so by providing a device name and its unique device identifier (UDID). You can register up to 100 devices at any time. Once registered, you may use that device for your development and ad hoc provisions. To begin, start by viewing the Devices screen at the portal and clicking Add Device. Enter a name, enter a UDID, and click Submit.

Finding UDIDs is not complicated: You can easily recover a device UDID from iTunes. When docked, select the device name from the sources list (the left iTunes column) and view the Summary tab. Click the words Serial Number. This changes the display from Serial Number to Identifier (UDID). Choose Edit > Copy (Command-C) and the UDID transfers to your system clipboard. You can then paste that number into a file.

Alternatively, have your users download a copy of Ad Hoc Helper (http://itunes.com/apps/adhochelper) to their iPhone. It is a free utility that I created to help people e-mail their device IDs directly to a developer. When launched, it automatically starts a new e-mail that is populated with the user's UDID. Users add your address as the recipient and tap Send.

Apple offers several ways to register several devices at once. The most reliable option is to enter several items into the Add Devices screen before clicking the Add Device button. You can also use Apple's iPhone Configuration Utility to manage UDIDs. It is available for download at the portal site but has had its ups and downs in terms of stability.

Please note that Unregister does not immediately free up slots on your 100-slot devices list. Due to some developers abusing the system there is a one-year time-out before a slot can be reused. You can contact Apple and ask them to override this setting if there is a valid reason that your slots need to be reused within the year.

Registering Application Identifiers

Each application you build should use an exclusive identifier. This string enables your application to uniquely present itself to SpringBoard and guarantees that it will not conflict with another application. Most typically, you build your identifiers using Apple's reverse domain notation, for example, com.sadun.myApplicationName, uk.co.sadun.myApplicationName, org.sadun.myApplicationName, and so on. Avoid using any special characters in your application identifiers.

You need not register each application at the portal, but you should register at least one "wild-card" identifier. By this, I mean an identifier that uses an asterisk as a wild-card matching character, for example, com.sadun.*. You can use this single identifier to create provisions that work with all your applications, regardless of whether they are used only during development or are destined for the App Store. A wild-card provision properly signs all applications whose identifiers match its pattern.

The sole exception to this wild-card rule are application identifiers meant to be used with push notifications. Chapter 16 details the difference, explaining why you must register applications individually and how you can do so. Push-based applications aside, most developers can get by with registering a single wild-card application ID at the program portal.

For the most part, the samples for this book use a single application identifier, com.sadun.helloworld. You need to replace this identifier with one that matches your provision profile. I mostly use just one identifier to avoid clogging up your iPhone with dozens of samples at once. Each sample replaces the previous one, ensuring that SpringBoard remains relatively uncluttered.

> **Note**
>
> If you're wondering what those random characters that precede your registered IDs are, they are *Bundle Seed IDs* and are meant to be used with applications that share keychain data. Consult Chapter 13, "Networking," and the Apple portal for more details about using seed IDs.

Provisioning

Provisioning profiles provide a way to associate registered developers and registered devices with a specific iPhone development team. They are used in Xcode to sign your code, authorizing the software to run on the device or to be allowed in the App Store. Most developers use two key provisions: a wild-card development provision and a wild-card distribution provision. In addition, most developers eventually build one or more ad hoc provisions, which allow you to distribute your application outside the App Store to devices you have registered at the portal.

Create your profiles at the Provisioning screen of the program portal. Choose the Development or Distribution tab, click Add Profile, check the certificate name box, and choose your wild-card application ID. For development and ad hoc provisions, you must select the devices that are included. Click Submit and then refresh the screen a few times. It usually takes less than minute for the provision to be generated and made available for download.

Should you need to add devices at a later time, you can easily do so. Expand the device user base by editing your already-issued provisions. Choose Edit > Modify, check the new devices, and click Submit. Re-download the updated provisioning profile by clicking Download.

To install provisions, drag them onto the Xcode icon or (for development and ad hoc provisions only) drop them into the Xcode Organizer window for the device. Xcode automatically reads them in and installs them into your home folder in ~/Library/MobileDevice/Provisioning Profiles. To remove a provision, use the Xcode organizer's Provisioning Profiles pane.

> **Note**
>
> If you'd rather manage your profiles from the command line, quit Xcode and delete them from the profiles folder. The provisions do not retain their original names so be sure to delete the correct file by using the command line grep utility (e.g. `grep -i firstpush *`) or by peeking at the files in a text editor to find the right one.

Xcode automatically installs provisions onto devices to ensure that applications compiled with those provisions can run properly. To remove a provision from a device, open Settings > General > Profiles on the iPhone or iPod touch in question. Select a profile, and click the red Remove button. When you remove a device provision, you won't be able to run any applications signed with that provision.

Assembling iPhone Projects

iPhone Xcode projects contain varied standard and custom components. Figure 1-2 shows a minimal project. Project elements include source code, linked frameworks, and media such as image and audio files. Xcode compiles your source, links it to the frameworks, and builds an application bundle suitable for iPhone installation. It adds your media to this application bundle, enabling your program to access that media as the application runs on the iPhone.

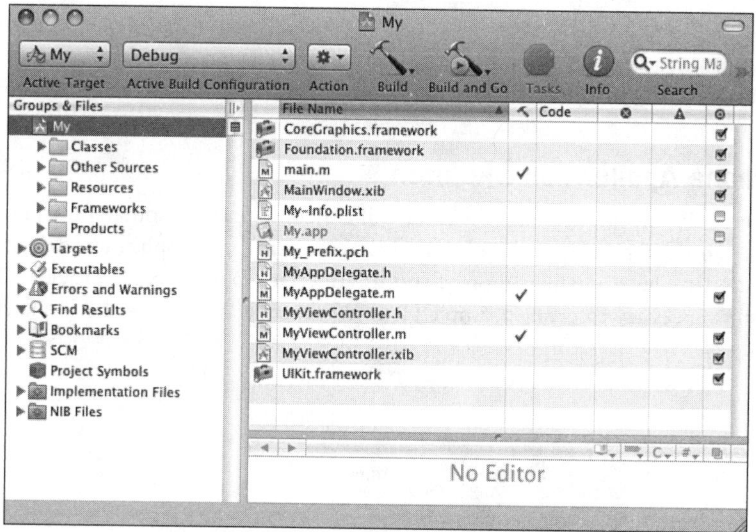

Figure 1-2 Xcode projects bring source code, frameworks, and media together to form the basis for iPhone applications.

iPhone code is normally written in Objective-C 2.0. This is an object-oriented superset of ANSI C, which was developed from a mix of C and Smalltalk. Chapter 3, "Objective-C Boot Camp," introduces the language on a practical level. If you're looking for more information about the language, Apple provides several excellent online tutorials at its iPhone developer site. Among these are an introduction to object-oriented programming with Objective-C and an Objective-C 2.0 reference (http://developer.apple.com/iphone/library/documentation/Cocoa/Conceptual/ObjectiveC/).

Frameworks are software libraries provided by Apple that supply the reusable class definitions for Cocoa Touch. Add frameworks to Xcode by dragging them onto your project's Frameworks folder. After including the appropriate header files (such as UIKit/UIKit.h or QuartzCore/QuartzCore.h), you call their routines from your program.

Associated media might include audio, image, and video files to be bundled with the package as well as text-based files that help define your application to the iPhone operating system. Drop media files into your project and reference them from your code.

roject shown in Figure 1-2 is both simple and typical despite its fairly cluttered :e. It consists of five source files (main.m, MyAppDelegate.h, MyAppDelegate.m, Controller.h, MyViewController.m) and two interface files (MyViewController.xib, MainWindow.xib) along with the default iPhone project frameworks (UIKit, Foundation, and Core Graphics) and a few supporting files (Default.png, icon.png, My-Info.plist). Together these items form all the materials needed to create an extremely basic application. As you discover in Chapter 2, "Building Your First Project," Xcode can generate most of these elements automatically for you. You can then edit them as needed to add functionality.

> **Note**
> The My_Prefix.pch file is created automatically by Xcode. It contains precompiled header files.

The iPhone Application Skeleton

Nearly every iPhone application you build will contain a few key source files. Figure 1-3 shows the most common source code pattern: a main.m file, an application delegate, and a view controller. These five files (more if you use Interface Builder .xibs) provide all the components necessary to create a simple Hello World style application that displays a view onscreen.

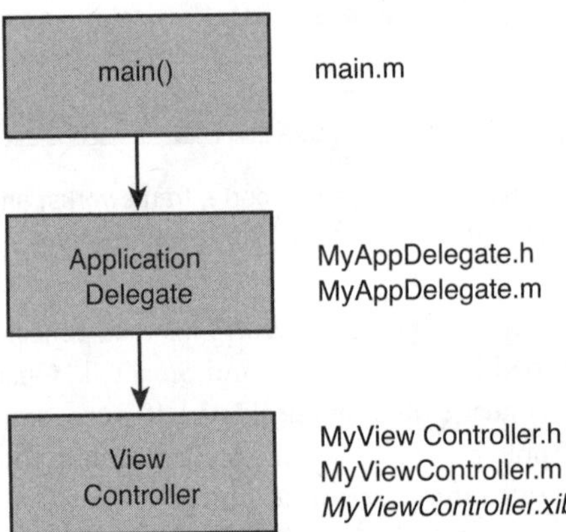

Figure 1-3 These files comprise the most common source code configuration for a minimal iPhone application. You may or may not choose to use a .xib file to define interfaces.

Some of these components may be familiar. Others may not. Here's a rundown of the file types:

- The implementation files use a .m extension and not a .c extension. These .m files contain Objective-C method implementations in addition to any C-style functions. The project in Figure 1-3 uses three .m files.
- iPhone source files use the standard C-style .h extension for the header files. Header files offer public declarations of class interfaces, constants, and protocols. You usually pair each class implementation file (in this case the application delegate and view controller .m files) with a header file, as you can see in Figure 1-3.
- XIB files (.xib) are created in Interface Builder. These XML-based user interface definition files are linked to your application and called by your app at runtime in their compiled .nib format. The project in Figure 1-3 uses a single .xib, which defines the contents of the primary view. A standard Xcode project may add a MainWindow.nib, which does little more than create a new, empty window.

Here is a quick rundown of those files, what they are and what role they play in the actual application.

main.m

The main.m file has two jobs. First, it creates a primary autorelease pool for your application. Second, it invokes the application event loop. These two elements provide critical elements to get your application started and running. Here is what those two items are and how they work.

```
int main(int argc, char *argv[])
{
      NSAutoreleasePool * pool = [[NSAutoreleasePool alloc] init];
      int retVal = UIApplicationMain(argc, argv, nil, @"MyAppDelegate");
      [pool release];
      return retVal;
}
```

> **Note**
>
> The `argc` and `argv` variables passed to `main()` refer to command-line arguments. Since the iPhone does not use a command-line to launch its programs (all applications are run from a common graphical user interface), these elements are not used. They are included for consistency with standard ANSI C practices.

Autorelease Pools

Autorelease pools are objects that support the iPhone's memory management system. This memory system is normally based on keeping track of reference counts, that is, counting how many objects refer to an allocated part of memory. Normally, you're responsible for releasing those objects. That's where the autorelease pool steps in. The pool automatically sends a release message to all the objects it owns at the end of every event loop cycle so you don't have to.

Autorelease objects are typically created with a pattern that looks like this:

```
[[[Someclass alloc] init] autorelease]
```

Once added to the autorelease pool, these objects pass their release responsibilities along to the pool. At the end of the event loop, the pool drains and sends the releases.

The iPhone expects that there will always be an autorelease pool available so memory can be recovered from these objects at the end of their lifetime. If you ever create a secondary thread in your application, you need to provide it with its own autorelease pool. Autorelease pools and the objects they contain are discussed further in Chapter 3.

The UIApplicationMain Function

The `UIApplicationMain` function provides the primary entry point for creating a new application object. It creates the new application instance and its delegate. The delegate is responsible for handling application status changes and providing program-specific responses to those changes.

The third and fourth arguments of the `UIApplicationMain` function specify the name of the principal application class and its delegate. If the third argument is omitted (set as nil), the iPhone defaults to using the standard `UIApplication` class.

`UIApplicationMain` also establishes the application's event loop. An event loop repeatedly looks for low-level user interactions such as touches on the screen or sensor triggers. Those events are captured by the iPhone's kernel and dispatch an event queue, which is forwarded to the application for handling.

Event loops let you design your program around callbacks. Callbacks are where you specify how the application should respond to these events. In Objective-C, this corresponds to method invocations. For example, you can build methods to determine how the application should reorient itself when the user moves the screen from portrait to landscape or how views should update when a finger is dragged onscreen. This style of programming is based on the underlying event loop, which is set up in main.m.

Application Delegate

An application delegate implements how your program should react at critical points in the application life cycle. The delegate is responsible for initializing a windowing system at launch and wrapping up business at termination. It also acts as the key player for handling memory warnings. Here are the more important delegate methods that your applications will implement:

- **The `applicationDidFinishLaunching:` method**—This method is the first thing triggered in your program after the application object has been instantiated. Upon launch, this is where you create a basic window, set its contents, and tell it to become the key responder for your application.
- **The `applicationWillTerminate:` method**—This method enables you to handle any status finalization before handing control back to SpringBoard. Use this to save defaults, update data, and close files.

- **The `applicationDidReceiveMemoryWarning` method**—When called, your application must free up memory to whatever extent possible. This method works hand in hand with the `UIViewController`'s `didReceiveMemoryWarning:` method. If your application is unable to release enough memory, the iPhone terminates it, causing your user to crash back to the SpringBoard. SpringBoard is the main iPhone GUI that presents the application icons, allowing users to launch programs.

The application delegate also handles responsibility for when your application suspends or resumes, such as when the user locks the screen.

After launching and loading the window, the application delegate takes a back seat. Nearly all application semantics move over to some child of a `UIViewController` class. The application delegate typically does not take a role again until the application is about to finish or if memory issues arise.

View Controller

In the iPhone programming paradigm, view controllers provide the heart of how an application runs. Here is where you normally implement how the application responds to selections, button presses, as well as sensor triggers. If you haven't used Interface Builder to create a precooked presentation, the view controller is where you load and lay out your views. While the main.m and application delegate files are typically small, view controller source code is normally extensive, defining all the ways your application accesses resources and responds to users. Some of key methods include the following:

- **The `loadView` and `viewDidLoad` methods**—Assuming you aren't using XIB files to lay out your views, the `loadView` method must set up the screen and lay out any subviews. Make sure to either call `[super loadView]` or, alternatively, implement `viewDidLoad`, whenever you inherit from a specialized subclass such as `UITableViewController` or `UITabBarController`. This allows the parent class to properly set up the screen before you add your customizations to that setup. Apple's documentation and sample code encourage the `viewDidLoad` approach when basing your code off specialized subclasses.
- **The `shouldAutorotateToInterfaceOrientation:` method**—Unless you have pressing reasons to force your user to remain in portrait orientation, add the `should-autorotate` method to allow the `UIViewController` method to automatically match your screen to the iPhone's orientation. You must define how the screen elements should update.
- **The `viewWillAppear:` and `viewDidAppear:` methods**—These methods get called whenever a view is ready to appear onscreen or a view has fully appeared onscreen. The `viewWillAppear:` method should update information for views that are about to display. When called, your view may not have been loaded yet. If you rely on accessing IBOutlets connected to subviews, poke `self.view` to ensure the view hierarchy gets loaded. Use `viewDidAppear:` to trigger behavior for once the view is fully transitioned onscreen, such as any animations.

The number and kind of XIB files varies with how you design your project. Figure 1-3 assumes you've created a single XIB for the view controller. You can use Interface Builder to design additional components or skip IB entirely and create your interfaces programmatically.

> **Note**
>
> Only `UIView` instances can directly receive touch calls; `UIViewController` objects cannot. See Chapter 8, "Gestures and Touches," to learn more about directly managing and interpreting touches and gestures in your application.

A Note About the Sample Code in This Book

For the sake of pedagogy, this book's sample code usually presents itself in a single main.m file. It's hard to tell a story when readers must look through five or seven or nine individual files at once. Offering a single file concentrates that story.

These samples are not intended as stand-alone applications. They are there to demonstrate a single recipe and a single idea. One main.m file with a central presentation reveals the implementation story in one place. Readers can study these concentrated ideas and transfer them into normal application structures, using the standard file system and layout.

There are two exceptions to this one-file rule. First, application-creation walk-throughs use the full file structure created by Xcode to mirror the reality of what you'd expect to build on your own. The walk-through folders may therefore contain a dozen or more files at once.

Second, standard implementation and header files are provided when the class itself *is* the recipe or provides a precooked utility class. Instead of highlighting a technique, some recipes offer these precooked class implementations and categories (that is, extensions to a preexisting class rather than a new class). For those recipes, look for separate .m and .h files in addition to the skeletal main.m that encapsulates the rest of the story.

iPhone Application Components

Compiled iPhone applications live in application bundles. Like their Macintosh cousins, these application bundles are just folders named with a .app extension. Your program's contents and resources reside in this folder, including the compiled executable, supporting media (such as images and audio), and a few special files that describe the application to the OS. The folder is treated by the operating system as a single bundle.

Application Folder Hierarchy

iPhone bundles are simple. Unlike the Mac, iPhone bundles do not use Contents and Resources folders to store data or a MacOS folder for the executable. All materials appear at the top level of the folder. For example, instead of putting a language support (.lproj) folder into Contents/Resources/, Xcode places it directly into the top .app folder. You can still use subfolders to organize your project, but these developer-defined folders do not follow any standard.

The iPhone SDK's core OS support includes the `NSBundle` class. This class offers access to the files stored in the application bundle. NSBundle makes it easy to locate your application's root folder and to navigate down to your custom subfolders to point to and load built-in resources like sounds, images, and data files.

> **Note**
>
> As on a Macintosh, user domains mirror system ones. Official Apple-distributed applications reside in the primary /Applications folder. Third-party applications live in /var/mobile/Applications. The underlying UNIX file system is obscured by the iPhone's sandbox, which is discussed later in this section.

The Executable

The executable application file of your application resides at the top-level folder of the application bundle. It carries executable permissions so it can run and is signed as part of the application bundle during the compilation process. You may only load and run applications that have been signed with an official developer certificate. Those certificates are issued by Apple via the iPhone developer program portal at the official developer Web site.

Apple offers several kinds of signing profiles called mobile provisions that vary by how the application will be deployed. You need separate provisions for applications that will be tested during development on a local device, for applications that will be sent out to registered devices for testing, and for those that will be distributed through App Store. You've already read about creating your provisions earlier in this chapter. The actual application signing process is discussed in further detail in Chapter 2.

The Info.plist File

As on a Macintosh, the iPhone application folder contains that all-important Info.plist file. Info.plist files are XML property lists that describe an application to the operating system. Property lists store key-value pairs for many different purposes and can be saved in readable text-based or compressed binary formats. In an Info.plist file, you specify where the application's executable (`CFBundleExecutable`, "Executable file") can be found, the text that appears under the application icon (`CFBundleDisplayName`, "Bundle display name"), and the application's unique identifier (`CFBundleIdentifier`, "Bundle identifier).

Be careful when setting the display name. Titles that are too long to display properly are truncated; the iPhone adds ellipses as needed. So your application named "My Very First iPhone App" may display as "My Very F..." This provides less information to your end user than a simpler title like "First App" would offer.

The application identifier typically uses Apple's reverse domain naming format (for example, com.sadun.appname). The identifier plays a critical role for proper behavior and execution; it must not duplicate any other identifier on App Store. In use, the product identifier registers your application with SpringBoard, the "Finder" of the iPhone. SpringBoard runs the home screen from which you launch your applications. The product identifier also forms the basis for the built-in preferences system called the user defaults.

The identifier is case sensitive and must be consistent with the provisions you generate at the developer portal. Problems with misnamed bundle identifiers have cost developers many hours of wasted time. Specify the identifier by editing your project's settings in Xcode (see Figure 1-4).

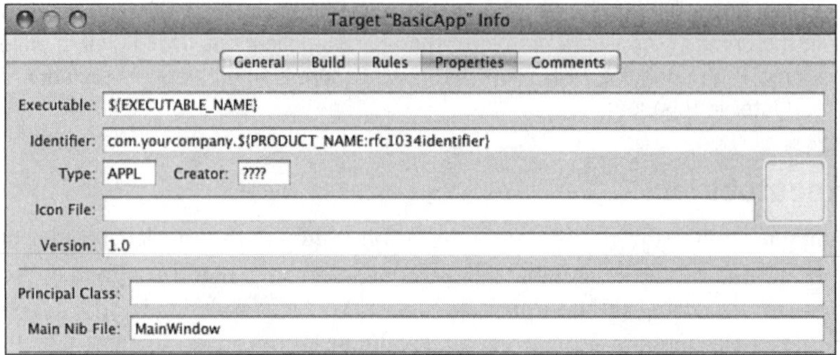

Figure 1-4 Customize your application's bundle identifier by editing target properties. Edits here are reflected in your application's Info.plist file. The PRODUCT_NAME identifier is specified in your project's settings.

> **Note**
>
> To change identifiers, open the Targets list in the Xcode project's left-hand column. Double-click Targets > *Your Application Name*. This opens the Target Info window. Click on the Properties tab and edit the Identifier from com.yourcompany to a reverse domain name that represents your actual company. Enter your personal domain and let Xcode append the application product name.

Application preferences are automatically stored in the application sandbox. The sandbox mimics the domains and folders normally found on the core OS. On the iPhone, preferences appear in a local Library folder and use the application identifier for naming. This identifier is appended with the .plist extension (for example, com.sadun.appname.plist), and the preferences are stored using a binary .plist format. You can read a binary .plist by transferring it to a Macintosh via Xcode's organizer.

> **Note**
>
> To copy application data from the iPhone to your Macintosh, open the Organizer window (Windows > Organizer). Select your device and then an item from the applications list. Click the arrow next to the name to reveal the Application Data bundle and then drag that bundle to the desktop. It expands to a standard folder named with the application identifier and the date and time the data was retrieved.

You can edit property list files directly in Xcode or use the Property List Editor that ships as part of Xcode's utilities. It's located in /Developer/Applications/Utilities and offers a user-friendly GUI. Use Apple's plutil utility to convert property lists from binary to a text-based XML format: `plutil —convert xml1 plistfile`. Apple uses binary plists to lower storage requirements and increase system performance.

As with the Macintosh, Info.plist files offer further flexibility and are highly customizable. With them, you can set application-specific variables (`UIRequiresPersistentWiFi`) or specify how your icon should display (`UIPrerenderedIcon`). These variables are powerful. They can define multiple roles for a single application although this functionality is not available to third-party development. For example, the Photos and Camera utilities are actually the same application, MobileSlideShow, playing separate "roles." Appendix A, "Info.plist Keys," lists these keys in detail.

Other standard Info.plist keys include `UIStatusBarStyle` for setting the look and color of the status bar and `UIStatusBarHidden` for hiding it altogether. `UIInterfaceOrientation` lets you override the accelerometer to create a landscape-only (`UIInterfaceOrientationLandscapeRight`) presentation. Register your custom application URL schemes (for example, myCustomApp://) by setting `CFBundleURLTypes`. See Chapter 21, "Accessibility and Other iPhone OS Services," for more information about URL schemes.

The Icon and Default Images

The icon.png image and Default.png are two key image files. Icon.png acts as your application's icon, the image used to represent the application on the SpringBoard home screen. Default.png (also known as your "launch image") provides the splash screen displayed during application launch.

Unlike Default.png, the icon filename is arbitrary. If you'd rather not use "icon.png," set the `CFBundleIconFile` key in your Info.plist file to whatever filename you want to use but be aware that this might cause trouble when submitting your application to App Store; iTunes Connects requires the application to use icon.png (or Icon.png) even if the Info.plist specifies another name. This key is not set by default, so be sure to add a value regardless of the art you use.

Apple recommends matching Default.png to your application's background. Many developers use Default.png to launch images for a logo splash or for a "Please wait" message. These go against Apple's human interface guidelines (launch images should provide visual continuity, not advertising or excuses for delays) but are perfectly understandable uses. Xcode lets you take screenshots of your application in action using its Organizer window (Window > Organizer). It also offers the option to set one of those shots as your Default.png image.

The official application icon size is 57-by-57 pixels. SpringBoard automatically scales larger art. Provide flat (not glossy) art with squared corners. SpringBoard smoothes and rounds those corners and adds an automatic gloss and shine effect. If for some compelling reason you need to use prerendered art, set `UIPrerenderedIcon` to `<true/>` in your Info.plist file.

As with all on/off Info.plist items, make sure to set the value for `UIPrerenderedIcon` to the Boolean value true (`<true/>`, the checked box in the Xcode GUI). Using a string for "true" (`<string>true</string>`) may work on the simulator while producing no effect on the iPhone. Also remember that the 3.0 Xcode property list editor hides the actual key name. Add a field for the "Icon already includes gloss and bevel effects" key and check the box that appears in the value column.

When submitting your application to App Store, you need to create a high-resolution (512-by-512 pixel) version of your icon. Although you can up sample your 57-by-57 icon.png art, it won't look good. Going the other way allows you to maintain high-quality art that you can compress to your icon as needed. Keep your art simple and compressible. An icon that looks stunning at 512x512 looks muddled and sloppy at 57x57 when overly detailed.

> **Note**
>
> You may include a 29-by-29 pixel image called Icon-settings.png in your project. This image represents your application in the Settings application. Most developers skip this option. If not included, Settings simply scales your icon.png image.

NIB Files

Interface Builder creates .xib files that store precooked addressable user interface layouts in XML format. (If you're curious, you can open these files in your favorite text editor and peek at the XML.) Most IB-based applications contain several .xib files that define various view components. Typical .xib contents might include window layouts, custom table cells, pop-up dialogs, and more.

When creating your application bundles, Xcode compiles the XML data into a NIB package, which is placed alongside the executable and any other application components. (NIB, somewhat archaically, stands for NeXT Interface Builder, which is the ancestor of the OS X Interface Builder used to build iPhone applications.) The .nib files appear at the top level of your application bundle and are used directly from your program when loading screens.

> **Note**
>
> When you develop programs that do not use XIB Interface-Builder bundles, remove the `NSMainNibFile` key from Info.plist and discard the automatically generated MainWindow.xib file from your project. This reduces clutter in your program and keeps your application from trying to load an interface file that you never fully defined. Set the fourth argument of `UIApplicationMain()` in `main()` to the class name of your application delegate.

Files Not Found in the Application Bundle

As with the Macintosh, things you do not find inside the application bundle include preferences files (generally stored in the application sandbox in Library/Preferences), application plug-ins (stored in /System/Library at this time and not available for general development), and documents (stored in the sandbox in Documents).

At this time, the iPhone SDK does not let you prepopulate these folders. Since your program cannot edit or overwrite any files in the application bundle, copy any files that need to be changed, such as database files, to another folder (Documents or Library) on the first run of your program.

Another thing that seems to be missing (at least from the Macintosh programmer point of view) is Application Support folders. You should copy your support data, which more rightfully would be placed into an Application Support structure, to your Documents or Library folders from the application bundle when your application is first launched. Thereafter, check to make sure that data is there and recopy the data if needed.

IPA Archives

When users purchase your application they download a .ipa file from iTunes. This file is actually a zipped archive. It contains a compressed payload, namely the app bundle you built from the components just described. iTunes stores .ipa archives in the Mobile Applications folder in the iTunes Library. If you rename a copy of any .ipa file to use the .zip extension, you can easily open it using standard compression software.

Each application is customized on download to ensure that it can only be installed and run on the iPhone devices authorized by your iTunes account. This prevents the application from being shared freely over the Internet. Although software pirates have created cracking tools, these are not widely used in the wild. Apple's basic protections ensure that for the most part only those who have purchased and downloaded the application from iTunes can run your software.

Sandboxes

The iPhone OS restricts all SDK development to application "sandboxes" for the sake of security. The iPhone sandbox limits your application's access to the file system to a minimal set of folders, network resources, and hardware. In some ways, it's like attending a restrictive school with a paranoid principal:

- Your application can play in its own sandbox, but it can't visit anyone else's sandbox.
- You cannot share toys. You cannot share data (except via the user-controlled system pasteboard). You cannot mess in the administrative offices. Your files must stay in the folders provided to you by the sandbox, and you cannot copy files to or from other application folders.
- You cannot peek over the fence. Reading from or attempting to write to files outside your sandbox is grounds for App Store rejection. Your application is prevented from writing to most folders outside the sandbox by the iPhone OS.
- Your application owns its own Library, Documents, and /tmp folders. These mimic the standard folders you'd use on a less-restrictive platform but specifically limit your capability to write and access this data.

In addition to these limitations, your application must be signed digitally and must authenticate itself to the operating system with a coded application identifier, which you must create at Apple's developer program site. Details on how to do this follow in Chapter 2.

On the bright side, sandboxing ensures that all program data gets synced whenever your device is plugged into its home computer. On the downside, at this time Apple has not clarified how that synced data can be accessed from a Windows- or Macintosh-based desktop application.

> **Note**
>
> Sandbox specification files (using the .sb extension) are stored in /var/mobile/Applications along with each actual sandbox folder. These files control privileges such as read-and-write access to various bits of the file system. As a developer, you will not be able to see or manipulate these files, but they are there, controlling the ways your app may or may not interact with the operating system.

Programming Paradigms

iPhone programming centers on two important paradigms: objected-oriented programming and the Model-View-Controller (MVC) design pattern. The iPhone SDK is designed around supporting these concepts in the programs you build. To do this, it has introduced delegation (controller) and data source methods (model) and customized view classes (view). Here is a quick rundown of some important iPhone/Cocoa Touch design vocabulary used through this book.

Object-Oriented Programming

Objective-C is heavily based on Smalltalk, one of the most historically important object-oriented languages. Object-oriented programming uses the concepts of encapsulation and inheritance to build reusable classes with published external interfaces and private internal implementation. You build your applications out of concrete classes that can be stacked together like LEGO toys, because it's always made clear which pieces fit together through class declarations.

Pseudo-multiple inheritance (via invocation forwarding and protocols) provides an important feature of Objective-C's approach to object-oriented programming. iPhone classes can inherit behaviors and data types from more than one parent. Take the class `UITextView`, for example. It's both text *and* a view. Like other view classes, it can appear onscreen. It has set boundaries and a given opacity. At the same time, it inherits text-specific behavior. You can easily change its display font, color, or text size. Objective-C and Cocoa Touch combine these behaviors into a single easy-to-use class.

Model-View-Controller

MVC separates the way an onscreen object looks from the way it behaves. An onscreen button (the view) has no intrinsic meaning. It's just a button that users can push. That view's controller acts as an intermediary. It connects user interactions such as button taps to targeted methods in your application, which is the model. The application supplies and stores meaningful data and responds to interactions such as these button taps by producing some sort of useful result. MVC is best described in the seminal 1988 paper by Glenn Krasner and Stephen Pope, which is readily available online.

Each MVC element works separately. You might swap out a pushbutton with, for example, a toggle switch without changing your model or controller. The program continues to work as before, but the GUI now has a different look. Alternatively, you might leave the interface as is and change your application where a button triggers a different kind of response in your model. Separating these elements enables you to build maintainable program components that can be updated independently.

The MVC paradigm on the iPhone breaks down into the following categories:

- **Model**—Model methods supply data through protocols such as data sourcing and meaning by implementing callback methods triggered by the controller.
- **View**—View components are provided by children of the `UIView` class and assisted by its associated (and somewhat misnamed) `UIViewController` class.
- **Controller**—The controller behavior is implemented through three key technologies: delegation, target action, and notification.

Together, these three elements form the backbone of the MVC programming paradigm. Let's look at each of these elements of the iPhone MVC design pattern in a bit more detail. The following sections introduce each element and its supporting classes.

View Classes

The iPhone builds its views based on two important classes: `UIView` and `UIViewController`. These two classes and their descendants are responsible for defining and placing all onscreen elements.

As views draw things on your screen, `UIView` represents the most abstract view class. Nearly all user interface classes descend from `UIView` and its parent `UIResponder`. Views provide all the visual application elements that make up your application. Important `UIView` classes include `UITextView`, `UIImageViews`, `UIAlertView`, and so forth. The `UIWindow` class, a kind of `UIView`, provides a viewport into your application and provides the root for your display.

Because of their onscreen nature, all views establish a frame of some sort. This frame is an onscreen rectangle that defines the space each view occupies. The rectangle is established by the view's origin and extent.

Views are arranged hierarchically and are built with trees of subviews. You can display a view by adding it to your main window or to another view by using the `addSubview` method to assign a child to a parent. You can think about views as attaching bits of transparent film to a screen, each piece of which has some kind of drawing on it. Views added last are the ones you see right away. Views added earlier may be obscured by other views sitting on top of them.

Despite the name, the `UIViewController` class does not act as controllers in the MVC sense. They more often act as view handlers and models than as controllers. Although some will disagree, Apple terminology does not always match the MVC paradigm taught in computer science classes.

View controllers are there to make your life easier. They take responsibility for rotating the display when a user reorients his or her iPhone. They resize views to fit within the boundaries when using a navigation bar or a toolbar. They handle all the interface's fussy bits and hide the complexity involved in directly managing interaction elements. You can design and build iPhone applications without ever using a `UIViewController` or one of its subclasses, but why bother? The class offers so much convenience it's hardly worth writing an application without them.

In addition to the base controller's orientation and view resizing support, two special controllers, the `UINavigationController` and `UITabBarController`, magically handle view shifting for you. The navigation version enables you to drill down between views, smoothly sliding your display between one view and the next. Navigation controllers remember which views came first and provide a full breadcrumb trail of "back" buttons to return to previous views without any additional programming.

The tabbed view controller lets you easily switch between view controller instances using a tabbed display. So if your application has a top ten list, a game play window, and a help sheet, you can add a three-buttoned tab bar that instantly switches between these views without any additional programming to speak of.

Every `UIViewController` subclass implements a method to load a view, whether through implementing a procedural `loadView` method or by pulling in an already-built interface from a .xib file and calling `viewDidLoad`. This is the method that lays out the controller's main view. It may also set up triggers, callbacks, and delegates if these have not already been set up in Interface Builder.

So in that sense alone, the `UIViewController` does act as a controller by providing these links between the way things look and how interactions are interpreted. And, because you almost always send the callbacks to the `UIViewController` itself, it often acts as your model in addition to its primary role as a controller for whatever views you create and want to display. It's not especially MVC, but it is convenient and easy to program.

Controller

When Apple designs interactive elements such as sliders and tables, they have no idea how you'll use them. The classes are deliberately general. With MVC, there's no programmatic meaning associated with row selection or button presses. It's up to you as a developer to provide the model that adds meaning. The iPhone provides several ways in which prebuilt Cocoa Touch classes can talk to your custom ones. Here are the three most important: delegation, target-action, and notifications.

Delegation

Many `UIKit` classes use delegation to hand off responsibility for responding to user interactions. When you set an object's delegate, you tell it to pass along any interaction messages and let that delegate take responsibility for them.

A `UITableView` is a good example of this. When a user taps on a table row, the `UITableView` has no built-in way of responding to that tap. The class is general purpose and it has no semantics associated with a tap. Instead, it consults its delegate—usually a view controller class or your main application delegate—and passes along the selection change through a delegate method. This enables you to add meaning to the tap at a point of time completely separate from when the table class was first implemented. Delegation lets classes be created without that meaning while ensuring that application-specific handlers can be added at a later time.

The `UITableView` delegate method `tableView: didSelectRowAtIndexPath:` is a typical example. Your model takes control of this method and implements how it should react to the row change. You might display a menu or navigate to a subview or place a check mark next to the current selection. The response depends entirely on how you implement the delegated selection change method.

To set an object's delegate, assign its delegate property (this is preferred) or use some variation on the `setDelegate:` method. This instructs your application to redirect interaction callbacks to the delegate. You let Xcode know that your object implements delegate calls by adding a mention of the delegate protocol it implements in the class declaration. This appears in angle brackets, to the right of the class inheritance. Listing 1-1 shows a kind of `UIViewController` that implements delegate methods for `UITableView` views. The `MergedTableController` class is, therefore, responsible for implementing all required table delegate methods.

Xcode's documentation exhaustively lists all standard delegate methods, both required and optional. Open Help > Documentation (Command-Option-Shift-?) and search for the delegate name, such as `UITableViewControllerDelegate`. The documentation provides a list of instance methods that your delegate method can or must implement.

Delegation isn't limited to Apple's classes. It's simple to add your own protocol declarations to your classes and use them to define callback vocabularies. Listing 1-1 creates the `FTPHostDelegate` protocol, which declares the `ftpHost` instance variable. When used, that object must implement all three (required) methods declared in the protocol. Protocols are an exciting and powerful part of Objective-C programming, letting you create client classes that are guaranteed to support all the functionality required by the primary class.

> **Note**
>
> If your application is built around a central table view, use `UITableViewController` instances to simplify table creation and use.

Listing 1-1 **Defining and Adding Delegate Protocol Declarations to a Class Definition**

```
@protocol FTPHostDelegate <NSObject>
- (void) percentDone: (NSString *) percent;
- (void) downloadDone: (id) sender;
- (void) uploadDone: (id) sender;
@end

@interface MergedTableController : UIViewController
    <UITableViewDelegate,UITableViewDataSource>
{
   UIView                    *contentView;
```

Listing 1-1 **Continued**

```
    UITableView              *subView;
    UIButton                 *button;
    id <FTPHostDelegate>     *ftpHost;
    SEL                      finishedAction;
}
@end
```

Target-Action

Target-actions are a lower-level way of redirecting user interactions. You encounter these almost exclusively for children of the UIControl class. With target-action, you tell the control to contact a given object when a specific user event takes place. For example, you'd specify which object to contact when users press a button.

Here is a typical example. This snippet defines a UIBarButtonItem instance, a typical buttonlike control used in iPhone toolbars. It sets the item's target to self and the action to @selector(trackNotifications:). When tapped, it triggers a call to the defining object sending the setHelvetica: message:

```
UIBarButtonItem *helvItem = [[[UIBarButtonItem alloc]
    initWithTitle:@"Helvetica" style:UIBarButtonItemStyleBordered
    target:self action:@selector(setHelvetica:)] autorelease];
```

As you can see, the name of the method (`setHelvetica:`) is completely arbitrary. Target-actions do not rely on an established method vocabulary the way delegates do. In use, however, they work exactly the same way. The user does something, in this case presses a button, and the target implements the selector to provide a meaningful response.

Whichever object defines this `UIBarButtonItem` instance must implement a `setHelvetica:` method. If it does not, the program crashes at runtime with an undefined method call error. Unlike delegates and their required protocols, there's no guarantee that `setHelvetica:` has been implemented at compile time. It's up to the programmer to make sure that the callback refers to an existing method.

Standard target-action pairs always pass either zero, one, or two arguments. These arguments are the interaction object and a `UIEvent` object that represents the user's input. Your selector can choose to pass any or all of these. In this case, the selector uses one argument, the `UIBarButtonItem` instance that was pressed. This self-reference, where the triggered object is included with the call, enables you to build more general action code. Instead of building separate methods for `setHelvetica:`, `setGeneva:`, and `setCourier:`, you could create a single `setFontFace:` method to update a font based on which button the user pressed.

> **Note**
>
> To build target-action into your own `UIControl`-style classes, add a target variable of type `id` (any object class) and an action variable of type `SEL` (method selector). At runtime, use `performSelector: withObject:` to send the method selector to the object. To use selectors without parameters, for example, `@selector(action)`, pass `nil` as the object.

Notifications

In addition to delegates and target-actions, the iPhone uses yet another way to communicate about user interactions between your model and your view—and about other events, for that matter. Notifications enable objects in your application to talk among themselves, as well as to talk to other applications on your system. By broadcasting information, notifications enable objects to send state messages: "I've changed," "I've started doing something," or "I've finished."

Other objects might be listening to these broadcasts, or they might not. For your objects to "hear" a notification, they must register with a notification center and start listening for messages. The iPhone implements many kinds of notification centers. For App Store development, only `NSNotificationCenter` is of general use.

The `NSNotificationCenter` class is the gold standard for in-application notification. You can subscribe to any or all notifications with this kind of notification center and listen as your objects talk to each other. The notifications are fully implemented and can carry data as well as the notification name. This name + data implementation offers great flexibility, and you can use this center to perform complex messaging.

It's easy to subscribe to a notification center. Register your application delegate or, more typically, your `UIViewController` as an observer. You supply an arbitrary selector to be called when a notification arrives, in this case `trackNotifications:`. The method takes one argument, an `NSNotification`. Ensure that your callback method hears all application notifications by setting the name and object arguments to `nil`.

```
[[NSNotificationCenter defaultCenter] addObserver:self
    selector:@selector(trackNotifications:) name:nil object:nil];
```

All notifications contain three data elements: the notification name, an associated object, and a user information dictionary. If you're unsure what notifications `UIKit` objects in your application produce, have your callback print out the name from all the notifications it receives—for example, `NSLog(@"% @", [notification name])`.

The kinds of notification vary by the task you are performing. For example, notifications when rotating an application include `UIApplicationWillChangeStatusBarOrientationNotification` and `UIDeviceOrientationDidChangeNotification`.

Make sure you implement the `trackNotifications:` method (or another callback method whose selector you supplied), which gets called in this case for all program notifications, regardless of name or object. Setting these to `nil` when listening acts as a wild card.

```
(void) trackNotifications: (NSNotification *) theNotification
{
    CFShow([theNotification name]);
    CFShow([theNotification object]);
    CFShow([[theNotification userInfo] description]);
}
```

te

recipes in this book use printf and CFShow as well as NSLog. Each debug feedback method has its advantages and disadvantages. The former have the advantage of not printing out the date and time, which results in cleaner output. How you choose to log information is strictly a matter of taste. There are no wrong or right ways to put print statements into your program. See Chapter 3 for more details about logging information.

Model

You're responsible for building all application semantics—the model portion of any MVC app. You create the callback methods triggered by your application's controller and provide the required implementation of any delegate protocol. For relatively simple programs, model details often are added to a `UIViewController` subclass. With more complex code, avoid shoehorning that implementation into a `UIViewController`. Custom-built classes can better help implement semantic details needed to support an application's model.

There's one place that the iPhone SDK gives you a hand with meaning, and that's with data sources. Data sources enable you to fill `UIKit` objects with custom content.

Data Sources

A data source refers to any object that supplies another object with on-demand data. Some UI objects are containers without any native content. When you set another object as its data source, by assigning its `dataSource` property (preferred) or via a call like `[uiobject setDataSource:applicationobject]`, you enable the UI object (the view) to query the data source (the model) for data such as table cells for a given `UITableView`. Usually the data source pulls its data in from a file such as a local database, from a Web service such as an XML feed, or from other scanned sources. `UITableView` and `UIPickerView` are two of the few Cocoa Touch classes that support or require data sources.

Data sources are like delegates in that you must implement their methods in another object, typically the `UITableViewController` that owns the table. They differ in that they create/supply objects rather than react to user interactions.

Listing 1-2 shows a typical data source method that returns a table cell for a given row. Like other data source methods, it enables you to separate implementation semantics that fill a given view from the Apple-supplied functionality that builds the view container.

Objects that implement data source protocols must declare themselves just as they would with delegate protocols. Listing 1-1 showed a class declaration that supports both delegate and data source protocols for `UITableViews`. Apple thoroughly documents data source protocols. You find this documentation in Xcode's Documentation window (Help > Documentation).

Listing 1-2 **Data Source Methods Fill Views with Meaningful Content**

```
// Return a cell for the ith row, labeled with its number
- (UITableViewCell *)tableView:(UITableView *)tableView
    cellForRowAtIndexPath:(NSIndexPath *)indexPath
{
```

Listing 1-2 **Continued**

```
    UITableViewCell *cell = [tableView
        dequeueReusableCellWithIdentifier:@"any-cell"];
    if (!cell) {
        cell = [[[UITableViewCell alloc] initWithFrame:CGRectZero
             reuseIdentifier:@"any-cell"] autorelease];
    }
    // Set up the cell
    cell.text = [tableTitles objectAtIndex:[indexPath row]];
    return cell;
}
```

The `UIApplication` Object

In theory, you'd imagine that the iPhone "model" component would center on the `UIApplication` class. In practice, it does not, at least not in any MVC sense of the word model. In the world of the Apple SDK, each program contains precisely one `UIApplication` instance, which you can refer to via `[UIApplication sharedInstance]`.

For the most part, unless you need to open a URL in Safari, recover the key window, or adjust the look of the status bar, you can completely ignore `UIApplication`. Build your program around a custom application delegate class that is responsible for setting things up when the application launches and closing things down when the application terminates. Otherwise, hand off the remaining model duties to methods in your custom `UIViewController` classes or to custom model classes.

> **Note**
>
> Use `[[UIApplication sharedInstance] keyWindow]` to locate your application's main window object.

Uncovering Data Source and Delegate Methods

In addition to monitoring notifications, message tracking can prove to be an invaluable tool. Add the following snippet to your class definitions to track all the optional methods that your class can respond to:

```
-(BOOL) respondsToSelector:(SEL)aSelector {
   printf("SELECTOR: %s\n", [NSStringFromSelector(aSelector)
       UTF8String]);
   return [super respondsToSelector:aSelector];
}
```

Summary

This chapter introduced you to the iPhone SDK, the developer portal, and the iPhone application. You saw how to choose a developer program and how to create provisions. You explored typical iPhone applications, from projects and source files to the application end product and learned about design limitations that should influence your development. Here are a few thoughts you may want to take away with you before leaving this chapter:

- Most developers end up choosing the $99/year standard iPhone developer program. This is the best, most general program to sign up for as it allows you to test on real devices and gives you access to the App Store.
- There are significant differences between each iPhone and iPod touch platform. Make sure your applications understand those differences to provide the best end-user experience.
- Developing for mobile platforms is not the same as developing for desktop systems. Keep this cardinal rule in mind: Fingers big, screen small, attention span short.
- The iPhone application bundle is much simpler and less structured than its Macintosh brother although it shares many common features such as Info.plist files and .lproj folders.
- If you come from a Cocoa background, you'll be prepared, if not overprepared, to create iPhone applications. Familiarity with Objective-C and Cocoa best practices will put you on a firm development footing.
- If you're more comfortable using C++ than Objective C, Apple has made it possible to create hybrid projects that leverage your C++ expertise with a minimum of Objective-C overhead.

2

Building Your First Project

Xcode and Interface Builder help you craft applications for the iPhone SDK. This chapter introduces you to the basics of using these tools in your projects. You see how to build a simple Hello World project, compile and test it in the simulator, and then learn how to compile for and deploy to the device. You also discover some basic debugging tools and walk through their use as well as pick up some tips about handy compiler directives. This chapter also looks at how to submit to App Store and distribute via ad hoc. By the time you finish this chapter, you'll have followed the application creation progress from start to finish and learned valuable tricks along the way.

Creating New Projects

If diving into SDK programming without a lifeline seems daunting, be reassured. Xcode makes getting started as simple as possible. It provides preconfigured projects that you can easily adapt while exploring the SDK. Since each of these projects is a fully working skeleton, all you need to do is add a little custom functionality to make that app your own.

To get started, launch Xcode and choose File > New Project (Command-Shift-N). The New Project template window (see Figure 2-1) opens, allowing you to select one of these application styles to get started.

These six project styles are chosen to match the most common development patterns for iPhone. Your choices are

- **Navigation-based Application**—Usually based around lists and tables, navigation applications offer a series of selection choices, each choice sliding to a new screen. The bar at the top of the screen offers a Back button, letting you return to previous screens. Apple's Contacts application is a navigation-based application.
- **OpenGL ES Application**—When programming with OpenGL ES, all you need is a view to draw into and a timer that offers an animation heartbeat. The OpenGL ES template provides these elements, letting you build your OpenGL ES graphics on top.
- **Tab Bar Application**—Apple's iPod and YouTube applications offer typical examples of Tab bar applications. In these applications, users can choose from a series of

screens by tapping buttons in a bar at the bottom of the application. For example, the YouTube application lets you choose from Featured videos, Most Viewed, Bookmarks, or the search pane. The Tab Bar Application template provides a skeleton that you can grow to add panes and their contents.

- **Utility Application**—Meant to be the simplest style of application, the Utility Application template creates a two-sided single-view presentation like the ones you see in the Stocks and Weather application. The template provides a main view and a flip view, which you can easily customize.
- **View-based Application**—The View-based template provides a skeleton that supports a single view. It provides a view controller to manage the view and an empty XIB to populate that view with custom GUI elements. This is the template you use later in this chapter to build your first Hello World application.
- **Window-based Application**—The window-based application offers the same template as the view-based one but without the view controller or view. You get an application delegate and a window and that's about it. One advantage of choosing this template is that it's relatively easy to strip out the Interface Builder elements should you prefer to build your iPhone applications completely from scratch.

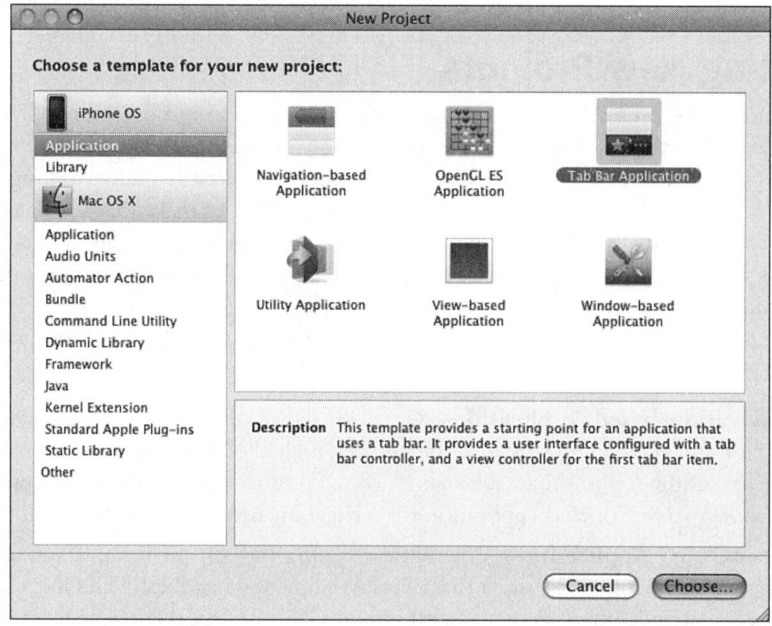

Figure 2-1 The Xcode New Project template selection window.

> **Note**
>
> Apple offers sample code and tutorials at the iPhone Reference Library. The library is located at http://developer.apple.com/iphone/library/navigation/index.html; you must use your developer credentials to access its contents. In addition to sample code, you'll find release notes, technical notes, Getting Started guides, Coding How-To's, and more.

Building Hello World the Template Way

Xcode's preconfigured template offers the easiest path to creating a Hello World-style sample application. In the following steps, you create a new project, edit it to say Hello World, and run it on the iPhone simulator. As you build your first Xcode project, you'll discover some of the key development pathways.

Create a New Project

With the iPhone SDK installed, launch Xcode. Close the Xcode news page; it's the window that says Welcome to Xcode and offers options like Create a new Xcode project. This window continues to appear until you uncheck Show at Launch before closing.

> **Note**
>
> If you ever change your mind about hiding the window, you can find it again by choosing Help > Welcome to Xcode.

To create the new project, choose File > New Project (Command-Shift-N). This opens the template selection window shown previously in Figure 2-1. Notice that there are currently just two sets of iPhone templates (called Application and Library in the left-hand column) available versus a dozen project styles available for the Macintosh. You can, in fact, add new iPhone templates to Xcode, and you learn how to do so later in this chapter. For now, choose Application if it has not already been selected for you.

Select View-based Application and click Choose. When Xcode prompts you to Save As, name the project HelloWorld and save it to your Desktop with Save. A new HelloWorld Xcode project window opens (see Figure 2-2). This project contains all the files you need to design an application centered on a primary view.

The style of the project window depends on an Xcode setting. Choose Xcode > Preferences (Command-,), select the General pane, and choose the layout from the pop-up. The samples in this chapter use the All-In-One layout that combines operations to a single window, as shown in Figure 2-2. Other options include Condensed, offering separate windows for most tasks, and Default, which has a core project window and separate tool windows.

> **Note**
>
> When creating new iPhone projects, some templates offer a Use Core Data for Storage check box. These projects offer a skeleton that creates a Core Data stack for persistent storage. See Chapter 19, "A Taste of Core Data," for more details about Core Data.

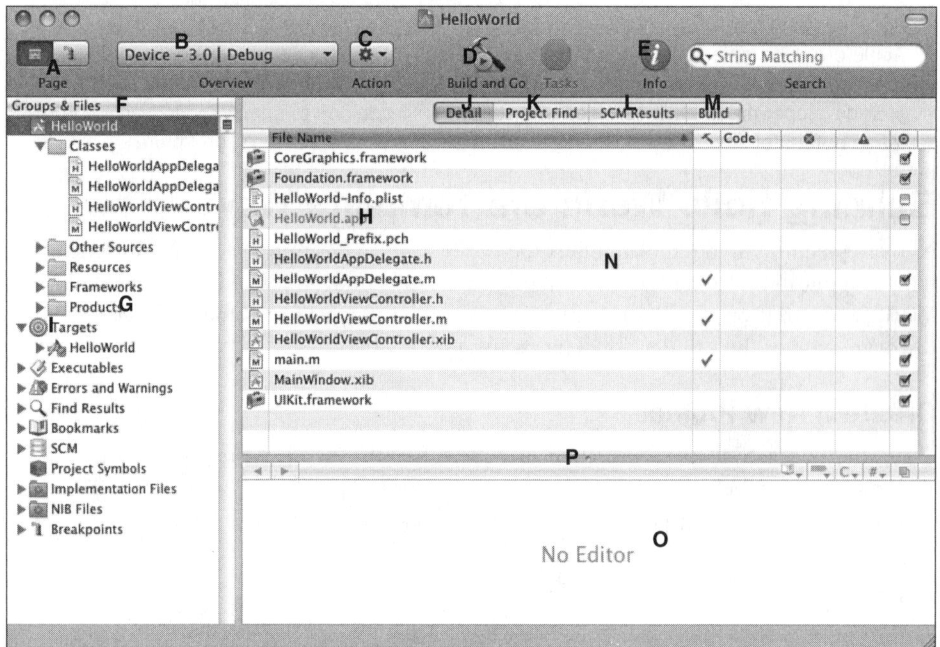

Figure 2-2 This brand-new HelloWorld project was created by choosing the View-based Application template.

Review the Project Window

The default Xcode project window is normally divided into three parts as you can see in Figure 2-2. These parts include the gray toolbar at top, the left-hand column, and the center-right portion of the window. Each part has a role to play in managing your project.

At the top, the gray toolbar provides a number of useful tools. The toggle on the very left (A) moves you between the project overview and the visual debugger. To its right, a pop-up (B) sets your targets and configuration. These control the application you intend to build and the way you intend to build it. The default iPhone templates provide two configurations, Debug and Release, which you can see from the pop-up choices. These configurations are actually a poor match for the realities of iPhone development, where better choices would have been Debug (for in-house development), Ad Hoc (for ad hoc distribution), and Distribution (for App Store release). Fortunately, the configurations are editable, and you discover how to create better choices later in this chapter.

To the right of the Configuration pop-up is Action (C), a pop-up that offers typical project functionality like adding new files and Reveal in Finder to locate those files on your Macintosh. To the right of that, you see the Build and Go button (D). Click it to compile your application and run it, whether on the device or in the simulator. The Info button (E) when clicked opens a window that you can use to customize parts of your project.

On the left side of the project window is the Groups and Files column (F). This column starts off with the source for your project. This list includes any files used to build the application plus any other files you've added to the project. The folder system shown is completely arbitrary. You can group with folders to organize your materials or skip the folders entirely. Groups provide an elegant way to organize your code and resources inside Xcode without touching the organization on the file system.

The Products folder (G), which is the last item in the folders list by default, contains the item you intend to build. In this case, that is the HelloWorld.app application (H). It is shown in red as it has not yet been built. Once built, it appears in black.

Below the first group of files is the Targets item (I). Click the gray disclosure triangle to reveal the HelloWorld entry under Targets. Locating your target is important. Select it and click the blue Info button at the top of the project window to open the Target "Hello World" Info window. This Target Info window is going to become one of your most important tools. Remember this sequence: Open the Target disclosure triangle, select the target, and click Info.

To the right of the Groups and Files column is a tabbed area. At the top, are four options: Detail (J), Project Find (K), SCM Results (L), and Build (M). Although they're stacked together, these four pane options have different roles and yet they all provide critical project information.

- Detail lists and previews files in your project. It helps you find files and open them to edit.
- Project Find searches through entire projects. You can match strings in files and frameworks. It mirrors and expands upon the single-file Find pop-up you access via Command-F.
- SCM Results shows the status of your files relative to a Source Code Management System. SCM systems track changes to your project both for single and multiple programmers. Xcode integrates with SVN, Perforce, or CVS, and displays the results of your syncs. Unfortunately, there is no support for the git version control system at this time.
- Build presents a results window for building your projects, showing any errors and their details.

The Detail Pane

You'll likely spend much of your time looking at the Detail pane (N), which is the default selection for the project window. The pane lists all the files in your project. Here you find all the individual elements listed by name. The Groups and Files column controls what you see. Click the HelloWorld group at the very top of the column to see all the files at once. Clicking on a group restricts the file list to just those files contained in that group.

The bottom pane (O) offers a preview of whichever element has been selected on the top. It's also a live editor, so any changes made in the bottom pane update the file in question. Click main.m and the bottom immediately updates with the contents of that file. A resize bar (P) sits between the top file list and the bottom editor/preview. Use this to adjust the proportions between the two elements. If you do not want to see a preview, drag the bar all the way down to the bottom.

Editor Windows

You will normally not want to edit your files in the tiny preview pane of the project window. Double-click any source file at the top, such as main.m, to open a stand-alone editor window (see Figure 2-3). This source code window offers some of the same options as the project window in the top gray bar. Below the top bar, it offers a standard Xcode source-code editing window. Make any changes you need by editing the text in the window. Be sure to regularly save your work using File > Save (Command-S).

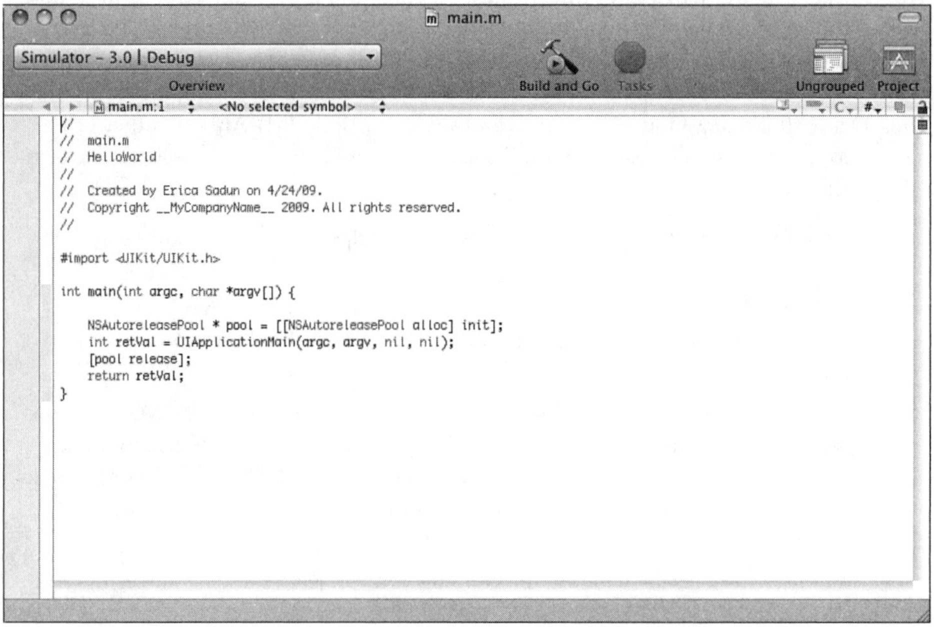

Figure 2-3 An Xcode source code editing window.

Xcode provides full undo support for a single session. You can even undo past a previous save so long as you do so within the same session. That is, you cannot close a project, reopen it, and then revert changes made before the project was closed.

> **Note**
>
> To add line numbers to your source code editing windows, open Preferences (Xcode > Preferences, Command-,). Scroll over to the Text Editing pane, check Show line numbers (on the left, under Display Options), click Apply, and then click OK.

Review the Project

When Xcode creates your new project, it populates it with all the basic elements and frameworks you need to build your first iPhone application. Items you see in this project include the following:

- **Foundation and Core Graphics frameworks**—These essential frameworks enable you to build your iPhone applications using the same fundamental classes and calls you are familiar with from the Macintosh.
- **UIKit framework**—This framework provides iPhone-specific user interface elements and is key to developing applications that can be seen and interacted with on the iPhone screen.
- **HelloWorld.app**—Displayed in red, this placeholder is used to store your finished application. Like on the Macintosh, iPhone applications are bundles and consist of many items stored in a central folder.
- **HelloWorld-Info.plist**—This file describes your application to the iPhone's system and enables you to specify its executable, its application identifier, and other key features. It works in the same way Info.plist files work on the Mac.
- **MainWindow.xib**—This Interface Builder file creates an unpopulated window. You will not use this for this first walk-through.
- **HelloWorldViewController.xib**—This Interface Builder file builds the view that displays in your first application. You edit this to customize how it looks.
- **main.m, HelloWorldAppDelegate.h, HelloWorldAppDelegate.m, HelloWorldViewController.h, and HelloWorldViewController.m**—These files contain a rough Objective-C skeleton that you can customize and expand to create your application. Feel free to browse through the code, but you will not edit these in this walk-through. Instead, you use the way that Xcode set them up and limit your modifications to the view controller .xib.

Open the View Controller .xib

In the HelloWorld project window, locate the HelloWorldViewController.xib file. As you read in Chapter 1, "Introducing the iPhone SDK," .xib files store Interface Builder layouts. Double-click the .xib file to launch Interface Builder so you can begin to edit the file. This may take a few seconds as the program opens and loads data. Once launched, locate the primary .xib window in Interface Builder shown in Figure 2-4.

The three icons in the .xib window represent three elements of the interface you're editing. To the very right is the View. The view is by default a member of the `UIView` class. It contains the onscreen elements that you want to display in your application.

On the left, the File's Owner represents the view controller. This is an abstract class, and its icon is called a *proxy* because it plays a role in IB, but the object is not itself embedded in the .xib archive.

Figure 2-4 The Interface Builder window for a view controller .xib

View controllers don't have a visual presentation. They manage views, but they don't display anything of their own. Each view controller has an instance variable called "view" which is set to some `UIView` (in this case, the one at the right) that is responsible for providing the actual onscreen presentation. So in the case of view controllers, the File's Owner proxy represents the object that loads and owns the .xib.

You can discover this for yourself by opening an inspector window. Choose Tools > Identity Inspector (Command-4). Click the File's Owner object and look at its class in the inspector. It is set to `HelloWorldViewController`. Then click the `View` object. Its class is `UIView`.

To see how the two are connected, click the File's Owner in the .xib window and then choose Tools > Connections Inspector (Command-2). You see that there is one Outlet listed. Outlet is IB-talk for instance variable. Move your mouse over the view-View listing in the Connections Inspector and you see the `View` object in the .xib window highlight. That's because the view outlet for your view controller is already connected to that view. Xcode prebuilt the file to work properly with the view.

The last icon, the one in the middle of Figure 2-4, is called First Responder. Like File's Owner, it's a proxy object. It represents the onscreen object that is currently responding to user touches. During the lifetime of an application, the first responder changes as users interact with the screen. For example, imagine a form. As the user touches each text field in that form, that field becomes active and assumes the first responder role.

Edit the View

To start customizing the view, double-click the `View` object in the .xib window. This opens a new editor window (see Figure 2-5, left). By default, the view is empty. It's up to you to customize it and add some content. To do so, you rely on two tools: the Interface Builder library and the inspector.

Select the view editor by clicking on it and then choose Tools > Attributes Inspector (Command-1). In the inspector, locate the Background swatch. Click on it and choose a new color from the Colors palette. The View automatically updates the background color. As you can see, the attributes inspector lets you adjust the properties of the currently selected object, in this case the view that you are editing.

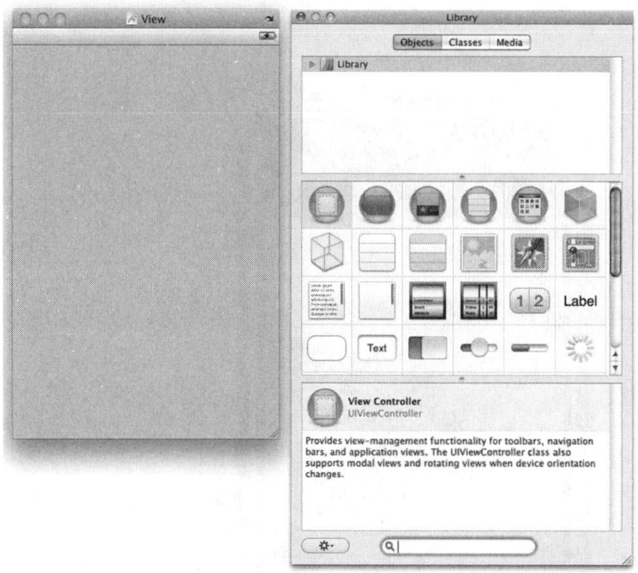

Figure 2-5 An empty view editor window (left); the Interface Builder Library (right).

Next, open the library by choosing Tools > Library (Command-Shift-L). The library (refer to Figure 2-5, right) presents a list of all the prebuilt Cocoa Touch elements you can use in your IB projects. These include both abstract elements like view controllers as well as visual components like buttons and sliders. Enter UILabel in the search field at the bottom of the library window. Drag the label from the middle pane, which is highlighted in Figure 2-5 (right) and drop it onto your view. Alternatively double-click the label in the middle pane. This automatically adds that item to your view. The bottom pane offers documentation of the selected class and you cannot drag from it.

Once dragged to the view, double-click the label and change the words from "Label" to "Hello World." You can also move the label around in the window to appeal to your aesthetic sensibilities or set its location in the Size Inspector (Command-3). Once satisfied, save your project with File > Save (Command-S). You have now customized your view with this content.

Run Your Application

Return to Xcode and to your project window. Choose Project > Set Active SDK > iPhone Simulator (3.0). This tells Xcode to compile your project for the Macintosh-based iPhone Simulator. Click Build and Go in the main project window and then wait as Xcode gets to work. It takes a few seconds to finish compiling and then Xcode automatically launches the simulator, installs your project, and runs it. Figure 2-6 shows the result, the Hello World application running on the simulator.

Figure 2-6 The customized Hello World application runs on the simulator.

Using the Simulator

The iPhone SDK Simulator makes it possible to test applications on the Macintosh using many of the same actions a user would perform on an actual device. Because the Macintosh is not a handheld touch-based unit, you must use menus, keyboard shortcuts, and the mouse to approximate iPhone-style interactions. Table 2-1 shows how to perform these tasks via the simulator.

Table 2-1 **Simulator Equivalents for iPhone Actions**

Action	Simulator Equivalent
Rotating the device	Hardware > Rotate Left (Command-left arrow) and Hardware > Rotate Right (Command-right arrow).
Shaking the device	Hardware > Shake Gesture (Command-Control-Z). This simulates a shake using a motion event but does not simulate other accelerometer actions.
Pressing the Home Key	Click the Home button on the Simulator screen or choose Hardware > Home (Command-Shift-H).
Locking the device	Hardware > Lock (Command-L).
Tapping and double-tapping	Click with the mouse, either a single- or double-click.
Tapping on the keyboard	Click the virtual keyboard or type on the Mac keyboard.
Dragging, swiping, and flicking	Click, drag, and release with the mouse. The speed of the drag determines the action. For flicks, drag very quickly.
Pinching in or out	Press and hold the Option key on your keyboard. When the two dots appear, drag them toward each other or away from each other.
Running out of memory	Hardware > Simulate Memory Warning.
In-progress phone call (visual display only)	Hardware > Toggle In-Call Status Bar. On the iPhone, you can run an application while on a phone call. The in-call bar appears at the top of the screen for the duration of the call.

Simulator: Behind the Scenes

Because the simulator runs on a Macintosh, Xcode compiles simulated applications for the Intel chip. Your application basically runs natively on the Macintosh within the simulator using a set of Intel-based frameworks that mirror the frameworks installed with the iPhone OS onto actual units. The simulator versions of these frameworks are located in the Xcode developer directory: /Developer/Platforms/iPhoneSimulator.platform/Developer/SDKs/iPhoneSimulator3.0.sdk/System/Library.

You can find your applications in your home's Library/Application Support folder. They are stored in iPhone Simulator/User/Applications/. It's helpful to visit this folder to peek under the hood and see how applications get deployed to the iPhone.

Each application is stored in an individual sandbox. The name of the sandbox is random, using a unique code (generated by `CFUUIDCreateString()`). Until OS 3.0, a sandbox file usually accompanied the sandbox folder. It used the same name with a .sb extension and stored the permissions associated with the file. Starting with 3.0, these sandbox permissions files no longer seem to be used. In the past, you had to zip up both the folder and the .sb file to share compiled simulator applications with others. Now you can zip up just the folder and still be able to share between Macintoshes.

Each sandbox name hides the application it's hosting, so you must peek inside to see what's there. Inside you find the application bundle (HelloWorld.app, for example), a Documents folder, a Library folder, and a /tmp folder. While running, each application is limited to accessing these local folders. They cannot use the main user Library as applications might on a Macintosh.

If you want to clean out your applications folder, you can delete files directly while the simulator is not running. Alternatively, use the press-and-hold-until-it-jiggles interface on the simulator that you're used to on the iPhone device itself. After pressing and holding any icon for a few seconds, the application icons start to jiggle. Once in this edit mode, you can move icons around or press the corner X icon to delete applications along with their data. Press the Home button to exit edit mode. You can also delete all of the simulator data by choosing iPhone Simulator > Reset Contents and Settings.

Although applications cannot access the user library folder, you can. If you want to edit the simulator's library, the files are stored in the `iPhone Simulator/User/Library` folder in your home Application Support folder. Editing your library lets you test applications that depend on the address book for example. You can load different address book sqlitedb files into Library/AddressBook to test your source with just a few or many contacts.

> **Note**
>
> The iPhone Simulator and Mac OS X use separate clipboards. The simulator stores its own clipboard data, which it gathers from the copy/paste features new to 3.0 firmware. Although you can use Edit > Paste (Command-V) to paste text from the Macintosh into simulator applications, this does not affect the simulator's onboard clipboard.

The Minimalist Hello World

While exploring the iPhone SDK, and in the spirit of Hello World, it helps to know how to build parsimonious applications. That is, it helps know how to build an application completely from scratch, without five source files and two interface files. So here is a walk-through showing you exactly that, a very basic Hello World that mirrors the `UIViewController` approach shown with the previous Hello World example but that manages to do so with one file and no .xibs.

Start by creating a new project (File > New Project, Command-Shift-N) in Xcode. Choose Window-based Application and save it as HelloWorld2 to your desktop. When the project window opens, select the Classes folder from the left column and click backspace to delete it. Choose Also Move to Trash when prompted. Next, delete MainWindow.xib.

Locate HelloWorld2-Info.plist (in the Resources folder) and double-click to open its editor. The last line should read Main nib file base name. Select this line and delete it. Save and close the file.

Open main.m and replace its contents with Listing 2-1. The source is included in the sample code for this book (see the preface for details), so you don't have to type it in by hand.

Listing 2-1 **Reductionist main.m**

```
#import <UIKit/UIKit.h>

@interface HelloWorldViewController : UIViewController
@end

@implementation HelloWorldViewController
- (void)loadView
{
    UIView *contentView = [[UIView alloc] initWithFrame:
        [[UIScreen mainScreen] applicationFrame]];

    contentView.backgroundColor = [UIColor lightGrayColor];

    UILabel *label = [[UILabel alloc] initWithFrame:
        CGRectMake(0.0f, 0.0f, 320.0f, 30.0f)];
    label.text = @"Hello World";
    label.center = contentView.center;
    label.textAlignment = UITextAlignmentCenter;
    label.backgroundColor = [UIColor clearColor];

    [contentView addSubview:label];
    [label release];

    self.view = contentView;
    [contentView release];
}
@end

@interface HelloWorldAppDelegate : NSObject <UIApplicationDelegate>
@end

@implementation HelloWorldAppDelegate
- (void)applicationDidFinishLaunching:(UIApplication *)application {
    UIWindow *window = [[UIWindow alloc] initWithFrame:
        [[UIScreen mainScreen] bounds]];

    HelloWorldViewController *hwvc;
    hwvc = [[HelloWorldViewController alloc] init];
    [window addSubview:hwvc.view];
    [window makeKeyAndVisible];
}
@end

int main(int argc, char *argv[])
{
    NSAutoreleasePool * pool = [[NSAutoreleasePool alloc] init];
    int retVal = UIApplicationMain(argc, argv, nil,
```

Listing 2-1 **Continued**

```
        @"HelloWorldAppDelegate");
    [pool release];
    return retVal;
}
```

So what does this application do? It builds a view, colors the background, and adds a label that says "Hello World." In other words, it does exactly what the first Hello World example did, but it does so by hand, without using Interface Builder.

It starts in main.m by establishing the autorelease pool and calling `UIApplicationMain`. From there, control passes to the application delegate, which is specified as the last argument of the call. This is a critical point for building a non-Interface Builder project, and one that has snagged many a new iPhone developer.

The delegate, receiving an application did launch message, builds a new window and creates a new instance of a custom view controller. It adds that controller's view to the window. The view controller waits for a request to load its view and when that request comes in, it runs `loadView`, which builds the view and adds the Hello World text.

Building views by hand means using this `loadView` method to set up the primary view and its children. This sample starts by creating a new view and telling it to fill the full space available to the application. It then sets the background color, in this case to light gray. Next, the sample builds a new instance of the `UILabel` class. Each of the label properties is set by hand.

In Interface Builder, the attributes inspector fills the same function. The inspector shows the label properties, offering interactive controls to choose settings like left, center, or right alignment. Here, that alignment is set programmatically to the constant `UITextAlignmentCenter`, the background color is set to clear, and the label programmatically moved into place via its `center` property. In the end, both the by-hand and Interface Builder approaches do the same thing, but here the programmer leverages specific knowledge of the SDK APIs to produce a series of equivalent commands.

As with other examples in this book, this code does not provide a `dealloc` method for the application delegate as it never gets called. The iPhone OS recovers all application memory during the application tear-down. Technically, the view controller leaks. In practice, this isn't a problem.

Browsing the SDK APIs

The iPhone SDK APIs are fully documented and accessible from within Xcode. Choose Help > Documentation (Command-Option-Shift-?) to open the Xcode Developer Documentation browser. Choose a documentation set from the top bar and search for `UILabel` from the top-right. This brings you to the full `UILabel` Class Reference (see Figure 2-7) where you can find all the class methods, properties, and instance methods as well as a general class overview.

Apple's Xcode-based documentation is thorough and clear. With it you have instant access to an entire SDK reference. You can look up anything you need without having to leave Xcode. When material goes out of date, a document subscription system lets you download updates directly within Xcode.

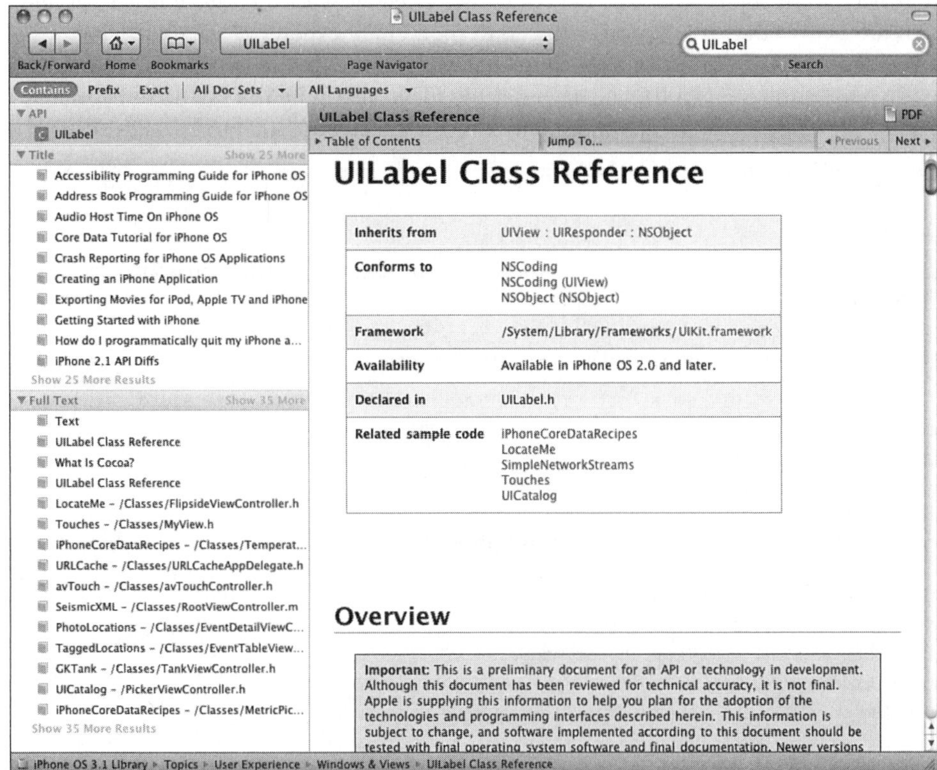

Figure 2-7 Apple offers complete developer documentation from within Xcode itself.

Interface Builder offers an extremely useful tool for developers at all expertise levels. Relying on it for many developer tasks, such as hooking up instance variables and crafting callbacks, may prove limiting. There is a lot more you can do in code that you cannot do in IB. Xcode's developer documentation helps you move past those limits and lets you focus your IB work on interface design, which is what the tool best offers. By understanding the SDK at a deeper level, you can craft more nuanced and powerful applications.

Converting Interface Builder Files to Their Objective-C Equivalents

A handy open source utility by Adrian Kosmaczewski allows you to convert Interface Builder files to Objective-C code. With it, you can extract all the layout information and properties of your visual design and see how that would be coded by hand. nib2objc does exactly what its name suggests. With it, you can generate converted code that takes into account the class constructors, method calls, and more.

Listing 2-2 shows the result of running nib2objc on the .xib file used in the first walk-through. Compare it to the far simpler (and less thorough) by-hand version in Listing 2-1. It performs more or less the same tasks. It creates a new view, then creates a new label, and adds the label to the view. However, this conversion utility exposes all the underlying properties, of which just a few were edited in Listing 2-1.

To peek at the original IB xml, open the .xib file in Text Edit. You can do so by issuing `open -e` from the Terminal command line while in the HelloWorld project folder.

```
open -e HelloWorldViewController.xib
```

Note

nib2obj is hosted at http://github.com/akosma/nib2objc/tree/master and issued under a general "Use this for good not evil" style of license.

Listing 2-2 **HelloWorldViewController.xib after Conversion to Objective-C**

```
UIView *view6 = [[UIView alloc] initWithFrame:CGRectMake(0.0, 0.0, 320.0, 460.0)];
view6.frame = CGRectMake(0.0, 0.0, 320.0, 460.0);
view6.alpha = 1.000;
view6.autoresizingMask = UIViewAutoresizingFlexibleWidth |
UIViewAutoresizingFlexibleHeight;
view6.backgroundColor = [UIColor colorWithRed:0.740 green:0.750 blue:0.638
   alpha:1.000];
view6.clearsContextBeforeDrawing = NO;
view6.clipsToBounds = NO;
view6.contentMode = UIViewContentModeScaleToFill;
view6.hidden = NO;
view6.multipleTouchEnabled = NO;
view6.opaque = YES;
view6.tag = 0;
view6.userInteractionEnabled = YES;

UILabel *view8 = [[UILabel alloc] initWithFrame:
    CGRectMake(100.0, 188.0, 89.0, 21.0)];
view8.frame = CGRectMake(100.0, 188.0, 89.0, 21.0);
view8.adjustsFontSizeToFitWidth = YES;
view8.alpha = 1.000;
view8.autoresizingMask = UIViewAutoresizingFlexibleRightMargin |
UIViewAutoresizingFlexibleBottomMargin;
view8.baselineAdjustment = UIBaselineAdjustmentAlignCenters;
view8.clearsContextBeforeDrawing = YES;
view8.clipsToBounds = YES;
view8.contentMode = UIViewContentModeScaleToFill;
view8.enabled = YES;
view8.font = [UIFont fontWithName:@"Helvetica" size:17.000];
view8.hidden = NO;
view8.lineBreakMode = UILineBreakModeTailTruncation;
view8.minimumFontSize = 10.000;
```

Listing 2-2 **Continued**

```
view8.multipleTouchEnabled = NO;
view8.numberOfLines = 1;
view8.opaque = NO;
view8.shadowOffset = CGSizeMake(0.0, -1.0);
view8.tag = 0;
view8.text = @"Hello World";
view8.textAlignment = UITextAlignmentLeft;
view8.textColor = [UIColor colorWithRed:0.000 green:0.000 blue:0.000 alpha:1.000];
view8.userInteractionEnabled = NO;

[view6 addSubview:view8];
```

Using the Debugger

Xcode's integrated debugger provides a valuable tool for iPhone application development. The following walk-through shows you where the debugger is and provides a simple grounding for using it with your program. In these steps, you discover how to set breakpoints and use the debugger console to inspect program details. These steps assume you are working on the second, minimalist Hello World example just described and that the project window is open and the main.m file displayed.

Set a Breakpoint

Locate the `loadView` method in the main.m file of your Hello World project. Click in the leftmost Xcode window column, just to the left of the `label.text` assignment line. A blue breakpoint indicator appears (see Figure 2-8). The dark blue color means the breakpoint is active. Tap once to deactivate—the breakpoint turns light blue—and once more to reactivate. You can remove breakpoints by dragging them offscreen and add them by clicking in the column, next to any line of code.

Open the Debugger

Click the Project/Debug toggle in the project window to view the debugger. The debugger provides a graphical front end for inspecting program objects, as well as a source window, and a log area with an interactive gdb shell. Locate the Activate/Deactivate button at the top-right of the debugger and make sure that it is activated, that is, that the button says "Deactivate."

Run the Program

Make sure the breakpoint is dark blue and that the button at the top of the debugger says "Deactivate" (which means that the breakpoint is active), and click Build and Go to run the program in the simulator. The program automatically stops when it hits the breakpoint.

The simulator window remains black and the debugger window updates to show the interactive interface of Figure 2-9.

```
@implementation HelloWorldViewController
- (void)loadView
{
    UIView *contentView = [[UIView alloc] initWithFrame:[[UIScreen mainScreen] applicationFrame]];
    contentView.backgroundColor = [UIColor lightGrayColor];

    UILabel *label = [[UILabel alloc] initWithFrame:CGRectMake(0.0f, 0.0f, 320.0f, 30.0f)];
    label.text = @"Hello World";
    label.center = contentView.center;
    label.backgroundColor = [UIColor clearColor];
    label.textAlignment = UITextAlignmentCenter;

    [contentView addSubview:label];
    [label release];

    self.view = contentView;
    [contentView release];
}
@end

@interface HelloWorldAppDelegate : NSObject <UIApplicationDelegate>
@end
```

Figure 2-8 Blue breakpoint indicators appear in the leftmost Xcode window column.

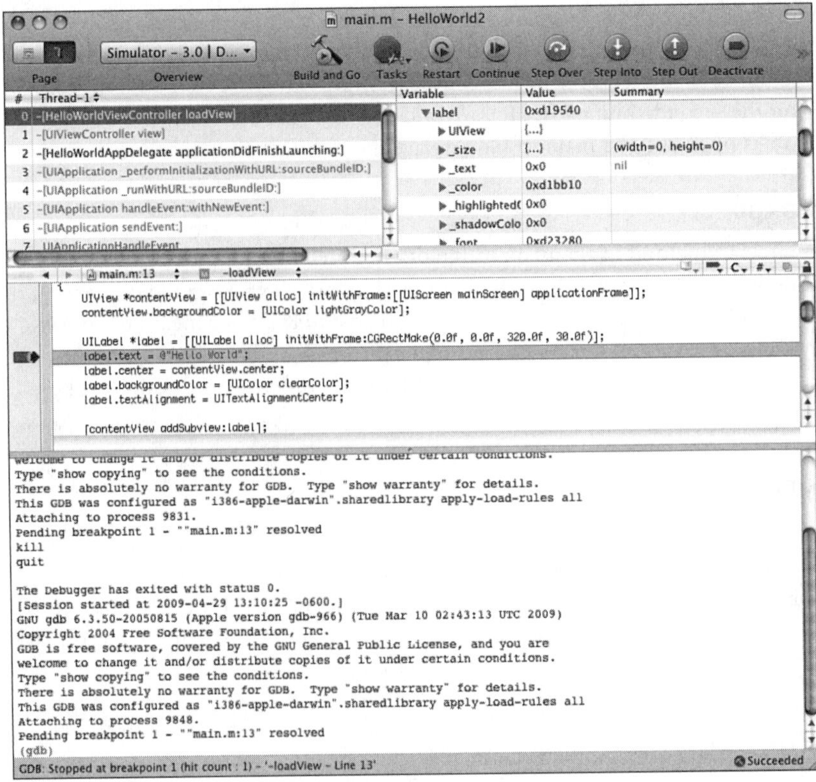

Figure 2-9 Xcode's graphical debugger enables you to interactively inspect program state. A command-line version of gdb runs concurrently in the console window, as shown by the (gdb) prompt. A red arrow appears at the active breakpoint.

Inspect the Label

Once stopped at the breakpoint, the interactive debugger and the gdb command line let you inspect objects in your program. For this example, navigate down the variable chain; the variable inspection pane appears at the top-right of the debugger window. Locate the Locals list of variables by scrolling down slightly below the Arguments list. Inside, click the disclosure triangle to the left of label to show the properties of the label object. Notice that text is labeled either nil or Invalid.

The gray Step Into button appears in the top toolbar of the window. Click it once. The text assignment executes and the red arrow moves down by one line. The summary of the `label.text` updates. It should now say Hello World.

Set Another Breakpoint

You can set additional breakpoints during a debugging session. For example, add a second breakpoint just after the line that sets the text alignment to center. You can do this in the middle pane; there's no need to reopen the original source window. Once again click in the leftmost column next to the line where you want to set the breakpoint.

Confirm that the current alignment is set to 0, the default value, by inspecting the label's textLabelFlags. You may have to scroll down a little and resize the variable column. Figure 2-10 shows the two breakpoints, the red arrow just after the assignment, and the alignment value defaulting to 0.

With the new breakpoint set, click the green Continue button. HelloWorld resumes execution until the next breakpoint, where it stops. The red arrow should now point to the `addSubview` line, and the alignment flag updates from 0 to 1 as that code has now run, changing the value for that variable.

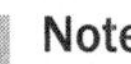

Note

Remove breakpoints by dragging them out from the left column.

Going Text

The bottom pane of the debugging window offers text-based GNU debugger (gdb) output that mirrors the results and data from the top two panes. For example, type backtrace at the gdb prompt to view the same trace shown in the top-left pane. After stopping at the second breakpoint, the backtrace should show that you are near line 19 in the source from main.m.

This bottom section is also known as the console. In Xcode, choose Run, Console (Command-Shift-R) to jump to the Xcode console. If the debugger is already open, the cursor jumps to the bottom pane. This pane is where your `printf`, `NSLog`, and `CFShow` messages are sent by default when running in tethered standard debug mode or when you use the simulator. You can resize the console by adjusting the resize bar at its top. If you want, you can drag it all the way to the top. This provides a full-window text-based console when needed.

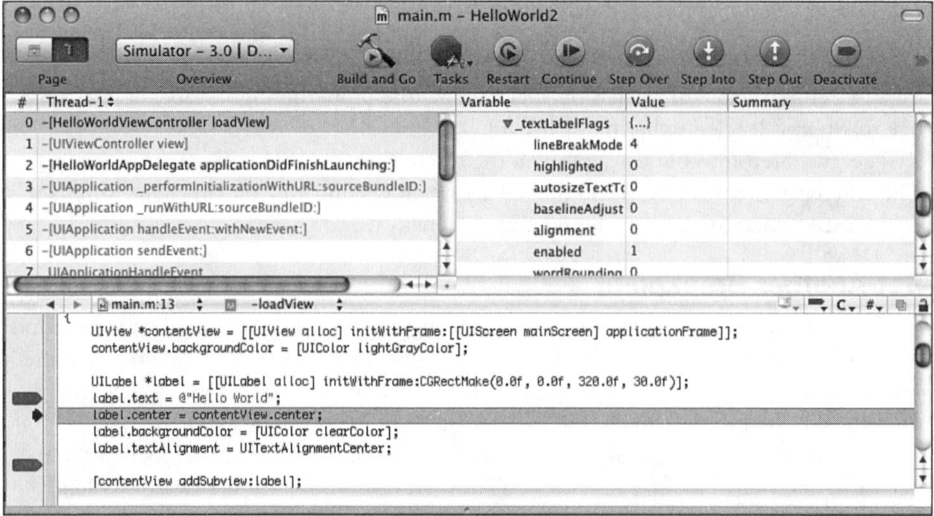

Figure 2-10 You can set additional breakpoints during the debugging session.

To test console logging, add a `NSLog(@"Hello World!");` line to your code; place it after the contentView release. Compile and run the application in the simulator. The log message appears in the console pane. The console keeps a running log of messages regardless of how many times you have tested your application. You can manually clear the log as needed.

You don't have to be running with gdb and the debugger console to see log messages. Tethered iPhones automatically send their NSLog output to the Xcode organizer (Window > Organizer > *Device Name* > Console). The Organizer console shows the output created by NSLog. For example, when run on an iPhone, that NSLog command displays like the following. It shows the date and time, the program name and the NSLog output (in this case, "Hello World!").

```
Sun May  3 09:08:11 unknown HelloWorld2[2198] <Warning>: Hello World!
```

Moving the Clear Log Button

In the current version of the iPhone SDK, the Clear Log button defaults to the very right of the toolbar. Because of this, Clear Log does not appear when the window is sized too small, as shown in Figure 2-10. You can access it by clicking the double-chevron at the top right of the window. I find this default location too much of a pain as I use the button constantly.

Fortunately, like most OS X toolbars, Xcode supports customization. To customize, Control- or right-click the toolbar. Choose Customize Toolbar from the contextual pop-up. From here you can drag Clear Log to a better location so less important buttons get sent to the chevron submenu and the Clear Log remains available at all times. To clear the console log via the keyboard, type the extremely awkward Control-Option-Command-R key combo. Alternatively, use Xcode's hotkey rebinding support. See the Key Bindings pane in Xcode preferences (Command-,).

You can also automatically clear the console, although this can sometimes erase content that you are still reviewing. Open Xcode Preferences (Xcode > Preferences, Command-,), and then check Debugging > Auto Clear Debug Console. This erases the console each time you execute the application.

Enabling Zombies

In the movies, a zombie is something dead that starts walking around. In Xcode vernacular, a zombie is an object that has been destroyed or released that you are still trying to send messages to. During debugging, you can set a special mode called `NSZombieEnabled`. This debug mode lets you gather information about messages sent to invalid objects. Say, for example, you create an instance variable called array. You set this and release it in the application's `loadView` method:

```
// Create and then release array
array = [[NSArray alloc] init];
[array release];
```

Should you attempt to access this object elsewhere in the program, the application will crash. The debugger will fail with `objc_msgSend` and at best you can view a backtrace to try to locate the error. Backtraces show a system stack, tracing the chain of messages that led to the current error.

```
- (void) accessArray
{
    CFShow([array self]);
}
```

`NSZombieEnabled` lets you locate the exact problem. In your project, select the Project view (as opposed to the Debug view). Locate Executables in the project list and open the disclosure triangle. Select your application, and click the blue Info button at the top toolbar. Click the Arguments tab and locate the Variables section at the bottom of the Arguments pane. Click +, add `NSZombieEnabled` as the name (zombie, not zombies) and `YES` as the value. Close the Executable Info window.

Now when you run the program, you receive a far more helpful message:

```
2009-05-03 13:20:31.014 HelloWorld[16603:20b] *** -[CFArray self]: message sent to
    deallocated instance 0xd32590
```

This message lets you use the interactive debugger window to match the instance value with the identity of the object; you'll know exactly which object went zombie on you. To disable zombies, delete the `NSZombieEnabled` from the variables section of the Executable Info. Make sure to do so before distributing the application.

> **Note**
>
> In Xcode 3.2 and newer, you can also use Run > Run with Performance Tool > Instruments > Zombies.

Memory Management

The iPhone does not offer garbage collection. It relies on a reference counted memory management system. As a developer that means you must control when objects are created, retained, and released from memory. Use too much memory and the iPhone warns your application delegate and UIViewControllers. Delegates receive `applicationDidReceive` ➥`MemoryWarning:` callbacks; view controllers get `didReceiveMemoryWarning`. Continue to use too much memory and the iPhone will terminate your application, crashing your user back to the SpringBoard. As Apple repeatedly points out, this is probably not the user experience you intend for your user, and it will keep your application from being accepted into App Store.

You must carefully manage memory in your programs and release that memory during low-memory conditions. Low memory is usually caused by one of two problems: leaks that allocate memory blocks that can't be accessed or reused and holding on to too much data at once.

> **Note**
>
> In addition to retain and release, Objective-C offers autorelease memory management. Sending autorelease to an object, typically at the time of its creation, says that you want it disposed of automatically at some time in the future. The method that requests the object can use the autoreleased object right away, and let it be disposed of at the end of the current run loop, or it can retain the object for future use. Chapter 3, "Objective-C Boot Camp," discusses memory management in further detail.

Leaks

Every object in Objective-C is created with an integer-based retain count. So long as that retain count remains at one or higher, objects will not be deallocated. It is up to you as a developer to implement strategies that ensure that objects get released at the time you will no longer use them.

Every object built with `alloc`, `new`, or `copy` starts with a retain value of 1. Sending a `retain` message to the object increases that count by one; sending `release` decreases the count. (Assigning the object to a retained property also increases the count.) If you lose access to an object without reducing the count to 0, that lost object creates a leak, that is, memory that is allocated and cannot be recovered. The following code leaks an array:

```
NSArray *leakyarray = [[NSMutableArray alloc] init];
leakyarray = nil;
```

Caching

When you load too much data at once, you can also run short of memory. Holding everything in your program when you are using memory-intense resources such as images, audio, or PDFs may cause problems. A strategy called *caching* lets you delay loads until resources are actually needed and release that memory when the system needs it.

The simplest approach involves building a cache from a `NSMutableDictionary` object. A basic object cache works like this. When queried, the cache checks to see whether the requested object has already been loaded. If it has not, the cache sends out a load request based on the object name. The object load method might retrieve data locally or from the Web. Once loaded, it stores the new information in memory for quick recall.

This code here performs the first part of a cache's duties. It delays loading new data into memory until that data is specifically requested. (In real life, you probably want to type your data and return objects of a particular class rather than use the generic `id` type.)

```
- (id) retrieveObjectNamed: (NSString *) someKey
{
    id object = [self.myCache objectForKey:someKey];
    if (!object)
    {
        object = [self loadObjectNamed:someKey];
        [self.myCache setObject:object forKey:someKey];
    }
    return object;
}
```

The second duty of a cache is to clear itself when the application encounters a low-memory condition. With a dictionary-based cache, all you have to do is remove the objects. When the next retrieval request arrives, the cache can reload the requested object.

```
- (void) respondToMemoryWarning
{
    [self.myCache removeAllObjects];
}
```

Combining the delayed loads with the memory-triggered clearing allows a cache to operate in a memory-friendly manner. Once objects are loaded into memory, they can be used and reused without loading delays. However, when memory is tight, the cache does its part to free up resources that are needed to keep the application running.

Recipe: Using Instruments to Detect Leaks

Instruments plays an important role in tuning your applications. It offers a suite of tools that lets you monitor performance. Its leak detection lets you track, identify, and resolve memory leaks within your program. Recipe 2-1 shows an application that creates two kinds of leaks on demands: a string built by `malloc()` that is not balanced by `free()`, and the `NSArray` example shown earlier in this chapter.

To see Instruments in action, first load the sample project for Recipe 2-1. Choose Run > Run with Performance Tool > Leaks in Xcode. This launches both Instruments and the simulator. The application begins to run in the simulator and Instruments watches over its progress.

Click either button in the application to leak memory. The string button leaks a 128-byte malloc'ed block. The array button leaks a 32-byte NSArray. Memory leaks appear in Instruments as an orange triangle. The size of the triangle indicates the size of the leak.

Be sure to click on the Leaks line to see the list of individual leaks as shown in Figure 2-11. By default, the ObjectAlloc line is selected. Each leak shows the amount of memory leaked, the address at which the leak starts, and the kind of object leaked.

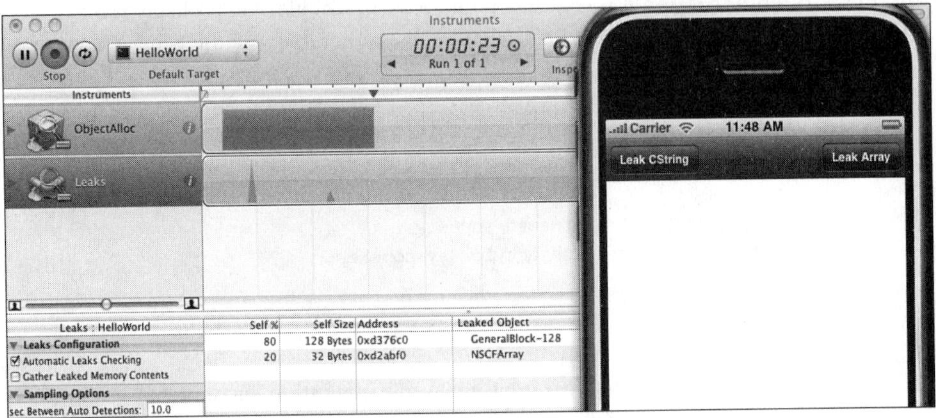

Figure 2-11 Instruments tracks leaks created by memory that cannot be recovered.

To track details about where the leak occurred, open the Extended Detail pane (View > Extended Detail, Command-E). Alternatively, click the detail button just to the left of the words "Leaked Blocks" at the bottom of the Instruments window. Click any item in the list of leaks. This opens a stack trace for that leak in the extended detail view, as shown in Figure 2-12.

Here, you find a stack trace that connects the leak to its creation. As this screenshot shows, the memory leak in question was allocated in `leakCString` after being malloc'ed. Finding the genesis of the object can help you track down where the leak occurs during its lifetime. Once discovered, hopefully you will be able to plug the leak and remove the memory issue from your application.

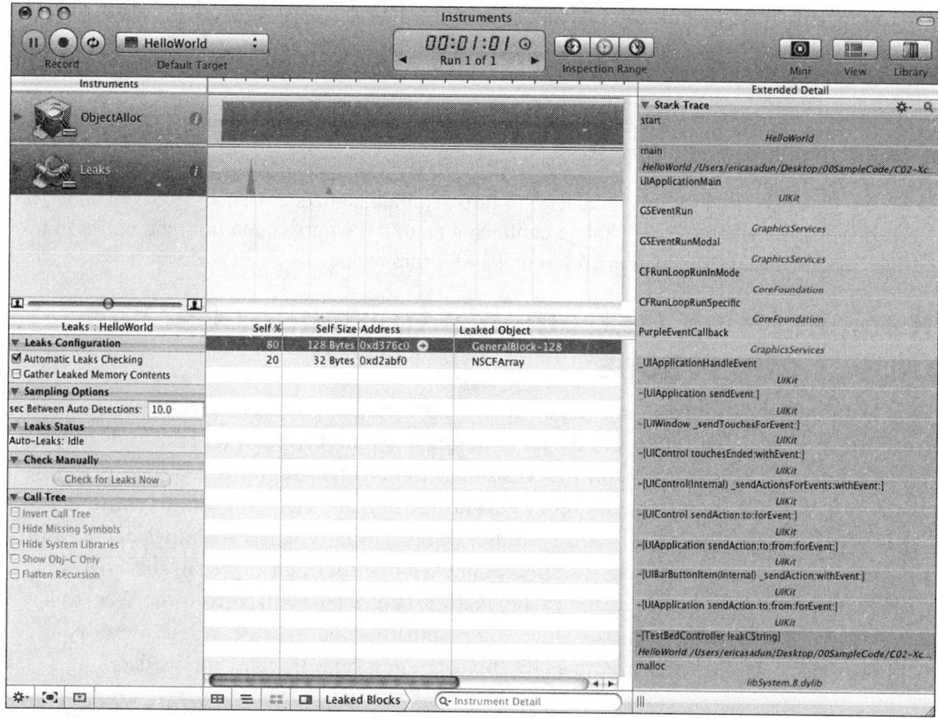

Figure 2-12 The stack trace in the Extended Detail view reveals where leaks occurred.

Recipe 2-1 **Creating Programmatic Leaks**

```
@implementation TestBedController
- (void) leakCString
{
    char *leakystring = malloc(sizeof(char)*128);
    leakystring = NULL;
}

- (void) leakArray
{
    NSArray *leakyarray = [[NSMutableArray alloc] init];
    leakyarray = nil;
}

- (void) viewDidLoad
{
    // set up buttons
    self.navigationController.navigationBar.tintColor =
          COOKBOOK_PURPLE_COLOR;
    self.navigationItem.rightBarButtonItem = BARBUTTON(@"Leak Array",
          @selector(leakArray));
```

```
    self.navigationItem.leftBarButtonItem =  BARBUTTON(@"Leak String",
        @selector(leakString));
}
@end
```

> **Get This Recipe's Code**
>
> To get the code used for this recipe, go to http://github.com/erica/iphone-3.0-cookbook-, or if you've downloaded the disk image containing all of the sample code from the book, go to the folder for Chapter 2, and open the project for this recipe.

Recipe: Using Instruments to Monitor Cached Object Allocations

One feature of the simulator allows you to test how your application responds to low-memory conditions. Selecting Hardware > Simulate Memory Warning sends calls to your application delegate and view controllers, asking them to release unneeded memory. Instruments, which lets you view memory allocations in real time, can monitor those releases. It ensures that your application handles things properly when warnings occur. With Instruments, you can test memory strategies like caches discussed earlier in this chapter.

Recipe 2-2 creates a basic image cache. Rather than retrieve data from the Web, this image cache builds empty `UIImage` objects to simulate a real use case. When memory warnings arrive, as shown in Figure 2-13, the cache responds by releasing its data.

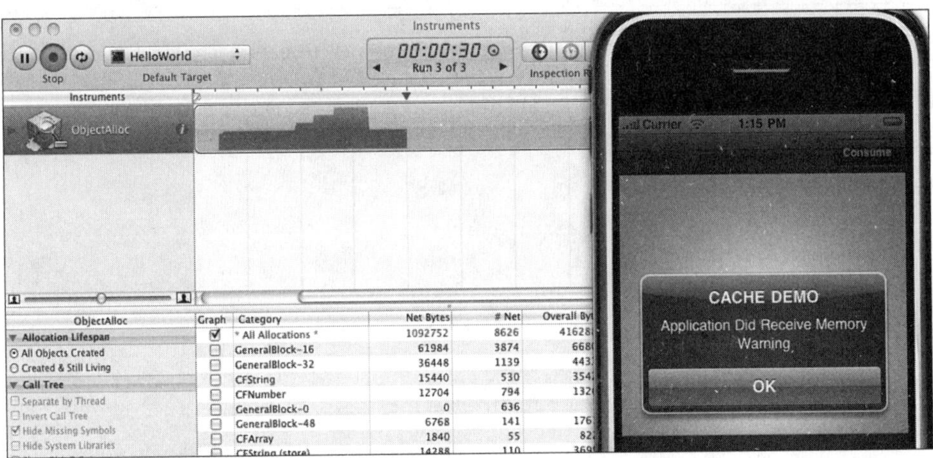

Figure 2-13 Instruments helps monitor object allocations, letting you test your release strategies during memory warnings.

The stair-step pattern shown here represents three memory allocations created by pressing the Consume button. After, the simulator issued a memory warning. In response, the cache did its job by releasing the images it had stored. The memory then jumped back down to its previous levels. Instruments lets you save your trace data, showing the application's performance over time. Choose File > Save to create a new trace file. By comparing runs, you can evaluate changes in performance and memory management between versions of your application.

Some SDK objects are automatically cached and released as needed. The `UIImage imageNamed:` method retrieves and caches images in this manner, although it has gained a deserved reputation for not operating as smoothly as it should and retaining memory that should rightly be released. Nibs used to build `UIViewControllers` are also cached, and reload as necessary when controllers need to appear.

Note

As a general rule of thumb for the first two generations of iPhones, an application can use up to about 20MB of memory before memory warnings occur and up to about 30MB until the iPhone OS kills your application.

Recipe 2-2 **Image Cache Demo**

```
// Build an empty image
UIImage *buildImage(int imgsize)
{
    UIGraphicsBeginImageContext(CGSizeMake(imgsize, imgsize));
    UIImage *image = UIGraphicsGetImageFromCurrentImageContext();
    UIGraphicsEndImageContext();
    return image;
}

@implementation ImageCache
@synthesize myCache;

- (id) init
{
    if (!(self = [super init])) return self;
    myCache = [[NSMutableDictionary alloc] init];
    return self;
}

- (UIImage *) loadObjectNamed: (NSString *) someKey
{
    // This demo doesn't actually use the key to retrieve
    // data from the web or locally.
    // It just returns another image to fill up memory
    return buildImage(320);
}

- (UIImage *) retrieveObjectNamed: (NSString *) someKey
{
    UIImage *object = [self.myCache objectForKey:someKey];
    if (!object)
    {
```

```
        object = [self loadObjectNamed:someKey];
        [self.myCache setObject:object forKey:someKey];
    }
    return object;
}

// Clear the cache at a memory warning
- (void) respondToMemoryWarning
{
    [self.myCache removeAllObjects];
}

- (void) dealloc
{
    self.myCache = nil;
    [super dealloc];
}
@end
```

Get This Recipe's Code

To get the code used for this recipe, go to http://github.com/erica/iphone-3.0-cookbook-, or if you've downloaded the disk image containing all of the sample code from the book, go to the folder for Chapter 2 and open the project for this recipe.

Using the Clang Static Analyzer

The LLVM/Clang static analyzer automatically helps detect bugs in Objective-C programs. It's a terrific tool for finding memory leaks and other issues. Starting with Xcode version 3.2, you can run the analyzer directly from Xcode. Choose Build > Build and Analyze (Command-Shift-A). The interactive screen shown in Figure 2-14 guides you through all suspected leaks and other potential problems.

Issues found by the static analyzer are not necessarily bugs. It's possible to write valid code that Clang identifies as incorrect. Always critically evaluate all reported issues before making any changes to your code.

A stand-alone version of Clang can be used with legacy Xcode. Here are the steps you can take to download, install, and use the static analyzer with your own projects:

1. Download a copy of the analyzer from http://clang-analyzer.llvm.org/. Unzip it and rename the folder. I use the name "analyzer"; adapt the script in step 3 to match your name.
2. Move the folder into place, typically into your home directory. I placed mine in ~/bin and the short shell script that follows uses this path.
3. I created and added the following script to ~/bin, naming it "clangit." Again, use your own judgment on placement and naming.

```
rm -rf /tmp/scan-build*
rm -rf build
~/bin/analyzer/scan-build —view xcodebuild
```

4. Open an Xcode project, choose the Simulator | Debug configuration, and then close Xcode.
5. From the command line, navigate to the project folder. Run the clangit script from that folder. Once analyzed, the analyzer report opens automatically in your Web browser.

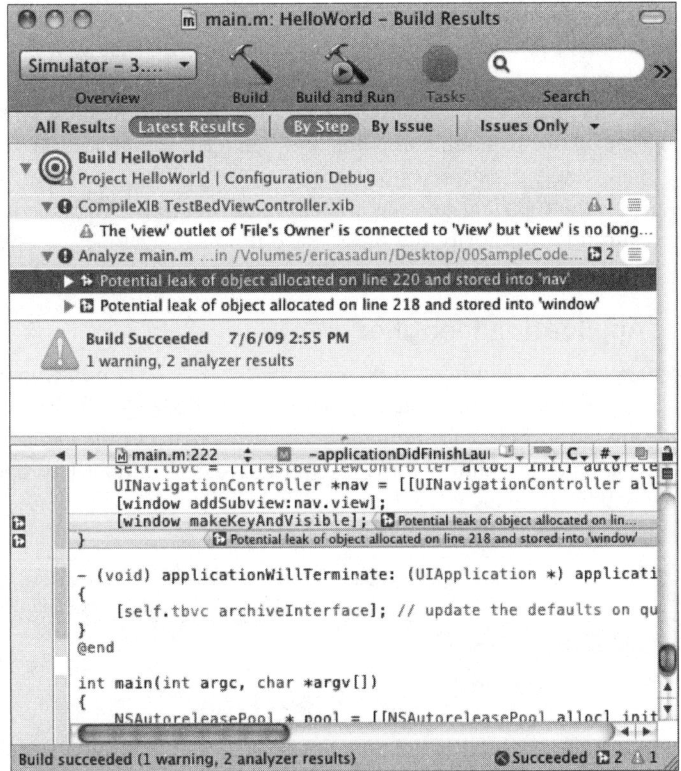

Figure 2-14 The Clang static analyzer creates bug reports for source code and displays them in an Xcode feedback window.

Building for the iPhone

Building for and testing in the simulator takes you only so far. The end goal of iPhone development is to create applications that run on actual devices. There are three ways to do so: building for development, for distribution, and for ad hoc distribution. These three, respectively, allow you to test locally on your device, to build for the App Store, and to build test and review versions of your applications that run on up to 100 registered devices. Chapter 1 introduced mobile provisions and showed how to create these in the Apple iPhone developer program portal. Now it's time to put these to use and deploy a program to the iPhone itself.

Install a Development Provision

At a minimum, a development provision is a prerequisite for iPhone deployment. So before going further, make sure you have created a wild-card dev provision and installed it into Xcode by dragging the mobileprovision file onto the Xcode application icon. (Alternatively, drop the provision onto iTunes.) After doing so, quit and restart Xcode to ensure that the provision is properly loaded and ready to use.

You may also want to review your keychain and ensure that the WWDR (Worldwide Developer Relations) and your developer identity certificates are available for use. During compilation, Xcode matches the provision against the keychain identity. These must match or Xcode will be unable to finish compiling and signing your application. To check your certificates, open Keychain Access (from /Applications/Utilities) and type "developer" in the search box on the top right. You see, at a minimum, an Apple Worldwide Developer Relations certifications Authority and one labeled iPhone Developer followed by your (company) name.

Edit Your Application Identifier

Your project application identifier can be set in the Target Info window under the Properties tab. To find this, open the disclosure triangle next to Targets in the left-hand column of your project window. Select the item inside. Its name matches the name of your project. Click the big blue Info button at the top of the project window. This opens the Target Info window with its five tabs. Click Properties, which is the fourth tab (see Figure 2-15).

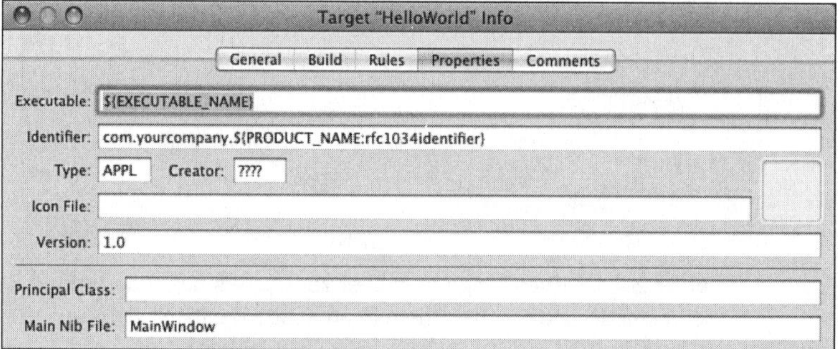

Figure 2-15 The Properties tab reveals the current application identifier settings.

Your wild-card development provision must match your actual application identifier. So if you registered a wild-card application identifier of, say, com.sadun.* and used that to generate your provisioning profile, your project's application identifier must match the registered identifier. You could use com.sadun.helloworld or com.sadun.testing, for example, but not helloworld or com.mycompany.helloworld.

By default, Xcode sets the application identifier to com.yourcompany.*productname*, where the product name is automatically filled in using the name you used to create your project. Edit com.yourcompany without touching the Xcode variable, which starts with the dollar sign, to match the values used in your wildcard identifier.

> **Note**
>
> You can change the default company name by editing the templates found at /Developer/Platforms/iPhoneOS.platform/Developer/Library/Xcode/Project Templates/Application or, better yet, by copying them and transforming them into custom templates. This process is described later in this chapter.

Set Your Code Signing Identity

After setting your identifier, click on the Build tab and confirm that the Configuration drop-down list at the top-left of the screen is set for the configuration type you want to modify (Debug or Release). Scroll down to find the Code Signing Identity entry. Click the triangle to disclose Any iPhone OS Device and click the pop-up to its right. This is where you select the provisioning profile identity you use to sign your application.

As you start to accumulate provisions and identities, the list of options can become long indeed. The sample shown in Figure 2-16 has been trimmed for narrative purposes. Normally, it's triple that size mostly due to third-party ad hoc provisions like the Polar Bear Farm Beta Program one.

Figure 2-16 Select a provisioning profile for your Code Signing Identity. To be used, provisions must match the application identifier.

You can see that there are items in black and items in gray. Gray items do not match the project's application identifier. They cannot be used to sign. In this example, these include a couple of push notification provisions, which are tied to specific application IDs that aren't equal to the current com.sadun.HelloWorld identifier.

The black items include my three matching provisions: my normal ad hoc provision, my wild-card distribution provision, and my wild-card development provision, which is selected in the image. Each of these three is listed with a certificate identity, namely iPhone Developer or iPhone Distribution followed by a colon, followed by my name. These match both the identities stored in the keychain and the certificates used in the portal to generate the provisions.

The two Automatic Profile Selectors automatically pick the first matching profile. This works well for the Developer identity. I have only one. This works poorly for the Distribution identity, which matches first to my ad hoc profile, which I rarely use. In day-to-day work, ignore the automatic profile selector and make sure you pick the item you actually intend to use by inspecting both the certificate name and the profile identity just above that name before choosing a profile.

Compile and Run the Hello World Application

Finally, it's time to test Hello World on an actual iPhone or iPod touch. Connect a unit that you will use for development. If this is your first time doing so, Xcode prompts you to confirm that you want to use it for development. Go ahead and agree, understanding that Apple always warns about possible dire consequences for doing so. First-time developers are sometimes scared that their device will be locked in some "development mode"; in reality, I have heard of no long-lasting issues. Regardless, do your homework before committing your device as a development unit. Read through the latest SDK release notes for details.

Before you compile, you must tell Xcode to build for the iPhone's ARM architecture rather than the Macintosh's Intel one. In the project window, choose iPhone Device as your Active SDK (see Figure 2-17). Then, check the Active Executable setting. If you have attached more than one development unit to your Macintosh, choose the one you want to test on. A check mark appears next to the unit name that will be used.

Click the Build and Go button in the project window. Assuming you have followed the directions earlier in this chapter properly, the Hello World project should compile without error, copy over to the iPhone, and start running.

If the project warns you about the absence of an attached provisioned device, open the Xcode Organizer window and verify that the dot next to your device is green. If this is not the case, you may need to reboot your device or your computer.

Signing Compiled Applications

You can sign already compiled applications at the command line using a simple shell script. This works for applications built for development. Signing applications directly helps developers share applications outside of ad hoc channels.

```
#! /bin/bash

export CODESIGN_ALLOCATE=/Developer/Platforms/iPhoneOS.platform/Developer/usr/
bin/codesign_allocate

codesign -f -s "iPhone Developer" $1.app
```

Figure 2-17 The Active Executable selection chooses which device to use. Two development units are connected to this Mac, with the Bologna unit chosen.

If you use several iPhone Developer profiles in your keychain, you may need to adapt this script so that it matches only one of those. Otherwise codesign complains about ambiguous matching.

I personally used this approach to distribute test versions of the sample code from this book. Using developer code-signing allowed me to skip the hassles of ad hoc distribution, allowing me to rapidly turn around applications to an arbitrary audience.

From Xcode to Your iPhone: The Organizer Interface

The Xcode Organizer helps manage your development units. Choose Window > Organizer (Control-Command-O). This window (see Figure 2-18) forms the control hub for access between your development computer and your iPhone or iPod testbed. This window allows you to add and remove applications, view midtest console results, examine crash logs, and snap screenshots of your unit while testing your application. Here's a quick rundown of the major features available to you through the Organizer.

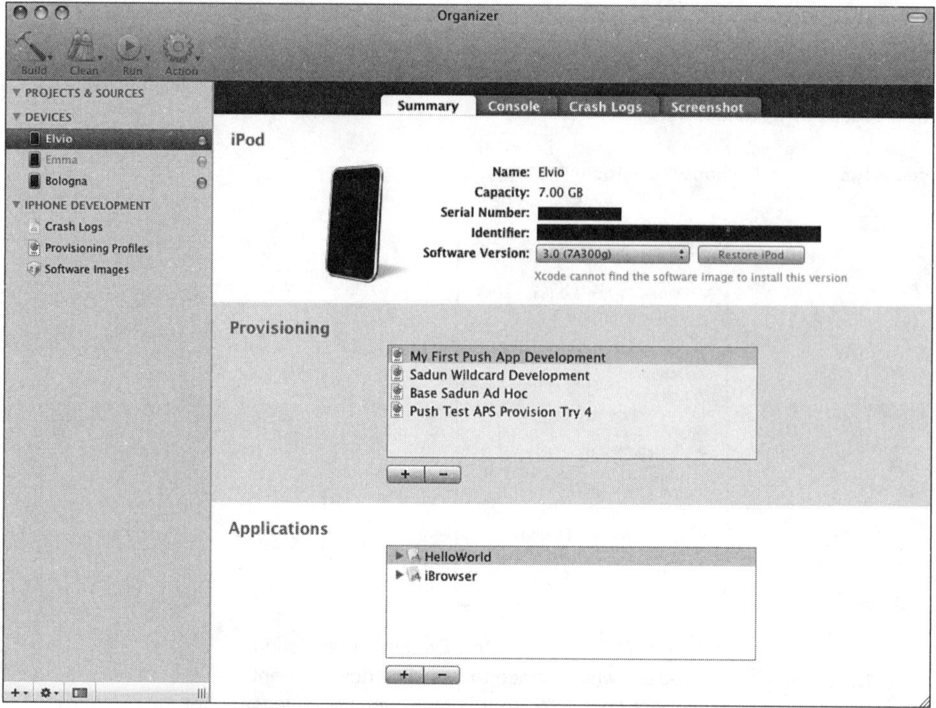

Figure 2-18 The Xcode-based iPhone Organizer window (Window > Organizer) provides a single control hub for most of your application testing needs. Here, you can load firmware, install and remove applications, read through crash logs, snap device-based screenshots, and more.

Projects and Sources List

Keep your current projects in easy reach by dragging them onto the Organizer. You can drag in the entire project folder. Once added, double-click the project file to open that project. You can add individual source files as well as complete projects. Use the Build, Clean, Run, and Action options at the top of the Organizer window, to perform even more development tasks directly from the Organizer.

In addition to storing files, the Projects and Sources list can be used for viewing the contents of sandboxes. When you download sandbox data from a device with the Summary tab, Xcode automatically adds that folder to this list, where you can browse through the file contents.

To remove items from this list, especially items that were added automatically and that you didn't choose to include, open the contextual pop-up. Right-click or control-click any item and choose Remove from Organizer, and then click OK. Doing so does not affect any files on your disk. You're not deleting files; you're just omitting the listing in the Projects and Sources list.

Devices List

The Devices list shows the name and status of those devices you've authorized as development platforms. The indicators to the right of each name show whether the device is attached (green light) or not (red light). A gray light indicates a unit that has not been set up for development or that it has been "ignored"—that is, removed from the active list. An amber light appears when a device has just been attached. Should the light remain amber-colored, you may have encountered a connection problem. This may be due to iTunes syncing, and the unit is not yet available, or there may be a problem connecting with the onboard services, in which case a reboot of your iPhone usually resolves any outstanding issues.

iPhone Development Tools

The items in this list offer Mac-based development resources. These include archival crash logs (i.e., not tied to a particular device but offloaded to your system), a Provisioning Profiles manager, and a Software Images list that shows the firmware bundles currently available on your system. The profile manager is particularly useful as it shows which device each profile is installed on, offers a profile identifier (so you can figure out which file in ~/Library/MobileDevice/Provisioning Profiles corresponds to which provision), and provides handy expiration date checks.

Summary Tab

The Summary tab tells you the name, capacity, serial number, and identifier of your iPhone or iPod touch. Here is where you can provision your unit (that is, authorize it to work with the projects you build in Xcode), add and remove applications, and load the latest firmware.

Each developer license allows you to provision your personal or corporate iPhones/iPod touches for testing. The Provisioning list shows a list of application provisions available to your unit. The provision determines which applications may or may not be run on the device. As a rule, only development and ad hoc distribution provisions are listed here, which makes sense. Distribution provisions are used to sign applications for the App Store, not for any specific device.

A list of installed applications appears at the bottom of the Summary tab. Use the – button to remove applications. To install an application, drag it onto the list or use the + button to browse for it. Make sure your application is compiled for the iPhone OS and that the device is provisioned to run that application. The application will immediately sync over. Applications installed from App Store are grayed out in the application list.

Open the disclosure triangle next to each application name to reveal the application data associated with that application. To download the application data, click the down-pointing arrow, choose a destination, and click Save. Xcode builds a dated folder and populates it with the contents of the sandbox, namely the Documents, Library, and tmp directories. Xcode also adds the folder to the Projects and Sources list, where you can browse the contents directly from the Organizer.

You can reverse this process and add edited sandboxes back to the device. Locate the folder you created (use Reveal in Finder from the contextual pop-up in Projects and Sources). Drop new items into any of the subfolders, and then drag the entire folder back onto the application name at the bottom of the Summary pane. Xcode reads the new items and instantly transfers them to the device. This is a great way to prepopulate your Documents folder with test material.

Console Tab

Use the console to view system messages from your connected units. This screen shows `NSLog()` calls as you're running software on the tethered iPhone. You need not be using Xcode's debugger to do this. The console listens in to any application currently running on the device.

In addition to the debugging messages you add to your iPhone applications, you also see system notices, device information, and debugging calls from Apple's system software. It's basically a text-based mess. Logged data also appears on the Xcode debugging console (Run > Console) along with any `printf` output. Click Save Log As to write the console contents out to disk.

Crash Logs Tab

Get direct access to your crash logs by selecting a particular crash (labeled with the iPhone application name and the date and time of the crash) from the scrolling list. The crash details, including a stack trace, thread information, exception types, and so forth, appear in the bottom pane.

In addition to crash logs that you generate yourself, you can also retrieve crash reports from users from their home computer and from iTunes Connect. The iPhone automatically syncs crash reports to computers when units back up to iTunes. These reports are stored in different locations depending on the platform used to sync the device:

- **Mac OS X**—~/Library/Logs/CrashReporter/MobileDevice/*DeviceName*
- **Windows XP**—C:\Documents and Settings*UserName*\Application Data\Apple Computer\Logs\CrashReporter\MobileDevice*DeviceName*
- **Windows Vista**—C:\Users*UserName*\AppData\Roaming\Apple Computer\Logs\CrashReporter\MobileDevice*DeviceName*

iTunes Connect collects crash log data from your App Store users and makes it available to you. Download reports by selecting Manage Your Applications > App Details > View Crash Report for any application. There you find a list of the most frequent crash types and Download Report buttons for each type.

Copy reports into the Mac OS X crash reporter folder and they load directly into the Organizer. Make sure to load them into the device folder for the currently selected device. The reports appear in IPHONE DEVELOPMENT > Crash Logs.

Once in the Organizer, Xcode uses the application binary and .dSYM file to replace the hexadecimal addresses normally supplied by the report with function and method names. This process is called *symbolication*. You don't have to manually locate these items; Xcode uses Spotlight and the application's unique identifier (UUID) to locate the original binary and .dSYM files so long as they exist somewhere in your home folder.

As with crash logs in the Organizer, the reports from users provide a stack trace that you can load into Xcode to detect where errors occurred. The trace always appears in reverse chronological order, so the first items in the list were the last ones executed.

In addition to showing you where the application crashed, Crash Reports also tell you why they crashed. The most common cause is EXC_BAD_ACCESS, which can be generated by accessing unmapped memory (KERN_INVALID_ADDRESS) or trying to write to read-only memory (KERN_PROTECTION_FAILURE).

Other essential items in the crash report include the OS version of the crash and the version of the application that crashed. Users do not always update software to the latest release, so it's important to distinguish which crashes arose from earlier, now potentially fixed, versions.

> **Note**
>
> See Apple Technical Note TN2151 for more details about iPhone OS Crash Reporting.

Screenshot Tab

Snap your tethered iPhone's screen by clicking the Capture button on the Screenshot tab. The screenshot feature takes a picture of whatever is running on the iPhone, whether your applications are open or not. So you can access shots of Apple's built-in software and any other applications running on the iPhone.

Once snapped, you can drag snapped images onto the desktop or save them as an open project's new Default.png image. Archival shots appear in a library on the left side of the window. To delete a screenshot, select one and press the Delete key to permanently remove it.

> **Note**
>
> Screenshots are stored in your home Library/Application Support/Developer/Shared/Xcode/Screenshots folder.

Using Compiler Directives

Xcode directives issue instructions to the compiler that can detect the platform and firmware you're building for. This lets you customize your application to safely take advantage of platform- or firmware-only features. Adding `#if` statements to your code lets you block or reveal functionality based on these options. To detect if your code is compiled for the simulator or for the iPhone, for example, use target defines: `TARGET_IPHONE_SIMULATOR` and `TARGET_OS_IPHONE`.

```
#if TARGET_IPHONE_SIMULATOR
    Code specific to simulator
#else
    Code specific to iPhone
#endif
```

The simple "OS 3 or later" version check lets you build OS-specific blocks. For example, you might want to include code specific to the 3.0 MapKit within these blocks so a program would still compile and run on 2.2.x devices. This approach lets you create version-specific builds. Your program will not adapt on the go to changing device conditions; as with the platform directive, this is a compile-time only check.

```
#ifdef _USE_OS_3_OR_LATER
    #import <MapKit/MapKit.h>
#endif
```

Another approach involves checking the minimum OS version required to run the application. For this, you can use any of the OS presets. This ensures that 3.0 code applies strictly to apps compiled for 3.0 and later.

```
#if __IPHONE_OS_VERSION_MIN_REQUIRED < 30000
    Pre-3.0 Code
#else
    3.0 Code
#endif
```

The values for the OS versions use the following basic naming pattern, which will presumably continue from 3.1 on. These definitions were pulled from a global set of iPhone defines. The next section shows you how to recover these for yourself.

```
#define __IPHONE_2_0 20000
#define __IPHONE_2_1 20100
#define __IPHONE_2_2 20200
#define __IPHONE_3_0 30000
```

Recovering iPhone-Specific Definitions

Although directive-specific definitions are not secret, they are not exactly well known. To check the current list of iPhone-specific defines, do the following. These steps dump a list from Xcode during compilation that you can use as a ready reference.

1. Open the Target Info window for the Hello World iPhone project from earlier in this chapter.
2. Add the following flags to the OTHER_CFLAGS in the Build tab: `-g3 -save-temps -dD`.

3. Build your project. It will compile with errors. Ignore these.

4. Open a Terminal shell and navigate to your project folder. Inside, you find a new file: main.mi.

5. Issue the following command: `grep -i iPhone main.mi | open -f`. This searches through the main.mi for all iPhone references and adds them to a new TextEdit document. This list contains all the currently defined macro elements. Save the list somewhere convenient.

6. Remove the custom flags from your project and save. You should now be able to rebuild without error.

> **Note**
>
> Platform-specific limitations like onboard camera or microphone access should also be addressed by your code. Read more about coding around these potential roadblocks in Chapter 14, "Device Capabilities."

Runtime Checks

Compiler directives allow you to build 2.x- and 3.x-specific versions of your applications. They do not, however, provide a way to run code that adapts to the current firmware.

To sell your application to the greatest number of customers, do not build for any SDK higher than your lowest desired customer. If your iPod customers are hesitant to pay for upgrades to newer firmware, you can still sell software that uses an older firmware specification so long as it has been thoroughly tested to run on newer firmware.

However, if you want to use more modern classes and calls, you either have to cut out older firmware customers entirely or you need to develop applications that provide those features while being compiled for earlier firmware. That means checking for compatibility at runtime rather than compile time.

You can accomplish this in a number of ways. First, you can check against the system running on the device, calling the firmware-appropriate methods. This sample does exactly that. It produces compile-time warnings for a 2.x build, letting you know that table cells may not respond to `textLabel`. This is not the preferred way of doing things. Apple recommends that you check for functionality and availability, not against specific firmware versions.

```
NSString *celltext = [[UIFont familyNames] objectAtIndex:
    [indexPath row]];
if ([[[UIDevice currentDevice] systemVersion] hasPrefix:@"2."])
    [cell setText:celltext];
else if ([[[UIDevice currentDevice] systemVersion] hasPrefix:@"3."])
    [[cell textLabel] setText:celltext];
return cell;
```

You can also test objects to see whether they respond to specific selectors. When 3.X versions of the frameworks are available, objects will report that they respond to those selectors, letting you call them without crashing the program. As with the previous approach, this too generates compile-time warnings about unimplemented selectors.

```
NSString *celltext = [[UIFont familyNames] objectAtIndex:
    [indexPath row]];
if (![cell respondsToSelector:@selector(textLabel)])
    [cell setText:celltext];
else
    [[cell textLabel] setText:celltext];
return cell;
```

To avoid those compile-time warnings, you can add 3.x specific interface declarations to your 2.x source.

```
@interface UITableViewCell (SDK3)
- (UILabel *) textLabel;
@end
```

A better approach, however, is to set the Base SDK and Deployment targets for your project. In Target Info > Build Settings, set Base SDK to the highest version of the OS you want to target, namely some 3.x version. Set the iPhone OS Deployment Target to the lowest OS version you intend to build for.

You can also use a variety of other workarounds like pulling the label out indirectly. This code retrieves the label and sets its text.

```
UILabel *label = (UILabel *)[cell valueForKey:@"textLabel"];
if (label) [label setText:celltext];
```

You can access 3.x classes from a 2.x build by using `NSClassFromString()`. Test to see whether the class returns nil. If not, the class is available for your use in the current firmware. Link against any framework you might use, regardless of whether it is available for the 2.x build.

```
Class MFMCVC = NSClassFromString(@"MFMailComposeViewController");
If (MFMVC) myMFMCViewController = [[MFMCVC alloc] init];
```

And if you really want to go hard core, you can build `NSInvocation` instances directly, as discussed in Chapter 3.

Pragma Marks

Pragma marks organize your source code by adding bookmarks into the method list pop-up button at the top of each Xcode window. This list shows all the methods and functions available in the current document. Adding pragma marks lets you group related items together, as shown in Figure 2-19. By clicking on these labels from the drop-down list, you can jump to a section of your file (for example, to `tag utilities`) as well as to a specific method (such as `-tagExists:`).

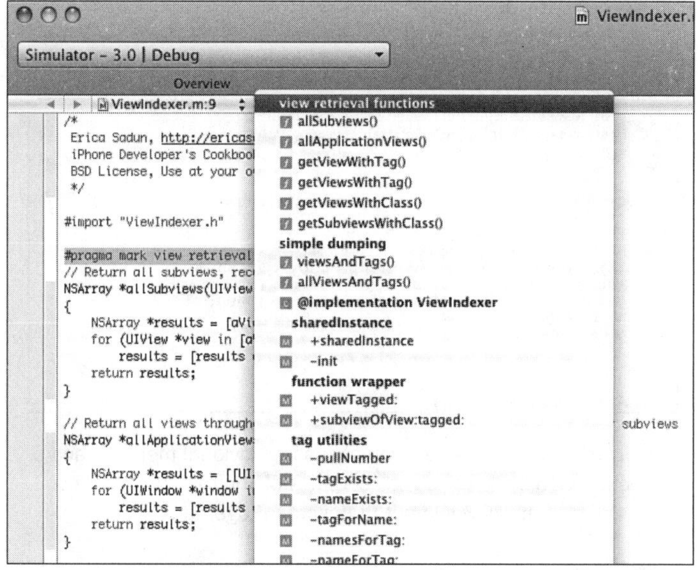

Figure 2-19 Use pragma marks to organize your method and function list.

To create a new bookmark, just add a simple pragma mark definition to your code. To replicate the first group in Figure 2-20, for example, add:

```
#pragma mark view retrieval functions
```

You can also add a separation line with a special pragma mark call. Do not add any text after the hyphen or Xcode will add a normal bookmark, not a spacer.

```
#pragma mark -
```

The marks have no functionality and otherwise do not affect your code. They are simply organizational tools that you choose to use or not.

Collapsing Methods

When you need to see more than one part of your code at once, Xcode lets you close and open method groups. Place your mouse in the gutter directly to the left of any method. A pair of disclosure triangles appears. Click a triangle and Xcode collapses the code for that method, as shown in Figure 2-20. The ellipsis indicates the collapsed method. Click again on the disclosure triangle, and Xcode reveals the collapsed code.

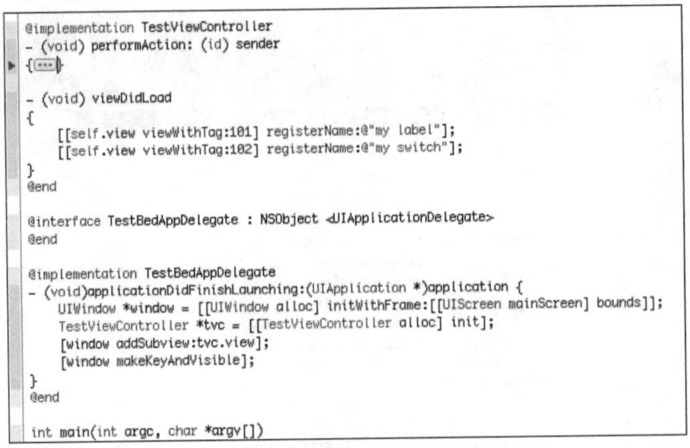

```
@implementation TestViewController
- (void) performAction: (id) sender
{...}

- (void) viewDidLoad
{
    [[self.view viewWithTag:101] registerName:@"my label"];
    [[self.view viewWithTag:102] registerName:@"my switch"];
}
@end

@interface TestBedAppDelegate : NSObject <UIApplicationDelegate>
@end

@implementation TestBedAppDelegate
- (void)applicationDidFinishLaunching:(UIApplication *)application {
    UIWindow *window = [[UIWindow alloc] initWithFrame:[[UIScreen mainScreen] bounds]];
    TestViewController *tvc = [[TestViewController alloc] init];
    [window addSubview:tvc.view];
    [window makeKeyAndVisible];
}
@end

int main(int argc, char *argv[])
```

Figure 2-20 Xcode lets you collapse individual methods and functions. This allows you to see parts of your program that normally would not fit onscreen together.

Building for Distribution

Building for distribution means creating a version of your application that can be submitted to Apple for sale in the App Store. Before you even think about building, know how to clean up builds, how to create a distribution configuration, and how to find your built product. You want to compile for the App Store with precision. Cleaning first, then compiling with a preset distribution configuration helps ensure that your application uploads properly. Locating the built application lets you compress and submit the right file. The following sections cover these skills and others needed for distribution compiles.

Creating and Editing Configurations

In Xcode, configurations store build settings. They act as a quick reference to the way you want to have everything set up, so you can be ready to compile for your device or for the App Store just by selecting a configuration. Standard Xcode projects offer Debug and Release configurations. You may want to create a few others, such as ones for regular or ad hoc distribution.

Assuming you've been following along in this chapter, you have already set up the HelloWorld project and edited its debug build settings. It uses your development wild-card provision to sign the application. Instead of editing the build settings each time you want to switch the signing provision, you can create a new configuration instead.

In the Project window, select the HelloWorld group at the top of the Groups & Files column. Click the blue Info button to open the Project Info window. This window contains four tabs: General, Build, Configurations, and Comments. Open the Configurations tab.

Select the Debug configuration that you have already customized and click the Duplicate button in the bottom-left of the window. Xcode creates a copy and opens a text entry field for its name, as shown in Figure 2-21. Edit the name from Debug copy to Distribution. For real world development, you may want to edit and/or duplicate the Release configuration rather than the Debug one. This example uses Debug as it's already customized.

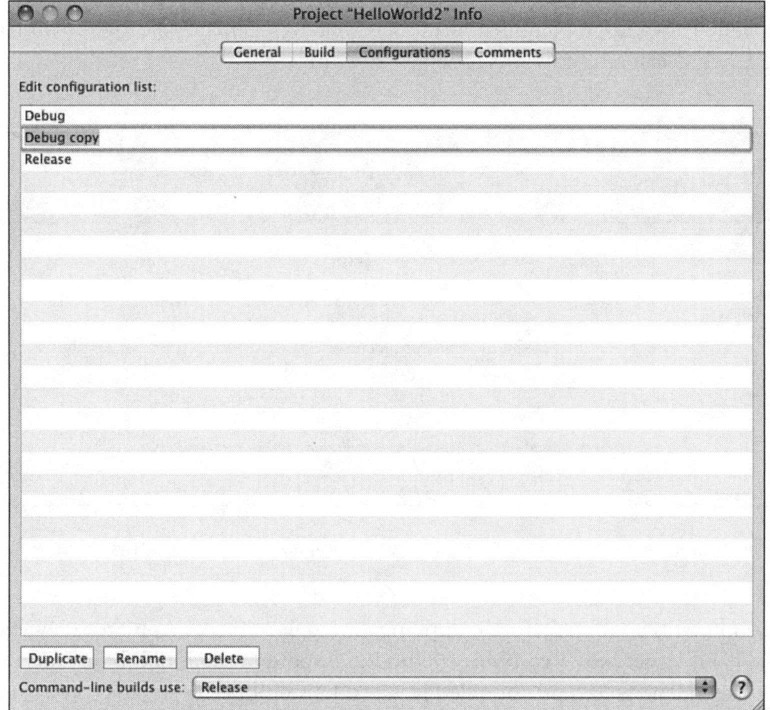

Figure 2-21 Use the Project Info configuration window to create new configurations so you can build with preset options such as signing identities.

Next, click the Build tab and choose the new Distribution option from the Configuration pop-up. It's important that you do so; otherwise, you'll be editing whatever configuration was last used. Locate the Code Signing Identity and set Any iPhone OS Device to your wild-card distribution profile. When you have done so, close the Project Info window.

Following these steps adds a distribution configuration to your project, allowing you to select it when you're ready to compile. Remember that you must create a separate configuration for each project. Configurations do not transfer from project to project and are stored as part of each project's settings.

Clean Builds

Clean builds ensure that every part of your project is recompiled from scratch. Doing a clean also ensures that your project build contains current versions of your project assets including images and sounds. You can force a clean build by deleting the build folder inside your project folder and you can use Xcode's built-in utility. Choose Build > Clean (Command-Shift-K). As Figure 2-22 shows, Xcode prompts you to choose whether to clean dependencies and precompiled headers as well. As a general rule, there's no harm in agreeing. Click Clean and wait as Xcode gets to work.

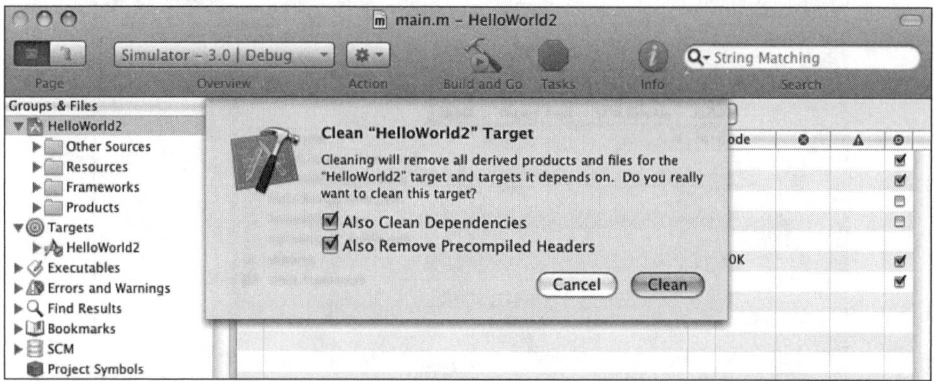

Figure 2-22 Xcode can thoroughly clean compiled artifacts from your project.

Apple recommends cleaning before compiling any application for App Store review, and it's a good habit to get into. I combine methods. I dispose of the build folder and then clean out dependencies and precompiled headers. This produces a single product that is easily located and won't be confused with other build versions.

Compiling for the App Store

To build your application in compliance with the App Store's submission policies, it must be signed by a valid distribution provision profile using an active developer identity. If you've properly set up a developer configuration, most of this is taken care of for you. Here's what's left.

- Select Device as the active SDK. I can't tell you how many people have attempted to submit simulator builds to App Store only to be frustrated for hours before discovering their error.
- Choose Distribution as the active configuration. You may want to open the Target Info window and confirm that your application identifier and code signing identity are set properly. Check that the Configuration at the top of the window is set to

Active (Distribution) or Distribution. The Overview pop-up in the project window should say Device | Distribution.

- Compile your application using Build > Compile (Command-K). Your application should compile without errors. If not, reconsider your readiness to submit to the App Store.
- Locate the compiled product. In the Groups & Files column, find the Products group. Open it and right-click/Control-click your compiled application. It should appear in black and not in red. Choose Reveal in Finder from the contextual pop-up.
- Use the Finder window to confirm that your build is located in a folder ending with the name iphoneos. (Again, you cannot submit simulator builds to the App Store.)
- Right-click (Control-click) the application and compress it. You will submit the zip file to the App Store through iTunes Connect.

If your application is larger than 10MB, use Apple's OS X application loader utility to submit your application to the App Store. This program is available for download through iTunes Connect on the Managing Your Applications page. Scroll to the very bottom and click Get Application Loader.

Debugging App Store Uploads

At times, it proves difficult to upload your application to the App Store. You log in to iTunes Connect. You set up your application details and get ready to upload your binary, but when you do, iTunes Connect rejects the binary. In a big pink message, the Web site tells you your upload has failed. Do you have a real signature problem? Are your certificates invalid? Sometimes you do have a signature problem and sometimes you don't. Here are a few steps that can help. Some of these you've just read about in the previous section; others are new. Make sure you go down the entire list until you've resolved your problem.

Start by visiting the program portal and make sure that your developer certificate is up to date. It expires after a certain period of time (typically one year) and if you haven't reissued a new one, you cannot submit software to App Store. If your certificate has expired, you need to request a new one and to build new provisioning profiles to match. For most people experiencing the "pink upload of doom," though, their certificates are already valid and Xcode is properly configured.

Return to Xcode and check that you've set the active SDK to one of the device choices, like Device - 3.0. Accidentally leaving the build settings set to Simulator can be a big reason for the pink rejection. Next, make sure that you've chosen a build configuration that uses your distribution (not your developer) certificate. Check this by double-clicking on your target in the Groups & Files column on the left of the project window. The Target Info window opens. Click the Build tab and review your Code Signing Identity. It should be iPhone Distribution: followed by your name or company name.

The top-left of your project window also confirms your settings and configuration. It should read something like "Device | Distribution," showing you the active SDK and the active configuration. If your settings are correct but you still aren't getting that upload finished properly, clean your builds. Choose Build > Clean (Command-Shift-K) and click Clean. Alternatively, you can manually trash the build folder in your Project from Finder. Once you've cleaned, build again fresh.

Avoid spaces and special characters in the name of the zip archive you upload to iTunes Connect. You cannot rename your app file but you can freely rename the zip archive. Name issues can cause problems with some application uploads. So long as the data inside the zip archive includes the proper application, the name of the zip file really doesn't matter.

If this does not produce an app that when zipped properly loads to iTunes Connect, do this: Quit and relaunch Xcode. This one simple trick solves more signing problems and "pink rejections of doom" than any other solution already mentioned. Quit, restart Xcode, clean your build, rebuild, zip, and submit. For most developers, this final step is all it takes to get past the invalid submission screen.

Assuming you are still having problems, download a copy of Apple's OS X Application Loader from iTunes Connect on the Manage Your Application page. Instead of uploading directly, check the box that says Check Here to Upload Your Binary Later and use the loader to submit the archive.

If you're still having trouble submitting to the App Store, consider compressing with a third-party archiver or try copying the application to the desktop before zipping it up. This sometimes solves the problem, creating an acceptable submission for an application that is otherwise properly signed. Some files rejected by the iTunes Connect Web site may be uploaded without error through the Application Loader.

Try launching Terminal and navigating to your compiled application. Run `codesign -vvv YourApplication.app`, substituting the actual application name to see whether any errors are reported about invalid signatures.

If you continue to have application submission problems even after walking through all these steps, contact Apple. Send an e-mail to iTunes Connect (they do not have a public phone) and explain your situation. Tell them that you've checked your certificates, that they are all valid, and mention the steps you've already tried. They may be able to help figure out why you're still getting pink-rejected when you try to submit your apps. For everybody else, the checklist items you've already seen are probably enough to help you move past your submission issues and get your app on the way to review.

Note

When renewing your developer and distribution certificates, you must reissue all your mobile provisions. Throw away the old ones and create new ones with your updated developer identity. Make sure to remove the outdated certificates from your keychain when replacing them with the new ones.

Building for Ad Hoc Distribution

Apple allows you to distribute your applications outside the App Store via ad hoc distribution. With ad hoc, you can send your applications to up to 100 registered devices and run those applications using a special kind of mobile provision that allows the applications to execute under the iPhone's FairPlay restrictions. Ad hoc distribution is especially useful for beta testing and for submitting review applications to news sites and magazines.

Register Devices

The ad hoc process starts with registering devices. Use the iPhone developer program portal to add device identifiers (Program Portal, Devices) and names to your account. Recover these identifiers from the iPhone directly (use the `UIDevice` calls from Chapter 9, "Building and Using Controls"), from Xcode's Organizer (copy the identifier from the Summary tab), from iTunes (click on Serial Number in the iPhone's Summary tab), from System Profiler (select USB, iPhone, Serial Number), or via Ad Hoc Helper from iTunes. Enter the identifier and a unique username.

Build the Ad Hoc Provision

If you have not done so already, build your Ad Hoc provision. To build a mobile provision, select Program Portal > Provisioning > Distribution. Click Add Profile. Select Ad Hoc, enter a profile name, your standard wildcard application identifier (for example, `com.yourname.*`), and select the device or devices to deploy on. Don't forget to check your identity and then click Submit and wait for Apple to build the new mobile provision. Download the provision file and drop it onto the Xcode application icon. You will use it to build your application. You may want to restart Xcode after adding the provision.

Add an Entitlement File to Your Project

A special entitlement file is needed in ad hoc projects. (See Apple Technical Note TN2242.) In Xcode, choose File > New File > Code Signing > Entitlements. Click Next. Create a new entitlement called dist.plist. Click Finish. This creates a new file and adds it to your project. The name of the entitlement file is arbitrary.

Locate the new entitlements file. The file contains a single property that you must edit. Double-click to open it in an editor and uncheck `get-task-allow` (that is, set it to a Boolean value of FALSE). Save your changes and close the file.

Add the Entitlement to Your Settings

After setting up your entitlement, you need to add it to your target settings. With the Ad Hoc configuration selected, open the Target Info window. Make sure that the configuration pop-up in the Target Info window also says Ad Hoc. If it does not, select it.

In the Build tab, choose your Ad Hoc provision for your Code Signing Identity. Then, double-click Code Signing Entitlements. This pops up an interactive dialog. Click + and add the filename dist.plist to the Code Signing Entitlement (see Figure 2-23) and click OK. Alternatively, you can drag the entitlements file onto the Code Signing Entitlements field.

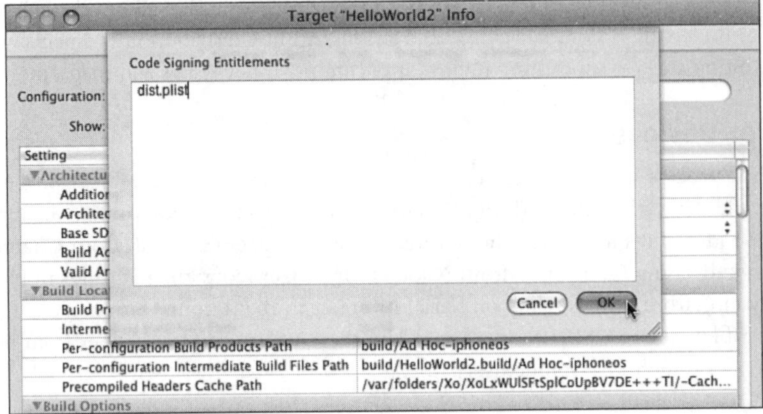

Figure 2-23 Add dist.plist as a new code signing entitlement for Ad Hoc distribution builds.

Build Your Ad Hoc Application

Now you're ready to build your application. Make sure your Code Signing Identity is set to your ad hoc provision. Select Build > Build (Command-B). You can find the newly compiled product via the Products group in the project window. Right-click (Control-click) it and choose Reveal in Finder. A Finder window opens, showing the compiled item.

Distribute a copy of this application, which you just compiled with the mobile ad hoc provision, along with the provision itself that you downloaded from Apple. Your user can drop the provision and the application into iTunes before syncing your application to his or her iPhone. The application runs only on those phones you registered, providing a secure way to distribute these apps directly to your user.

Adding Artwork to Ad Hoc Distributions

Normally, iTunes does not display artwork for ad hoc programs. By default, it shows a stylized "A" instead. Fortunately, you can work around this. iPhone developer Malcolm Hall taught me how to set up ad hoc applications so they display the proper image.

Create a folder in Finder and populate it with two items. The first is a 512x512 JPEG image called iTunesArtwork. The second is a folder called Payload. Add the application bundle (do not compress it) into the Payload subfolder. Then zip up the entire folder and rename the zip file to *Appname*.ipa, where the name of the application matches the bundle you included in the Payload subfolder.

This IPA package (IPA stands for *iPhone application*) mimics the way that Apple provides applications for iTunes. When iTunes sees the iTunesArtwork file, it uses it to create the image seen in the Applications library.

Add the iTunesArtwork file without an explicit extension. If needed, remove any existing extension by renaming the file at the command line. Although the file needs to be in JPEG format, it should not use the standard .jpg or .jpeg naming.

> **Note**
>
> When distributing ad hoc builds to Windows Vista clients, instruct users to unzip the IPA first and then add the unzipped folder into iTunes. Vista apparently unzips the file incorrectly, resulting in application verification errors.

Customizing Xcode Identities

By definition, Xcode builds the following header into all your source code. Each of the items contained within the double chevrons is a variable and is set at the time the code gets created. Your user and organization names are retrieved from your Address Book, where they correspond to your personal contact information. The icon for this contact is marked with "me"—as shown in Figure 2-24.

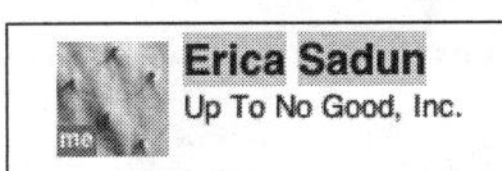

Figure 2-24 In OS X's address book, the contact used for personalizing Xcode files is marked with a "me" in the corner of the user's icon.

```
/*
 *  main.m
 *  <<PROJECTNAME>>
 *
 *  Created by <<FULLUSERNAME>> on <<DATE>>.
 *  Copyright (c) <<YEAR>> <<ORGANIZATIONNAME>>. All rights reserved.
 *
 */
```

You can override these settings with a pair of defaults that you assign at the command line. The following `defaults` command sets the organization and username to values different from those found in the address book. When used, these custom settings override the address book entry.

```
defaults write com.apple.Xcode PBXCustomTemplateMacroDefinitions
'{ORGANIZATIONNAME = "Apple, Inc." ; FULLUSERNAME = "Jonathan I.}'
```

You can also update the Organization Name in the Project Info > General settings on a project-by-project basis.

Unfortunately, the one string most iPhone developers want to override cannot be set by defaults. The `com.yourcompany` identifier that appears in new projects is hard coded into Xcode templates. If you want to change that identifier, you must edit Apple's built-in templates or, better yet, create copies of those templates and edit them in your own user library.

Creating Custom Xcode Templates

When you create new projects in Xcode, the program lets you select a template. You can choose from iPhone and Mac OS X options that let you craft your application from any number of predesigned program skeletons. For the iPhone, these include view-based applications and applications built with OpenGL ES. On the Mac, you can build dynamic libraries, command-line utilities, and apps built with Cocoa, among many others.

Sometimes, though, you find yourself taking the same steps over and over to customize your projects to your own particular in-house design including updating that company identifier. Fortunately, Xcode lets you add user templates that you can precustomize so you can always start your new projects off where you really need to begin, not just where Apple left off. Jay Abbott of TinyPlay.com first showed me how to do this. His instructions involve making a copy of one of Apple's templates, dragging it to a folder in your application support library, and customizing it.

Apple stores its project templates in Xcode's /Developer directory. iPhone project templates are found in /Developer/Platforms/iPhoneOS.platform/Developer/Library/Xcode/Project Templates/Application. Each folder in that directory corresponds to a single template.

Overriding com.yourcompany

Replacing com.yourcompany is one of the simplest patches you can make. To start, copy the entire Application folder from the developer templates to your desktop. Search each folder for instances of com.yourcompany inside Info.plist files and edit them to match the actual identifier for your wild-card provisions. Make sure you look in subfolders in the templates to locate all Info.plist files. Use caution when editing and avoid changing any of the normal formatting information.

Once patched, locate the Library/Application Support/Developer/Shared/Xcode folder in your home directory. Create a Project Templates folder there and move the Application folder from the Desktop into that folder. When you next launch Xcode, it adds a new User Templates section and lists your version of the Application templates there, as shown in Figure 2-25.

Selecting a template from User Templates rather than from iPhone OS loads your customized version, complete with the patched Info.plist. When you create new projects this way, you ensure that the application identifier has been preset to match your provisions.

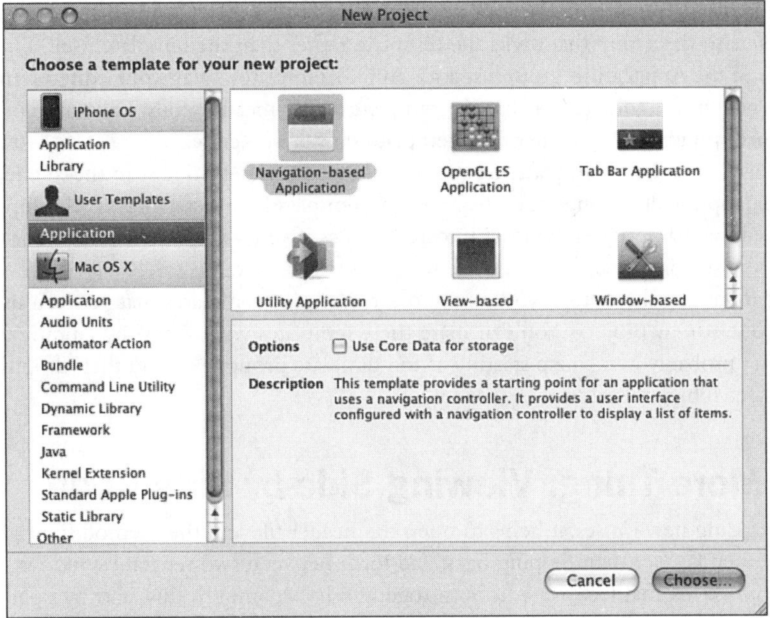

Figure 2-25 Xcode lets you create new projects from custom User Templates. These templates are stored in your home library folder in a special Xcode directory.

Building Other Templates

There's a lot more you can do with custom templates than just editing a single string. Think of user templates as a jumping off point for any project development you can think of. You can add custom images like your company logo or often-used classes. Any materials added to a template become available to Xcode to clone into new projects. If you find yourself repeating the same customization tasks again and again with Apple's templates, a custom template will save you those steps. Custom templates can save you a lot of work. By carefully going through the project initialization process once, you can build on that well-executed start for all your projects.

Survey the existing templates. Copy whichever template best matches your goal onto your desktop. Adapt the folder by editing, trimming, and/or augmenting the files within. You need to update the project in Xcode to set it up. You might add Distribution and ad hoc configurations including your ad hoc entitlement file. Avoid setting provisioning profiles in the Target Info window, however. Once a template hard codes a signing identity, it becomes difficult to switch to other configurations. Perform however many edits you need.

Make sure that the template actually compiles and, if working with iPhone source, that it runs properly in the simulator. Save your work and then delete the build folder. Also delete the user-specific files in the xcodeproj subdirectory that contain your username. (You need to delete these files again should you ever reedit your project.)

Decide on a group name for your new template such as My Custom Templates. This name refers to the group that owns the template rather than the template itself. This corresponds to the Application group used for Apple's templates. Drag your edited template into the new group folder. Rename the template folder meaningfully. The name of the folder corresponds to the name of the template shown in Xcode.

To finish, update the template description in the TemplateInfo.plist in the xcodeproj folder and, optionally, change the images in the TemplateIcons.icns file. Xcode ships with an icon editor that lets you paste art into ICNS files if you want. Otherwise, the icon defaults to the standard image used by the template you copied.

After following these steps, you'll have created custom templates that you can use in Xcode to start new projects. You can share these templates with others by zipping up their folders. It's probably best to zip starting at the template group level and then drop them into Project Templates folders.

One More Thing: Viewing Side-by-Side Code

When building new classes, it helps to open the header file and the method file right next to each other. Rather than flipping back and forth between two separate windows, Xcode offers a nifty trick that lets you edit both together. To accomplish this, start by opening the .m file in a standard editor.

Locate the top-right corner of the edit area, just under the Ungrouped and Project buttons. There, you see several icons in the corner. The corner is shaped like a lock and just underneath it is a bifurcated square. Hover your mouse over that square and confirm that the tool tip says Click to Split the Editor View.

Press the Option key and with the key pressed, click that square. The Option-click combination creates a vertical split rather than the default horizontal split normally introduced by the button. Once split, notice the new button that appears under the split button. It's a merge button, and when you're ready to do so, clicking it returns the window to a single unsplit display. For now, leave the display split.

Next, move your mouse up and to the left of the lock corner square. The tool tip for this button should read Go to Counterpart. This is used to switch between .h and .m views. Click it. (Alternatively, press Command-Option-Up Arrow.) After doing so, the screen updates, as shown in Figure 2-26, to display both the .m (at the left) and .h (at the right) versions of a class definition file in a single editor. This provides you with both items in a single window, making it simple to refer back and forth.

If you need to, you can resize the window and reapportion the two panes. The resize bar occurs just to the right of the scrollbar for the left-hand view. It's hard to see at first, but when you move your mouse onto the right spot, the cursor updates to the double-arrowed resizer. Click and drag to perform the resize.

> **Note**
>
> Command-double-click on any class or method to automatically load the associated header file.

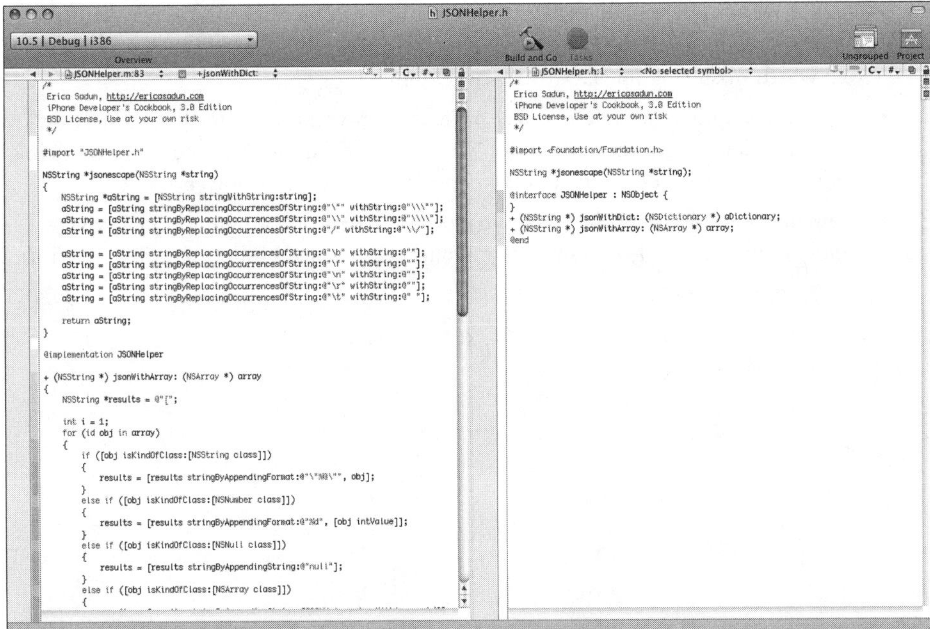

Figure 2-26 Xcode lets you edit header and method class sources in a single window.

Summary

This chapter covered a lot of ground. From start to finish, you saw how to create, compile, and debug Xcode projects. You were introduced to most of the major Xcode components that you'll use on a day-to-day basis, and you read about many of the different ways you can produce and run iPhone projects. Here are some thoughts to take away from this chapter.

- Although Xcode provides easy-to-use templates, think of them as a jumping off point not an endpoint. You can customize and edit projects however you want, and, as you read in this chapter, you can turn those edited projects into new templates.
- Interface Builder makes it really easy to lay out views. Although technically, you're producing the same method calls and property assignments as if you'd designed by hand, IB's elegant GUI transforms those design tasks into the visual domain, which is a welcome place for many developers.
- Learning to navigate through Xcode's in-program reference documentation is an essential part of becoming an iPhone developer. No one can keep all that information in his or her head. The more you master the documentation interface, the better you'll be at finding the class, method, or property you need to move forward.
- Everything changes. Subscribe to iPhone OS documentation in Xcode and ensure that your documentation remains as up-to-date as possible.

- Xcode's built-in debugger and Instruments tools help you fix bugs faster than trying to figure out everything by hand. The tools may seem complex at first but are well worth mastering for day-to-day development.
- Get to know and love the Organizer pane. It gives you critical feedback for knowing which devices are connected and what state they are in. And the other tools, including the screenshot utility and the console, just add to its power.
- Configurations help prevent repetitive work. Once set, a configuration lets you choose how to compile and sign your application with a minimum of further effort.

3

Objective-C Boot Camp

Most iPhone development centers on Objective-C. It is the standard programming language for both the iPhone and for Mac OS X. It offers a powerful object-oriented language that lets you build applications that leverage Apple's Cocoa and Cocoa Touch frameworks. In this chapter, you learn basic Objective-C skills that help you get started with iPhone programming. You learn about interfaces, methods, properties, memory management, and more. To round things out, this chapter takes you beyond Objective-C into Cocoa to show you the core classes you'll use in day-to-day programming and offers you concrete examples of how these classes work.

The Objective-C Programming Language

Objective-C is a strict superset of ANSI C. C is a compiled, procedural programming language developed in the early 1970s at AT&T. Objective-C, which was developed by Brad J. Cox, adds object-oriented features to C, blending C language constructs with concepts that originated in Smalltalk-80. Smalltalk is one of the earliest and best-known object-oriented languages, which was developed at Xerox PARC. Cox layered Smalltalk's object and message passing system on top of standard C to create his new language. This allowed programmers to continue using familiar C-language development while accessing object-based features from within that language. In the late 1980s, Objective-C was adopted as the primary development language for the NeXTStep operating system by Steve Jobs's startup computer company NeXT. NeXTStep became both the spiritual and literal ancestor of OS X. The current version of Objective-C is 2.0, which was released in October 2007 along with OS X Leopard.

Object-oriented programming brings features to the table that are missing in standard C. Objects refer to data structures that are associated with a preset list of function calls. Every object in Objective-C has *instance variables*, which are the fields of the data structure, and *methods*, which are the function calls the object can execute. Object-oriented code uses these objects and methods to introduce programming abstractions that increase code readability and reliability.

Object-oriented programming lets you build reusable code units that can be decoupled from the normal flow of procedural development. Instead of relying on process flow, object-oriented programs are developed around smart data structures provided by objects and their methods. Cocoa Touch on the iPhone and Cocoa on Mac OS X offer a massive library of these smart objects. Objective-C unlocks that library and lets you build on Apple's toolbox to create effective, powerful applications with a minimum of effort and code.

> **Note**
>
> The iPhone's Cocoa Touch class names that start with NS, such as `NSString` and `NSArray`, hearken back to NeXT. NS stands for NeXTStep, the operating system that ran on NeXT computers.

Classes and Objects

Objects are the heart of object-oriented programming. You define objects by building classes, which act as object creation templates. In Objective-C, a class definition specifies how to build new objects that belong to the class. So to create a "widget" object, you define the Widget class and then use that class to create new objects on demand.

Each class lists its instance variables and methods in a public header file using the standard C .h convention. For example, you might define a `Car` object like the one shown in Listing 3-1. The Car.h header file shown here contains the interface that declares how a `Car` object is structured. Note that all classes in Objective-C should be capitalized.

Listing 3-1 **Declaring the Car Interface (Car.h)**

```
#import <Foundation/Foundation.h>
@interface Car : NSObject
{
    int year;
    NSString *make;
    NSString *model;
}
- (void) setMake:(NSString *) aMake andModel:(NSString *) aModel
    andYear: (int) aYear;
- (void) printCarInfo;
- (int) year;
@end
```

In Objective-C, the `@` symbol is used to indicate certain keywords. The two items shown here (`@interface` and `@end`) delineate the start and end of the class interface definition. This class definition describes an object with three instance variables: year, make, and model. These three items are declared between the braces at the start of the interface.

The year instance variable is declared as an integer (using `int`). Make and model are strings, specifically instances of `NSString`. Objective-C uses this object-based class for the most part rather than the byte-based C strings defined with `char *`. As you see throughout this book, `NSString` offers far more power than C strings. With this class, you can find out a string's length, search for and replace substrings, reverse strings, retrieve file extensions, and more. These features are all built into the base Cocoa Touch object library.

This class definition also declares three public methods. The first is called `setMake:andModel:andYear:`. This entire three-part declaration, including the colons, is the name of that single method. That's because Objective-C places parameters inside the method name. In C, you'd use a function like `setProperties(char *c1, char *c2, int i)`. Objective-C's approach, although heftier than the C approach, provides much more clarity and self-documentation. You don't have to guess what `c1`, `c2`, and `i` mean because their use is declared directly within the name:

```
[myCar setMake:c1 andModel:c2 andYear:i];
```

The three methods are typed as `void`, `void`, and `int`. As in C, these refer to the type of data returned by the method. The first two do not return data, the third returns an integer. In C, the equivalent function declaration to the second and third method would be `void printCarInfo()` and `int year();`.

Using Objective-C's method-name-interspersed-with-arguments approach can feel odd to new programmers but quickly becomes a much-loved feature. There's no need to guess which argument to pass when the method name itself tells you what items go where. In Objective-C, method names are also interchangeably called *selectors*. You see this a lot in iPhone programming, especially when you use calls to `performSelector:`, which lets you send messages to objects at runtime.

Notice that this header file uses `#import` to load headers rather than `#include`. Importing headers in Objective-C automatically skips files that have already been added. This lets you add duplicate `#import` directives to your various source files without any penalties.

Note

The code for this example, and all the examples in this chapter, is found in the sample code for this book. See the Preface for details about downloading the book sample code from the Internet.

Creating Objects

To create an object, you tell Objective-C to allocate the memory needed for the object and return a pointer to that object. Because Objective-C is an object-oriented language, its syntax looks a little different from regular C. Instead of just calling functions, you ask an object to do something. This takes the form of two elements within square brackets, the object receiving the message followed by the message itself, `[object message]`.

Here, the source code sends the message `alloc` to the `Car` class, and then sends the message `init` to the newly allocated `Car` object. This nesting is typical in Objective-C.

```
Car *myCar = [[Car alloc] init];
```

The "allocate followed by init" pattern you see here represents the most common way to instantiate a new object. The class `Car` performs the `alloc` method. It allocates a new block of memory sufficient to store all the instance variables listed in the class definition, zeroes out any instance variables, and returns a pointer. The newly allocated block is called an *instance* and represents a single object in memory.

Some classes, like views, use specialized initializers such as `initWithFrame:`. You can write custom ones like `initWithMake: andModel: andYear:`. The pattern of allocation followed by initialization to create new objects holds universally. You create the object in memory and then you preset any critical instance variables.

Memory Allocation

In this example, the memory allocated is 16 bytes in size. Notice that both make and model are pointers, as indicated by the asterisk. In Objective-C, object variables point to the object itself. The pointer is 4 bytes in size. So `sizeof(myCar)` returns 4. The object consists of two 4-byte pointers, one integer, plus one additional field that does not derive from the `Car` class.

That extra field is from the `NSObject` class. Notice NSObject at the right of the colon next to the word Car in the class definition of Listing 3-1. `NSObject` is the parent class of `Car`, and `Car` inherits all instance variables and methods from this parent. That means that `Car` is a type of `NSObject` and any memory allocation needed by `NSObject` instances is inherited by the `Car` definition. So that's where the extra 4 bytes come from.

The final size of the allocated object is 16 bytes in total. That size includes two 4-byte NSString pointers, one 4-byte int, and one 4-byte allocation inherited from NSObject. You can easily print out the size of objects using C's `sizeof` function. This code uses standard C `printf` statements to send text information to the console. `printf` commands work just as well in Objective-C as they do in ANSI C.

```
NSObject *object = [[NSObject alloc] init];
Car *myCar = [[Car alloc] init];

// This returns 4, the size of an object pointer
printf("object pointer: %d\n", sizeof(object));

// This returns 4, the size of an NSObject object
printf("object itself: %d\n", sizeof(*object));

// This returns 4, again the size of an object pointer
printf("myCar pointer: %d\n", sizeof(myCar));

// This returns 16, the size of a Car object
printf("myCar object: %d\n", sizeof(*myCar));
```

Releasing Memory

In C, you allocate memory with `malloc()` or a related call and free that memory with `free()`. In Objective-C, you allocate memory with `alloc` and free it with `release`. (In Objective-C, you can also allocate memory a few other ways, such as by copying other objects.)

```
[object release];
[myCar release];
```

As discussed in Chapter 2, "Building Your First Project," releasing memory is a little more complicated than in standard C. That's because Objective-C uses a reference-counted memory system. Each object in memory has a retain count associated with it. You can see that retain count by sending `retainCount` to the object. Every object is created with a retain count of 1. Sending `release` reduces that retain count by one. When the retain count for an object reaches zero, it is released into the general memory pool.

```
Car *myCar = [[Car alloc] init];

// The retain count is 1 after creation
printf("The retain count is %d\n", [myCar retainCount]);

// This reduces the retain count to 0
[myCar release];

// This causes an error. The object has already been freed
printf("Retain count is now %d\n", [myCar retainCount]);
```

Sending messages to freed objects will crash your application. When the second `printf` executes, the `retainCount` message is sent to the already-freed `myCar`. This creates a memory access violation, terminating the program.

```
The retain count is 1
objc[10754]: FREED(id): message retainCount sent to freed
object=0xd1e520
```

There is no garbage collection on the iPhone. As a developer, you must manage your objects. Keep them around for the span of their use and free their memory when you are finished. Read more about basic memory management strategies later in this chapter.

Methods, Messages, and Selectors

In standard C, you'd perform two function calls to allocate and initialize data. Here is how that might look, in contrast to Objective-C's `[[Car alloc] init]` statement.

```
Car *myCar = malloc(sizeof(Car));
init(myCar);
```

Objective-C doesn't use `function_name(argument)` syntax. Instead, you send messages to objects using square brackets. Messages tell the object to perform a method. It is the object's responsibility to implement that method and produce a result. The first item within the brackets is the receiver of the message, the second item is a method name, and possibly some arguments to that method that together define the message you want sent. In C, you might write

```
printCarInfo(myCar);
```

but in Objective-C, you say:

```
[myCar printCarInfo];
```

Despite the difference in syntax, methods are basically functions that operate on objects. They are typed using the same types available in standard C. Unlike function calls, Objective-C places limits on who can implement and call methods. Methods belong to classes. And the class interface defines which of these are declared to the outside world.

Dynamic Typing

Objective-C uses dynamic typing in addition to static typing. Static typing restricts a variable declaration to a specific class at compile time. With dynamic typing, the runtime system, not the compiler, takes responsibility for asking objects what methods they can perform and what class they belong to. That means you can choose what messages to send and which objects to send them to as the program runs. This is a powerful feature, one that is normally identified with interpreted systems like Lisp. You can choose an object, programmatically build a message, and send the message to the object all without knowing which object will be picked and what message will be sent at compile time.

With power, of course, comes responsibility. You can only send messages to objects that actually implement the method described by that selector (unless that class can handle messages that don't have implementations by implementing Objective-C invocation forwarding, which is discussed at the end of this chapter). Sending `printCarInfo` to an array object, for example, causes a runtime error and crashes the program. Arrays do not define that method. Only objects that implement a given method can respond to the message properly and execute the code that was requested.

```
2009-05-08 09:04:31.978 HelloWorld[419:20b] *** -[NSCFArray printCarInfo]:
➥unrecognized selector sent to instance 0xd14e80
2009-05-08 09:04:31.980 HelloWorld[419:20b] *** Terminating app due to uncaught
➥exception 'NSInvalidArgumentException', reason: '*** -[NSCFArray
➥printCarInfo]: unrecognized selector sent to instance 0xd14e80'
```

During compilation, Objective-C performs object message checks using static typing. The array definition in Figure 3-1 is declared statically, telling the compiler that the object in question is of type `(NSArray *)`. When the compiler finds objects that may not be able to respond to the requested methods, it issues warnings.

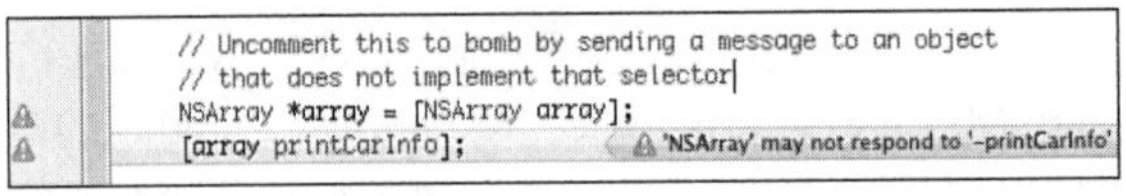

```
// Uncomment this to bomb by sending a message to an object
// that does not implement that selector
NSArray *array = [NSArray array];
[array printCarInfo];                'NSArray' may not respond to '-printCarInfo'
```

Figure 3-1 Xcode's Objective-C issues warnings when it finds a method that does not appear to be implemented by the receiver.

These warnings do not make the compilation fail, and it's possible that this code could run without error if NSArray implemented printCarInfo and did not declare that implementation in its published interface. Since NSArray does not, in fact, implement this method, running this code produces the actual runtime crash shown previously.

Objective-C's dynamic typing means you can point to the same kind of object in several different ways. Although array was declared as a statically typed (NSArray *) object, that object uses the same internal object data structures as an object declared as id. The id type can point to any object, regardless of class, and is equivalent to (NSObject *). This following assignment is valid and does not generate any warnings at compile time.

```
NSArray *array = [NSArray array];
// This assignment is valid
id untypedVariable = array;
```

To further demonstrate, consider a mutable array. The NSMutableArray class is a subclass of NSArray. The mutable version offers arrays that you can change and edit. Creating and typing a mutable array but assigning it to an array pointer compiles without error. Although anotherArray is statically typed as NSArray, creating it in this way produces an object at runtime that contains all the instance variables and behaviors of the mutable array class.

```
NSArray *anotherArray = [NSMutableArray array];
// This mutable-only method call is valid but
// produces a compile-time warning
[anotherArray addObject:@"Hello World"];
```

What produces a warning here is not the creation and assignment. It's the use. Sending addObject: to anotherArray uses our knowledge that the array is, in fact, mutable despite the fact that it is statically typed as (NSArray *). That's something the compiler does not understand. This use generates a compile-time warning, namely "'NSArray' may not respond to '-addObject:'" At runtime, however, the code works without error.

While assigning a child class object to a pointer of a parent class generally works at runtime, it's far more dangerous to go the other way. A mutable array is a kind of array. It can receive all the messages that arrays do. Not every array, on the other hand, is mutable. Sending the addObject: message to a regular array is lethal. Doing so bombs at runtime, as arrays do not implement that method.

```
NSArray *standardArray = [NSArray array];
NSMutableArray *mutableArray;
// This line produces a warning
mutableArray = standardArray;
// This will bomb at run-time
[mutableArray addObject:@"Hello World"];
```

The code seen here produces just one warning, at the line where the standard array object is assigned to the mutable array pointer, namely "assignment from distinct Objective-C type." Parent-to-child assignments do not generate this warning. Child-to-parent assignments do.

So do assignments between completely unrelated classes. Do not ignore this warning; fix your code. Otherwise, you're setting yourself up for a runtime crash. Because Objective-C is a compiled language that uses dynamic typing, it does not perform many of the runtime checks that interpreted object-oriented languages do.

> **Note**
>
> In Xcode, you can set the compiler to treat warnings as errors by setting the GCC_TREAT_WARNINGS_AS_ERRORS flag in the Project Info > Build > User-Defined panel. Because Objective-C is so dynamic, the compiler cannot catch every problem that might crash at runtime the way static language compilers can. So pay special attention to warnings and try to eliminate them.

Inheriting Methods

As with data, objects inherit method implementations as well as instance variables. A `Car` is a kind of `NSObject`, so it can respond to all the messages that an `NSObject` responds to. That's why myCar can be allocated and initialized with `alloc` and `init`. These methods are defined by `NSObject`. Therefore, they can be used by any instance of `Car`, which is derived from the `NSObject` class.

Similarly, `NSMutableArray` instances are a kind of `NSArray`. All array methods can be used by mutable arrays, their child class. You can count the items in the array, pull an object out by its index number, and so forth.

A child class may override a parent's method implementation, but it can't negate that the method exists. Child classes always inherit the full behavior and state package of their parents.

Declaring Methods

As Listing 3-1 showed, a class interface defines the instance variables and methods that a new class adds to its parent class. This interface is normally placed into a header file, which is named with a .h extension. The interface from Listing 3-1 declared three methods, namely

```
- (void) setMake:(NSString *) aMake andModel:(NSString *) aModel
    andYear: (int) aYear;
- (void) printCarInfo;
- (int) year;
```

These three methods, respectively, return `void`, `void`, and `int`. Notice the dash that starts the method declaration. It indicates that the methods are implemented by object instances. For example, you call `[myCar year]` and not `[Car year]`. The latter sends a message to the `Car` class rather than an actual car object. A discussion about class methods (indicated by "+" rather than "-") follows later in this section.

As mentioned earlier, methods calls can be complex. The following invocation sends a method request with three parameters. The parameters are interspersed inside the method invocation. The name for the method, that is, its selector, is `setMake: andModel: andYear:`. The three colons indicate where parameters should be inserted. The types for each parameter are specified in the interface after the colons, namely `(NSString *)`, `NSString *)`, and `(int)`. As this method returns `void`, the results are not assigned to a variable.

```
[myCar setMake:@"Ford" andModel:@"Prefect" andYear:1946];
```

Implementing Methods

Together, a method file and a header file pair store all the information needed to implement a class and announce it to the rest of an application. The implementation section of a class definition provides the code that implements functionality. This source is usually placed in a .m (m is for "method") file.

Listing 3-2 shows the implementation for the Car class example. It codes all three methods declared in the header file from Listing 3-1 and adds a fourth. This extra method redefines `init`. The Car version of `init` sets the make and model of the car to nil, which is the `NULL` pointer for Objective-C objects. It also initializes the year of the car to 1901.

The special variable `self` refers to the object that is implementing the method. That object is also called the receiver, that is, the object that receives the message. This variable is made available by the underlying Objective-C runtime system. In this case, self refers to the current instance of the Car class. Calling `[self` *`message`*`]` tells Objective-C to send a message to the object that is currently executing the method.

Several things are notable about the `init` method seen here. First, the method returns a value, which is typed to `(id)`. As mentioned earlier in this chapter, the `id` type is more or less equivalent to `(NSObject *)`, although it's theoretically slightly more generic than that. It can point to any object of any class (including Class objects themselves). You return results the same way you would in C, using `return`. The goal of `init` is to return a properly initialized version of the receiver via `return self`.

Second, the method calls `[super init]`. This tells Objective-C to send a message to a different implementation, namely the one defined in the object's superclass. The superclass of `Car` is `NSObject`, as shown in Listing 3-1. This call says "please perform the initialization that is normally done by my parent class before I add my custom behavior."

Finally, notice the check for `if (!self)`. In rare instances, memory issues arise. In such a case, the call to `[super init]` returns nil. If so, this `init` method returns before setting any instance variables. Since a nil object does not point to allocated memory, you cannot access instance variables within nil.

As for the other methods, they use year, make, and model as if they were locally declared variables. As instance variables, they are defined within the context of the current object and can be set and read as shown in this example. The `UTF8String` method that is sent to the make and model instance variables converts these `NSString` objects into C strings, which can be printed using the `%s` format specifier.

> **Note**
>
> You can send any message to nil, for example, `[nil anyMethod]`. The result of doing so is, in turn, nil. (Or, more accurately, 0 casted as nil.) In other words, there is no effect. This behavior lets you nest method invocations with a failsafe should any of the individual methods fail and return nil. If you were to run out of memory during an allocation with `[[Car alloc] init]`, the `init` message would be sent to nil, allowing the entire `alloc/init` request to return nil in turn.

Listing 3-2 **The Car Class Implementation (Car.m)**

```
#import "Car.h"

@implementation Car
- (id) init
{
    self = [super init];
    if (!self) return nil;

    make = nil;
    model = nil;
    year = 1901;

    return self;
}

- (void) setMake:(NSString *) aMake andModel:(NSString *) aModel
    andYear: (int) aYear
{
    make = [NSString stringWithString:aMake];
    model = [NSString stringWithString:aModel];
    year = aYear;
}

- (void) printCarInfo
{
    if (!make) return;
    if (!model) return;

    printf("Car Info\n");
    printf("Make: %s\n", [make UTF8String]);
    printf("Model: %s\n", [model UTF8String]);
    printf("Year: %d\n", year);
}

- (int) year
{
    return year;
}
@end
```

Class Methods

Class methods are defined using a plus (+) prefix rather than a hyphen (-). They are declared and implemented in the same way as instance methods. For example, you might add the following method declaration to your interface:

```
+ (NSString *) motto;
```

and code it up in your implementation:

```
+ (NSString *) motto
{
    return(@"Ford Prefects are Mostly Harmless");
}
```

Class methods differ from instance methods in that they generally cannot use state. That is, they have no access to instance variables because those elements are only created when objects are allocated from memory.

So why use class methods at all? The answer is threefold. First, class methods produce results without having to instantiate an actual object. This `motto` method produces a hard-coded result that does not depend on access to variables. Convenience methods like this often have a better place as classes rather than instance methods.

You might imagine a class that handles geometric operations. The class could implement a conversion between radians and angles without needing an instance, for example, `[GeometryClass convertAngleToRadians:theta];`. Simple C functions declared in header files also provide a good match to this need.

The second reason is that class methods can hide a singleton. Singletons refer to statically allocated instances. The iPhone SDK is full of these. For example, `[UIApplication sharedApplication]` returns a pointer to the singleton object that is your application. `[UIDevice currentDevice]` retrieves an object representing the hardware platform you're working on.

Combining a class method with a singleton lets you access that static instance anywhere in your application. You don't need a pointer to the object or an instance variable that stores it. The class method pulls that object's reference for you and returns it on demand.

Third, class methods tie into memory management schemes. Consider allocating a new `NSArray`. You do so via `[[NSArray alloc] init]`, or you can use `[NSArray array]`. This latter class method returns an array object that has been initialized and set for autorelease. As you read about later in this chapter, Apple has provided a standard about class methods that create objects. They always return those objects to you already autoreleased. Because of that, this class method pattern is a fundamental part of the standard iPhone memory management system.

Fast Enumeration

Fast enumeration was introduced in Objective-C 2.0 and offers a simple and elegant way to enumerate through collections like arrays and sets. It adds a for-loop that iterates through the collection using concise for/in syntax. The enumeration is very efficient, running quickly. It is also safe. Attempts to modify the collection as it's being enumerated raise a runtime exception.

```
NSArray *colors = [NSArray arrayWithObjects:
    @"Black", @"Silver", @"Gray", nil];
for (NSString *color in colors)
    printf("Consider buying a %s car", [color UTF8String]);
```

> **Note**
>
> Use caution when using methods like arrayWithObjects: or dictionaryWithKeysAndValues: as being unnecessarily error-prone. Developers often use these methods with instance variables without first checking that these values are non-nil.

Class Hierarchy

In Objective-C, each new class is derived from an already-existing class. The Car class described in Listings 3-1 and 3-2 is formed from NSObject, the root class of the Objective-C class tree. Each subclass adds or modifies state and behavior that it inherits from its parent, also called its superclass. The Car class adds several instance variables and methods to the vanilla NSObject it inherits.

Figure 3-2 shows some of the classes found on the iPhone and how they relate to each other in the class hierarchy. Strings and arrays descend from NSObject as does the UIResponder class. UIResponder is the ancestor of all onscreen iPhone elements. Views, labels, text fields, and sliders are children, grandchildren, or other descendants of UIResponder and NSObject.

Every class other than NSObject descends from other classes. UITextField is a kind of UIControl, which is in turn a kind of UIView, which is a UIResponder, which is an NSObject. Building into this object hierarchy is what Objective-C is all about. Child classes can

- Add new instance variables that are not allocated by their parent, also called the superclass. The Car class adds three: the make and model strings, and the year integer.
- Add new methods that are not defined by the parent. Car defines several new methods, letting you set the values of the instance variables and print out a report about the car.
- Override methods that the parents have already defined. The Car class's init method overrides NSObject's version. When sent an init message, a car object runs its version, not NSObject's. At the same time, the code for init makes sure to call

NSObject's init method via [super init]. Referencing a parent's implementation, while extending that implementation, is a core part of the Objective-C design philosophy.

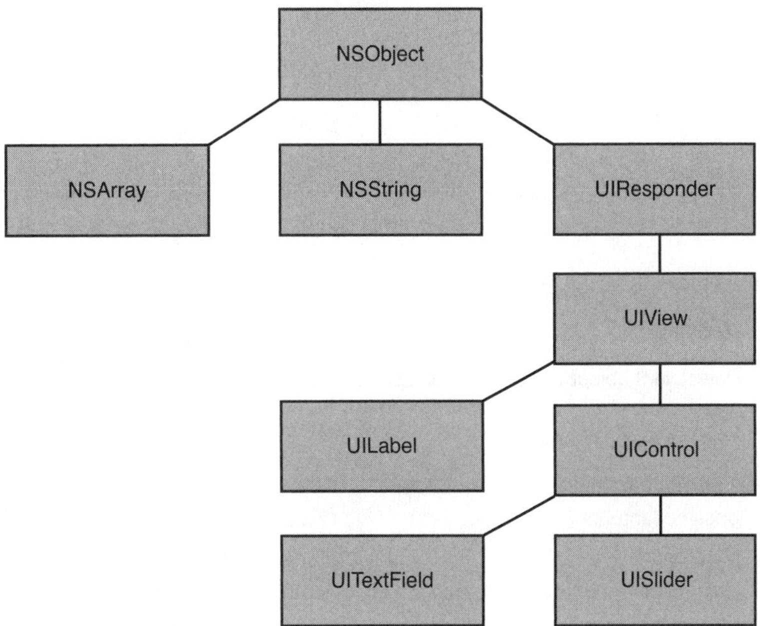

Figure 3-2 All Cocoa Touch classes are descended from NSObject, the root of the class hierarchy tree.

Logging Information

Now that you've read the basics about classes and objects, it's important to understand how to log information about them. In addition to printf, Objective-C offers a fundamental logging function called NSLog. This function works like printf and uses a similar format string, but it outputs to stderr instead of stdout. NSLog also uses an NSString format string rather than a C string one.

NSStrings are declared differently than C strings. They are prepended with the @ (at) symbol. A typical NSString looks @"like this"; the equivalent C string looks "like this", omitting the @. Whereas C strings refer to a pointer to a string of bytes, NSStrings are objects. You can manipulate a C string by changing the values stored in each byte. NSStrings are immutable; you cannot access the bytes to edit them, and the actual string data is not stored within the object.

```
// This is 12 bytes of addressable memory
printf("%d\n", sizeof("Hello World"));
```

```
// This 4-byte object points to non-addressable memory
NSString *string = @"Hello World";
printf("%d\n", sizeof(*string));
```

In addition to using the standard C format specifiers, `NSLog` introduces an object specifier, `%@`, which lets you print objects. This allows you to transform

```
printf("Make: %s\n", [make UTF8String]);
```

into

```
NSLog(@"Make: %@", make);
```

Table 3-1 shows some of the most common format specifiers. This is far from an exhaustive list, so consult Apple's String Programming Guide for Cocoa for more details.

Table 3-1 **Common String Format Specifiers**

Specifier	Meaning
`%@`	Objective-C object using the `description` or `descriptionWithLocale:` results
`%%`	The "%" literal character
`%d`	Signed integer (32-bit)
`%u`	Unsigned integer (32-bit)
`%f`	Floating-point (64-bit)
`%e`	Floating-point printed using exponential (scientific) notation (64-bit)
`%c`	Unsigned char (8-bit)
`%C`	Unicode char (16-bit)
`%s`	Null-terminated char array (string, 8-bit)
`%S`	Null-terminated Unicode char array (16-bit)
`%p`	Pointer address using lowercase hex output, with a leading 0x
`%x`	Lowercase unsigned hex (32-bit)
`%X`	Uppercase unsigned hex (32-bit)

Notice that NSLog does not require a hard-coded return character. It automatically appends a new line when used. What's more it adds a time stamp to every log, so the results of the NSLog invocation shown previously look something like this:

```
2009-05-07 14:19:08.792 HelloWorld[11197:20b] Make: Ford
```

Nearly every object converts itself into a string via the `description` message. `NSLog` uses `description` to show the contents of objects formatted with `%@`. This returns an NSString with a textual description of the receiver object. You can describe objects outside of `NSLog` by sending them the same `description` method. This is particularly handy for use with `printf` and `fprintf`, which cannot otherwise print objects.

```
fprintf(stderr, "%s\n", [[myCar description] UTF8String]);
```

Another useful logging function is called `CFShow()`. It takes one argument, an object, and prints out a snapshot description of that object to stderr.

```
CFShow(make);
```

Like `NSLog`, `CFShow` sends `description` to the objects it displays. Unlike `NSLog`, however, `CFShow` does not clutter your debugging console with time stamps, so it appeals to anyone who prefers to skip that extra information. `CFShow` doesn't require format strings, which simplifies adding them to code, but they can only be used with objects. You cannot `CFShow` an integer or float.

Properties

Properties expose class variables and methods to outside use through what are called *accessor methods*, that is, methods that access information. Using properties might sound redundant. After all, the class definition shown in Listing 3-1 already announces public methods. So why use properties? It turns out that there are advantages to using properties over hand-built methods, not the least of which are dot notation and memory management.

Dot Notation

Dot notation allows you to access object information without using brackets. Instead of calling `[myCar year]` to recover the year instance variable, you use `myCar.year`. While this may look as if you're directly accessing the year instance variable, you're not. Properties always invoke methods. These in turn can access an object's data. So you're not, strictly speaking, breaking an object's encapsulation as properties rely on these methods to bring data outside the object.

Due to method hiding, properties simplify the look and layout of your code. For example, you can access properties to set a table's cell text via

```
myTableViewCell.textLabel.text = @"Hello World";
```

rather than the more cumbersome

```
[[myTableViewCell textLabel] setText:@"Hello World"];
```

The property version of the code is more readable and ultimately easier to maintain.

Properties and Memory Management

Properties simplify memory management. You can create properties that automatically retain instance variables for the lifetime of your objects and release them when you set those variables to nil. Setting a retained property ensures that memory will not be released until you say so.

The `arrayWithObjects:` method normally returns an autoreleased object, whose memory is deallocated at the end of the event loop cycle. (See Chapter 1, "Introducing the iPhone SDK," for details about autorelease pools. A deeper discussion about memory

follows later in this chapter.) Assigning the array to a retained property
e array will stick around indefinitely.

```
[NSArray arrayWithObjects:
@"Gray", @"Silver", @"Black"];
```

When you're done using the array and want to release its memory, set the property to nil. This approach works because Objective-C knows how to synthesize accessor methods, creating properly managed ways to change the value of an instance variable. You're not really setting a variable to nil. You're actually telling Objective-C to run a method that releases any previously set object and then sets the instance variable to nil. All this happens behind the scenes. From a coding point of view, it simply looks as if you're assigning a variable to nil.

```
self.colors = nil;
```

As a rule, do not send release directly to retained properties, that is, `[self.colors release]`. This does not affect the colors instance variable assignment, which now points to memory that is likely deallocated. When you next assign an object to the retained property, the memory pointed to by self.colors will receive an additional release message, likely causing a crash due to a double-free exception.

Creating Properties

There are two basic styles of properties, `readwrite` and `readonly`. Read-write properties, which are the default, let you modify the values you access; read-only properties do not. The two kinds of accessor methods you must provide are called setters and getters.

Setters set information; getters retrieve information. You can define these with arbitrary method names or you can use the standard Objective-C conventions: The name of the instance variable retrieves the object, while the name prefixed with set, sets it. Objective-C can even synthesize these methods for you. For example, if you declare a property such as the Car class's `year` in your class interface as such

```
@property int year;
```

and then synthesize it in your class implementation with

```
@synthesize year;
```

you can read and set the instance variable with no further coding. Objective-C builds two methods that get the current value (that is, `[myCar year]`) and sets the current value (that is, `[myCar setYear:1962]`) and adds the two dot notation shortcuts:

```
myCar.year = 1962;
NSLog(@"%d", myCar.year);
```

To build a read-only property, declare it in your interface using the `readonly` attribute. Read-only properties use getters without setters. For example, here's a property that returns a formatted text string with car information:

```
@property (readonly) NSString *carInfo;
```

Although Objective-C can synthesize read-only properties, you can also build the getter method by hand and add it to your Class implementation. This method returns a description of the car via `stringWithFormat:`, which uses a format string a la `sprintf` to create a new string.

```
- (NSString *) carInfo
{
    if (!self.make) return @"";
    if (!self.model) return @"";
    return [NSString stringWithFormat:
        @"Car Info\nMake: %@nYear: % %d",
        self.make, self.model, self.year];
}
```

This method now becomes available for use via dot notation, for example, `CFShow(myCar.carInfo);`.

If you choose to synthesize a getter for a read-only property, you should use care in your code. Inside your implementation file, make sure you assign the instance variable for that property without dot notation. Imagine that you declared `model` as a read-only property. You could assign `model` with

```
model = @"Prefect";
```

but not with

```
self.model = @"Prefect";
```

The latter use attempts to call `setModel:`, which is not defined for a read-only property.

Creating Custom Getters and Setters

Although Objective-C automatically builds methods when you `@synthesize` properties, you may skip the synthesis. You can create those methods yourself. For example, you could build methods as simple as these. Notice the capitalization of the second word in the set method. By convention, Objective-C expects setters to use a method named `set`*`Instance`*`:` where the first letter of the instance variable name is capitalized.

```
-(int) year
{
    return year;
}

- (void) setYear: (int) aYear
{
    year = aYear;
}
```

When building your own setters and getters, you might add some basic memory management. The following methods retain new items and release previous values.

```
- (NSString *) model
{
```

```
    return model;
}

- (void) setModel: (NSString *) newModel
{
    if (newModel != model) {
        [model release];
        model = [newModel retain];
    }
}
```

> **Note**
>
> In the remote case that `newModel` is somehow a child of model, calling `[model release]` may free the memory of new model. For that reason, a more complete setter method retains `newModel` before calling `[model release]`.

Or you could go even further by building more complicated routines that generate side effects upon assignment and retrieval. For example, you might keep a count of the number of times the value has been retrieved or changed, or send in-app notifications to other objects. The Objective-C compiler remains happy so long as it finds, for any property, a getter (typically named the same as the property name) and a setter (usually `set`*`Name`*`:` where name is the name of the property). What's more, you can bypass any Objective-C naming conventions by specifying setter and getter names in the property declaration. This declaration creates a new Boolean property called `forSale` and declares a custom getter/setter pair. As always, you add any property declarations to the class interface.

```
@property (getter=isForSale, setter=setSalable:) BOOL forSale;
```

Then synthesize the methods as normal in the class implementation. The implementation is typically stored in the .m file that accompanies the .h header file.

```
@synthesize forSale;
```

Using this approach creates both the normal setter and getter via dot notation plus the two custom methods, `isForSale` and `setSalable:`. Oddly, while you can use dot notation to assign and retrieve `forSale`, you cannot use the equivalent methods, and you cannot use the customized setter in dot notation. Here is how the usage breaks down.

```
Car *myCar = [Car car];

// You can use the synthesized setter and getter of course
[myCar setSalable:YES];
printf("The car %s for sale\n",
    myCar.isForSale ? "is" : "is not");

// The normal getter and setter still work in dot notation
myCar.forSale = NO;
```

```
printf("The car %s for sale\n",
    myCar.forSale ? "is" : "is not");

// But not the method versions.
// These produce run-time errors
// [myCar setForSale:YES];
// printf("The car %s for sale\n",
//     [myCar forSale] ? "is" : "is not");

// You cannot use the customized setter via dot notation.
// This produces a compile-time error
// myCar.setSalable = YES;
```

Property Attributes

In addition to `readwrite` and `readonly` attributes, you can specify whether a property is retained and/or atomic. The default behavior for properties is `assign`. Assignment acts exactly as if you'd assigned a value to an instance variable. There's no special retain/release behavior associated with the property, but by making it a property you expose the variable outside the class via dot notation. A property that's declared

```
@property NSString *make;
```

uses the `assign` behavior.

Setting the property's attribute to `retain` does two things. First, it retains the passed object upon assignment. Second, it releases the previous value before a new assignment is made. Using the `retain` attribute introduces the memory management advantages discussed in the previous section. To create a retained property, add the attribute between parentheses in the declaration:

```
@property (retain) NSString *make;
```

A third attribute called `copy` sends a copy message to the passed object, retains it, and releases any previous value.

```
@property (copy) NSString *make;
```

You can also retain the object as you assign it.

```
myCar.make = @"Ford";
[myCar.make retain];
```

When you develop in a multithreaded environment, you want to use atomic methods. Xcode synthesizes atomic methods to automatically lock objects before they are accessed or modified and unlock them after. This ensures that setting or retrieving an object's value is performed fully regardless of concurrent threads. There is no `atomic` keyword. All methods are synthesized atomically by default. You can, however, state the opposite, allowing Objective-C to create accessors that are nonatomic.

```
@property (nonatomic, retain) NSString *make;
```

Marking your properties nonatomic does speed up access, but you might run into problems should two competing threads attempt to modify the same property at once. Atomic properties, with their lock/unlock behavior, ensure that an object update completes from start to finish before that property is released to another read or change.

Simple Memory Management

Memory management comes down to two simple rules. At creation, every object has a retain count of one. At release, every object has a retain count of zero. It is up to you as a developer to manage an object's retention over its lifetime. You should ensure that it moves from start to finish without being prematurely released and guarantee that it does finally get released when it is time to do so. Complicating matters is Objective-C's autorelease pool. If some objects are autoreleased and others must be released manually, how do you best control your objects? Here's a quick and dirty guide to getting your memory management right.

Creating Objects

Any time you create an object using the alloc/init pattern, you build it with a retain count of one. It doesn't matter which class you use or what object you build, alloc/init produces a +1 count.

```
id myObject = [[SomeClass alloc] init];
```

For locally scoped variables, if you do not release the object before the end of a method, the object leaks. Your reference to that memory goes away, but the memory itself remains allocated. The retain count remains at +1.

```
- (void) leakyMethod
{
   // This is leaky
    NSArray *array = [[NSArray alloc] init];
}
```

The proper way to use an alloc/init pattern is to create, use, and then release. Releasing brings the retain count down to 0. When the method ends, the object is deallocated.

```
- (void) properMethod
{
    NSArray *array = [[NSArray alloc] init];
    // use the array here
    [array release];
}
```

Autorelease objects do not require an explicit release statement for locally scoped variables. (In fact, avoid doing so to prevent double-free errors that will crash your program.) Sending the `autorelease` message to an object marks it for autorelease. When the autorelease pool drains at the end of each event loop, it sends release to all the objects it owns.

```
- (void) anotherProperMethod
{
    NSArray *array = [[[NSArray alloc] init] autorelease];
    // This won't crash the way release would
    printf("Retain count is %d\n", [array retainCount]);
    // use the array here
}
```

By convention, all class object-creation methods return an autoreleased object. The `NSArray` class method `array` returns a newly initialized array that is already set for autorelease. The object can be used throughout the method, and its release is handled when the autorelease pool drains.

```
- (void) yetAnotherProperMethod
{
    NSArray *array = [NSArray array];
    // use the array here
}
```

At the end of this method, the autoreleased array can return to the general memory pool.

Creating Autoreleased Objects

As a rule, whenever you ask another method to create an object, it's good programming practice to return that object autoreleased. Doing so consistently lets you follow a simple rule: "If I didn't allocate it, then it was built and returned to me as an autorelease object."

```
- (Car *) fetchACar
{
    Car *myCar = [[Car alloc] init];
    return [myCar autorelease];
}
```

This holds especially true for class methods. By convention all class methods that create new objects return autorelease objects. These are generally referred to as convenience methods. Any object that you yourself allocate is not set as autorelease unless you specify it yourself.

```
// This is not autoreleased
Car *car1 = [[Car alloc] init];

// This is autoreleased
Car *car2 = [[[Car alloc] init] autorelease];

// By convention, this *should* be an autoreleased object
Car *car3 = [Car car];
```

To create a convenience method at the class level, make sure to define the class with the + prefix instead of - and return the object after sending `autorelease` to it.

```
+ (Car *) car
{
    return [[[Car alloc] init] autorelease];
}
```

Autorelease Object Lifetime

So how long can you use an autorelease object? What guarantees do you have? The hard and fast rule is that the object is yours until the next item in the event loop gets processed. The event loop is triggered by user touches, by button presses, by "time passed" events, and so forth. In human reckoning these times are impossibly short; in the iPhone's processor frame of reference, they're quite large. As a more general rule, you can assume that an autoreleased object should persist throughout the duration of your method call.

Once you return from a method, guarantees go out the window. When you need to use an array beyond the scope of a single method or for extended periods of time (for example, you might start a custom run-loop within a method, prolonging how long that method endures), the rules change. You must retain autorelease objects to increase their count and prevent them from getting deallocated when the pool drains; when the autorelease pool calls release on their memory, they'll maintain a count of at least +1.

> **Note**
>
> Avoid assigning properties to themselves, for example, `myCar.colors = myCar.colors`. The release-then-retain behavior of properties may cause the object to deallocate before it can be reassigned and re-retained.

Retaining Autorelease Objects

You can send `retain` to autorelease objects just like any other object. Retaining objects set to autorelease allows them to persist beyond a single method. Once retained, an autorelease object is just as subject to memory leaks as one that you created using alloc/init. For example, retaining an object that's scoped to a local variable might leak, as shown here.

```
- (void)anotherLeakyMethod
{
    // After returning, you lose the local reference to
    // array and cannot release.
    NSArray *array = [NSArray array];
    [array retain];
}
```

Upon creation, `array` has a retain count of +1. Sending retain to the object brings that retain count up to +2. When the method ends and the autorelease pool drains, the object receives a single `release` message; the count returns to +1. From there, the object is stuck. It cannot be deallocated with a +1 count and with no reference left to point to the object, it cannot be sent the final release message it needs to finish its life cycle. This is why it's critical to build references to retained objects.

By creating a reference, you can both use a retained object through its lifetime and be able to release it when you're done. Set references via an instance variable (preferred) or a static variable defined within your class implementation. If you want to keep things simple and reliable, use retained properties built from those instance variables. The next section shows you how retained properties work and demonstrates why they provide a solution of choice for developers.

Retained Properties

Retained properties hold onto data that you assign to them and properly relinquish that data when you set a new value. Because of this, they tie in seamlessly to basic memory management. Here's how you create and use retained properties in your iPhone applications.

First, declare your retained property in the class interface by including the `retain` keyword between parentheses.

```
@property (retain) NSArray *colors;
```

Then synthesize the property methods in your implementation.

```
@synthesize colors;
```

When given the `@synthesize` directive, Objective-C automatically builds routines that manage the retained property. The routines automatically retain an object when you assign it to the property. That behavior holds regardless of whether the object is set as autorelease. When you reassign the property, the previous value is automatically released.

Assigning Values to Retained Properties

When working with retained properties, you need to be aware of two patterns of assignment. These patterns depend on whether you're assigning an autorelease object. For autorelease style objects, use a simple single assignment. This assignment sets the `colors` property to the new array and retains it.

```
myCar.colors = [NSArray arrayWithObjects:
    @"Black", @"Silver", @"Gray", nil];
```

The array is created and returned as an autorelease object with a count of +1. The assignment to the retained `colors` property brings the count to +2. Once the current event loop ends, the autorelease pool sends release to the array, and the count drops back to +1.

For normal (nonautorelease) objects, release the object after assigning it. Upon creation, the retain count for a normally allocated object is +1. Assigning the object to a retained property increases that count to +2. Releasing the object returns the count to +1.

```
// Non-autorelease object. Retain count is +1 at creation
NSArray *array = [[NSArray alloc]
    initWithObjects:@"Black", @"Silver", @"Gray", nil];

// Count rises to +2 via assignment to a retained property
myCar.colors = array;
```

```
// Now release to get that retain count back to +1
[array release];
```

You often see this pattern of create, assign, release in iPhone development. You might use it when assigning a newly allocated view to a view controller object. For example:

```
UIView *mainView = [[UIView alloc] initWithFrame:aFrame];
self.view = mainView;
[mainView release];
```

These three steps move the object's retain count from +1 to +2 and back to +1.

A final count of +1 guarantees you that can use an object indefinitely. At the same time, you're assured that the object deallocates properly when the property is set to a new value and release is called on its prior value. That release brings the count down from +1 to 0, and the object automatically deallocates.

Reassigning a Retained Property

When you're done using a retained property, regardless of the approach used to create that object, set the property to nil or to another object. This sends a release message to the previously assigned object.

```
myCar.colors=nil;
```

If the `colors` property had been set to an array, as just shown, that array would automatically be sent a release message. Since each pattern of assignment produced a +1 retained object, this reassignment would bring that retain count down from +1 to 0. The object's life would be over.

Avoiding Assignment Pitfalls

Within a class implementation, it's handy to use properties to take advantage of this memory management behavior. To take advantage of this, avoid using instance variables directly. Direct assignment like this won't retain the array or release any previous value. This is a common pitfall for new iPhone developers. Remember the dot notation when accessing the instance variables.

```
colors = [NSArray arrayWithObjects:
    @"Black", @"Silver", @"Gray", nil];
```

This same caution holds true for properties defined as `assign`. Note the following behavior carefully. Although both

```
@property NSArray *colors;
```

and

```
@property (assign) NSArray *colors;
```

allow you to use dot notation, assignment via these properties does not retain or release objects. `Assign` properties expose the colors instance variable to the outside world, but they do not provide the same memory management that `retain` properties do.

Note

As a general rule of thumb, Apple recommends you avoid using properties in your `init` functions. Instead, use instance variables directly.

High Retain Counts

Retain counts that go and stay above +1 do not necessarily mean you've done anything wrong. Consider the following code segment. It creates a view and starts adding it to arrays. This raises the retain count from +1 up to +4.

```
// On creation, view has a retain count of +1;
UIView *view = [[[UIView alloc] init] autorelease];
printf("Count: %d\n", [view retainCount]);

// Adding it to an array increases that retain count to +2
NSArray *array1 = [NSArray arrayWithObject:view];
printf("Count: %d\n", [view retainCount]);

// Another array, retain count goes to +3
NSArray *array2 = [NSArray arrayWithObject:view];
printf("Count: %d\n", [view retainCount]);

// And another +4
NSArray *array3 = [NSArray arrayWithObject:view];
printf("Count: %d\n", [view retainCount]);
```

Notice that each array was created using a class convenience method and returns an autoreleased object. The view is set as autorelease, too. Some collection classes like `NSArray` automatically retain objects when you add them into an array and release them when either the object is removed (mutable objects only) or when the collection is released. This code has no leaks because every one of the four objects is set to properly release itself and its children when the autorelease pool drains.

When release is sent to the three arrays, each one releases the view, bringing the count down from +4 to +1. The final release, sent to the object, brings the count from +1 down to 0, allowing the view to deallocate when this method finishes: no leaks, no further retains, no problems.

Other Ways to Create Objects

You've seen how to use `alloc` to allocate memory. Objective-C offers other ways to build new objects. You can discover these by browsing class documentation as the methods vary by class and framework. As a rule of thumb, if you build an object using any method whose name includes `alloc`, `new`, `create`, or `copy`, you maintain responsibility for releasing the object. Unlike class convenience methods, methods that include these words generally do not return autoreleased objects.

Sending a `copy` message to an object, for example, duplicates it. Copy returns an object with a retain count of +1 and no assignment to the autorelease pool. Use `copy` when you want to duplicate and make changes to an object while preserving the original. Note that for the most part, Objective-C produces shallow copies of collections like arrays and dictionaries. It copies the structure of the collection, and maintains the addresses for each pointer, but does not perform a deep copy of the items stored within.

C-Style Object Allocations

As a superset of C, Objective-C programs for the iPhone often use APIs with C-style object-creation and management. Core Foundation (CF) is a Cocoa Touch framework with C-based function calls. When working with CF objects in Objective-C, you build objects with `CFAllocators` and often use the `CFRelease()` function to release object memory.

There are, however, no simple rules. As the following code shows, you may end up using `free()`, `CFRelease()`, and custom methods like `CGContextRelease()` all in the same scope, side-by-side with standard Objective-C class convenience methods like `imageWithCGImage:`. The function used to create the context object used here is `CGBitmapContextCreate()` and like most Core Foundation function calls, it does not return an autoreleased object. This code snippet builds a `UIImage`, the iPhone class that stores image data.

```
UIImage *buildImage(int imgsize)
{
    // Create context with allocated bits
    CGContextRef context  =
        MyCreateBitmapContext(imgsize, imgsize);
    CGImageRef myRef =
        CGBitmapContextCreateImage(context);
    free(CGBitmapContextGetData(context));
    CGContextRelease(context);
    UIImage *img = [UIImage imageWithCGImage:myRef];
    CFRelease(myRef);
    return img;
}
```

Carbon and Core Foundation

Working with Core Foundation comes up often enough that you should be aware of its existence and be prepared to encounter its constructs, specifically as regards to its frameworks. Frameworks are libraries of classes that you can utilize in your application.

Table 3-2 explains the key terms involved. To summarize the issue, early OS X used a C-based framework called Core Foundation to provide a transitional system for developing applications that could run on both Classic Mac systems as well as Mac OS X. Although Core Foundation uses object-oriented extensions to C, its functions and constructs are all C-based, not Objective-C-based.

Table 3-2 **Key OS X Development Terms**

Term	Definition
Foundation	The core classes for Objective-C programming, offering all the fundamental data types and services needed for Cocoa and Cocoa Touch. A section at the end of this chapter introduces some of the most important Foundation classes you'll use in your applications.
Core Foundation	A library of C-based classes that are based on Foundation APIs but that are implemented in C. Core Foundation uses object-oriented data but is not built using the Objective-C classes.
Carbon	An early set of libraries provided by Apple that use a procedural API. Carbon offered event handling support, a graphics library, and many more frameworks. Some Carbon APIs live on through Core Foundation. Carbon was introduced for the Classic Mac OS, first appearing in Mac OS 8.1.
Cocoa	Apple's collection of frameworks, APIs, and runtimes that make up the modern Mac OS X runtime system. Frameworks are primarily written in Objective-C although some continue to use C/C++.
Cocoa Touch	Cocoa's equivalent for the iPhone OS, where the frameworks are tuned for the touch-based mobile iPhone user experience. Some iPhone frameworks such as Core Audio and Open GL are considered to reside outside Cocoa Touch.
Toll Free Bridging	A method of Cocoa/Carbon integration. Toll Free Bridging refers to sets of interchangeable data types. For example, Cocoa's Foundation (`NSString *`) object can be used interchangeably with Carbon's Core Foundation's `CFStringRef`. Bridging connects the C-based Core Foundation with the Objective-C Foundation world.

Core Foundation technology lives on through Cocoa. You can and will encounter C-style Core Foundation when programming iPhone applications using Objective-C. The specifics of Core Foundation programming fall outside the scope of this chapter, however, and are best explored separately from learning how to program in Objective-C.

Deallocating Objects

The iPhone uses reference-count managed Objective-C. On the iPhone, there's no garbage collection and little likelihood there ever will be. Every object cleans up after itself. So what does that mean in practical terms? Here's a quick rundown of how you end an object's life, cleaning up its instance variables and preparing it for deallocation.

Instance variables must release retained objects before deallocation. You as the developer must ensure that those objects return to a retain count of 0 before the parent object is itself released. To do this, you implement `dealloc`, a method automatically called by the runtime system when an object is about to be released. If you use a class with object instance variables (i.e., not just floats, ints, and Bools), you probably need to implement a deallocation method. The basic `dealloc` method structure looks like this:

```
- (void) dealloc
{
    // Class-based clean-up
    clean up my own instance variables here

    // Clean up superclass
    [super dealloc]
}
```

The method you write should work in two stages. First, clean up any instance variables from your class. Then ask your superclass to perform its cleanup routine. The special `super` keyword refers to the superclass of the object that is running the `dealloc` method. How you clean up depends on whether your instance variables are automatically retained.

You've read about creating objects, building references to those objects, and ensuring that the objects' retain counts stay at +1 after creation. Now, you see the final step of the object's lifetime, namely reducing that count back to 0 so the objects can be deallocated.

Retained Properties

In the case of retained properties, set those properties to nil using dot notation assignment. This calls the custom setter method synthesized by Objective-C and releases any prior object the property has been set to. Assuming that prior object had a retain count of +1, this release brings the count to 0.

```
self.make = nil;
```

Variables

When using plain (nonproperty) instance variables or assign style properties, send release at deallocation time. Say, for example, you've defined an instance variable called salesman. It might be set at any time during the lifetime of your object. The assignment of salesman might look like this:

```
// release any previous value
[salesman release];

// make the new assignment. Retain count is +1
salesman = [[SomeClass alloc] init];
```

This assignment style means that salesman could point to an object with a +1 retain count at any time during the object's lifetime. Therefore in your dealloc method, you must release any object currently assigned to salesman, setting the count to 0.

```
[salesman release];
```

A Sample Deallocation Method

Keeping with an expanded `Car` class that uses retained properties for `make`, `model`, and `colors`, and that has a simple instance variable for salesman, the final deallocation method would look like this. The integer year and the Boolean forSale instance variables are not objects and do not need to be managed this way.

```
- (void) dealloc
{
    self.make = nil;
    self.model = nil;
    self.colors = nil;
    [salesman release];
    [super dealloc];
}
```

Setting a retain count upper limit proves key to making Objective-C memory management work. Few objects should continue to have a retain count greater than +1 after their creation and assignment. By guaranteeing a limit, your final releases in `dealloc` are assured to bring those counts down to 0.

Cleaning Up Other Matters

The `dealloc` method offers a perfect place to clean up shop. For example, you might need to dispose of an Audio Toolbox sound or perform other maintenance tasks before the class is released. These tasks almost always relate to legacy Core Foundation, Core Graphics, Core Audio, or similar C-style frameworks.

```
if (snd) AudioServicesDisposeSystemSoundID(snd);
```

Think of `dealloc` as your last chance to tidy up loose ends before your object goes away forever. Whether this involves shutting down open sockets, closing file pointers, or releasing resources, use this method to make sure your code returns state as close to pristine as possible.

Crafting Singletons

The `UIApplication` and `UIDevice` classes let you access information about the currently running application and the device hardware it is running on. They do so by offering singletons, that is, a sole instance of a class in the current process. For example, `[UIApplication sharedApplication]` returns a singleton that can report information about the delegate it uses, whether the application supports shake-to-edit features, what windows are defined by the program, and so forth.

Most singleton objects act as control centers. They coordinate services, provide key information, and direct external access, among other functionality. If you have a need for centralized functionality, like a manager that accesses a Web service, a singleton approach ensures that all parts of your application coordinate with the same central manager.

Building a singleton takes very little code. You define a static shared instance inside the class implementation and add a class method pointing to that instance. In this snippet, which is taken from the tagging example of Chapter 6, "Assembling Views and Animations," the instance is built the first time it is requested.

```
@implementation ViewIndexer
static ViewIndexer *sharedInstance = nil;

+(ViewIndexer *) sharedInstance {
    if(!sharedInstance)
        sharedInstance = [[self alloc] init];
    return sharedInstance;
}

// Class behavior defined here

@end
```

To use this singleton, call `[ViewIndexer sharedInstance]`. This returns the shared object and lets you access any behavior that the singleton provides. You can prevent any class from creating a second instance by overriding `allocWithZone:`. (For most uses this is paranoid overkill.) The `@synchronized()` directive used here prevents this code from being executed by more than one thread at a time.

```
+ (id)allocWithZone:(NSZone *)zone
{
    @synchronized(self) {
        if (sharedInstance == nil) {
            sharedInstance = [super allocWithZone:zone];
            return sharedInstance;
        }
    }
    return nil;
}
```

Categories (Extending Classes)

Objective-C's built-in capability to expand already-existing classes is one of its most powerful features. This behavioral expansion is called a *category*. Categories extend class functionality without subclassing. You choose a descriptive expansion name, build a header, and then implement the functionality in a method file. Categories add methods to existing classes even if you did not define that class in the first place and do not have the source code for that class.

To build a category, you declare a new interface. Specify the category name (it's arbitrary) within parentheses, as you see here. List any new public methods and properties and save the header file. This Orientation category expands the `UIDevice` class, which is the

SDK class responsible for reporting device characteristics including orientation, battery level, and the proximity sensor state. This interface adds a single property to `UIDevice`, returning a read-only Boolean value. The new `isLandscape` property reports back whether the device is currently using a landscape orientation.

```
@interface UIDevice (Orientation)
@property (nonatomic, readonly) BOOL isLandscape;
@end
```

You cannot add new instance variables to a category interface as you could when subclassing. You are instead expanding a class's behavior, as shown in the source code of Listing 3-3. The code implements the landscape check by looking at the standard `UIDevice` orientation property.

You might use the new property like this.

```
NSLog(@"The device orientation is%@landscape",
      [UIDevice currentDevice].isLandscape ? @" " : @" not ");
```

Here, the landscape orientation check integrates seamlessly into the SDK-provided `UIDevice` class via a property that did not exist prior to expanding the class. Just FYI, `UIKit` does offer device orientation macros (`UIDeviceOrientationIsPortrait` and `UIDeviceOrientationIsLandscape`), but you must pass these an orientation value, which you have to poll from the device.

> **Note**
>
> In addition to adding new behavior to existing classes, categories also let you group related methods into separate files for classes you build yourself. For large, complex classes, this helps increase maintainability and simplifies the management of individual source files. Please note that when you add a category method that duplicates an existing method signature, the Objective-C runtime uses your implementation and overrides the original.

Listing 3-3 **Building an Orientation Category for the UIDevice Class**

```
@interface UIDevice (Orientation)
@property (nonatomic, readonly) BOOL isLandscape;
@end

@implementation UIDevice (Orientation)
- (BOOL) isLandscape
{
    return (self.orientation == UIDeviceOrientationLandscapeLeft) ||
        (self.orientation == UIDeviceOrientationLandscapeRight);
}
@end
```

Protocols

Chapter 1 introduced the notion of delegates. Delegates implement details that cannot be determined when a class is first defined. For example, a table knows how to display rows of cells, but it can't know what to do when a cell is tapped. The meaning of a tapped row changes with whatever application implements that table. A tap might open another screen, or send a message to a Web server, or perform any other imaginable result. Delegation lets the table communicate with a smart object that is responsible for handling those taps but whose behavior is written at a completely separate time from when the table class itself is created.

Delegation basically provides a language that mediates contact between an object and its handler. A table tells its delegate "I have been tapped," "I have scrolled," and other status messages. The delegate then decides how to respond to these messages, producing updates based on its particular application semantics.

Data sources operate the same way, but instead of mediating action responses, data sources provide data on demand. A table asks its data source, "What information should I put into cell 1 and cell 2?" The data source responds with the requested information. Like delegation, data sourcing lets the table place requests to an object that is built to understand those demands.

In Objective-C, both delegation and data sourcing are produced by a system called *protocols*. Protocols define a priori how one class can communicate with another. They contain a list of methods that are defined outside any class. Some of these methods are required. Others are optional. Any class that implements the required methods is said to conform to the protocol.

Defining a Protocol

Imagine, if you would, a jack-in-the box toy. This is a small box with a handle. When you turn the crank, music plays. Sometimes a puppet (called the "jack") jumps out of the box. Now imagine implementing that toy (or a rough approximation) in Objective-C. The toy provides one action, turning the crank, and there are two possible outcomes: the music or the jack.

Now consider designing a programmatic client for that toy. It could respond to the outcomes, perhaps, by gradually increasing a boredom count when more music plays or reacting with surprise when the jack finally bounces out. From an Objective-C point of view, your client needs to implement two responses: one for music, another for the jack. Here's a client protocol you might build.

```
@protocol JackClient <NSObject>
- (void) musicDidPlay;
- (void) jackDidAppear;
@end
```

This protocol declares that to be a client of the toy, you must respond to music playing and the jack jumping out of the box. Listing these methods inside an `@protocol` container defines the protocol. All the methods listed here are required unless you specifically declare them as `@optional`, as you read about in the next sections.

Incorporating a Protocol

Next, imagine designing a class for the toy itself. It offers one action, turning the crank, and requires a second object that implements the protocol, in this case called client. This class interface specifies that the client needs to be some kind of object (`id`) that conforms to the JackClient protocol (`<JackClient>`). Beyond that, the class does not know at design time what kind of object will provide these services.

```
@interface JackInTheBox : NSObject
{
    id <JackClient> client;
}
- (void) turnTheCrank;
@property (retain)      id <JackClient> client;
@end
```

Adding Callbacks

Callbacks connect the toy class to its client. Since the client must conform to the JackClient protocol, you can send `jackDidAppear` and `musicDidPlay` messages to the object and they will compile without error. The protocol ensures that the client implements these methods. In this code, the callback method is selected randomly. The music plays approximately nine out of every ten calls, sending `musicDidPlay` to the client.

```
- (void) turnTheCrank
{
    // You need a client to respond to the crank
    if (!self.client) return;

    // Randomly respond to the crank turn
    int action = random() % 10;
    if (action < 1)
        [self.client jackDidAppear];
    else
        [self.client musicDidPlay];
}
```

Declaring Optional Callbacks

Protocols include two kinds of callbacks, required and optional. By default, callbacks are required. A class that conforms to the protocol must implement those methods or they produce a compiler warning. You can use the `@required` and `@optional` keywords to declare a protocol to be of one form or the other. Any methods listed after an `@required` keyword are required; after an `@optional` keyword, they are optional. Your protocol can grow complex accordingly.

```
@protocol JackClient <NSObject>
- (void) musicDidPlay; // required
@required
- (void) jackDidAppear; // also required
@optional
- (void) nothingDidHappen; // optional
@end
```

In practice, using more than a single `@optional` keyword is overkill. The same protocol can be declared more simply. When you don't use any optional items, skip the keyword entirely. Notice the `<NSObject>` declaration here. It's required to effectively implement optional protocols. It says that a `JackClient` object conforms to and will be a kind of `NSObject`.

```
@protocol JackClient <NSObject>
- (void) musicDidPlay;
- (void) jackDidAppear;
@optional
- (void) nothingDidHappen;
@end
```

Implementing Optional Callbacks

Optional methods let the client choose whether to implement a given protocol method. They reduce the implementation burden on whoever writes that client but add a little extra work to the class that hosts the protocol definition. When you are unsure whether a class does or does not implement a method, you must test before you send a message. Fortunately, Objective-C and the `NSObject` class make it easy to do so.

```
// optional client method
if ([self.client  respondsToSelector: @selector(nothingDidHappen)])
    [self.client nothingDidHappen];
```

`NSObject` provides a `respondsToSelector:` method, which returns a Boolean YES if the object implements the method or NO otherwise. By declaring the client with `<NSObject>`, you tell the compiler that the client can handle this method, allowing you to check the client for conformance before sending the message.

Conforming to a Protocol

Classes include protocol conformance in interface declarations. A view controller that implements the JackClient protocol announces it between angle brackets. A class might conform to several protocols. Combine these within the brackets, separating protocol names with commas.

```
@interface TestBedViewController :
    UIViewController <JackClient>
{
    JackInTheBox *jack;
}
@property (retain) JackInTheBox *jack;
@end
```

Declaring the JackClient protocol lets you assign the host's client property. The following code compiles without error because the class for `self` was declared in conformance with JackClient.

```
self.jack = [JackInTheBox jack];
self.jack.client = self;
```

Had you omitted the protocol declaration in your interface, this assignment would produce an error at compile time.

Once you include that protocol between the angle brackets, you *must* implement all required methods in your class. Omitting any of them produces the kind of compile-time warnings shown in Figure 3-3. The compiler tells you which method is missing and what protocol that method belongs to.

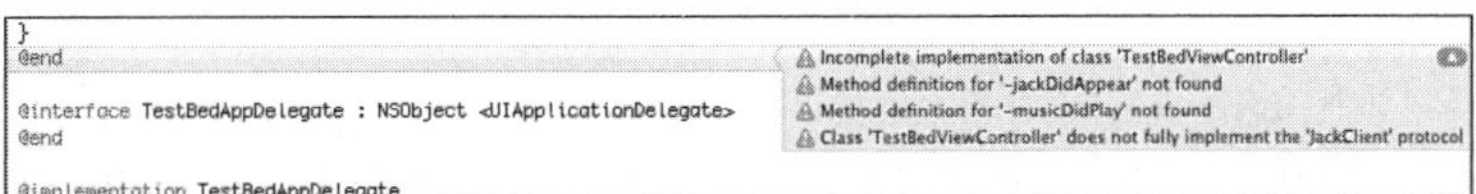

Figure 3-3 You must implement all required methods to conform to a protocol. Objective-C warns about incomplete implementations.

The majority of protocol methods in the iPhone SDK are optional. Both required and optional methods are detailed exhaustively in the developer documentation. Note that protocols are documented separately from the classes they support. For example, Xcode documentation provides three distinct UITableView reference pages: one for the `UITableView` class, one for the UITableViewDelegate protocol, and another for the UITableViewDataSource protocol.

Foundation Classes

If you're new to Objective-C, there are a few key classes you absolutely need to be familiar with before moving forward. These include strings, numbers, and collections, and they provide critical application building blocks. The `NSString` class, for example, provides the workhorse for nearly all text manipulation in Objective-C. However it, like other fundamental classes, is not defined in Objective-C itself. It is part of the Foundation framework, which offers nearly all the core utility classes you use on a day-to-day basis.

Foundation provides over a dozen kinds of object families and hundreds of object classes. These range from value objects that store numbers and dates, to strings that store character data, and collections that store other objects, to classes that access the file system and retrieve data from URLs. Foundation is often referred to (slightly inaccurately) as Cocoa. (Cocoa and its iPhone equivalent Cocoa Touch actually include all the frameworks for OS X programming.) To master Foundation is to master Objective-C programming, and thorough coverage of the subject demands an entire book of its own.

As this section cannot offer an exhaustive introduction to Foundation classes, you're about to be introduced to a quick and dirty survival overview. Here are the classes you need to know about and the absolutely rock-core ways to get started using them. You find extensive code snippets that showcase each of the classes to give you a jumping-off point if, admittedly, not a mastery of the classes involved.

Strings

Cocoa strings store character data, just as their cousins the `(char *)` C strings do. They are, however, objects and not byte arrays. Unlike C, the core `NSString` class is immutable in Cocoa. That is, you can use strings to build other strings, but you can't edit the strings you already own. String constants are delineated by quote marks and the @ character. Here is a typical string constant, which is assigned to a string variable.

```
NSString *myString = @"A string constant";
```

Building Strings

You can build strings using formats, much as you would using sprintf. If you're comfortable creating printf statements, your knowledge transfers directly to string formats. Use the `%@` format specifier to include objects in your strings. String format specifiers are thoroughly documented in the Cocoa String Programming Guide, available via Xcode's documentation window (Command-Option-?). The most common formats are listed in Table 3-1.

```
NSString *myString = [NSString stringWithFormat:
    @"The number is %d", 5];
```

To create new strings, you can append strings together. This call outputs "The number is 522". It creates a new instance built from other strings.

```
NSLog(@"%@", [myString stringByAppendingString:@"22"]);
```

Appending formats provides even more flexibility. You specify the format string and the components that build up the result.

```
NSLog(@"%@", [myString stringByAppendingFormat:@"%d", 22]);
```

Length and Indexed Characters

Every string can report its length (via `length`) and produce an indexed character on demand (via `characterAtIndex:`). The two calls shown here output 15 and e, respectively, based on the previous @"The number is 5" string. Cocoa characters use the `unichar` type, which store Unicode-style characters.

```
NSLog(@"%d", myString.length);
printf("%c", [myString characterAtIndex:2]);
```

Converting to and from C Strings

The realities of normal C programming often crop up despite working in Objective-C. Being able to move back and forth between C strings and Cocoa strings is an important skill. Convert an NSString to a C string either by sending `UTF8String` or `cStringUsingEncoding:`. These are equivalent, producing the same C-based bytes.

```
printf("%s\n", [myString UTF8String]);
printf("%s\n", [myString cStringUsingEncoding: NSUTF8StringEncoding]);
```

You can also go the other way and transform a C string into an NSString by using `stringWithCString: encoding:`. The samples here use UTF-8 encoding, but Objective-C supports a large range of options, including ASCII, Japanese, Latin, Windows-CP1251, and so forth.

```
NSLog(@"%@", [NSString stringWithCString:"Hello World"
    encoding: NSUTF8StringEncoding]);
```

Writing Strings to and Reading Strings from Files

Writing to and reading strings from the local file system offers a handy way to save and retrieve data. This snippet shows how to write a string to a file.

```
NSString *myString = @"Hello World";
NSError *error;
NSString *path = [NSHomeDirectory()
    stringByAppendingPathComponent:@"Documents/file.txt"];
if (![myString writeToFile:path atomically:YES
    encoding:NSUTF8StringEncoding error:&error])
{
    NSLog(@"Error writing to file: %@", [error localizedDescription]);
    return;
}
NSLog(@"String successfully written to file");
```

The path for the file is NSHomeDirectory(), a function that returns a string with a path pointing to the application sandbox. Notice the special append method that properly appends the Documents/file.txt subpath.

In Cocoa, most file access routines offer an atomic option. When you set the atomically parameter to YES, the iPhone writes the file to a temporary auxiliary and then renames it into place. Using an atomic write ensures that the file avoids corruption.

The request shown here returns a Boolean, namely YES if the string was written, or NO if it was not. Should the write request fail, this snippet logs the error using a language-localized description. It uses an instance of the `NSError` class to store that error information and sends the `localizedDescription` selector to convert the information into a human-readable form. Whenever iPhone methods return errors, use this approach to determine which error was generated.

Reading a string from a file follows a similar form but does not return the same Boolean result. Instead, check to see whether the returned string is nil, and if so display the error that was returned.

```
NSString *inString = [NSString stringWithContentsOfFile:path
    encoding:NSUTF8StringEncoding error:&error];
if (!inString)
{
    NSLog(@"Error reading from file % %@", [path lastPathComponent],
        [error localizedDescription]);
    return;
}
NSLog(@"String successfully read from file");
NSLog(@"%@", inString);
```

Accessing Substrings

Cocoa offers a number of ways to extract substrings from strings. Here's a quick review of some typical approaches. As you'd expect, string manipulation is a large part of any flexible API, and Cocoa offers many more routines and classes to parse and interpret strings than the few listed here. This quick `NSString` summary skips any discussion of `NSScanner`, `NSXMLParser`, and so forth.

Converting Strings to Arrays

You can convert a string into an array by separating its components across some repeated boundary. This sample chops the string into individual words by splitting around spaces. The spaces are discarded, leaving an array that contains each number word.

```
NSString *myString = @"One Two Three Four Five Six Seven";
NSArray *wordArray = [myString componentsSeparatedByString: @" "];
NSLog(@"%@", wordArray);
```

Requesting Indexed Substrings

You can request a substring from the start of a string to a particular index, or from an index to the end of the string. These two examples return @"One Two" and @"Two Three Four Five Six Seven", respectively, using the to and from versions of the indexed substring request. As with standard C, array and string indices start at 0.

```
NSString *sub1 = [myString substringToIndex:7];
NSLog(@"%@", sub1);

NSString *sub2 = [myString substringFromIndex:4];
NSLog(@"%@", sub2);
```

Generating Substrings from Ranges

Ranges let you specify exactly where your substring should start and stop. This snippet returns @"Tw", starting at character 4 and extending 2 characters in length. `NSRange` provides a structure that defines a section within a series. You use ranges with indexed items like strings and arrays.

```
NSRange r;
r.location = 4;
r.length = 2;
NSString *sub3 = [myString substringWithRange:r];
NSLog(@"%@", sub3);
```

Search and Replace with Strings

With Cocoa, you can easily search a string for a substring. Searches return a range, which contain both a location and a length. Always check the range location. The location `NSNotFound` means the search failed. This returns a range location of 18, with a length of 4.

```
NSRange searchRange = [myString rangeOfString:@"Five"];
if (searchRange.location != NSNotFound)
    NSLog(@"Range location: %d, length: %d", searchRange.location, searchRange.length);
```

Once you've found a range, you can replace a subrange with a new string. The replacement string does not need to be the same length as the original, thus the result string may be longer or shorter than the string you started with.

```
NSLog(@"%@", [myString stringByReplacingCharactersInRange:
    searchRange withString: @"New String"]);
```

A more general approach lets you replace all occurrences of a given string. This snippet produces @"One * Two * Three * Four * Five * Six * Seven" by swapping out each space for a space-asterisk-space pattern.

```
NSString *replaced = [myString stringByReplacingOccurrencesOfString:
    @" " withString: @" * "];
NSLog(@"%@", replaced);
```

Changing Case

Cocoa provides three simple methods that change a string's case. Here, these three examples produce a string all in uppercase, all in lowercase, and one where every word is capitalized ("Hello World. How Do You Do?"). Because Cocoa supports case-insensitive comparisons, you rarely need to apply case conversions when testing strings against each other.

```
NSString *myString = @"Hello world. How do you do?";
NSLog(@"%@",[myString uppercaseString]);
NSLog(@"%@",[myString lowercaseString]);
NSLog(@"%@",[myString capitalizedString]);
```

Testing Strings

The iPhone offers many ways to compare and test strings. The three simplest check for string equality and match against the string prefix (the characters that start the string) and suffix (those that end it). More complex comparisons use `NSComparisonResult` constants to indicate how items are ordered compared with each other.

```
NSString *s1 = @"Hello World";
NSString *s2 = @"Hello Mom";
NSLog(@"%@ %@ %@", s1, [s1 isEqualToString:s2] ?
    @"equals" : @"differs from", s2);
NSLog(@"%@ %@ %@", s1, [s1 hasPrefix:@"Hello"] ?
    @"starts with" : @"does not start with", @"Hello");
NSLog(@"%@ %@ %@", s1, [s1 hasSuffix:@"Hello"] ?
    @"ends with" : @"does not end with", @"Hello");
```

Extracting Numbers from Strings

Convert strings into numbers by using a value method. These examples return 3, 1, 3.141592, and 3.141592, respectively.

```
NSString *s1 = @"3.141592";
NSLog(@"%d", [s1 intValue]);
NSLog(@"%d", [s1 boolValue]);
NSLog(@"%f", [s1 floatValue]);
NSLog(@"%f", [s1 doubleValue]);
```

Mutable Strings

The `NSMutableString` class is a subclass of `NSString`. It offers you a way to work with strings whose contents can be modified. Once instantiated, you can append new contents to the string, allowing you to grow results before returning from a method. This sample displays "Hello World. The results are in now."

```
NSMutableString *myString = [NSMutableString stringWithString:
    @"Hello World. "];
[myString appendFormat:@"The results are %@ now.", @"in"];
NSLog(@"%@", myString);
```

Numbers and Dates

Foundation offers a large family of value classes. Among these are numbers and dates. Unlike standard C floats, integers, and so forth, these elements are all objects. They can be allocated and released, and used in collections like arrays, dictionaries, and sets. The following examples show numbers and dates in action, providing a basic overview of these classes.

Working with Numbers

The `NSNumber` class lets you treat numbers as objects. You can create new `NSNumber` instances using a variety of convenience methods, namely `numberWithInt:`, `numberWithFloat:`, `numberWithBool:`, and so forth. Once set, you extract those values via `intValue`, `floatValue`, `boolValue`, and so on, and use normal C-based math to perform your calculations.

You are not limited to extracting the same data type an object was set with. You can set a float and extract the integer value, for example. Numbers can also convert themselves into strings.

```
NSNumber *number = [NSNumber numberWithFloat:3.141592];
NSLog(@"%d", [number intValue]);
NSLog(@"%@", [number stringValue]);
```

One of the biggest reasons for using `NSNumber` objects rather than ints, floats, and so forth, is that you can use them with Cocoa routines and classes. For example, you cannot set a user default (that is, a preference value) to, say, the integer 23, as in "You have used this program 23 times." You can, however, store an object `[NSNumber numberWithInt:23]` and later recover the integer value from that object to produce the same user message.

> **Note**
>
> The `NSDecimalNumber` class provides a handy object-oriented wrapper for base-10 arithmetic.

Working with Dates

As with standard C and time(), `NSDate` objects use the number of seconds since an epoch, that is a standardized universal time reference, to represent the current date. The iPhone epoch was at midnight on January 1, 2001. The standard Unix epoch took place at midnight on January 1, 1970.

Each `NSTimeInterval` represents a span of time in seconds, stored with subsecond floating-point precision. The following code shows how to create a new date object using the current time and how to use an interval to reference some time in the future (or past).

```
// current time
NSDate *date = [NSDate date];

// time 10 seconds from now
date = [NSDate dateWithTimeIntervalSinceNow:10.0f];
```

You can compare dates by setting or checking the time interval between them. This snippet forces the application to sleep until 5 seconds into the future and then compares the date to the one stored in `date`.

```
// Sleep 5 seconds and check the time interval
[NSThread sleepUntilDate:[NSDate dateWithTimeIntervalSinceNow:5.0f]];
NSLog(@"Slept %f seconds", [[NSDate date] timeIntervalSinceDate:date]);
```

The standard description method for dates returns a somewhat human-readable string, showing the current date and time.

```
// Show the date
NSLog(@"%@" [date description]);
```

To convert dates into fully formatted strings rather than just using the default description, use an instance of `NSDateFormatter`. You specify the format (for example, YY for two-digit years, and YYYY for four-digit years) using the object's date format property. A full list of format specifiers is offered in the built-in Xcode documentation. In addition to producing formatted output, this class can also be used to read preformatted dates from strings, although that is left as an exercise for the reader.

```
// Produce a formatted string representing the current date
NSDateFormatter *formatter = [[[NSDateFormatter alloc] init]
    autorelease];
formatter.dateFormat = @"MM/dd/YY HH:mm:ss";
NSString *timestamp = [formatter stringFromDate:[NSDate date]];
NSLog(@"%@", timestamp);
```

Timers

When working with time, you may need to request that some action occur in the future. Cocoa offers an easy-to-use timer that triggers at an interval you specify; use the `NSTimer` class. The timer shown here triggers after one second and repeats until the timer is disabled.

```
[NSTimer scheduledTimerWithTimeInterval: 1.0f target: self
    selector: @selector(handleTimer:) userInfo: nil repeats: YES];
```

Each time the timer activates, it calls its target sending the selector message it was initialized with. The callback method takes one argument (notice the single colon), which is the timer itself. To disable a timer, send it the `invalidate` message; this releases the timer object and removes it from the current runloop.

```
- (void) handleTimer: (NSTimer *) timer
{
    printf("Timer count: %d\n", count++);
    if (count > 3)
    {
        [timer invalidate];
        printf("Timer disabled\n");
    }
}
```

Recovering Information from Index Paths

The `NSIndexPath` class is used with iPhone tables. It stores the section and row number for a user selection, that is, when a user taps on the table. When provided with index paths, you can recover these numbers via the `myIndexPath.row` and `myIndexPath.section` properties. Learn more about this class and its use in Chapter 11, "Creating and Managing Table Views."

Collections

The iPhone primarily uses three kinds of collections: arrays, dictionaries, and sets. Arrays act like C arrays. They provide an indexed list of objects, which you can recover by specifying which index to look at. Dictionaries, in contrast, store values that you can look up by keys. For example, you might store a dictionary of ages, where Dad's age is the NSNumber 57, and a child's age is the NSNumber 15. Sets offer an unordered group of objects and are usually used on the iPhone in connection with recovering user touches from the screen. Each of these classes offers regular and mutable versions, just as the `NSString` class does.

Building and Accessing Arrays

Create arrays using the `arrayWithObjects:` convenience method, which returns an autoreleased array. When calling this method, list any objects you want added to the array and finish the list with nil. (If you do not include nil in your list, you'll experience a runtime crash.) You can add any kind of object to an array, including other arrays and dictionaries. This sample showcases the creation of a three-item array.

```
NSArray *array = [NSArray arrayWithObjects:@"One", @"Two", @"Three", nil];
```

The `count` property returns the number of objects in an array. Arrays are indexed starting with 0, up to one less than the count. Attempting to access `[array objectAtIndex: array.count]` causes an "index beyond bounds" exception and crashes. So always use care when retrieving objects, making sure not to cross either the upper or lower boundary for the array.

```
NSLog(@"%d", array.count);
NSLog(@"%@", [array objectAtIndex:0]);
```

Mutable arrays are editable. The mutable form of `NSArray` is `NSMutableArray`. With mutable arrays, you can add and remove objects at will. This snippet copies the previous array into a new mutable one and then edits the array by adding one object and removing another one. This returns an array of [@"One", @"Two", @"Four].

```
NSMutableArray *marray = [NSMutableArray arrayWithArray:array];
[marray addObject:@"Four"];
[marray removeObjectAtIndex:2];
NSLog(@"%@", marray);
```

Whether or not you're working with mutable arrays, you can always combine arrays to form a new version containing the components from each. No checks are done about duplicates. This code produces a six-item array including one, two, and three from the original array, and one, two, and four, from the mutable array.

```
NSLog(@"%@", [array arrayByAddingObjectsFromArray:marray]);
```

Checking Arrays

You can test whether an array contains an object and recover the index of a given object. This code searches for the first occurrence of "Four" and returns the index for that object. The test in the if statement ensures that at least one occurrence exists.

```
if ([marray containsObject:@"Four"])
      NSLog(@"The index is %d",
        [marray indexOfObject:@"Four"]);
```

Converting Arrays into Strings

As with other objects, sending `description` to an array returns an `NSString` that describes an array. In addition, you can use `componentsJoinedByString` to transform an `NSArray` into a string. The following code returns @"One Two Three".

```
NSArray *array = [NSArray arrayWithObjects:@"One", @"Two", @"Three", nil];
NSLog(@"%@", [array componentsJoinedByString:@" "]);
```

Building and Accessing Dictionaries

`NSDictionary` objects store keys and values, enabling you to look up objects using strings. The mutable version of dictionaries, `NSMutableDictionary`, lets you modify these dictionaries by adding and removing elements on demand. In iPhone programming, you use the mutable class more often the static one, so these examples showcase mutable versions.

Creating Dictionaries

Use the `dictionary convenience` method to create a new mutable dictionary, as shown here. This returns a new initialized dictionary that you can start to edit. Populate the dictionary using `setObject: forKey:`.

```
NSMutableDictionary *dict = [NSMutableDictionary dictionary];
[dict setObject:@"1" forKey:@"A"];
[dict setObject:@"2" forKey:@"B"];
[dict setObject:@"3" forKey:@"C"];
NSLog(@"%@", [dict description]);
```

Searching Dictionaries

Searching the dictionary means querying the dictionary by key name. Use `objectForKey:` to find the object that matches a given key. When a key is not found, the dictionary returns nil. This returns `@"1"` and `nil`.

```
NSLog(@"%@", [dict objectForKey:@"A"]);
NSLog(@"%@", [dict objectForKey:@"F"]);
```

Replacing Objects

When you set a new object for the same key, Cocoa replaces the original object in the dictionary. This code replaces "3" with "foo" for the key "C".

```
[dict setObject:@"foo" forKey:@"C"];
NSLog(@"%@", [dict objectForKey:@"C"]);
```

Removing Objects

You can also remove objects from dictionaries. This snippet removes the object associated with the "B" key. Once removed, both the key and the object no longer appear in the dictionary.

```
[dict removeObjectForKey:@"B"];
```

Listing Keys

Dictionaries can report the number of entries they store plus they can provide an array of all the keys currently in use. This key list lets you know what keys have already been used. It lets you test against the list before adding an item to the dictionary, avoiding overwriting an existing key/object pair.

```
NSLog(@"The dictionary has %d objects", [dict count]);
NSLog(@"%@", [dict allKeys]);
```

Accessing Set Objects

Sets store unordered collections of objects. You encounter sets almost exclusively when working with the iPhone's multitouch screen. The `UIView` class receives finger movement updates that deliver touches as an `NSSet`. To work with touches, you almost always issue `allObjects` and work with the array that gets returned. Once converted, use standard array calls to list, query, and iterate through the touches.

Memory Management with Collections

Arrays, sets and dictionaries automatically retain objects when they are added and release those objects when they are removed from the collection. Releases are also sent when the collection is deallocated. Collections do not copy objects. Instead, they rely on retain counts to hold onto objects and use them as needed.

Writing Out Collections to File

Both arrays and dictionaries can store themselves into files using `writeToFile:atomically:` methods so long as the types within the collections belong to the set of `NSData`, `NSDate`, `NSNumber`, `NSString`, `NSArray`, and `NSDictionary`. Pass the path as the first argument, and a Boolean as the second. As when saving strings, the second argument determines whether the file is first stored to a temporary auxiliary and then renamed. The method returns a Boolean value: YES if the file was saved, NO if not. Storing arrays and dictionaries create standard property lists files.

```
NSString *path = [NSHomeDirectory()
stringByAppendingPathComponent:@"Documents/ArraySample.txt"];
if ([array writeToFile:path atomically:YES])
    NSLog(@"File was written successfully");
```

To recover an array or dictionary from file, use the convenience methods `arrayWithContentsOfFile:` and `dictionaryWithContentsOfFile:`. If the methods return nil, the file could not be read.

```
NSArray *newArray = [NSArray arrayWithContentsOfFile:path];
NSLog(@"%@", newArray);
```

Building URLs

`NSURL` objects point to resources. These resources can refer to both local files and to URLs on the Web. Create url objects by passing a string to class convenience functions. Separate functions have been set up to interpret each kind of URL. Once built, however, `NSURL` objects are interchangeable. Cocoa does not care if the resource is local or points to an object only available via the Net. This code demonstrates building URLs of each type, path, and Web.

```
NSString *path = [NSHomeDirectory()
    stringByAppendingPathComponent:@"Documents/foo.txt"];
NSURL *url1 = [NSURL fileURLWithPath:path];
NSLog(@"%@", url1);

NSString *urlpath = @"http://ericasadun.com";
NSURL *url2 = [NSURL URLWithString:urlpath];
NSLog(@"%d characters read",
    [[NSString stringWithContentsOfURL:url2] length]);
```

Working with NSData

If `NSString` objects are analogous to zero-terminated C strings, then `NSData` objects correspond to buffers. `NSData` provides data objects that store and manage bytes. Often, you fill `NSData` with the contents of a file or URL. The data returned can report its length, letting you know how many bytes were retrieved. This snippet retrieves the contents of a URL and prints the number of bytes that were read.

```
NSData *data = [NSData dataWithContentsOfURL:url2];
NSLog(@"%d", [data length]);
```

To access the core byte buffer that underlies an `NSData` object, use `bytes`. This returns a `(const void *)` pointer to actual data.

As with many other Cocoa objects, you can use the standard `NSData` version of the class or its mutable child, `NSMutableData`. Most Cocoa programs that access the Web, particularly those that perform asynchronous downloads, pull in a bit of data at a time. For those cases, `NSMutableData` objects prove useful. You can keep growing mutable data by issuing `appendData:` to add the new information as it is received.

File Management

The iPhone's file manager is a singleton provided by the `NSFileManager` class. It can list the contents of folders to determine what files are found and perform basic file system tasks. The following snippet retrieves a file list from two folders. First it looks in the sandbox's Documents folder and then inside the application bundle itself.

```
NSFileManager *fm = [NSFileManager defaultManager];


// List the files in the sandbox Documents folder
NSString *path = [NSHomeDirectory() stringByAppendingPathComponent:@"Documents"];
NSLog(@"%@",[fm directoryContentsAtPath:path]);

// List the files in the application bundle
path = [[NSBundle mainBundle] bundlePath];
NSLog(@"%@",[fm directoryContentsAtPath:path]);
```

Note the use here of `NSBundle`. It lets you find the application bundle and pass its path to the file manager. You can also use `NSBundle` to retrieve the path for any item included in your app bundle. (You cannot, however, write to the application bundle at any time.) This code returns the path to the application's Default.png image. Note that the file and extension names are separated and that each is case sensitive.

```
NSBundle *mb = [NSBundle mainBundle];
NSLog(@"%@", [mb pathForResource:@"Default" ofType:@"png"]);
```

The file manager offers a full suite of file-specific management. It can move, copy, and remove files as well as query the system for file traits and ownership. Here are some examples of the simpler routines you may use in your applications.

```
// Create a file
NSString *docspath = [NSHomeDirectory()
    stringByAppendingPathComponent:@"Documents"];
NSString *filepath = [NSHomeDirectory()
    stringByAppendingPathComponent:@"Documents/testfile"];
NSArray *array = [@"One Two Three" componentsSeparatedByString:@" "];
[array writeToFile:filepath atomically:YES];
NSLog(@"%@", [fm directoryContentsAtPath:docspath]);

// Copy the file
NSString *copypath = [NSHomeDirectory()
    stringByAppendingPathComponent:@"Documents/copied"];
if (![fm copyItemAtPath:filepath toPath:copypath error:&error])
{
    NSLog(@"Copy Error: %@", [error localizedDescription]);
    return;
}
NSLog(@"%@", [fm directoryContentsAtPathdocspath]);

// Move the file
NSString *newpath = [NSHomeDirectory()
    stringByAppendingPathComponent:@"Documents/renamed"];
if (![fm moveItemAtPath:filepath toPath:newpath error:&error])
```

```
{
    NSLog(@"Move Error: %@", [error localizedDescription]);
    return;
}
NSLog(@"%@", [fm directoryContentsAtPath:docspath]);

// Remove a file
if (![fm removeItemAtPath:copypath error:&error])
{
    NSLog(@"Remove Error: %@", [error localizedDescription]);
    return;
}
NSLog(@"%@", [fm directoryContentsAtPath:docspath]);
```

Note

As another convenient file trick, use tildes in path names, for example, "~/Library/Preferences/foo.plist" and apply the `NSString` method `stringByExpandingTildeInPath`.

One More Thing: Message Forwarding

Although Objective-C does not provide true multiple-inheritance, it offers a workaround that lets objects respond to messages that are implemented in other classes. If you want your object to respond to another class's messages, you can add message forwarding to your applications and gain access to that object's methods.

Normally, sending an unrecognized message produces a runtime error, causing an application to crash. But before the crash happens, the iPhone's runtime system gives each object a second chance to handle a message. Catching that message lets you redirect it to an object that understands and can respond to that message.

Consider the Car example used throughout this chapter. The `carInfo` property introduced midway through these examples returns a string that describes the car's make, model, and year. Now imagine if a `Car` instance could respond to `NSString` messages by passing them to that property. Send `length` to a `Car` object and instead of crashing, the object would return the length of the `carInfo` string. Send `stringByAppendingString:` and the object adds that string to the property string. It would be as if the `Car` class inherited (or at least borrowed) the complete suite of string behavior.

Objective-C provides this functionality through a process called *message forwarding*. When you send a message to an object that cannot handle that selector, the selector gets forwarded to a `forwardInvocation:` method. The object sent with this message, namely an `NSInvocation` instance stores the original selector and arguments that were requested. You can override `forwardInvocation:` and send that message on to another object.

Implementing Message Forwarding

To add message forwarding to your program, you must override two methods, namely, `methodSignatureForSelector:` and `forwardInvocation:`. The former creates a valid method signature for messages implemented by another class. The latter forwards the selector to an object that actually implements that message.

Building a Method Signature

This first method returns a method signature for the requested selector. For this example, a `Car` instance cannot properly create a signature for a selector implemented by another class, in this case `NSString`. Adding a check for a malformed signature (i.e., returning nil) gives this method the opportunity to iterate through each pseudo-inheritance and attempt to build a valid result. This example draws methods from just one other class via `self.carInfo`.

```
- (NSMethodSignature*) methodSignatureForSelector:(SEL)selector
{
    // Check if car can handle the message
    NSMethodSignature* signature = [super
        methodSignatureForSelector:selector];

    // If not, can the car info string handle the message?
    if (!signature)
        signature = [self.carInfo methodSignatureForSelector:selector];

    return signature;
}
```

Forwarding

The second method you need to override is `forwardInvocation:`. This method only gets called when an object has been unable to handle a message. This method gives the object a second chance, allowing it to redirect that message. The method checks to see whether the `self.carInfo` string responds to the selector. If it does respond, it tells the invocation to invoke itself using that object as its receiver.

```
- (void)forwardInvocation:(NSInvocation *)invocation
{
    SEL selector = [invocation selector];

    if ([self.carInfo respondsToSelector:selector])
    {
        printf("[forwarding from %s to %s] ", [[[self class] description]
            UTF8String], [[NSString description] UTF8String]);
        [invocation invokeWithTarget:self.carInfo];
    }
}
```

Using Forwarded Messages

Calling nonclass messages like UTF8String and length produces compile-time warnings, which you can ignore. The code shown in Figure 3-4 causes two compiler warnings. The code, however, compiles and (more importantly) runs without error. As the figure shows, you can send a `Car` instance methods that are defined by the class itself and also those implemented by `NSString`.

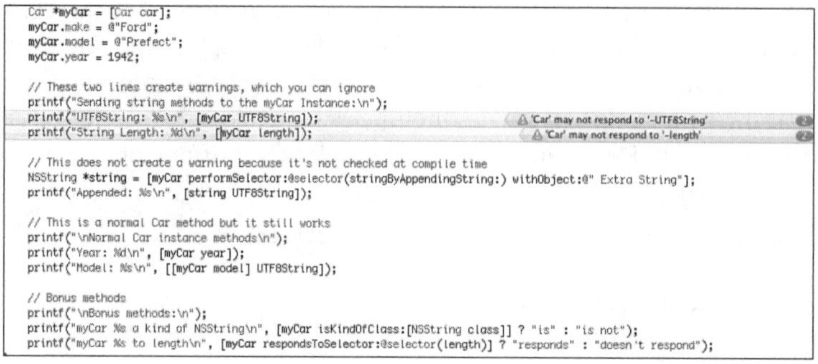

```
Car *myCar = [Car car];
myCar.make = @"Ford";
myCar.model = @"Prefect";
myCar.year = 1942;

// These two lines create warnings, which you can ignore
printf("Sending string methods to the myCar Instance:\n");
printf("UTF8String: %s\n", [myCar UTF8String]);          'Car' may not respond to '-UTF8String'
printf("String Length: %d\n", [myCar length]);            'Car' may not respond to '-length'

// This does not create a warning because it's not checked at compile time
NSString *string = [myCar performSelector:@selector(stringByAppendingString:) withObject:@" Extra String"];
printf("Appended: %s\n", [string UTF8String]);

// This is a normal Car method but it still works
printf("\nNormal Car instance methods\n");
printf("Year: %d\n", [myCar year]);
printf("Model: %s\n", [[myCar model] UTF8String]);

// Bonus methods
printf("\nBonus methods:\n");
printf("myCar %s a kind of NSString\n", [myCar isKindOfClass:[NSString class]] ? "is" : "is not");
printf("myCar %s to length\n", [myCar respondsToSelector:@selector(length)] ? "responds" : "doesn't respond");
```

Figure 3-4 The compiler issues warnings for forwarded methods, but the code runs without error.

House Cleaning

Although invocation forwarding mimics multiple inheritance, NSObject never confuses the two. Methods like `respondsToSelector:` and `isKindOfClass:` only look at the inheritance hierarchy and not at the forwarding change.

A couple of optional methods allow your class to better express its message compliance to other classes. Reimplementing `respondsToSelector:` and `isKindOfClass:` lets other classes query your class. In return, the class announces that it responds to all string methods (in addition to its own) and that it is a "kind of" string, further emphasizing the pseudo-multiple inheritance approach.

```
// Extend selector compliance
- (BOOL)respondsToSelector:(SEL)aSelector
{
    // Car class can handle the message
    if ( [super respondsToSelector:aSelector] )
        return YES;

    // CarInfo string can handle the message
    if ([self.carInfo respondsToSelector:aSelector])
        return YES;
```

```
    // Otherwise...
    return NO;
}

// Allow posing as class
- (BOOL)isKindOfClass:(Class)aClass
{
    // Check for Car
    if (aClass == [Car class]) return YES;
    if ([super isKindOfClass:aClass]) return YES;

    // Check for NSString
    if ([self.carInfo isKindOfClass:aClass]) return YES;

    return NO;
}
```

Supereasy Forwarding

The method signature/forward invocation pair of methods provides a robust and approved way to add forwarding to your classes. A simpler approach is also available on the iPhone, which you can use at your own risk. You can replace both those methods with this single one, which does all the same work with less coding.

```
- (id)forwardingTargetForSelector:(SEL)sel
{
    if ([self.carInfo respondsToSelector:sel]) return self.carInfo;
    return nil;
}
```

Summary

This chapter provided an abridged, high-octane introduction to Objective-C and Foundation. In it, you read about the way that Objective-C extends C and provides support for object-oriented programming. You discovered properties and memory management and were subjected to a speedy review of the most important Foundation classes. So what can you take away from this chapter? Here are a few final thoughts.

- The sample code for this chapter contains all the examples used throughout this introduction. Try testing this material directly in Xcode. Mess around with the material, add your own samples, or expand the ones you've been given. Hands-on offers the best way to gain critical skills you need for iPhone development.

- Learning Objective-C and Cocoa takes more than just a chapter. If you're serious about learning iPhone programming, and these concepts are new to you, consider seeking out single-topic books that are dedicated to introducing these technologies to developers new to the platform. Consider Aaron Hillegass's *Cocoa Programming for Mac OS X*, 3rd Edition, or Stephen Kochan's *Programming in Objective-C 2.0*, 2nd Edition, or Fritz Anderson's *Xcode 3 Unleashed.*
- This chapter mentioned Core Foundation and Carbon but did not delve into these technologies in any depth. You can and will experience C-based APIs on the iPhone, particularly when you work with the address book, with Quartz 2-D graphics, and with Core Audio, among other frameworks. Each of these specific topic areas are documented exhaustively at Apple's developer Web site, complete with sample code. A strong grounding in C (and sometimes C++) programming will help you work through the specific implementation details.

4
Designing Interfaces

The iPhone SDK helps you craft user interfaces. This chapter introduces the visual classes you'll work with and discusses their roles in the interface design process. You read about controllers that work with these visual classes and discover how they handle tasks like device reorientation. Then you move on to solutions for laying out and customizing interfaces. You learn about hybrid solutions that rely both on IB-created interfaces and Objective-C-centered ones. By the time you finish this chapter, you'll have discovered many approaches that you can apply to your own application design.

UIView and UIWindow

Nearly everything that appears on the iPhone's screen is a child of the `UIView` class. Views act like little canvases that you can draw on with colors, pictures, and buttons. You can drag them around the screen. You can resize them. You can layer them. Views provide the basic component of user interfaces.

The iPhone rule goes like this: one window, many views. If you keep that idea in mind, the iPhone interface design scenario simplifies. Metaphorically speaking, `UIWindow` is the TV set, and `UIViews` are the actors on your favorite show. They can move around the screen, appear, and disappear, and may change the way they look and behave over time.

The TV set, on the other hand, normally stays still. It has a set screen size that doesn't change even if the virtual world you see through it is practically unlimited. You may even own several TVs in the same household (just like you can create several `UIWindow` instances in the same application), but you can watch just one at a time.

`UIViews` are user interface building blocks. They provide visual elements that are shown onscreen and invite user interaction. Every iPhone user interface is built from `UIViews` displayed within one `UIWindow`, which is a specialized kind of `UIView`. The window acts a container; it is the root of the display hierarchy. It holds all the visible application components within itself.

Beyond `UIView` and `UIWindow`, you find a wealth of specialized views, such as `UIImageView` and `UITextView`, that allow you to build your interfaces from predesigned components. This section provides a rundown of those views. The Interface Builder library makes these views available to you, allowing you to place them in your application interfaces to build your GUIs.

Note

The UI at the beginning of certain classes (like `UIView`) stands for User Interface.

Views That Display Data

One of the most important things that a view can do is provide a visual representation of data. In Cocoa Touch, the following classes show information onscreen.

- The `UITextView` class presents passages of text to your users and/or allows them to type in their own text using the keyboard. You choose whether to set the view text as editable. Text views use a single font with a single text size throughout.
- `UILabel` instances present short, read-only text views. As the name implies, this class is used to statically label items on your screen. You choose the color, font size, and font face for your labels by setting view properties. The words "Fahrenheit" and "Celsius" shown in Figure 4-8, later in the chapter, are created by `UILabels`.
- `UIImageViews` show pictures. You load them with `UIImage` objects, which are instances of an abstract image storing class. Once loaded, you specify the view's location and size. The `UIImageView` automatically scales its contents to fit those bounds. A special feature of this class allows you to load a sequence of images rather than a single picture and animate them on demand.
- When you want to display HTML, PDFs, or other advanced Web content, the `UIWebView` class provides all the functionality you need. `UIWebView` instances offer a powerhouse of display capabilities, allowing you to present nearly any data type supported by the built-in Safari browser. These views offer simple Web browsing with a built-in history, essentially giving you a canned, usable Safari-style object you can insert into your programs. Sometimes developers use `UIWebView` instances to present blocks of stylized text. As a bonus, these support zoom and scroll with no additional work.
- `MKMapViews` (MK stands for Map Kit) embed maps into your applications. Users can view map information and interact with the map contents, much as they would with the Maps application. This class, which was introduced in the 3.0 SDK, lets you annotate the map with custom information using the `MKAnnotationView` and `MKPinAnnotationView` classes.
- `UIScrollView` instances allow you to present content that is larger than the normal size of an application window. Users can scroll through that content to view it all, using horizontal and/or vertical scrolling. Scroll views support zooming, so you can use standard iPhone pinch and spread gestures to resize content.

Views for Making Choices

The iPhone offers two core classes that offer choices to users. The `UIAlertView` class produces those blue pop-up windows you've seen in many applications. You choose the message and customize their buttons to ask users questions. For example, you might ask a user to confirm or cancel an action in your program. In addition to questions, you can present information. By offering just one button (typically "Okay"), alert views provide a simple way to show text to users.

The second choice-based class is `UIActionSheet`, which offers menus that scroll up from the bottom of the screen. Action sheets display a message and present buttons for the user to choose from. Although these sheets look different from alert views, functionally they perform in a similar manner. As a rule, use action sheets when you have a number of options to choose from and alert views when you are presenting just two or three choices at most.

Both these presentations are modal. They require users to make a selection before proceeding. For this reason, it's polite to offer a cancel option among the other choices.

Controls

Controls are onscreen objects that transform user touches into callback triggers. They may also provide numeric or text values consumed by your application. Controls include buttons, switches, and sliders, among others. They correspond closely to the same kinds of control classes used in desktop programming. Here's a quick rundown of the major classes provided by Cocoa Touch and what each control offers:

- `UIButton` instances provide onscreen buttons. Users can push them to trigger a callback via target/action programming. You specify how the button looks, the text it displays, and how the button triggers. The most typical trigger used is "touch up inside," where the user touch ends inside the button's bounds. If it seems strange to trigger with touch up rather than touch down, consider that the de facto standard on the iPhone allows users to cancel a button press by sliding their finger away from the button before lifting it.

  In Interface Builder, buttons are called Round Rect Buttons. In IB, you also encounter buttons that look like views and act like views but are not, in fact, views. Bar button items (`UIBarButtonItem`) store the properties of toolbar and navigation bar buttons but are not buttons themselves. The bars use these descriptions to build themselves; the actual button views are not generally accessible to you as a developer.

> **Note**
>
> In Interface Builder, you can search the view library by class name (e.g., `UIButton`) or by IB's description (e.g., `round` or `button`).

- The `UISegmentedControl` offers a row of equally sized buttons that act like the old-fashioned radio buttons in a car, namely that only one button can be selected at a time. You can present these buttons as images or text. An option (called "momentary") lets you replace the radio-button behavior with a style that prevents the buttons from showing which button was last selected.
- In Cocoa Touch, the `UISwitch` class provides a simple binary control. This class presents On/Off choices and looks like a standard light switch you'd see on a wall.
- The `UISlider` class lets users choose a value from a specified range by sliding an indicator along a horizontal bar. The indicator (called the "thumb") represents the current setting for the control. The value is set by the thumb's relative placement. The iPhone's onscreen volume slider in the iPod/Music application represents a typical slider instance.
- Page controls let users move between pages, usually as part of a `UIScrollView` implementation. The `UIPageControl` class offers a series of small dots (like the ones you see on the iPhone's home page) showing the current page and letting users navigate to the next or previous pages.
- `UITextFields` are a kind of control that let you enter text. These fields offer just a single line for input and are meant to solicit short text items (like usernames and passwords) from users. Figure 4-8, later in the chapter, includes two text fields.

Tables and Pickers

Tables present a scrolling list of choices. The `UITableView` class provides the most commonly used table style, which you see, for example, in the Contacts, YouTube, and iPod/Music applications. Tables offer rows of information (provided by the `UITableViewCell` class), which users scroll through and can select.

The `UIPickerView` class offers a kind of table, where users can select choices by scrolling individual wheels. A specialized version of this class is the `UIDatePicker`, which comes preloaded with date- and time-specific behavior and is used extensively in the Calendar and Clock applications.

Bars

The iPhone offers four kinds of bar-style views. Bars are compact views (typically shorter than 50 pixels in height) that extend from one side of the screen to the other. The most commonly used view is the `UINavigationBar` (see Figure 4-2, later in the chapter), which is presented on top of many interfaces to provide navigation state. As a developer, you almost never work directly with class instances. Instead, the view is generated and managed by `UINavigationController` instances, which you read about in chapter sections that follow this one.

Tab bars offer the kinds of choices you see at the bottom of the YouTube and iPod/Music applications, like Featured, Most Viewed, Albums, and Podcasts. Later in the chapter, Figure 4-3 (top) shows a typical `UITabBar` instance. Search bars (UISearchBar) add a text-based view meant to be shown on the top navigation bar of a table, as used in the Contacts application. As with navigation bars, you normally work through `UITabBarControllers` and `UISearchDisplayControllers` instead of building and managing the view directly.

Of all the iPhone bars, only the `UIToolbar` class is meant for direct use. It provides a series of buttons similar to segmented controls but with a different look (see Figure 4-3, bottom). Toolbars are limited to a momentary highlighting style. The role of toolbars is to provide a vocabulary of actions that act on the current view. The toolbar used in the Mail application allows you to delete messages or to reply to messages. Toolbars present monochrome images on each button.

If your design ideas include tab bars and toolbars, take the time to read Apple's Human Interface Guidelines, available as part of the standard iPhone documentation library. Apple regularly rejects applications that use bars in a manner inconsistent with these guidelines.

> **Note**
>
> As with bar button Items, navigation items appear in Interface Builder and can be placed in your projects as you would place views. Like their cousins, navigation items are not views themselves. They store information about what items go on navigation bars and are used to build the bar that does appear.

Progress and Activity

Cocoa Touch provides two classes meant to communicate an ongoing activity to the user. The `UIActivityIndicatorView` offers a spinning-style wheel, which is shown during an ongoing task. The wheel tells the user that the task may finish at some point, but it does not determine when that time will end. When you want to communicate progress to a user, use the `UIProgressView` class. Instances offer a bar that fills from left to right, indicating how far a task has progressed.

UIViewControllers

On the iPhone, view controllers centralize certain kinds of view management. They provide practical utility by linking views into the pragmatic reality of your device. View controllers handle reorientation events such as when users tip the iPhone on its side to landscape mode and navigation issues such as when users need to move their attention from view to view.

View controllers aren't views. They are abstract classes with no visual representation; only views offer visual canvases. Instead, they help your views live in a larger application design environment. Do not set a frame the way you would with a normal `UIView`. `UIViews` use `initWithFrame:`; `UIViewControllers` use `init`.

The iPhone SDK offers many view controller classes. These classes range from the general to the specific. In a way, specialized controllers are both a blessing and a curse. On the positive side, they introduce enormous functionality, essentially with no additional programming burden. On the downside, they're so specialized that they often hide core features that developers might prefer to work with.

For example, there's no simple camera access class. You must work through the `UIImagePickerController` class to snap photos. This class with its prebuilt GUI is elegant and well designed, but it denies developers direct access to the camera and to custom user interfaces that they might prefer to build. You cannot pull live data from the camera and store it to a time-lapse database. Instead, your user must shoot the image, agree that the image is what he or she wanted, and then pass the control back to your application.

Here's a quick guide to some of the view controllers you'll encounter while building your iPhone application interfaces.

UIViewController

`UIViewController` is the parent class for view controllers and the one you use to manage your primary views. It's the workhorse of view controllers. You may spend a large part of your time customizing this one class. The basic `UIViewController` class manages each primary view's lifetime from start to finish and takes into account the changes that the view must react to along the way.

For example, `UIViewControllers` handle reorientation tasks, letting you program for both landscape and portrait orientation. `UIViewControllers` decide whether to change their orientation when a user tilts the iPhone, and specify how that orientation change occurs. They do this via instance methods like `shouldAutorotateToInterface➥Orientation:`. Without a view controller, your interface won't support automatic orientation updates. Many developers have found it difficult trying to rotate `UIViews` directly without the help of a view controller class.

`UIViewController` instances are responsible for setting up how a view looks and what subviews it displays. Often they rely on loading that information from .xib files. A variety of instance methods such as `loadView` and `viewDidLoad` let you add behavior while or after a view sets up.

Reacting to views being displayed or dismissed is another job that view controllers handle. These are the realities of belonging to a larger application. Methods like `viewDidAppear:` and `viewWillDisappear:` let you finish any bookkeeping associated with your view management. You might preload data in anticipation of being presented or clean up memory that won't be used when the view is not onscreen.

Each of the tasks mentioned here specifies how a view fits into an enveloping application and works on a particular device. The `UIViewController` mediates between views and these external demands, allowing the view to change itself to meet these needs.

UINavigationController

As the name suggests, navigation controllers allow you to navigate up and down through tree-based view hierarchies. They create the solid-colored navigation bars that appear at the top of many standard iPhone applications. You see navigation controllers in use whenever you drill through some sort of hierarchy, whether using the Contacts application or the on-iPhone App Store. Both of these applications are built using navigation controllers.

Navigation controllers let you push new views into place and automatically generate "back" buttons showing the title of the calling view controller. All navigation controllers use a "root" view controller to establish the top of their navigation tree, letting those back buttons lead you back to a primary view. Navigation controllers and their trees are discussed in greater detail later in this chapter.

Handing off responsibility to a navigation controller lets you focus your design work on creating individual view controller screens. You don't have to worry about specific navigation details other than telling the navigation controller which view to move to next. The history stack and the navigation buttons are handled for you. Chapter 5, "Working with View Controllers," discusses navigation controllers in further detail and offers recipes for their use.

UITabBarController

Parallel views are like stations on a radio. A tab bar helps users select which `UIViewController` to "tune in to," without there being a specific navigation hierarchy. You see this best in applications like YouTube and iPod, where users choose whether to see a "Top 25" list or decide between viewing albums or playlists. Each parallel world operates independently, and each can have its own navigation hierarchy. You build the view controller or navigation controller that inhabits each tab, and Cocoa Touch handles the multiple-view details.

For example, when tab bar instances offer more than five view controller choices at a time, users can customize them through the More > Edit screen. The More > Edit screen lets users drag their favorite controllers down to the button bar at the bottom of the screen. No extra programming is involved. You gain editable tabs for free. All you have to do is request them via the `customizableViewControllers` property. See Chapter 5 to read more about implementing tab bar-based applications and setting the images that adorn each button.

Table Controllers

Table view controllers simplify using tables in your iPhone projects. The `UITableViewController` class provides a standard already-connected `UITableView` instance and automatically sets delegation and data sources to point to itself. All you have to do is supply those delegate and data source methods to fill up the table with data and react to user taps. `UITableViewController` is discussed at length in Chapter 11, "Creating and Managing Table Views."

The search display controller is a kind of table view but one that offers a built-in search bar via `UISearchBar`. With it, you allow users to search data that is provided by another view controller, called its *contents controller*. As users update the search information, the contents controller adjusts its data source to include only those items that match the search query.

It may seem odd to force another controller to perform that work, but in practice, it works out very neatly. The contents controller is almost always a table view controller, which displays the search controller on demand. The search then weeds through the original table's data and shows a subset of that information until the search is dismissed.

The `NSFetchedResultsController` also provides a kind of table-based controller. Although strictly speaking, not a view controller, this class helps populate a UITableView with objects fetched from a Core Data store. See Chapter 19, "A Taste of Core Data," for an example that shows this class in action.

Address Book Controllers

The Address Book user interface framework (AddressBookUI.framework) provides several view controllers that let you select a person from your address book, view his or her details, and add a new person or modify an existing person's entry. These view controllers tie into the C-based ABAddressBook framework, which provides functions that query and update the iPhone's built-in address book. Chapter 18, "Connecting to the Address Book," discusses the Address Book and its UI controllers in greater detail.

UIImagePickerController

This utility controller allows users to select images from onboard albums or to snap a photo or shoot video using the iPhone camera. With it, you gain full access to most of the organizational features made available to users via the Camera and Photos applications. In truth, there are not two separate applications. There is just one application that poses as those two utilities, just as the single controller offers access to both camera and photo selection features.

When selecting pictures, Apple has added an advanced image-selection interface. Users can navigate up and down the photo album hierarchy until they find the image they want to use. The picker automatically handles access to the onboard photo album leaving you little more to do than decide how to use the picture it picks.

The photo/video interface is equally impressive. The controller even lets the users optionally orient and zoom an image before finishing, providing user-defined "edits" on the picture they snap. Full discussions of this class, including how-to's for both the selection and camera versions, appear in Chapter 7, "Working with Images," and Chapter 15, "Audio, Video, and MediaKit."

Mail Composition

The `MFMailComposeViewController` lets you create mail messages that users can customize from directly in your program. Although the iPhone has long supported `mailto:` URLs to send mail messages, this new class introduced in the 3.0 SDK offers far more control over mail contents and attachments. What's more, users can continue working within your program without being forced to leave to access the Mail application.

The mail composition controller is simple to use and is used in Chapter 7 to mail photographs. It is part of the MessageUI framework; the MF prefix apparently stands for Message Framework.

GKPeerPickerController

The GameKit peer picker provides a standard GUI for discovering and connecting to other iPhones. It offers a slick interface listing other iPhones that are available and can be linked to. Although this controller is part of GameKit, its technology is readily adaptable to nongame uses including file transfer, messaging, and so forth.

You can configure the picker to select whether to use Bluetooth or Internet connections. When presented to the user, only the supported connections appear. Note that users cannot control that choice themselves using this interface.

Read more about using the peer picker controller in Chapter 12, "Making Connections with GameKit and Bonjour."

Media Player Controllers

The Media Player framework offers several controllers that allow you to choose and play music and movies. The `MPMediaPickerController` provides a media-selection GUI that allows users to choose music, podcasts, and audio books. You choose which media to present, and you can play back that media via an `MPMusicPlayerController` instance.

When your user needs to watch a movie or listen to audio, an `MPMoviePlayerController` instance does the trick. Just supply it with a path to the media resource and push the controller into view. The controller provides a Done button for the user or automatically returns a delegate call when playback finishes.

If you want to read more about picking and playing back media, refer to Chapter 15.

View Design Geometry

The iPhone hardware is not theoretically limited to a 320-by-480 display. Design your applications as resolution-independently as possible. That having been said, certain facts of geometry play a role in the design of current generation iPhone applications, particularly when you need to hand specs to a graphic designer to take to Photoshop.

Here is a rundown of the onscreen elements whose geometry can mostly be counted on to stay set when building your interfaces. Try not to rely on these sizes where possible, but rather design around them while keeping their proportions and aspect ratios in mind.

Keep in mind that future iPhone models and related iPhone OS devices may not use the same screen size or shape. All the measurements in this section apply specifically to the first five members of the iPhone OS family, all of which use a 320x480 screen: the first generation iPhone, the iPhone 3G/3G S, and the various generations of iPod touch.

Status Bar

The status bar at the very top of the iPhone screen shows the time, connectivity, battery status, and carrier (iPhones) or model (iPods) of the unit. This bar is 20 pixels in height for normal use. It zooms to 40 pixels high during phone calls or when displaying messages;

note that double-height status bars appear to be a portrait-only feature. Unfortunately the SDK does not offer any public hooks into the message display system so you can't display your own messages. You can see these 40-pixel colorful status displays when you pause a Voice Memo recording, use Nike+, or tether the iPhone on 3G or later units.

Figure 4-1 shows the status bar for portrait, landscape, and 40-pixel-high message modes. You can hide the status bar from your users, but doing so at a minimum eliminates their access to seeing the time and battery information unless you supply that information elsewhere in your application's user interface. You can set the status bar to display in gray, black, or translucent black. The latter allows the view behind it to bleed through to better coordinate colors with your application.

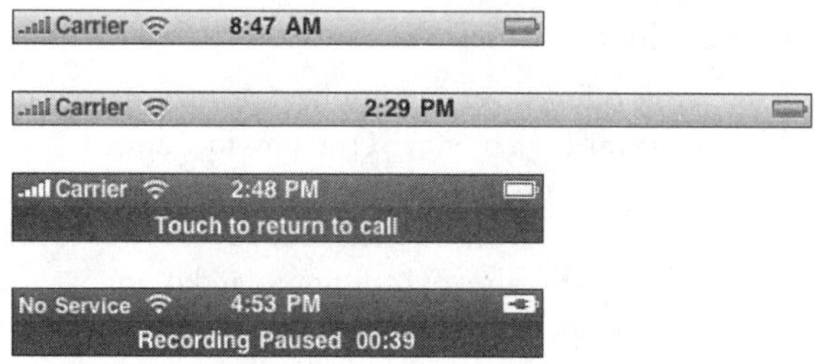

Figure 4-1 The status bar is normally 20 pixels high, regardless of whether the iPhone is using portrait or landscape orientation. At times the status bar zooms to 40 pixels in height to indicate ongoing system operations like a phone call or a paused recording.

If you'd rather free up those 20 pixels of screen space for other use, you can hide the status bar entirely. Use this `UIApplication` call: `[UIApplication sharedApplication] setStatusBarHidden:YES animated:NO]`. Alternatively, set the `UIStatusBarHidden` key to `<true/>` in your application Info.plist file.

With the status bar displayed, your application has 320x460 pixels to work with in portrait mode, and 480x300 pixels in landscape mode for the standard iPhone. These numbers change depending on whatever other elements you add into the interface such as navigation bars, tab bars, and so forth. And as already mentioned, the standard iPhone pixel dimensions may change over time as Apple releases new models and new related touch-based products that run iPhone OS.

The status bar plays a role in both landscape and portrait orientations, adjusting to fit as needed. To run your application in landscape-only mode, set the status bar orientation to landscape. Do this even if you plan to hide the status bar (that is, `[[UIApplication sharedApplication] setStatusBarOrientation: UIInterfaceOrientation LandscapeRight]`). Alternatively, set `UIInterfaceOrientation` in your Info.plist to the string `UIInterfaceOrientationLandscapeLeft` or `UIInterfaeOrientationLandscapeRight`. These options force windows to display side to side and produce a proper landscape keyboard.

> **Note**
>
> Use Hardware > Toggle In Call Status Bar to test your interfaces in the simulator using the 40-pixel-high status bar.

Navigation Bars, Toolbars, and Tab Bars

By default, `UINavigationBar` objects (see Figure 4-2) are 44 pixels in height in portrait mode and 32 pixels high in landscape. They stretch from one side of the screen to the other, so their full dimensions are 320x44 pixels and 480x32 pixels.

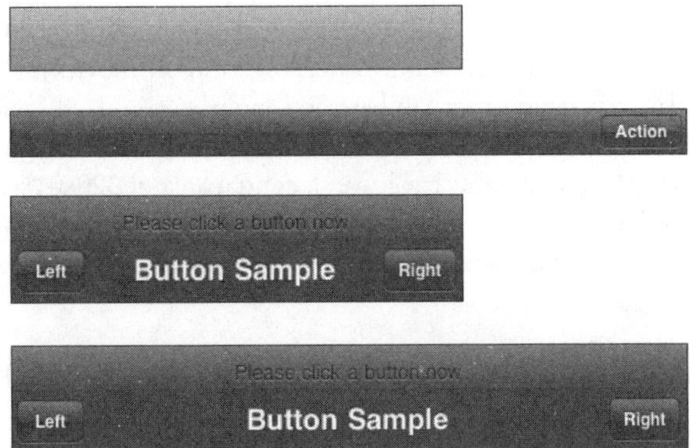

Figure 4-2 Navigation bars stretch from one side of the screen to the other. Their height is fixed at 44 pixels for portrait mode and 32 pixels for landscape on the standard iPhone. The rarely used prompt feature shown in the bottom two images zoom the bar to 74 pixels high.

Navigation bars offer a seldom-used "prompt" mode that extends the height by 30 pixels. In portrait mode, the bar occupies 320x74 pixels and in landscape, 480x74, using a 44 pixel high navigation bar rather than the normal 32 pixel high version.

> **Note**
>
> To add a prompt to a navigation bar, edit the view controller's navigation item, that is, `self.navigationItem.prompt = @"Please click a button now";`.

Tab bars are 48 pixels high in both orientations, 320x48 pixels and 480x48 pixels. According to Apple, the individual items on tab bars should be designed with a minimum 44x44 hit region to provide sufficient space for users to tap. That corresponds to individual art of about 30x30 pixels.

Figure 4-3 shows a typical tab bar and its near-cousin class, the toolbar. Toolbars use the same 44 pixel spacing as navigation bars but, like tab bars, they're meant to be displayed at the bottom of the screen.

Figure 4-3 Tab bars are 48 pixels high for 320x480-pixel iPhone units (top). Toolbars use the same 44-pixel spacing as navigation bars.

These two UI elements aren't generally meant for landscape mode use. You can see this with both the iPod and YouTube applications. These apps swap out a toolbar-based portrait view for a completely separate landscape presentation: Coverflow for iPod, movies for YouTube.

Between status bars, navigation bars, tab bars, and toolbars, you need to apply some basic math to calculate the remaining proportions available to background design. A typical application with a navigation bar and status bar leaves a central area of 320x416 for portrait display and 480x268 for landscape. Using tab bars or toolbars effectively diminishes the available height by another 48 or 44 pixels and the resulting proportions change accordingly.

Keyboards and Pickers

The standard iPhone keyboard uses 320x216 pixels for landscape presentation and 480x162 for portrait. Figure 4-4 shows the keyboard in its default configuration in both its orientations. When a text element becomes active in your application, the keyboard displays over any elements at the bottom of the screen leaving a shortened space at the top for interaction. Complex keyboard layouts may use even more onscreen room.

Figure 4-4 Both the portrait and landscape keyboards occupy a large part of the iPhone screen. Design your applications accordingly.

As a rule, resize your main view when the keyboard displays. When you have several on-screen elements to edit, a shortened scrolling view works best. This lets your users access all possible areas by scrolling and won't leave text fields or text views hidden behind the keyboard. Change the background view's frame, shortening it by 216 or 162 pixels, depending on orientation.

Make sure you provide a way for the user to dismiss the keyboard, by pressing the Return key or tapping a Done button, to make sure you can return to your normal display. Don't leave users caught with the keyboard displayed. See Chapter 9, "Building and Using Controls," for a discussion about dismissing keyboards for more details.

> **Note**
>
> Both the `UIPickerView` and `UIDatePicker` use the same geometry as the standard Keyboard. `UISwitches` default to 94 by 28 pixels, and `UISegmentedControls` are typically 44 pixels high in their standard text-based form.

Text Fields

When working with `UITextField` instances, allocate at least 30 pixels in height. This allows users enough room to enter text using the default font size without clipping.

The UIScreen Class

The `UIScreen` object acts as a stand-in for the iPhone's physical screen, which you can access via `[UIScreen mainScreen]`. This object maps standard window layout boundaries into pixel space. It takes into account any toolbars, status bars, and navigation bars in use.

To recover the size of the entire screen, use `[[UIScreen mainScreen] bounds]`. This returns a rectangle defining the full pixel size of the iPhone's screen. As mentioned earlier in this chapter, the iPhone screen may not always be 320x480 pixels in size should Apple introduce new units.

Another method call returns the central application space. Call `[[UIScreen mainScreen] applicationFrame]` to query this value. On a first or second generation unit, for an application that uses a status bar and a navigation bar, this might return a size of 320x416 pixels, taking into account the 20-pixel status bar and 44-pixel navigation bar.

Use these numbers to calculate the available space on your iPhone screen and lay out your application views when not using Interface Builder.

Building Interfaces

There's more than one way to build an interface. With the iPhone SDK, you can build a GUI by hand using Objective-C, or you can lay it out visually in Interface Builder. When coding, you programmatically specify where each element appears onscreen and how it behaves. With Interface Builder, you lay out those same elements using a visual editor.

Both approaches offer benefits. As a developer, it's up to you to decide how to balance these benefits.

In the end, both technologies take you to the same place. The code used in Objective-C corresponds directly to the layout used in Interface Builder, and the callback behavior set up in Interface Builder produces identical results to those designed in Objective-C.

Yes, the implementation details differ. A hand-built version uses `loadView` to create the main view and add its interface elements. In contrast, an xib-based view controller finishes setting itself up in `viewDidLoad` after loading the prebuilt interface from a .xib file. Cocoa Touch supports both these approaches, plus you can use a hybrid approach, loading .xib files via direct Objective-C commands.

The next few sections show you various ways to use these tools. You walk through a full IB approach and then a full Xcode one. After, you'll find two further hybrid solutions. All four of these walk-throughs produce identical end products offering identical functionality.

Walk-Through: Building a Temperature Converter with IB

Interface Builder, with its interactive GUI layout tools, helps lay out visual content. It makes it possible for you to add interactive controls, moving them around the screen by hand to design custom interfaces. This first example creates a classic Fahrenheit to Celsius converter using absolutely standard Xcode/IB design templates. The interface is laid out entirely in Interface Builder with a minimum of coding in Xcode.

> **Note**
>
> Make sure that you have worked through the Hello World examples in Chapter 2, "Building Your First Project," so you have a starting off point for understanding Xcode and Interface Builder. The samples in this chapter go into greater depth but assume you've already learned some of the basic vocabulary for using these tools.

Create a New Project

Launch Xcode and create a new project. Choose File > New Project > iPhone OS > Application > Navigation-based Application and click Choose. Name it HelloWorld and save it to your Desktop. Once created, a new project window opens in Xcode. This new project contains two .xib files, MainWindow.xib and RootViewController.xib, as well as classes for your application delegate and the root view controller.

Any time you use a navigation-style project, you must assign it a root view controller. This is the view controller that lives at the top of the navigation tree. All other view controllers branch out from this one. The name of the .xib file and its class reflect this design necessity.

Add Media

Before moving forward, you need to add some basic media to the project. Copy the icon.png and Default.png artwork—they're in the sample code folder—to the project by dropping them into the Resources group in the Groups & Files column. Make sure to check Copy Items into Destination Group's Folder (If Needed) before clicking Add.

> **Note**
>
> When you use a single asset in multiple projects, you can add that file without copying. This maintains a single source version that you can update, and its changes are reflected in each of the projects that use it. On the downside, if you remove the file from any project, you might accidentally delete the original, which can affect multiple projects.

These two items provide the image used for the application icon on the iPhone's SpringBoard (icon.png) and the image displayed as the application launches (Default.png). Each application you build should contain art for these. The roles of these two items are discussed in further detail in Chapter 1, "Introducing the iPhone SDK."

Next, add cover320x416.png in the same manner and add it to the Resources group. This file provides a backsplash image, which you use in this project. The art is sized for a portrait-style interface that uses a status bar and a navigation bar.

Interface Builder

Locate MainWindow.xib and double-click it to open the file in Interface Builder. Bring the MainWindow.xib window to the front. It is listed in the Windows menu if you have trouble finding it. Here, you find five items, as shown in Figure 4-5. The first two, File's Owner and First Responder, you saw in Chapter 2. The others, a Hello World application delegate (labeled Hello World A...), the Window, and the navigation controller (labeled Navigation Co...) are new.

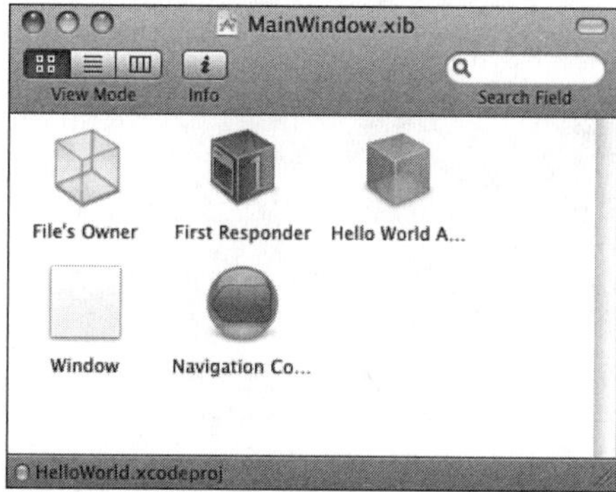

Figure 4-5 The standard MainWindow.xib components generated by Xcode's Navigation Application.

The identity inspector (Command-4) lets you explore the classes for each object. Click on each object with the inspector open. The File's Owner is a `UIApplication` instance, and its delegate is the Hello World application delegate. This matches the design pattern previously discussed in Chapter 1.

The Window is a `UIWindow` instance. The window provides a full-screen view that owns all application views once they are added. You will not work with this instance directly because it has already been set up to show the view contents defined by the navigation controller.

The role of the navigation controller is a little tricky. That's because it provides a navigation bar showing an optional title and maybe some buttons while another class provides the actual interface elements below the bar. Every `UINavigationController` must be initialized with a single root view controller. That view controller provides the view that fills the rest of the screen. Navigation controllers are discussed in greater detail later in this chapter.

Double-click the navigation controller object and an editor window opens, as shown in Figure 4-6. As you can see from this screenshot, the MainWindow .xib does not define the root directly. Instead, it loads that view from RootViewController.xib, the second .xib file that was created when you built the Navigation Application template.

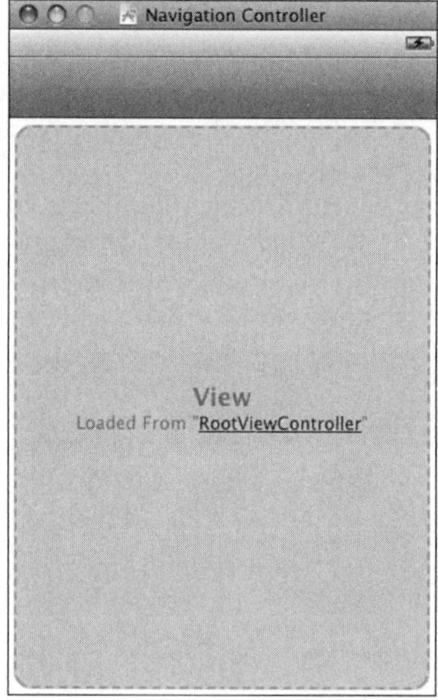

Figure 4-6 The Navigation Controller loads its root view controller from a secondary .xib file.

In theory, loading that view controller from a secondary file lets you design components orthogonally, designing the view separately from the window and navigation bar. (In reality, this is not a universally loved feature of Interface Builder.) Open the Attributes Inspector (Command-1). Here you see the pop-up that lets you choose a .xib to set as the root view controller. Do not change the selection, as you have no other UIViewController .xib items to choose from.

Edit the Navigation Bar

Return to the editor shown in Figure 4-6, and make the following changes. First double-click the middle of the blue bar and type the word "Converter." This adds a title to your navigation bar. Second, drag a bar button item from the library (Tools > Library, Command-Shift-L) onto the right side of the bar. Double-click and change the word "Item" to "Convert." Figure 4-7 shows the bar after performing these actions.

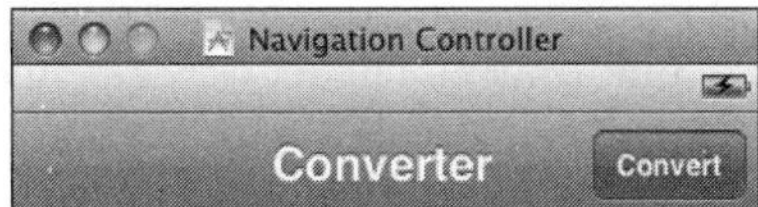

Figure 4-7 You can edit the navigation controller bar directly and add buttons to it.

Replace the Main View

When using standard templates, sometimes Apple doesn't quite deliver what you really need. To see this problem in action, open RootViewController.xib in Interface Builder. This file includes a File's Owner, a First Responder, and a Table View. Xcode's default Navigation Application project assumes you will use a table view controller, but this walk-through requires a `UIViewController` instead. Quit IB. You're about to replace the table-based controller with a view-based one.

In Xcode, select RootViewController.xib, RootViewController.h, and RootViewController.m. Delete these files by pressing Delete on your keyboard. Choose Also Move to Trash. This eliminates the table-based defaults you started with.

Choose File > New (Command-N) > iPhone OS > Cocoa Touch Class > UIViewController subclass. Check With XIB for User Interface and click Next. Name the file RootViewController.m, check Also Create RootView Controller.h, set the location to your main project folder, and click Finish. This builds a new view-based version of the three RootViewController files you need for the project: the .xib file, the .h header file, and the .m implementation file. At this point, you may want to drag the new class files into the Classes group and the new .xib file into the Resources group.

> **Note**
>
> I use navigation controller-based projects often enough that I created my own template rather than fix up the table-based version each time. Directions for building your own Xcode user templates appear in Chapter 2.

Enable Simulated Elements

Locate the new RootViewController.xib file and double-click it to open it in IB. In Interface Builder, double-click View. This opens the view editor, which starts as basically a blank view, possibly with a status bar. Before going any further, you need to add a simulated element; this ensures that the design space matches the components that show onscreen.

Open the attributes inspector (Command-1). The status bar should already be selected as Gray. If it is not, go ahead and do so. Then choose Top Bar > Navigation Bar. This adds a basic navigation bar placeholder to the view. Leave the bottom bar unselected. These simulated elements block off parts of the screen, limiting your design space to the remaining area.

Create an Image Backdrop

Drag an image view into the editor. It automatically zooms to fill all available space in the view below the navigation bar. Let the image view automatically snap into place and completely cover that below-bar area.

In the attributes inspector, locate the Image drop-down. Choose cover320x416.png. This drop-down lists all available art from your Xcode project. (To add more images, drop them into the project in Xcode.) After selecting the png image, the editor's image view updates to show the art you chose.

Remaining in the attributes inspector, check Interaction > User Interaction Enabled. This is a vital step, allowing users to interact with any subviews. Whenever you use an image backdrop, always be sure to enable interactions. This little "gotcha" frequently snags developers who forget.

Add Labels and Views

Drag two text fields and two labels into the view from the library. Set up these elements to roughly match the layout in Figure 4-8. Then double-click the labels and edit the text, labeling the top one Fahrenheit and the bottom Celsius.

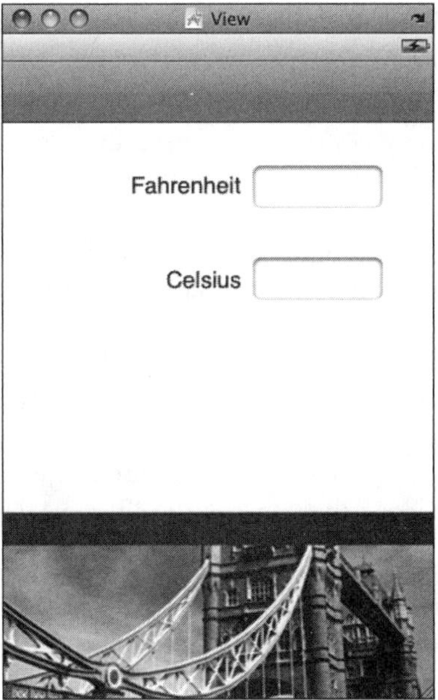

Figure 4-8 Lay out your text fields and labels to match this design.

It's important to specify how you want each text field to interact with users. Among other features, you can choose which keyboard to display, whether a prompt appears in the text box, whether words are autocorrected, autocapitalized, and so forth.

Select the top text field. In the attributes inspector, choose Text Input Traits > Keyboard > Numbers & Punctuation. This ensures that a numeric keyboard is presented when the user taps the top field.

Select the bottom field. Uncheck Control > Content > Enabled. The bottom field shows results and should not be editable by users.

> **Note**
>
> As you add more elements to your Interface Builder view, it becomes difficult to select the correct one by clicking on it. One handy tip is to Control+Shift+click on any view in an Interface Builder edit window to display a list of all views stacked at that point. You can choose an item from that list to select it.

Test the Interface

Save your changes and return to Xcode. Choose Project > Set Active SDK > iPhone Simulator, and then Run > Run to compile the project as-is and run it in the simulator. While running, make sure that the top field opens a numbers-based keyboard and that the bottom field cannot be edited. You can click on the Convert button, but it does not do anything yet. So long as your project can be compiled, you can always check your current progress in the simulator and/or on a device.

Although you can test an interface directly in Interface Builder (use File > Simulate Interface, Command-R), the IB implementation is far less reliable than actual Xcode testing.

Add Outlets and an Action

Outlets and actions play important roles in Interface Builder design. Outlets connect interfaces to objects; they essentially act as instance variable stand-ins. Actions are methods that your IB-created interfaces can invoke. They specify target/action pairs, sending callbacks from control views to objects. For this project you need to create two outlets and one action.

Return to Interface Builder and open the Library > Classes pane. Type RootViewController into the search field at the bottom of the pane. Then tap on RootViewController in the search results and click the Outlets tab. Add two outlets by clicking the + button. Name them `field1` and `field2`. By default, the outlets are typed to id. Edit each type to change id to `UITextField`. Typing limits how outlets can connect to view objects. When typed to `UITextField`, the outlets can connect to the two fields you placed in the view but not, for example, to the labels.

Next, add an action, again using +. Edit the default action name to `convert:`, making sure to add the colon. Figure 4-9 shows the Library pane after making these changes.

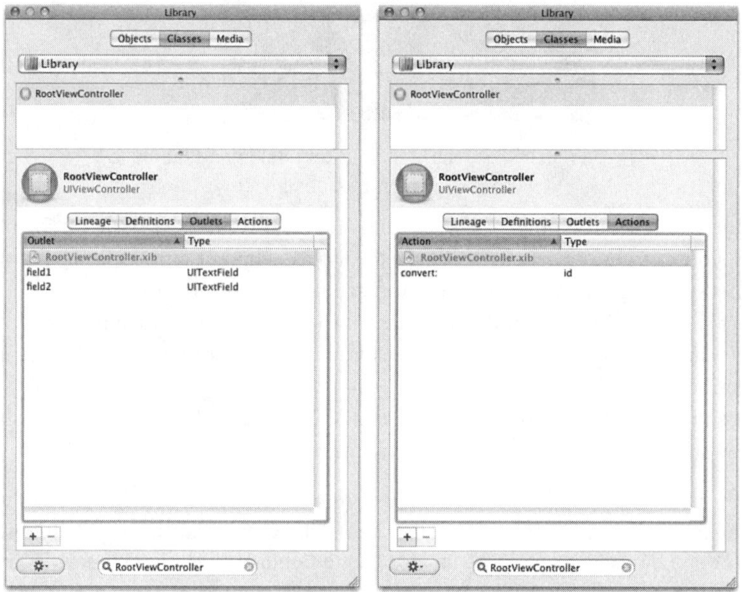

Figure 4-9 Use the Library's Classes pane to add outlets and actions to your classes.

Interface Builder can generate class files from the action and outlet changes you made. Save the project, select File's Owner, and choose File > Write Class Files. Keep the filename as RootViewController (no extensions) and save into your main folder, not the Classes subfolder. When you re-created RootViewController, both the .xib file and the class files were added to the main project folder. Click Replace to replace those files. Take note that this action could cause data loss if you've already customized the `RootViewController` class and then use IB to overwrite those changes.

> **Note**
>
> Interface Builder can read class header files from Xcode (File > Read Class Files), or yo drop header files into your IB document. This lets you add instances of custom classes ...d assign objects to those classes with the identity inspector. If your .xib file "forgets" which class the file owner belongs to (usually indicated by a warning about the view outlet being connected but no longer defined), just reimport the custom view controller class header.

Inspect the New Class Header

Return to Xcode and open RootViewController.h. The newly generated class interface includes the outlets and action you defined in IB. Both `field1` and `field2` are typed, as you requested, as `UITextField` instances and they are declared using the `IBOutlet` keyword. This keyword specifies that the instance variable will be set to match an IB element when the view controller loads. The single convert action is typed to `IBAction`, which is basically the same as `(void)`.

```
@interface RootViewController : UIViewController {
    IBOutlet UITextField *field1;
    IBOutlet UITextField *field2;
}
- (IBAction)convert:(id)sender;
@end
```

Although you have now defined these two outlets and the action in your `RootViewController` class, you have not made any assignments that would connect these to elements in your view object. It's time to do so.

Add Your Connections

Return to IB, select File's Owner, and open the connections inspector (Command-2). This inspector (shown in Figure 4-10) lists each available outlet and action. The empty circles on the right show that the three elements you added have not yet been assigned.

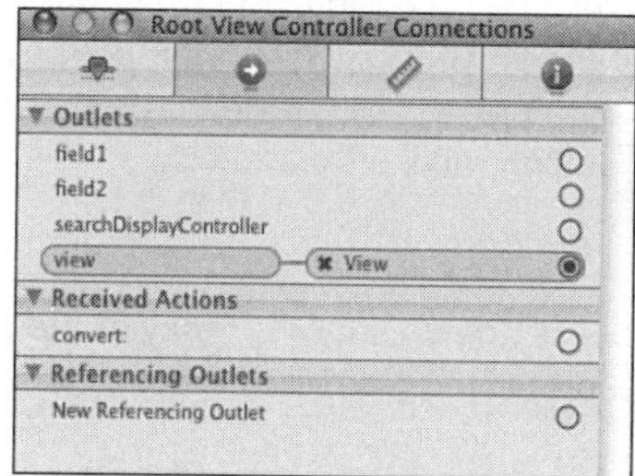

Figure 4-10 Empty circles indicate outlets and actions that have yet to be connected to real world objects.

Drag from the field1 circle to the top text field. Then drag from the field2 circle to the bottom text field. These connections define the real objects that each IBOutlet refers to. Save your work.

Open MainWindow.xib. Double-click Navigation Controller to open the editor window shown in Figure 4-6. While holding down the Control key, drag from the Convert button to the view in the middle. The Control-drag shortcut creates connections in the same way as dragging from the circles shown in Figure 4-10. When the central view turns slightly darker, release the mouse. A Sent Actions pop-up appears, as shown in Figure 4-11. Select `convert:`, the only available action currently defined by the RootViewController. Save.

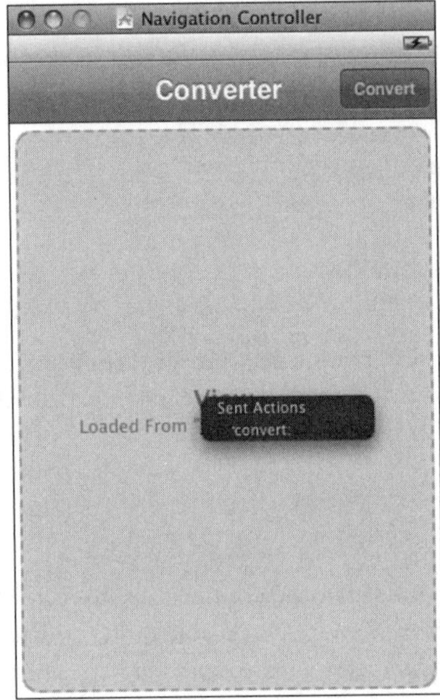

Figure 4-11 Dragging from the bar button item to the central view allows you to connect the button action to a method defined by the view's view controller.

> **Note**
>
> Control-click (right-click) objects to open a pop-up showing many of the same details that normally display in the connections inspector.

It may seem counterintuitive to connect a button's action to a view, when the actual method being called is defined by the view's view controller and not by the view itself. It may also seem odd to connect a button in one .xib file to an object that's defined in another. These are, unfortunately, Interface Builder quirks that must be lived with.

Capture Purple

The design for this project specifies a navigation bar that is tinted to match the art in the backsplash. To make this happen, you must capture the right shade of purple. Return to RootViewController.xib and open the View editor, which displays the cover320x416.png art.

Open the Color Inspector (Font > Show Colors). Click the magnifying glass and drag it over to the purple bar in the View art and click. This measures the purple from that view and sets it as the current color for the color inspector.

Close RootViewController.xib and return to MainWindow.xib. In the project window, locate the view-mode options at the top-left of the window, above the File's Owner icon. Click the middle of these three view mode buttons. The window switches from icon display to a list.

Open the disclosure triangle to the left of Navigation Controller and select Navigation Bar, as shown in Figure 4-12.

Figure 4-12 To edit the navigation bar's tint color, you must navigate down to items not directly available in the editor window.

With Navigation Bar selected, open the attributes inspector (Command-1). Make sure the View from RootViewController.xib is visible onscreen. Drag the purple you sampled from the top bar of the Colors palette into the tint well of the attributes inspector. Save the file and close MainWindow.xib.

Defining the Conversion Method

Your project is now fully laid out and wired. The outlets are connected to the text field, the button to the `convert:` action. That action, however, does not yet do anything. Return to Xcode and open RootViewController.m. The method is still just a skeleton that does nothing.

```
@implementation RootViewController
- (IBAction) convert: (id) sender {
```

```
}
@end
```

For this project, the method should recover any text typed into the top field, convert it to a float value, and then transform it from a Fahrenheit value to a Celsius one. The resulting value gets placed into the second field. The following method does exactly that. What's more, it dismisses the keyboard after performing the conversion by calling `resignFirstResponder`. Add this full method to your code, and save.

```
- (IBAction) convert: (id) sender
{
    float invalue = [[field1 text] floatValue];
    float outvalue = (invalue - 32.0f) * 5.0f / 9.0f;
    [field2 setText:[NSString stringWithFormat:@"%3.2f", outvalue]];
    [field2 resignFirstResponder];
}
```

Run the Application

Now that you have fully edited your project, once again, run the program with Run > Run. The program now converts Fahrenheit values into Celsius. Test with values of 32 (0 Celsius), 98.6 (37 Celsius), and 212 (100 Celsius).

Walk-Through: Building a Converter Interface by Hand

Anything that can be designed in Interface Builder can be implemented directly using Objective-C and Cocoa Touch. The code in Listing 4-1 duplicates the sample project you just built. Instead of loading an interface from a .xib file, it manually lays out the elements in the `loadView` method.

The code takes the same approach in doing so. First after creating a background view (corresponding to View in the IB project), it adds an image view on top. The image view uses the same art (cover320x416.png) and, as in IB, has its userInteractionEnabled flag set to YES.

Next, it adds two labels and two text fields. It sets the label texts to Fahrenheit and Celsius, tells the first field to use a numbers and punctuation keyboard, and disables the second. The locations and sizes for these items use view frames derived from the previous walk-through.

To finish the layout, the code tints the navigation bar purple and adds a Convert button. The button uses the same `convert:` callback as the IB project and calls the same code.

Listing 4-1 **Code-Based Temperature Converter**

```
#import <UIKit/UIKit.h>

#define COOKBOOK_PURPLE_COLOR    [UIColor colorWithRed:0.20392f ➥
green:0.19607f blue:0.61176f alpha:1.0f]
#define BARBUTTON(TITLE, SELECTOR)     [[[UIBarButtonItem alloc]➥
initWithTitle:TITLE style:UIBarButtonItemStylePlain target:self action:SELECTOR]➥
autorelease]

@interface HelloWorldController : UIViewController {
    UITextField *field1;
    UITextField *field2;
}
-(void) convert: (id)sender;
@end

@implementation HelloWorldController
- (void) convert: (id) sender
{
    float invalue = [[field1 text] floatValue];
    float outvalue = (invalue - 32.0f) * 5.0f / 9.0f;
    [field2 setText:[NSString stringWithFormat:@"%3.2f", outvalue]];
    [field1 resignFirstResponder];
}
- (void)loadView
{
    UIView *contentView = [[UIView alloc] initWithFrame:
        [[UIScreen mainScreen] applicationFrame]];
    self.view = contentView;
    contentView.backgroundColor = [UIColor whiteColor];
    [contentView release];

    UIImageView *iv = [[UIImageView alloc] initWithImage:
        [UIImage imageNamed:@"cover320x416.png"]];
    [self.view addSubview:iv];
    iv.userInteractionEnabled = YES;

    field1 = [[UITextField alloc] initWithFrame:
        CGRectMake(185.0, 31.0, 97.0, 31.0)];
    field1.borderStyle = UITextBorderStyleRoundedRect;
    field1.keyboardType = UIKeyboardTypeNumbersAndPunctuation;
    field1.contentVerticalAlignment =
        UIControlContentVerticalAlignmentCenter;

    field2 = [[UITextField alloc] initWithFrame:
        CGRectMake(185.0, 97.0, 97.0, 31.0)];
    field2.borderStyle = UITextBorderStyleRoundedRect;
```

Listing 4-1 **Continued**

```
    field2.enabled = NO;
    field2.contentVerticalAlignment =
        UIControlContentVerticalAlignmentCenter;

    UILabel *label1 = [[UILabel alloc] initWithFrame:
        CGRectMake(95.0, 34.0, 82.0, 21.0)];
    label1.text = @"Fahrenheit";
    label1.textAlignment = UITextAlignmentLeft;
    label1.textColor = [UIColor colorWithRed:0.000 green:0.000
        blue:0.000 alpha:1.000];
    label1.backgroundColor = [UIColor clearColor];

    UILabel *label2 = [[UILabel alloc] initWithFrame:CGRectMake(121.0,
        102.0, 56.0, 21.0)];
    label2.text = @"Celsius";
    label2.textAlignment = UITextAlignmentLeft;
    label2.textColor = [UIColor colorWithRed:0.000 green:0.000
        blue:0.000 alpha:1.000];
    label2.backgroundColor = [UIColor clearColor];

    [iv addSubview:field1];
    [iv addSubview:field2];
    [iv addSubview:label1];
    [iv addSubview:label2];

    [field1 release];
    [field2 release];
    [label1 release];
    [label2 release];

    [iv release];

    self.title = @"Converter";
    self.navigationItem.rightBarButtonItem = BARBUTTON(@"Convert",
        @selector(convert:));
    self.navigationController.navigationBar.tintColor =
        COOKBOOK_PURPLE_COLOR;
}
@end

@interface TestBedAppDelegate : NSObject <UIApplicationDelegate>
@end

@implementation TestBedAppDelegate
- (void)applicationDidFinishLaunching:(UIApplication *)application {
    UIWindow *window = [[UIWindow alloc] initWithFrame:
        [[UIScreen mainScreen] bounds]];
```

Listing 4-1 **Continued**

```
    UINavigationController *nav = [[UINavigationController alloc]
        initWithRootViewController:[[HelloWorldController alloc]
            init]];
    [window addSubview:nav.view];
    [window makeKeyAndVisible];
}
@end

int main(int argc, char *argv[])
{
    NSAutoreleasePool * pool = [[NSAutoreleasePool alloc] init];
    int retVal = UIApplicationMain(argc, argv, nil,
        @"TestBedAppDelegate");
    [pool release];
    return retVal;
}
```

Putting the Project Together

Building this project means adapting one of Xcode's built-in templates. Start by selecting File > New Project (Command-Shift-N) > iPhone OS > Application > Window-based Application. Click Choose. Name the new project HelloWorld2 and save it to the Desktop.

This template-based project demands a little file bookkeeping. Delete MainWindow.xib, and choose Also Move to Trash. Next, open HelloWorld-Info.plist. Locate the line that says "Main nib file base name". Delete this and save your change. This removes the project's dependency on an xib-based interface.

Similarly, locate the Classes group. Delete this group including the two source files contained within. Choose Also Move to Trash. This removes the code associated with the original .xib file, leaving you free to introduce your own code.

As with the previous walk-through Copy in the three image files from the sample code: icon.png, Default.png, and cover320x416.png. Make sure to check Copy Items into Destination Group's Folder (If Needed) before clicking Add. Move these files to the Resources group in your project.

To finish, open the main.m file, paste in the code from Listing 4-1 (it's in the sample code folder), compile the project and run it in the simulator. What you'll find is an application that both looks and acts identical to the IB version. Instead of loading the interface from a .xib file, this version creates it programmatically in the view controller class implementation.

Walk-Through: Creating a Hybrid Converter

One of the great things about Cocoa Touch is that you don't have to program entirely by hand or entirely using Interface Builder. You can leverage IB's visual layout and combine it with Xcode-based programming for a better, hybrid solution. This combines the static loading of .xib files provided by IB with a more reusable programmatic dynamic loading approach. You can use one of two approaches. Either create entire IB-centered `UIViewController`-based classes or code your own view controller class and load an IB-designed `UIView`. This walk-through shows you the former; the next walk-through describes the latter.

Whenever Xcode finds a .xib file whose name matches a class derived from `UIViewController`, it automatically loads that .xib when initializing an instance. For example, say you create a new navigation controller and initialize its root view controller as follows:

```
UINavigationController *nav = [[UINavigationController alloc]
➥initWithRootViewController:[[RootViewController alloc] init]];
```

When a file named RootViewController.xib is included in the project, Xcode uses that .xib to set up the view controller's view. The actual name of the view controller class does not matter. What matters is that that name has a matching .xib file. This walk-through uses this behavior to initialize an interface.

Clean Up a Basic Template

As with the previous project, you need to adapt a built-in template to get started. Select File > New Project (Command-Shift-N) > iPhone OS > Application > Window-based Application. Click Choose. Name the new project HelloWorld3 and save it to the Desktop.

Delete MainWindow.xib, and choose Also Move to Trash. Open HelloWorld-Info.plist. Locate the line that says "Main nib file base name". Delete this and save your change. In the project window, locate the Classses group and delete it, including the two source files contained within. Choose Also Move to Trash.

Finally, copy in the three image files from the sample code: icon.png, Default.png, and cover320x416.png. Make sure to check Copy Items into Destination Group's Folder (If Needed) before clicking Add. Move these files to the Resources group in your project.

Add a New View Controller Class with .xib

In Xcode, choose File > New (Command-N) > iPhone OS > Cocoa Touch Class > UIViewController subclass. Check With XIB for User Interface and click Next. Name the file RootViewController.m, check Also Create RootView Controller.h, set the location to your main project folder, and click Finish.

The class name is arbitrary. I use `RootViewController` here because it describes the role of the view controller, and it matches the name used in the previous walk-throughs.

Design the Interface

As you did with the first walk-through, locate the new RootViewController.xib file and double-click it to open it in IB. In Interface Builder, double-click View to open the view editor, and then perform the following steps:

1. With View selected, open the attributes inspector (Command-1), and choose Top Bar > Navigation Bar.

2. Drag an image view into the editor. Let it snap to fill the view below the navigation bar.
3. In the attributes inspector, set the Image drop-down to Choose cover320x416.png. Also check Interaction > User Interaction Enabled.
4. Drag two text fields and two labels into the view from the library. As before, set up these elements to roughly match the layout in Figure 4-8.
5. Select the top text field. In the attributes inspector, choose Text Input Traits > Keyboard > Numbers & Punctuation.
6. Select the bottom field. Uncheck Control > Content > Enabled.
7. Open the Library (Command-Shift-L). Search for and select the RootViewController class and then click Outlets. Add two outlets by clicking the + button. Name them `field1` and `field2`. Edit each type to change `id` to `UITextField`.
8. Click Actions and add an action, again using +. Edit the default action name to `convert:`, making sure to add the colon.
9. Open the connections inspector (Command-2). Drag from the field1 circle to the top text field. Then drag from the field2 circle to the bottom text field.
10. Save the project with your changes.
11. Select File's Owner, and choose File > Write Class Files. Keep the file name as RootViewController (no extensions) and save into your main folder. Agree to replace the existing files.
12. Close the RootViewController.xib file and return to Xcode.

Edit the View Controller Implementation

In Xcode, open RootViewController.m and replace the contents of that file with this code. This code adds the `convert:` method used in the previous two walk-throughs but also adds a new method called `viewDidLoad`. This method is called after the .xib loads and gives the view controller a chance to finish any initialization details. Here it sets the title ("Converter"), adds the navigation bar's bar button item ("convert"), sets its callback (`convert:`), and tints the bar purple.

```
#import "RootViewController.h"


#define COOKBOOK_PURPLE_COLOR [UIColor colorWithRed:0.20392f
➥green:0.19607f blue:0.61176f alpha:1.0f]
#define BARBUTTON(TITLE, SELECTOR) [[[UIBarButtonItem alloc] initWithTitle:TITLE
➥style:UIBarButtonItemStylePlain target:self action:SELECTOR] autorelease]
```

```
@implementation RootViewController
- (IBAction) convert: (id) sender
{
    float invalue = [[field1 text] floatValue];
    float outvalue = (invalue - 32.0f) * 5.0f / 9.0f;
    [field2 setText:[NSString stringWithFormat:@"%3.2f", outvalue]];
    [field1 resignFirstResponder];
}

- (void) viewDidLoad
{
    self.title = @"Converter";
    self.navigationItem.rightBarButtonItem = BARBUTTON(@"Convert",
        @selector(convert:));
    self.navigationController.navigationBar.tintColor =
        COOKBOOK_PURPLE_COLOR;
}
@end
```

Edit main.m

As a final step edit main.m, replacing its contents with the following. This code sets up the main window and navigation controller, and assigns a new instance of `RootViewController` as the navigation controller's root view controller.

```
#import <UIKit/UIKit.h>
#import "RootViewController.h"

@interface HelloWorldAppDelegate : NSObject <UIApplicationDelegate>
@end

@implementation HelloWorldAppDelegate
- (void)applicationDidFinishLaunching:(UIApplication *)application {
    UIWindow *window = [[UIWindow alloc] initWithFrame:
        [[UIScreen mainScreen] bounds]];
    UINavigationController *nav = [[UINavigationController alloc]
        initWithRootViewController:[[RootViewController alloc] init]];
    [window addSubview:nav.view];
    [window makeKeyAndVisible];
}
@end

int main(int argc, char *argv[])
{
    NSAutoreleasePool * pool = [[NSAutoreleasePool alloc] init];
    int retVal = UIApplicationMain(argc, argv, nil,
        @"HelloWorldAppDelegate");
```

```
    [pool release];
    return retVal;
}
```

Run the Application

Now that you have fully edited your project, once again, run the program with Run > Run. The compiled application loads its interface from the .xib file. Once loaded, it finalizes the details regarding the navigation bar, its button, its title, and its tint. The application's look and behavior remains identical to those built in the previous walk-throughs.

Walk-Through: Loading .xib Files Directly from Code

Cocoa Touch lets you recover objects from any .xib file by calling `loadNibNamed: owner: options:`. This returns an array of objects initialized from the .xib bundle, which you can then grab and use in your program. In this walk-through, you use this feature to load an IB-designed interface from an otherwise hand-built application. To get started, copy the project from the second walk-through, the one built entirely by code. You adapt this hand-built code to use a xib-designed view.

The view you use is from the first project. Copy the RootViewController.xib file from that project and add it into your new project folder. This .xib file contains the original layout, with the image view backsplash, the two text fields, and so on. Rename the file to mainview.xib. This renaming is important because you need to use a .xib file whose name does not match the name of the primary view controller class. If you forget, the application attempts to load that view causing all kinds of runtime misery.

Open the project in Xcode and drop the copied mainview.xib file from the folder into the project. You can leave the Copy check box checked although it is not needed here; the file is already in the folder. Click Add.

Clean Up the .xib

Open mainview.xib in Interface Builder. Here you perform a few maintenance tasks that allow the .xib file to load properly from `loadView`, and allow you to access subviews that normally would be assigned to `IBOutlet` instance variables.

Tagging views assigns numbers to them. All view classes provide a tag field. Tags are integers that you can utilize to identify view instances. You choose what number to use. Select the top text field, open the attributes inspector (Command-1), and edit the View > Tag field to 101. (You may have to scroll down to find this field.) Select the bottom field and edit its tag field to 102. Once tagged, you can retrieve views from a parent view by calling `viewWithTag:`.

Remove any previous connections set up in Interface Builder. Select the File's Owner and open the connections inspector (Command-2). Delete all the connections (there are three) by clicking the small X on each. Save and close the .xib file. This ensures that your application does not attempt to make any outlet or action connections at compile time.

Update loadView

Open main.m and replace the `loadView` method with the following code. This code loads a view from a .xib file and assigns it as the main view for the view controller. This approach relies on the fact that there is just one actual view object in that .xib. For this .xib that is the main `UIView` that is named View in Interface Builder. Neither the File's Owner nor First Responder is a view.

```
- (void)loadView
{
    self.view = [[[NSBundle mainBundle] loadNibNamed:@"mainview"
        owner:self options:NULL] lastObject];
    field1 = (UITextField *)[self.view viewWithTag:101];
    field2 = (UITextField *)[self.view viewWithTag:102];
    self.title = @"Converter";
    self.navigationItem.rightBarButtonItem = BARBUTTON(@"Convert",
    @selector(convert:));
    self.navigationController.navigationBar.tintColor =
        COOKBOOK_PURPLE_COLOR;
}
```

More complicated .xib files may include several view objects. When loading views from .xibs, you may want to use tagging and class confirmation to check which object is which, ensuring you retrieve the correct object from the returned array.

> **Note**
>
> The order of the items in the .xib file array mirrors the order of the items in Interface Builder's project window. Since this .xib contains exactly one top-level item, the code could just as easily use `objectAtIndex:0` as `lastObject`.

Objects from a .xib file are created with a retain count of 1 and autoreleased. When loading items directly from a .xib file, you must retain any objects from within the returned array that you need to stick around. Using the `self.view` setter automatically retains a view. Be aware that the default memory warning logic for view controllers relies on releasing and setting to nil all views that are not displayed at that moment. This effectively disposes any .xib files from memory.

Designing for Rotation

On the iPhone, device orientation changes are a fact of life. How you decide your application should respond to those changes presents a common design challenge. Do you resize onscreen elements, letting them grow and shrink in place like Safari does? Do you move them to new locations to accommodate the different view proportions? Or do you present an entirely different view, like the YouTube and iPod/Music apps do? Each of these choices presents a possible design solution. The one you pick depends on your application's needs and the visual elements in play.

The following sections explore these design approaches. You learn about autosizing and manual view placement as well as view swapping approaches. Apple has indicated it will eventually support separate landscape and portrait views in the SDK. At the time of writing, this functionality has not yet been implemented.

Enabling Reorientation

`UIViewController` instances decide whether to respond to iPhone orientation by implementing the optional `shouldAutorotateToInterfaceOrientation:` method. This method returns either YES or NO, depending on whether you want to support autorotation to a given orientation. To allow autorotation to all possible orientations, simply return YES.

```
- (BOOL)shouldAutorotateToInterfaceOrientation:
        (UIInterfaceOrientation)interfaceOrientation
{

    return YES;
}
```

Possible iPhone orientations passed to this method include

- `UIDeviceOrientationUnknown`
- `UIDeviceOrientationPortrait`
- `UIDeviceOrientationPortraitUpsideDown`
- `UIDeviceOrientationLandscapeLeft`
- `UIDeviceOrientationLandscapeRight`
- `UIDeviceOrientationFaceUp`
- `UIDeviceOrientationFaceDown`

Of these orientations, only the portrait and landscape varieties influence how a view autorotates. If your application is portrait only or landscape only, it might allow flipping between the two available orientations. This code uses the logical OR symbol "||" to combine tests into a single return value.

```
- (BOOL)shouldAutorotateToInterfaceOrientation:
    (UIInterfaceOrientation) interfaceOrientation
{
    return ((interfaceOrientation == UIDeviceOrientationPortrait) ||
            (interfaceOrientation ==
                UIDeviceOrientationPortraitUpsideDown))
}
```

When returning YES, the view controller uses several flags to determine how the autorotation takes place. For example, you might want to stretch subviews both horizontally and vertically.

```
contentView.autoresizesSubviews = YES;
contentView.autoresizingMask = (UIViewAutoresizingFlexibleWidth |
    UIViewAutoresizingFlexibleHeight);
```

These flags correspond exactly to settings made available in Interface Builder's size inspector (Command-3), which is discussed in the next section.

Autosizing

When you tilt the iPhone on its side in Safari, the browser view adjusts its proportions to match the new orientation. It does this through autosizing. Autosizing adds rules to a view telling it how to reshape itself. It can stretch, stay the same size, and/or be pinned a certain distance from the edge of its parent. These properties can be set by hand in code or in Interface Builder's size inspector (Command-3), which is shown in Figure 4-13.

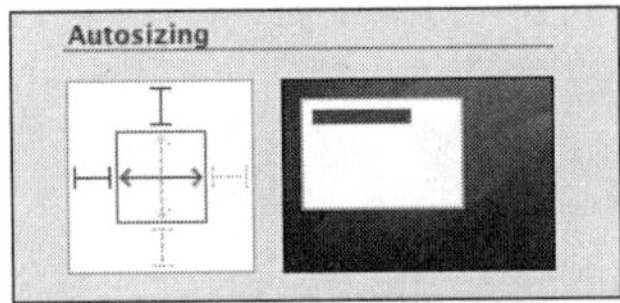

Figure 4-13 Interface Builder's Autosizing pane sets a view's autoresizingMask.

This pane adjusts a view's autosizing rules. The control consists of an inner square with two double-arrowed lines and an outer square with four blunt-ended lines. Each item can be set or unset via a click. When enabled, they appear in bright red; when disabled they are dim red in color.

The four outer lines are called *struts*. They establish a fixed distance between a view and its parent's edge. Imagine setting a view at 40 pixels from the top and left of the superview. Enabling the top and left struts (as shown in Figure 4-13) fixes that view at that position. It basically pins the view in place. When you use a right or bottom strut, those distances are also maintained. The view must either move or resize to stay the same pixel distance from those sides.

The two inner lines are called *springs*. They control how a view resizes itself. The sample shown in Figure 4-13 has its horizontal spring set, allowing the view to resize horizontally in proportion to the parent view's size.

To allow a view to float, that is, to set it as both unpinned and without automatic resizing, unset all six struts and springs. This option is only available for subviews. The primary view defined in Interface Builder must be set with both springs on.

If you prefer to set these traits by hand, the two properties involved are `autoresizesSubviews`, a Boolean value that determines whether the view provides subview resizing, and `autoresizingMask`, an integer composed of the following flags, which are combined using the bitwise OR operator "|" to produce a value for the property.

- `UIViewAutoresizingNone` means the view does not resize.
- `UIViewAutoresizingFlexibleLeftMargin`, `UIViewAutoresizingFlexibleRightMargin`, `UIViewAutoresizingFlexibleTopMargin`, and `UIViewAutoresizingFlexibleBottomMargin` allow a view to resize by expanding or shrinking in the direction of a given margin without affecting the size of any items inside. These correspond to the four struts of Interface Builder's Autosizing pane (refer to Figure 4-13) but act in the opposite way. In IB, struts fix the margins; the flags allow flexible resizing along those margins.
- `UIViewAutoresizingFlexibleWidth` and `UIViewAutoresizingFlexibleHeight` control whether a view shrinks or expands along with a view. These correspond directly with Interface Builder's springs. Springs allow flexible resizing, as do these flags.

Autosizing Example

Consider the view shown in Figure 4-14. It consists of one main view and three subviews, namely the title, a white background splash, and a small piece of art. These subviews represent three typical scenarios you'll encounter while designing applications. The title wants to stay in the same place and maintain its size regardless of orientation. The white splash needs to stretch or shrink to match its parent's geometry, and the butterfly art should float within its parent.

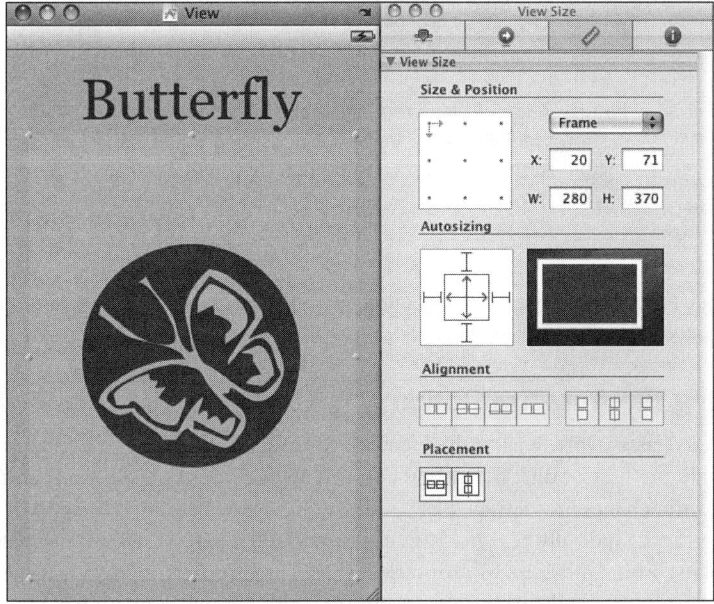

Figure 4-14 Setting view autosizing in Interface Builder.

The autosizing behavior of each subview is set in the size inspector (Command-3). The title requires only a single strut at the top. The splash needs to resize while maintaining its distance from each edge. Setting all six struts and springs (shown in Figure 4-14) produces this result. The art subview uses the opposite setting, with none of the six struts or springs in use.

Test the view in its opposite orientation by clicking the small curved arrow at the top-right of the view editor window. In Figure 4-14, this arrow appears just above the battery indicator in the simulated status bar. Figure 4-15 shows the landscape version of this view using these settings. Switching between portrait and landscape presentation helps preview how your autoresizing choices work.

Figure 4-15 This is the landscape version of the view shown in Figure 4-14 using the described autosizing choices. Click the arrow at the right of the title bar to rotate the view in Interface Builder.

> **Note**
> The iPhone loads the last saved .xib orientation on launch. Make sure to return to the portrait view before saving your .xib file.

Evaluating the Autosize Option

Some iPhone classes work well with autosizing. Some do not. Large presentation-based views provide the best results. Web views and text views autosize well. Their content easily adapts to the change in view shape.

Small controls, especially text fields, fare more poorly. These views are not naturally elastic. Moving from landscape to portrait, or portrait to landscape, often leaves either too much room or not enough room to accommodate the previous layout. For these views you might place each item in a custom position rather than depend on autosizing. That's not to say that autosize solutions cannot work for simple layouts just that as a general rule more complex views with many subviews do not always lend themselves to autosizing.

Image views are another class that doesn't work well with autosizing. Most pictures need to maintain their original aspect ratios. A 320x480 image shown originally in portrait orientation must shrink to 213x320 for landscape. That leaves you with just 45% of the portrait size. Consider swapping out art to a landscape-appropriate version rather than trying to stretch or resize portrait-based originals.

When working with autosizing, always take the keyboard into account. If your main view does not scroll or provide provisions for moving its views into accessible places, a keyboard may hide some of the views it's trying to service. Test your interfaces as you design them, both with Interface Builder's flip button and in the simulator, to ensure that all elements remain well placed and accessible.

Moving Views

If autosizing provides a practically no-work solution to orientation changes, moving views offers a fix with higher-bookkeeping responsibilities. The idea works like this. After a view controller finishes its orientation, it calls the delegate method `didRotateFromInterfaceOrientation:`. You can implement a method that manually moves each view into place, producing the kinds of results seen in Figure 4-16. As you can see, this approach quickly gets tedious, especially when you are dealing with more than four subviews at a time.

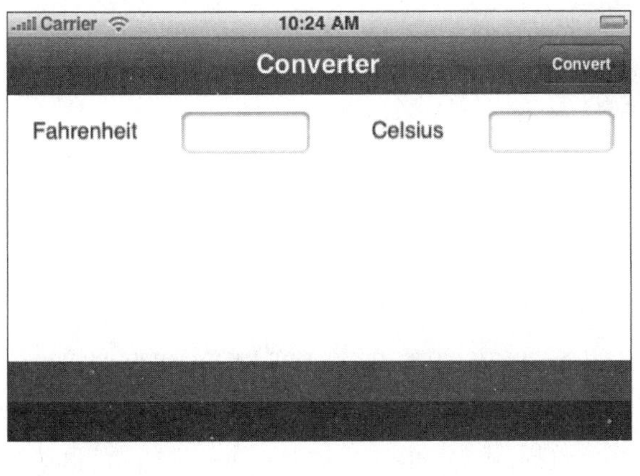

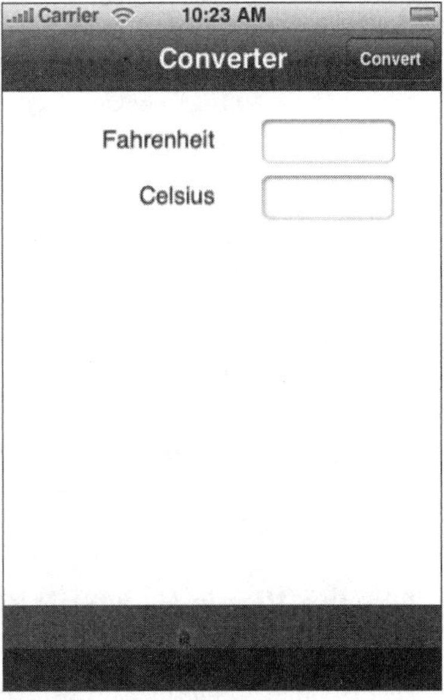

Figure 4-16 Moving views allows you to adjust layouts after orientation changes.

```
- (void)didRotateFromInterfaceOrientation:
    (UIInterfaceOrientation) fromInterfaceOrientation
{
    UIInterfaceOrientation orientation = [[UIDevice currentDevice]
        orientation];

    UILabel *flabel = (UILabel *) [self.view viewWithTag:11];
    UILabel *clabel = (UILabel *) [self.view viewWithTag:12];
    UITextField *ffield = (UITextField *) [self.view viewWithTag:101];
    UITextField *cfield = (UITextField *) [self.view viewWithTag:102];

    switch (orientation)
    {
        case UIInterfaceOrientationLandscapeLeft:
        case UIInterfaceOrientationLandscapeRight:
        {
            flabel.center = CGPointMake(61,114);
            clabel.center = CGPointMake(321, 114);
            ffield.center = CGPointMake(184, 116);
            cfield.center = CGPointMake(418, 116);
            break;
        }
        case UIInterfaceOrientationPortrait:
        case UIInterfaceOrientationPortraitUpsideDown:
        {
            flabel.center = CGPointMake(113, 121);
            clabel.center = CGPointMake(139, 160);
            ffield.center = CGPointMake(236, 123);
            cfield.center = CGPointMake(236, 162);
            break;
        }
        default:
            break;
    }
}
```

The big advantage of this moving-subviews approach over presenting two separate views is that you maintain access to your original subviews. Any instance variables in your view controller that point, say, to a text field, continue to do so regardless of where that field is placed onscreen. The data structure of your view controller remains unchanged and independent of location, which is very model-view-controller compliant.

Moving Views by Mimicking Templates

There's a much simpler way to accomplish the same movement with less work. In Interface Builder, duplicate your primary view twice. Edit those two copies to create landscape and portrait versions using the same view elements. Since the views were copied from the original, all the subviews retain their original tags. Figure 4-17 shows what those views might look like.

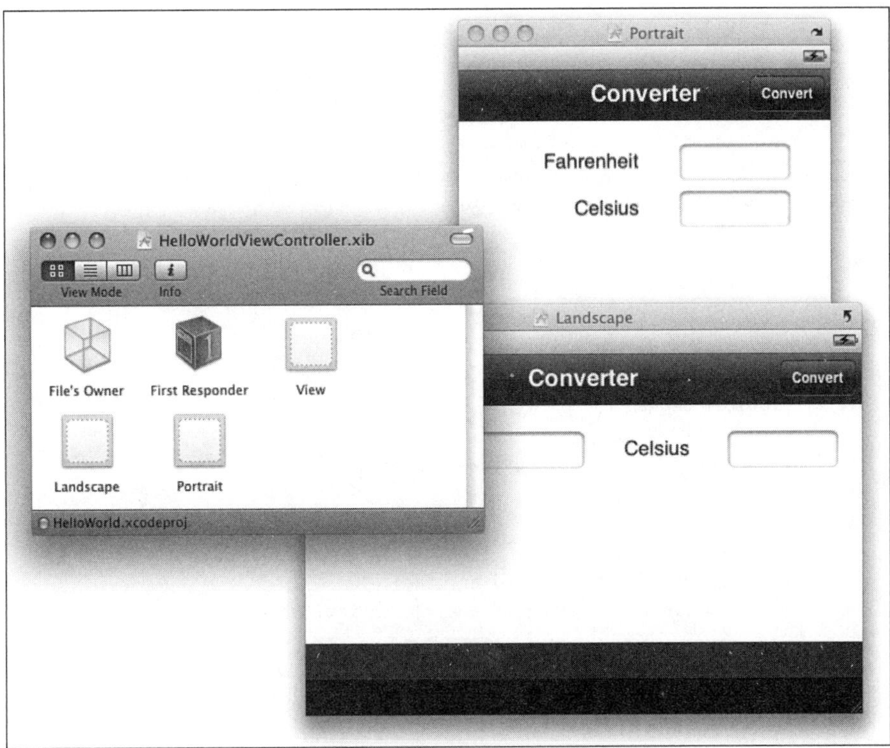

Figure 4-17 Duplicating views in Interface Builder creates templates for moving subviews.

This example continues to use your original view and subviews after orientation changes. (Please note that allSubviews() is defined in Recipe 6-2, "Subview Utility Functions.") What you do is use those extra two views as templates to determine where to place each subview. You move objects into position based on matching the template. This approach introduces two enormous advantages. You don't hard-code locations, and you can adjust the layouts in Interface Builder as needed.

```
- (void)didRotateFromInterfaceOrientation:
    (UIInterfaceOrientation) fromInterfaceOrientation
{
    UIView *template = nil;
```

```
    switch ([[UIDevice currentDevice] orientation])
    {
        case UIInterfaceOrientationLandscapeLeft:
        case UIInterfaceOrientationLandscapeRight:
        {
            template = landscapeTemplate;
            break;
        }
        case UIInterfaceOrientationPortrait:
        case UIInterfaceOrientationPortraitUpsideDown:
        {
            template = portraitTemplate;
            break;
        }
        default:
            break;
    }

    if (!template) return;

    for (UIView *eachView in allSubviews(template))
    {
        int tag = eachView.tag;
        if (tag < 10) continue;
        printf("About to move view %d\n", tag);
        [self.view viewWithTag:tag].frame = eachView.frame;
    }
}
```

Here are a few points about this approach:

- This code ignores untagged views and tags with a value under 10. Apple rarely tags views, but when it does so, it uses small numbers like 1, 2, and 3. Make sure to tag your views starting with numbers from 10 and up.
- This example uses two instance variables (`portraitTemplate` and `landscapeTemplate`) to provide immediate access to the templates. These are defined as `IBOutlets` in the view controller header file and are connected via Interface Builder. When the .xib loads, these two outlets are automatically set.
- If you decide to edit your portrait layout, do so in your original view in Interface Builder. Discard the previous Portrait view and replace it with a copy of your edited View. Reconnect the outlet from the File's Owner to the new Portrait view. This ensures that your portrait and primary views remain identical in the .xib file. Unfortunately, you cannot just use the main view as your portrait template. Once rotated, it loses all memory of the proper portrait view positions.

Swapping Views

The iPod/Music application does not attempt to restructure its table when you flip the iPhone into landscape. Instead it displays an entirely different view, namely a Coverflow presentation of albums. To create your own swap, add two views into your view controller's .xib, one portrait and one landscape. Assign `IBOutlets` to each and, to start, set your view controller's `view` property to the portrait version.

In your view controller implementation, make sure to set the `autoresizesSubviews` flag for each primary view to `NO`. This ensures that the view appears exactly as you laid it out in Interface Builder. (If you want, you can amuse yourself by commenting out those lines and performing a few flips in the simulator. The results are often startling.)

```
@implementation HelloWorldViewController
- (void)viewDidLoad
    {
    self.view.frame = [[UIScreen mainScreen] applicationFrame];
    landscapeView.autoresizesSubviews = NO;
    portraitView.autoresizesSubviews = NO;
}
```

When the view rotates to landscape or portrait, switch `self.view` to point to the proper view. This code first checks for landscape and then uses `else if` and checks for portrait orientations. This guards against matching unknown orientations and face up/face down ones to the portrait view.

```
- (BOOL)shouldAutorotateToInterfaceOrientation:
    (UIInterfaceOrientation) interfaceOrientation
    {
    if ((interfaceOrientation == UIInterfaceOrientationLandscapeLeft)
         || (interfaceOrientation == UIInterfaceOrientationLandscapeRight))
        self.view = landscapeView;
    else if ((interfaceOrientation == UIInterfaceOrientationPortrait)
         || (interfaceOrientation == UIInterfaceOrientationPortraitUpsideDown))
        self.view = portraitView;
    return YES;
}
@end
```

When run, this code responds to interface changes by reassigning the view controller's `view` property either to the landscape or the portrait version based on the new orientation.

One More Thing: A Half Dozen Great Interface Builder Tips

It never hurts to have a few extra tricks up your sleeve when developing with Interface Builder and Xcode. Here are six favorite IB tricks that I use on a regular basis:

- **Selecting from stacked views**—Figure 4-12 showed you how to drill down into Interface Builder's object hierarchy to reveal subviews. Another way to find and select subviews is by Control-Shift-clicking a view. This exposes all the views layered at that point (see Figure 4-18) and lets you select whichever item you want, regardless of whether it is the top view.

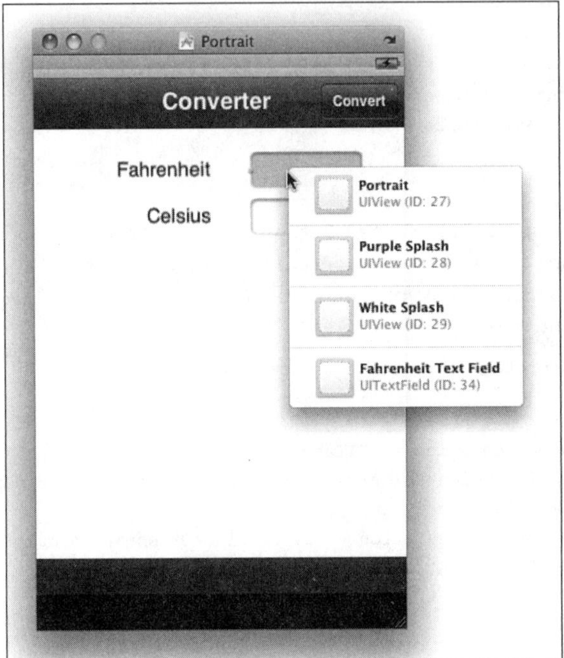

Figure 4-18 Shift-Control-click a view to pop up a view-selection dialog.

- **Naming views**—Give your views names like the ones used in Figure 4-18 in the identity inspector (Command-4). Edit the Interface Builder Identity > Name field.
- **Pulling in media**—Interface Builder's library offers a Media tab, listing the media currently available in your Xcode project (see Figure 4-19, left). You can drag artwork from there and drop it onto a view. Interface Builder automatically creates a new `UIImageView` instance, adding the art (as a `UIImage`) to that view.
- **Adding custom guides**—Interface Builder offers the same kind of layout guides used in programs like Photoshop. Use the Layout menu to add horizontal and

Figure 4-19 You can drag media from the Library into your IB projects (left). Custom guides add attraction points for laying out views (right).

vertical guides. As Figure 4-19 (right) shows, IB provides live position feedback as you drag the guide into place, offering pixel-precise placement.

- **Moving objects**—When moving subviews, the arrow keys move you one pixel in any direction. Hold down the Shift key to move by 5 pixels at a time.
- **Show object layout**—Hold down the option key and hover the mouse over any object to reveal the pixel-accurate layout information shown in Figure 4-20.

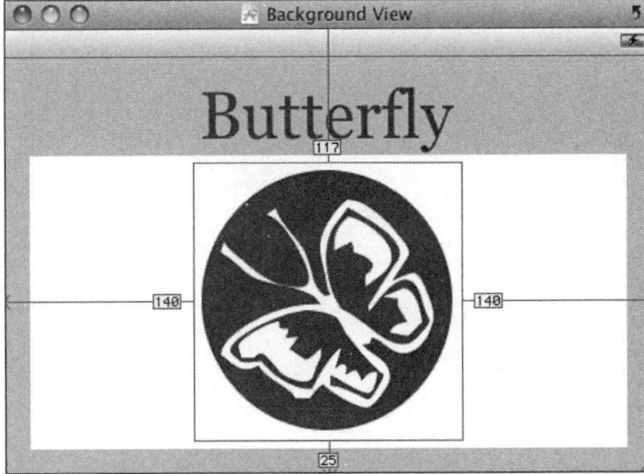

Figure 4-20 Holding the option key while moving the mouse over views reveals how each view is placed in the view container.

Summary

This chapter introduced the basics of iPhone interface design. You discovered not one but four ways to build interfaces: using Interface Builder, using Xcode, and blending the two approaches. You saw reorientation in action and learned about different ways to update your views to live in both portrait and landscape worlds.

Before moving on to the next chapter, here are a few points to consider about laying out interfaces:

- Interface Builder excels at laying out the content of `UIView` instances. Use its tools to connect those instances to the view controllers in your program and use Interface Builder to refine WYSIWYG-style interfaces like the temperature converter example covered in this chapter.
- Know when Interface Builder isn't the right solution. When you're building tab bars and navigation controllers with minimal window design (such as for table-based or text-based applications), you don't especially need IB's view layout tools. When skipping IB, make sure to delete the .xib file from your project and remove the Main NIB Window key from Info.plist. Also edit your main.m file to substitute the application delegate class name for the fourth UIApplicationMain() argument. Failing to do so produces an application that shows a black screen and provides no further interaction.
- Some views work beautifully under multiple orientations. Some do not. Don't feel that you must provide a landscape version of your application that exactly matches either the look or the functionality of the portrait one.
- Always, always save your work in Interface Builder. Until you do so, your project will not be updated with the current version of your .xib files.
- There's no "right" way to design and implement portrait and landscape layouts. Choose the approach that works best for your needs and provides the best experience for your users.

5

Working with View Controllers

UIViewControllers handle view management for many iPhone applications. In the previous chapter you saw how to build view controller-based applications using Xcode and Interface Builder. Now it's time to dive into more advanced view controller-based classes and learn how to apply them to real-world situations. In this chapter you discover how to build simple menus, create view navigation trees, design tab bar-based applications, and more. This chapter offers hands-on recipes for working with a variety of controller classes.

Developing with Navigation Controllers

The `UINavigationController` class provides all the high-calorie goodness of a `UINavigationBar`-based interface with minimal navigation-specific programming. Navigation controllers let users move smoothly between views (or, more accurately, view controllers) using built-in animation. They provide history control for free without any programming effort. Navigation controllers automatically handle Back button functionality. The titles of each parent view controller appear as Back buttons, letting users "pop the stack," so to speak, without any further programming effort.

And if that weren't enough, the navigation controller also offers a simple menu bar. You can add buttons—or even more complicated controls—into the bar to build actions into your application. Between these three features of navigation, history, and menus, navigation controllers build a lot of wow into a simple-to-program package.

The following recipes introduce these core navigation controller features, from building menus to building a history stack. In these examples, you see how to use the `UINavigationController` class to create a variety of novel and useful interfaces.

Setting Up a Navigation Controller

Whether you plan to use a navigation controller to simplify moving between views—its intended use—or use it as a convenient menu button holder you should understand how the navigation controller works. At their simplest level, navigation controllers manage view controller stacks.

Every navigation controller owns a root view controller. This controller forms the base of the stack. You can programmatically push other controllers onto the stack. This extends the navigation breadcrumb trail and automatically builds a Back button each time a new view controller gets pushed.

Tap one of these Back buttons to pop controllers off the stack. Users can pop back until reaching the root. Then you can go no further. The root is the root, and you cannot pop beyond that root.

This stack-based design lingers even when you plan to use just one view controller. You might want to leverage the `UINavigationController`'s built-in navigation bar to build a two-button menu, for example. This would disregard any navigational advantage of the stack. You still need to set that one controller as the root via `initWithRootViewController:`.

You can use Interface Builder and Xcode templates to build navigation-based interfaces, as introduced in Chapter 4, "Designing Interfaces," or you can create those same interfaces by hand. The easiest way to do so is by building your navigation controller in the `applicationDidFinishLaunching:` method that gets called at the start of your application run. Here, you set up the window, create the navigation controller, and assign its root.

```
- (void)applicationDidFinishLaunching:(UIApplication *)application {
    UIWindow *window = [[UIWindow alloc] initWithFrame:
        [[UIScreen mainScreen] bounds]];
    UINavigationController *nav = [[UINavigationController alloc]
        initWithRootViewController:[[HelloWorldController alloc]
        init]];
    [window addSubview:nav.view];
    [window makeKeyAndVisible];
}
```

This is one of the few places you don't really have to worry about memory management and leaky calls. An application delegate's `dealloc` method is never called at application termination, so while you can assign the window and the navigation controller to instance variables and use those variables in a deallocation method, it doesn't really matter if you'd rather not do so.

Pushing and Popping View Controllers

Add new items onto the navigation stack by pushing a new controller with `pushViewController: animated:`. Send this call to the navigation controller that owns a `UIViewController`. This is normally called on `self.navigationController`. When pushed, the new controller slides onscreen from the right (assuming you set animated to `YES`). A left-pointing Back button appears, leading you one step back on the stack. The Back button uses the title of the previous view controller.

There are many reasons you'd push a new view. Typically, these involve navigating to subviews like detail views or drilling down a file structure. You can push controllers onto the navigation controller stack after your user taps a button, a table item, or a disclosure accessory.

Perform push requests and navigation bar customization (like setting up a bar's right-hand button) inside `UIViewController` subclasses. As a rule, there's no reason or need to ever subclass `UINavigationController`. And, for the most part, you need never access the navigation controller directly. The two exceptions to this rule include managing the navigation bar's buttons and when you change the bar's look.

You might change a bar style or its tint color by accessing the `navigationBar` property directly.

```
self.navigationController.navigationBar.barStyle =
    UIBarStyleBlackTranslucent;
```

To add a new button you modify your `navigationItem`, which provides an abstract class that describes the content shown on the navigation bar. To remove a button, assign the item to nil.

```
self.navigationItem.rightBarButtonItem = [[[UIBarButtonItem alloc]
    initWithTitle:@"Action" style:UIBarButtonItemStylePlain target:self
    action:@selector(performAction:)] autorelease];
```

The Navigation Item Class

The objects that populate the navigation bar are put into place using the `UINavigationItem` class, which is an abstract class that stores information about those objects. Navigation item properties include the left and right bar button items, the title shown on the bar, the view used to show the title, and any Back button used to navigate back from the current view.

This class basically enables you to attach buttons, text, and other UI objects into three key locations: the left, the center, and the right of the navigation bar. Typically, this works out to be a regular button on the right, some text (usually the `UIViewController`'s title) in the middle, and a Back-styled button on the left. But you're not limited to that layout. You can add custom controls to any of these three locations You can build navigation bars with search fields, segment controls, toolbars, pictures, and more.

You've already seen how to add custom bar button items to the left and right of a navigation item. Adding a custom view to the title is just as simple. Instead of adding a control, assign a view. This code adds a custom `UILabel`, but this could be a `UIImageView`, a `UISwitch`, or anything else.

```
self.navigationItem.titleView = [[[UILabel alloc]
    initWithFrame:CGRectMake(0.0f,0.0f, 120.0f, 36.0f)] autorelease];
```

The simplest way to customize the actual title is to use the `title` property of the child view controller rather than the navigation item.

```
self.title = @"Hello";
```

When you want the title to automatically reflect the name of the running application, here is a little trick you can use. This returns the short display name defined in the bundle's Info.plist file.

```
self.title = [[[NSBundle mainBundle] infoDictionary]
    objectForKey:@"CFBundleName"];
```

Modal Presentation

With normal navigation controllers, you push your way along views, stopping occasionally to pop back to previous views. That approach assumes that you're drilling your way up and down a set of data that matches the tree-based view structure you're using. Modal presentation offers another way to show a view controller. After sending the `presentModalViewController: animated:` message, a new view controller slides up into the screen and takes control until it's dismissed with `dismissModalViewController➥Animated:`. This enables you to add special-purpose dialogs into your applications that go beyond alert views.

Typically, modal controllers are used to pick data such as contacts from the Address Book or photos from the Library, but you can use modal controllers in any setting where it makes sense to perform a task that lies outside the normal scope of the active view controller.

You can present a modal dialog in any of three ways, controlled by the `modalTransitionStyle` property of the presented view controller. The standard, `UIModalTransitionStyleCoverVertical`, slides the modal view up and over the current view controller. When dismissed it slides back down. `UIModalTransitionStyleFlip➥Horizontal` performs a back-to-front flip from right-to-left. It looks as if you're revealing the back side of the currently presented view. When dismissed, it flips back left-to-right. The final style is `UIModalTransitionStyleCrossDissolve`. It fades the new view in over the previous one. On dismissal, it fades back to the original view.

Utility Function

Some of the recipes in this book use this `showAlert()` macro/function combination. This function acts as a visual version of `NSLog()`, and it displays a message and information about where the call originated. This function can be called using the same parameters as NSLog, complete with format string and arguments. For space considerations, this alert code is not listed in individual recipes. Invoking the alert code is shown in Figure 5-1, which follows later in this chapter.

```
#define showAlert(format, ...) myShowAlert(__LINE__, (char *)__FUNCTION__,
➥format, ##__VA_ARGS__)

// Simple Alert Utility
void myShowAlert(int line, char *functname, id formatstring,...)
```

```
{
    va_list arglist;
    if (!formatstring) return;
    va_start(arglist, formatstring);
    id outstring = [[[NSString alloc] initWithFormat:formatstring
        arguments:arglist] autorelease];
    va_end(arglist);

    NSString *filename = [[NSString stringWithCString:__FILE__]
        lastPathComponent];
    NSString *debugInfo = [NSString stringWithFormat:@"%@:%d\n%s",
        filename, line, functname];

    UIAlertView *av = [[[UIAlertView alloc] initWithTitle:outstring
        message:debugInfo delegate:nil
        cancelButtonTitle:@"OK"otherButtonTitles:nil] autorelease];
    [av show];
}
```

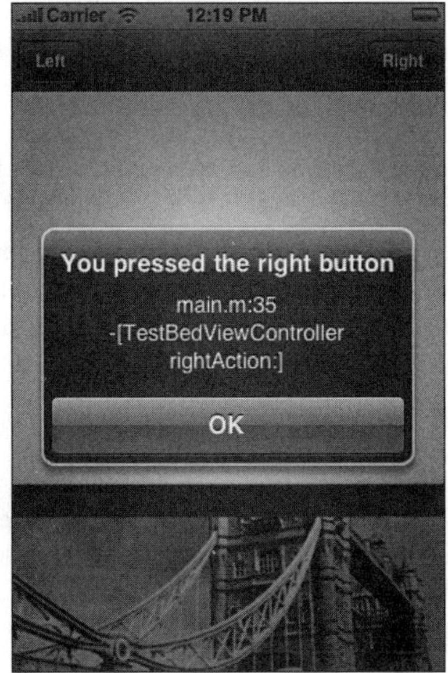

Figure 5-1 Create a basic two-button menu for iPhone applications by adding custom buttons to a `UINavigationController`-based interface.

Recipe: Building a Simple Two-Item Menu

Although many applications demand serious user interfaces, sometimes you don't need complexity. A simple one- or two-button menu can accomplish a lot. Use these steps to create a hand-built interface for simple utilities:

1. Create a `UIViewController` subclass that you use to populate your primary interaction space.
2. Allocate a navigation controller and assign an instance of your custom view controller to its root view.
3. In the custom view controller, create one or two buttons and add them to the view's navigation item.
4. Build the callback routines that get triggered when a user taps a button.

Recipe 5-1 demonstrates these steps. It creates a simple view controller called `TestBedViewController` and assigns it as the root view for a `UINavigationController`. In the `loadView` method, two buttons populate the left and right custom slots for the view's navigation item. When tapped, these show an alert, indicating which button was pressed. This recipe is not feature rich, but it provides an easy-to-build two-item menu. Figure 5-1 shows the interface in action.

This code uses a handy bar button creation macro. When passed a title and a selector, this macro returns a properly initialized autoreleased bar button item ready to be assigned to a navigation item.

```
#define BARBUTTON(TITLE, SELECTOR) [[[UIBarButtonItem alloc] initWithTitle:
➥TITLE style:UIBarButtonItemStylePlain target:self action:SELECTOR] autorelease]
```

If you're looking for more complexity than two items can offer, consider having the buttons trigger `UIActionSheet` menus. Action sheets, which are discussed in Chapter 10, "Alerting Users," let users select actions from a short list of options (usually between two and five options, although longer scrolling sheets are possible) and can be seen in use in the Photos and Mail applications for sharing and filing data.

> **Note**
>
> You can add images instead of text to the `UIBarButtonItem` instances used in your navigation bar. Use `initWithImage: style: target: action:` instead of the text-based initializer.

Recipe 5-1 **Creating a Two-Item Menu Using a Navigation Controller**

```
@implementation TestBedViewController
- (void) rightAction: (id) sender
{
    showAlert(@"You pressed the right button");
}
```

Recipe 5-1 **Continued**

```
- (void) leftAction: (id) sender
{
    showAlert(@"You pressed the left button");
}

- (void) loadView
{
    self.view = [[[NSBundle mainBundle] loadNibNamed:@"mainview"
                    owner:self options:nil] lastObject];
    self.navigationItem.rightBarButtonItem =
        BARBUTTON(@"Right",@selector (rightAction:));
    self.navigationItem.leftBarButtonItem = BARBUTTON(@"Left",selector(leftAction:));
}
@end

@implementation TestBedAppDelegate
- (void)applicationDidFinishLaunching:(UIApplication *)application
{
    UIWindow *window = [[UIWindow alloc]
              initWithFrame:[[UIScreen mainScreen] bounds]];
    UINavigationController *nav = [[UINavigationController alloc]
      initWithRootViewController:[[TestBedViewController alloc] init]];
    [window addSubview:nav.view];
    [window makeKeyAndVisible];
}
@end
```

Get This Recipe's Code

To get the code used for this recipe, go to http://github.com/erica/iphone-3.0-cookbook-, or if you've downloaded the disk image containing all of the sample code from the book, go to the folder for Chapter 5 and open the project for this recipe.

Recipe: Adding a Segmented Control

The preceding recipe showed how to use the two available button slots in your navigation bar to build mini menus. Recipe 5-2 expands on that idea by introducing a six-item `UISegmentedControl` and adding it to a navigation bar's custom title view, as shown in Figure 5-2. When tapped, each item updates the main view with its number.

The key thing to pay attention to in this recipe is the `momentary` attribute assigned to the segmented control. This transforms the interface from a radio button style into an actual menu of options, where items can be selected independently and more than once. So after tapping item three, for example, you can tap it again. That's an important behavior for menu interaction.

Figure 5-2 Adding a segmented control to the custom title view allows you to build a multi-item menu. Notice that no items remain highlighted even after an action takes place. (In this case, the One button was pressed.)

Unlike Recipe 5-1, all items in the segmented control trigger the same action (in this case, `segmentAction:`). Determine which action to take by querying the control for its `selectedSegmentIndex` and use that value to create the needed behavior. This recipe updates a central text label. You might want to choose different options based on the segment picked.

> **Note**
>
> If you want to test this code with the momentary property disabled, set the `selectedSegmentIndex` property to match the initial data displayed. In this case, segment 0 corresponds to the displayed number 1.

Segmented controls use styles to specify how they should display. The sample here, shown in Figure 5-2, uses a bar style. It is designed for use with bars, as it is in this example. The other two styles (`UISegmentedControlStyleBordered` and `UISegmentedControlStylePlain`) offer larger, more metallic-looking presentations. Of these three styles, only `UISegmentedControlStyleBar` can respond to the `tintColor` changes used in this recipe.

Recipe 5-2 **Adding a Segmented Control to the Navigation Bar**

```
-(void) segmentAction: (UISegmentedControl *) sender
{
    // Update the label with the segment number
    UILabel *label = (UILabel *)[self.view viewWithTag:101];
    [label setText:[NSString stringWithFormat:
        @"%0d", sender.selectedSegmentIndex + 1]];
}

- (void) loadView
{
    self.view = [[[NSBundle mainBundle] loadNibNamed:@"mainview"
        downer:self options:nil] lastObject];

    // Create the segmented control
    NSArray *buttonNames = [NSArray arrayWithObjects:@"One", @"Two",
        @"Three", @"Four", @"Five", @"Six", nil];
    UISegmentedControl* segmentedControl = [[UISegmentedControl alloc]
        initWithItems:buttonNames];
    segmentedControl.segmentedControlStyle =
        UISegmentedControlStyleBar;
    segmentedControl.momentary = YES;
    @selector(segmentAction:[segmentedControl addTarget:self action:)
        forControlEvents:UIControlEventValueChanged];

    // Add it to the navigation bar
    self.navigationItem.titleView = segmentedControl;
    [segmentedControl release];
}
```

Get This Recipe's Code

To get the code used for this recipe, go to http://github.com/erica/iphone-3.0-cookbook-, or if you've downloaded the disk image containing all of the sample code from the book, go to the folder for Chapter 5 and open the project for this recipe.

Recipe: Navigating Between View Controllers

In addition to providing menus, navigation controllers do the job they are designed to do: managing hierarchy as you navigate between views. Recipe 5-3 introduces the navigation controller as an actual navigation controller, pushing views on the stack.

These views consist of the same number-display stand-ins you've seen in earlier recipes. An instance variable stores the current depth number, which is used to show the current level and decide whether to display a further push option. The maximum depth here is 6. In real use, you'd use more meaningful view controllers or contents. This sample demonstrates things at their simplest level.

The navigation controller automatically creates the Level 2 Back button shown in Figure 5-3 (left) as an effect of pushing the new Level 3 controller onto the stack. The rightmost button (Push 4) triggers navigation to the next controller by calling `pushViewController: animated:`. When pushed, the next Back button reads Level 3, as shown in Figure 5-3 (right).

Figure 5-3 The navigation controller automatically creates properly labeled Back buttons. After selecting the Push 4 button in the left interface, the navigation controller pushes the Level 4 view controller and creates the Level 3 Back button in the right interface.

Back buttons pop the controller stack for you. You do not need to program any popping behavior yourself. Note that Back buttons are automatically created for pushed view controllers but not for the root controller itself, as it is not applicable.

Recipe 5-3 **Drilling Through Views with UINavigationController**

```
@interface TestBedViewController : UIViewController
{
    int depth;
}
@end

@implementation TestBedViewController
- (id) initWithDepth: (int) theDepth
{
    self = [super init];
```

Recipe 5-3 **Continued**

```
    if (self) depth = theDepth;
    return self;
}

- (void) push
{
    TestBedViewController *tbvc = [[[TestBedViewController alloc]
        initWithDepth:(depth + 1)] autorelease];
    [self.navigationController pushViewController:tbvc animated:YES];
}

- (void) loadView
{
    self.view = [[[NSBundle mainBundle] loadNibNamed:@"mainview"
        owner:self options:nil] lastObject];
    NSString *valueString = [NSString stringWithFormat:@"%d", depth];
    NSString *nextString = [NSString stringWithFormat:@"Push %d",
        depth + 1];

    // set the title
    self.title = [@"Level " stringByAppendingString:valueString];

    // Set the main label
    ((UILabel *)[self.view viewWithTag:101]).text = valueString;

    // Add the "next" bar button item. Max depth is 6
    if (depth < 6) self.navigationItem.rightBarButtonItem =
        BARBUTTON(nextString, @selector(push));
}
@end
```

Get This Recipe's Code

To get the code used for this recipe, go to http://github.com/erica/iphone-3.0-cookbook-, or if you've downloaded the disk image containing all of the sample code from the book, go to the folder for Chapter 5 and open the project for this recipe.

Recipe: Using Creative Popping Options

Although you usually want to pop to the previous view controller upon hitting the Back button, be aware that there are times you want to pop the entire stack instead. For example, you might have just given an interactive quiz, or a museum visitor might have finished his walking tour. For these cases, it makes little sense to move back up a long complex tree a screen at a time. Instead, use `popToRootViewControllerAnimated:`. This empties the stack, popping all view controllers except the root, updating the display accordingly.

To pop back to a specific controller other than the root, use `popToViewController:animated:`. This pops the stack until the top view matches the view controller specified.

To pop back just one item, as if the user had tapped the back button, use `popViewControllerAnimated:`.

Loading a View Controller Array

You can create and assign an array of `UIViewController` objects to a UINavigationController's `viewControllers` property. The array represents the current controller stack. The top (that is, active) view controller occupies the last position (n -1) in the array; the root object lives at index 0.

There are various reasons you might want to set the array property. Controller arrays help restore previous states after quitting and then returning to an application. You might store a state list to user defaults and then re-create the same array on launch, returning your user to the same place in the controller hierarchy that he or she left from.

Arrays are also handy when jumping within a conceptual tree. For example, you might be navigating directories and then need to jump through a symbolic link to somewhere else. By setting the entire array, you avoid the detail work of popping and then pushing the stack.

Pushing Momentary Views

Every now and then, I run into developers who want to be able to push UIViewControllers that do not remain in the navigation controller stack. For example, you might start at view 1, push on view 2, and then push on view 3 while letting the Back button from view 3 link back to the first view.

This situation comes up more often than you might imagine. The most common reason is that you're introducing the action that will take place in the third view with the second. Typically, the second screen contains instructions, general "read me" content, or a visual splash. These are meant to display once and then be gone from the user experience and yet, you want the navigation controller experience to remain as standard as possible. To make this work, the Back button needs to ignore the second, temporary view.

Recipe 5-4 demonstrates how to do this. When the second view is ready to transition to the third, the navigation controller goes ahead and performs the push. This creates the proper animation for the viewer, from view two to view three. Then, without animation, the code pops the last two views, leaving the stack at view one. To finish, the code performs a delayed animated push, adding view three behind view one, creating the proper "back" button.

Although the main view animation properly shows a push from view two to view three, be aware that the navigation bar animation shows a push from root to Level 3. This should not be enough to get your application booted from the App Store for violating human interaction guidelines but you might want to use smart interface design to minimize visual discontinuities.

Recipe 5-4 **Pushing Momentary Views**

```
- (void) doPush: (id) nc
{
    // With the stack back at view 1, push on view #depth+1
    [nc pushViewController:[[TestBedViewController alloc]
        initWithDepth:depth+1] animated:YES];
}

- (void) push
{
    if (depth < 2)
    {
        [self.navigationController
            pushViewController:[[TestBedViewController alloc]
            initWithDepth:depth+1] animated:YES];
        return;
    }

    // Push from current view to view #depth+1, showing the animation
    [self.navigationController
        pushViewController:[[TestBedViewController alloc]
        initWithDepth:depth+1] animated:YES];

    // Get ready to push from view #1 to view #depth+1
    [self performSelector:@selector(doPush:)
        withObject:self.navigationController afterDelay:0.05f];

    // Pop off view #depth+1 and then view #depth
    [[self.navigationController topViewController] autorelease];
    [self.navigationController popViewControllerAnimated:NO];
    [[self.navigationController topViewController] autorelease];
    [self.navigationController popViewControllerAnimated:NO];

}
```

Get This Recipe's Code

To get the code used for this recipe, go to http://github.com/erica/iphone-3.0-cookbook-, or if you've downloaded the disk image containing all of the sample code from the book, go to the folder for Chapter 5 and open the project for this recipe.

Recipe: Presenting a Custom Modal Information View

Modal view controllers slide onscreen without being part of your standard view controller stack. Modal views are useful for picking data or presenting information, tasks that might not match well to your normal hierarchy. Any view controller or navigation controller can present a modal controller:

```
[self presentModalViewController:[[[InfoViewController alloc] init]
    autorelease] animated:YES];
```

The controller that is presented can be either a view controller or navigation controller. Either way, it helps to provide a Done button to allow the user to dismiss the controller. Figure 5-4 shows a modal presentation built around a UIViewController instance. The navigation bar at the top of the view was added via a UINavigationBar instance, making this view especially easy to construct in Interface Builder.

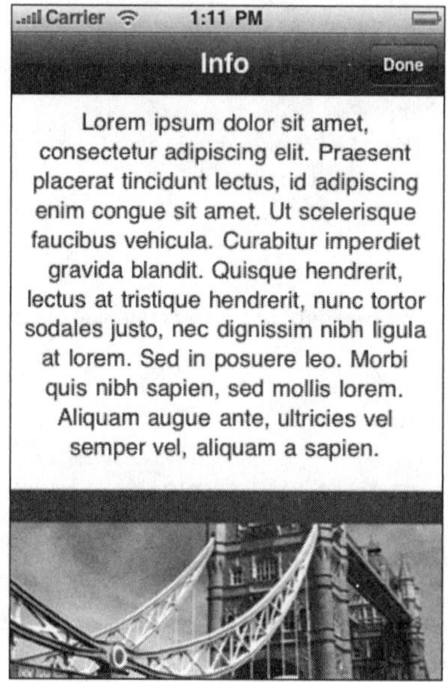

Figure 5-4 This modal view is built using UIViewController with a UINavigationBar.

Normally, a navigation controller-based view requires two .xib files and extra work, as shown in the Chapter 4 walk-throughs that built a navigation-based interface. Using the bar directly avoided the hassle and provided an elegant solution that mimics the normal look of a UINavigationController presentation.

Recipe 5-5 shows the two key pieces for this presentation. The presentation is done in the main view controller, with the presentation style set by a segmented control. The `InfoViewController`, that is, the class that was presented, handles dismissal. Its Done button was connected via IB to the `doneReading` method. This method asks the view controller's parent to dismiss the modally presented view controller.

Recipe 5-5 **Presenting and Dismissing a Modal Controller**

```
// Presenting the controller
- (void) info
{
    int segment = [(UISegmentedControl *)self.navigationItem.titleView
        selectedSegmentIndex];
    int styles[3] = {UIModalTransitionStyleCoverVertical,
        UIModalTransitionStyleCrossDissolve,
        UIModalTransitionStyleFlipHorizontal};
    InfoViewController *ivc = [[[InfoViewController alloc] init]
        autorelease];
    ivc.modalTransitionStyle = styles[segment];
    [self presentModalViewController:ivc animated:YES];
}
```

And...

```
// Dismissing the controller
- (IBAction) doneReading
{
    [[self parentViewController]
        dismissModalViewControllerAnimated:YES];
}
```

> **Get This Recipe's Code**
>
> To get the code used for this recipe, go to http://github.com/erica/iphone-3.0-cookbook-, or if you've downloaded the disk image containing all of the sample code from the book, go to the folder for Chapter 5 and open the project for this recipe.

Recipe: Tab Bars

The `UITabBarController` class allows users to move between multiple view controllers and to customize the bar at the bottom of the screen. This is best seen in the YouTube and iPod applications. Both offer one-tap access to different views, and both offer a More button leading to user selection and editing of the bottom bar.

With tab bars, you don't push views the way you do with navigation bars. Instead, you assemble a collection of controllers (they can individually be `UIViewControllers`, `UINavigationControllers`, or any other kind of view controllers) and add them into a tab bar by setting the bar's `viewControllers` property. It really is that simple. Cocoa Touch does all the rest of the work for you. Set `allowsCustomizing` to `YES` to enable user reordering of the bar.

Recipe 5-6 creates 11 simple view controllers of the `BrightnessController` class. This class uses a `UIView` embedded into mainview.xib and sets its background to a specified gray level, in this case from 0% to 100% in steps of 10%. Figure 5-5 (left) shows the interface in its default mode, with the first four items and a More button displayed.

Reorder these tabs by selecting the More option and then tapping Edit. This opens the Configure panel shown in Figure 5-5 (right). These 11 view controllers are the options a user can navigate through and select from.

Figure 5-5 Tab bar controllers allow users to pick view controllers from a bar at the bottom of the screen (left side of the figure) and to customize the bar from a list of available view controllers (right side of the figure).

Notice that this recipe adds those 11 controllers twice. The first time assigns them to the list of view controllers available to the user:

```
tbarController.viewControllers = controllers;
```

The second time specifies that the user can select from the entire list when interactively customizing the bottom tab bar:

```
tbarController.customizableViewControllers = controllers;
```

The second line is optional, the first mandatory. After setting up the view controllers, you can add all or some to the customizable list. If you don't, you still can see the extra view controllers using the More button, but users won't be able to include them in the main tab bar on demand.

Tab art appears inverted in color on the More screen. According to Apple, this is the expected and proper behavior. They have no plans to change this. It does provide an interesting view contrast when your 100% white swatch appears as pure black on that screen.

Note that this recipe uses a convenience class called `GraphicsUtilities`, which I created for this book. This and other goodies are looked at in detail in later chapters.

Recipe 5-6 **Creating a Tab View Controller**

```
@implementation BrightnessController
- (UIImage*) buildSwatch: (float) tint
{
    CGContextRef context  = [GraphicsUtilities
        newBitmapContextWithWidth:30 andHeight:30];
    [GraphicsUtilities addRoundedRect:
        CGRectMake(0.0f, 0.0f, 30.0f, 30.0f) toContext:context
        withWidth:4.0f andHeight:4.0f];
    CGFloat gray[4] = {tint, tint, tint, 1.0f};
    CGContextSetFillColor(context, gray);
    CGContextFillPath(context);

    CGImageRef myRef = CGBitmapContextCreateImage (context);
    free(CGBitmapContextGetData(context));
    CGContextRelease(context);
    UIImage *img = [UIImage imageWithCGImage:myRef];
    CFRelease(myRef);
    return img;
}

-(BrightnessController *) initWithBrightness: (int) aBrightness
{
    self = [super init];
    brightness = aBrightness;
    self.title = [NSString stringWithFormat:@"%d%%", brightness * 10];
    [self.tabBarItem initWithTitle:self.title image:[self
        buildSwatch:(((float)brightness) / 10.0f)] tag:0];
    return self;
}

- (void) loadView
{
    self.view = [[[NSBundle mainBundle] loadNibNamed:@"mainview"
        owner:self options:nil] lastObject];
    UIView *bigSwatch = [self.view viewWithTag:101];
    bigSwatch.backgroundColor = [UIColor colorWithWhite:
        (brightness / 10.0f) alpha:1.0f];
}
@end

@interface TestBedAppDelegate : NSObject <UIApplicationDelegate,
    UITabBarControllerDelegate>
@end

@implementation TestBedAppDelegate
- (void)applicationDidFinishLaunching:(UIApplication *)application {
    NSMutableArray *controllers = [NSMutableArray array];
```

Recipe 5-6 **Continued**

```
    for (int i = 0; i <= 10; i++)
    {
        BrightnessController *bControl = [[BrightnessController alloc]
            initWithBrightness:i];
        UINavigationController *nav = [[UINavigationController alloc]
            initWithRootViewController:bControl];
        nav.navigationBar.barStyle = UIBarStyleBlackTranslucent;
        [bControl release];

        [controllers addObject:nav];
        [nav release];
    }

    // Create the toolbar and add the view controllers
    UITabBarController *tbarController = [[UITabBarController alloc]
        init];
    tbarController.viewControllers = controllers;
    tbarController.customizableViewControllers = controllers;
    tbarController.delegate = self;

    // Set up the window
    UIWindow *window = [[UIWindow alloc] initWithFrame:[[UIScreen
        mainScreen] bounds]];
    [window addSubview:tbarController.view];
    [window makeKeyAndVisible];
}
@end
```

Get This Recipe's Code

To get the code used for this recipe, go to http://github.com/erica/iphone-3.0-cookbook-, or if you've downloaded the disk image containing all of the sample code from the book, go to the folder for Chapter 5 and open the project for this recipe.

Recipe: Remembering Tab State

On the iPhone, persistence is golden. When starting or resuming your application from termination or interruption, always return users to a state that closely matches where they left off. This lets your users pick up with whatever tasks they were involved with and provides a user interface that matches the previous session. Recipe 5-7 introduces an example of doing exactly that.

This recipe stores both the current tab order and the currently selected tab, and does so whenever those items are updated. When a user launches the application, the code searches for previous settings and applies them when they are found.

The approach used here depends on two delegate methods. The first, `tabBarController:didEndCustomizingViewControllers:` provides the current array of view controllers after the user has customized them with the More > Edit screen. This code snags their titles (10%, 20%, and so on) and uses that information to relate a name to each view controller.

The second delegate method is `tabBarController: didSelectViewController:`. The tab bar controller sends this method each time a user selects a new tab. By capturing the `selectedIndex`, this code stores the controller number relative to the current array.

Setting these values depends on using the iPhone's built-in user defaults system, `NSUserDefaults`. This preferences system works very much as a large mutable dictionary. You can set values for keys using `setObject: forKey:`

```
[[NSUserDefaults standardUserDefaults] setObject:titles
    forKey:@"tabOrder"];
```

and retrieve them with `objectForKey:`.

```
NSArray *titles = [[NSUserDefaults standardUserDefaults]
    objectForKey:@"tabOrder"];
```

Always make sure to `synchronize` your settings as shown in this code to ensure that the defaults dictionary matches your changes. If you do not synchronize, the defaults will not get set until the program terminates. If you do synchronize, your changes are updated immediately. Any other parts of your application that rely on checking these settings will then be guaranteed to access the latest values.

When the application launches, it checks for previous settings for the last selected tab order and selected tab. If it finds them, it uses these to set up the tabs and select a tab to make active. Since the titles contain the information about what brightness value to show, this code converts the stored title from text to a number and divides that number by ten to send to the initialization function.

Most applications aren't based on such a simple numeric system. Should you use titles to store your tab bar order, make sure you name your view controllers meaningfully and in a way that lets you match a view controller with the tab ordering.

> **Note**
>
> You could also store an array of the view tags as NSNumbers or, better yet, use the `NSKeyedArchiver` class that is introduced in Chapter 8, "Gestures and Touches." Keyed archiving lets you rebuild views using state information that you store on termination.

Recipe 5-7 **Storing Tab State to User Defaults**

```
@implementation TestBedAppDelegate

- (void)tabBarController:(UITabBarController *)tabBarController
didEndCustomizingViewControllers:(NSArray *)viewControllers changed:(BOOL)changed
{
    // Store the titles from the tabs in order
    NSMutableArray *titles = [NSMutableArray array];
    for (UIViewController *vc in viewControllers) [titles
        addObject:vc.title];
    [[NSUserDefaults standardUserDefaults] setObject:titles
```

Recipe 5-7 **Continued**

```
        forKey:@"tabOrder"];
    [[NSUserDefaults standardUserDefaults] synchronize];
}

- (void)tabBarController:(UITabBarController *)tabBarController
        didSelectViewController:(UIViewController *)viewController
{
    // Update the currently selected tab number
    NSNumber *tabNumber = [NSNumber numberWithInt:[tabBarController
        selectedIndex]];
    [[NSUserDefaults standardUserDefaults] setObject:tabNumber
        forKey:@"selectedTab"];
    [[NSUserDefaults standardUserDefaults] synchronize];
}

- (void)applicationDidFinishLaunching:(UIApplication *)application {
    NSMutableArray *controllers = [NSMutableArray array];
    NSArray *titles = [[NSUserDefaults standardUserDefaults]
        objectForKey:@"tabOrder"];

    if (titles)
    {
        // titles retrieved from user defaults
        for (NSString *theTitle in titles)
        {
            BrightnessController *bControl = [[BrightnessController
                alloc] initWithBrightness:([theTitle intValue] / 10)];
            UINavigationController *nav = [[UINavigationController
                alloc] initWithRootViewController:bControl];
            nav.navigationBar.barStyle = UIBarStyleBlackTranslucent;
            [bControl release];

            [controllers addObject:nav];
            [nav release];
        }
    } else {
        // generate all new controllers
        for (int i = 0; i <= 10; i++)
        {
            BrightnessController *bControl = [[BrightnessController
                alloc] initWithBrightness:i];
            UINavigationController *nav = [[UINavigationController
                alloc] initWithRootViewController:bControl];
            nav.navigationBar.barStyle = UIBarStyleBlackTranslucent;
            [bControl release];
```

Recipe 5-7 **Continued**

```
            [controllers addObject:nav];
            [nav release];
        }
    }

    // Create the toolbar and add the view controllers
    UITabBarController *tbarController = [[UITabBarController alloc]
        init];
    tbarController.viewControllers = controllers;
    tbarController.customizableViewControllers = controllers;
    tbarController.delegate = self;

    NSNumber *tabNumber = [[NSUserDefaults standardUserDefaults]
        objectForKey:@"selectedTab"];
    if (tabNumber)
        tbarController.selectedIndex = [tabNumber intValue];

    // Set up the window
    UIWindow *window = [[UIWindow alloc] initWithFrame:[[UIScreen
        mainScreen] bounds]];
    [window addSubview:tbarController.view];
    [window makeKeyAndVisible];
}
@end
```

Get This Recipe's Code

To get the code used for this recipe, go to http://github.com/erica/iphone-3.0-cookbook-, or if you've downloaded the disk image containing all of the sample code from the book, go to the folder for Chapter 5 and open the project for this recipe.

One More Thing: Interface Builder and Tab Bar Controllers

Xcode offers an easy to customize Tab Bar Application template that gets you started building tab-bar-based GUIs in Interface Builder. The tab bar controller's attribute inspector lets you add new tabs, as shown in Figure 5-6. Click the + button. The class column lets you select what kind of view controller you're working with, namely View Controller, Table View Controller, Navigation Controller, or Image Picker Controller.

You'll likely want to create a new view controller class for each tab. Create your class (and its associated .xib file) in Xcode and then choose the .xib from within Interface Builder. Tap any of the black tabs in the MainWindow .xib, and tap the gray View presentation. Select the .xib from the attributes inspector (Command-1). The first tab comes prepopulated with a view (as shown in Figure 5-6), but all the other tabs require a .xib to be assigned to them.

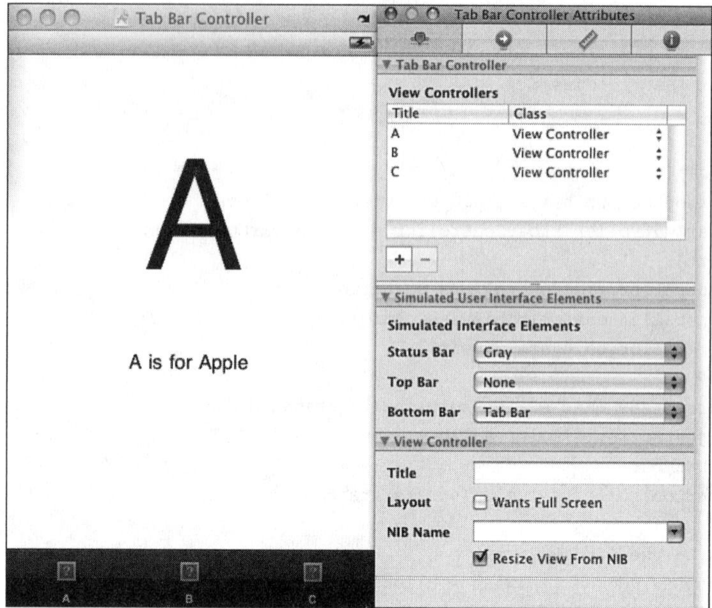

Figure 5-6 Interface Builder provides tools for laying out tab bar controllers but offers few advantages for building what is essentially a logical and not a visual class.

To add art to the tabs in IB, drag 20x20 png images from the Library > Media pane onto each tab button. The Media pane lists the images you have added to your Xcode project. Design your images using a transparent background and a white foreground.

While Interface Builder offers a friendly way to lay out individual views, you may find yourself forgoing it for tab bars and navigation bars. These classes provide what can be argued is more of a logical construct than a visual presentation. After all, you cannot drag the tab bar or the navigation bar around the screen and any customizations can easily be done in code.

Further, once you start taking advantage of the delegate callbacks that are leveraged directly from code, the IB overhead may no longer be worth the trouble. IB works best with view design. Its support for navigation controllers and tab bar controllers is relatively weak.

Summary

This chapter showed the `UIViewController`, `UINavigationController`, and `UITabBarController` classes in action. You learned how to use them to handle view presentation and user navigation. With these classes, you discovered how to expand virtual interaction space and create multipage interfaces as demanded by applications. Before moving on to the next chapter, here are a few points to consider about view controllers:

- Use navigation trees to build hierarchical interfaces. They work well for looking at file structures or building a settings tree. When you think "disclosure view" or "preferences," consider pushing a new controller onto a navigation stack.
- Don't be afraid to use conventional UI elements in unconventional ways so long as you respect the overall Apple human interface guidelines. Parts of this chapter covered innovative uses for the `UINavigationController` that didn't involve any navigation. The tools are there for the using.
- Be persistent. Let your users return to the same GUI state that they last left from. NSUserDefaults provides a built-in system for storing information between application runs. Use these defaults to re-create the prior interface state.
- Interface Builder works best for visual layout. Many developers use it for designing views but give it a pass when building navigation controllers and tab bar controllers.

6

Assembling Views and Animations

UIView and its subclasses populate the iPhone's screen. This chapter introduces views from the ground up. You learn how to build, inspect, and break down view hierarchies and understand how views work together. You discover the role geometry plays in creating and placing views into your interface, and you read about animating views so they move and transform onscreen. This chapter covers everything you need to know to work with views from the lowest levels up.

View Hierarchies

A tree-based hierarchy orders what you see on your iPhone screen. Starting with the main window, views are laid out in a specifically hierarchical way. All views may have children, called subviews. Each view, including the window, owns an ordered list of these subviews. Views might own many subviews; they might own none. Your application determines how views are laid out and who owns whom.

Subviews display onscreen in order, always from back to front. This works something like a stack of animation cells—those transparent sheets used to create cartoons. Only the parts of the sheets that have been painted show through. The clear parts allow any visual elements behind that sheet to be seen. Views too can have clear and painted parts, and can be layered to build a complex presentation.

Figure 6-1 shows a little of the layering used in a typical window. Here the window owns a `UINavigationController`-based hierarchy. The elements layer together. The window (represented by the empty, rightmost element) owns a navigation bar, which in turn owns two subview buttons (one left and one right). The window also owns a table with its own subviews. These items stack together to build the GUI.

Listing 6-1 shows the actual view hierarchy of the window in Figure 6-1. The tree starts at the top `UIWindow` and shows the classes for each of the child views. If you trace your way down the tree, you can see the navigation bar (at level 2) with its two buttons (each at level 3) and the table view (level 4) with its two cells (each at level 5). Some of the items in this listing are private classes, automatically added by the SDK when laying out views. For example, the UILayoutContainerView is never used directly by developers. It's part of the SDK's UIWindow implementation.

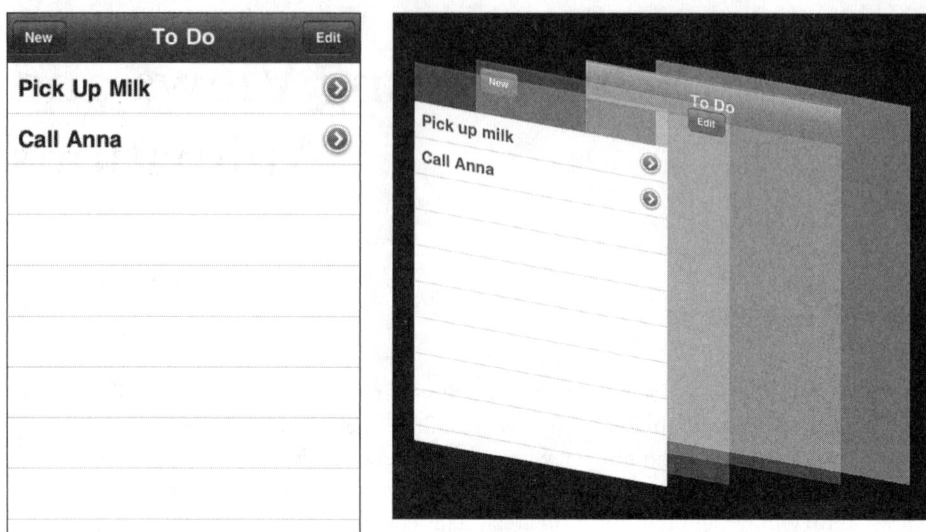

Figure 6-1 Subview hierarchies combine to build complex GUIs.

The only parts missing from this listing are the dozen or so line separators for the table, omitted for space considerations. Each separator is actually a UITableViewSeparatorView instance. They belong to the UITableView and would normally display at a depth of 5.

Listing 6-1 **To Do List View Hierarchy**

```
[ 0] UIWindow
--[ 1] UILayoutContainerView
----[ 2] UINavigationTransitionView
------[ 3] UIViewControllerWrapperView
--------[ 4] UITableView
----------[ 5] UITableViewCell
------------[ 6] UIView
--------------[ 7] UILabel
------------[ 6] UIButton
--------------[ 7] UIImageView
------------[ 6] UIView
----------[ 5] UITableViewCell
------------[ 6] UIView
--------------[ 7] UILabel
------------[ 6] UIButton
--------------[ 7] UIImageView
```

Listing 6-1 **Continued**

```
------------[ 6] UIView
----------[ 5] UIImageView
----------[ 5] UIImageView
----[ 2] UINavigationBar
------[ 3] UINavigationItemView
------[ 3] UINavigationButton
--------[ 4] UIImageView
--------[ 4] UIButtonLabel
------[ 3] UINavigationButton
--------[ 4] UIImageView
--------[ 4] UIButtonLabel
```

Recipe: Recovering a View Hierarchy Tree

Each view knows both its parent (`[aView superview]`) and its children (`[aView subviews]`). Build a view tree like the one shown in Listing 6-1 by recursively walking through a view's subviews. Recipe 6-1 does exactly that. It builds a visual tree by noting the class of each view and increasing the indentation level every time it moves down from a parent view to its children. The results are stored into a mutable string and returned from the calling method.

The code shown in Recipe 6-1 was used to create the tree shown in Listing 6-1. The same interface and recipe appear as part of the sample code that accompanies this book. You can use this routine to duplicate the results of Listing 6-1, or you can copy it to other applications to view their hierarchies.

Recipe 6-1 **Extracting a View Hierarchy Tree**

```
// Recursively travel down the view tree, increasing the
// indentation level for children
 - (void) dumpView: (UIView *) aView atIndent: (int) indent
    into:(NSMutableString *) outstring
{
    for (int i = 0; i < indent; i++)
        [outstring appendString:@"-"];
    [outstring appendFormat:@"[%2d] %@\n", indent,
        [[aView class] description]];
    for (UIView *view in [aView subviews])
        [self dumpView:view atIndent:indent + 1 into:outstring];
}

// Start the tree recursion at level 0 with the root view
- (NSString *) displayViews: (UIView *) aView
{
    NSMutableString *outstring = [[NSMutableString alloc] init];
    [self dumpView:aView atIndent:0 into:outstring];
    return [outstring autorelease];
}
```

> **Get This Recipe's Code**
>
> To get the code used for this recipe, go to http://github.com/erica/iphone-3.0-cookbook-, or if you've downloaded the disk image containing all of the sample code from the book, go to the folder for Chapter 6 and open the project for this recipe.

Recipe: Querying Subviews

Views store arrays of their children. Retrieve this array by calling `[aView subviews]`. Onscreen, the child views are always drawn after the parent, in the order that they appear in the subviews array. These views draw in order from back to front, and the subviews array mirrors that drawing pattern. Views that appear later in the array are drawn after views that appear earlier.

The `subviews` method returns just those views that are immediate children of a given view. At times, you may want to retrieve a more exhaustive list of subviews including the children's children. Recipe 6-2 introduces `allSubviews()`, a simple recursive function that returns a full list of descendants for any view. Call this function with view.window to return a complete set of views appearing in the `UIWindow` that hosts that view. This list proves useful when you want to search for a particular view, like a specific slider or button.

Although it is not typical, iPhone applications may include several windows, each of which can contain many views. Recover an exhaustive list of all application views by iterating through each available window. The `allApplicationSubviews()` function in Recipe 6-2 does exactly that. A call to `[[UIApplication sharedApplication] windows]` returns the array of application windows. The function iterates through these, adding their subviews to the collection.

In addition to knowing its subviews, each view knows the window it belongs to. The view's `window` property points to the window that owns it. Recipe 6-2 also includes a simple function called `pathToView()` that returns an array of superviews, from the window down to the view in question. It does this by calling `superview` repeatedly until arriving at that window.

Views can also check their superview ancestry in another way. The `isDescendantOfView:` method determines whether a view lives within another view, even if that view is not its direct superview. This method returns a simple Boolean value. `YES` means the view descends from the view passed as a parameter to the method.

Recipe 6-2 **Subview Utility Functions**

```
// Return an exhaustive descent of the view's subviews
NSArray *allSubviews(UIView *aView)
{
    NSArray *results = [aView subviews];
    for (UIView *eachView in [aView subviews])
    {
        NSArray *riz = allSubviews(eachView);
```

Recipe 6-2 **Continued**

```
        if (riz) results = [results arrayByAddingObjectsFromArray:riz];
    }
    return results;
}

// Return all views throughout the application
NSArray *allApplicationViews()
{
    NSArray *results = [[UIApplication sharedApplication] windows];
    for (UIWindow *window in [[UIApplication sharedApplication]
        windows])
    {
        NSArray *riz = allSubviews(window);
        if (riz) results = [results arrayByAddingObjectsFromArray:
            riz];
    }
    return results;
}

// Return an array of parent views from the window down to the view
NSArray *pathToView(UIView *aView)
{
    NSMutableArray *array = [NSMutableArray arrayWithObject:aView];
    UIView *view = aView;
    UIWindow *window = aView.window;
    while (view != window)
    {
        view = [view superview];
        [array insertObject:view atIndex:0];
    }
    return array;
}
```

Get This Recipe's Code

To get the code used for this recipe, go to http://github.com/erica/iphone-3.0-cookbook-, or if you've downloaded the disk image containing all of the sample code from the book, go to the folder for Chapter 6 and open the project for this recipe.

Managing Subviews

The `UIView` class offers numerous methods that help build and manage views. These methods let you add, order, remove, and query the view hierarchy. Since this hierarchy controls what you see onscreen, updating the way that views relate to each other changes what you see on the iPhone. Here are some approaches for typical view-management tasks.

Adding Subviews

Call `[parentView addSubview:child]` to add new subviews to a parent. Newly added subviews are always placed frontmost on your screen; the iPhone adds them on top of any existing views. To insert a subview into the view hierarchy at a particular location other than the front, the SDK offers a trio of utility methods:

- `insertSubview:atIndex:`
- `insertSubview:aboveSubview:`
- `insertSubview:belowSubview:`

These methods control where view insertion happens. That insertion can remain relative to another view, or it can move into a specific index of the subviews array. The above and below methods add subviews in front of or behind a given child. Insertion pushes other views forward and does not replace any views that are already there.

Reordering and Removing Subviews

Applications often need to reorder and remove views as users interact with the screen. The iPhone SDK offers several easy ways to do this, allowing you to change the view order and contents.

- Use `[parentView exchangeSubviewAtIndex:i withSubviewAtIndex:j]` to exchange the positions of two views.
- Move subviews to the front or back using `bringSubviewToFront:` and `sendSubviewToBack`.
- To remove a subview from its parent, call `[childView removeFromSuperview]`. If the child view had been onscreen, it disappears. Removing a child from the superview calls a release on the subview, allowing its memory to be freed if its retain count has returned to zero.

When you reorder, add, or remove views, the screen automatically redraws to show the new view presentation.

View Callbacks

When the view hierarchy changes, callbacks can be sent to the views in question. The iPhone SDK offers six callback methods. These callbacks may help your application keep track of views that are moving and changing parents.

- `didAddSubview:` is sent to a view after a successful invocation of `addSubview:` lets subclasses of `UIView` perform additional actions when new views are added.
- `didMoveToSuperview:` informs views that they've been re-parented to a new superview. The view may want to respond to that new parent in some way. When the view was removed from its superview, the new parent is `nil`.
- `willMoveToSuperview:` is sent before the move occurs.

- `didMoveToWindow:` provides the callback equivalent of didMoveToSuperview but when the view moves to a new Window hierarchy instead of to just a new superview.
- `willMoveToWindow:` is, again, sent before the move occurs.
- `willRemoveSubview:` informs the parent view that the child view is about to be removed.

Recipe: Tagging and Retrieving Views

The iPhone SDK offers a built-in search feature that lets you recover views by tagging them. Tags are just numbers, usually positive integers, that identify a view. Assign them using the view's tag property, for example, `myView.tag = 101`. In Interface Builder, you can set a view's tag in the attributes inspector. As Figure 6-2 shows, you specify the tag in the View section.

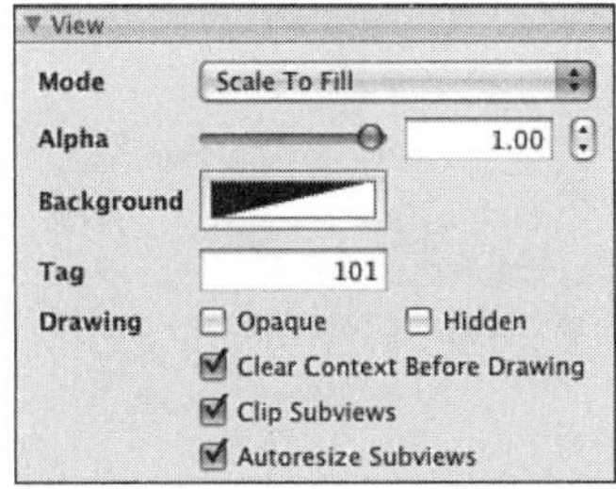

Figure 6-2 Set the tag for any view in Interface Builder's attributes inspector.

Tags are completely arbitrary. The only "reserved" tag is 0, which is the default property setting for all newly created views. It's up to you to decide how you want to tag your views and which values to use. You can tag any instance that is a child of `UIView`, including windows and controls. So if you have many onscreen buttons and switches, adding tags helps tell them apart when users trigger them. You can add a simple switch statement to your callback methods that looks at the tag and determines how to react.

Apple rarely tags subviews. The only instance I have ever found of their view tagging has been in UIAlertViews where the buttons use tags of 1, 2, and so forth. (I'm half convinced they left this tagging in there as a mistake.) If you worry about conflicting with Apple tags, start your numbering at 10 or 100, or some other number higher than any value Apple might use.

Using Tags to Find Views

Tags let you avoid passing user interface elements around your program by making them directly accessible from any parent view. The `viewWithTag:` method recovers a tagged view from a child hierarchy. The search is recursive, so the tagged item need not be an immediate child of the view in question. You can search from the window with `[window` `viewWithTag:101]` and find a view that is several branches down the hierarchy tree. When more than one view uses the same tag, `viewWithTag:` returns the first item it finds.

The problem with `viewWithTag:` is that it returns a `UIView` object. This means you often have to cast it to the proper type before you can use it. Say you want to retrieve a label and set its text.

```
UILabel *label = (UILabel *)[self.view.window viewWithTag:101];
label.text = @"Hello World";
```

It would be far easier to use a call that returned an already typed object and then be able to use that object right away, as these calls do:

```
- (IBAction)updateTime:(id)sender
{
    // set the label to the current time
    [self.view.window labelWithTag:LABEL_TAG].text =
        [[NSDate date] description];
}

- (IBAction)updateSwitch:(id)sender
{
    // toggle the switch from its current setting
    UISwitch *s = [self.view.window switchWithTag:SWITCH_TAG];
    [s setOn:!s.isOn];
}
```

Recipe 6-3 extends the behavior of `UIView` to introduce a new category, TagExtensions. This category adds just two typed tag methods, for `UILabel` and `UISwitch`. The sample code for this book extends this to include a full suite of typed tag utilities. The additional classes were omitted for space considerations; they follow the same pattern of casting from `viewWithTag:`. Access the full collection by including the UIView-TagExtensions files in your projects.

Recipe 6-3 **Recovering Tagged Views with Properly Cast Objects**

```
@interface UIView (TagExtensions)
- (UILabel *) labelWithTag: (NSInteger) aTag;
- (UISwitch *) switchWithTag: (NSInteger) aTag;
@end

@implementation UIView (TagExtensions)
- (UILabel *) labelWithTag: (NSInteger) aTag
{
    return (UILabel *)[self viewWithTag:aTag];
}

- (UISwitch *) switchWithTag: (NSInteger) aTag
{
```

Recipe 6-3 **Continued**

```
    return (UISwitch *)[self viewWithTag:aTag];
}
@end
```

Get This Recipe's Code

To get the code used for this recipe, go to http://github.com/erica/iphone-3.0-cookbook-, or if you've downloaded the disk image containing all of the sample code from the book, go to the folder for Chapter 6 and open the project for this recipe.

Recipe: Naming Views

Although tagging offers a thorough approach to identifying views, some developers may prefer to work with names rather than numbers. Using names adds an extra level of meaning to your view identification schemes. Instead of referring to "the view with a tag of 101," a switch named "Ignition Switch" describes its role and adds a level of self-documentation missing from a plain number.

```
// Toggle switch
UISwitch *s = [self.view switchNamed:@"Ignition Switch"];
[s setOn:!s.isOn];
```

It's relatively easy to design a class that associates strings with view tags. This custom class needs to store a dictionary that matches names with tags, allowing views to register and unregister those names. Recipe 6-4 shows how to build that view name manager, which uses a singleton instance (`[ViewIndexer sharedInstance]`) to store its tag and name dictionary.

The class demands unique names. If a view name is already registered, a new registration request will fail. If a view was already registered under another name, a second registration request will unregister the first name. There are ways to fool this of course. If you change a view's tag and then register it again, the indexer has no way of knowing that the view had been previously registered. So if you decide to use this approach, set your tags in Interface Builder or let the registration process automatically tag the view but otherwise leave the tags be.

If you build your views by hand, register them at the same point you create them and add them into your overall view hierarchy. When using an IB-defined view, register your names in `viewDidLoad` using the tag numbers you set in the attributes inspector.

```
- (void) viewDidLoad
{
    [[self.view viewWithTag:LABEL_TAG] registerName:@"my label"];
    [[self.view viewWithTag:SWITCH_TAG] registerName:@"my switch"];
}
```

Recipe 6-4 hides the view indexer class from public view. It wraps its calls inside a `UIView` category for name extensions. This allows you to register, retrieve, and unregister views without using `ViewIndexer` directly. For reasons of space, the recipe omits typed name retrievals like `labelNamed:` and `textFieldNamed:`, but these are included in the sample code for the chapter.

Recipe 6-4 **Creating a View Name Manager**

```
@interface ViewIndexer : NSObject {
    NSMutableDictionary *tagdict;
    NSInteger count;
}
@property (nonatomic, retain) NSMutableDictionary *tagdict;
@end

@implementation ViewIndexer
@synthesize tagdict;

static ViewIndexer *sharedInstance = nil;

+(ViewIndexer *) sharedInstance {
    if(!sharedInstance) sharedInstance = [[self alloc] init];
    return sharedInstance;
}

- (id) init
{
    if (!(self = [super init])) return self;
    self.tagdict = [NSMutableDictionary dictionary];
    count = 10000;
    return self;
}

- (void) dealloc
{
    self.tagdict = nil;
    [super dealloc];
}

// Pull a new number and increase the count
- (NSInteger) pullNumber
{
    return count++;
}

// Check to see if name exists in dictionary
- (BOOL) nameExists: (NSString *) aName
{
    return [self.tagdict objectForKey:aName] != nil;
}
```

Recipe 6-4 **Continued**

```
// Pull out first matching name for tag
- (NSString *) nameForTag: (NSInteger) aTag
{
    NSNumber *tag = [NSNumber numberWithInt:aTag];
    NSArray *names = [self.tagdict allKeysForObject:tag];
    if (!names) return nil;
    if ([names count] == 0) return nil;
    return [names objectAtIndex:0];
}

// Return the tag for a registered name. 0 if not found
- (NSInteger) tagForName: (NSString *)aName
{
    NSNumber *tag = [self.tagdict objectForKey:aName];
    if (!tag) return 0;
    return [tag intValue];
}

// Unregistering reverts tag to 0
- (BOOL) unregisterName: (NSString *) aName forView: (UIView *) aView
{
    NSNumber *tag = [self.tagdict objectForKey:aName];

    // tag not found
    if (!tag) return NO;

    // tag does not match registered name
    if (aView.tag != [tag intValue]) return NO;

    aView.tag = 0;
    [self.tagdict removeObjectForKey:aName];
    return YES;
}

// Register a new name. Names will not re-register. (Unregister first,
// please). If a view is already registered, it is unregistered and
// re-registered
- (NSInteger) registerName:(NSString *)aName forView: (UIView *) aView
{
    // You cannot re-register an existing name
    if ([[ViewIndexer sharedInstance] nameExists:aName]) return 0;

    // Check to see if the view is named already. If so, unregister.
    NSString *currentName = [self nameForTag:aView.tag];
    if (currentName) [self unregisterName:currentName forView:aView];
```

Recipe 6-4 **Continued**

```
    // Register the existing tag or pull a new tag if aView.tag is 0
    if (!aView.tag) aView.tag = [[ViewIndexer sharedInstance]
        pullNumber];
    [self.tagdict setObject:[NSNumber numberWithInt:aView.tag]
        forKey: aName];
    return aView.tag;
}
@end

@implementation UIView (NameExtensions)

- (NSInteger) registerName: (NSString *) aName
{
    return [[ViewIndexer sharedInstance] registerName: aName
        forView: self];
}

- (BOOL) unregisterName: (NSString *) aName
{
    return [[ViewIndexer sharedInstance] unregisterName: aName
        forView:self];
}

- (UIView *) viewNamed: (NSString *) aName
{
    NSInteger tag = [[ViewIndexer sharedInstance] tagForName: aName];
    return [self viewWithTag: tag];
}
@end
```

> **Get This Recipe's Code**
>
> To get the code used for this recipe, go to http://github.com/erica/iphone-3.0-cookbook-, or if you've downloaded the disk image containing all of the sample code from the book, go to the folder for Chapter 6 and open the project for this recipe.

View Geometry

As you'd expect, geometry plays an important role when working with views. Geometry defines where each view appears onscreen, what its size is, and how it is oriented. The `UIView` class provides two built-in properties that define these aspects.

Every view uses a `frame` to define its boundaries. The frame specifies the outline of the view: its location, width, and height. If you change a view's frame, the view updates to match the new frame. Use a bigger width and the view stretches. Use a new location and the view moves. The view's frame delineates each view's onscreen outline. View sizes are not limited to the screen size. A view can be smaller than the screen or larger. It can also be smaller or larger than its parent.

Views also use a `transform` property that sets the view's orientation and any geometric transformations that have been applied to it. For example, a view might be stretched or squashed by applying a transform, or it might be rotated away from vertical. Together the frame and transform fully define a view's geometry.

Frames

Frame rectangles use a `CGRect` structure, which is defined as part of the Core Graphics framework as its CG prefix suggests. A `CGRect` is made up of an origin (a `CGPoint`, x and y) and a size (a `CGSize`, width and height). When you create views, you normally allocate them and initialize them with a frame, for example:

```
CGRect rect = CGRectMake(0.0f, 0.0f, 320.0f, 416.0f);
myView = [[UIView alloc] initWithFrame: rect];
```

The `CGRectMake` function creates a new rectangle using four parameters, the origin's x and y locations, the width of the rectangle, and its height. In addition to `CGRectMake`, there are several other convenience functions you may want to be aware of that help you work with rectangles and frames.

- `NSStringFromCGRect(aCGRect)` converts a `CGRect` structure to a formatted string. This function makes it easy to log a view's frame when you're debugging.
- `CGRectFromString(aString)` recovers a rectangle from its string representation. It proves useful when you've stored a view's frame as a string in user defaults and want to convert that string back to a `CGRect`.
- `CGRectInset(aRect, xinset, yinset)` enables you to create a smaller or larger rectangle that's centered on the same point as the source rectangle. Use a positive inset for smaller rectangles, negative for larger ones.
- `CGRectIntersectsRect(rect1, rect2)` lets you know whether rectangle structures intersect. Use this function to know when two rectangular onscreen objects overlap.
- `CGRectCreateDictionaryRepresentation(aRect)` transforms a rectangle structure into a standard `CFDictionaryRef`, also known (via the magic of toll-free bridging) as `(NSDictionary *)` instances. Transform the dictionary back to a rectangle by using `CGRectMakeWithDictionaryRepresentation(aDict, aRect)`.
- `CGRectZero` is a rectangle constant located at `(0,0)` whose width and height are zero. You can use this constant when you're required to create a frame but are still unsure what that frame size or location will be at the time of creation.

The `CGRect` structure is made up of two substructures: `CGPoint`, which defines the rectangle's origin, and `CGSize`, which defines its bounds. Points refer to locations defined with x and y coordinates; sizes have width and height. Use `CGPointMake(x, y)` to create points. `CGSizeMake(width, height)` creates sizes. Although these two structures appear to be the same (two floating-point values), the iPhone SDK differentiates between them. Points refer to locations. Sizes refer to extents. You cannot set `myFrame.origin` to a size.

As with rectangles, you can convert them to and from strings: `NSStringFromCGPoint()`, `NSStringFromCGSize()`, `CGSizeFromString()`, and `CGPointFromString()` perform these functions. You can also transform points and sizes to and from dictionaries.

Transforms

The iPhone supports standard affine transformations as part of its Core Graphics implementation. Affine transforms allow points in one coordinate system to transform into another coordinate system. These functions are widely used in both 2D and 3D animations. The version used in the iPhone SDK uses a 3-by-3 matrix to define `UIView` transforms, making it a 2D-only solution. With affine transforms, you can scale, translate, and rotate your views in real time. You do so by setting the view's `transform` property, for example:

```
float angle = theta * (PI / 100);
CGAffineTransform transform = CGAffineTransformMakeRotation(angle);
myView.transform = transform;
```

The transform is always applied with respect to the view's center. So when you apply a rotation like this, the view rotates around its center. If you need to rotate around another point, you must first translate the view, then rotate, and then return from that translation.

To revert any changes, set the `transform` property to the identity transform. This restores the view back to the last settings for its frame.

```
myView.transform = CGAffineTransformIdentity;
```

Coordinate Systems

Views live in two worlds. Their frames are defined in the coordinate system of their parents. Their bounds and subviews are defined in their own coordinate system. The iPhone SDK offers several utilities that allow you move between these coordinate systems so long as the views involved live within the same UIWindow. To convert a point from another view into your own coordinate system, use `convertPoint: fromView:`, for example:

```
myPoint = [myView convertPoint:somePoint fromView:otherView];
```

If the original point indicated the location of some object, the new point retains that location but gives the coordinates with respect to `myView`'s origin. To go the other way, use `convertPoint: toView:` to transform a point into another view's coordinate system. Similarly, `convertRect: toView:` and `convertRect: fromView:` work with `CGRect` structures rather than `CGPoint` ones.

Recipe: Working with View Frames

When you change a view's frame, you update its size (i.e., its width and height) and its location. For example, you might move a frame as follows. This code creates a subview located at (0,0) and then moves it down 30 pixels to (0,30).

```
CGRect initialRect = CGRectMake(0.0f, 0.0f, 320.0f, 50.0f);
myView = [[UIView alloc] initWithFrame:initialRect];
[topView addSubview:myView];
myView.frame = CGRectMake(0.0f, 30.0f, 320.0f, 50.0f);
```

This approach is fairly uncommon. The iPhone SDK does not expect you to move a view by changing its frame. Instead, it provides you with a way to update a view's position. The preferred way to do this is by setting the view's center. `center` is a built-in view property, which you can access directly:

```
myView.center = CGPointMake(160.0f, 55.0f);
```

Although you'd expect the SDK to offer a way to move a view by updating its origin, no such option exists. It's easy enough to build your own class extension. Retrieve the view frame, set the origin to the requested point, and then update the frame with change. This snippet creates a new origin property letting you retrieve and change the view's origin.

```
@interface UIView (ViewFrameGeometry)
@property CGPoint origin;
@end

@implementation UIView (ViewFrameGeometry)
- (CGPoint) origin
{
    return self.frame.origin;
}

- (void) setOrigin: (CGPoint) aPoint
{
    CGRect newframe = self.frame;
    newframe.origin = aPoint;
    self.frame = newframe;
}
@end
```

When you move a view, you don't need to worry about things such as rectangular sections that have been exposed or hidden. The iPhone takes care of the redrawing. This lets you treat your views like tangible objects and delegate rendering issues to Cocoa Touch.

Adjusting Sizes

A view's frame and bounds control its size. Frames, as you've already seen, define the location of a view in its parent's coordinate system. If the frame's origin is set to (0, 30), the view appears in the superview flush with the left side of the view and offset 30 pixels from the top. Bounds define a view within its own coordinate system. That means the origin for a view's bounds, that is, `myView.bounds`, is always (0,0), and its size matches its normal extent, that is, the frame's `size` property.

Change a view's size onscreen by adjusting either its frame or its bounds. In practical terms, you're updating the size component of those structures. As with moving origins, it's simple to create your own utility method to do this directly.

```
- (void) setSize: (CGSize) aSize
{
    CGRect newframe = self.frame;
    newframe.size = aSize;
    self.frame = newframe;
}
```

When a view's size changes, the view itself updates live onscreen. Depending how the elements within the view are defined and the class of the view itself, subviews may shrink to fit or they may get cropped. There's no single rule that covers all circumstances. Interface Builder's size inspector offers interactive resizing options that define how subviews respond to changes in a superview's frame. See Chapter 4, "Designing Interfaces," for more details about laying out items in Interface Builder.

Sometimes, you need to resize a view before adding it to a new parent. For example, you might have an image view to place into an alert. To fit that view into place without changing its aspect ratio, you might use a method like this to ensure that both the height and width scale appropriately.

```
- (void) fitInSize: (CGSize) aSize
{
    CGFloat scale;
    CGRect newframe = self.frame;

    if (newframe.size.height > aSize.height)
    {
        scale = aSize.height / newframe.size.height;
        newframe.size.width *= scale;
        newframe.size.height *= scale;
    }

    if (newframe.size.width >= aSize.width)
    {
        scale = aSize.width / newframe.size.width;
        newframe.size.width *= scale;
        newframe.size.height *= scale;
    }

    self.frame = newframe;
}
```

CGRects and Centers

As you've seen, UIViews use CGRect structures composed of an origin and a size to define their frames. This structure contains no references to a center point. At the same time, UIViews depend on their `center` property to update a view's position when you move a view to a new point. Unfortunately Core Graphics doesn't use centers as a primary rectangle concept. As far as centers are concerned, Core Graphics' built-in utilities are limited to recovering a rectangle's midpoint along the X- or Y-axis.

You can bridge this gap by constructing functions that coordinate between the origin-based CGRect struct and center-based `UIView` objects. This function retrieves the center from a rectangle by building a point from the X- and Y- midpoints. It takes one argument, a rectangle, and returns its center point.

```
CGPoint CGRectGetCenter(CGRect rect)
{
    CGPoint pt;
    pt.x = CGRectGetMidX(rect);
    pt.y = CGRectGetMidY(rect);
    return pt;
}
```

Moving a rectangle by its center point is another function that may prove helpful, and one that mimics the way UIViews work. Say you need to move a view to a new position but need to keep it inside its parent's frame. To test before you move, you'd use a function like this to offset the view frame to a new center. You could then test that offset frame against the parent (use `CGRectContainsRect()`) and ensure that the view won't stray outside its container.

```
CGRect CGRectMoveToCenter(CGRect rect, CGPoint center)
{
    CGRect newrect = CGRectZero;
    newrect.origin.x = center.x-CGRectGetMidX(rect);
    newrect.origin.y = center.y-CGRectGetMidY(rect);
    newrect.size = rect.size;
    return newrect;
}
```

Other Utility Methods

As you've seen, it's convenient to expose a view's origin and size in parallel to its center, allowing you to work more natively with Core Graphics calls. You can build on this idea to expose other properties of the view including its `width` and `height`, as well as basic geometry like its `left`, `right`, `top`, and `bottom` points.

In some ways, this breaks Apple's design philosophy. This exposes items that normally fall into structures without reflecting the structures. At the same time, it can be argued that these elements are true view properties. They reflect fundamental view characteristics and deserve to be exposed as properties.

Recipe 6-5 provides a full view frame utility category for `UIView`, letting you make the choice of whether to use these properties.

Recipe 6-5 UIView Frame Geometry Category

```
@interface UIView (ViewFrameGeometry)
@property CGPoint origin;
@property CGSize size;
@property (readonly) CGPoint bottomLeft;
@property (readonly) CGPoint bottomRight;
@property (readonly) CGPoint topRight;
@property CGFloat height;
@property CGFloat width;
@property CGFloat top;
@property CGFloat left;
@property CGFloat bottom;
@property CGFloat right;
- (void) moveBy: (CGPoint) delta;
- (void) scaleBy: (CGFloat) scaleFactor;
- (void) fitInSize: (CGSize) aSize;
@end

@implementation UIView (ViewGeometry)
// Retrieve and set the origin
- (CGPoint) origin
{
    return self.frame.origin;
}

- (void) setOrigin: (CGPoint) aPoint
{
    CGRect newframe = self.frame;
    newframe.origin = aPoint;
    self.frame = newframe;
}

// Retrieve and set the size
- (CGSize) size
{
    return self.frame.size;
}

- (void) setSize: (CGSize) aSize
{
    CGRect newframe = self.frame;
    newframe.size = aSize;
    self.frame = newframe;
}
```

Recipe 6-5 **Continued**

```
// Query other frame locations
- (CGPoint) bottomRight
{
    CGFloat x = self.frame.origin.x + self.frame.size.width;
    CGFloat y = self.frame.origin.y + self.frame.size.height;
    return CGPointMake(x, y);
}

- (CGPoint) bottomLeft
{
    CGFloat x = self.frame.origin.x;
    CGFloat y = self.frame.origin.y + self.frame.size.height;
    return CGPointMake(x, y);
}

- (CGPoint) topRight
{
    CGFloat x = self.frame.origin.x + self.frame.size.width;
    CGFloat y = self.frame.origin.y;
    return CGPointMake(x, y);
}


// Retrieve and set height, width, top, bottom, left, right
- (CGFloat) height
{
    return self.frame.size.height;
}

- (void) setHeight: (CGFloat) newheight
{
    CGRect newframe = self.frame;
    newframe.size.height = newheight;
    self.frame = newframe;
}

- (CGFloat) width
{
    return self.frame.size.width;
}

- (void) setWidth: (CGFloat) newwidth
{
    CGRect newframe = self.frame;
    newframe.size.width = newwidth;
```

Recipe 6-5 **Continued**

```
    self.frame = newframe;
}

- (CGFloat) top
{
    return self.frame.origin.y;
}

- (void) setTop: (CGFloat) newtop
{
    CGRect newframe = self.frame;
    newframe.origin.y = newtop;
    self.frame = newframe;
}

- (CGFloat) left
{
    return self.frame.origin.x;
}

- (void) setLeft: (CGFloat) newleft
{
    CGRect newframe = self.frame;
    newframe.origin.x = newleft;
    self.frame = newframe;
}

- (CGFloat) bottom
{
    return self.frame.origin.y + self.frame.size.height;
}

- (void) setBottom: (CGFloat) newbottom
{
    CGRect newframe = self.frame;
    newframe.origin.y = newbottom - self.frame.size.height;
    self.frame = newframe;
}

- (CGFloat) right
{
    return self.frame.origin.x + self.frame.size.width;
}

- (void) setRight: (CGFloat) newright
{
    CGFloat delta = newright - (self.frame.origin.x + self.frame.size.width);
```

Recipe 6-5 **Continued**

```
    CGRect newframe = self.frame;
    newframe.origin.x += delta;
    self.frame = newframe;
}
@end
```

Get This Recipe's Code

To get the code used for this recipe, go to http://github.com/erica/iphone-3.0-cookbook-, or if you've downloaded the disk image containing all of the sample code from the book, go to the folder for Chapter 6 and open the project for this recipe.

Recipe: Randomly Moving a Bounded View

When you move a view to a random point, you must take into account several things. Often a view must fit entirely within its parent's view container so there aren't parts of the view clipped off. You may also want to add a boundary to that container so the view does not quite touch the parent's edge at any time. Finally, if you're working with out-of-the-box SDK versions of the `UIView` class, you need to work with random centers, not random positions, as discussed earlier in this chapter. Just picking a point somewhere in the parent view fails some or all of these qualifications.

Recipe 6-6 approaches this problem by creating a series of insets. It uses the `UIEdgeInset` structure to define the boundaries for the view. This structure contains four inset values, corresponding to the amount to inset a rectangle at its top, left, bottom, and right.

```
typedef struct {
CGFloat top, left, bottom, right;
} UIEdgeInsets;
```

This method uses the `UIEdgeInsetsInsetRect()` function to narrow a `CGRect` rectangle to create an inner container, which is called `innerRect` in this method.

It then narrows the container even further. It insets that rectangle by half the child's height and width. This leaves enough room around any point in the subrectangle to allow the placement of the child view, guaranteeing that the view can do so without overlapping the inner bounded rectangle. Select any point in that subrectangle to return a valid center for the child view.

Recipe 6-6 **Randomly Moving a Bounded View**

```
- (CGPoint) randomCenterInView: (UIView *) aView withInsets: (UIEdgeInsets) insets
{
    // Move in by the inset amount and then by size of the subview
    CGRect innerRect = UIEdgeInsetsInsetRect([aView bounds], insets);
    CGRect subRect = CGRectInset(innerRect,
        self.frame.size.width / 2.0f, self.frame.size.height / 2.0f);
```

Recipe 6-6 **Continued**

```
    // Return a random point
    float rx = (float)(random() % (int)floor(subRect.size.width));
    float ry = (float)(random() % (int)floor(subRect.size.height));
    return CGPointMake(rx + subRect.origin.x, ry + subRect.origin.y);
}

- (CGPoint) randomCenterInView: (UIView *) aView
        withInset: (float) inset
{
    UIEdgeInsets insets = UIEdgeInsetsMake(inset, inset, inset, inset);
    return [self randomCenterInView:aView withInsets:insets];
}

- (void) moveToRandomLocationInView: (UIView *) aView {
    self.center = [self randomCenterInView:aView withInset:5];
    return;
}
```

Get This Recipe's Code

To get the code used for this recipe, go to http://github.com/erica/iphone-3.0-cookbook-, or if you've downloaded the disk image containing all of the sample code from the book, go to the folder for Chapter 6 and open the project for this recipe.

Recipe: Transforming Views

Affine transforms enable you to change an object's geometry by mapping that object from one view coordinate system into another. The iPhone SDK fully supports standard affine 2D transforms. With them, you can scale, translate, rotate, and skew your views however your heart desires and your application demands.

Transforms are defined in Core Graphics and consist of calls such as `CGAffineTransformMakeRotation` and `CGAffineTransformScale`. These build and modify the 3-by-3 transform matrices. Once built, use `UIView`'s `setTransform` call to apply 2D affine transformations to `UIView` objects.

Recipe 6-7 demonstrates how to build and apply an affine transform of a `UIView`. To create the sample, I kept things simple. I build an `NSTimer` that ticks every 1/30th of a second. On ticking, it rotates a view by 1% of pi and scales over a cosine curve. I use the cosine's absolute value for two reasons. It keeps the view visible at all times, and it provides a nice bounce effect when the scaling changes direction. This produces a rotating bounce animation.

This is one of those samples that it's best to build and view as you read through the code. You are better able to see how the `handleTimer:` method correlates to the visual effects you're looking at.

> **Note**
>
> This recipe uses the standard C math library, which provides both the cosine function and the M_PI constant.

Recipe 6-7 Example of an Affine Transform of a `UIView`

```
#import <math.h>
#define BARBUTTON(TITLE, SELECTOR)      [[[UIBarButtonItem alloc]
➥initWithTitle:TITLE style:UIBarButtonItemStylePlain target:self action:SELECTOR]
➥autorelease]

@interface TestBedViewController : UIViewController
{
    NSTimer *timer;
    int      theta;
}
@end

@implementation TestBedViewController
- (void) move: (NSTimer *) aTimer
{
    // Rotate each iteration by 1% of PI
    CGFloat angle = theta * (M_PI / 100.0f);
    CGAffineTransform transform = CGAffineTransformMakeRotation(angle);

    // Theta ranges between 0% and 199% of PI, i.e. between 0 and 2*PI
    theta = (theta + 1) % 200;

    // For fun, scale by the absolute value of the cosine
    float degree = cos(angle);
    if (degree < 0.0) degree *= -1.0f;
    degree += 0.5f;

    // Create add scaling to the rotation transform
    CGAffineTransform scaled = CGAffineTransformScale(transform,
        degree, degree);

    // Apply the affine transform
    [[self.view viewWithTag:999] setTransform:scaled];
}

- (void) start: (id) sender
{
    // The timer is automatically retained by the runloop
    // You can start and stop it without being the owner
    // or messing with its retain count.
```

Recipe 6-7 **Continued**

```
    timer = [NSTimer scheduledTimerWithTimeInterval:0.03f target:self
        @selector(move:selector:) userInfo:nil repeats:YES];
    [self move:nil];
    self.navigationItem.rightBarButtonItem = BARBUTTON(@"Stop",
        @selector(stop:));
}

- (void) stop: (id) sender
{
    [timer invalidate];
    timer = nil;
    self.navigationItem.rightBarButtonItem = BARBUTTON(@"Start",
        @selector(start:));
}

- (void) viewDidLoad
{
    self.navigationItem.rightBarButtonItem = BARBUTTON(@"Start",
         @selector(start:));
    UIImageView *imgView = [[UIImageView alloc] initWithImage:[UIImage
        imageNamed:@"BflyCircle.png"]];
    imgView.tag = 999;
    imgView.center = CGPointMake(160.0f, 143.0f);
    [self.view addSubview:imgView];
    [imgView release];

    timer = nil;
    theta = 0;
}
@end
```

Get This Recipe's Code

To get the code used for this recipe, go to http://github.com/erica/iphone-3.0-cookbook-, or if you've downloaded the disk image containing all of the sample code from the book, go to the folder for Chapter 6 and open the project for this recipe.

Centering Landscape Views

Use the same affine transform approach to center landscape-oriented views. This snippet creates a 480-by-320 pixel view, centers it at [160, 240] (using portrait view coordinates), and then rotates it into place. Half of pi corresponds to 90 degrees, creating a landscape-right rotation. Centering keeps the entire view onscreen. All subviews, including text fields, labels, switches, and so on rotate into place along with the parent view.

```
#define PI 3.141592f

- (void)loadView
{
    contentView = [[UIView alloc] initWithFrame:
        CGRectMake(0.0f, 0.0f, 480.0f, 320.0f)];
    [contentView setCenter:CGPointMake(160.0f, 240.0f)];
    [contentView setBackgroundColor:[UIColor blackColor]];
    [contentView setTransform:CGAffineTransformMakeRotation(PI/2.0f)];
    self.view = contentView;
    [contentView release];
}
```

For the most part, it's far easier using `UIViewControllers` to work with reorientation events than manually rotating and presenting views. Additionally, manual view rotation does not change the status bar orientation nor the keyboard orientation. Chapter 4 discusses view controllers and reorientation in depth.

Display and Interaction Traits

In addition to physical screen layout, the `UIView` class provides properties that control how your view appears onscreen and whether users can interact with it. Every view uses a translucency factor (`alpha`) that ranges between opaque and transparent. Adjust this by issuing `[myView setAlpha:value]`, where the alpha values falls between 0.0 (fully transparent) and 1.0 (fully opaque). This is a great way to hide views and to fade them in and out onscreen.

You can assign a color to the background of any view. `[myView setBackgroundColor: [UIColor redColor]]` colors your view red, for example. This property affects different view classes in different ways depending on whether those views contain subviews that block the background. Create a transparent background by setting the view's background color to clear (i.e. `[UIColor clearColor]`).

Every view, however, offers a background color property regardless of whether you can see the background. Using bright, contrasting background colors is great way to visually see the true extents of views. When you're new to iPhone development, coloring in views offers a concrete sense of what is and is not onscreen and where each component is located.

The `userInteractionEnabled` property controls whether users can touch and interact with a given view. For most views, this property defaults to `YES`. For `UIImageView`, it defaults to `NO`, which can cause a lot of grief among beginning developers. They often place a `UIImageView` as their backsplash and don't understand why their switches, text entry fields, and buttons do not work. Make sure to enable the property for any view that needs to accept touches, whether for itself or for its subviews, which may include buttons, switches, pickers, and other controls. If you're experiencing trouble with items that seem unresponsive to touch, you should check the `userInteractionEnabled` property value for that item and for its parents.

Disable this property for any display-only view you layer over your interaction area. To show a noninteractive clock via a transparent full-screen view, unset interaction. This allows touches to pass through the view and fall below to the actual interaction area of your application.

UIView Animations

`UIView` animation provides one of the odd but lovely perks of working with the iPhone as a development platform. It enables you to slow down changes when updating views, producing smooth animated results that enhance the user experience. Best of all, this all occurs without you having to do much work.

`UIView` animations are perfect for building a visual bridge between a view's current and changed states. With them, you emphasize visual change and create an animation that links those changes together. Animatable changes include the following:

- **Changes in location**—Moving a view around the screen
- **Changes in size**—Updating the view's frame and bounds
- **Changes in stretching**—Updating the view's content stretch regions
- **Changes in transparency**—Altering the view's alpha value
- **Changes in states**—Hidden versus showing
- **Changes in view order**—Altering which view is in front
- **Changes in rotation**—Or any other affine transforms that you apply to a view

Building UIView Animation Blocks

`UIView` animations work as blocks, that is, a complete transaction that progresses at once. Start the block by issuing `beginAnimations:context:`. End the block with `commitAnimations`. Send these class methods to `UIView` and not to individual views. In the block between these two calls, you define the way the animation works and perform the actual view updates. The animation controls you'll use are as follows:

- **`beginAnimations:context`**—Marks the start of the animation block.
- **`setAnimationCurve`**—Defines the way the animation accelerates and decelerates. Use ease-in/ease-out (`UIViewAnimationCurveEaseInOut`) unless you have some compelling reason to select another curve. The other curve types are ease in (accelerate into the animation), linear (no animation acceleration), and ease out (accelerate out of the animation). Ease-in/ease-out provides the most natural-feeling animation style.
- **`setAnimationDuration`**—Specifies the length of the animation, in seconds. This is really the cool bit. You can stretch out the animation for as long as you need it to run. Be aware of straining your user's patience and keep your animations below a second or two in length. As a point of reference, the keyboard animation, when it slides on or offscreen, lasts 0.3 seconds.
- **`commitAnimations`**—Marks the end of the animation block.

Sandwich your actual view change commands after setting up the animation details and before ending the animation.

```
CGContextRef context = UIGraphicsGetCurrentContext();
[UIView beginAnimations:nil context:context];
[UIView setAnimationCurve:UIViewAnimationCurveEaseInOut];
[UIView setAnimationDuration:1.0];

// View changes go here
[contentView setAlpha:0.0f];

[UIView commitAnimations];
```

This snippet shows `UIView` animations in action by setting an animation curve and the animation duration (here, one second). The actual change being animated is a transparency update. The alpha value of the content view goes to zero, turning it invisible. Instead of the view simply disappearing, this animation block slows down the change and fades it out of sight. Notice the call to `UIGraphicsGetCurrentContext()`, which returns the graphics context at the top of the current view stack. A graphics context provides a virtual connection between your abstract drawing calls and the actual pixels on your screen (or within an image). As a rule, you can pass `nil` for this argument without ill effect in the latest SDKs.

Animation Callbacks

View animations can notify an optional delegate about state changes, namely that an animation has started or ended. This proves helpful when you need to catch the end of an animation to start the next animation in a sequence. To set the delegate, use `setAnimationDelegate:`, for example:

```
[UIView setAnimationDelegate:self];
```

To set up an end-of-animation callback, supply the selector sent to the delegate.

```
[UIView setAnimationDidStopSelector:@selector(animationDidStop:finished:context:)];
```

You see animation callbacks in action later in this chapter in Recipe 6-9, which animates a view swap.

Recipe: Fading a View In and Out

At times, you want to add information to your screen that overlays your view but does not of itself do anything. For example, you might show a top scores list or some instructions or provide a context-sensitive tooltip. Recipe 6-8 demonstrates how to use a `UIView` animation block to fade a view into and out of sight. This recipe follows the most basic animation approach. It creates a surrounding view animation block and then adds the single line of code that sets the `alpha` property.

One thing this recipe does not do is wait for the animation to finish. The change in the bar button item gets called as soon as the animations are committed, nearly a second before they end. If you tap the Fade In/Fade Out button quickly (you may want to slow the animation duration to see this better), you discover that the new animation starts up, replacing the old one, creating a visual discontinuity.

To address this, you might want to add a call to `UIView` with `setAnimationBegins` ➥`FromCurrentState:`, setting the argument to `YES`. This tells the iPhone to use the current state of the ongoing animation to start the next animation, avoiding that jump.

Recipe 6-8 Animating Transparency Changes to a View's Alpha Property

```
@implementation TestBedViewController

- (void) fadeOut: (id) sender
{
    CGContextRef context = UIGraphicsGetCurrentContext();
    [UIView beginAnimations:nil context:context];
    [UIView setAnimationCurve:UIViewAnimationCurveEaseInOut];
    [UIView setAnimationDuration:1.0];
    [[self.view viewWithTag:999] setAlpha:0.0f];
    [UIView commitAnimations];
    self.navigationItem.rightBarButtonItem =
       BARBUTTON(@"Fade In",@selector(fadeIn:));
}

- (void) fadeIn: (id) sender
{
    CGContextRef context = UIGraphicsGetCurrentContext();
    [UIView beginAnimations:nil context:context];
    [UIView setAnimationCurve:UIViewAnimationCurveEaseInOut];
    [UIView setAnimationDuration:1.0];
    [[self.view viewWithTag:999] setAlpha:1.0f];
    [UIView commitAnimations];
    self.navigationItem.rightBarButtonItem =
       BARBUTTON(@"Fade Out",@selector(fadeOut:));
}

- (void) viewDidLoad
{
    self.navigationItem.rightBarButtonItem =
       BARBUTTON(@"Fade Out",@selector(fadeOut:));
}
@end
```

Get This Recipe's Code

To get the code used for this recipe, go to http://github.com/erica/iphone-3.0-cookbook-, or if you've downloaded the disk image containing all of the sample code from the book, go to the folder for Chapter 6 and open the project for this recipe.

Recipe: Swapping Views

The `UIView` animation block doesn't limit you to a single change. Recipe 6-9 combines size transformations with transparency changes to create a more compelling animation. It does this by adding several directives at once to the animation block. This recipe performs five actions at a time. It zooms and fades one view into place while zooming out and fading away another and then exchanges the two in the subview array list.

Notice how the `viewDidLoad` method prepares the `back` object for animation by shrinking it and making it transparent. When the `swap:` method first executes, that view will be ready to appear and zoom to size.

Unlike Recipe 6-8, this recipe does wait for the animation to finish by providing a delegate and a simplified callback that ignores the parameters of the default callback invocation (`animationDidStop:finished:context:`). This code hides the bar button after it is pressed and does not return it to view until the animation completes.

Recipe 6-9 **Combining Multiple View Changes in Animation Blocks**

```
- (void) animationFinished: (id) sender
{
    self.navigationItem.rightBarButtonItem =
       BARBUTTON(@"Swap",@selector(swap:));
}

- (void) swap: (id) sender
{
    self.navigationItem.rightBarButtonItem = nil;

    UIView *frontObject = [[self.view subviews] objectAtIndex:2];
    UIView *backObject = [[self.view subviews] objectAtIndex:1];

    CGContextRef context = UIGraphicsGetCurrentContext();
    [UIView beginAnimations:nil context:context];
    [UIView setAnimationCurve:UIViewAnimationCurveEaseInOut];
    [UIView setAnimationDuration:1.0];

    frontObject.alpha = 0.0f;
    backObject.alpha = 1.0f;
    frontObject.transform = CGAffineTransformMakeScale(0.25f, 0.25f);
    backObject.transform = CGAffineTransformIdentity;
    [self.view exchangeSubviewAtIndex:1 withSubviewAtIndex:2];
```

Recipe 6-9 **Continued**

```
    [UIView setAnimationDelegate:self];
    [UIView setAnimationDidStopSelector:@selector(animationFinished:)];
    [UIView commitAnimations];
}

- (void) viewDidLoad
{
    UIView *backObject = [self.view viewWithTag:998];
    backObject.transform = CGAffineTransformMakeScale(0.25f, 0.25f);
    backObject.alpha = 0.0f;

    self.navigationItem.rightBarButtonItem = BARBUTTON(@"Swap",@selector(swap:));
}
```

Get This Recipe's Code

To get the code used for this recipe, go to http://github.com/erica/iphone-3.0-cookbook-, or if you've downloaded the disk image containing all of the sample code from the book, go to the folder for Chapter 6 and open the project for this recipe.

Recipe: Flipping Views

Transitions extend `UIView` animation blocks to add even more visual flair. Two transitions—`UIViewAnimationTransitionFlipFromLeft` and `UIViewAnimationTransitionFlip` ➥`FromRight`—do just what their names suggest. You can flip views left or flip views right like the Weather and Stocks applications do. Recipe 6-10 demonstrates how to do this.

First, you add the transition as a block parameter. Use `setAnimationTransition:` to assign the transition to the enclosing `UIView` animation block. Second, rearrange the view order while inside the block. This is best done `with exchangeSubviewAtIndex:` ➥`withSubviewAtIndex:`. Recipe 6-10 creates a simple flip view using these techniques.

What this code does not show you is how to set up your views. UIKit's flip transition more or less expects a black background to work with. And the transition needs to be performed on a parent view while exchanging that parent's two subviews. Figure 6-3 reveals the view structure used with this recipe.

Here, you see a black and white backdrop, both using the same frame. The white backdrop contains the two child views, again using identical frames. When the flip occurs, the white backdrop "turns around," as shown in Figure 6-4, to reveal the second child view.

Do not confuse the `UIView` animation blocks with the Core Animation `CATransition` class. Unfortunately, you cannot assign a `CATransition` to your `UIView` animation. To use a `CATransition`, you must apply it to a `UIView`'s layer, which is discussed next.

Recipe 6-10 **Using Transitions with UIView Animation Blocks**

```
@interface FlipView : UIImageView
@end

@implementation FlipView
- (void) touchesEnded:(NSSet*)touches withEvent:(UIEvent*)event
{
    // Start Animation Block
    CGContextRef context = UIGraphicsGetCurrentContext();
    [UIView beginAnimations:nil context:context];
    [UIView setAnimationTransition:
          UIViewAnimationTransitionFlipFromLeft
          forView:[self superview] cache:YES];
    [UIView setAnimationCurve:UIViewAnimationCurveEaseInOut];
    [UIView setAnimationDuration:1.0];

    // Animations
    [[self superview] exchangeSubviewAtIndex:0 withSubviewAtIndex:1];

    // Commit Animation Block
    [UIView commitAnimations];
}
@end
```

Get This Recipe's Code

To get the code used for this recipe, go to http://github.com/erica/iphone-3.0-cookbook-, or if you've downloaded the disk image containing all of the sample code from the book, go to the folder for Chapter 6 and open the project for this recipe.

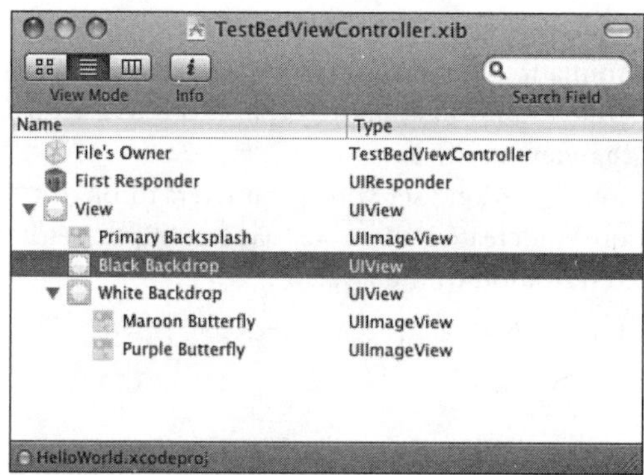

Figure 6-3 Use two backdrops when building a flip transition.

Figure 6-4 Create a black backdrop when using flip transition animations.

Recipe: Using Core Animation Transitions

In addition to `UIView` animations, the iPhone supports Core Animation as part of its QuartzCore framework. The Core Animation API offers highly flexible animation solutions for your iPhone applications. Specifically, it offers built-in transitions that offer the same kind of view-to-view changes you've been reading about in the previous recipe.

Core Animation Transitions expand your `UIView` animation vocabulary with just a few small differences in implementation. CATransitions work on layers rather than on views. Layers are the Core Animation rendering surfaces associated with each `UIView`. When working with Core Animation, you apply CATransitions to a view's default layer (`[myView layer]`) rather than the view itself.

With these transitions, you don't set your parameters through `UIView` the way you do with `UIView` animation. You create a `Core Animation` object, set its parameters, and then add the parameterized transition to the layer.

```
CATransition *animation = [CATransition animation];
animation.delegate = self;
animation.duration = 1.0f;
animation.timingFunction = UIViewAnimationCurveEaseInOut;
animation.type = kCATransitionMoveIn;
animation.subtype = kCATransitionFromTop;

// Perform some kind of view exchange or removal here

[myView.layer addAnimation:animation forKey:@"move in"];
```

Animations use both a *type* and a *subtype*. The type specifies the kind of transition used. The subtype sets its direction. Together the type and subtype tell how the views should act when you apply the animation to them.

Core Animation Transitions are distinct from the `UIViewAnimationTransitions` discussed in previous recipes. Cocoa Touch offers four types of Core Animation transitions, which are highlighted in Recipe 6-11. These available types include cross fades, pushes (one view pushes another offscreen), reveals (one view slides off another), and covers (one view slides onto another). The last three types enable you to specify the direction of motion for the transition using their subtypes. For obvious reasons, cross fades do not have a direction and they do not use subtypes.

Because Core Animation is part of the QuartzCore framework, you must add the Quartz Core framework to your project and import `<QuartzCore/QuartzCore.h>` into your code when using these features.

> **Note**
>
> Apple's Core Animation features 2D and 3D routines built around Objective-C classes. These classes provide graphics rendering and animation for your iPhone and Macintosh applications. Core Animation avoids many low-level development details associated with, for example, direct OpenGL while retaining the simplicity of working with hierarchical views.

Recipe 6-11 **Animating Transitions with Core Animation**

```
- (void) animate: (id) sender
{
    // Set up the animation
    CATransition *animation = [CATransition animation];
    animation.delegate = self;
    animation.duration = 1.0f;
    animation.timingFunction = UIViewAnimationCurveEaseInOut;

    switch ([(UISegmentedControl *)self.navigationItem.titleView
            selectedSegmentIndex])
    {
        case 0:
            animation.type = kCATransitionFade;
            break;
        case 1:
            animation.type = kCATransitionMoveIn;
            break;
        case 2:
            animation.type = kCATransitionPush;
            break;
```

Recipe 6-11 **Continued**

```
        case 3:
            animation.type = kCATransitionReveal;
        default:
            break;
    }

    if (isLeft)
        animation.subtype = kCATransitionFromRight;
    else
        animation.subtype = kCATransitionFromLeft;

    // Perform the animation
    UIView *whitebg = [self.view viewWithTag:10];
    NSInteger purple = [[whitebg subviews] indexOfObject:[whitebg
        viewWithTag:99]];
    NSInteger white = [[whitebg subviews] indexOfObject:[whitebg
        viewWithTag:100]];
    [whitebg exchangeSubviewAtIndex:purple withSubviewAtIndex:white];
    [[whitebg layer] addAnimation:animation forKey:@"animation"];

    // Allow or disallow user interaction (otherwise you can
    // touch "through" the cover view to enable/disable the switch)
    if (purple < white)
        [self.view viewWithTag:99].userInteractionEnabled = YES;
    else
        [self.view viewWithTag:99].userInteractionEnabled = NO;

    isLeft = !isLeft;
}
```

Get This Recipe's Code

To get the code used for this recipe, go to http://github.com/erica/iphone-3.0-cookbook-, or if you've downloaded the disk image containing all of the sample code from the book, go to the folder for Chapter 6 and open the project for this recipe.

Recipe: General Core Animation Calls

The iPhone provides partial support for Core Animation calls. By partial, I mean that some standard classes are missing in action, although they're slowly showing up as the iPhone SDK evolves. Core Image's `CIFilter` is one such class. It's not included in Cocoa Touch, although the `CALayer` and `CATransition` classes are both filter-aware. If you're willing to work through these limits, you can freely use standard Core Animation calls in your programs.

Recipe 6-12 shows iPhone native Core Animation code based on a sample from Lucas Newman (http://lucasnewman.com). When run, this method scales down and fades away the contents of a `UIImageView`.

This code remains virtually unchanged from the Mac OS X sample it was based on. More complex Core Animation samples may offer porting challenges, but for simple reflections, shadows, and transforms, all the functionality you need can be had at the native iPhone level.

Recipe 6-12 **Using Standard Core Animation Calls on the iPhone**

```
- (void) action: (id) sender
{
    self.navigationItem.rightBarButtonItem = nil;

    UIView *theView = [self.view viewWithTag:101];
    [CATransaction begin];
    [CATransaction setValue: [NSNumber numberWithFloat: 8.0f]
        forKey:kCATransactionAnimationDuration];

    // scale it down
    CABasicAnimation *shrinkAnimation = [CABasicAnimation
        animationWithKeyPath:@"transform.scale"];
    shrinkAnimation.delegate = self;
    shrinkAnimation.timingFunction = [CAMediaTimingFunction
        functionWithName:kCAMediaTimingFunctionEaseIn];
    shrinkAnimation.toValue = [NSNumber numberWithFloat:0.0];
    [[theView layer] addAnimation:shrinkAnimation
        forKey:@"shrinkAnimation"];

    // fade it out
    CABasicAnimation *fadeAnimation = [CABasicAnimation
        animationWithKeyPath:@"opacity"];
    fadeAnimation.toValue = [NSNumber numberWithFloat:0.0];
    fadeAnimation.timingFunction = [CAMediaTimingFunction
        functionWithName:kCAMediaTimingFunctionEaseIn];
    [[theView layer] addAnimation:fadeAnimation
        forKey:@"fadeAnimation"];

    // make it jump a couple of times with a keyframe animation
    CAKeyframeAnimation *positionAnimation = [CAKeyframeAnimation
        animationWithKeyPath:@"position"];
    CGMutablePathRef positionPath =
        CGAutorelease(CGPathCreateMutable());

    CGPathMoveToPoint(positionPath, NULL,
        [theView layer].position.x, [theView layer].position.y);
    CGPathAddQuadCurveToPoint(positionPath, NULL,
        [theView layer].position.x, - [theView layer].position.y,
        [theView layer].position.x, [theView layer].position.y);
    CGPathAddQuadCurveToPoint(positionPath, NULL,
        [theView layer].position.x, - [theView layer].position.y *
        1.5, [theView layer].position.x, [theView layer].position.y);
    CGPathAddQuadCurveToPoint(positionPath, NULL,
        [theView layer].position.x, - [theView layer].position.y *
```

Recipe 6-12 **Continued**

```
        2.0, [theView layer].position.x, [theView layer].position.y);
    positionAnimation.path = positionPath;
    positionAnimation.timingFunction = [CAMediaTimingFunction
        functionWithName:kCAMediaTimingFunctionEaseIn];

    // Add the animation
    [[theView layer] addAnimation:positionAnimation
        forKey:@"positionAnimation"];

    [CATransaction commit];
}
```

Get This Recipe's Code

To get the code used for this recipe, go to http://github.com/erica/iphone-3.0-cookbook-, or if you've downloaded the disk image containing all of the sample code from the book, go to the folder for Chapter 6 and open the project for this recipe.

Curl Transitions

The previous two recipes introduced two important concepts: `UIView` animation transitions and Core Animation transitions. These approaches allow you to animate the way your application moves from displaying one view to showing another. In addition to the two flip transitions, the `UIView` class supports a pair of curl transitions, namely `UIViewAnimationTransitionCurlUp` and `UIViewAnimationTransitionCurlDown`. These curl-based transitions offer another way to change views, in this case curling up the view until the new view gets revealed. Figure 6-5 shows the page curl in action.

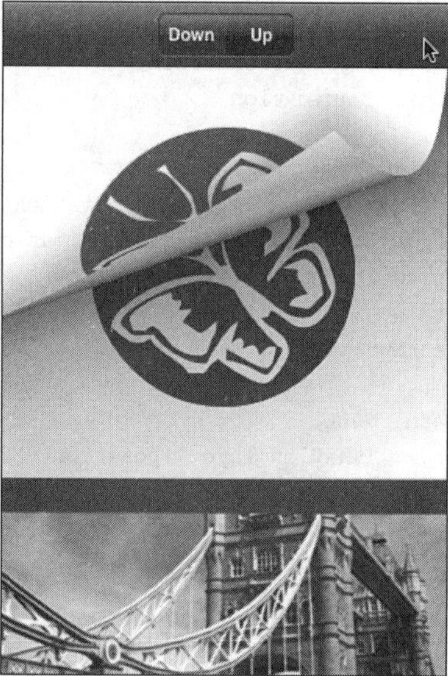

Figure 6-5 Using UIView curl animations

You build and apply the animation the same way you did with the built-in flip transition. Apply the transition to a backdrop that owns the two views you want to animate and exchange those views. Table 6-1 lists the transitions available on the iPhone.

```
CGContextRef context = UIGraphicsGetCurrentContext();
[UIView beginAnimations:nil context:context];
[UIView setAnimationCurve:UIViewAnimationCurveEaseInOut];
[UIView setAnimationDuration:1.0];

// Apply the animation to the backdrop
UIView *whiteBackdrop = [self.view viewWithTag:100];n
[UIView setAnimationTransition: UIViewAnimationTransitionCurlUp
    forView:whiteBackdrop cache:YES];

// Exchange the two foreground views
NSInteger purple = [[whiteBackdrop subviews]
    indexOfObject:[whiteBackdrop viewWithTag:999]];
NSInteger maroon = [[whiteBackdrop subviews]
    indexOfObject:[whiteBackdrop viewWithTag:998]];
[whiteBackdrop exchangeSubviewAtIndex:purple
    withSubviewAtIndex:maroon];

[UIView commitAnimations];
```

Table 6-1 **Cocoa Touch Transitions**

Transition Key	Usage
`UIViewAnimationTransition` ➥`FlipFromLeft`	UIView transition that flips from left to right, replacing the old view with the new.
`UIViewAnimationTransition` ➥`FlipFromRight`	UIView transition that flips from right to left, hiding the old view, revealing the new.
`UIViewAnimationTransition` ➥`CurlUp`	UIView transition that curls up from the bottom to reveal the new view.
`UIViewAnimationTransition` ➥`CurlDown`	UIView transition where the new view curls down onto the old view.
`kCATransitionFade`	Core Animation cross fade transition where the new view fades into place and the old one fades out.
`kCATransitionMoveIn`	Core Animation transition where the new view moves in over the old view, as if a piece of paper were being pushed over. Use with up, down, left, and right styles.
`kCATransitionPush`	Core Animation transition where the new view pushes the old view out of the way. Can be used with up, down, left, and right styles.
`kCATransitionReveal`	Core Animation transition pulls the old view out of the way to reveal the new underneath. Works with up, down, left, and right styles.

Recipe: Bouncing Views as They Appear

Apple often uses two animation blocks one called after another finishes to add bounce to their animations. For example, they might zoom into a view a bit more than needed and then use a second animation to bring that enlarged view down to its final size. Using "bounces" adds a little more life to your animation sequences, adding an extra physical touch.

When calling one animation after another, be sure that the animations do not overlap. There are two "standard" ways to create sequential `UIView` animation blocks without using CAKeyframeAnimation. (Core Animation keyframe animation is the preferred and more straightforward approach to doing this and is demonstrated later in this chapter.)

Neither of these is ideal; they create a bit of a programming nightmare, as control needs to keep moving between methods. Standard solutions include adding a delay so that the second animation does not start until the first ends (`performSelector:withObject:afterDelay:`) and assigning an animation delegate callback (`animationDidStop:finished:context:`) or, if you ignore the callback arguments, a simpler method like `animationFinished:`) to catch the end of the first animation before starting the second.

From a simple programming point of view, it's a lot easier to build an animation that blocks until it finishes. Listing 6-2 does exactly that. It extends the `UIView` class to introduce a new class method called `commitModalAnimations`. You call this instead of `commitAnimations`. It creates a new runloop, running it until the animation finishes. This ensures that the `commitModalAnimations` method does not return control to the calling method until the animation completes. With this extension, you can place blocks sequentially in your code and need no further work to avoid overlaps.

Listing 6-2 **Creating a Modal Animation by Using a Run Loop**

```
@interface UIView (ModalAnimationHelper)
+ (void) commitModalAnimations;
@end

@interface UIViewDelegate : NSObject
{
    CFRunLoopRef currentLoop;
}
@end

@implementation UIViewDelegate
-(id) initWithRunLoop: (CFRunLoopRef)runLoop
{
    if (self = [super init]) currentLoop = runLoop;
    return self;
}
```

Listing 6-2 **Continued**

```
-(void) animationFinished: (id) sender
{
    CFRunLoopStop(currentLoop);
}
@end

@implementation UIView (ModalAnimationHelper)
+ (void) commitModalAnimations
{
    CFRunLoopRef currentLoop = CFRunLoopGetCurrent();

    UIViewDelegate *uivdelegate = [[UIViewDelegate alloc]
        initWithRunLoop:currentLoop];
    [UIView setAnimationDelegate:uivdelegate];
    [UIView setAnimationDidStopSelector:@selector(animationFinished:)];
    [UIView commitAnimations];

    CFRunLoopRun();

    [uivdelegate release];
}
@end
```

This modal approach allows you to create the bounced presentation demonstrated in Recipe 6-13. Here, each animation block ends with the modal commit. That method's runloop prevents the next block from starting until the previous block finishes.

Recipe 6-13 **Bouncing Views**

```
- (void) animate: (id) sender
{
    // Hide the bar button and show the view
    self.navigationItem.rightBarButtonItem = nil;
    [self.view viewWithTag:101].alpha = 1.0f;

    // Bounce to 115% of the normal size
    [UIView beginAnimations:nil context:UIGraphicsGetCurrentContext()];
    [UIView setAnimationCurve:UIViewAnimationCurveEaseInOut];
    [UIView setAnimationDuration:0.4f];
    [self.view viewWithTag:101].transform =
        CGAffineTransformMakeScale(1.15f, 1.15f);
    [UIView commitModalAnimations];

    // Return back to 100%
    [UIView beginAnimations:nil context:UIGraphicsGetCurrentContext()];
```

Recipe 6-13 **Continued**

```
    [UIView setAnimationCurve:UIViewAnimationCurveEaseInOut];
    [UIView setAnimationDuration:0.3f];
    [self.view viewWithTag:101].transform =
        CGAffineTransformMakeScale(1.0f, 1.0f);
    [UIView commitModalAnimations];

    // Pause for a second and appreciate the presentation
    [NSThread sleepUntilDate:[NSDate
        dateWithTimeIntervalSinceNow:1.0f]];

    // Slowly zoom back down and hide the view
    [UIView beginAnimations:nil context:UIGraphicsGetCurrentContext()];
    [UIView setAnimationCurve:UIViewAnimationCurveEaseInOut];
    [UIView setAnimationDuration:1.0f];
    [self.view viewWithTag:101].transform =
        CGAffineTransformMakeScale(0.01f, 0.01f);
    [UIView commitModalAnimations];

    [self.view viewWithTag:101].alpha = 0.0f;

    // Restore the bar button
    self.navigationItem.rightBarButtonItem = BARBUTTON(@"Bounce",
    @selector(animate:));
}
```

Get This Recipe's Code

To get the code used for this recipe, go to http://github.com/erica/iphone-3.0-cookbook-, or if you've downloaded the disk image containing all of the sample code from the book, go to the folder for Chapter 6 and open the project for this recipe.

Recipe: Image View Animations

In addition to displaying static pictures, the `UIImageView` class supports built-in animation. After loading an array of images, you can tell instances to animate them. Recipe 6-14 shows you how.

Start by creating an array populated by individual images loaded from files and assign this array to the `UIImageView` instance's `animationImages` property. Set the `animationDuration` to the total loop time for displaying all the images in the array. Finally, begin animating by sending the `startAnimating` message. (There's a matching `stopAnimating` method available for use as well.)

Once you add the animating image view into your interface, you can place it into a single location, or you can animate it just as you could animate any other `UIView` instance.

Recipe 6-14 **Using UIImageView Animation**

```
NSMutableArray *bflies = [NSMutableArray array];
// Load the butterfly images
for (int i = 1; i <= 17; i++)
    [bflies addObject:[UIImage imageWithContentsOfFile:
         [[NSBundle mainBundle]
             pathForResource: [NSString stringWithFormat:@"bf_%d", i]
             ofType:@"png"]]];

// Create the view
UIImageView *butterflyView = [[UIImageView alloc]
    initWithFrame:CGRectMake(40.0f, 300.0f, 60.0f, 60.0f)];

// Set the animation cells, and duration
butterflyView.animationImages = bflies;
butterflyView.animationDuration = 0.75f;
[butterflyView startAnimating];

// Add the view to the parent and release
[self.view addSubview:butterflyView];
[butterflyView release];
```

Get This Recipe's Code

To get the code used for this recipe, go to http://github.com/erica/iphone-3.0-cookbook-, or if you've downloaded the disk image containing all of the sample code from the book, go to the folder for Chapter 6 and open the project for this recipe.

One More Thing: Adding Reflections to Views

Reflections enhance the reality of onscreen objects. They provide a little extra visual spice beyond the views-floating-over-a-backsplash, which prevails as the norm. Reflections aren't hard to implement, depending on how particular you want the results to be.

The simplest reflections involve nothing more than a flipped copy of the original view and, perhaps, adjusting the reflection's alpha levels to offer a more ethereal presentation. Listing 6-3 shows a basic Core Animation-based reflection that copies the view into a new layer, flips it via a scale transform, and displaces it a set distance. Figure 6-6 shows this kind of basic reflection in action.

With this approach, the reflection layer travels with the view. When you move the view, the reflection moves with it.

Listing 6-3 **Creating Reflections**

```
const CGFloat kReflectPercent = -0.25f;
const CGFloat kReflectOpacity = 0.3f;
const CGFloat kReflectDistance = 10.0f;

+ (void) addSimpleReflectionToView: (UIView *) theView
{
```

Listing 6-3 **Continued**

```
    CALayer *reflectionLayer = [CALayer layer];
    reflectionLayer.contents = [theView layer].contents;
    reflectionLayer.opacity = kReflectOpacity;
    reflectionLayer.frame = CGRectMake(0.0f, 0.0f,
        theView.frame.size.width, theView.frame.size.height *
        kReflectPercent);
    CATransform3D stransform = CATransform3DMakeScale(1.0f, -1.0f,
        1.0f);
    CATransform3D transform = CATransform3DTranslate(stransform, 0.0f,
        -(kReflectDistance + theView.frame.size.height), 0.0f);
    reflectionLayer.transform = transform;
    reflectionLayer.sublayerTransform = reflectionLayer.transform;
    [[theView layer] addSublayer:reflectionLayer];
}
```

Figure 6-6 A basic Core Animation reflection uses scaling, transparency, and a slight vertical offset.

Better Reflections

Although full-size reflections work well in simple interfaces, a better reflection fades away at its bottom. This provides a slicker, more "Apple-y" presentation. Core Graphics functions allow you to create these flipped, masked reflections shown in Figure 6-7.

Figure 6-7 Masking away the bottom of a reflected image creates a more Apple-like reflection.

This solution comes admittedly at a slightly higher cost than the basic solution from Listing 6-3. The faded-reflection solution, which you can see in Listing 6-4, relies on copying the view contents to a shortened bitmap and applying a gradient-based mask. These results, which are returned as a `UIImage`, are added to the original view as a new `UIImageView`. Using this subview approach provides another simple solution that allows the reflection to stick to its parent.

To make this reflection effect work, it's vital that you disable view clipping. Set the view's `clipsToView` to `NO`. That ensures the parent view won't clip away the reflection; it remains completely viewable, even those parts that fall outside the parent's bounds.

Listing 6-4 **Masking Reflections with Core Graphics**

```
+ (CGImageRef) createGradientImage: (CGSize)size
{
    CGFloat colors[] = {0.0, 1.0, 1.0, 1.0};

    // Create gradient in gray device color space
    CGColorSpaceRef colorSpace = CGColorSpaceCreateDeviceGray();
    CGContextRef context = CGBitmapContextCreate(nil, size.width,
        size.height, 8, 0, colorSpace, kCGImageAlphaNone);
    CGGradientRef gradient =
        CGGradientCreateWithColorComponents(colorSpace, colors,
```

Listing 6-4 **Continued**

```
            NULL, 2);
    CGColorSpaceRelease(colorSpace);

    // Draw the linear gradient
    CGPoint p1 = CGPointZero;
    CGPoint p2 = CGPointMake(0, size.height);
    CGContextDrawLinearGradient(context, gradient, p1, p2,
        kCGGradientDrawsAfterEndLocation);

    // Return the CGImage
    CGImageRef theCGImage = CGBitmapContextCreateImage(context);
    CFRelease(gradient);
    CGContextRelease(context);
    return theCGImage;
}

// Create a shrunken frame for the reflection
+ (UIImage *) reflectionOfView: (UIView *)theView
        withPercent: (CGFloat) percent
{
    // Retain the width but shrink the height
    CGSize size = CGSizeMake(theView.frame.size.width,
        theView.frame.size.height * percent);

    // Shrink the view
    UIGraphicsBeginImageContext(size);
    CGContextRef context = UIGraphicsGetCurrentContext();
    [theView.layer renderInContext:context];
    UIImage *partialimg =
        UIGraphicsGetImageFromCurrentImageContext();
    UIGraphicsEndImageContext();

    // build the mask
    CGImageRef mask = [ImageHelper createGradientImage:size];
    CGImageRef ref = CGImageCreateWithMask(partialimg.CGImage, mask);
    UIImage *theImage = [UIImage imageWithCGImage:ref];
    CGImageRelease(ref);
    CGImageRelease(mask);
    return theImage;
}

const CGFloat kReflectDistance = 10.0f;

+ (void) addReflectionToView: (UIView *) theView
{
    theView.clipsToBounds = NO;
```

Listing 6-4 **Continued**

```
    UIImageView *reflection = [[UIImageView alloc] initWithImage:
        [ImageHelper reflectionOfView:theView withPercent: 0.45f]];
    CGRect frame = reflection.frame;
    frame.origin = CGPointMake(0.0f, theView.frame.size.height +
        kReflectDistance);
    reflection.frame = frame;

    // add the reflection as a simple subview
    [theView addSubview:reflection];
    [reflection release];
}
```

Summary

`UIViews` provide the onscreen components your users see and interact with. As this chapter showed, even in their most basic form, they offer incredible flexibility and power. You discovered how to use views to build up elements on a screen, retrieve views by tag or name, and introduce eye-catching animation. Here's a collection of thoughts about the recipes you saw in this chapter that you might want to ponder before moving on:

- When dealing with multiple onscreen views, hierarchy should always remain in your mind. Use your view hierarchy vocabulary (`bringSubviewToFront:`, `sendSubviewToBack:`, `exchangeSubviewAtIndex:withSubviewAtIndex:`) to take charge of your views and always present the proper visual context to your users.
- Don't let the Core Graphics `frame`/UIKit `center` dichotomy stand in your way. Use functions that help you move between these structures to produce the results you need.
- Make friends with tags. They provide immediate access to views in the same way that your program's symbol table provides access to variables.
- Animate everything. Animations don't have to be loud, splashy, or bad design. The iPhone's strong animation support enables you to add smooth transitions between user tasks. The essence of the iPhone experience is subtle, smooth transitions. Short, smooth, focused changes are the iPhone's bread and butter.

7

Working with Images

On the iPhone, images and views play two distinct roles. Unlike views, images have no onscreen presence. Although views can use and display images, they are not themselves images, not even `UIImageView` objects. This chapter introduces images, specifically the `UIImage` class, and teaches you all the basic know-how you need for working with iPhone images. You learn how to load, store, and modify image data in your applications. You see how to add images to views and how to convert views into images. You discover how to process image data to create special effects, how to access images on a byte-by-byte basis, and how to take photos with your iPhone's built-in camera.

Recipe: Finding and Loading Images

iPhone images are generally stored in one of four places. These four sources allow you to access image data and display that data in your programs. These sources include the photo album, the application bundle, the sandbox, and the Internet:

- **Photo album**—The iPhone's photo album contains both a camera roll (for camera-able units) and photos synced from the user's computer. Users can request images from this album using the interactive dialog supplied by the `UIImagePicker` ➥`Controller` class. The dialog lets users browse through stored photos and select the image they want to work with.
- **Application bundle**—Your application bundle may store images along with your application executable, Info.plist file, and other resources. You can read these bundle-based images using their local file paths and display them in your application.
- **Sandbox**—Your application can also write image files into your sandbox and read them back as needed. The sandbox lets you store files to the Documents, Library, and tmp folders. Each of these folders is readable by your application, and you can create new images by supplying a file path. Although parts of the iPhone outside the sandbox are technically readable, Apple has made it clear that these areas are off-limits for App Store applications.
- **Internet**—Your application can download images from the Net using URL resources to point to web-based files. To make this work, the iPhone needs an active

web connection, but once connected the data from a remote image is just as accessible as data stored locally.

Reading Image Data

An image's file location controls how you can read its data. You'd imagine that you could just use a method like `UIImage`'s `imageWithContentsOfFile:` to load all four types. In reality, you cannot. Photo album pictures and their paths are (at least officially) hidden from direct application access. Only end users are allowed to browse and choose images, making the chosen image available to the application. Images also cannot be directly initialized with URLs, although this is easy to work around. Here's a roundup that discusses how to read data from each source type with details on doing so.

Loading Images from the Application Bundle

The `UIImage` class offers a simple method that loads any image stored in the application bundle. Call `imageNamed:` with a filename, including its extension, for example:

```
myImage = [UIImage imageNamed:@"icon.png"];
```

This method looks for an image with the supplied name in the top-level folder of the application bundle. If found, the image loads and is cached by the iPhone system. That means the image is (theoretically) memory managed by that cache.

In reality, the `imageNamed:` method cannot be used as freely as that. The image cache does not, in fact, respond properly to memory warnings and release its objects. This isn't a problem for simple applications. It's not a problem for small images that get reused over and over within an application. It is a huge problem, however, for large apps that must carefully allocate and release memory with little room to spare. In response to the built-in cache issues, many developers have chosen to design their own image caches as demonstrated in the sample code in Chapter 2, "Building Your First Project."

Substitute `imageWithContentsOfFile:` for `imageNamed:` This method returns an image loaded from the path supplied as an argument. To retrieve an image path from the bundle, query the `NSBundle` class to find the path for a given resource. This snippet loads icon.png from the top level of the application bundle. Notice how the filename and file extension are supplied as separate arguments.

```
NSString *path = [[NSBundle mainBundle]
    pathForResource:@"icon" ofType:@"png"];
myImage = [UIImage imageWithContentsOfFile:path];
```

> **Note**
>
> The iPhone supports the following image types: PNG, JPG, THM, JPEG, TIF, TIFF, GIF, BMP, BMPF, ICO, CUR, XBM, and PDF.

Loading Images from the Sandbox

By default, each sandbox contains three folders: Documents, Library, and tmp. Application-generated data such as images normally reside in the Documents folder. This folder does exactly what the name suggests. You store documents to and access them from this directory. Apple recommends you keep file data here that is created by or browsed from your program.

The Library folder stores user defaults and other state information for your program. The tmp folder provides a place to create transient files on-the-fly. Unlike tmp, files in Documents and Library are not transient. iTunes backs up all Documents and Library files whenever the iPhone syncs. In contrast the iPhone discards any tmp files when it reboots.

These directories demonstrate one of the key differences between Macintosh and iPhone programming. You're free to use both standard and nonstandard file locations on the Macintosh. The iPhone with its sandbox is far more structured—rigidly so by Apple's dictates; its files appear in better-defined locations. On the Macintosh, locating the Documents folder usually means searching the user domain. This is the standard way to locate Documents folders:

```
NSArray *paths = [NSSearchPathForDirectoriesInDomains(
    NSDocumentDirectory, NSUserDomainMask, YES);
return [paths lastObject];
```

The iPhone is more constrained. You can reliably locate the top sandbox folder by calling a utility home directory function. The result of `NSHomeDirectory()` lets you navigate down one level to Documents with full assurance of reaching the proper destination. The following function provides a handy way to return a path to the Documents folder.

```
NSString *documentsFolder()
{
    return [NSHomeDirectory()
        stringByAppendingPathComponent:@"Documents"];
}
```

To load your image, append its filename to the returned path and tell `UIImage` to create a new image with those contents. This code loads a file named image.png from the top level of the documents folder and returns a `UIImage` instance initialized with that data.

```
path = [documentsFolder() stringByAppendingPathComponent:@"image.png"];
return [UIImage imageWithContentsOfFile:path];
```

Loading Images from URLs

The `UIImage` class can load images from `NSData` instances, but it cannot do so directly from URL strings or `NSURL` objects. So supply `UIImage` with data already downloaded from a URL. This snippet downloads the latest United States weather map from weather.com and then creates a new image using the weather data. First, it constructs an `NSURL` object, and then creates an `NSData` instance initialized with the contents of that URL. The data returned helps build the `UIImage` instance.

```
NSURL *url = [NSURL URLWithString:
    @"http://image.weather.com/images/maps/current/curwx_600x405.jpg"];
UIImage *img = [UIImage imageWithData:
    [NSData dataWithContentsOfURL:url]];
```

It's easy enough to write a method that handles this process for you, letting you supply a URL string to retrieve a `UIImage`. This method takes one argument, a URL string, and returns a `UIImage` built from that resource.

```
+ (UIImage *) imageFromURLString: (NSString *) urlstring
{
    // This call is synchronous and blocking
    return [UIImage imageWithData:[NSData
        dataWithContentsOfURL:[NSURL URLWithString:urlstring]]];
}
```

This is a synchronous method, with certain drawbacks. It may fail without feedback and doesn't have a built-in time-out. See Chapter 13, "Networking," for an in-depth discussion about retrieving resources from URLs.

Loading Data from the Photo Album

The `UIImagePickerController` class helps users select images from the iPhone photo album. It provides a stand-alone view controller that you present modally. The controller sends back delegate messages reflecting the image choice made by the user.

Loading Image Files

Recipe 7-1 introduces a class that will be used throughout this chapter, namely `ImageHelper`. This helper class provides handy image routines. All routines are implemented as class methods, letting you avoid allocating an actual `ImageHelper` object. Just query the class to retrieve the results you need.

`ImageHelper`'s version of `imageNamed:` loads files using `UIImage`'s `imageWithContents` ➥`OfFile:` method, avoiding the caching hazards of the native `imageNamed:` method. The method searches through the application bundle first, and then if the file is not found, performs a second search in the sandbox documents folder. Both searches are deep. They exhaustively descend through all subfolders. The search ends upon finding the first match or when the completed search is unsuccessful.

Recipe 7-1's `imageFromURLString:` method implements an image retrieval request from a URL as discussed earlier in this section. No checks are done here to test whether the unit is currently connected to the Internet. If you need to add such checks, use a persistent Wi-Fi flag in Info.plist (see Appendix A, "Info.plist Keys") or perform a connection test (see Chapter 13, "Networking").

Recipe 7-1 **Loading Image Files Using ImageHelper**

```
NSString *documentsFolder()
{
    // Return the sandbox documents folder
    return [NSHomeDirectory()
```

```
        stringByAppendingPathComponent:@"Documents"];
}

NSString *bundleFolder()
{
    // Return the app bundle folder
    return [[NSBundle mainBundle] bundlePath];
}

@implementation ImageHelper (Files)

+ (NSString *) pathForItemNamed: (NSString *) fname
    inFolder: (NSString *) path
{
    // Return a complete path for the named item
    NSString *file;
    NSDirectoryEnumerator *dirEnum =
        [[NSFileManager defaultManager] enumeratorAtPath:path];
    while (file = [dirEnum nextObject])
        if ([[file lastPathComponent] isEqualToString:fname])
            return [path stringByAppendingPathComponent:file];
    return nil;
}

// Searches bundle first then documents folder
+ (UIImage *) imageNamed: (NSString *) aName
{
    // Return a UIImage for the named item
    NSString *path = [ImageHelper pathForItemNamed:aName
        inFolder:bundleFolder()];
    path = path ? path : [ImageHelper pathForItemNamed:aName
        inFolder:documentsFolder()];
    if (!path) return nil;
    return [UIImage imageWithContentsOfFile:path];
}

+ (UIImage *) imageFromURLString: (NSString *) urlstring
{
    // Download the image located at the URL
    // This method is blocking
    NSURL *url = [NSURL URLWithString:urlstring];
    if (!url) return nil;
    return [UIImage imageWithData:
        [NSData dataWithContentsOfURL: url]];
}
```

Get This Recipe's Code

To get the code used for this recipe, go to http://github.com/erica/iphone-3.0-cookbook-, or if you've downloaded the disk image containing all of the sample code from the book, go to the folder for Chapter 7 and open the project for this recipe.

Recipe: Accessing Photos from the iPhone Photo Album

The `UIImagePickerController` class offers a highly specialized interface with relatively few public methods and some modest quirks. It's designed to operate solely as a modal dialog, and it has its own navigation controller built in. If you push it onto an existing navigation controller-based view scheme, it adds a second navigation bar below the first. That means that although you can use it with a tab bar and as an independent view system, you can't really push it onto an existing navigation stack and have it look right.

Recipe 7-2 shows the picker in its simplest mode. It enables users to select an image from any of the onboard albums; this operation is seen in Figure 7-1. Set the picker to use any of the legal source types. The three kinds of sources follow.

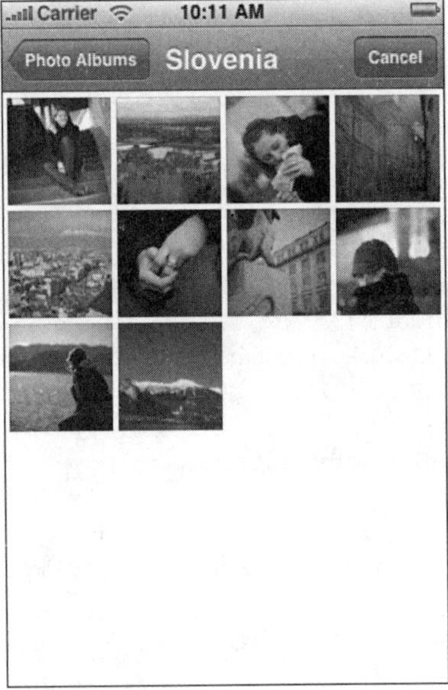

Figure 7-1 Apple supplies several prebuilt albums, including this trip to Slovenia, for in-simulator testing.

- **`UIImagePickerControllerSourceTypePhotoLibrary`**—All images synced to the iPhone plus any camera roll including pictures snapped by the user

- **`UIImagePickerControllerSourceTypeSavedPhotosAlbum`**—Also called the camera roll
- **`UIImagePickerControllerSourceTypeCamera`**—Allows users to shoot pictures with the built-in iPhone camera

Working with the Image Picker

Recipe 7-2 follows a basic work path. Select an album, select an image, display the selected image, and then repeat. This simple flow works because there's no image editing involved. That's because the picker's image editing property defaults to `NO`. This property, which is `allowsImageEditing` for SDKs prior to 3.1, and `allowsEditing` for the 3.1 SDK and later, tells the image picker whether to allow users to frame and stretch an image. When disabled, any selection (basically any image tap) redirects control to the `UIImagePickerControllerDelegate` object via the finished picking image method.

The delegate for an image picker must conform to two protocols, namely `UINavigationControllerDelegate` and `UIImagePickerControllerDelegate`. Be sure to declare these in the interface for the object you set as the picker delegate.

This recipe includes not one but two callbacks, a 3.x version and a 2.x version. If you intend to deploy your software to both 2.x and 3.x systems, increasing your user base to the highest audience possible, your code must respond to callbacks for both OS versions. That's because the 2.x callback has been deprecated in 3.0.

Adding 2.x Support

For simple image selection, 2.x support proves trivial. The 2.x callback redirects to the 3.x one, passing a constructed dictionary with the selected image. As you see in Recipe 7-3, that callback redirection becomes a little more complicated when the image picker returns editing information.

The image sent by the delegate method is basically guaranteed to be non-nil, although you can add a check in the 2.x method before attempting to construct a dictionary. Should the user cancel, the delegate receives an `imagePickerControllerDidCancel:` callback. When users cancel, the picker automatically dismisses and is released.

You can see this, along with the general memory consuming behavior of the image picker, by running Instruments; the memory levels return down after cancelling. When you choose to implement this callback (Apple describes it as optional but "expected"), make sure to dismiss and release the controller manually.

For nontrivial applications, make sure you've implemented memory management in your program and can respond to memory warnings when using the image picker. It's a memory hog in any of its basic forms: image picking or camera use.

Adding 3.1 Support

The `allowsImageEditing` property was deprecated in the 3.1 SDK. At the time of writing this book, it remains available for use in your applications. It will likely remain so for a while but not forever. Deprecated methods may disappear without warning in future SDKs.

If you plan to deploy to a mix of firmware, both earlier than 3.1 as well as 3.1 and later, make sure to check whether your image picker instances respond to `setAllowsImageEditing:` and/or `setAllowsEditing:`. Use the `NSObject` `respondsToSelector:` method to test.

> **Note**
>
> The `NSObject` utility category at http://github.com/erica addresses this issue by scanning through a list of selectors until it finds one that an object can respond to. See the sample code that accompanies the category for examples of use.

Picking Video

Despite its name, the `UIImagePickerController` is not limited to picking images. You can configure it to select both images and videos from your onboard media library. See Chapter 15, "Audio, Video, and MediaKit," for details on configuring the picker's media types. You'll also read about selecting, recording, and editing video resources.

Recipe 7-2 **Simple UIImagePickerController Image Selection**

```
#define SETIMAGE(X) [(UIImageView *)self.view setImage:X];

@interface TestBedViewController : UIViewController
➥<UINavigationControllerDelegate, UIImagePickerControllerDelegate>
@end

@implementation TestBedViewController

// 3.x callback
- (void) imagePickerController:(UIImagePickerController *)picker
    didFinishPickingMediaWithInfo:(NSDictionary *)info
{
    SETIMAGE([info objectForKey:
        @"UIImagePickerControllerOriginalImage"]);
    [self dismissModalViewControllerAnimated:YES];
    [picker release];
}

// 2.x callback, which redirects to 3.x callback
- (void)imagePickerController:(UIImagePickerController *)picker
        didFinishPickingImage:(UIImage *)image
        editingInfo:(NSDictionary *)editingInfo
{
    NSDictionary *dict = [NSDictionary dictionaryWithObject:image
        forKey:@"UIImagePickerControllerOriginalImage"];
    [self imagePickerController:picker
        didFinishPickingMediaWithInfo:dict];
}
```

```
// Optional but "expected" dismiss
- (void) imagePickerControllerDidCancel:
        (UIImagePickerController *)picker
{
      [self dismissModalViewControllerAnimated:YES];
      [picker release];
}

// Present the image picker
- (void) pickImage: (id) sender
{
    UIImagePickerController *ipc = [[UIImagePickerController alloc]
        init];
    ipc.sourceType =  UIImagePickerControllerSourceTypePhotoLibrary;
    ipc.delegate = self;
    ipc.allowsImageEditing = NO; // allowsEditing in 3.1
    [self presentModalViewController:ipc animated:YES];
}

- (void) viewDidLoad
{
    self.navigationItem.rightBarButtonItem = BARBUTTON(@"Pick",
        @selector(pickImage));
    self.title = @"Image Picker";
}
@end
```

Get This Recipe's Code

To get the code used for this recipe, go to http://github.com/erica/iphone-3.0-cookbook-, or if you've downloaded the disk image containing all of the sample code from the book, go to the folder for Chapter 7 and open the project for this recipe.

Recipe: Selecting and Customizing Images from the Camera Roll

Recipe 7-3 extends image picker interaction to add user-controlled edits. To enable image editing in a `UIImagePickerController`, set the `allowsImageEditing` (3.0 and earlier) or `allowsEditing` (3.1 and later) property to `YES`. This allows users to scale and position images after selection, or in the case of camera shots, after snapping a photo. You can see this editor in action on the iPhone when using the Set Wallpaper feature of Settings. Figure 7-2 shows the post-selection editor for the 3.x and 2.x firmware.

This window allows users to move and scale the image as desired. Pinching and unpinching changes the image scale. Dragging resets the image origin.

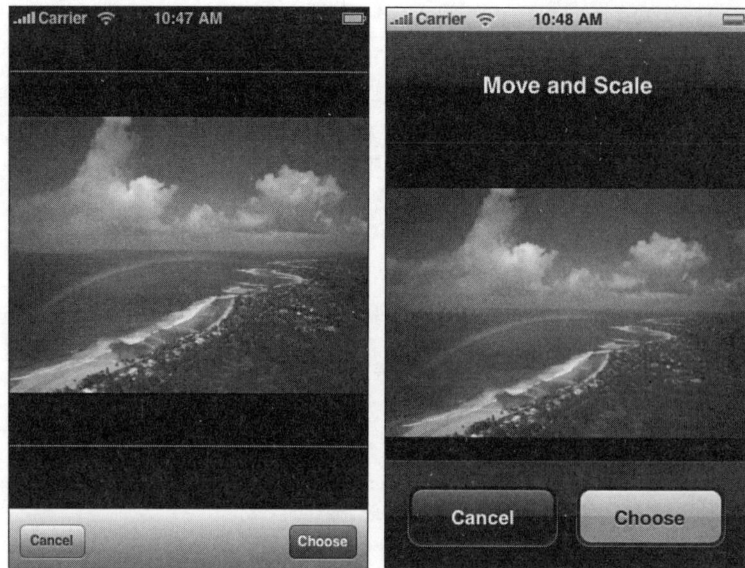

Figure 7-2 The interactive image editor allows users to move, scale, and choose their final presentation. The 3.x editor appears on the left, the 2.x editor on the right. As the left image shows, the words "Move and Scale" do not always appear, even when the iPhone is in edit mode.

When the user taps Choose, control moves to the picker delegate, and your program picks up from there. Something different happens when users tap Cancel. Control returns to the album view, allowing the user to select another image and start over.

Recovering Image Edit Information

The 3.x callback returns a dictionary containing information about the selected image. The info dictionary returned by the 3.x firmware contains four keys that provide access to important dictionary data:

- **`UIImagePickerControllerMediaType`**—Defines the kind of media selected by the user, normally `public.image`. Media types are defined in the UTCoreTypes.h header file, which is part of the Mobile Core Services framework and is new to 3.0. Media types are primarily used for adding items to the system pasteboard.
- **`UIImagePickerControllerCropRect`**—Returns the section of the image selected by the user. Oddly enough, this returns as an `NSRect`, a data type equivalent to `CGRect` but more normally used on the Macintosh rather than the iPhone.
- **`UIImagePickerControllerOriginalImage`**—Stores a `UIImage` instance with the original (nonedited) image contents.

- **`UIImagePickerControllerEditedImage`**—Provides the edited version of the image, containing the portion of the picture selected by the user. The `UIImage` returned is small, sized to fit the iPhone screen.

When working with 2.x firmware, the delegate method `imagePickerController: didFinishPickingImage: editingInfo:` returns the edited version of the image as its second argument. This image reflects the scaling and translation specified by the user. The third argument, the `editingInfo` dictionary, contains the copy of the original image and the rectangle that represents the image cropping. Recipe 7-3 provides 2.x compliance by adding the edited image into the info dictionary and passing that to the 3.x delegate method.

> **Note**
>
> To populate the camera roll on the iPhone simulator, locate the mobile user file system in ~/Library/Application Support/iPhone Simulator/User. Navigate down to Media/DCIM and copy a 100APPLE folder from a real iPhone to that folder. Make sure to copy both the JPG images and the small THM thumbnail files.

Recipe 7-3 **Allowing Users to Edit Selected Images**

```
- (void)imagePickerController:(UIImagePickerController *)picker
    didFinishPickingMediaWithInfo:(NSDictionary *)info
{
    CFShow(info); // review the info dictionary
    SETIMAGE([info objectForKey:
        @"UIImagePickerControllerEditedImage"]);
    [self dismissModalViewControllerAnimated:YES];
    [picker release];
}

// Provide 2.x compliance
- (void)imagePickerController:(UIImagePickerController *)picker
        didFinishPickingImage:(UIImage *)image
        editingInfo:(NSDictionary *)editingInfo
{
    NSMutableDictionary *dict = [NSMutableDictionary
        dictionaryWithDictionary:editingInfo];
    [dict setObject:image
        forKey:@"UIImagePickerControllerEditedImage"];
    [self imagePickerController:picker
        didFinishPickingMediaWithInfo:dict];
}

- (void) pickImage: (id) sender
{
```

```
    // Present the photo library image picker
    UIImagePickerController *ipc = [[UIImagePickerController alloc]
        init];
    ipc.sourceType =  UIImagePickerControllerSourceTypePhotoLibrary;
    ipc.delegate = self;
    ipc.allowsImageEditing = YES; // allowsEditing 3.1 and later
    [self presentModalViewController:ipc animated:YES];
}
```

Get This Recipe's Code

To get the code used for this recipe, go to http://github.com/erica/iphone-3.0-cookbook-, or if you've downloaded the disk image containing all of the sample code from the book, go to the folder for Chapter 7 and open the project for this recipe.

Recipe: Snapping Photos and Writing Them to the Photo Album

Recipes 7-2 and 7-3 showed how to select and edit images using the image picker controller. Recipe 7-4 introduces a different mode, snapping photos with the iPhone's built-in camera. The image picker lets users shoot a picture and decide whether to use that image. Because cameras are not available on all iPhone units (specifically, the first generations of the iPod touch), begin by checking whether the system running the application supports camera usage. This snippet checks for a camera, limiting access to the "Snap" button.

```
if ([UIImagePickerController isSourceTypeAvailable:
    UIImagePickerControllerSourceTypeCamera])
    self.navigationItem.rightBarButtonItem =
        BARBUTTON(@"Snap", @selector(snapImage));
else
    showAlert(CAMERA_NOT_AVAILABLE_STRING);
```

As with other modes, you can allow or disallow image editing as part of the photo-capture process. One feature the camera interaction brings that has no parallel is the Preview screen. This displays after the user taps the camera icon, which is shown in Figure 7-3. The Preview screen lets users retake the photo or use the photo as is. On tapping Use (or Use Photo under 2.x), control passes to the next phase. If you've enabled image editing, the user can do so next. If not, control moves to the standard "did finish picking" method.

The sample code that accompanies this recipe assigns the returned image to the `UIImageView` that forms the application background. Notice that just a part of the image is shown. That's because the captured picture is much larger than the iPhone screen. Recipes for resizing a large image follow later in this chapter.

This code also saves the snapped image to the photo album by calling `UIImageWriteToSavedPhotosAlbum()`. This function can save any image, not just those from the onboard camera. Its second and third arguments specify a callback target and selector. The selector must take three arguments itself, as shown in Recipe 7-4; these are an image, an error, and a pointer to context information. Photos snapped from applications do not contain geotagging information.

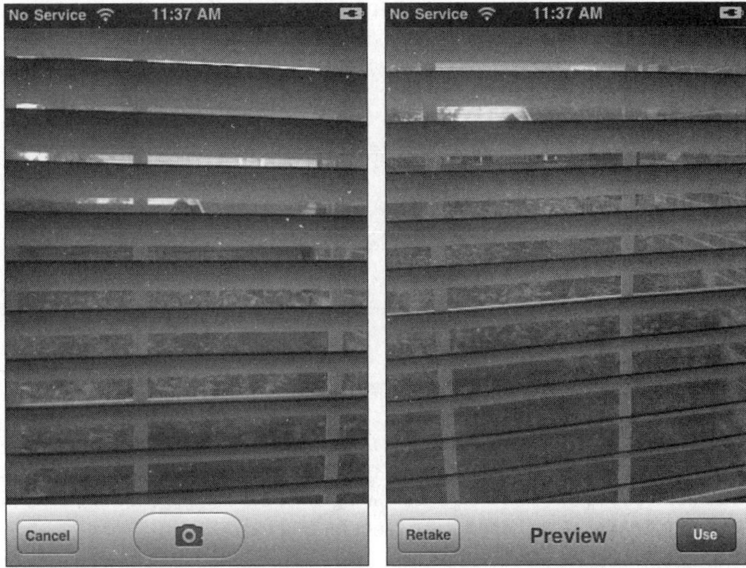

Figure 7-3 After pressing the snap button (Camera icon, left), the Preview screen lets users chose whether to use or retake the image.

Recipe 7-4 **Snapping Images with the Onboard Camera**

```
- (void) snapImage: (id) sender
{
    // Present the camera interface
    UIImagePickerController *ipc = [[UIImagePickerController alloc]
        init];
    ipc.sourceType =  UIImagePickerControllerSourceTypeCamera;
    ipc.delegate = self;
    ipc.allowsImageEditing = NO; // allowsEditing in 3.1
    [self presentModalViewController:ipc animated:YES];
}

- (void)image:(UIImage *)image didFinishSavingWithError:
        (NSError *)error contextInfo:(void *)contextInfo;
{
    // Handle the end of the image write process
    if (!error)
        showAlert(@"Image written to photo album");
    else
        showAlert(@"Error writing to photo album: %@",
```

```
            [error localizedDescription]);
}

- (void) imagePickerController:(UIImagePickerController *)picker
    didFinishPickingMediaWithInfo:(NSDictionary *)info
{
    // Recover the snapped image
    UIImage *image = [info
        objectForKey:@"UIImagePickerControllerOriginalImage"];
    SETIMAGE(image);
    // Save the image to the album
    UIImageWriteToSavedPhotosAlbum(image, self,
        @selector(imagedidFinishSavingWithError:contextInfo:), nil);
    [self dismissModalViewControllerAnimated:YES];
    [picker release];
}
```

> **Get This Recipe's Code**
>
> To get the code used for this recipe, go to http://github.com/erica/iphone-3.0-cookbook-, or if you've downloaded the disk image containing all of the sample code from the book, go to the folder for Chapter 7 and open the project for this recipe.

Recipe: Saving Pictures to the Documents Folder

Each `UIImage` can convert itself into JPEG or PNG data. Two built-in `UIKit` functions produce the necessary `NSData` from `UIImage` instances. These functions are `UIImageJPEGRepresentation()` and `UIImagePNGRepresentation()`. The JPEG version takes two arguments—the image and a compression quality that ranges from 0.0 (lowest quality, maximum compression) to 1.0 (highest quality, minimum compression). The PNG version takes one argument—the image.

To write the image to file, use the `NSData` object that is returned by either function and call the `writeToFile: atomically:` method. This stores the image data to a path that you specify. Setting the second argument to `YES` ensures that the entire file gets written before being placed into that path. This guarantees that you won't have to handle the consequences of partial writes.

Recipe 7-5 uses an image picker controller to select items already in the iPhone library. The code stores whatever item was selected to the application's Documents folder in the sandbox. The `findUniqueSavePath` method defined in the recipe returns a unique name. It searches until it generates a name that does not match an existing file. The picker delegate method uses that name to save the image.

At the end of the callback, a list of files is printed to the debugging console. This allows you to see which items have been created, which is handy when you're running this recipe on an iPhone device rather than in the simulator.

File-writing speed varies. On the simulator, it runs very fast. On older, first generation iPhones, it may proceed far more slowly especially for full-size photos that have been snapped by the camera. Saving a photo may take up to 5 or 10 seconds, which is a good time to display an ongoing activity alert like the one used in Recipe 7-11 later in this chapter.

Recipe 7-5 **Saving Images to File**

```
// Return a unique save path in the Documents folder
- (NSString *) findUniqueSavePath
{
    int i = 1;
    NSString *path;
    do {
        // iterate until a name does not match an existing file
        path = [NSString stringWithFormat:
            @"%@/Documents/IMAGE_%04d.PNG", NSHomeDirectory(), i++];
    } while ([[NSFileManager defaultManager] fileExistsAtPath:path]);

    return path;
}

- (void)imagePickerController:(UIImagePickerController *)picker
        didFinishPickingMediaWithInfo:(NSDictionary *)info
{
    // Retrieve the selected image
    UIImage *image = [info objectForKey:
        @"UIImagePickerControllerOriginalImage"];
    [self dismissModalViewControllerAnimated:YES];
    [picker release];

    // Write it to file
    [UIImageJPEGRepresentation(image, 1.0f) writeToFile:
        [self findUniqueSavePath] atomically:YES];

    // Set the background
    SETIMAGE(image);

    // Show the current contents of the documents folder
    CFShow([[NSFileManager defaultManager]
         directoryContentsAtPath:[NSHomeDirectory()
         stringByAppendingString:@"/Documents"]]);
}
```

Get This Recipe's Code

To get the code used for this recipe, go to http://github.com/erica/iphone-3.0-cookbook-, or if you've downloaded the disk image containing all of the sample code from the book, go to the folder for Chapter 7 and open the project for this recipe.

Recipe: E-Mailing Pictures

New to the 3.0 SDK, the Message UI framework allows users to compose e-mail directly within applications. Add this to your applications by setting up and initializing instances of `MFMailComposeViewController`. Recipe 7-6 shows you how to set up a composition view and initialize its contents.

The mail composition controller operates in a similar fashion to the image picker controller. Your primary view controller presents it as a modal controller and waits for results via a delegate callback. Make sure to declare the `MFMailComposeViewController➥Delegate` protocol and implement the single callback that is responsible for dismissing the controller. Be sure to give the image picker time to finish shutting down before presenting the composition controller.

Set the composition controller's mostly optional properties to build the message. The subject and bodies are defined via `setSubject:` and `setMessageBody:`. These methods take strings as their arguments. Creating the attachment requires slightly more work.

To add an attachment, you need to provide all the file components expected by the mail client. Supply data (via an `NSData` object), a MIME type (a string), and a filename (another string). Retrieve the image data using the same `UIImageJPEGRepresentation()` function discussed in Recipe 7-5. Like that recipe, this function takes some time, often several seconds, to work. So expect a delay before the message view appears.

This example uses a MIME type of `image/jpeg`. If you want to send other data types, search on the Internet for the proper MIME representations. The receiving e-mail uses the file name you specify to store the data you send. Use any arbitrary name you like.

Recipe 7-6 **Sending Images by E-Mail**

```
- (void)mailComposeController:(MFMailComposeViewController*)controller
        didFinishWithResult:(MFMailComposeResult)result
        error:(NSError*)error
{
    // Dismiss the e-mail controller once the user is done
    [self dismissModalViewControllerAnimated:YES];
}

- (void) emailImage: (UIImage *) image
{
    // Requires 3.0 or later, set the base SDK accordingly
    if ([MFMailComposeViewController canSendMail])
    {
        // Customize the e-mail
        MFMailComposeViewController *mcvc =
            [[[MFMailComposeViewController alloc] init] autorelease];
        mcvc.mailComposeDelegate = self;
        [mcvc setSubject:@"Here's a great photo!"];
        NSString *body = @"<h1>Check this out</h1>\
            <p>I selected this image from the\
```

```
            <code><b>UIImagePickerController</b></code>.</p>";
        [mcvc setMessageBody:body isHTML:YES];
        [mcvc addAttachmentData:UIImageJPEGRepresentation(image, 1.0f)
             mimeType:@"image/jpeg" fileName:@"pickerimage.jpg"];

        // Present the e-mail composition controller
        [self presentModalViewController:mcvc animated:YES];
    }
}
```

Get This Recipe's Code

To get the code used for this recipe, go to http://github.com/erica/iphone-3.0-cookbook-, or if you've downloaded the disk image containing all of the sample code from the book, go to the folder for Chapter 7 and open the project for this recipe.

Recipe: Capturing Time Lapse Photos

There are times that you just want to use the camera to take a quick shot without user interaction. For example, you might write a utility that does time lapse photography as you're biking, or you may want to build an application that builds stop motion animation. Recipe 7-7 demonstrates how to achieve this by using new 3.1 SDK features with the camera from the `UIImagePickerController`.

Two 3.1 API changes enable this kind of capture. The `showsCameraControls` property allows you to hide the normal camera GUI, presenting a full-screen camera preview instead. Set this property to `NO`.

```
ipc.showsCameraControls = NO;
```

To programmatically capture an image rather than depend on user input, call the `takePicture` method. This begins the photo acquisition process, just as if a user had pressed the snap button. When the photo is ready, the picker sends the `imagePickerController:didFinishPickingMediaWithInfo:` callback to its delegate. You cannot capture another picture until after this method is called.

Recipe 7-7 takes a series of three pictures, one after another. It saves each image to the photo album and then snaps the next shot. Each image is a full-resolution photo, taking up 2 or 3 megabytes of memory each. You could easily add a timer to space out the photos for longer delays.

When using the iPhone in a dock to snap photos over a long period of time, make sure to disable the `UIApplication`'s idle timer as follows. This code ensures that the device will not sleep even though a user has not interacted with it for a while.

```
[UIApplication sharedApplication].idleTimerDisabled = YES;
```

Note

Consider combining Recipe 7-7's time-lapse photography with Recipe 13-11's Twitpic uploader to create a security camera system with a spare iPhone.

Recipe 7-7 **Time Lapse Photos**

```
@implementation TestBedViewController
- (void)image:(UIImage *)image
    didFinishSavingWithError:(NSError *)error
    contextInfo:(void *)contextInfo;
{
    // Respond to the file save results
    if (!error)
        NSLog(@"Image written to photo album");
    else
        NSLog(@"Error writing to photo album: %@",
            [error localizedDescription]);

    // Take three photos and then stop
    if (count++ == 3)
    {
        [self dismissModalViewControllerAnimated:YES];
        [ipc release];
        ipc = nil;
    }
    else [ipc takePicture];
}

- (void) imagePickerController:(UIImagePickerController *)picker
    didFinishPickingMediaWithInfo:(NSDictionary *)info
{
    // Save snapped image to photo album
    UIImage *image = [info objectForKey:
        @"UIImagePickerControllerOriginalImage"];
    UIImageWriteToSavedPhotosAlbum(image, self,
        @selector(imagedidFinishSavingWithError:contextInfo:), nil);
}

- (void) snapImage: (id) sender
{
    count = 0; // will take a total of 3 snaps

    // initialize the image picker
    ipc = [[UIImagePickerController alloc] init];
    ipc.sourceType =  UIImagePickerControllerSourceTypeCamera;
    ipc.delegate = self;
    ipc.allowsEditing = NO;
    ipc.showsCameraControls = NO;
    [self presentModalViewController:ipc animated:YES];
```

```
    // Wait for camera set up and then snap a picture
    [NSTimer scheduledTimerWithTimeInterval:2.0f target:ipc
        selector:@selector(takePicture) userInfo:nil repeats:NO];
}

- (void) viewDidLoad
{
    if ([UIImagePickerController isSourceTypeAvailable:
        UIImagePickerControllerSourceTypeCamera])
        self.navigationItem.rightBarButtonItem =
            BARBUTTON(@"Snap", @selector(snapImage));
    else
        showAlert(@"This demo relies on camera access.");
    self.title = @"Image Picker";
}
@end
```

Get This Recipe's Code

To get the code used for this recipe, go to http://github.com/erica/iphone-3.0-cookbook-, or if you've downloaded the disk image containing all of the sample code from the book, go to the folder for Chapter 7 and open the project for this recipe.

Recipe: Using a Custom Camera Overlay

With the 3.1 firmware, you can now add custom overlays to the camera interface. Use this feature to create a GUI that floats over the live camera preview. You can add buttons and other user interface controls to snap photographs and dismiss the controller. Figure 7-4 shows a rudimentary overlay with two buttons: one for snapping a photo, the other (the small circled "X") for dismissing the image picker controller.

The light gray bar behind the Snap button was added in Interface Builder when laying out the overlay. In Figure 7-4, this bar sits partway in the image area and partway in the black control area, which is left blank for your use.

Set the overlay by assigning a view to the picker's `cameraOverlayView` property and hide the normal controls. When you present the picker, the custom overlay, not the built-in one, appears.

Another 3.1 feature, the `cameraViewTransform` property, provides a way to change how the camera view is shown. Recipe 7-8 uses this property to spin the preview while an image is being saved. In normal use, this property comes in handy for videoconferencing should Apple ever release a front-mounted iPhone or (more likely) iPod camera.

Recipe 7-8 highlights these two features and demonstrates how to use them in your iPhone applications.

Figure 7-4 Snapping photos with a custom image picker overlay.

Recipe 7-8 **Custom Camera Overlays and Transforms**

```
@implementation TestBedViewController
- (void)image:(UIImage *)image didFinishSavingWithError:
    (NSError *)error contextInfo:(void *)contextInfo;
{
    // Respond to the file save success
    if (!error)
        NSLog(@"Image written to photo album");
    else
        NSLog(@"Error writing to photo album: %@",
            [error localizedDescription]);

    // Restore the picker controller standards
    overlay.alpha = 1.0f;
    [timer invalidate];
    ipc.cameraViewTransform = CGAffineTransformIdentity;
}

- (void) imagePickerController:(UIImagePickerController *)picker
    didFinishPickingMediaWithInfo:(NSDictionary *)info
{
    // Retrieve and save the image
    UIImage *image = [info objectForKey:
        @"UIImagePickerControllerOriginalImage"];
    UIImageWriteToSavedPhotosAlbum(image, self,
```

```
        @selector(imagedidFinishSavingWithError:contextInfo:), nil);
}

- (void) rotate
{
    // Rotate the camera view
    ipc.cameraViewTransform =
        CGAffineTransformMakeRotation(2.0f*M_PI*((float)count/100.0f));
    count = (count + 10) % 100;
}

- (void) snap: (id) sender
{
    // Prepare to snap a photo
    overlay.alpha = 0.0f;
    [ipc takePicture];
    count = 0;
    timer = [NSTimer scheduledTimerWithTimeInterval:0.1f
       target:self selector:@selector(rotate) userInfo:nil
       repeats:YES];
}

- (void) dismiss: (id) sender
{
    // Dismiss the image picker interface
    [self dismissModalViewControllerAnimated:YES];
    [ipc release];
    ipc = nil;
}

- (void) takePics: (id) sender
{
    // Create and present the image picker interface
    ipc = [[UIImagePickerController alloc] init];
    ipc.sourceType =  UIImagePickerControllerSourceTypeCamera;
    ipc.delegate = self;
    ipc.allowsEditing = NO;
    ipc.showsCameraControls = NO;
    ipc.cameraOverlayView = overlay;
    [self presentModalViewController:ipc animated:YES];
}

- (void) viewDidLoad
{
    if ([UIImagePickerController
        isSourceTypeAvailable:
        UIImagePickerControllerSourceTypeCamera])
            self.navigationItem.rightBarButtonItem =
                BARBUTTON(@"Camera", @selector(takePics));
```

```
    else
        showAlert(@"This demo relies on camera access.");
    self.title = @"Image Picker";
}
@end
```

> **Get This Recipe's Code**
>
> To get the code used for this recipe, go to http://github.com/erica/iphone-3.0-cookbook-, or if you've downloaded the disk image containing all of the sample code from the book, go to the folder for Chapter 7 and open the project for this recipe.

Recipe: Displaying Images in a Scrollable View

Image display is all about memory. Treat large and small image display as separate problems. The `UIWebView` class easily handles memory-intense data. You might load a larger image into a web view using a method like this. This approach works well with bulky PDF images. `UIWebViews` offer a complete package of image presentation including built-in scrolling and resizing.

```
- (void) loadImageIntoWebView: (NSString *) path
{
    // Automatically fit the image to the view
    self.webView.scalesPageToFit = YES;

    // Load the image by creating a request
    NSURL *fileURL = [NSURL fileURLWithPath:path];
    NSURLRequest *request = [NSURLRequest requestWithURL:fileURL];
    [self.webView loadRequest:request];
}
```

With smaller images, say less than half a megabyte in size when compressed, you can load them directly to `UIImageViews` and add them to your interface. Apple recommends that `UIImage` images never exceed 1024-by-1024 pixels due to memory concerns.

The problem with basic image views is that they are static. Unlike web views, they do not respond to user scrolls and pinches. Embedding into a `UIScrollView` solves this problem. Scroll views provide those user interactions, allowing users to manipulate any image placed on the scroll view surface.

Recipe 7-9 demonstrates how to do this. It adds a scroll view to the interface and a weather map to the scroll view, as shown in Figure 7-5. Then it calculates a pair of minimum values based on the core size of the image, namely the least degree of zoom that allows the image to be fully seen in the scroll view. It assigns this value to the scroll view's `minimumZoomScale`. The maximum scale is set, arbitrarily to three times the image size. These settings allow full user interaction with the image while limiting that interaction to a reasonable scope.

The delegate method shown in the recipe identifies which view responds to zooming. For this recipe, that corresponds to the single image view placed onto the scroll view.

Scroll views do not automatically know anything about any subviews you add to them. Defining this delegate method binds the zoom to your image.

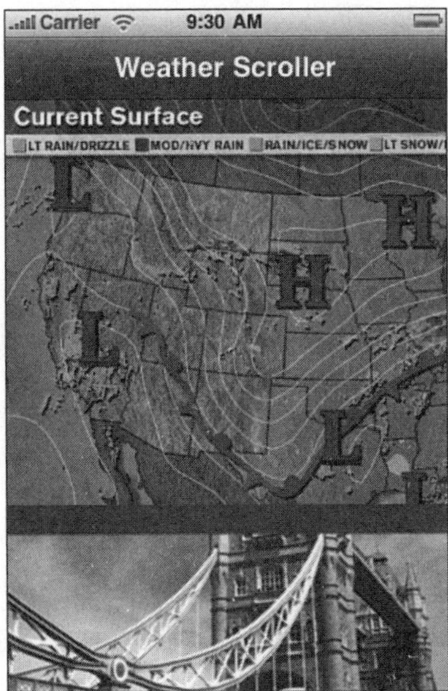

Figure 7-5 This live weather map is downloaded from a World Wide Web URL and layered onto a scroll view that allows users to scale and pan through the image.

Note

As with other views, you can set a `UIImageView`'s properties in Interface Builder. IB's inspectors enable you to change the view's alpha setting, size, location, and so forth. There's one quirk though. When you use an image view as your primary view, IB balks at adding subviews. If you run into this problem, create another view as your main view, and edit your image view as needed. After, delete the main view. Control-drag from your application delegate and assign the edited image view to the view outlet.

Recipe 7-9 **Embedding an Image onto a Scroller**

```
@implementation TestBedViewController
@synthesize weathermap;

- (UIView *)viewForZoomingInScrollView:(UIScrollView *)scrollView
{
    return [self.view viewWithTag:201];
}

- (void) viewDidLoad
```

```
{
    // Create the scroll view and set its content size and delegate
    UIScrollView *sv = [[[UIScrollView alloc]
        initWithFrame:CGRectMake(0.0f, 0.0f, 320.0f, 284.0f)]
        autorelease];
    sv.contentSize = self.weathermap.size;
    sv.delegate = self;

    // Create an image view and add it to the scroll view
    self.weathermap = URLIMAGE(MAP_URL);
    UIImageView *iv = [[[UIImageView alloc]
        initWithImage:self.weathermap] autorelease];
    iv.userInteractionEnabled = YES;
    iv.tag = 201;

    // Calculate and set the zoom scale values
    float minzoomx = sv.frame.size.width/self.weathermap.size.width;
    float minzoomy = sv.frame.size.height/self.weathermap.size.height;
    sv.minimumZoomScale = MIN(minzoomx, minzoomy);
    sv.maximumZoomScale = 3.0f;

    // Add in the subviews
    [sv addSubview:iv];
    [self.view addSubview:sv];
}
@end
```

Get This Recipe's Code

To get the code used for this recipe, go to http://github.com/erica/iphone-3.0-cookbook-, or if you've downloaded the disk image containing all of the sample code from the book, go to the folder for Chapter 7 and open the project for this recipe.

Recipe: Creating a Multiimage Paged Scroll

Scroll views aren't just about zooming. The `UIScrollView`'s paging property allows you to place images (or other views, for that matter) in a scroll view and move through them one view-width at a time. The key lies in ensuring that each image loaded exactly matches the width of the scroll view frame for horizontal presentations or its height for vertical ones.

Set the `pagingEnabled` property to `YES`. This allows users to flick their way from one image to another. Recipe 7-10 demonstrates how to do this. What this recipe offers is a page-by-page presentation of several image views. You can use this same approach to present views that aren't just images.

> **Note**
>
> Adding zooming to a paged view presents a more difficult problem than the simple scrolling shown here. It's a problem that has been solved ably and extensively by Joe Hewitt, developer of the iPhone Facebook application. His open source three20 project (http://github.com/joehewitt/three20) offers photo-album style interactions including image zooming from within a paged scroller. The repository provides a wide range of useful and beautiful view utility classes.

Recipe 7-10 **Creating a Paged Image Presentation**

```
- (void) viewDidLoad
{
    // Create the scroll view and set its content size and delegate
    UIScrollView *sv = [[[UIScrollView alloc]
        initWithFrame:CGRectMake(0.0f, 0.0f, 320.0f, BASEHEIGHT)]
        autorelease];
    sv.contentSize = CGSizeMake(NPAGES * 320.0f, sv.frame.size.height);
    sv.pagingEnabled = YES;
    sv.delegate = self;

    // Load in all the pages
    for (int i = 0; i < NPAGES; i++)
    {
        NSString *filename = [NSString stringWithFormat:@"image%d.png",
                              i+1];
        UIImageView *iv = [[UIImageView alloc] initWithImage:
                              [UIImage imageNamed:filename]];
        iv.frame = CGRectMake(i * 320.0f, 0.0f, 320.0f, BASEHEIGHT);
        [sv addSubview:iv];
        [iv release];
    }

    [self.view addSubview:sv];
}
```

> **Get This Recipe's Code**
>
> To get the code used for this recipe, go to http://github.com/erica/iphone-3.0-cookbook-, or if you've downloaded the disk image containing all of the sample code from the book, go to the folder for Chapter 7 and open the project for this recipe.

Recipe: Creating New Images from Scratch

In addition to loading images from files and from the Web, Cocoa Touch allows you to create new images on-the-fly. This blends UIKit functions with standard Quartz 2D graphics to build new `UIImage` instances.

So why would build new images from scratch? The answers are many. You might create a thumbnail by shrinking a full-size picture into a new image. You could programmatically lay out a labeled game piece. You might generate a semitransparent backsplash for custom alert views. You can also add effects to existing images like the reflection discussed in Chapter 6, "Assembling Views and Animations," or you might just want to customize an image in some other way. Each of these examples builds a new image in code, whether that image is based on another or built entirely from new elements.

Cocoa Touch provides a simple way to build new images. As this code shows, you just create a new image context, draw to it, and then transform the context into a `UIImage` object.

```
UIGraphicsBeginImageContext(CGSizeMake(40.0f, 40.0f));
CGContextRef context = UIGraphicsGetCurrentContext();

// Draw to the context here

UIImage *theImage = UIGraphicsGetImageFromCurrentImageContext();
UIGraphicsEndImageContext();
```

The drawing commands you use may consist of a combination of UIKit calls (like `drawAtPoint:` and `drawInRect:`) and Core Graphics Quartz calls like the ones used in Recipe 7-11. Recipe 7-11 builds new image views and populates them with images drawn from scratch. As Figure 7-6 shows, these images are circles with random colors, labeled with a number. These numbers are drawn directly into the image; they are not added with a separate `UILabel`.

Recipe 7-11 **Creating UIImage Instances from Scratch**

```
// Draw centered text into the context
void centerText(CGContextRef context, NSString *fontname,
    float textsize, NSString *text, CGPoint point, UIColor *color)
{
    CGContextSaveGState(context);
    CGContextSelectFont(context, [fontname UTF8String], 24.0f,
        kCGEncodingMacRoman);

    // Retrieve the text width without actually drawing anything
    CGContextSaveGState(context);
    CGContextSetTextDrawingMode(context, kCGTextInvisible);
    CGContextShowTextAtPoint(context, 0.0f, 0.0f, [text UTF8String],
        text.length);
    CGPoint endpoint = CGContextGetTextPosition(context);
    CFShow(NSStringFromCGPoint(endpoint));
    CGContextRestoreGState(context);
```

```
    // Query for size to recover height. Width is less reliable
    CGSize stringSize = [text sizeWithFont:
        [UIFont fontWithName:fontname size:textsize]];

    // Draw the text
    CGContextSetShouldAntialias(context, true);
    CGContextSetTextDrawingMode(context, kCGTextFill);
    CGContextSetFillColorWithColor(context, [color CGColor]);
    CGContextSetTextMatrix (context,
        CGAffineTransformMake(1, 0, 0, -1, 0, 0));
    CGContextShowTextAtPoint(context, point.x - endpoint.x / 2.0f,
        point.y + stringSize.height / 3.0f, [text UTF8String],
        text.length);
    CGContextRestoreGState(context);
}

- (UIImage *) createImageWithColor: (UIColor *) color
{
    // Create a new 40x40 image context
    UIGraphicsBeginImageContext(CGSizeMake(40.0f, 40.0f));
    CGContextRef context = UIGraphicsGetCurrentContext();

    // Create a filled circle
    CGContextSetFillColorWithColor(context, [color CGColor]);
    CGContextAddEllipseInRect(context,
        CGRectMake(0.0f, 0.0f, 40.0f, 40.0f));
    CGContextFillPath(context);
    CGContextClip(context);

    // Label with a number
    CGContextSetFillColorWithColor(context,
        [[UIColor whiteColor] CGColor]);
    NSString *numstring = [NSString stringWithFormat:@"%d", count++];
    centerText(context, @"Georgia", 18.0f, numstring,
        CGPointMake(20.0f, 20.0f), [UIColor whiteColor]);

    // Outline the circle with a slight (2-pixel) inset
    CGContextSetStrokeColorWithColor(context,
        [[UIColor whiteColor] CGColor]);
    CGContextAddEllipseInRect(context,
        CGRectMake(2.0f, 2.0f, 36.0f, 36.0f));
    CGContextStrokePath(context);

    // Return the new image
    UIImage *theImage = UIGraphicsGetImageFromCurrentImageContext();
    UIGraphicsEndImageContext();
    return theImage;
}
```

```
- (void) add: (id) sender
{
    // Create a random color
    CGFloat red = (random() % 128) / 256.0f;
    CGFloat green = (random() % 128) / 256.0f;
    CGFloat blue = (random() % 128) / 256.0f;
    UIColor *color = [UIColor colorWithRed:red green:green
        blue:blue alpha:1.0f];

    // Request the new image and place it into a UIImageView
    UIImage *newimage = [self createImageWithColor:color];
    UIImageView *newview = [[UIImageView alloc]
        initWithImage:newimage];

    // Randomly position the image view
    newview.center = [newview randomCenterInView:
        [self.view viewWithTag:101] withInset:0];
    [[self.view viewWithTag:101] addSubview:newview];
    [newview release];
}
```

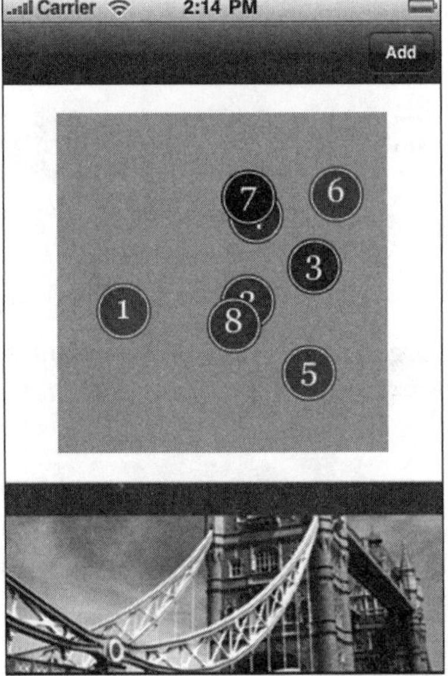

Figure 7-6 Each circle represents an image created entirely with Core Graphics/Quartz calls.

> **Get This Recipe's Code**
>
> To get the code used for this recipe, go to http://github.com/erica/iphone-3.0-cookbook-, or if you've downloaded the disk image containing all of the sample code from the book, go to the folder for Chapter 7 and open the project for this recipe.

Recipe: Building Thumbnails from Images

Thumbnails play an important role in any application that uses images. Often you need to resize an image to fit into a smaller space. Sure, you can load up a `UIImageView` with the fully leaded original and resize its frame, but you can save a lot of memory by redrawing that image into fewer bytes Thumbnails can use one of three approaches, which are demonstrated in Figure 7-7. You can

- Resize the image while retaining its proportions. Depending on the image's aspect ratio, you'll need to either letterbox or pillarbox some extra area, matting the image with transparent pixels.
- Punch out part of the image to match the available space. The example in Figure 7-7 chooses a centered subimage and crops any elements that fall outside the pixel area.
- Fill the image by matching the height and width to the available space. Every pixel gets used, but the image will get cropped, either horizontally or vertically. This corresponds to the full-screen film presentation shown on nonwidescreen TVs, which tend to lose details at either side of the movie.

Figure 7-7 These screenshots represent three ways to create image thumbnails. Fitting (left) preserves original aspect ratios, padding the image as needed with extra space. Centering (center) uses the original image pixels, cropping from the center out. Filling (right) ensures that every available pixel is filled, cropping only those portions that fall outside the frame.

Recipe 7-12 shows how to create these three thumbnail effects. The methods in this code allow you to pass an image and a size. They return a new thumbnail respectively using the fit, center, or fill technique.

Recipe 7-12 **Creating Thumbnails**

```
// Calculate a size that fits in another size while retaining its
// original proportions
+ (CGSize) fitSize: (CGSize)thisSize inSize: (CGSize) aSize
{
    CGFloat scale;
    CGSize newsize = thisSize;

    if (newsize.height && (newsize.height > aSize.height))
    {
        scale = aSize.height / newsize.height;
        newsize.width *= scale;
        newsize.height *= scale;
    }

    if (newsize.width && (newsize.width >= aSize.width))
    {
        scale = aSize.width / newsize.width;
        newsize.width *= scale;
        newsize.height *= scale;
    }

    return newsize;
}

// Proportionately resize, completely fit in view, no cropping
+ (UIImage *) image: (UIImage *) image fitInSize: (CGSize) viewsize
{
    // calculate the fitted size
    CGSize size = [ImageHelper fitSize:image.size inSize:viewsize];

    UIGraphicsBeginImageContext(viewsize);

    // Calculate any matting needed for image spacing
    float dwidth = (viewsize.width - size.width) / 2.0f;
    float dheight = (viewsize.height - size.height) / 2.0f;

    CGRect rect = CGRectMake(dwidth, dheight, size.width, size.height);
    [image drawInRect:rect];

    UIImage *newimg = UIGraphicsGetImageFromCurrentImageContext();
    UIGraphicsEndImageContext();
```

```
    return newimg;
}

// No resize, may crop
+ (UIImage *) image: (UIImage *) image centerInSize: (CGSize) viewsize
{
    CGSize size = image.size;

    UIGraphicsBeginImageContext(viewsize);

    // Calculate the offset to ensure that the image center is set
    // to the view center
    float dwidth = (viewsize.width - size.width) / 2.0f;
    float dheight = (viewsize.height - size.height) / 2.0f;

    CGRect rect = CGRectMake(dwidth, dheight, size.width, size.height);
    [image drawInRect:rect];

    UIImage *newimg = UIGraphicsGetImageFromCurrentImageContext();
    UIGraphicsEndImageContext();

    return newimg;
}

// Fill every view pixel with no black borders,
// resize and crop if needed
+ (UIImage *) image: (UIImage *) image fillSize: (CGSize) viewsize

{
    CGSize size = image.size;

    // Choose the scale factor that requires the least scaling
    CGFloat scalex = viewsize.width / size.width;
    CGFloat scaley = viewsize.height / size.height;
    CGFloat scale = MAX(scalex, scaley);

    UIGraphicsBeginImageContext(viewsize);

    CGFloat width = size.width * scale;
    CGFloat height = size.height * scale;


    // Center the scaled image
    float dwidth = ((viewsize.width - width) / 2.0f);
    float dheight = ((viewsize.height - height) / 2.0f);
```

```
    CGRect rect = CGRectMake(dwidth, dheight,
        size.width * scale,
        size.height * scale);
    [image drawInRect:rect];

    UIImage *newimg = UIGraphicsGetImageFromCurrentImageContext();
    UIGraphicsEndImageContext();

    return newimg;
}
```

Get This Recipe's Code

To get the code used for this recipe, go to http://github.com/erica/iphone-3.0-cookbook-, or if you've downloaded the disk image containing all of the sample code from the book, go to the folder for Chapter 7 and open the project for this recipe.

Fixing Photo Orientation

Any photo snapped with a digital camera may be tagged with an intrinsic orientation; this orientation reflects how the camera was held during shooting. For example, if the user positioned the camera to the left or right to snap a landscape picture, the EXIF metadata stored with that image may contain an orientation property. The `UIImage` class reads in this metadata along with the image and uses it to set its `imageOrientation` property.

Cocoa Touch handles eight kinds of `UIImageOrientation` values. These correspond to up, down, left, right plus four more values that provide mirrored versions of the same orientation. These orientations are

- `UIImageOrientationUp`
- `UIImageOrientationLeft`
- `UIImageOrientationRight`
- `UIImageOrientationDown`
- `UIImageOrientationUpMirrored`
- `UIImageOrientationLeftMirrored`
- `UIImageOrientationRightMirrored`
- `UIImageOrientationDownMirrored`

Mirrored images are typically captured when using webcams. The webcam software reverses the image automatically; mirrored images feel more natural when looking at a live webcam feed of yourself.

This issue can be important when loading images from files in byte order, without regard to orientation. That means a picture snapped with some alternate orientation may load sideways, upside down, or mirrored into a bitmap. Fixing image orientation allows you to ensure that the displayed image matches the photographer's perception.

Listing 7-1 demonstrates how to return an unrotated version of any `UIImage`. It works by recovering the `imageOrientation` property and drawing the image into a graphics context that has been transformed to match the original camera properties. For the most part you won't need to use this approach unless you're dealing directly with bits. The `UIImageView` class automatically handles most image orientation issues for you.

Listing 7-1 **Unrotating UIImage Instances**

```
// Orientation convenience macros
#define MIRRORED ((image.imageOrientation ==
    UIImageOrientationUpMirrored) || (image.imageOrientation ==
    UIImageOrientationLeftMirrored) || (image.imageOrientation ==
    UIImageOrientationRightMirrored) || (image.imageOrientation ==
    UIImageOrientationDownMirrored))
#define ROTATED90    ((image.imageOrientation ==
    UIImageOrientationLeft) || (image.imageOrientation ==
    UIImageOrientationLeftMirrored) || (image.imageOrientation ==
    UIImageOrientationRight) || (image.imageOrientation ==
    UIImageOrientationRightMirrored))

// Return an unrotated version of the image
+ (UIImage *) doUnrotateImage: (UIImage *) image
{
    CGSize size = image.size;
    if (ROTATED90) size = CGSizeMake(image.size.height,
                                     image.size.width);

    UIGraphicsBeginImageContext(size);
    CGContextRef context = UIGraphicsGetCurrentContext();
    CGAffineTransform transform = CGAffineTransformIdentity;

    // Rotate as needed
    switch(image.imageOrientation)
    {
        case UIImageOrientationLeft:
        case UIImageOrientationRightMirrored:
            transform = CGAffineTransformRotate(transform,
                                        M_PI / 2.0f);
            transform = CGAffineTransformTranslate(transform,
                                        0.0f, -size.width);
            size = CGSizeMake(size.height, size.width);
            CGContextConcatCTM(context, transform);
            break;
        case UIImageOrientationRight:
        case UIImageOrientationLeftMirrored:
            transform = CGAffineTransformRotate(transform,
                -M_PI / 2.0f);
```

```
            transform = CGAffineTransformTranslate(transform,
                -size.height, 0.0f);
            size = CGSizeMake(size.height, size.width);
            CGContextConcatCTM(context, transform);
            break;
        case UIImageOrientationDown:
        case UIImageOrientationDownMirrored:
            transform = CGAffineTransformRotate(transform, M_PI);
            transform = CGAffineTransformTranslate(transform,
                -size.width, -size.height);
            CGContextConcatCTM(context, transform);
            break;
        default:
            break;
    }

    if (MIRRORED)
    {
        // de-mirror
        transform = CGAffineTransformMakeTranslation(size.width, 0.0f);
        transform = CGAffineTransformScale(transform, -1.0f, 1.0f);
        CGContextConcatCTM(context, transform);
    }

    // Draw the image into the transformed context and return the image
    [image drawAtPoint:CGPointMake(0.0f, 0.0f)];
    UIImage *newimg = UIGraphicsGetImageFromCurrentImageContext();
    UIGraphicsEndImageContext();
    return newimg;
}
```

Adding Test Images

It's simple enough to a snap a set of test pictures using the four main orientations (left, right, up, down) using your built-in iPhone camera. Add them to the simulator by copying them to your home Library/Application Support/iPhone Simulator/User/Media/ DCIM/100APPLE/ folder. You'll need to create the DCIM/100APPLE subfolder.

Taking Screenshots

As Listing 7-2 demonstrates, you can draw views into image contexts and transform those contexts into `UIImage` instances. This code works by using Core Graphic's `renderInContext` call for `CALayer` instances. It produces a screenshot not only of the view but all the views that view owns.

There are, of course, limits. You cannot screenshot the entire window (the status bar will be missing in action) and you cannot screenshot videos or the camera previews. OpenGLES views may also not be captured.

Listing 7-2 **Screenshotting a View**

```
+ (UIImage *) imageFromView: (UIView *) theView
{
    // Draw a view's contents into an image context
    UIGraphicsBeginImageContext(theView.frame.size);
    CGContextRef context = UIGraphicsGetCurrentContext();
    [theView.layer renderInContext:context];
    UIImage *theImage = UIGraphicsGetImageFromCurrentImageContext();
    UIGraphicsEndImageContext();
    return theImage;
}
```

Recipe: Working Directly with Bitmaps

Although Cocoa Touch provides excellent resolution-independence tools for working with many images, there are times you need to reach down to the bits that underlie a picture and access data on a bit-by-bit basis. For example, you might apply edge detection or blurring routines. These functions calculate their results by convolving matrices against actual byte values.

Figure 7-8 shows the result of Canny Edge Detection on an iPhone image. The Canny operator in its most basic form is one of the first algorithms taught in image processing classes. The version used to produce the image shown here uses a hardwired 3x3 mask.

Drawing into a Bitmap Context

To get started with image processing, draw an image into a bitmap context and then retrieve bytes as a char * buffer. This code does exactly that, retrieving the bits from the context once the image has been drawn.

```
+ (unsigned char *) bitmapFromImage: (UIImage *) image
{
    // Create bitmap data for the given image
    CGContextRef context = CreateARGBBitmapContext(image.size);
    if (context == NULL) return NULL;

    CGRect rect = CGRectMake(0.0f, 0.0f,
        image.size.width, image.size.height);
    CGContextDrawImage(context, rect, image.CGImage);
    unsigned char *data = CGBitmapContextGetData (context);
    CGContextRelease(context);
    return data;
}
```

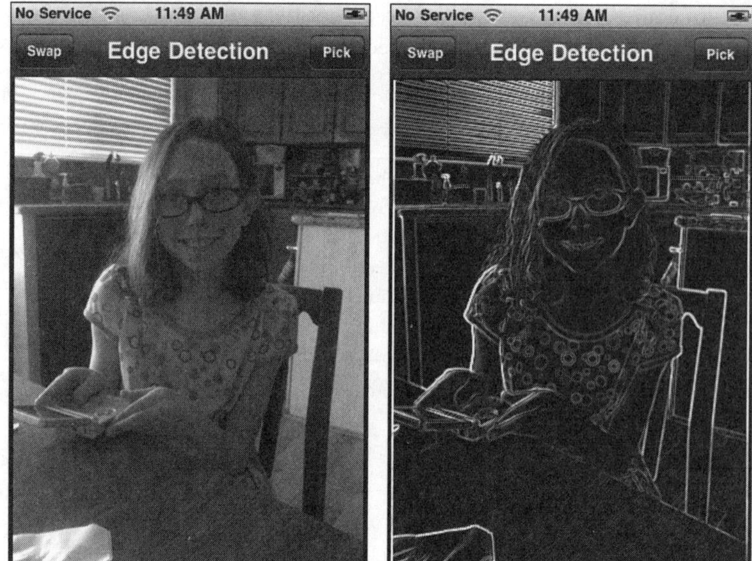

Figure 7-8 Applying edge detection to an image produces a result that outlines areas where byte values experience the greatest changes.

This routine relies on a special bitmap context that allocates memory for the bitmap data. Here is the function that creates that context. It produces an ARGB bitmap context using an Alpha-Red-Green-Blue representation, one byte per channel, 256 levels per unsigned byte.

```
CGContextRef CreateARGBBitmapContext (CGSize size)
{
    // Create the new color space
    CGColorSpaceRef colorSpace = CGColorSpaceCreateDeviceRGB();
    if (colorSpace == NULL)
    {
        fprintf(stderr, "Error allocating color space\n");
        return NULL;
    }

    // Allocate memory for the bitmap data
    void *bitmapData = malloc(size.width * size.height * 4);
    if (bitmapData == NULL)
    {
        fprintf (stderr, "Error: Memory not allocated!");
        CGColorSpaceRelease(colorSpace);
        return NULL;
    }
```

```
    // Build an 8-bit per channel context
    CGContextRef context = CGBitmapContextCreate (bitmapData,
        size.width, size.height, 8, size.width * 4, colorSpace,
        kCGImageAlphaPremultipliedFirst);
    CGColorSpaceRelease(colorSpace );
    if (context == NULL)
    {
        fprintf (stderr, "Error: Context not created!");
        free (bitmapData);
        return NULL;
    }

    return context;
}
```

Once the image bytes are available, you can access them directly. The following functions return offsets for any point (x,y) inside an ARGB bitmap using width w. The height is not needed for these calculations; the width of each row allows you to determine a two-dimensional point in what is really a one-dimensional buffer. Notice how the data is interleaved. Each 4-byte sequence contains a level for alpha, red, green, and then blue. Each byte ranges from 0 (0%) to 255 (100%). Convert to a float and divide by 255.0 to retrieve the ARGB value.

```
NSUInteger alphaOffset(NSUInteger x, NSUInteger y, NSUInteger w)
    {return y * w * 4 + x * 4 + 0;}
NSUInteger redOffset(NSUInteger x, NSUInteger y, NSUInteger w)
    {return y * w * 4 + x * 4 + 1;}
NSUInteger greenOffset(NSUInteger x, NSUInteger y, NSUInteger w)
    {return y * w * 4 + x * 4 + 2;}
NSUInteger blueOffset(NSUInteger x, NSUInteger y, NSUInteger w)
    {return y * w * 4 + x * 4 + 3;}
```

Applying Image Processing

It's relatively easy then to convolve an image by recovering its bytes and applying some image-processing algorithm. This routine uses the basic Canny edge detection mentioned earlier. It calculates both the vertical and horizontal edge results for each color channel, and then scales the sum of those two results into a single value that falls within [0, 255]. The output alpha value preserves the original level.

```
+ (UIImage *) convolveImageWithEdgeDetection: (UIImage *) image
{
    // Dimensions
    int theheight = (int) image.size.height;
    int thewidth = (int) image.size.width;
```

```
// Get input and create output bits
unsigned char *inbits = (unsigned char *)[ImageHelper
    bitmapFromImage:image];
unsigned char *outbits = (unsigned char *)malloc(theheight *
    thewidth * 4);

int radius = 1;

// Iterate through each available pixel (leaving a radius-sized
// boundary)
for (int y = radius; y < (theheight - radius); y++)
    for (int x = radius; x < (thewidth - radius); x++)
    {
        int sumr1 = 0, sumr2 = 0;
        int sumg1 = 0, sumg2 = 0;
        int sumb1 = 0, sumb2 = 0;

        // Basic Canny Edge Detection
        int matrix1[9] = {-1, 0, 1, -2, 0, 2, -1, 0, 1};
        int matrix2[9] = {-1, -2, -1, 0, 0, 0, 1, 2, 1};
        int offset = 0;
        for (int j = -radius; j <= radius; j++)
            for (int i = -radius; i <= radius; i++)
            {
                sumr1 += inbits[redOffset(x+i, y+j, thewidth)] *
                    matrix1[offset];
                sumr2 += inbits[redOffset(x+i, y+j, thewidth)] *
                    matrix2[offset];

                sumg1 += inbits[greenOffset(x+i, y+j, thewidth)] *
                    matrix1[offset];
                sumg2 += inbits[greenOffset(x+i, y+j, thewidth)] *
                    matrix2[offset];

                sumb1 += inbits[blueOffset(x+i, y+j, thewidth)] *
                    matrix1[offset];
                sumb2 += inbits[blueOffset(x+i, y+j, thewidth)] *
                    matrix2[offset];

                offset++;
            }

        // Assign the outbits
        int sumr = MIN(((ABS(sumr1) + ABS(sumr2)) / 2), 255);
        int sumg = MIN(((ABS(sumg1) + ABS(sumg2)) / 2), 255);
        int sumb = MIN(((ABS(sumb1) + ABS(sumb2)) / 2), 255);
```

```
            outbits[redOffset(x, y, thewidth)] = (unsigned char) sumr;
            outbits[greenOffset(x, y, thewidth)] = (unsigned char)
                sumg;
            outbits[blueOffset(x, y, thewidth)] = (unsigned char) sumb;
            outbits[alphaOffset(x, y, thewidth)] =
               (unsigned char) inbits[alphaOffset(x, y, thewidth)];
        }

    // Release the original bitmap. imageWithBits frees outbits
    free(inbits);
    return [ImageHelper imageWithBits:outbits withSize:image.size];
}
```

Image Processing Realities

The iPhone is not a number-crunching powerhouse. Routines like these may slow down applications significantly. Use them judiciously. Recipe 7-13 demonstrates how to balance image-processing demands with iPhone limitations. It follows three main rules of iPhone implementation:

- Provide meaningful feedback to the user when dealing with unavoidable delays.
- Perform processor-heavy functionality on a secondary thread.
- Only ever perform GUI updates on the main thread.

The flow for this solution is shown in Figure 7-9. A "Please Wait" Heads Up Display (HUD) appears with a spinning activity indicator. It remains in view until a separate processing thread finishes:

This indicator cannot display properly when all the processing happens in the main thread. Heavy processing blocks GUI updates, causing the `UIAlertView` that the HUD is based on to delay its appearance until after the processing finishes. That counters the "provide meaningful feedback" directive so important to iPhone application development. That's why a two-thread approach is so important.

The `process` routine was designed to run on its own thread. It provides a separate `NSAutorelease` pool and is spawned by the did-finish-picking method. Although it works with image contexts, nothing in the method actually changes any GUI elements. Its job is to redraw an image into a 320-by-416-pixel space and then perform Canny edge detection on that image.

When the thread finishes its heavy lifting, it calls a `finish` method on the main thread. That method cleans up the GUI by dismissing the HUD, adding a Swap button, and setting the displayed image.

Recipe 7-13 **Providing an iPhone-Friendly GUI for Image Processing**

```
@implementation TestBedViewController
@synthesize original;
@synthesize processed;
```

```
#define SETIMAGE(X) [UIImageView*)self.view setImage:X];
// Allow user to swap between original and processed image
- (void) swap
{
    // SETIMAGE works with 2.2 and later
    if ([(UIImageView *)self.view image] == self.original)
        SETIMAGE(self.processed)
    else
        SETIMAGE(self.original);
}

// Handle main thread GUI cleanup
- (void) finish
{
    SETIMAGE(self.processed);
    self.navigationItem.leftBarButtonItem = BARBUTTON(@"Swap",
        @selector(swap));
    [ModalHUD dismiss];
}

// Perform calculation-heavy processing on a second thread
- (void) process
{
    NSAutoreleasePool *pool = [[NSAutoreleasePool alloc] init];
    CGSize coreSize = CGSizeMake(320.0f, 416.0f);

    // Scale image
    UIGraphicsBeginImageContext(coreSize);
    [self.original drawInRect:[ImageHelper frameSize:self.original.size
        inSize:coreSize]];
    UIImage *newimg = UIGraphicsGetImageFromCurrentImageContext();
    UIGraphicsEndImageContext();
    self.original = newimg;

    // Calculate edge detection image
    self.processed = [ImageHelper convolveImageWithEdgeDetection:
        self.original];

    // Clean up on the main thread
    [self performSelectorOnMainThread:@selector(finish) withObject:nil
        waitUntilDone:NO];
    [pool release];
}
```

```
// Display the HUD and start the processing thread
- (void)imagePickerController:(UIImagePickerController *)picker
    didFinishPickingMediaWithInfo:(NSDictionary *)info
{
    [ModalHUD showHUD:@"Processing\nPlease wait."];
    self.original = [info objectForKey:
        @"UIImagePickerControllerOriginalImage"];
    [self dismissModalViewControllerAnimated:YES];
    [picker release];

    [NSThread detachNewThreadSelector:@selector(process)
        toTarget:self withObject:nil];
}

// Provide 2.x compliance
- (void)imagePickerController:(UIImagePickerController *)picker
    didFinishPickingImage:(UIImage *)image
    editingInfo:(NSDictionary *)editingInfo
{
    NSDictionary *dict = [NSDictionary dictionaryWithObject:image
        forKey:@"UIImagePickerControllerOriginalImage"];
    [self imagePickerController:picker
        didFinishPickingMediaWithInfo:dict];
}

// Allow user to pick a new image to work on
- (void) pickImage: (id) sender
{
    UIImagePickerController *ipc = [[UIImagePickerController alloc]
        init];
    ipc.sourceType =  UIImagePickerControllerSourceTypePhotoLibrary;
    ipc.delegate = self;
    ipc.allowsImageEditing = NO; // .allowsEditing in 3.1
    [self presentModalViewController:ipc animated:YES];
}

// Initialize title and bar button
- (void) viewDidLoad
{
    self.navigationController.navigationBar.tintColor =
        COOKBOOK_PURPLE_COLOR;
    self.navigationItem.rightBarButtonItem = BARBUTTON(@"Pick",
        @selector(pickImage));
    self.title = @"Edge Detection";
}
@end
```

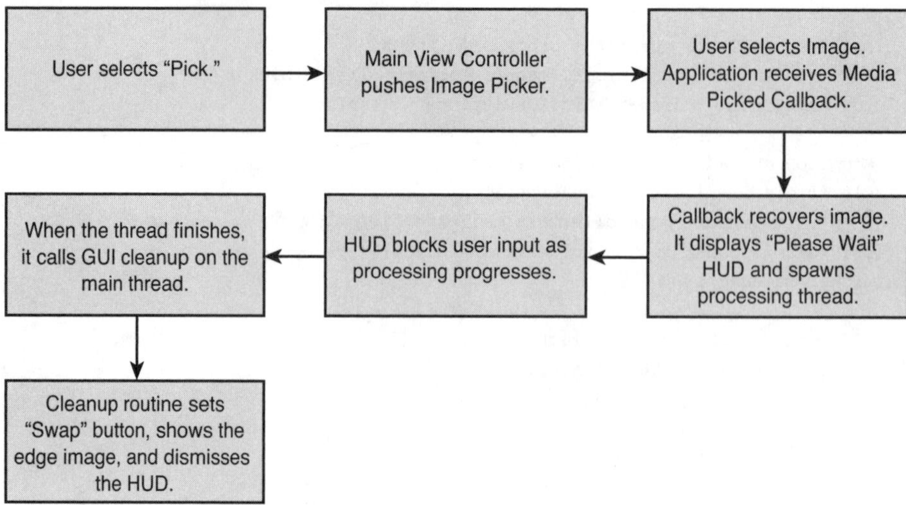

Figure 7-9 Using two threads allows a "Please Wait" Heads Up Display (HUD) to block user input until the image processing finishes.

> **Get This Recipe's Code**
>
> To get the code used for this recipe, go to http://github.com/erica/iphone-3.0-cookbook-, or if you've downloaded the disk image containing all of the sample code from the book, go to the folder for Chapter 7 and open the project for this recipe.

One More Thing: Going Grayscale

As Recipe 7-12 suggests, you can easily create a grayscale version of any image, not just black and white masks. Listing 7-3 provides a general utility method that produces an image drawn into a grayscale color space. Unlike the `CreateMaskImage()` function you just saw, this method does not need to match the `UIImage` coordinate system with the Quartz one, so it does not flip the context. It simply draws the image into the context and returns the grayscale version.

Combine this function with the screenshot `renderInContext:` functionality described earlier in this chapter and you can create an "inactive" backsplash that copies the current GUI. Use this to provide a visual context that moves a user's focus onto an ongoing operation such as a file download. This provides a creative alternative to the normal screen-darkening overlay.

Listing 7-3 **Returning the Grayscale Version of an Image**

```
+ (UIImage *) grayscaleImage: (UIImage *) image
{
    CGSize size = image.size;
    CGRect rect = CGRectMake(0.0f, 0.0f, image.size.width,
        image.size.height);
```

```
    // Create a mono/gray color space
    CGColorSpaceRef colorSpace = CGColorSpaceCreateDeviceGray();
    CGContextRef context = CGBitmapContextCreate(nil, size.width,
        size.height, 8, 0, colorSpace, kCGImageAlphaNone);
    CGColorSpaceRelease(colorSpace);

    // Draw the image into the grayscale context
    CGContextDrawImage(context, rect, [image CGImage]);
    CGImageRef grayscale = CGBitmapContextCreateImage(context);
    CGContextRelease(context);

    // Recover the image
    UIImage *img = [UIImage imageWithCGImage:grayscale];
    CFRelease(grayscale);
    return img;
}
```

Summary

This chapter introduced many ways to handle images, including picking, reading, modifying, and saving. You saw recipes that showed you how to use the iPhone's built-in editor selection process and how to snap images with the camera. You also read about adding images to the `UIScrollView` class and how to send pictures as e-mail attachments. Before moving on from this chapter, here are some thoughts about the recipes you saw here:

- The built-in image picker is a memory hog. Develop your code around that basic fact of life.
- Always provide user feedback when working with long processing delays. Most image manipulation is slow. The simulator always outperforms the iPhone so test your applications on the device as well as the simulator and provide a mechanism like the HUD display used in this chapter that lets users know that ongoing operations may take some time.
- Sending image e-mail attachments from in-program is a great new 3.0 feature. Make sure that you check that e-mail is available on your device before attempting to use the controller and be aware that sending images can be very, very slow.
- Paged scrollers offer a handy GUI foundation. Use them for showing multiple images or for presenting multiscreened, scrollable interfaces.
- Thumbnails use far less memory than loading all images at once. Consider precomputing icon versions of your pictures in addition to using the thumbnail-sizing routines shown in this chapter.

8

Gestures and Touches

The touch represents the heart of iPhone interaction; it provides the most important way that users communicate their intent to an application. Touches are not limited to button presses and keyboard interaction. You can design and build applications that work directly with users' taps and other gestures. This chapter introduces direct manipulation interfaces that go far beyond prebuilt controls. You see how to create views that users can drag around the screen. You also discover how to distinguish and interpret gestures and how to work with the iPhone's built-in multitouch sensors. By the time you finish reading this chapter, you'll have read about many different ways you can implement gesture control in your own applications.

Touches

Cocoa Touch implements direct manipulation in the simplest way possible. It sends touch events to the view you're working with. As an iPhone developer, you tell the view how to respond to each touch.

Touches convey information: where the touch took place (both the current and previous location), what phase of the touch was used (essentially mouse down, mouse moved, mouse up in the desktop application world, corresponding to finger or touch down, moved, and up in the direct manipulation world), a tap count (for example, single-tap/double-tap), and when the touch took place (through a time stamp). Touches and their information are stored in `UITouch` objects. Each object represents a single touch event. Your applications receive these in the view class, which is where you need to process and respond to them.

This may seem counterintuitive. You probably expect to separate the way an interface looks (its view) from the way it responds to touches (its controller). In the iPhone world, direct touch interaction follows a fairly primitive design pattern, offering little or no Model-View-Controller design orthogonality. The rule for this is that you program in the `UIView` class and not in the `UIViewController` class. This is an important point. Trying to implement low-level gesture control in the wrong class has tripped up many new iPhone developers.

When working with low-level touch interaction, gesture interpretation and visual display become tightly intertwined. There are benefits to this organization. View controllers can own multiple views, all of which can use touches differently. If the view controller handled all touches directly, its response routines would have to choose between responses appropriate for each view. The code would quickly become complicated. Keeping that programming at the view level simplifies each implementation. As a second benefit, programming at the view level makes it possible for you to create custom user interface objects that are completely self-contained.

In the following sections and recipes, you discover how touches work, how you can incorporate them into your apps, and how you connect what a user sees with how that user interacts with the screen.

Phases

Touches have life cycles. Each touch can pass through any of five phases that represent the progress of the touch within an interface. These phases are as follows:

- **`UITouchPhaseBegan`**—Starts when users touch the screen.
- **`UITouchPhaseMoved`**—Means a touch has moved on the screen.
- **`UITouchPhaseStationary`**—Indicates that a touch remains on the screen surface but that there has not been any movement since the previous event.
- **`UITouchPhaseEnded`**—Gets triggered when the touch is pulled away from the screen.
- **`UITouchPhaseCancelled`**—Occurs when the iPhone OS system stops tracking a particular touch. This usually occurs due to a system interruption, such as when the application is no longer active or the view is removed from the window.

Taken as a whole, these five phases form the interaction language for a touch event. They describe all the possible ways that a touch can progress or fail to progress within an interface and provide the basis for control for that interface. It's up to you as the developer to interpret those phases and provide reactions to them. You do that by implementing a series of view methods.

Touches and View Methods

All members and children of the `UIResponder` class, including `UIView`, respond to touches. Each class decides whether and how to respond. When choosing to do so, they implement customized behavior when a user touches one or more fingers down in a view or window.

Predefined callback methods handle the start, movement, and release of touches from the screen. Corresponding to the phases you've already seen, the methods involved are as follows. Notice that `UITouchPhaseStationary` does not generate a callback.

- **`touchesBegan:withEvent:`**—Gets called at the starting phase of the event, as the user starts touching the screen.
- **`touchesMoved:withEvent:`**—Handles the movement of the fingers over time.
- **`touchesEnded:withEvent:`**—Concludes the touch process, where the finger or fingers are released. It provides an opportune time to clean up any work that was handled during the movement sequence.
- **`touchesCancelled:WithEvent:`**—Called when Cocoa Touch must respond to a system interruption of the ongoing touch event.

Each of these is a `UIResponder` method, typically implemented in a `UIView` subclass. All views inherit basic nonfunctional versions of the methods. When you want to add touch behavior to your application, you override these methods and add a custom version that provides the responses your application needs.

The recipes in this chapter implement some but not all of these methods. For real-world deployment, you may want to add a touches cancelled event to handle the case of incoming phone calls, which cancels an ongoing touch sequence. Apple recommends overriding all four methods in `UIView` subclasses as a best practice.

> **Note**
>
> Views have a mode called exclusive touch that prevents touches from being delivered to other views. When enabled, this property blocks other views from receiving touch events. The primary view handles all touch events exclusively.

Touching Views

When dealing with many onscreen views, the iPhone automatically decides which view the user touched and passes any touch events to the proper view for you. This helps you write concrete direct manipulation interfaces where users touch, drag, and interact with onscreen objects.

Just because a touch is passed to a view doesn't mean that a view has to respond. Each view can choose whether to handle a touch or to let that touch fall through to views beneath it. As you see in the recipes that follow, you can use clever response strategies to decide when your view should respond, particularly when you're using irregular art with partial transparency.

Multitouch

The iPhone supports both single and multitouch interfaces. For single touch GUIs, you handle just one touch at any time. This relieves you of any responsibility of trying to determine which touch you were tracking. The one touch you receive is the only one you need to work with. You look at its data, respond to it, and wait for the next event.

When working with multitouch, that is, when you respond to multiple onscreen touches at once, you receive an entire set of touches. It is up to you to order and respond to that set. You can track each touch separately and see how it changes over time, providing a richer set of possible user interaction. Recipes for both single touch and multitouch interaction follow in this chapter.

Recipe: Adding a Simple Direct Manipulation Interface

The design focus moves from the `UIViewController` to the `UIView` when you work with direct manipulation. The view, or more precisely the `UIResponder`, forms the heart of direct manipulation development. Create touch-based interfaces by customizing methods that derive from the `UIResponder` class.

Recipe 8-1 centers on touches in action. This example creates a child of `UIImageView` called `DragView` and adds touch responsiveness to the class. Being an image view, it's important to enable user interaction, that is, set `setUserInteractionEnabled` to `YES`. This property affects all the view's children as well as the view itself.

The recipe works by updating a view's center to match the movement of an onscreen touch. When a user first touches any `DragView`, the object stores the start location as an offset from the view's origin. As the user drags, the view moves along with the finger—always maintaining the same origin offset so that the movement feels natural. Movement occurs by updating the object's center. Recipe 8-1 calculates x- and y-offsets and adjusts the view center by those offsets after each touch movement.

Upon being touched, the view pops to the front. That's due to a call in the `touchesMoved:withEvent:` method. The code tells the superview that owns the `DragView` to bring that view to the front. This allows the active element to always appear foremost in the interface.

This recipe does not implement touches-ended or touches-cancelled methods. Its interests lie only in the movement of onscreen objects. When the user stops interacting with the screen, the class has no further work to do.

Recipe 8-1 **Creating a Draggable View**

```
@interface DragView : UIImageView
{
    CGPoint startLocation;
}
@end

@implementation DragView
- (id) initWithImage: (UIImage *) anImage
{
    if (self = [super initWithImage:anImage])
        self.userInteractionEnabled = YES;
```

```
    return self;
}

- (void) touchesBegan:(NSSet*)touches withEvent:(UIEvent*)event
{
    // Calculate and store offset, and pop view into front if needed
    CGPoint pt = [[touches anyObject] locationInView:self];
    startLocation = pt;
    [[self superview] bringSubviewToFront:self];
}

- (void) touchesMoved:(NSSet*)touches withEvent:(UIEvent*)event
{
    // Calculate offset
    CGPoint pt = [[touches anyObject] locationInView:self];
    float dx = pt.x - startLocation.x;
    float dy = pt.y - startLocation.y;
    CGPoint newcenter = CGPointMake(self.center.x + dx,
        self.center.y + dy);

    // Set new location
    self.center = newcenter;
}
@end
```

Get This Recipe's Code

To get the code used for this recipe, go to http://github.com/erica/iphone-3.0-cookbook-, or if you've downloaded the disk image containing all of the sample code from the book, go to the folder for Chapter 8 and open the project for this recipe.

Recipe: Constraining Movement

The problem with the simple approach of Recipe 8-1 is that it's entirely possible to drag a view offscreen to the point where the user cannot see or easily recover it. That recipe uses completely unconstrained movement. There is no check to test whether the object remains in view and is touchable. Recipe 8-2 fixes this problem by constraining a view's movement to within its parent.

It achieves this by limiting movement in each direction, splitting its checks into separate x and y constraints. This two-check approach allows the view to continue to move even when one direction has passed its maximum. If the view has hit the rightmost edge of its parent, for example, it can still move up and down.

Figure 8-1 shows this interface. The flowers are constrained into the black rectangle in the center of the interface and cannot be dragged off-view. The code is general and can adapt to parent bounds and child views of any size.

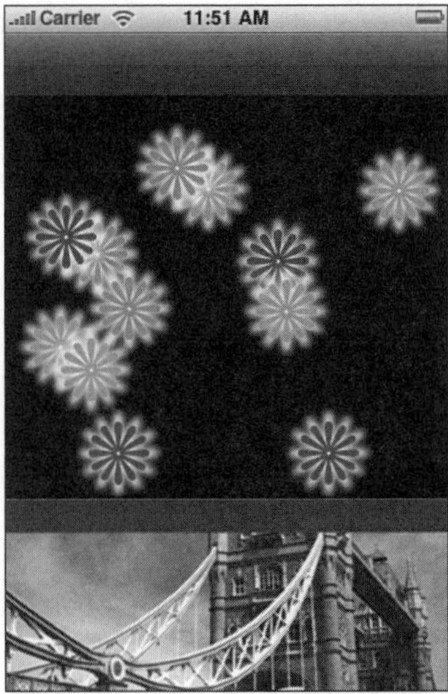

Figure 8-1 The movement of these flowers is bounded into the black rectangle.

Recipe 8-2 **Bounded Movement**

```
- (void) touchesMoved:(NSSet*)touches withEvent:(UIEvent*)event
{
    // Calculate offset
    CGPoint pt = [[touches anyObject] locationInView:self];
    float dx = pt.x - startLocation.x;
    float dy = pt.y - startLocation.y;
    CGPoint newcenter = CGPointMake(self.center.x + dx,
        self.center.y + dy);

    // Constrain movement into parent bounds
    float halfx = CGRectGetMidX(self.bounds);
    newcenter.x = MAX(halfx, newcenter.x);
    newcenter.x = MIN(self.superview.bounds.size.width - halfx,
        newcenter.x);

    float halfy = CGRectGetMidY(self.bounds);
    newcenter.y = MAX(halfy, newcenter.y);
    newcenter.y = MIN(self.superview.bounds.size.height - halfy,
        newcenter.y);
```

```
    // Set new location
    self.center = newcenter;
}
```

Get This Recipe's Code

To get the code used for this recipe, go to http://github.com/erica/iphone-3.0-cookbook-, or if you've downloaded the disk image containing all of the sample code from the book, go to the folder for Chapter 8 and open the project for this recipe.

Recipe: Testing Touches

Most onscreen view elements for direct manipulation interfaces are not rectangular. This complicates touch detection because parts of the actual view rectangle may not correspond to actual touch points. Figure 8-2 shows the problem in action. The screenshot on the right shows the interface with its touch-based subviews. The shot on the left shows the actual view bounds for each subview. The light gray areas around each onscreen circle fall within the bounds, but touches to those areas should not "hit" the view in question.

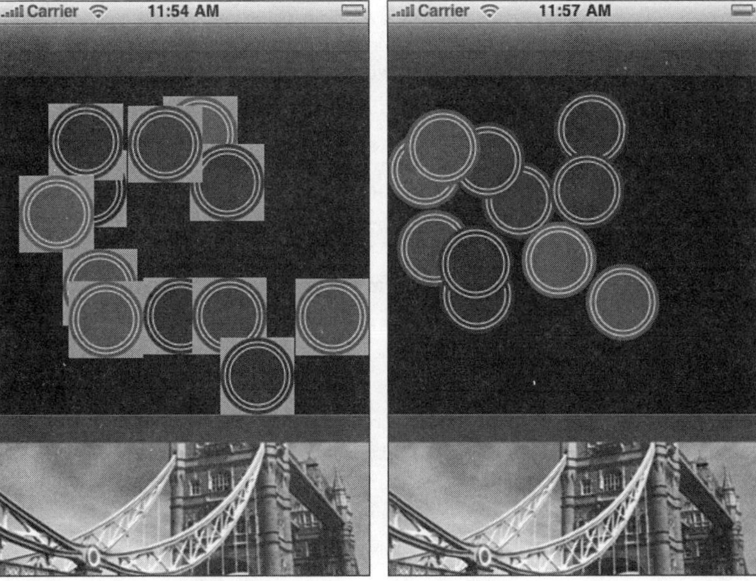

Figure 8-2 The application should ignore touches to the gray areas that surround each circle (left). The actual interface (right) uses zero alpha values to hide the parts of the view that are not used.

The iPhone senses user taps throughout the entire view frame. This includes the undrawn area such as the corners of the frame outside the actual circles of Figure 8-2 just as much as the primary presentation. That means that unless you add some sort of hit test, users may attempt to tap through to a view that's "obscured" by the clear portion of the `UIView` frame.

Visualize your actual view bounds by setting a view's background color, for example:

```
dragger.backgroundColor = [UIColor lightGrayColor];
```

This adds the backsplashes shown in Figure 8-2 (left) without affecting the actual onscreen art. In this case, the art consists of a centered circle with a transparent background. Unless you add some sort of test, all taps to any portion of this frame are captured by the view in question. Enabling background colors offers a convenient debugging aid to visualize the true extent of each view; don't forget to comment out the background color assignment in production code.

Recipe 8-3 adds a simple hit test to the views, determining whether touches fall within the circle. This test overrides the standard `UIView pointInside:withEvent:` method. This method returns either `YES` (the point falls inside the view) or `NO` (it does not). The test here uses basic geometry, checking whether the touch lies within the circle's radius. You can provide any test that works with your onscreen views. As you see in Recipe 8-4, that test can be expanded for much finer control.

Recipe 8-3 **Providing a Circular Hit Test**

```
- (BOOL) pointInside:(CGPoint)point withEvent:(UIEvent *)event
{
    CGPoint pt;
    float HALFSIDE = SIDELENGTH / 2.0f;

    // normalize with centered origin
    pt.x = (point.x - HALFSIDE) / HALFSIDE;
    pt.y = (point.y - HALFSIDE) / HALFSIDE;

    // x^2 + y^2 = radius
    float xsquared = pt.x * pt.x;
    float ysquared = pt.y * pt.y;

    // If the radius <= 1, the point is within the clipped circle
    if ((xsquared + ysquared) <= 1.0) return YES;
    return NO;
}
```

Get This Recipe's Code

To get the code used for this recipe, go to http://github.com/erica/iphone-3.0-cookbook-, or if you've downloaded the disk image containing all of the sample code from the book, go to the folder for Chapter 8 and open the project for this recipe.

Recipe: Testing Against a Bitmap

Unfortunately, most views don't fall into the simple geometries that make the hit test from Recipe 8-3 so straightforward. The flowers shown in Figure 8-1, for example, offer irregular boundaries and varied transparencies. For complicated art, it helps to test touches against a bitmap. Bitmaps provide byte-by-byte information about the contents of an image-based view, allowing you to test whether a touch hits a solid portion of the image or should pass through to any views below.

Recipe 8-4 extracts an image bitmap from a `UIImageView`. It assumes that the image used provides a pixel-by-pixel representation of the view in question. When you distort that view (normally by resizing a frame or applying a transform), update the math accordingly. Keeping the art at a 1:1 proportion to the actual view pixels simplifies lookup. You can recover the pixel in question, test its alpha level, and determine whether the touch has hit a solid portion of the view.

This example uses a cutoff of 85. That corresponds to a minimum alpha level of 33% (that is, 85 / 255). The `pointInside:` method considers any pixel with an alpha level below 33% to be transparent. This is arbitrary. Use any level (or other test for that matter) that works with the demands of your actual GUI.

Recipe 8-4 **Testing Touches Against Bitmap Alpha Levels**

```
// Return the offset for the alpha pixel at (x,y) for RGBA
// 4-bytes-per-pixel bitmap data
NSUInteger alphaOffset(NSUInteger x, NSUInteger y, NSUInteger w)
    {return y * w * 4 + x * 4;}

// Return the bitmap from a provided image
unsigned char *getBitmapFromImage (UIImage *image)
{

    CGColorSpaceRef colorSpace = CGColorSpaceCreateDeviceRGB();
    if (colorSpace == NULL)
    {
        fprintf(stderr, "Error allocating color space\n");
        return NULL;
    }

    CGSize size = image.size;
    void *bitmapData = malloc(size.width * size.height * 4);
    if (bitmapData == NULL)
    {
        fprintf (stderr, "Error: Memory not allocated!");
        CGColorSpaceRelease(colorSpace);
        return NULL;
    }
```

```
    CGContextRef context = CGBitmapContextCreate (bitmapData,
        size.width, size.height, 8, size.width * 4, colorSpace,
        kCGImageAlphaPremultipliedFirst);
    CGColorSpaceRelease(colorSpace );
    if (context == NULL)
    {
        fprintf (stderr, "Error: Context not created!");
        free (bitmapData);
        return NULL;
    }

    CGRect rect = CGRectMake(0.0f, 0.0f, size.width, size.height);
    CGContextDrawImage(context, rect, image.CGImage);
    unsigned char *data = CGBitmapContextGetData(context);
    CGContextRelease(context);

    return data;
}

@interface DragView : UIImageView
{
    CGPoint startLocation;
    unsigned char *bytes;
}
@end

@implementation DragView
- (id) initWithImage: (UIImage *) anImage
{
    if (self = [super initWithImage:anImage])
    {
        self.userInteractionEnabled = YES;
        bytes = getBitmapFromImage(anImage);
    }
    return self;
}

- (void) dealloc
{
    free(bytes);
    [super dealloc];
}

// Does the point hit the view?
- (BOOL) pointInside:(CGPoint)point withEvent:(UIEvent *)event
{
    if (!CGRectContainsPoint(self.bounds, point)) return NO;
```

```
    return (bytes[alphaOffset(point.x, point.y,
        self.image.size.width)] > 85);
}

- (void) touchesBegan:(NSSet*)touches withEvent:(UIEvent*)event
{
    // Calculate and store offset, and pop view into front if needed
    CGPoint pt = [[touches anyObject] locationInView:self];
    startLocation = pt;
    [[self superview] bringSubviewToFront:self];
}

- (void) touchesMoved:(NSSet*)touches withEvent:(UIEvent*)event
{
    // Calculate offset
    CGPoint pt = [[touches anyObject] locationInView:self];
    float dx = pt.x - startLocation.x;
    float dy = pt.y - startLocation.y;
    CGPoint newcenter = CGPointMake(self.center.x + dx,
        self.center.y + dy);

    // Bound movement into parent bounds
    float halfx = CGRectGetMidX(self.bounds);
    newcenter.x = MAX(halfx, newcenter.x);
    newcenter.x = MIN(self.superview.bounds.size.width - halfx, newcenter.x);

    float halfy = CGRectGetMidY(self.bounds);
    newcenter.y = MAX(halfy, newcenter.y);
    newcenter.y = MIN(self.superview.bounds.size.height - halfy, newcenter.y);

    // Set new location
    self.center = newcenter;
}
@end
```

Get This Recipe's Code

To get the code used for this recipe, go to http://github.com/erica/iphone-3.0-cookbook-, or if you've downloaded the disk image containing all of the sample code from the book, go to the folder for Chapter 8 and open the project for this recipe.

Recipe: Adding Persistence to Direct Manipulation Interfaces

Persistence represents a key iPhone design touch point. After users leave a program, Apple strongly recommends that they return to a state that matches as closely to where they left off as possible. Adding persistence to a direct manipulation interface, in the simplest approach, involves storing a representation of the onscreen data when an application terminates and restoring that state on startup.

Storing State

Every view knows its position because you can query its frame or center. This enables you to easily recover and store positions for each onscreen flower. The flower type (green, pink, or blue) is another matter. For each view to report its current flower, the `DragView` class must store that value, too. Adding a string instance variable enables the view to return the image name used. Extending the `DragView` interface lets you do that.

```
@interface DragView : UIImageView
{
    CGPoint startLocation;
    NSString *whichFlower;
}
@property (retain) NSString *whichFlower;
@end
```

Adding this extra property lets the view controller that owns the flowers store both a list of colors and a list of locations to its defaults file. Here, a simple loop collects both values from each draggable view and then stores them.

```
- (void) updateDefaults
{
    NSMutableArray *colors =  [[NSMutableArray alloc] init];
    NSMutableArray *locs = [[NSMutableArray alloc] init];

    for (DragView *dv in [[self.view viewWithTag:201] subviews])
    {
        [colors addObject:dv.whichFlower];
        [locs addObject:NSStringFromCGRect(dv.frame)];
    }

    [[NSUserDefaults standardUserDefaults] setObject:colors
        forKey:@"colors"];
    [[NSUserDefaults standardUserDefaults] setObject:locs
        forKey:@"locs"];
    [[NSUserDefaults standardUserDefaults] synchronize];

    [colors release];
    [locs release];
}
```

Defaults, as you can see, work like a dictionary. Just assign an object to a key and the iPhone updates the preferences file associated with your application ID. Defaults are stored in Library/Preferences inside your application's sandbox. Calling the synchronize function updates those defaults immediately instead of waiting for the program to terminate.

The `NSStringFromCGRect()` function provides a tight way to store frame information as a string. To recover the rectangle, issue `CGRectFromString()`. Each call takes one argument: a `CGRect` in the first case, an `NSString` object in the second. The UIKit framework provides functions that translate points and sizes as well as rectangles to and from strings.

This `updateDefaults` method, which saves the current state to disk, should be called in the application delegate's `applicationWillTerminate:` method, just before the program ends. The defaults are stored to reflect the final application state.

```
- (void) applicationWillTerminate: (UIApplication *) application
{
    [self.tbvc updateDefaults]; // update the defaults on quit
}
```

Recovering State

To bring views back to life, re-create them in either the `loadView` or `viewDidLoad` methods of your view controller. (Persistence awareness can also reside in the view controller's `init` method if you're not working with actual views.) Your methods should find any previous state information and update the interface to match that state.

When querying user defaults, Recipe 8-5 checks whether state data is unavailable (for example, the value returned is nil). When state data goes missing, the method creates random flowers at random points.

> **Note**
>
> When working with large data sources, you may want to initialize and populate your saved object array in the `UIViewController`'s `init` method, and then draw them in `loadView` or `viewDidLoad`. Where possible, use threading when working with many objects to avoid too much processing on the main thread. This can make the program laggy or unresponsive by blocking GUI updates.

Recipe 8-5 **Checking for Previous State**

```
- (void) loadFlowersInView: (UIView *) backdrop
{
    // Attempt to read in previous colors and locations
    NSMutableArray *colors = [[NSUserDefaults standardUserDefaults]
        objectForKey:@"colors"];
    NSMutableArray *locs = [[NSUserDefaults standardUserDefaults]
        objectForKey:@"locs"];

    // Add the flowers to random points on the screen
    for (int i = 0; i < MAXFLOWERS; i++)
    {

        NSString *whichFlower = [[NSArray
            arrayWithObjects:@"blueFlower.png", @"pinkFlower.png",
            @"orangeFlower.png", nil] objectAtIndex:(random() % 3)];
```

```
        if (colors && ([colors count] == MAXFLOWERS)) whichFlower =
            [colors objectAtIndex:i];

        DragView *dragger = [[DragView alloc] initWithImage:[UIImage
            imageNamed:whichFlower]];
        dragger.center = randomPoint();
        dragger.userInteractionEnabled = YES;
        dragger.whichFlower = whichFlower;
        if (locs && ([locs count] == MAXFLOWERS)) dragger.frame =
            CGRectFromString([locs objectAtIndex:i]);

        [backdrop addSubview:dragger];
        [dragger release];
    }
}
```

Get This Recipe's Code

To get the code used for this recipe, go to http://github.com/erica/iphone-3.0-cookbook-, or if you've downloaded the disk image containing all of the sample code from the book, go to the folder for Chapter 8 and open the project for this recipe.

Recipe: Persistence Through Archiving

Recipe 8-5 created persistence via the user defaults system. It stored descriptions of the onscreen views and built those views from the recovered description. Recipe 8-6 takes things to the next level. Instead of storing descriptions, it archives the objects themselves, or at least as much of the objects as is necessary to reconstruct them at launch time.

Two classes—`NSKeyedArchiver` and `NSKeyedUnarchiver`—provide an elegant solution for archiving objects into a file for later retrieval. These archive classes provide an object persistence API that allows you to restore objects between successive application sessions. The example you're about to see uses the simplest archiving approach. It stores a single root object, which in this case is an array of `DragViews`, that is, the flowers.

To create an archivable object class, you must define a pair of methods. The first, `encodeWithCoder:`, stores any information needed to rebuild the object. In this case, that is the view's frame and its flower. Both are stored as NSString objects. The second method, `initWithCoder:`, recovers that information and initializes objects using saved information. Here are the two methods defined for the `DragView` class, allowing objects of this class to be encoded and retrieved from an archive.

```
- (void) encodeWithCoder: (NSCoder *)coder
{
    [coder encodeCGRect:self.frame forKey:@"viewFrame"];
    [coder encodeObject:self.whichFlower forKey:@"flowerType"];
}
```

```
- (id) initWithCoder: (NSCoder *)coder
{
    [super initWithFrame:CGRectZero];
    self.frame = [coder decodeCGRectForKey:@"viewFrame"];
    self.whichFlower = [coder decodeObjectForKey:@"flowerType"];
    self.image = [UIImage imageNamed:self.whichFlower];
    self.userInteractionEnabled = YES;
    return self;
}
```

Each element is stored with a key name. Keys let you recover stored data in any order. Special UIKit extensions to the `NSCoder` class add storage methods for points, sizes, rectangles, affine transforms, and edge insets. This example takes advantage of the rectangle method for encoding and decoding the view frame.

Data is saved to an actual file. You supply an archive path to that file. This example stores its data in the Documents folder in the sandbox in a file called flowers.archive.

```
#define DATAPATH [NSString stringWithFormat:
    @"%@/Documents/flowers.archive", NSHomeDirectory()]
```

So for this direct manipulation interface, how do you actually perform the archiving and unarchiving? Recipe 8-6 shows the exact calls, which in this case are implemented in the view controller. Here are two custom methods that collect the DragViews and archive them to the file, and that retrieve the views from the file.

Notice that the latter method returns a Boolean value. This indicates whether the views could be read in correctly. On fail, a fallback method generates a new set of subviews. It's assumed that either the data was corrupted or that this is the first time running the application. Either way, the application generates new data to populate the backdrop.

Recipe 8-6 **Archiving Interfaces**

```
- (void) archiveInterface
{
    NSArray *flowers = [[self.view viewWithTag:201] subviews];
    [NSKeyedArchiver archiveRootObject:flowers toFile:DATAPATH];
}

- (BOOL) unarchiveInterfaceInView: (UIView *) backdrop
{
    NSArray *flowers = [NSKeyedUnarchiver
        unarchiveObjectWithFile:DATAPATH];
    if (!flowers) return NO;

    for (UIView *aView in flowers)
        [backdrop addSubview:aView];
    return YES;
}
```

> **Get This Recipe's Code**
>
> To get the code used for this recipe, go to http://github.com/erica/iphone-3.0-cookbook-, or if you've downloaded the disk image containing all of the sample code from the book, go to the folder for Chapter 8 and open the project for this recipe.

Recipe: Adding Undo Support

Undo support provides another important component of direct manipulation interfaces. For a simple GUI, this involves little more than returning each object to a previous onscreen position. Cocoa Touch offers the `NSUndoManager` class to provide a way to reverse user actions.

Creating an Undo Manager

Define your undo manager in the most central location possible. You want to use just one instance of this class for each primary view controller, sharing it with any child views in your interface. The `viewDidLoad` or `loadView` methods provide a good place to allocate a new undo manager.

```
// Initialize the undo manager for this application
self.undoManager = [[NSUndoManager alloc] init];
[self.undoManager setLevelsOfUndo:999];
[self.undoManager release];
```

The manager can store an arbitrary number of undo actions. You specify how deep that stack goes. Each action can be complex, involving groups of undo activities, or the action can be simple as in the example shown here. These undos do one thing: move a view to a previous location.

Child-View Undo Support

All children of the `UIResponder` class can find the nearest undo manager in the responder chain. This means that if you add `DragView` instances to a view whose view controller has an undo manager, each `DragView` automatically knows about that manager through its `undoManager` property. This is enormously convenient as you can add undo support in your main view controller, and all your child views basically pick up that support for free.

Working with Navigation Bars

When working with the navigation bar in any way, child views should store a pointer to their view controller. A pointer to their view controller lets the children coordinate with any navigation controller bar button items. You only want an Undo button to appear when items are available on the undo stack.

```
@interface DragView : UIImageView
{
    CGPoint startLocation;
    NSString *whichFlower;
    UIViewController *viewController;
```

```
}
@property (retain) NSString *whichFlower;
@property (assign) UIViewController *viewController;
@end
```

Upon adding an undo item to the manager, you may want to display an Undo button as this example does. The Undo button calls the manager's `undo` method, which in turn uses the target, action, and object set stored at the top of the undo stack to perform the actual reversion. When the undo manager has no more undos to perform, the Undo button should hide.

```
- (void) checkUndoAndUpdateNavBar
{
    while ([self.undoManager isUndoing]);

    // Don't show the undo button if the undo stack is empty
    if (!self.undoManager.canUndo)
        self.navigationItem.leftBarButtonItem = nil;
    else
        self.navigationItem.leftBarButtonItem =
            BARBUTTON(@"Undo", @selector(undo));
}

- (void) undo
{
    [self.undoManager undo];
}
```

Notice that this method waits for the undo manager to finish any ongoing undo actions before proceeding to update the navigation bar.

Registering Undos

Here is the simplest call to register an undo. It stores the object location at the start of a touch sequence, specifying that upon undo, the object should reset its position to this start location. This call is made from the child view, and not from the view controller. This approach tells the undo manager how to reset an object to its previous attributes.

```
[self.undoManager registerUndoWithTarget:self
    selector:@selector(resetPosition)
    object:NSStringFromCGPoint(self.center)];
```

An alternative, preferred approach uses an invocation instead of a target and selector. The invocation records a message for reverting state, that is, it stores a way that it can jump back to the previous state. Perform this preparation before you change the object's state.

```
[[self.undoManager prepareWithInvocationTarget:self] setPosition:self.center];
```

With invocations, you can use a method with any number of arguments and argument types. This invocation simplifies adding redo support, which is why it is preferred.

There are several ways to approach the undo registration process in a direct manipulation interface. Placing a call to a setter/unsetter method from the `touchesBegan:` ➥`withEvent:` provides the easiest solution, as shown in Recipe 8-7.

Be aware that if users touch an object and release without moving it, undo results may be imperceptible. You may want to add a check into the touches ended routine to make sure that an object was actually moved. If not, remove the last item from the undo stack by issuing `undo`.

Recipe 8-7 lists the actual undo code. The `setPosition:` method provides both a set and reset solution for the undo manager. Upon registration, it stores the position of a view into the undo stack. Upon undo, it animates the view back to that position, providing a visual connection between the new value and the old. Although redo support is not used in this recipe (see Recipe 8-8), the `setPosition:` method is redo compliant. When called by the undo manager, the repeat `prepareWithInvocationTarget:` call gets added to the redo stack.

The delayed selector in this method, `checkUndoAndUpdateNavBar:`, triggers after the animation has completed. This allows the `setPosition`: method to finish before any checks are made against the undo stack.

The stack will not decrease its count until after the registered method returns. If you call the method directly, the Undo button on the navigation controller will not dismiss even though there are no further undos to perform. The while loop that checks for `isUndoing` would never clear and `setPosition:` would never return.

Recipe 8-7 **Creating a Custom Undo Routine**

```
- (void) setPosition: (CGPoint) pos
{
    [[self.undoManager prepareWithInvocationTarget:self]
        setPosition:self.center];

    [self.viewController
        performSelector:@selector(checkUndoAndUpdateNavBar)
        withObject:nil afterDelay:0.2f];

    [UIView beginAnimations:@"" context:nil];
    [UIView setAnimationCurve:UIViewAnimationCurveEaseInOut];
    [UIView setAnimationDuration:0.1f];

    self.center = pos; // animate

    [UIView commitAnimations];
}

- (void) touchesBegan:(NSSet*)touches withEvent:(UIEvent*)event
{
    [self setPosition:self.center];
```

```
    // Calculate and store offset, and pop view into front if needed
    CGPoint pt = [[touches anyObject] locationInView:self];
    startLocation = pt;
    [[self superview] bringSubviewToFront:self];
}
```

Get This Recipe's Code

To get the code used for this recipe, go to http://github.com/erica/iphone-3.0-cookbook-, or if you've downloaded the disk image containing all of the sample code from the book, go to the folder for Chapter 8 and open the project for this recipe.

Recipe: Adding Shake-Controlled Undo Support

New to the 3.0 SDK, shake-to-undo support offers a whimsical feature that automatically produces an undo/redo menu. When users shake the phone, this menu appears, connected to the current undo manager. The menu allows users to undo the previous action or redo an action that has been undone. Figure 8-3 shows the shake-to-undo menu.

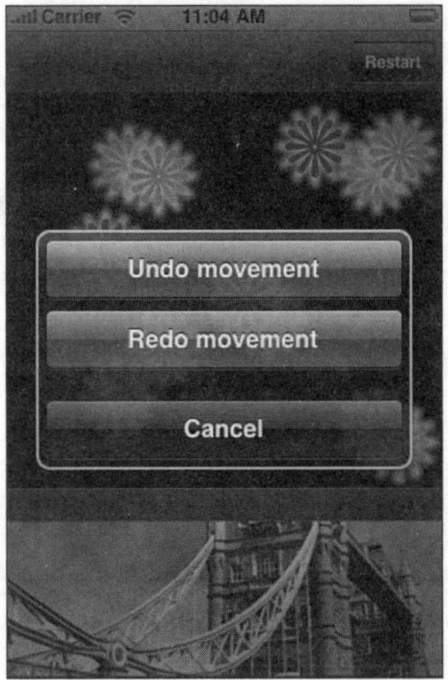

Figure 8-3 Shake-to-undo provides an undo/redo menu for users.

Shake-to-edit is a clever concept, but it's not entirely practical in application. Training your users to shake the phone rather than press an Undo button presents a real-world hurdle. Even trained, it's a pain to keep shaking the phone to process a series of undo events. If you plan to include this feature in your applications, consider using it to enhance and extend an existing undo setup rather than replace it.

Adding support for shake-to-edit takes just a few steps. Here is an item-by-item list of the changes you make to offer this feature in your application.

Add an Action Name for Undo and Redo

Action names provide the word or words that appear after "Undo" and "Redo," as shown in Figure 8-3. Here, the action name is set to "movement." The undo menu option is therefore Undo Movement. Extend the `setPosition:` method to provide this name by adding this line right after you prepare the invocation target.

```
if (![self.undoManager isUndoing])
    [self.undoManager setActionName:@"movement"];
```

Provide Shake-To-Edit Support

Locate the `applicationDidFinishLaunching:` method of your application delegate. In that method add this line. Setting the `applicationSupportsShakeToEdit` property explicitly adds shake-to-edit support to the application as a whole.

```
application.applicationSupportsShakeToEdit = YES;
```

Force First Responder

For a view controller to handle undo/redo, it must always be first responder. Since each application may be handling several undo manager clients, the application must match each undo manager to a particular view controller. Only the first responder receives undo/redo calls.

As the undo manager typically lives inside a `UIViewController` instance, make sure to add the routines from Recipe 8-8 to your view controller. These ensure that it becomes first responder whenever it appears onscreen and that its undo manager is used.

Recipe 8-8 **Providing Shake-to-Edit Support by Becoming First Responder**

```
- (BOOL)canBecomeFirstResponder {
    return YES;
}

- (void)viewDidAppear:(BOOL)animated {
    [super viewDidAppear:animated];
    [self becomeFirstResponder];
}
```

```
- (void)viewWillDisappear:(BOOL)animated {
    [super viewWillDisappear:animated];
    [self resignFirstResponder];
}
```

Get This Recipe's Code

To get the code used for this recipe, go to http://github.com/erica/iphone-3.0-cookbook-, or if you've downloaded the disk image containing all of the sample code from the book, go to the folder for Chapter 8 and open the project for this recipe.

Recipe: Drawing Onscreen

As with gestures, the `UIView` hosts the realm of direct onscreen drawing. Its `drawRect:` method offers a low-level way to draw content directly, letting you create and display arbitrary elements using Quartz 2D calls. These two elements can join together to build concrete, manipulatable interfaces.

Recipe 8-9 combines gestures with `drawRect` to create touch-based painting. As a user touches the screen, the `TouchView` class collects a series of points. At each touch movement, the `touchesMoved:withEvent:` method calls `setNeedsDisplay`. This, in turn, triggers a call to `drawRect:`, where the view draws a series of line segments from those points to create a visual onscreen path. Figure 8-4 shows the interface with a user-created path.

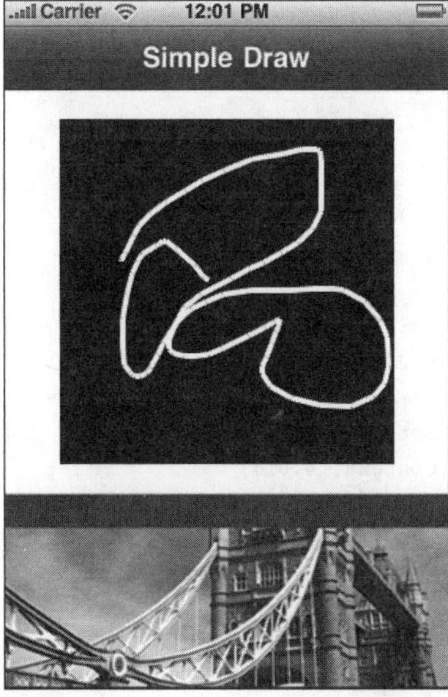

Figure 8-4 A simple painting tool for the iPhone requires little more than collecting touches along a path and painting that path with Quartz 2D calls.

Recipe 8-9 **Touch-Based Painting in a UIView**

```
@interface TouchView : UIView
{
    NSMutableArray *points;
}
@property (retain) NSMutableArray *points;
@end

@implementation TouchView
@synthesize points;

- (BOOL) isMultipleTouchEnabled {return NO;}

// Start new array
- (void) touchesBegan:(NSSet *) touches withEvent:(UIEvent *) event
{
    self.points = [NSMutableArray array];
    CGPoint pt = [[touches anyObject] locationInView:self];
    [self.points addObject:[NSValue valueWithCGPoint:pt]];
}

// Add each point to array
- (void) touchesMoved:(NSSet *) touches withEvent:(UIEvent *) event
{
    CGPoint pt = [[touches anyObject] locationInView:self];
    [self.points addObject:[NSValue valueWithCGPoint:pt]];
    [self setNeedsDisplay];
}

// Draw all points
- (void) drawRect: (CGRect) rect
{
    if (!self.points) return;
    if (self.points.count < 2) return;

    [[UIColor whiteColor] set];
    CGContextSetLineWidth(context, 4.0f);

    CGContextRef context = UIGraphicsGetCurrentContext();

    for (int i = 0; i < (self.points.count - 1); i++)
    {
        CGPoint pt1 = POINT(i);
        CGPoint pt2 = POINT(i+1);
        CGContextMoveToPoint(context, pt1.x, pt1.y);
```

```
        CGContextAddLineToPoint(context, pt2.x, pt2.y);
        CGContextStrokePath(context);
    }
}
@end
```

Get This Recipe's Code

To get the code used for this recipe, go to http://github.com/erica/iphone-3.0-cookbook-, or if you've downloaded the disk image containing all of the sample code from the book, go to the folder for Chapter 8 and open the project for this recipe.

Recipe: Calculating Lines

When user input relies primarily on touches, applied geometry can help interpret those gestures. In this recipe and the next, computational solutions filter user input to create simpler data sets that are more application appropriate. Recipe 8-10 collects the same touch array that was shown in Recipe 8-9. When the gesture finishes, that is, at touch-up, this code analyzes that array and creates a minimized set of line segments to match the freeform points.

A reduced point set accomplishes two things. First, it creates a straighter, better-looking presentation. The right image in Figure 8-5 is much cleaner than the one on the left. Second, it produces a set of points that are better matched to interpretation. The six-point line segments shown in Figure 8-5 on the right are far easier to analyze than the more than 50 points on the left.

The extra line segments are due to a slight finger squiggle at the top-right of the triangle. Converting a freeform gesture into meaningful user intent can be a significantly hard problem. Although it's obvious to a human that the user meant to draw a triangle, computational algorithms are never perfect. When you need to interpret gestures, a certain amount of hand waving accommodation is necessary.

Recipe 8-10 works by analyzing sets of three points at a time. For each triplet, it centers the first and third points around the origin of the second. It then takes the dot product of the vectors to the first and third points. The dot product returns a value that is the cosine of the angle between the two vectors. If those points are collinear, that is, the angle between them is roughly 180 degrees (give or take), the algorithm discards the middle point.

The cosine of 180 degrees is -1. This code discards all points where the vector cosine falls below -0.75. Increasing the tolerance (by raising the cosine check, say to -0.6 or -0.5) produces flatter results but may also discard intentional direction changes from users. If your goal is to check for triangles, squares, and other simple polygons, the tolerance can be quite robust. To produce "prettier" line drawings, use a tighter tolerance to retain user-provided detail.

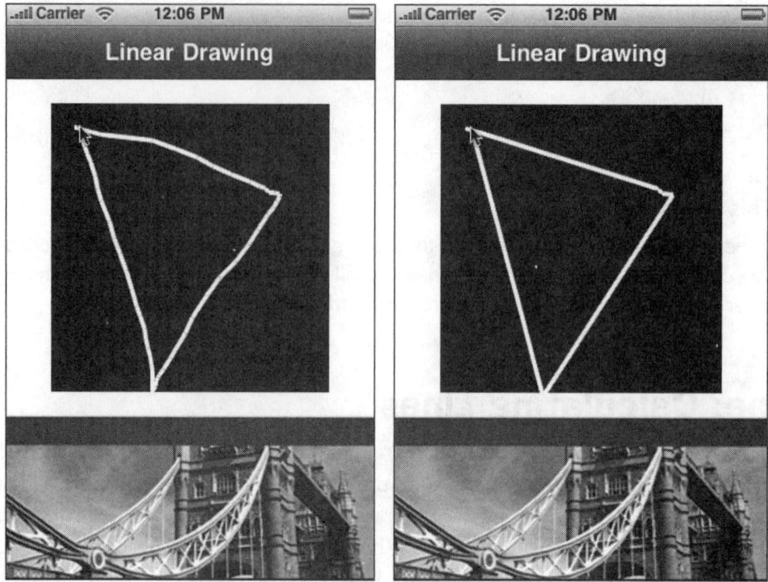

Figure 8-5 Computational solutions can manage user input. Here, a line detection algorithm reduces the number of input points by converting user intent into a better geometric representation.

Recipe 8-10 **Creating Line Segments from Freeform Gestures**

```
// Return dot product of two vectors normalized
float dotproduct (CGPoint v1, CGPoint v2)
{
    float dot = (v1.x * v2.x) + (v1.y * v2.y);
    float a = ABS(sqrt(v1.x * v1.x + v1.y * v1.y));
    float b = ABS(sqrt(v2.x * v2.x + v2.y * v2.y));
    dot /= (a * b);

    return dot;
}

// remove all intermediate points that are approximately colinear
- (void) touchesEnded:(NSSet *) touches withEvent:(UIEvent *) event
{
    if (!self.points) return;
    if (self.points.count < 3) return;

    // Create the filtered array
    NSMutableArray *newpoints = [NSMutableArray array];
    [newpoints addObject:[self.points objectAtIndex:0]];
    CGPoint p1 = POINT(0);
```

```
    // Add only those points that are inflections
    for (int i = 1; i < (self.points.count - 1); i++)
    {
        CGPoint p2 = POINT(i);
        CGPoint p3 = POINT(i+1);

        // Cast vectors around p2 origin
        CGPoint v1 = CGPointMake(p1.x - p2.x, p1.y - p2.y);
        CGPoint v2 = CGPointMake(p3.x - p2.x, p3.y - p2.y);
        float dot = dotproduct(v1, v2);

        // Colinear items need to be as close as possible
        // to 180 degrees
        if (dot < -0.75f) continue;
        p1 = p2;
        [newpoints addObject:[self.points objectAtIndex:i]];
    }

    // Add final point
    if ([newpoints lastObject] != [self.points lastObject])
        [newpoints addObject:[self.points lastObject]];

    // Report initial and final point counts
    NSLog(@"%@",[NSString stringWithFormat@"%d points to %d points",
        self.points.count, newpoints.count]);

    // Update with the filtered points and draw
    self.points = newpoints;
    [self setNeedsDisplay];
}
```

Get This Recipe's Code

To get the code used for this recipe, go to http://github.com/erica/iphone-3.0-cookbook-, or if you've downloaded the disk image containing all of the sample code from the book, go to the folder for Chapter 8 and open the project for this recipe.

Recipe: Detecting Circles

In a direct manipulation interface like the iPhone, you'd imagine that most people could get by just pointing to items onscreen. And yet, circle detection remains one of the most requested gestures. Developers like having people circle items onscreen with their fingers. In the spirit of providing solutions that readers have requested, Recipe 8-11 offers a relatively simple circle detector, which is shown in Figure 8-6.

In this implementation, detection uses a two-step test. First, there's a convergence test. The circle must start and end close enough together that the points are somehow related. A fair amount of leeway is needed because when you don't provide direct visual feedback, users tend to undershoot or overshoot where they began. The pixel distance used here is a generous 60 pixels, approximately a third of the view size.

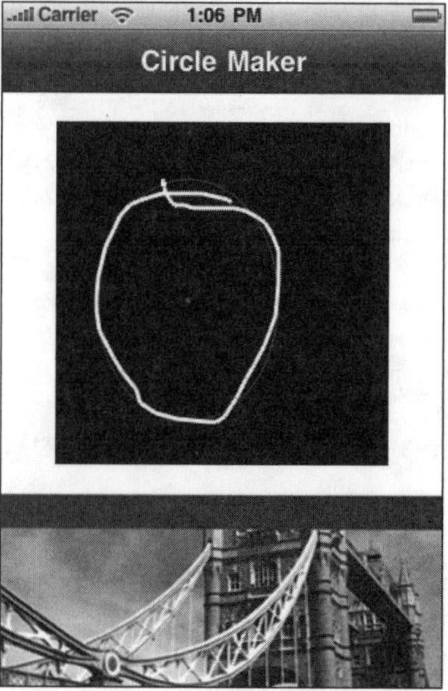

Figure 8-6 The dot and the outer ellipse show the key features of the detected circle.

The second test looks at movement around a central point. It adds up the arcs traveled, which should equal 360 degrees in a perfect circle. This sample allows any movement that falls within 45 degrees of that number.

Upon passing the two tests, the algorithm produces a least bounding rectangle and centers that rectangle on the geometric mean of the points from the original gesture. This result is assigned to the circle instance variable. It's not a perfect detection system (you can try to fool it when testing the sample code), but it's robust enough to provide reasonably good circle checks for many iPhone applications.

Recipe 8-11 **Detecting Circles**

```
// At the end of touches, determine whether a circle was drawn
- (void) touchesEnded:(NSSet *) touches withEvent:(UIEvent *) event
{
    if (!self.points) return;
    if (self.points.count < 3) return;

    // Test 1: The start and end points must be between
    // 60 pixels of each other
    CGRect tcircle;
    if (distance(POINT(0), POINT(self.points.count - 1)) < 60.0f)
```

```
        tcircle = [self centeredRectangle];

    // Test 2: Count the distance traveled in degrees. Must fall
    // within 45 degrees of 2 PI
    CGPoint center = CGPointMake(CGRectGetMidX(tcircle),
        CGRectGetMidY(tcircle));
    float distance = ABS(acos(dotproduct(centerPoint(POINT(0), center),
        centerPoint(POINT(1), center))));
    for (int i = 1; i < (self.points.count - 1); i++)
        distance += ABS(acos(dotproduct(centerPoint(POINT(i), center),
            centerPoint(POINT(i+1), center))));
    if ((ABS(distance - 2 * M_PI) < (M_PI / 4.0f))) circle = tcircle;

    [self setNeedsDisplay];
}
```

Get This Recipe's Code

To get the code used for this recipe, go to http://github.com/erica/iphone-3.0-cookbook-, or if you've downloaded the disk image containing all of the sample code from the book, go to the folder for Chapter 8 and open the project for this recipe.

Recipe: Detecting Multitouch

Enabling multitouch interaction in your UIViews lets the iPhone recover and respond to more than one finger touch at a time. Set the `UIView` property `multipleTouchEnabled` to `YES` or override `isMultipleTouchEnabled` for your view. When multitouch is enabled, each touch callback returns an entire set of touches. When that set's count exceeds one, you know you're dealing with multitouch.

In theory, the iPhone could support an arbitrary number of touches. On the iPhone, multitouch is limited to five finger touches at a time. Even five at a time goes beyond what most developers need. There aren't many meaningful gestures you can make with five fingers at once. This particularly holds true when you grasp the iPhone with one hand and touch with the other.

Touches are not grouped. If, for example, you touch the screen with two fingers from each hand, there's no way to determine which touches belong to which hand. The touch order is arbitrary. Although grouped touches retain the same finger order for the lifetime of a single touch event (down, move, up), the order may change the next time your user touches the screen. When you need to distinguish touches from each other, build a touch dictionary indexed by the touch objects.

Perhaps it's a comfort to know that if you need to, the extra finger support has been built in. Unfortunately, when you are using three or more touches at a time, the screen has a pronounced tendency to lose track of one or more of those fingers. It's hard to programmatically track smooth gestures when you go beyond two finger touches.

Recipe 8-12 adds multitouch to a UIView (via the `isMultipleToucheEnabled` method) and draws lines between each touch location onscreen. When you limit your input to two touches, it produces a reasonably steady response, maintaining a line between those two fingers. Add a third touch to the screen and the lines start to flicker. That's because the iPhone does not steadily detect all the touches.

Unfortunately, multitouch detection is not nearly as stable and dependable as single touch interaction. You see that in this recipe and see an even more pronounced example in Recipe 8-13. While multitouch is available and, admittedly, an exciting technology, its limits mean you should use it cautiously and with heavy testing before deployment to real-world applications.

Recipe 8-12 **Adding Basic Multitouch**

```
@implementation TouchView
@synthesize points;

- (BOOL) isMultipleTouchEnabled {return YES;}

- (void) touchesBegan:(NSSet *) touches withEvent: (UIEvent *) event
{
    self.points = [touches allObjects];
    [self setNeedsDisplay];
}

- (void) touchesMoved:(NSSet *) touches withEvent: (UIEvent *) event
{
    self.points = [touches allObjects];
    [self setNeedsDisplay];
}

- (void) drawRect: (CGRect) rect
{
    if (!self.points) return;
    if (self.points.count < 2) return;

    CGContextRef context = UIGraphicsGetCurrentContext();
    CGContextSetLineWidth(context, 4.0f);
    [[UIColor redColor] set];

    // Draw lines between each point
    CGPoint pt1 = POINT(0);
    CGContextMoveToPoint(context, pt1.x, pt1.y);

    for (int i = 1; i < self.points.count; i++)
    {
        pt1 = POINT(i % self.points.count);
        CGPoint pt2 = POINT((i + 1) % self.points.count);
        CGContextAddLineToPoint(context, pt2.x, pt2.y);
    }
```

```
    CGContextStrokePath(context);
}
@end
```

Get This Recipe's Code

To get the code used for this recipe, go to http://github.com/erica/iphone-3.0-cookbook-, or if you've downloaded the disk image containing all of the sample code from the book, go to the folder for Chapter 8 and open the project for this recipe.

Note

Apple provides many Core Graphics/Quartz 2D resources on its developer Web site. Although many of these forums, mailing lists, and source code samples are not iPhone specific, they offer an invaluable resource for expanding your iPhone Core Graphics knowledge.

Recipe: Gesture Distinction

Standard Apple iPhone applications support a variety of gestures that have become a basic language for touch interaction. Users can tap, double-tap, swipe, and drag the screen, and Apple applications interpret those gestures accordingly. Unfortunately, Apple does not offer a public API that performs the heavy lifting. You need to interpret your own gestures. Recipe 8-13 offers a gesture detection system that waits for user input and then evaluates that input.

Distinguishing gestures is not trivial, particularly when you add multitouch into the equation. As Recipe 8-12 demonstrated, iPhone touch sensors are less reliable in multitouch mode. A two-touch drag, for example, might flip back and forth between detecting two fingers and one.

The solution in Recipe 8-13 for working with this inconsistency is twofold. First, the code tries to find the most immediate solution for matching input to a known gesture as quickly as possible. When matched, it sets a "finished" flag so the first gesture matched wins. Second, this code may invalidate a match should user input continue beyond a reasonable limit. For example, taps are short; a tap should not involve 20 or 30 UITouch instances. Here are the gestures that Recipe 8-13 handles, and how it interprets them:

- **Swipes**—Swipes are short, single-touch gestures that move in a single cardinal direction: up, down, left, or right. They cannot move too far off course from that primary direction. The code here checks for touches that travel at least 16 pixels in X or Y, without straying more than 8 pixels in another direction.
- **Pinches**—To pinch or unpinch, a user must move two fingers together or apart in a single movement. That gesture must compress or expand by at least 8 pixels to register with this code.
- **Taps**—Although a tap should ideally represent a single touch to the screen, extra callbacks may register. Recipe 8-13 uses a point limit of 3 for single-touch taps, and 10 for double-touch taps. And yes, that high tolerance is needed. Empirical testing

set the levels used in this recipe. Users touched one or two fingers to the screen at once, and the code counted the UITouch instances produced.

- **Double-taps**—Each touch object provides a tap count, letting you check whether users tapped once or twice. However, a double-tap is not counted until a single-tap has already been processed. When looking to distinguish between single- and double-taps, be aware of this behavior.
- **Drags**—For the purpose of this example, a drag refers to any single-touch event that is not a tap, a double-tap, or a swipe.

Recipe 8-13 **Interpreting Gestures**

```
@interface TouchView : UIView
{
    BOOL multitouch;
    BOOL finished;
    CGPoint startPoint;
    NSUInteger touchtype;
    NSUInteger pointCount;
    UIViewController *vc;
}
@property (assign) UIViewController *vc;
@end

@implementation TouchView
@synthesize vc;

#define SWIPE_DRAG_MIN 16
#define DRAGLIMIT_MAX 8
#define POINT_TOLERANCE 16
#define MIN_PINCH    8

- (BOOL) isMultipleTouchEnabled {return YES;}

- (void) touchesBegan:(NSSet *) touches withEvent: (UIEvent *) event
{
    finished = NO;
    startPoint = [[touches anyObject] locationInView:self];
    multitouch = (touches.count > 1);
    pointCount = 1;
}

- (void) touchesMoved:(NSSet *) touches withEvent: (UIEvent *) event
{
    pointCount++;
    if (finished) return;
```

```
// Handle multitouch
if (touches.count > 1)
{
    // get touches
    UITouch *touch1 = [[touches allObjects] objectAtIndex:0];
    UITouch *touch2 = [[touches allObjects] objectAtIndex:1];

    // find current and previous points
    CGPoint cpoint1 = [touch1 locationInView:self];
    CGPoint ppoint1 = [touch1 previousLocationInView:self];
    CGPoint cpoint2 = [touch2 locationInView:self];
    CGPoint ppoint2 = [touch2 previousLocationInView:self];

    // calculate distances between the points
    CGFloat cdist = distance(cpoint1, cpoint2);
    CGFloat pdist = distance(ppoint1, ppoint2);

    multitouch = YES;

    // The pinch has to exceed a minimum distance to trigger
    if (ABS(cdist - pdist) < MIN_PINCH) return;

    if (cdist < pdist)
        touchtype = UITouchPinchIn;
    else
        touchtype = UITouchPinchOut;

    finished = YES;
    return;
}
else
{
    // Check single touch for swipe
    CGPoint cpoint = [[touches anyObject] locationInView:self];
    float dx = DX(cpoint, startPoint);
    float dy = DY(cpoint, startPoint);
    multitouch = NO;

    finished = YES;
    if ((dx > SWIPE_DRAG_MIN) && (ABS(dy) < DRAGLIMIT_MAX))
        touchtype = UITouchSwipeLeft;
    else if ((-dx > SWIPE_DRAG_MIN) && (ABS(dy) < DRAGLIMIT_MAX))
        touchtype = UITouchSwipeRight;
    else if ((dy > SWIPE_DRAG_MIN) && (ABS(dx) < DRAGLIMIT_MAX))
        touchtype = UITouchSwipeUp;
    else if ((-dy > SWIPE_DRAG_MIN) && (ABS(dx) < DRAGLIMIT_MAX))
        touchtype = UITouchSwipeDown;
```

```
        else
            finished = NO;
    }
}

- (void) touchesEnded:(NSSet *) touches withEvent: (UIEvent *) event
{
    // was not detected as a swipe
    if (!finished && !multitouch)
    {
        // tap or double tap
        if (pointCount < 3)
        {
            if ([[touches anyObject] tapCount] == 1)
                touchtype = UITouchTap;
            else
                touchtype = UITouchDoubleTap;
        }
        else
            touchtype = UITouchDrag;
    }

    // did points exceeded proper swipe?
    if (finished && !multitouch)
    {
        if (pointCount > POINT_TOLERANCE) touchtype = UITouchDrag;
    }

    // Is this properly a tap/double tap?
    if (multitouch || (touches.count > 1))
    {
        // tolerance is *very* high
        if (pointCount < 10)
        {
            if ([[touches anyObject] tapCount] == 1)
                touchtype = UITouchMultitouchTap;
            else
                touchtype = UITouchMultitouchDoubleTap;
        }
    }

    NSString *whichItem = nil;
    if (touchtype == UITouchUnknown)
        whichItem = @"Unknown";
    else if (touchtype == UITouchTap)
        whichItem = @"Tap";
    else if (touchtype == UITouchDoubleTap)
```

```
        whichItem = @"Double Tap";
    else if (touchtype == UITouchDrag)
        whichItem = @"Drag";
    else if (touchtype == UITouchMultitouchTap)
        whichItem = @"Multitouch Tap";
    else if (touchtype == UITouchMultitouchDoubleTap)
        whichItem = @"Multitouch Double Tap";
    else if (touchtype == UITouchSwipeLeft)
        whichItem = @"Swipe Left";
    else if (touchtype == UITouchSwipeRight)
        whichItem = @"Swipe Right";
    else if (touchtype == UITouchSwipeUp)
        whichItem = @"Swipe Up";
    else if (touchtype == UITouchSwipeDown)
        whichItem = @"Swipe Down";
    else if (touchtype == UITouchPinchIn)
        whichItem = @"Pinch In";
    else if (touchtype == UITouchPinchOut)
        whichItem = @"Pinch Out";

    [self.vc performSelector:@selector(updateStatewithPoints:)
         withObject:whichItem
         withObject:[NSNumber numberWithInt:pointCount]];
}
@end
```

Get This Recipe's Code

To get the code used for this recipe, go to http://github.com/erica/iphone-3.0-cookbook-, or if you've downloaded the disk image containing all of the sample code from the book, go to the folder for Chapter 8 and open the project for this recipe.

One More Thing: Interactive Resize and Rotation

As the recipes in this chapter have shown, if you're willing to bring math to the table, the iPhone can respond in powerful ways. Listing 8-1 demonstrates that power by combining the `DragView` class shown throughout this chapter with Apple sample code. This code creates a touchable, interactive view that responds to single and double touches by translating, rotating, and zooming.

This implementation, whose features are due to Apple and whose mistakes are down solely to me, stores a set of points at the beginning of each touch. It then creates incremental affine transforms based on touch progress, comparing the touch locations to their starting positions and updating the view transform in real time.

It's a complicated way to approach direct manipulation, but the results are outstanding. This class responds directly to user interaction to match the view to its touches.

Listing 8-1 **Resizing and Rotating Views**

```
@implementation DragView

// Prepare the drag view
- (id) initWithImage: (UIImage *) anImage
{
    if (self = [super initWithImage:anImage])
    {
        self.userInteractionEnabled = YES;
        self.multipleTouchEnabled = YES;
        self.exclusiveTouch = NO;
        originalSize = anImage.size;
        originalTransform = CGAffineTransformIdentity;
        touchBeginPoints = CFDictionaryCreateMutable(NULL, 0,
            NULL, NULL);
    }
    return self;
}

// Create an incremental transform matching the current touch set
- (CGAffineTransform)incrementalTransformWithTouches:(NSSet *)touches
{
    // Sort the touches by their memory addresses
    NSArray *sortedTouches = [[touches allObjects]
        sortedArrayUsingSelector:@selector(compareAddress)];
    NSInteger numTouches = [sortedTouches count];

    // If there are no touches, simply return identify transform.
    if (numTouches == 0) return CGAffineTransformIdentity;

    // Handle single touch as a translation
    if (numTouches == 1) {
        UITouch *touch = [sortedTouches objectAtIndex:0];
        CGPoint beginPoint = *(CGPoint *)
            CFDictionaryGetValue(touchBeginPoints, touch);
        CGPoint currentPoint = [touch locationInView:self.superview];
        return CGAffineTransformMakeTranslation(currentPoint.x -
            beginPoint.x, currentPoint.y - beginPoint.y);
    }

    // If two or more touches, go with the first two
    UITouch *touch1 = [sortedTouches objectAtIndex:0];
    UITouch *touch2 = [sortedTouches objectAtIndex:1];

    CGPoint beginPoint1 = *(CGPoint *)
        CFDictionaryGetValue(touchBeginPoints, touch1);
```

```
    CGPoint currentPoint1 = [touch1 locationInView:self.superview];
    CGPoint beginPoint2 = *(CGPoint *)
        CFDictionaryGetValue(touchBeginPoints, touch2);
    CGPoint currentPoint2 = [touch2 locationInView:self.superview];

    double layerX = self.center.x;
    double layerY = self.center.y;

    double x1 = beginPoint1.x - layerX;
    double y1 = beginPoint1.y - layerY;
    double x2 = beginPoint2.x - layerX;
    double y2 = beginPoint2.y - layerY;
    double x3 = currentPoint1.x - layerX;
    double y3 = currentPoint1.y - layerY;
    double x4 = currentPoint2.x - layerX;
    double y4 = currentPoint2.y - layerY;

    // Solve the system:
    //   [a b t1, -b a t2, 0 0 1] * [x1, y1, 1] = [x3, y3, 1]
    //   [a b t1, -b a t2, 0 0 1] * [x2, y2, 1] = [x4, y4, 1]

    double D = (y1-y2)*(y1-y2) + (x1-x2)*(x1-x2);
    if (D < 0.1) {
        return CGAffineTransformMakeTranslation(x3-x1, y3-y1);
    }

    double a = (y1-y2)*(y3-y4) + (x1-x2)*(x3-x4);
    double b = (y1-y2)*(x3-x4) - (x1-x2)*(y3-y4);
    double tx = (y1*x2 - x1*y2)*(y4-y3) - (x1*x2 + y1*y2)*(x3+x4) +
        x3*(y2*y2 + x2*x2) + x4*(y1*y1 + x1*x1);
    double ty = (x1*x2 + y1*y2)*(-y4-y3) + (y1*x2 - x1*y2)*(x3-x4) +
        y3*(y2*y2 + x2*x2) + y4*(y1*y1 + x1*x1);

    return CGAffineTransformMake(a/D, -b/D, b/D, a/D, tx/D, ty/D);
}

// Cache where each touch started
- (void)cacheBeginPointForTouches:(NSSet *)touches
{
    for (UITouch *touch in touches) {
        CGPoint *point = (CGPoint *)
            CFDictionaryGetValue(touchBeginPoints, touch);
        if (point == NULL) {
            point = (CGPoint *)malloc(sizeof(CGPoint));
            CFDictionarySetValue(touchBeginPoints, touch, point);
        }
```

```
            *point = [touch locationInView:self.superview];
        }
    }

    // Clear out touches from the cache
    - (void)removeTouchesFromCache:(NSSet *)touches
    {
        for (UITouch *touch in touches) {
            CGPoint *point = (CGPoint *)
                CFDictionaryGetValue(touchBeginPoints, touch);
            if (point != NULL) {
                free((void *)CFDictionaryGetValue(touchBeginPoints,
                    touch));
                CFDictionaryRemoveValue(touchBeginPoints, touch);
            }
        }
    }

    // Limit zoom to a max and min value
    - (void) setConstrainedTransform: (CGAffineTransform) aTransform
    {
        self.transform = aTransform;
        CGAffineTransform concat;
        CGSize asize = self.frame.size;

        if (asize.width > MAXZOOM * originalSize.width)
        {
            concat = CGAffineTransformConcat(self.transform,
                CGAffineTransformMakeScale((MAXZOOM * originalSize.width /
                asize.width), 1.0f));
            self.transform = concat;
        }
        else if (asize.width < MINZOOM * originalSize.width)
        {
            concat = CGAffineTransformConcat(self.transform,
                CGAffineTransformMakeScale((MINZOOM * originalSize.width /
                asize.width), 1.0f));
            self.transform = concat;
        }
        if (asize.height > MAXZOOM * originalSize.height)
        {
            concat = CGAffineTransformConcat(self.transform,
                CGAffineTransformMakeScale(1.0f, (MAXZOOM *
                originalSize.height / asize.height)));
            self.transform = concat;
        }
```

```
    else if (asize.height < MINZOOM * originalSize.height)
    {
        concat = CGAffineTransformConcat(self.transform,
            CGAffineTransformMakeScale(1.0f, (MINZOOM *
            originalSize.height / asize.height)));
        self.transform = concat;
    }
}

// Apply touches to create transform
- (void)updateOriginalTransformForTouches:(NSSet *)touches
{
    if ([touches count] > 0) {
        CGAffineTransform incrementalTransform = [self
            incrementalTransformWithTouches:touches];
        [self setConstrainedTransform:
            CGAffineTransformConcat(originalTransform,
            incrementalTransform)];
        originalTransform = self.transform;
    }
}

// At start, store the touch begin points and set an original transform
- (void)touchesBegan:(NSSet *)touches withEvent:(UIEvent *)event
{
    [[self superview] bringSubviewToFront:self];
    NSMutableSet *currentTouches = [[[event touchesForView:self]
        mutableCopy] autorelease];
    [currentTouches minusSet:touches];
    if ([currentTouches count] > 0) {
        [self updateOriginalTransformForTouches:currentTouches];
        [self cacheBeginPointForTouches:currentTouches];
    }
    [self cacheBeginPointForTouches:touches];
}

// During movement, update the transform to match the touches
- (void)touchesMoved:(NSSet *)touches withEvent:(UIEvent *)event
{
    CGAffineTransform incrementalTransform = [self
        incrementalTransformWithTouches:[event touchesForView:self]];
    [self setConstrainedTransform:
        CGAffineTransformConcat(originalTransform,
        incrementalTransform)];
}
```

```
// Finish by removing touches, handling double-tap requests
- (void)touchesEnded:(NSSet *)touches withEvent:(UIEvent *)event
{
    [self updateOriginalTransformForTouches:[event
        touchesForView:self]];
    [self removeTouchesFromCache:touches];

    for (UITouch *touch in touches) {
        if (touch.tapCount >= 2) {
            [self.superview bringSubviewToFront:self];
        }
    }

    NSMutableSet *remainingTouches = [[[event touchesForView:self]
        mutableCopy] autorelease];
    [remainingTouches minusSet:touches];
    [self cacheBeginPointForTouches:remainingTouches];
}

// Redirect cancel to ended
- (void)touchesCancelled:(NSSet *)touches withEvent:(UIEvent *)event
{
    [self touchesEnded:touches withEvent:event];
}

- (void)dealloc {
    if (touchBeginPoints) CFRelease(touchBeginPoints);
    [super dealloc];
}
@end
```

Summary

UIViews provide the onscreen components your users see. Gestures give views the ability to interact with those users via the `UITouch` class. As this chapter has shown, even in their most basic form, touch-based interfaces offer easy-to-implement flexibility and power. You discovered how to move views around the screen and how to bound that movement. You read about testing touches to see whether views should or should not respond to them. Several recipes covered both persistence and undo support for direct manipulation interfaces. You saw how to "paint" on a view and how to process user touches to interpret and respond to gestures. Here's a collection of thoughts about the recipes in this chapter that you might want to ponder before moving on:

- Be concrete. The iPhone has a perfectly good touch screen. Why not let your users drag items around the screen with their fingers? It adds to the reality and the platform's interactive nature.
- Users typically have five fingers per hand. Don't limit yourself to a one-finger interface when it makes sense to expand your interaction into multitouch territory.
- A solid grounding in Quartz graphics and Core Animation will be your friend. Using `drawRect:`, you can build any kind of custom `UIView` presentation you'd like, including text, Bézier curves, scribbles, and so forth.
- Explore! This chapter only touched lightly on the ways you can use direct manipulation in your applications. Use this material as a jumping-off point to explore the full vocabulary of the `UITouch` class.

9

Building and Using Controls

The `UIControl` class provides the basis for many iPhone interactive elements, including buttons, text fields, sliders, and switches. These onscreen objects have more in common than their ancestor class. Controls all use similar layout and target-action approaches. This chapter introduces controls and their use. You discover how to build and customize controls in a variety of ways. From the prosaic to the obscure, this chapter introduces a range of control recipes you can reuse in your programs.

The UIControl Class

On the iPhone, controls refer to a library of prebuilt onscreen objects designed for user interaction. Controls include buttons and text fields, sliders and switches, along with other Apple-supplied objects. A control's role is to transform user interactions into callbacks. Users touch and manipulate controls and in doing so communicate with your application.

The `UIControl` class lies at the root of the control class tree. All controls define a visual interface and implement ways to dispatch messages when users interact with that interface. Controls send those messages using target-action. When you define a new onscreen control, you tell it who receives messages, what messages to send, and when to send those messages.

Kinds of Controls

The members of the `UIControl` family include buttons, segmented controls, switches, sliders, page controls, and text fields. Each of these controls can be found in Interface Builder's Object Library (Tools > Library > Objects) in the Inputs & Values section, as shown in Figure 9-1. Control objects correspond to Inputs. The label, progress indicator, and activity indicator represent the Values.

Control Events

Controls respond primarily to three kinds of events: those based on touch, those based on value, and those based on edits. Table 9-1 lists the full range of event types available to controls.

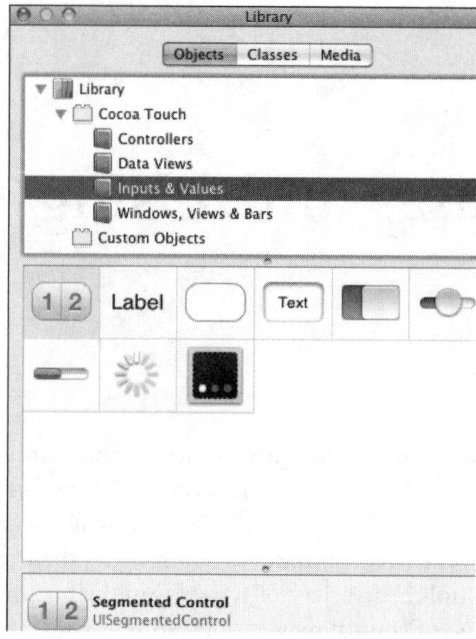

Figure 9-1 Interface Builder groups controls together in the Inputs & Values section of the Object Library.

Table 9-1 **UIControl** Event Types

Event	Type	Use
`UIControlEventTouchDown`	Touch	A touch down event anywhere within a control's bounds.
`UIControlEventTouchUpInside`	Touch	A touch up event anywhere within a control's bounds. This is the most common event type used for buttons.
`UIControlEventTouchUpOutside`	Touch	A touch up event that falls strictly outside a control's bounds.
`UIControlEventTouchDragEnter` `UIControlEventTouchDragExit`	Touch	Events corresponding to drags that cross into or out from the control's bounds.
`UIControlEventTouchDragInside` `UIControlEventTouchDragOutside`	Touch	Drag events limited to inside the control bounds or to just outside the control bounds.

Table 9-1 **Continued**

Event	Type	Use
UIControlEvent TouchDownRepeat	Touch	A repeated touch down event with a tapCount above 1, i.e., a double-tap.
UIControlEvent TouchCancel	Touch	A system event that cancels the current touch. See Chapter 8, "Gestures and Touches," for more details about touch phases and life cycles.
UIControlEvent AllTouchEvents	Touch	A mask that corresponds to all the touch events listed above, used to catch any touch event.
UIControlEvent ValueChanged	Value	A user-initiated event that changes the value of a control such as moving a slider's thumb or toggling a switch.
UIControlEvent EditingDidBegin UIControlEvent EditingDidEnd	Editing	Touches inside or outside a UITextField. A touch inside begins the editing session. A touch outside ends it.
UIControlEvent EditingChanged	Editing	An editing change to the contents of the UITextField contents.
UIControlEvent EditingDidEndOn Exit	Editing	An event that ends an editing session but not necessarily a touch outside its bounds.
UIControlEvent AllEditingEvents	Editing	A mask of all editing events.
UIControlEvent Application Reserved	Application	Application-specific event range (rarely if ever used).
UIControlEvent SystemReserved	System	System-specific event range (rarely if ever used).
UIControlEvent AllEvents	Touch, Value, Editing, Application, System	A mask of all touch, value, editing, application, and system events.

For the most part, Event types break down along the following lines. Buttons use touch events; the single `UIControlEventTouchUpInside` event accounts for nearly all button interaction. Value events (i.e., `UIControlEventValueChanged`) correspond to user-initiated adjustments to segmented controls, switches, sliders, and page controls. When users switch, slide, or tap those objects, the control value changes. `UITextField` objects trigger editing events. Users cause these events by tapping into (or out from) the text field, or by changing the text field contents.

As with all iPhone GUI elements, you can lay out controls in Interface Builder or build them directly in Xcode. This chapter discusses IB approaches but focuses more intently on code-based solutions. IB layout, once mastered, remains pretty much the same regardless of the item involved. You place an object into the interface, customize it with inspectors, and connect it to other IB objects.

Buttons

`UIButton` instances provide simple onscreen buttons. Users can tap them to trigger a callback via target-action programming. You specify how the button looks, what art it uses, and what text it displays.

The iPhone offers two ways to build buttons. You can use a precooked button type or build a custom button from scratch. The current iPhone SDK offers the following precooked types. As you can see, the buttons available are not general purpose. They were added to the SDK primarily for Apple's convenience, not yours. Nonetheless, you can use these in your programs as needed. Figure 9-2 shows each button.

Figure 9-2 The iPhone SDK offers five precooked button types, which you can access in Interface Builder or build directly into your applications. From left to right, these are the Detail Disclosure button, the Info Light and Info Dark buttons, the Contact Add button, and the Rounded Rectangle.

- **Detail Disclosure**—This is the same round, blue circle with the chevron you see when you add a detail disclosure accessory to table cells. Detail disclosures are used in tables to lead to a screen that shows details about the currently selected cell.
- **Info Light and Info Dark**—These two buttons offer a small circled *i* like you see on a Macintosh's Dashboard widget and are meant to provide access to an information or settings screen. These are used in the Weather and Stocks application to flip the view from one side to the other.
- **Contact Add**—This round, blue circle has a white + in its center and can be seen in the Mail application for adding new recipients to a mail message.
- **Rounded Rectangle**—This button provides a simple onscreen rounded rectangle that surrounds the button text. In its default state it is not an especially attractive

button (that is, it's not very "Apple" looking), but it is simple to program and use in your applications.

To use a precooked button in code, allocate it, set its frame, and add a target. Don't worry about adding custom art or creating the overall look of the button. The SDK takes care of all that. For example, here's how to build a simple rounded rectangle button. Note that `buttonWithType:` returns an autoreleased object.

```
UIButton *button = [UIButton buttonWithType:UIButtonTypeRoundedRect];
[button setFrame:CGRectMake(0.0f, 0.0f, 80.0f, 30.0f)];
[button setCenter:CGPointMake(160.0f, 208.0f)];
[button setTitle:@"Beep" forState:UIControlStateNormal];
[button addTarget:self action:@selector(playSound)
     forControlEvents:UIControlEventTouchUpInside];
[contentView addSubview:button];
```

To build one of the other standard button types, omit the title line. Rounded rectangles is the only precooked button type that uses a title.

Most buttons use the "touch up inside" trigger, where the user touch ends inside the button's bounds. iPhone UI standards allow users to cancel button presses by pulling their fingers off a button before releasing the finger from the screen. The `UIControlEventTouchUpInside` event choice mirrors that standard.

When using a precooked button, you *must* conform to Apple's Human Interface Guidelines on how those buttons can be used. Adding a detail disclosure, for example, to lead to an information page can get your application rejected from the App Store. It might seem a proper extrapolation of the button's role, but if it does not meet the exact wording of how Apple expects the button to be used, it may not pass review. To avoid potential issues, you may want to use rounded rectangle and custom buttons wherever possible.

Adding Buttons in Interface Builder

Buttons appear in the Interface Builder library as Rounded Rect Button objects. To use them, drag them into your interface. You can then change them to another button type via the Attribute Inspector (Command-1). A button-type pop-up appears at the top of the inspector, as shown in Figure 9-3. Use this pop-up menu to select the button type.

If your button uses text (such as the word "Button" in Figure 9-2), you can enter that text in the Title field. The Image and Background pull-downs let you choose a primary and background image for the button.

Each button provides four configuration settings, which can be seen in Figure 9-3 (right). The four button states are default (the button in its normal state), highlighted (when a user is currently touching the button), selected (an "on" version of the button for buttons that support toggled states), and disabled (when the button is unavailable for user interaction).

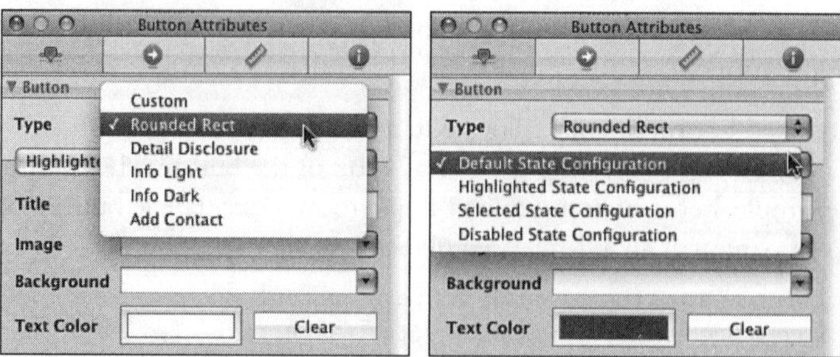

Figure 9-3 Choose your button type from the Type pop-up in the attributes inspector (left). Changes in the Button section apply to the current configuration (right).

Changes in the Button Attributes > Button > Configuration section (i.e., the darkened rectangle below the configuration pop-up) apply to the currently selected configuration. You might, for example, use a different button text color for a button in its default state versus its disabled state.

To preview each state, locate the three check boxes in Button Attributes > Control > Content. The Highlighted, Selected, and Enabled options let you set the button state. After previewing, and before you compile, make sure you returned the button to the actual state it needs to be in when you first run the application.

Art

Apart from the precooked button types (disclosure, info, and add contact), you'll likely want to create buttons using custom art. Figure 9-4 shows a variety of buttons built around the Rounded Rect and Custom button classes.

Figure 9-4 shows that when working with Rounded Rect buttons, you are not limited to just text (Button A). You can add an image along with text (Button B), use an image instead of text (Button F), or even replace the background rounded rectangle style with custom art (Button E), although this latter case does not make a lot of sense in the day-to-day design process.

Custom buttons have no built-in look. You can make buttons with any size you like (Buttons C and G) and add text (Button D) using the attributes inspector. What Figure 9-4 does not show is that these three buttons also represent other custom design decisions.

Button D uses the same art from Button B. Being a custom button, its text is centered and not displayed on a rounded backsplash. Beyond that, there's no big difference between the B layout and the D layout. The button relies on the default highlighting provided by Interface Builder and the `UIButton` class.

Button C represents a button created for highlighting on touch. Its relatively small size allows it to work with Button Attributes > Button > Shows Touch On Highlight. When touched, the button reveals a glowing halo. This halo is approximately 55-by-55 pixels in size. Buttons larger than about 40-by-40 pixels cannot effectively use this visual pop.

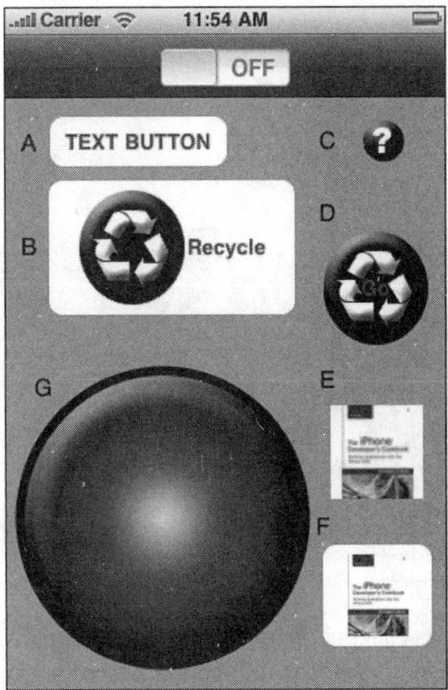

Figure 9-4 These examples show a variety of custom art options for both Rounded Rect Buttons and Custom Buttons.

What can't be seen in this static screenshot is that Button G was built to display an alternate image when pushed. Setting a second image in Button Attributes > Button > Highlighted State Configuration lets a button change its look on touch. For Button G, that image shows the same button but pushed into an indented position.

Connecting Buttons to Actions

When you Control-drag (right-drag) from a button to an IB object like the File's Owner view controller, IB presents a pop-up menu of actions to choose from. These actions are polled from the target object's available IBActions. Connecting to an action creates a target-action pair for the button's touch up inside event.

Alternatively, as Figure 9-5 shows, you can Control-click (right-click) the button, scroll down to Touch Up Inside, and drag from the unfilled dot to the target you want to connect to. The same pop-up menu appears with its list of available actions. Select the one you want to use to finish defining the target-action callback.

Buttons That Are Not Buttons

In Interface Builder, you also encounter buttons that look like views and act like views but are not, in fact, views. Bar button items (`UIBarButtonItem`) store the properties of toolbar and navigation bar buttons but are not buttons themselves. See Chapter 5, "Working with View Controllers," for more information about using bar button items.

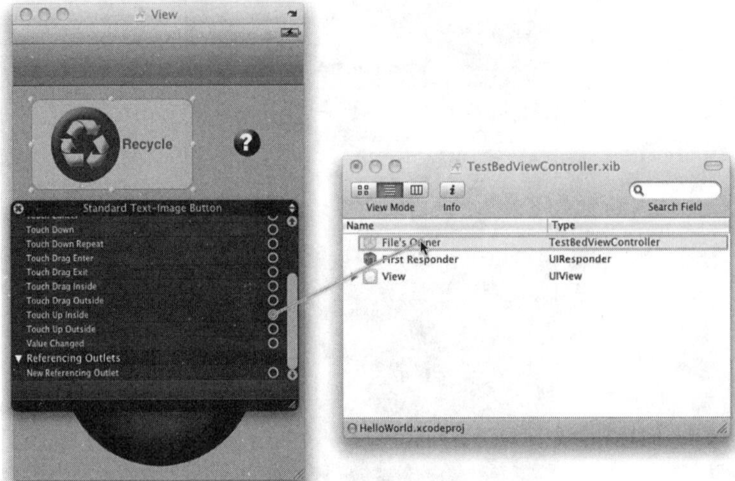

Figure 9-5 Control-clicking (right-clicking) a UIControl in Interface Builder reveals a table of events that you can connect to a target. Available actions appear in a pop-up menu after dragging out the connection.

Building Custom Buttons in Xcode

When using the `UIButtonTypeCustom` style, you supply all button art. The number of images depends on how you want the button to work. For a simple pushbutton, you might add a single background image and vary the label color to highlight when the button is pushed. For a toggle-style button, you might use four images: for the "off" state in a normal presentation, the "off" state when highlighted (that is, pressed), and two more for the "on" state. You choose and design the interaction details.

Recipe 9-1 builds a button that toggles on and off, demonstrating the detail that goes into building custom buttons. When tapped, the button switches its art from green (on) to red (off), or from red to green. This allows your (noncolorblind) users to instantly identify a current state. The displayed text reinforces the state setting. Figure 9-6 (left) shows the button created by this recipe.

The `UIImage` stretchable image calls in this recipe play an important role in button creation. Stretchable images enable you to create buttons of arbitrary width, turning circular art into lozenge-shaped buttons. You specify the caps at either end (that is, the art that should not be stretched). In this case, the cap is 110 pixels wide. If you were to change the button width from the 300 pixels used in this recipe to 220, the button loses the middle stretch, as shown in Figure 9-6 (right).

Figure 9-6 Use **UIImage** stretching to resize art for arbitrary button widths. Set the left cap width to specify where the stretching can take place.

> **Note**
>
> The `UIView contentStretch` property provides view-specific stretching. The rectangle stored in the property defines the portion of the view that can be stretched. The rectangle values are normalized between 0.0 and 1.0, so to make only the middle portion of a view stretchable, you might set that rectangle to (0.25, 0.25, 0.5, 0.5). Using a `contentStretch` property lets a view maintain the kind of crisp borders seen in Figure 9-6.

Recipe 9-1 **Building a UIButton That Toggles On and Off**

```
- (void) toggleButton: (UIButton *) button
{
    if (isOn = !isOn)
    {
        [button setTitle:@"On" forState:UIControlStateNormal];
        [button setTitle:@"On" forState:UIControlStateHighlighted];
        [button setBackgroundImage:baseGreen
            forState:UIControlStateNormal];
        [button setBackgroundImage:altGreen
            forState:UIControlStateHighlighted];
    }
    else
    {
        [button setTitle:@"Off" forState:UIControlStateNormal];
        [button setTitle:@"Off" forState:UIControlStateHighlighted];
```

```
        [button setBackgroundImage:baseRed
            forState:UIControlStateNormal];
        [button setBackgroundImage:altRed
            forState:UIControlStateHighlighted];
    }
}


- (void) viewDidLoad
{
    self.title = @"Toggle Button";

    baseGreen = [[[UIImage imageNamed:@"green.png"]
        stretchableImageWithLeftCapWidth:110.0f topCapHeight:0.0f]
        retain];
    baseRed = [[[UIImage imageNamed:@"red.png"]
        stretchableImageWithLeftCapWidth:110.0f topCapHeight:0.0f]
        retain];
    altGreen = [[[UIImage imageNamed:@"green2.png"]
        stretchableImageWithLeftCapWidth:110.0f topCapHeight:0.0f]
        retain];
    altGreen = [[[UIImage imageNamed:@"red2.png"]
        stretchableImageWithLeftCapWidth:110.0f topCapHeight:0.0f]
        retain];

    // Create a button sized to our art
    UIButton *button = [UIButton buttonWithType:UIButtonTypeCustom];
    button.frame = CGRectMake(0.0f, 0.0f, 300.0f, 233.0f);
    button.center = CGPointMake(160.0f, 140.0f);

    // Set up the button alignment properties
    button.contentVerticalAlignment =
        UIControlContentVerticalAlignmentCenter;
    button.contentHorizontalAlignment =
        UIControlContentHorizontalAlignmentCenter;

    // Set the font and color
    [button setTitleColor:[UIColor whiteColor]
        forState:UIControlStateNormal];
    [button setTitleColor:[UIColor lightGrayColor]
        forState:UIControlStateHighlighted];
    button.titleLabel.font = [UIFont boldSystemFontOfSize:24.0f];

    // Add action
    [button addTarget:self action:@selector(toggleButton)
        forControlEvents: UIControlEventTouchUpInside];
```

```
    // For tracking the two states
    isOn = NO;
    [self toggleButton:button];

    // Place the button into the view. The button is autoreleased.
    [self.view addSubview:button];
}
```

> **Get This Recipe's Code**
>
> To get the code used for this recipe, go to http://github.com/erica/iphone-3.0-cookbook-, or if you've downloaded the disk image containing all of the sample code from the book, go to the folder for Chapter 9 and open the project for this recipe.

Multiline Button Text

New to the 3.0 SDK, UIButtons now offer access to their title label via the `titleLabel` property. By exposing this property, the SDK allows you to modify the title attributes directly, including its font and line break mode. Here, the font is set to a very large value (basically ensuring that the text needs to wrap to display correctly) and used with word wrap and centered alignment.

```
button.titleLabel.font = [UIFont boldSystemFontOfSize:36.0f];
[button setTitle:@"Lorem Ipsum Dolor Sit" forState:
    UIControlStateNormal];
button.titleLabel.textAlignment = UITextAlignmentCenter;
button.titleLabel.lineBreakMode = UILineBreakModeWordWrap;
```

Be aware that the default label stretches from one end of your button to the other. This means that text may extend farther out than you might otherwise want, possibly beyond the edges of your button art. To fix this problem, you can force carriage returns in word wrap mode by embedding new line literals (i.e., \n) into the text. This allows you to control how much text appears on each line of the button title.

Adding Animated Elements to Buttons

When working with buttons, you can creatively layer art in front of or behind them. Use the standard `UIView` hierarchy to do this, making sure to disable user interaction for any view that might otherwise obscure your button (`setUserInteractionEnabled:NO`). Figure 9-7 shows what happens when you combine semitranslucent button art with an animated UIImageView behind it. The image view contents "leak" through to the viewer, enabling you to add live animation elements to the button.

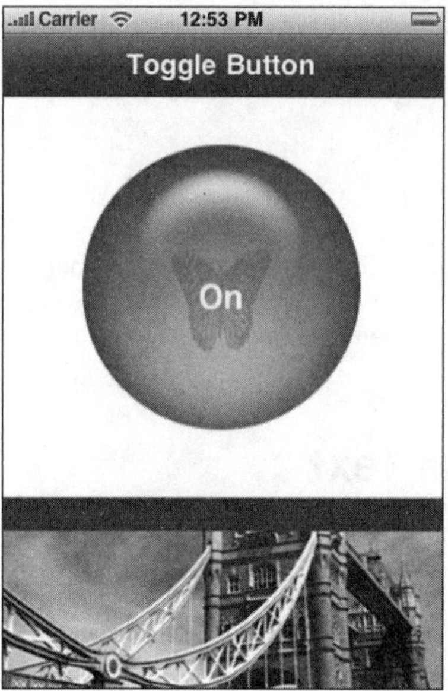

Figure 9-7 Combine semitranslucent button art with animated UIImageViews to build eye-catching UI elements. In this concept, the butterfly flaps "within" the button.

Recipe: Animating Button Responses

There's more to UIControl instances than frames and target-action. All controls inherit from the UIView class. This means you can use UIView animation blocks when working with controls just as you would with standard views. Recipe 9-2 builds a toggle switch that flips around using UIViewAnimationTransitionFlipFromLeft to spin the button while changing states.

Unlike Recipe 9-1, this code doesn't switch art. Instead, it switches buttons. There are two: an on button and an off button, both of which rest on a clear UIView backdrop. Giving the two buttons a see-through parent enables you to apply the flip to just those buttons without involving the rest of the user interface. Skip the clear background, and you end up spinning the entire window—not a good UI choice.

As this recipe uses the same semitranslucent art as the previous recipes, it's important that only one button appears onscreen at any time. To make this happen, the current button hides (sets its alpha value to 0.0) while in the animation block. The button with the opposite state takes its place. Figure 9-8 shows the flipping button in midflip.

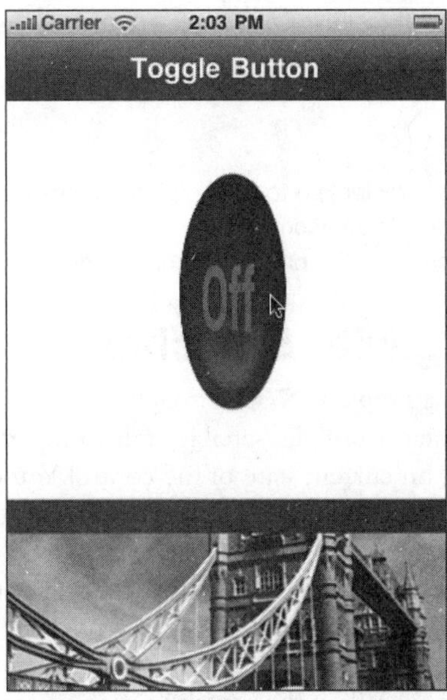

Figure 9-8 Use **UIView** animation blocks to flip between control states. Here, a button twirls around to move between Off and On.

Recipe 9-2 **Adding `UIView` Animation Blocks to Controls**

```
- (IBAction) flip: (UIButton *) button
{
    // Hide the view that's going away
    [self.view viewWithTag:BUTTON1].alpha = 1.0f;
    [self.view viewWithTag:BUTTON2].alpha = 1.0f;
    [button setAlpha:0.0f];

    // Decide which animation to use
    UIViewAnimationTransition trans;
    trans = (button.tag == BUTTON1) ?
        UIViewAnimationTransitionFlipFromLeft :
        UIViewAnimationTransitionFlipFromRight;

    // Animate the flip
    [UIView beginAnimations:nil context:NULL];
    [UIView setAnimationDuration:1.0f];
    [UIView setAnimationTransition:trans forView:[self.view
        viewWithTag:CLEARVIEW] cache:YES];
    [[self.view viewWithTag:CLEARVIEW] exchangeSubviewAtIndex:0
        withSubviewAtIndex:1];
```

```
    [UIView commitAnimations];
}
```

Get This Recipe's Code

To get the code used for this recipe, go to http://github.com/erica/iphone-3.0-cookbook-, or if you've downloaded the disk image containing all of the sample code from the book, go to the folder for Chapter 9 and open the project for this recipe.

Recipe: Working with Switches

The `UISwitch` object offers a simple ON/OFF toggle that lets users choose a Boolean value. The switch object contains a single (settable) value property, called `on`. This returns either `YES` or `NO`, depending on current state of the control. You can programmatically update a switch's value by changing the property value directly or calling `setOn:animated:`, which offers a way to animate the change.

Interface Builder offers relatively few options for working with switches. You can enable it and set its initial value, but beyond that there's not much to customize. Switches produce a value-changed event when a user adjusts them. Recipe 9-3 uses that behavior to trigger an `IBAction` callback. When the switch updates, it enables or disables an associated button.

As with all IB work, make sure you've defined your outlets and actions in the Library > Classes pane before you make your connections. The switch should trigger on Value Changed and send the `doSwitch:` action to the File's Owner, that is, the main view controller. The controller then sets the enabled property for the button. Unfortunately, you cannot connect the switch directly to the button inside IB to tie the switch value to the button's enabled property. If you are a longtime IB user, you will recall that there was a time when such connections were allowed.

This recipe builds on the modal animations introduced in Chapter 6, "Assembling Views and Animations," and the control animation shown in Recipe 9-2. When the switch activates, it calls one or more animation requests that transform the button into its active or inactive state.

Note

Do not name `UISwitch` instances as `switch`. Recall that `switch` is a reserved C word; it is used for conditional statements. This simple oversight has tripped up many iPhone developers.

Recipe 9-3 **Using a Switch State to Enable/Disable a Guarded Button**

```
@implementation TestBedViewController
- (void) expand: (NSNumber *) aFactor
{
    // Cause the button to zoom to the given factor
    dangerButton.transform =
```

```
        CGAffineTransformMakeScale(aFactor.intValue, aFactor.intValue);
}

- (void) rotate
{
    // Rotate the button by 90 degrees
    dangerButton.transform =
        CGAffineTransformRotate(dangerButton.transform, M_PI_2);
}

- (void) updateAlpha: (NSNumber *) level
{
    // Set the button's transparency to the given level
    dangerButton.alpha = level.floatValue;
}

- (IBAction) doSwitch: (UISwitch *) aSwitch
{
    dangerButton.enabled = aSwitch.isOn;

    // Adjust button alpha level to match the enabled/disabled state
    NSNumber *aLevel = NUMBER((dangerButton.enabled) ? 1.0f : 0.25f);
    [UIView modalAnimationWithTarget:self
        selector:@selector(updateAlpha)
        object:aLevel duration:0.3f];
    dangerButton.transform = CGAffineTransformIdentity;

    if (!dangerButton.enabled) return;

    // When the switch enables the button, add a little animation to
    // introduce the change
    [UIView modalAnimationWithTarget:self
        selector:@selector(expand)
        object:NUMBER(2.0f) duration:0.3f];
    [UIView modalAnimationWithTarget:self
        selector:@selector(expand)
        object:NUMBER(1.0f) duration:0.3f];
    for (int i = 0; i < 4; i++)
        [UIView modalAnimationWithTarget:self
            selector:@selector(rotate)
            object:nil duration:0.3f];
}

- (void) boom
{
    // Display a "Boom" alert, as the consequence of tapping
    // the danger button
```

```
    UIAlertView *av = [[[UIAlertView alloc] initWithTitle:@"Boom"
        message:nil delegate:nil
        cancelButtonTitle:@"OK"otherButtonTitlesnil] autorelease];
    [av show];
}

- (void) viewDidLoad
{
    // Initialize the danger button as semi-transparent
    dangerButton.alpha = 0.25f;
    [dangerButton addTarget:self action:@selector(boom)
        forControlEvents:UIControlEventTouchUpInside];
}
@end
```

Get This Recipe's Code

To get the code used for this recipe, go to http://github.com/erica/iphone-3.0-cookbook-, or if you've downloaded the disk image containing all of the sample code from the book, go to the folder for Chapter 9 and open the project for this recipe.

Recipe: Adding Custom Slider Thumbs

`UISlider` instances provide a control allowing users to choose a value by sliding a knob (called its "thumb") between its left and right extent. You'll have seen UISliders in the iPod/Music application, where the class is used to control volume.

Slider values default to 0.0 for the minimum and 1.0 for the maximum, although you can easily customize this in the Interface Builder attributes inspector or by setting the `minimumValue` and `maximumValue` properties. If you want to stylize the ends of the control, you can add in a related pair of images (`minimumValueImage` and `maximumValueImage`) that reinforce those settings. For example, you might show a snowman on one end and a steaming cup of tea on the other for a slider that controls temperature settings.

The slider's `continuous` property controls whether a slider continually sends value updates as a user drags the thumb. When set to `NO` (the default is `YES`), the slider only sends an action event when the user releases the thumb.

Customizing UISlider

In addition to setting minimum and maximum images, the `UISlider` class lets you directly update its thumb component. You can set a thumb to whatever image you like by calling `setThumbImage:forState:`. Recipe 9-4 takes advantage of this option to dynamically build thumb images on the fly, as shown in Figure 9-9. The indicator bubble appears above the user's finger as part of the custom-built thumb. This bubble provides instant feedback both textually (the number inside the bubble) and graphically (the shade of the bubble reflects the slider value, moving from black to white as the user drags).

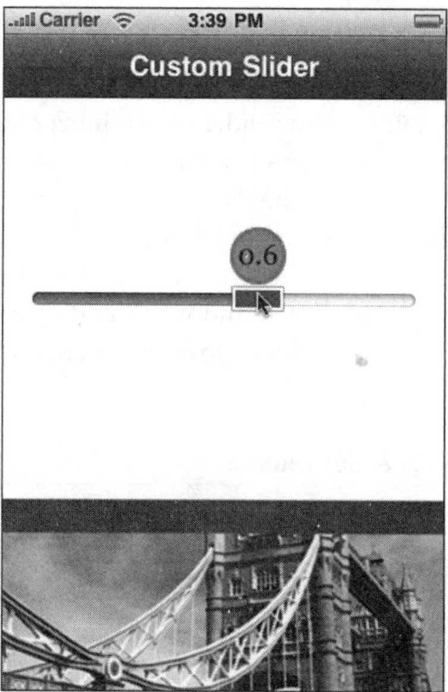

Figure 9-9 Core Graphics/Quartz calls enable this slider's thumb image to dim or brighten based on the current slider value. The text inside the thumb bubbles mirrors that value.

This kind of dynamically built feedback could be based on any kind of data. You might grab values from onboard sensors or make calls out to the Internet just as easily as you use the user's finger movement with a slider. No matter what live update scheme you use, dynamic updates are certainly graphics intensive—but it's not as expensive as you might fear. The Core Graphics calls are fast, and the memory requirements for the thumb-sized images are minimal.

This particular recipe assigns two thumb images to the slider. The bubble appears only when the slider is in use, for its `UIControlStateHighlighted`. In its normal state, namely `UIControlStateNormal`, only the smaller rectangular thumb appears. Users can tap on the thumb to review the current setting. The context-specific feedback bubble mimics the letter highlights on the standard iPhone keyboard.

To accommodate these changes in art, the slider updates its frame at the start and end of each gesture. On being touched (`UIControlEventTouchDown`), the frame expands by sixty pixels in height to the `thumbFrame`. This extra space provides enough room to show the expanded thumb during interaction.

When the finger is removed from the screen (`UIControlEventTouchUpInside` or `UIControlEventTouchUpOutside`), the slider returns to its previous dimensions, the `baseFrame`. This restores space to other onscreen objects, ensuring that the slider will not activate unless a user directly touches it.

Adding Efficiency

This recipe stores a previous value for the slider to minimize the overall computational burden on the iPhone. It updates the thumb with a new custom image when the slider has changed by at least 0.1, or 10% in value. You can omit this check, if you want, and run the recipe with full live updating. When tested, this provided reasonably fast updates, even on a first generation iPod touch unit. It also avoids any issues at the ends of the slider, namely when the thumb gets caught at 0.9 and won't update properly to 1.0. In this recipe, a hard-coded workaround for values above 0.98 handles that particular situation by forcing updates.

Recipe 9-4 **Building Dynamic Slider Thumbs**

```
@implementation TestBedViewController

// Draw centered text into the context
void centerText(CGContextRef context,
    NSString *fontname, float textsize,
    NSString *text, CGPoint point, UIColor *color)
{
    CGContextSaveGState(context);
    CGContextSelectFont(context, [fontname UTF8String], textsize,
        kCGEncodingMacRoman);

    // Retrieve the text width without actually drawing anything
    CGContextSaveGState(context);
    CGContextSetTextDrawingMode(context, kCGTextInvisible);
    CGContextShowTextAtPoint(context, 0.0f, 0.0f, [text UTF8String],
        text.length);
    CGPoint endpoint = CGContextGetTextPosition(context);
    CGContextRestoreGState(context);

    // Query for size to recover height. Width is less reliable
    CGSize stringSize = [text sizeWithFont:[UIFont
        fontWithName:fontname size:textsize]];

    // Draw the text
    [color setFill];
    CGContextSetShouldAntialias(context, true);
    CGContextSetTextDrawingMode(context, kCGTextFill);
    CGContextSetTextMatrix (context, CGAffineTransformMake(1, 0, 0, -1,
        0, 0));
```

```
    CGContextShowTextAtPoint(context, point.x - endpoint.x / 2.0f,
        point.y + stringSize.height / 4.0f, [text UTF8String],
        text.length);
    CGContextRestoreGState(context);
}

// Create a thumb image using a grayscale/numeric level
- (UIImage *) createImageWithLevel: (float) aLevel
{
    UIGraphicsBeginImageContext(CGSizeMake(40.0f, 100.0f));
    CGContextRef context = UIGraphicsGetCurrentContext();

    float INSET_AMT = 1.5f;

    // Create a filled rect for the thumb
    [[UIColor darkGrayColor] setFill];
    CGContextAddRect(context, CGRectMake(INSET_AMT, 40.0f + INSET_AMT,
        40.0f - 2.0f * INSET_AMT, 20.0f - 2.0f * INSET_AMT));
    CGContextFillPath(context);

    // Outline the thumb
    [[UIColor whiteColor] setStroke];
    CGContextSetLineWidth(context, 2.0f);
    CGContextAddRect(context, CGRectMake(2.0f * INSET_AMT,
        40.0f + 2.0f * INSET_AMT, 40.0f - 4.0f * INSET_AMT,
        20.0f - 4.0f * INSET_AMT));
    CGContextStrokePath(context);

    // Create a filled ellipse for the indicator
    [[UIColor colorWithWhite:aLevel alpha:1.0f] setFill];
    CGContextAddEllipseInRect(context, CGRectMake(0.0f, 0.0f, 40.0f,
        40.0f));
    CGContextFillPath(context);

    // Label with a number
    NSString *numstring = [NSString stringWithFormat:@"%0.1f", aLevel];
    UIColor *textColor = (aLevel > 0.5f) ? [UIColor blackColor] :
        [UIColor whiteColor];
    centerText(context, @"Georgia", 20.0f, numstring,
        CGPointMake(20.0f, 20.0f), textColor);

    // Outline the indicator circle
    [[UIColor grayColor] setStroke];
    CGContextSetLineWidth(context, 3.0f);
    CGContextAddEllipseInRect(context, CGRectMake(INSET_AMT, INSET_AMT,
        40.0f - 2.0f * INSET_AMT, 40.0f - 2.0f * INSET_AMT));
    CGContextStrokePath(context);
```

```
    // Build and return the image
    UIImage *theImage = UIGraphicsGetImageFromCurrentImageContext();
    UIGraphicsEndImageContext();
    return theImage;
}

// Return a base thumb image without the bubble
UIImage *createSimpleThumb()
{
    float INSET_AMT = 1.5f;
    UIGraphicsBeginImageContext(CGSizeMake(40.0f, 100.0f));
    CGContextRef context = UIGraphicsGetCurrentContext();

    // Create a filled rect for the thumb
    [[UIColor darkGrayColor] setFill];
    CGContextAddRect(context, CGRectMake(INSET_AMT, 40.0f + INSET_AMT,
        40.0f - 2.0f * INSET_AMT, 20.0f - 2.0f * INSET_AMT));
    CGContextFillPath(context);

    // Outline the thumb
    [[UIColor whiteColor] setStroke];
    CGContextSetLineWidth(context, 2.0f);
    CGContextAddRect(context, CGRectMake(2.0f * INSET_AMT,
        40.0f + 2.0f * INSET_AMT, 40.0f - 4.0f * INSET_AMT,
        20.0f - 4.0f * INSET_AMT));
    CGContextStrokePath(context);

    UIImage *theImage = UIGraphicsGetImageFromCurrentImageContext();
    UIGraphicsEndImageContext();
    return theImage;
}

// Update the thumb images as needed
- (void) updateThumb: (UISlider *) aSlider
{
    // Only update the thumb when registering significant changes
    if ((aSlider.value < 0.98) &&
        (ABS(aSlider.value - previousValue) < 0.1f)) return;

    // create a new custom thumb image and use for highlighted state
    UIImage *customimg = [self createImageWithLevel:aSlider.value];
    [aSlider setThumbImage: simpleThumbImage forState:
        UIControlStateNormal];
    [aSlider setThumbImage: customimg forState:
        UIControlStateHighlighted];
    previousValue = aSlider.value;
```

```
}

// Expand the slider to accommodate the bigger thumb
- (void) startDrag: (UISlider *) aSlider
{
    aSlider.frame = thumbFrame;
    aSlider.center = CGPointMake(160.0f, 140.0f);
}

// At release, shrink the frame back to normal
- (void) endDrag: (UISlider *) aSlider
{
    aSlider.frame = baseFrame;
    aSlider.center = CGPointMake(160.0f, 140.0f);
}

- (void) viewDidLoad
{
    self.title = @"Custom Slider";

    // Initialize slider settings
    previousValue = -99.0f;
    simpleThumbImage = [createSimpleThumb() retain];
    thumbFrame = CGRectMake(0.0f, 0.0f, 280.0f, 100.0f);
    baseFrame = CGRectMake(0.0f, 0.0f, 280.0f, 40.0f);

    // Create slider
    UISlider *slider = [[UISlider alloc] initWithFrame:baseFrame];
    slider.center = CGPointMake(160.0f, 140.0f);
    slider.value = 0.0f;

    // Create the callbacks for touch, move, and release
    [slider addTarget:self action:@selector(startDrag)
        forControlEvents:UIControlEventTouchDown];
    [slider addTarget:self action:@selector(updateThumb)
        forControlEvents:UIControlEventValueChanged];
    [slider addTarget:self action:@selector(endDrag)
        forControlEvents:UIControlEventTouchUpInside |
        UIControlEventTouchUpOutside];

    // Present the slider
    [self.view addSubview:slider];
    [self performSelector:@selector(updateThumb) withObject:slider
        afterDelay:0.1f];
}
@end
```

Get This Recipe's Code

To get the code used for this recipe, go to http://github.com/erica/iphone-3.0-cookbook-, or if you've downloaded the disk image containing all of the sample code from the book, go to the folder for Chapter 9 and open the project for this recipe.

Recipe: Creating a Twice-Tappable Segmented Control

The `UISegmentedControl` class presents a multiple button interface, where users can choose one choice out of a group. The control provides two styles of use. In its normal radio-button style mode, a button once selected remains selected. Users can tap on other buttons, but they cannot generate a new event by re-tapping their existing choice. The alternative momentary style lets users tap on each button as many times as desired but stores no state about a currently selected item. It provides no highlights to indicate the most recent selection.

Recipe 9-5 builds a hybrid approach. It allows users to see their currently selected option and to reselect that choice if needed. This is not the way segmented controls normally work. There are times, though, that you want to generate a new result on reselection (as in momentary mode) while visually showing the most recent selection (as in radio button mode).

Unfortunately, "obvious" solutions to create this desired behavior don't work. You cannot add target-action pairs that detect `UIControlEventTouchUpInside`. `UIControlEventValueChanged` is the only control event generated by `UISegmentedControl` instances. (You can easily test this yourself by adding a target-action pair for touch events.)

Here is where subclassing comes in to play. It's relatively simple to create a new class based on `UISegmentedControl` that does respond to that second tap. Recipe 9-5 defines that class. Its code works by detecting when a touch has occurred, operating independently of the segmented control's internal touch handlers that are subclassed from `UIControl`.

Segment switches remain unaffected; they'll continue to update and switch back and forth as users tap them. Unlike the parent class, here touches on an already-touched segment continue to do something. In this case, they request that the object's delegate produce the `performSegmentAction` method.

Don't add target-action pairs to your segmented controllers the way you'd normally do. Since all touch down events are detected, target-actions for value-changed events would add a second callback and trigger twice whenever you switched segments. Instead, implement the delegate callback and let object delegation handle the updates.

Recipe 9-5 **Creating a Segmented Control Subclass That Responds to a Second Tap**

```
@class DoubleTapSegmentedControl;

@protocol DoubleTapSegmentedControlDelegate <NSObject>
- (void) performSegmentAction: (DoubleTapSegmentedControl *) aDTSC;
@end

@interface DoubleTapSegmentedControl : UISegmentedControl
{
    id <DoubleTapSegmentedControlDelegate> delegate;
}
@property (nonatomic, retain) id delegate;
@end

@implementation DoubleTapSegmentedControl
@synthesize delegate;

- (void) touchesBegan:(NSSet *)touches withEvent:(UIEvent *)event
{
    [super touchesBegan:touches withEvent:event];
    if (self.delegate)
        [self.delegate performSegmentAction:self];
}
@end
```

Get This Recipe's Code

To get the code used for this recipe, go to http://github.com/erica/iphone-3.0-cookbook-, or if you've downloaded the disk image containing all of the sample code from the book, go to the folder for Chapter 9 and open the project for this recipe.

Recipe: Subclassing UIControl

Apple provides several prebuilt controls that you can use directly in your applications. But you don't have to limit yourself to Apple-supplied items. Recipe 9-6 demonstrates how to subclass `UIControl` and build new controls. This example creates a touch wheel, like the ones used on older model iPods.

Touch wheels provide an infinitely scrollable input. Users can rotate their finger clockwise or counterclockwise, and the object's value increases or decreases accordingly. Each complete turn around the wheel, that is, a traversal of 360 degrees, corresponds to a value change of 1.0. Clockwise changes are positive; counterclockwise changes are negative. The value accumulates on each touch, although it can be reset; simply assign the control's `value` property back to 0.0. This property is not a standard part of `UIControl` instances even though many controls use values.

This recipe computes user changes by casting out vectors from the control's center. The code adds differences in the angle as the finger moves, updating the current value accordingly. For example, three spins around the touch wheel adds or subtracts 3 to the current value, depending on the direction of movement.

Tracking Touches

`UIControl` instances use an embedded method set to work with touches. These methods allow the control to track touches throughout their interaction with the control object:

- **`beginTrackingWithTouch:withEvent:`**—Gets called when a touch enters a control's bounds.
- **`continueTrackingWithTouch:withEvent:`**—Follows the touch with repeated calls as the touch remains within the control bounds.
- **`endTrackingWithTouch:withEvent:`**—Handles the last touch for the event.
- **`cancelTrackingWithEvent:`**—Manages a touch cancellation.

Add your custom control logic by implementing any or all of these methods in a `UIControl` subclass. Recipe 9-6 uses the begin and continue versions to locate the user touch and track it until the touch is lifted or otherwise leaves the control.

Dispatching Events

Controls use target-action pairs to communicate changes triggered by events. When you build a new control, you must decide what kind of events your object will generate and add code to trigger those events.

Add a dispatch message to your custom control by calling `sendActionsFor➥ControlEvents:`. This method lets you send an event, in this case `UIControlEvent➥ValueChanged` to the specified target. Controls transmit these updates by messaging the `UIApplication` singleton. As Apple notes, the application acts as the centralized dispatch point for all messages.

> **Note**
>
> The basic wheel defined in Recipe 9-6 tracks touch rotation but does little else. The original iPod scroll wheel offered five click points: in the center circle and at the four cardinal points of the wheel. Adding click support and the associated button-like event support (for `UIControlEventTouchUpInside`) are left as an exercise for the reader.

Recipe 9-6 **Building a Touch Wheel Control**

```
@implementation ScrollWheel
@synthesize value;
@synthesize theta;

- (id) initWithFrame: (CGRect) aFrame
{
    if (self = [super initWithFrame:aFrame])
    {
        // This control uses a fixed 200x200 sized frame
        self.frame = CGRectMake(0.0f, 0.0f, 200.0f, 200.0f);
```

```
        self.center = CGPointMake(CGRectGetMidX(aFrame),
            CGRectGetMidY(aFrame));

        // Add the touchwheel art
        UIImageView *iv = [[UIImageView alloc] initWithImage:[UIImage
            imageNamed:@"wheel.png"]];
        [self  addSubview:iv];
        [iv release];
    }

    return self;
}

- (id) init
{
    return [self initWithFrame:CGRectZero];
}

+ (id) scrollWheel
{
    return [[[self alloc] init] autorelease];
}

- (BOOL)beginTrackingWithTouch:(UITouch *)touch
        withEvent:(UIEvent *)event
{
    CGPoint p = [touch locationInView:self];
    CGPoint cp = CGPointMake(self.bounds.size.width / 2.0f,
        self.bounds.size.height / 2.0f);
    // self.value = 0.0f; // Uncomment for separate event values

    // First touch must touch the gray part of the wheel
    if (!pointInsideRadius(p, cp.x, cp)) return NO;
    if (pointInsideRadius(p, 30.0f, cp)) return NO;

    // Set the initial angle
    self.theta = getangle([touch locationInView:self], cp);
    return YES;
}

- (BOOL)continueTrackingWithTouch:(UITouch *)touch
        withEvent:(UIEvent *)event
{

    CGPoint p = [touch locationInView:self];
    CGPoint cp = CGPointMake(self.bounds.size.width / 2.0f,
        self.bounds.size.height / 2.0f);
```

```
    // falls outside too far, with boundary of 50 pixels.
    // Inside strokes treated as touched
    if (!pointInsideRadius(p, cp.x + 50.0f, cp)) return NO;

    float newtheta = getangle([touch locationInView:self], cp);
    float dtheta = newtheta - self.theta;

    // correct for edge conditions
    int ntimes = 0;
    while ((ABS(dtheta) > 300.0f)  && (ntimes++ < 4))
        if (dtheta > 0.0f) dtheta -= 360.0f; else dtheta += 360.0f;

    // Update current values
    self.value -= dtheta / 360.0f;
    self.theta = newtheta;

    // Send value changed alert
    [self sendActionsForControlEvents:UIControlEventValueChanged];

    return YES;
}
@end
```

Get This Recipe's Code

To get the code used for this recipe, go to http://github.com/erica/iphone-3.0-cookbook-, or if you've downloaded the disk image containing all of the sample code from the book, go to the folder for Chapter 9 and open the project for this recipe.

Recipe: Dismissing a UITextField Keyboard

The most commonly asked question about the `UITextField` control is, "How do I dismiss the keyboard?" There's no built-in way to automatically detect this. When users finish editing the contents of a `UITextField`, the keyboard should go away.

Fortunately, it takes little work to respond to the end of edits. By watching for the Return key, you can resign first-responder status. This moves the keyboard out of sight, as Recipe 9-7 shows. Here are a few key points about doing this:

- Optionally, set the Return key type to `UIReturnKeyDone`. You can do this in Interface Builder's Attribute Inspector or by assignment to the text field's `returnKeyType` property. Using a "Done"-style Return key tells the user how to finish editing. Figure 9-10 shows a keyboard using the Done key style.
- Be the delegate. You must set the text field's `delegate` property to your view controller in code. Interface Builder does not provide a way to make that assignment

graphically. Make sure your view controller implements the `UITextFieldDelegate` protocol.

- Implement `textFieldShouldReturn:`. This method catches all Return key presses—no matter how they are named. Use the method to resign first responder. This hides the keyboard until the user touches another text field or text view.

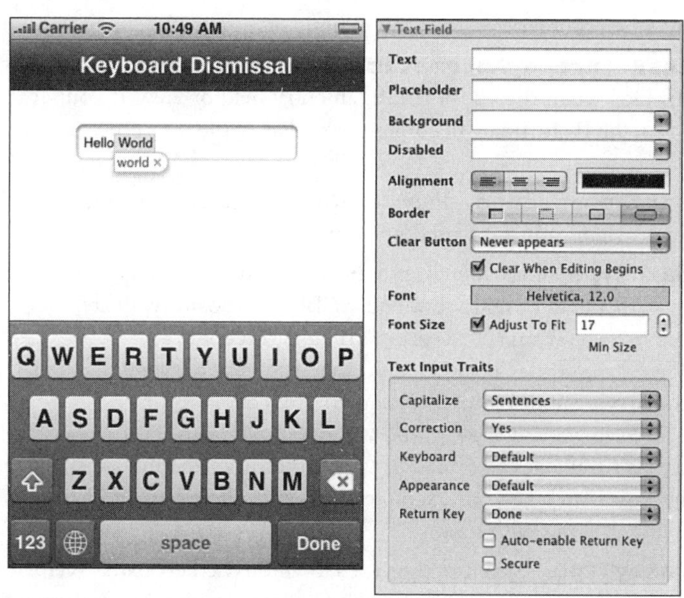

Figure 9-10 Setting the name of the Return key to Done (left) tells your user how to finish editing the field. Specify this directly in code or use Interface Builder's text field attributes inspector (right) to customize the way the text field looks and acts.

> **Note**
>
> You can also use `textFieldShouldReturn:` to perform an action when the Return key is pressed as well as dismissing the keyboard.

Your code needs to handle each of these points to create a smooth interaction process for your `UITextField` instances.

Text Trait Properties

Text fields implement the `UITextInputTraits` protocol. This protocol provides seven properties that you can set to define the way the field handles text input. Those traits are as follows:

- **`autocapitalizationType`**—Defines the text autocapitalization style. Available styles use sentence capitalization (`UITextAutocapitalizationTypeSentences`), word capitalization (`UITextAutocapitalizationTypeWords`), all caps (`UITextAutocapitalizationTypeAllCharacters`), and no capitalization (`UITextAutocapitalizationTypeNone`). Avoid capitalizing when working with account name entry. Use word capitalization for proper names and street address entry.

- **`autocorrectionType`**—Specifies whether the text is subject to the iPhone's autocorrect feature like the bubble shown in Figure 9-10. When enabled (set to `UITextAutocorrectionTypeYes`), the iPhone suggests replacement words to the user.
- **`enablesReturnKeyAutomatically`**—Helps control whether the Return key is disabled when there's no text in an entry field or view. If you set this property to `YES`, the Return key becomes enabled after the user types in at least one character.
- **`keyboardAppearance`**—Provides two keyboard presentation styles: the default style and a style meant to be used with an alert panel.
- **`keyboardType`**—Lets you choose the keyboard that first appears when a user interacts with a field or text view. The available keyboard types are `UIKeyboardTypeDefault`, `UIKeyboardTypeASCIICapable`, `UIKeyboardTypeNumbersAndPunctuation`, `UIKeyboardTypeURL`, `UIKeyboardTypeNumberPad`, `UIKeyboardTypePhonePad`, `UIKeyboardTypeNamePhonePad`, and `UIKeyboardTypeEmailAddress`. Each keyboard has its advantages and disadvantages in terms of the mix of characters it presents. The Email keyboard, for example, is meant to help enter addresses and includes the @ symbol, along with text.
- **`returnKeyType`**—Specifies the text shown on the keyboard's Return key. You can choose from the default ("Return"), Go, Google, Join, Next, Route, Search, Send, Yahoo, Done, and Emergency Call.
- **`secureTextEntry`**—Toggles a text hiding feature meant to provide more secure text entry. When enabled, you can see the last character typed, but all other characters are shown as a series of dots. Switch this feature for password text fields.

Other Text Field Properties

In addition to the standard text traits, text fields offer several other properties that control how the field is presented. The `placeholder` text is shown in light gray when the text field is empty, providing a user prompt. Use the placeholder to provide usage hints like "User Name" or "E-mail address."

Text fields allow you to control the type of `borderStyle` displayed around the text area. You can choose from a simple line, a bezel, and a rounded rectangle presentation. These are best seen in Interface Builder, where the attributes inspector lets you toggle between each style.

The text field clear button appears as an X in the right side of the entry area. Set the `clearButtonMode` to specify if and when this button appears: always, never, when editing, or unless editing is ongoing.

Recipe 9-7 **Using the Done Key to Dismiss a Text Field Keyboard**

```
@interface TestBedViewController : UIViewController <UITextFieldDelegate>
@end

@implementation TestBedViewController
- (BOOL)textFieldShouldReturn:(UITextField *)textField
{
    [textField resignFirstResponder];
    return YES;
}


- (void) viewDidLoad
{
    self.title = @"Keyboard Dismissal";

    // Customize text field from Interface Builder
    UITextField *tf = (UITextField *)[self.view viewWithTag:101];
    tf.delegate = self;

    // Create a text field by hand
    tf = [[UITextField alloc] initWithFrame:CGRectMake(0.0f, 0.0f,
        100.0f, 30.0f)];
    tf.center = CGPointMake(160.0f, 120.0f);
    tf.borderStyle = UITextBorderStyleRoundedRect;
    tf.autocorrectionType = UITextAutocorrectionTypeNo;
    tf.placeholder = @"Name";
    tf.returnKeyType = UIReturnKeyDone;
    tf.clearButtonMode = UITextFieldViewModeWhileEditing;
    tf.delegate = self;
    [self.view addSubview:tf];
    [tf release];
}
@end
```

Get This Recipe's Code

To get the code used for this recipe, go to http://github.com/erica/iphone-3.0-cookbook-, or if you've downloaded the disk image containing all of the sample code from the book, go to the folder for Chapter 9 and open the project for this recipe.

Recipe: Dismissing UITextView Keyboards

When dismissing keyboards, `UITextView` instances require a slightly different approach than `UITextField` ones. Users should be able to tap Return in the text view, adding carriage returns without dismissing the keyboard. Instead, add a Done button to the general interface when the text view becomes active, as shown in Figure 9-11. Use this key to resign first-responder status when the user finishes his or her edits.

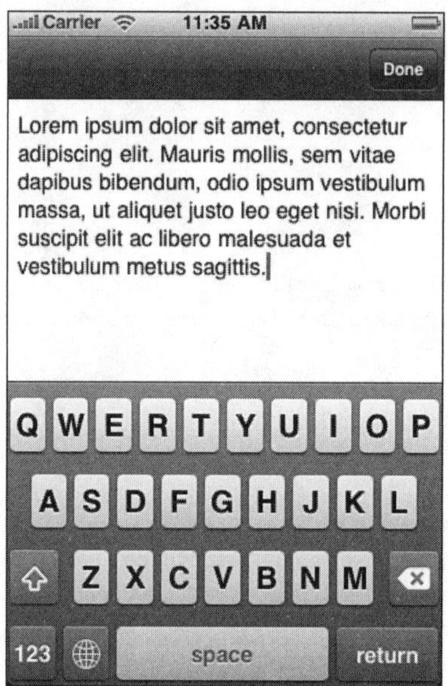

Figure 9-11 Add a Done key to the navigation bar when users start interacting with a text view. This offers users an obvious way to finish editing and dismiss the keyboard.

To sense text view activity, your view controller must implement the `UITextView` ➥`Delegate` protocol, and it must be set as the text view's delegate. The `textView` ➥`DidBeginEditing:` delegate method triggers whenever a user taps the view. Detecting this enables you to either add or enable the Done button. Users can then tap on Done after they've finished editing. The Done button offers an obvious way to finish editing and dismiss the keyboard.

Recipe 9-8 demonstrates how to add the navigation item button in the delegate method call and how to remove it when the user is done editing. Reveal the Done button when the view becomes active. Hide it when resigning the view's first-responder status.

Recipe 9-8 **Adding a Done Button to Active `UITextView` Sessions**

```
@interface TestBedViewController : UIViewController <UITextViewDelegate>
@end

@implementation TestBedViewController

// Reveal a Done button when editing starts
- (void) textViewDidBeginEditing: (UITextView *) textView
{
    self.navigationItem.rightBarButtonItem = BARBUTTON(@"Done",
        @selector(doneEditing));
}

// Remove the Done button and dismiss the keyboard
- (void) doneEditing: (id) sender
{
    [self.view resignFirstResponder];
    self.navigationItem.rightBarButtonItem = nil;
}


- (void) viewDidLoad
{
    [(UITextView *)self.view setDelegate:self];
    [(UITextView *)self.view setFont:[UIFont systemFontOfSize:16.0f]];
}
@end
```

> **Get This Recipe's Code**
>
> To get the code used for this recipe, go to http://github.com/erica/iphone-3.0-cookbook-, or if you've downloaded the disk image containing all of the sample code from the book, go to the folder for Chapter 9 and open the project for this recipe.

Recipe: Building a Better Text Editor

Recipe 9-8 showed how to catch user interactions within a text view. Recipe 9-9 expands upon this notion to add a number of critical features that make a better text editor. These features are easy to implement in your own programs.

First, the view controller adds undo support. Users can shake the iPhone to load the undo/redo editor that was first introduced in Chapter 8. `UITextView` objects ship in an undo-ready state. They provide built-in support that works hand-in-hand with select, cut, copy, and paste. The undo manager understands these actions, so possible user messages might include "Undo Paste," "Redo Cut," and so forth. All the view controller needs to do is instantiate an undo manager; it leaves the rest of the work to the built-in objects.

Second, the view uses persistence. It archives its contents to file in the `performArchive` method. The application delegate calls this method right before the application is due to quit.

```
- (void) applicationWillTerminate: (UIApplication *) application
{
    // update the defaults on quit by calling
    // the test bed view controller's archive method
    [self.tbvc performArchive];
}
```

On launch, any data in that file is read in to initialize the text view instance.

Finally, the text view automatically updates its size when the keyboard appears. This ensures that the keyboard does not hide any part of the text. That's especially important when you want to edit the end of a long text entry. By shrinking the text view so it appears fully above the keyboard, users can access every part of the text.

To make this happen, Recipe 9-9 listens for two standard notifications that are sent when the keyboard is about to show or hide. The code adds observers that can respond to the keyboard state and adjust the text view height to match the keyboard presentation.

Recipe 9-9 **Adding Undo Support, Persistence, and Autoresizing to Text Views**

```
@interface TestBedViewController : UIViewController <UITextViewDelegate>
{
    NSUndoManager *undoManager;
    IBOutlet UITextView *textView;
}
@property (retain) NSUndoManager *undoManager;
@end

@implementation TestBedViewController
@synthesize undoManager;

- (void) performArchive
{
    [[textView text] writeToFile:DATAPATH atomically:YES
        encoding:NSUTF8StringEncoding error:nil];
}

// Reveal a Done button when editing starts
- (void) textViewDidBeginEditing: (UITextView *) aTextView
{
    self.navigationItem.rightBarButtonItem = BARBUTTON(@"Done",
        @selector(doneEditing));
}

// Remove the Done button and dismiss the keyboard
- (void) doneEditing: (id) sender
{
    [textView resignFirstResponder];
    self.navigationItem.rightBarButtonItem = nil;
```

```
}

// Prepare to resize for keyboard. Courtesy of August Joki
- (void)keyboardWillShow:(NSNotification *)notification
{
    NSDictionary *userInfo = [notification userInfo];
    CGRect bounds;
    [(NSValue *)[userInfo objectForKey:UIKeyboardBoundsUserInfoKey]
        getValue:&bounds];

    // Resize text view
    CGRect aFrame = textView.frame;
    aFrame.size.height -= bounds.size.height;
    textView.frame = aFrame;
}

// Expand textview on keyboard dismissal.
- (void)keyboardWillHide:(NSNotification *)notification
{
    // Resize text view
    CGRect aFrame = CGRectMake(0.0f, 0.0f, 320.0f, 416.0f);
    textView.frame = aFrame;
}

- (void) viewDidLoad
{
    // Initialize text view
    textView.delegate = self;
    textView.font = [UIFont systemFontOfSize:16.0f];
    textView.text = [NSString stringWithContentsOfFile:DATAPATH];

    // Prepare undo manager
    [[UIApplication sharedApplication]
        setApplicationSupportsShakeToEdit:YES];
    self.undoManager = [[NSUndoManager alloc] init];
    [self.undoManager setLevelsOfUndo:99];
    [self.undoManager release];

    // Listen for keyboard
    [[NSNotificationCenter defaultCenter] addObserver:self
        selector:@selector(keyboardWillShow)
        name:UIKeyboardWillShowNotification object:nil];
    [[NSNotificationCenter defaultCenter] addObserver:self
        selector:@selector(keyboardWillHide)
        name:UIKeyboardWillHideNotification object:nil];
}
```

```
- (void) dealloc
{
    // Clean up
    [[NSNotificationCenter defaultCenter] removeObserver:self];
    self.undoManager = nil;
    [super dealloc];
}
@end
```

Get This Recipe's Code

To get the code used for this recipe, go to http://github.com/erica/iphone-3.0-cookbook-, or if you've downloaded the disk image containing all of the sample code from the book, go to the folder for Chapter 9 and open the project for this recipe.

Recipe: Text Entry Filtering

At times you want to ensure that a user enters only a certain subset of characters. For example, you might want to create a numeric-only text field that does not handle letters. Although you can use predicates to test the final entry against a regular expression (the `NSPredicate` class's `MATCH` operator supports regex values), for filtered data it's easier to check each new character as it's typed against a legal set.

A `UITextField` delegate can catch those characters as they are typed and decide whether to add the character to the active text field. The optional `textField:`
`➥shouldChangeCharactersInRange:replacementString:` delegate method returns either `YES`, allowing the newly typed character(s) or `NO`, disallowing it or them. In practice, this works on a character-by-character basis being called after each user keyboard tap. However, with 3.0's new pasteboard support, the replacement string could theoretically be longer when text is pasted to a text field.

Recipe 9-10 works by looking for any disallowed characters within the new string. When it finds them, it rejects the entry leaving the text field unedited. So a paste of mixed allowed and disallowed text would be rejected entirely.

This recipe considers four scenarios: alphabetic text entry only, numeric, numeric with an allowed decimal point, and a mix of alphanumeric characters. You can adapt this example to any set of legal characters you want.

The third entry type, numbers with a decimal point, uses a little trick to ensure that only one decimal point gets typed. Once it finds a period character in the associated text field, it switches the characters it accepts from a set with the period to a set without it. Yes, you can sneak your way around this using paste, although it's unlikely that users will resort to doing so.

Recipe 9-10 **Filtering User Text Entry**

```
#define ALPHA @"ABCDEFGHIJKLMNOPQRSTUVWXYZabcdefghijklmnopqrstuvwxyz "
#define NUMBERS @"0123456789"
#define ALPHANUM \
```

```
    @"ABCDEFGHIJKLMNOPQRSTUVWXYZabcdefghijklmnopqrstuvwxyz0123456789 "
#define NUMBERSPERIOD    @"0123456789."

@implementation TestBedViewController
- (BOOL)textField:(UITextField *)textField
        shouldChangeCharactersInRange:(NSRange)range
        replacementString:(NSString *)string
{
    NSCharacterSet *cs;

    switch (SEGMENT)
    {
        case 0:
            cs = [[NSCharacterSet characterSetWithCharactersInString:
                ALPHA] invertedSet];
            break;
        case 1:
            cs = [[NSCharacterSet characterSetWithCharactersInString:
                NUMBERS] invertedSet];
            break;
        case 2:
            cs = [[NSCharacterSet characterSetWithCharactersInString:
                NUMBERS] invertedSet];
            if ([textField.text rangeOfString:@"."].location ==
                NSNotFound)
                cs = [[NSCharacterSet
                    characterSetWithCharactersInString:NUMBERSPERIOD]
                    invertedSet];
            break;
        case 3:
            cs = [[NSCharacterSet characterSetWithCharactersInString:
                ALPHANUM] invertedSet];
            break;
        default:
            break;
    }

    NSString *filtered = [[string componentsSeparatedByCharactersInSet:
        cs] componentsJoinedByString:@""];
    BOOL basicTest = [string isEqualToString:filtered];
    return basicTest;
}

- (void) segmentChanged: (UISegmentedControl *) seg
{
    [(UITextField *)[self.view viewWithTag:101] setText:@""];
}
```

```
- (void) viewDidLoad
{
    // Text field defined in interface builder
    [(UITextField *)[self.view viewWithTag:101] setDelegate:self];

    // Add segmented control with entry options
    UISegmentedControl *seg = [[UISegmentedControl alloc]
        initWithItems:[@"ABC 123 2.3 A2C"
        componentsSeparatedByString:@" "]];
    seg.segmentedControlStyle = UISegmentedControlStyleBar;
    seg.selectedSegmentIndex = 0;
    [seg addTarget:self action:@selector(segmentChanged)
        forControlEvents:UIControlEventValueChanged];
    self.navigationItem.titleView = seg;
    [seg release];
}
@end
```

Get This Recipe's Code

To get the code used for this recipe, go to http://github.com/erica/iphone-3.0-cookbook-, or if you've downloaded the disk image containing all of the sample code from the book, go to the folder for Chapter 9 and open the project for this recipe.

Recipe: Adding a Page Indicator Control

The `UIPageControl` class provides a line of dots that indicates which item of a multipage view is currently displayed. The dots at the bottom of the SpringBoard home page present an example of this kind of control in action. Sadly, the `UIPageControl` class is a disappointment in action. The `UIPageControl` class is awkward to handle, hard to tap, and will generally annoy your users. So when using it, make sure you add alternative navigation options so that the page control acts more as an indicator and less as a control.

Figure 9-12 shows a page control with three pages. Taps to the left or right of the bright-colored current page indicator trigger `UIControlEventValueChanged` events, launching whatever method you set as the control's action. You can query the control for its new value by calling `currentPage` and set the available page count by adjusting the `numberOfPages` property. SpringBoard limits the number of dots representing pages to nine, but your application can use a higher number, particularly in landscape mode.

Recipe 9-11 uses a `UIScrollView` instance to display three pages of images. Users can scroll through the pictures using swipes, and the page indicator updates to reflect the current page shown. Similarly, users can tap on the page control and the scroller animates the selected page into place. This two-way relationship is built by adding a target-action callback to the page control and a delegate callback to the scroller. Each callback updates the other object, providing a tight coupling between the two.

Figure 9-12 The `UIPageControl` class offers an interactive indicator for multipage presentations. Taps to the left or right of the active dot enable users to select new pages. At least they do in theory. The page control is hard to tap, requires excessive user precision, and offers poor response performance.

Recipe 9-11 Using the `UIPageControl` Indicator

```
@implementation TestBedViewController
- (void) pageTurn: (UIPageControl *) aPageControl
{
    // Update the scroller to match the page turn
    int whichPage = aPageControl.currentPage;

    [UIView beginAnimations:nil context:NULL];
    [UIView setAnimationDuration:0.3f];
    [UIView setAnimationCurve:UIViewAnimationCurveEaseInOut];

    sv.contentOffset = CGPointMake(320.0f * whichPage, 0.0f);

    [UIView commitAnimations];
}

- (void) scrollViewDidScroll: (UIScrollView *) aScrollView
{
```

```
    // Update the page control to match the scroller
    CGPoint offset = aScrollView.contentOffset;
    pageControl.currentPage = offset.x / 320.0f;
}

- (void) viewDidLoad
{
    // Create the scroll view and set its content size and delegate
    sv = [[UIScrollView alloc] initWithFrame:
        CGRectMake(0.0f, 0.0f, 320.0f, BASEHEIGHT)];
    sv.contentSize = CGSizeMake(NPAGES * 320.0f, sv.frame.size.height);
    sv.pagingEnabled = YES;
    sv.delegate = self;
    [sv release];

    // Load in all the pages
    for (int i = 0; i < NPAGES; i++)
    {
        NSString *filename = [NSString stringWithFormat:
            @"image%d.png", i+1];
        UIImageView *iv = [[UIImageView alloc] initWithImage:[UIImage
            imageNamed:filename]];
        iv.frame = CGRectMake(i * 320.0f, 0.0f, 320.0f, BASEHEIGHT);
        [sv addSubview:iv];
        [iv release];
    }

    [self.view addSubview:sv];

    // Initialize the page control, which was added in IB
    pageControl.numberOfPages = 3;
    pageControl.currentPage = 0;
    [pageControl addTarget:self action:@selector(pageTurn)
        forControlEvents:UIControlEventValueChanged];
}
@end
```

Get This Recipe's Code

To get the code used for this recipe, go to http://github.com/erica/iphone-3.0-cookbook-, or if you've downloaded the disk image containing all of the sample code from the book, go to the folder for Chapter 9 and open the project for this recipe.

Recipe: Creating a Customizable Paged Scroller

Recipe 9-11 introduced a basic paged scroller but didn't add any dynamic interaction to the equation. That sample started and ended with three pages. In real life, page controls are far more useful when you can add and delete pages on the fly. Recipe 9-12 does exactly that. It adds buttons that build and remove views for the UIScrollView.

This approach uses not two but four separate controls to produce the add-and-remove interface of Figure 9-13. The four buttons include an add button built using the standard Contacts Add button style, a delete button that mimics that style, a confirm button that looks like an "X," which is built to fit over the delete button, and a full-screen, completely clear cancel button.

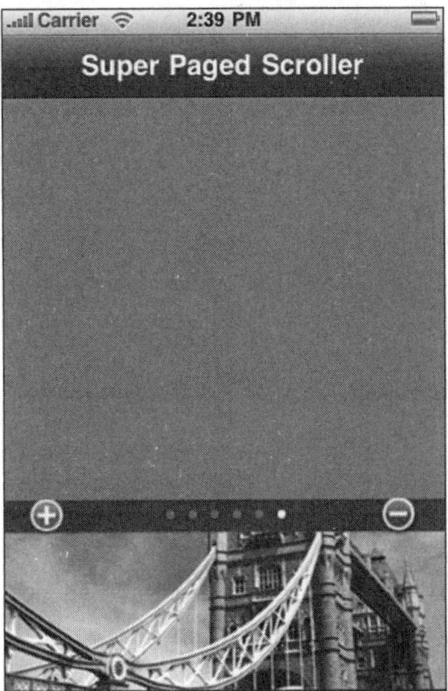

Figure 9-13 The + and - buttons let users add and remove paged views from the scroller. Deletion requires an extra step as a confirm button animates into place.

The buttons work like this. So long as there are fewer than eight buttons, the user can tap Add to create a new view in the UIScrollView. On add, the number of pages for the page control updates, and the new view scrolls into place. There's also a check for the current page count; when that page count hits the maximum, the code disables the add button. The eight-page limit is arbitrary. You can adjust the code for a larger or smaller number.

Upon tapping Delete, a confirm button animates into place and the invisible cancel button is enabled, covering the rest of the screen. If the user taps Confirm, the page deletes. A tap anywhere else causes the action to cancel, hiding the confirm button without performing a page deletion.

This confirm/cancel approach mirrors Apple's delete-with-caution policy that's seen in table edits and in other user interfaces. It takes two taps to delete a page and the user can cancel out without penalty. This prevents accidental page deletion and provides a safe exit route should the user decide not to continue.

Recipe 9-12 **Adding and Deleting Pages On the Fly**

```
@implementation TestBedViewController
- (void) pageTurn: (UIPageControl *) aPageControl
{
    // Update the page control and animate the new page into place
    int whichPage = aPageControl.currentPage;
    [UIView beginAnimations:nil context:NULL];
    [UIView setAnimationDuration:0.3f];
    [UIView setAnimationCurve:UIViewAnimationCurveEaseInOut];
    sv.contentOffset = CGPointMake(320.0f * whichPage, 0.0f);
    [UIView commitAnimations];
}

- (void) scrollViewDidScroll: (UIScrollView *) aScrollView
{
    // Mirror user scrolls on the page control
    CGPoint offset = aScrollView.contentOffset;
    pageControl.currentPage = offset.x / 320.0f;
}

- (UIColor *)randomColor
{
    // Return a random color
    float red = (64 + (random() % 191)) / 256.0f;
    float green = (64 + (random() % 191)) / 256.0f;
    float blue = (64 + (random() % 191)) / 256.0f;
    return [UIColor colorWithRed:red green:green blue:blue alpha:1.0f];
}

- (void) addPage
{
    // All new pages are added to the end of the scroll view
    pageControl.numberOfPages = pageControl.numberOfPages + 1;
    pageControl.currentPage = pageControl.numberOfPages - 1;

    // Increase the scroll view size and add the new page
    sv.contentSize = CGSizeMake(pageControl.numberOfPages * 320.0f,
        BASEHEIGHT);
```

```
    UIView *aView = [[UIView alloc] initWithFrame:
        CGRectMake(pageControl.currentPage * 320.0f, 0.0f, 320.0f,
        BASEHEIGHT)];
    aView.backgroundColor = [self randomColor];
    [sv addSubview:aView];
    [aView release];
}

- (void) requestAdd: (UIButton *) button
{
    // Add the page and update the buttons as needed
    [self addPage];
    addButton.enabled = (pageControl.numberOfPages < 8) ? YES : NO;
    deleteButton.enabled = YES;
    [self pageTurn:pageControl];
}

- (void) deletePage
{
    // Always delete the currently displayed page
    int whichPage = pageControl.currentPage;
    pageControl.numberOfPages = pageControl.numberOfPages - 1;

    // Remove the view in question
    NSMutableArray *properViews = [NSMutableArray array];
    for (UIView *view in sv.subviews)
        if ([[[view class] description] isEqualToString:@"UIView"] &&
            (view.frame.size.width == 320.0f))
            [properViews addObject:view];

    [UIView beginAnimations:nil context:NULL];
    [UIView setAnimationDuration:0.3f];
    [UIView setAnimationCurve:UIViewAnimationCurveEaseInOut];

    UIView *whichView = [properViews objectAtIndex:whichPage];

    // Move other pages into place
    for (int i = whichPage + 1; i < [properViews count]; i++)
    {
        UIView *aView = [properViews objectAtIndex:i];
        CGRect frame = aView.frame;
        frame.origin.x = frame.origin.x - 320.0f;
        aView.frame = frame;
    }

    [UIView commitAnimations];
```

```
    // Remove the page after the animation finishes
    [whichView performSelector:@selector(removeFromSuperview)
        withObject:nil afterDelay:0.3f];

    sv.contentSize = CGSizeMake(sv.contentSize.width - 320.0f,
        BASEHEIGHT);
}

// Animate the confirm button away and hide cancel
- (void) hideConfirmAndCancel
{
    cancelButton.enabled = NO;

    [UIView beginAnimations:nil context:NULL];
    [UIView setAnimationDuration:0.3f];
    [UIView setAnimationCurve:UIViewAnimationCurveEaseInOut];
    confirmButton.center = CGPointMake(deleteButton.center.x + 100.0f,
        deleteButton.center.y);
    [UIView commitAnimations];
}

// Perform delete on confirm and update the buttons
- (void) confirmDelete: (UIButton *) button
{
    [self deletePage];
    addButton.enabled = YES;
    deleteButton.enabled = (pageControl.numberOfPages > 1) ? YES : NO;
    [self pageTurn:pageControl];
    [self hideConfirmAndCancel];
}

// On cancel, simply hide confirm and cancel
- (void) cancelDelete: (UIButton *) button
{
    [self hideConfirmAndCancel];
}

// Respond to a delete request by showing the confirmation button
- (void) requestDelete: (UIButton *) button
{
    // Bring forth the cancel and confirm buttons
    [cancelButton.superview bringSubviewToFront:cancelButton];
    [confirmButton.superview bringSubviewToFront:confirmButton];
    cancelButton.enabled = YES;

    // Animate the confirm button into place
    confirmButton.center = CGPointMake(deleteButton.center.x + 100.0f,
```

```
        deleteButton.center.y);
    [UIView beginAnimations:nil context:NULL];
    [UIView setAnimationDuration:0.3f];
    [UIView setAnimationCurve:UIViewAnimationCurveEaseInOut];
    confirmButton.center = deleteButton.center;
    [UIView commitAnimations];
}

- (void) viewDidLoad
{
    // Create the scroll view and set its content size and delegate
    sv = [[UIScrollView alloc] initWithFrame:CGRectMake(0.0f, 0.0f,
        320.0f, BASEHEIGHT)];
    sv.contentSize = CGSizeZero;
    sv.pagingEnabled = YES;
    sv.delegate = self;
    [self.view addSubview:sv];
    [sv release];

    pageControl.numberOfPages = 0;
    [pageControl addTarget:self action:@selector(pageTurn)
        forControlEvents:UIControlEventValueChanged];

    // Load in all the pages
    for (int i = 0; i < INITPAGES; i++) [self addPage];
    pageControl.currentPage = 0;

    // Move the confirm button off screen
    confirmButton.center = CGPointMake(deleteButton.center.x + 100.0f,
        deleteButton.center.y);

    // Set up the target-action pairs for all the buttons
    [addButton addTarget:self action:@selector(requestAdd)
        forControlEvents:UIControlEventTouchUpInside];
    [cancelButton addTarget:self action:@selector(cancelDelete)
        forControlEvents:UIControlEventTouchUpInside];
    [deleteButton addTarget:self action:@selector(requestDelete)
        forControlEvents:UIControlEventTouchUpInside];
    [confirmButton addTarget:self action:@selector(confirmDelete)
        forControlEvents:UIControlEventTouchUpInside];
}
@end
```

Get This Recipe's Code

To get the code used for this recipe, go to http://github.com/erica/iphone-3.0-cookbook-, or if you've downloaded the disk image containing all of the sample code from the book, go to the folder for Chapter 9 and open the project for this recipe.

Building a Toolbar

You can build toolbars in Interface Builder and in Xcode, but when push comes to shove, it's often a lot easier in Xcode. That's because the IB user interface for adding and customizing a toolbar's bar button items is pretty dreadful. You need to keep switching between palettes and inspectors, and things quickly get messy.

After dragging a toolbar into an IB view, you must add and then customize each bar button item. Drag in one bar button item for each element you plan to add. Toolbar elements include both view items like buttons and spacers that lie between those buttons, as shown in Figure 9-14 (left).

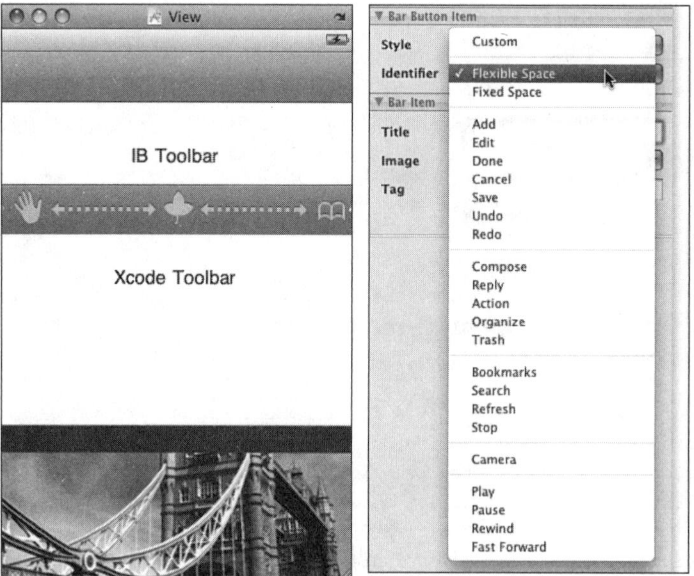

Figure 9-14 Adding bar button items in Interface Builder can be a complex process.

Once added, the bar button item attributes inspector (Command-1) shown in Figure 9-14 (right) lets you choose which kind of item each bar button represents. Use the Custom style to create custom text- and image-based items. Otherwise, pick from the list of system-defined icons. These include icons for playing media, accessing the camera, editing a list, and more.

When using a system item, make sure your application uses that item in a manner that complies with Apple's Human Interface Guidelines. App Store reviewers take a dim view of "creative" icon interpretations.

On a similar note, avoid creating your own buttons that look like any Apple products or trademarks. Apps have been rejected for using icons that look like the iPhone and Apple's logo.

Building Toolbars in Xcode

It's easy to define and lay out toolbars in Xcode provided that you've supplied yourself with a few handy macro definitions. The following macros return proper bar button items for the four available styles of items.

```
#define BARBUTTON(TITLE, SELECTOR) [[[UIBarButtonItem alloc] initWithTitle:TITLE
➥style:UIBarButtonItemStylePlain target:self action:SELECTOR] autorelease]
#define IMGBARBUTTON(IMAGE, SELECTOR) [[[UIBarButtonItem alloc]
➥initWithImage:IMAGE style:UIBarButtonItemStylePlain target:self action:SELECTOR]
➥autorelease]
#define SYSBARBUTTON(ITEM, SELECTOR) [[[UIBarButtonItem alloc]
➥initWithBarButtonSystemItem:ITEM target:self action:SELECTOR] autorelease]
#define CUSTOMBARBUTTON(VIEW) [[[UIBarButtonItem alloc] initWithCustomView:VIEW]
➥autorelease]
```

Those styles are text items, image items, system items, and custom view items. Each of these macros provides an autoreleased `UIBarButtonItem` that can be placed into a `UIToolbar`. Recipe 9-13 demonstrates these macros in action, showing how to add each style including spacers. You can even add a custom view to your toolbars, as Recipe 9-13 does. It inserts a `UISwitch` instance as one of the bar button items, as shown in Figure 9-15.

The fixed space bar button item represents the only instance where you need to move beyond these handy macros. You must set the item's `width` property to define how much space the item occupies.

Recipe 9-13 **Creating Toolbars in Xcode**

```
@implementation TestBedViewController
- (void) action
{
    // no action actually happens
}

- (void) viewDidLoad
{
    UIToolbar *tb = [[UIToolbar alloc] initWithFrame:
        CGRectMake(0.0f, 0.0f, 320.0f, 44.0f)];
    tb.center = CGPointMake(160.0f, 200.0f);
    NSMutableArray *tbitems = [NSMutableArray array];
```

```
    // Set up the items for the toolbar
    [tbitems addObject:BARBUTTON(@"Title", @selector(action))];
    [tbitems addObject:SYSBARBUTTON(UIBarButtonSystemItemAdd,
        @selector(action))];
    [tbitems addObject:IMGBARBUTTON([UIImage
        imageNamed:@"TBUmbrella.png"], @selector(action))];
    [tbitems addObject:CUSTOMBARBUTTON([[[UISwitch alloc] init]
        autorelease])];
    [tbitems addObject:SYSBARBUTTON(UIBarButtonSystemItemFlexibleSpace,
        nil)];
    [tbitems addObject:IMGBARBUTTON([UIImage
        imageNamed:@"TBPuzzle.png"], @selector(action))];

    // Add fixed 20 pixel width
    UIBarButtonItem *bbi = [[[UIBarButtonItem alloc]
        initWithBarButtonSystemItem:UIBarButtonSystemItemFixedSpace
        target:nil action:nil] autorelease];
    bbi.width = 20.0f;
    [tbitems addObject:bbi];

    tb.items = tbitems;
    [self.view addSubview:tb];
    [tb release];
}
@end
```

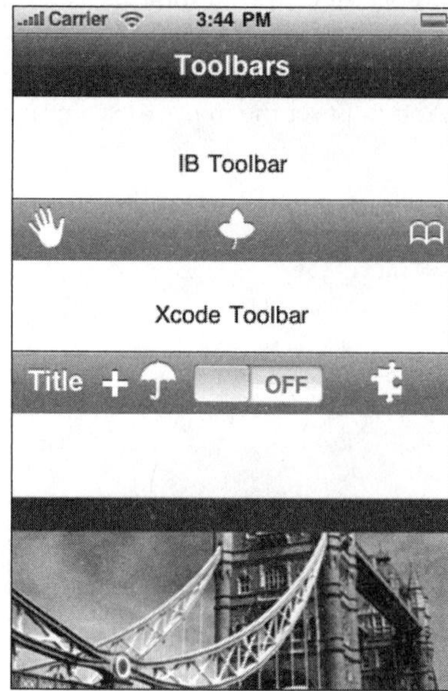

Figure 9-15 Custom toolbar items can include views like this switch.

> **Get This Recipe's Code**
>
> To get the code used for this recipe, go to http://github.com/erica/iphone-3.0-cookbook-, or if you've downloaded the disk image containing all of the sample code from the book, go to the folder for Chapter 9 and open the project for this recipe.

Toolbar Tips

When working with toolbars, here are a few tricks of the trade that might come in handy:

- **Fixed spaces can have widths**—Of all UIBarButtonItems, only `UIBarButtonSystemItemFixedSpace` items can be assigned a width. So create the spacer item, set its width, and only then add it to your items array.
- **Use a single flexible space for left or right alignment**—Adding a single `UIBarButtonSystemItemFlexibleSpace` at the start of an items list right-aligns all the remaining items. Adding one to the end, left-aligns. Use two, one at the start and one at the end, to create center alignments.
- **Take missing items into account**—When hiding bar button items due to context, don't just use flexible spacing to get rid of the item. Instead, replace the item with a fixed-width space that matches the item's original size. That preserves the layout and leaves all the other icons in the same position both before and after the item disappears.

One More Thing: Smart Labels

Unfortunately, the built-in `UILabel` class isn't very smart when it comes to providing clickable elements like phone numbers and Web addresses. That's where the `UITextView` class can step in. Text views offer a new 3.0 property called `dataDetectorTypes`, which specifies which data types get converted to clickable URLs. The available types are phone numbers (`UIDataDetectorTypePhoneNumber`) and links (`UIDataDetectorTypesLink`). To enable all types, choose the all flag (`UIDataDetectorTypeAll`) as used here.

```
- (void) viewDidLoad
{
    UITextView *tv = (UITextView *)[self.view viewWithTag:101];
    tv.dataDetectorTypes = UIDataDetectorTypeAll;
}
```

You also find individual check boxes for links and phone numbers in the Interface Builder text view attributes inspector.

When replacing `UILabel` instances with `UITextView` instances make sure to disable scrolling. Set the view's `editable` property to `NO`, either in code or in Interface Builder. Use carriage return constants (\n) to provide line breaks and carefully consider your text alignment choices. Figure 9-16 shows a `UITextView` stepping in and acting like a label while offering automatic URL creation.

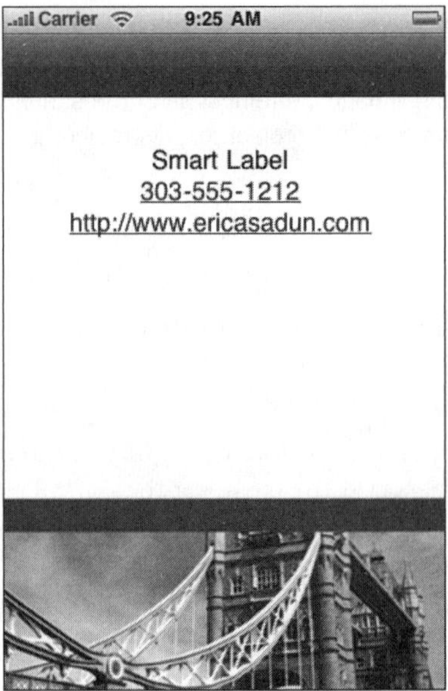

Figure 9-16 This "label" is actually a text view with its data detectors enabled.

When working with embedded URLs be aware that links take users to the requested resource without any further confirmation. In contrast, telephone numbers require user confirmation before dialing.

> **Note**
>
> Ever need to work with fonts outside those supplied with Cocoa Touch? A an open source iPhone project called FontLabel (http://github.com/zynga/FontLabel), developed by iPhone guru Kevin Ballard, uses the Core Graphics `CGFont` class to bypass the iPhone's `UIFont` limitations. FontLabel is in active development at the time this book was written, with regular updates.

Summary

This chapter introduced many ways to interact with and get the most from the controls in your applications. Before you move on to the next chapter, here are a few thoughts for you to ponder:

- Just because an item belongs to the `UIControl` class doesn't mean you can't treat it like a `UIView`. Give it subviews, resize it, animate it, move it around the screen, or tag it for later.

- Core Graphics and Quartz 2D let you build visual elements as needed. Combine the comfort of the SDK classes with a little real-time wow to add punch to your presentation.
- If the iPhone SDK hasn't delivered the control you need, consider adapting an existing control or building a new control from scratch.
- Apple provides top-notch examples of user interface excellence. Consider mimicking their examples when creating new interaction styles like the confirm button used in this chapter to safeguard a delete action.
- Interface Builder doesn't always provide the best solution for creating interfaces. With toolbars, you may save time in Xcode rather than customizing each element by hand in IB.

10

Alerting Users

At times, you need to grab your user's attention. New messages might arrive or the system status might change. You might want to tell your user that there's going to be a wait before anything more happens—or that the wait is over and it's time to come back and pay attention. The iPhone offers many ways to provide that heads-up to the user: from alerts and progress bars to audio pings. In this chapter, you discover how to build these indications into your applications and expand your user-alert vocabulary. You see real-life examples that showcase these classes and discover how to make sure your user pays attention at the right time.

Talking Directly to Your User Through Alerts

Alerts speak to your user. Members of the `UIAlertView` and `UIActionSheet` classes pop up or scroll in above other views to deliver their messages. These lightweight classes add two-way dialog to your apps. Alerts visually "speak" to users and can prompt them to reply. You present your alert onscreen, get user acknowledgment, and then dismiss the alert to move on with other tasks.

If you think that alerts are nothing more than messages with an attached OK button, think again. Alert objects provide incredible versatility. With alert sheets, you can actually build menus, text input, queries, and more. In this chapter's recipes, you see how to create a wide range of useful alerts that you can use in your own programs.

Building Simple Alerts

To create alert sheets, allocate a `UIAlertView` object. Initialize it with a title and a button array. The title is an NSString, and the button array includes NSStrings, where each string represents a single button that should be shown.

The method snippet shown here creates and displays the simplest alert scenario. It shows a message with a single OK button. The alert is autoreleased, avoiding any requirements for a delegate and callbacks. When you use non-autorelease alerts, make sure a delegate takes responsibility for releasing the alert after a user taps a button.

```
- (void) showAlert: (NSString *) theMessage
{
```

```
    UIAlertView *av = [[[UIAlertView alloc] initWithTitle:@"Title"
        message:theMessage delegate:nil
        cancelButtonTitle:@"OK" otherButtonTitles:nil] autorelease];
    [av show];
}
```

To add more buttons, introduce them as parameters to `otherButtonTitles:`. Make sure you end your list of buttons with `nil`. This argument takes an arbitrary number of parameters. Adding `nil` tells the method where your list finishes.

The following snippet creates an alert with three buttons (Cancel, Option, and OK). Since this code does not declare a delegate, there's no way to recover the alert and determine which of the three buttons was pushed. The alert displays until a user tap and then it automatically dismisses without any further effect.

```
- (void) showAlert: (NSString *) theMessage
{
    UIAlertView *av = [[[UIAlertView alloc] initWithTitle:@"Title"
        message:theMessage delegate:nil cancelButtonTitle:@"Cancel"
        otherButtonTitles: @"Option", @"OK", nil] autorelease];
    [av show];
}
```

When working with alerts, space is often at a premium. Adding more than two buttons causes the alert to display in multiline mode. Figure 10-1 shows a pair of alerts depicting both two-button (side-by-side display) and three-button (line-by-line display) presentations. Limit the number of alert buttons you add at any time to no more than three or four. Fewer buttons work better; one or two is ideal. If you need to use more buttons, consider using action sheet objects, which are discussed later in this chapter, rather than alert views.

`UIAlertView` objects provide no visual "default" button highlights. The only highlighting is for the Cancel button, as you can see in Figure 10-1. As a rule, Cancel buttons appear at the bottom or left of alerts.

Alert Delegates

Alerts use delegates to recover user choices. Unless you have some compelling reason to do otherwise, set the delegate to your primary (active) `UIViewController` object. The delegate implements the `UIAlertViewDelegate` protocol. `UIAlertView` instances require this delegate support to respond to button taps, at a minimum.

Delegate methods enable you to customize your responses when different buttons are pressed. As you've already seen, you can omit that delegate support if all you need to do is show some message with an OK button.

After the user has seen and interacted with your alert, they raise the following delegate method call: `alertView:clickedButtonAtIndex:`. This call indicates which button was pressed with its second argument. Button numbering begins with zero. The Cancel button, when defined, is always button 0. Even though it appears at the left in some views and the bottom at others, its button numbering remains the same. This is not true for action sheet objects, which are discussed later in this chapter.

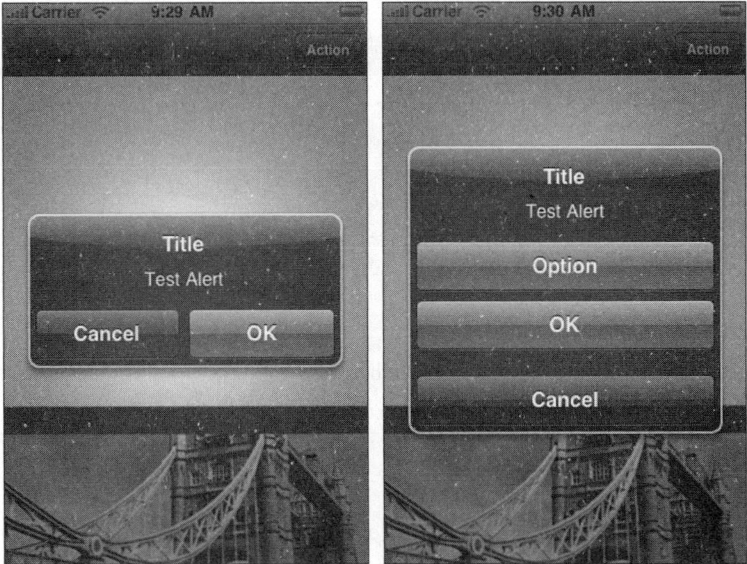

Figure 10-1 Alerts work best with one or two buttons (left). Alerts with more than two buttons stack the buttons as a list, producing a less elegant presentation (right).

Here is a simple example of an alert presentation and callback, which prints out the selected button number to the debugging console:

```
@interface TestBedViewController : UIViewController <UIAlertViewDelegate>
@end

@implementation TestBedViewController

- (void) alertView:(UIAlertView *) alertView
    clickedButtonAtIndex: (int) index
{
    printf("User selected button %d\n", index);
    [alertView release];
}

- (void) showAlert: (NSString *) message
{
    UIAlertView *av = [[UIAlertView alloc] initWithTitle:@"Title"
        message:message delegate:self cancelButtonTitle:@"Cancel"
        otherButtonTitles:@"One", @"Two", @"Three", nil];
    av.tag = MAIN_ALERT;
```

```
    [av show];
}
@end
```

When working with many alerts at once, tag your objects. Tags help you identify which alert produced a given callback. Unlike controls that use target-action pairs, all alerts trigger the same methods. Adding an alert-tag-based switch statement lets you differentiate your responses to each alert.

> **Note**
>
> Notice that this snippet does not use an autorelease alert. The object is released in the callback.

Displaying the Alert

As you've seen, the `show` method is used to tell your alert to appear onscreen. When shown, the alert works in a modal fashion. That is, it dims the screen behind it and blocks user interaction with your application behind the modal window. This modal interaction continues until your user acknowledges the alert through a button tap, typically by selecting OK or Cancel.

After creating the alert sheet, you may customize the alert by updating its `message` property. That's the optional text that appears below the alert title and above its buttons. As you see in recipes later in this chapter, you can also change the alert's frame and add subviews.

Alert Classes

In early releases of the iPhone firmware, `UIActionSheet` and `UIAlertView` were implemented by the same class, `UIAlertView`. This one class provided both pop-up alert and menu functionality. Then Apple replaced alert sheets with `UIModalView` and subclassed these new objects from that base class.

Later, Apple removed `UIModalView`, and in new versions of the SDK, `UIActionSheet` and `UIAlertView` are no longer derived from that class. (They both descend from `UIView`.) Like their predecessors, they remain siblings in their behavior and use similar underlying technology to present themselves onscreen.

This history presents an important lesson. Although Apple stands behind its APIs and published methods, you cannot depend on the underlying classes to remain stable. The iPhone is a rapidly evolving platform.

Recipe: No-Button Alerts

When you want to display an asynchronous message without involving user interaction, you can create a `UIAlertView` instance without buttons. You can build this alert and show it just as you would a normal buttoned version. No-button alerts provide an excellent way to throw up a "Please Wait" message, as shown in Figure 10-2.

Figure 10-2 Removing buttons from an alert lets you create heads-up displays about ongoing actions.

No-button alerts present a special challenge because they do not properly call back to a delegate method. They do not autodismiss, even when tapped. Instead, you must manually dismiss the alert when you are done displaying it. Call `dismissWithClickedButtonIndex:animated:` to do so.

Recipe 10-1 adds a `UIActivityIndicator` instance below the alert title. This creates the progress wheel you see at the bottom of the alert in Figure 10-2. This provides visual feedback to the user that some activity or process is ongoing that prevents user interaction. In Recipe 10-1 that "activity" is simply a three-second wait. In real applications, you'd use this kind of alert more meaningfully.

Once an alert is created, it works like any other view and you can add subviews and otherwise update its look. Unfortunately, Interface Builder does not offer alert views in its library so all customization must be done in code, as shown here. Recipe 10-1 builds the subview and adds it to the alert after first presenting the alert with `show`. Showing the alert allows it to build a real onscreen view that you can modify and customize.

Be aware that alerts display in a separate window. The view is not part of your main window's hierarchy. Another thing to note is that removing buttons can create an imbalance in the overall presentation geometry. The space that the buttons normally occupy does not go away. In Recipe 10-1, that space is used for the activity indicator. When just using text, adding a carriage return (`@"\n"`) to the start of your message helps balance the bottom where buttons normally go with the spacing at the top.

Recipe 10-1 **Displaying and Dismissing a No-Button Alert**

```
- (void) performDismiss
{
    [baseAlert dismissWithClickedButtonIndex:0 animated:NO];
}

- (void) action: (UIBarButtonItem *) item
{
    baseAlert = [[[UIAlertView alloc] initWithTitle:@"Please Wait"
        message:nil delegate:self cancelButtonTitle:nil
        otherButtonTitles: nil] autorelease];
    [baseAlert show];

    // Create and add the activity indicator
    UIActivityIndicatorView *aiv = [[UIActivityIndicatorView alloc]
        initWithActivityIndicatorStyle:
        UIActivityIndicatorViewStyleWhiteLarge];
    aiv.center = CGPointMake(baseAlert.bounds.size.width / 2.0f,
        baseAlert.bounds.size.height - 40.0f);
    [aiv startAnimating];
    [baseAlert addSubview:aiv];
    [aiv release];

    // Auto dismiss after 3 seconds for this example
    [self performSelector:@selector(performDismiss) withObject:nil
        afterDelay:3.0f];
}
```

Get This Recipe's Code

To get the code used for this recipe, go to http://github.com/erica/iphone-3.0-cookbook-, or if you've downloaded the disk image containing all of the sample code from the book, go to the folder for Chapter 10 and open the project for this recipe.

Recipe: Creating Modal Alerts with Run Loops

The indirect nature of the alert, namely its delegate callback approach, can produce unnecessarily complex code. It's relatively easy to build a custom class that directly returns a button choice value. Consider the following code. It requests an answer from the alert shown in Figure 10-3 (left) and then uses the answer that the class method returns.

```
- (void) confirm: (id) sender
{
    NSUInteger answer = [ModalAlert confirm:@"Are you sure?"];
    [self showAlert:[NSString stringWithFormat:@"You %@ confirm",
        answer ? @"did" : @"did not"]];
}
```

Figure 10-3 These modal alerts return immediate answers because they are built using their own run loops.

To create an alert that returns an immediate result requires a bit of ingenuity. The `ModalAlert` class in Recipe 10-2 introduces a second run loop. It creates the alert as you'd normally do but after presentation, the code calls `CFRunLoopRun()`. This makes the method sit and wait until the user finishes interacting with the alert. The method goes no further as the run loop runs.

It's up to the custom modal alert delegate class (`ModalAlertDelegate`) to cancel that run loop on a button click and return the value of the selected item. When the user finishes interacting, the calling method can finally proceed past the run loop.

This `ModalAlert` class offers two class methods that display the Cancel/OK and Yes/No styles shown in Figure 10-3. These return either 0 or 1, or 1 and 0, respectively. (Cancel and No are the 0-value choices.)

This recipe could easily be generalized for other button counts and titles. When you're unsure of how many buttons you need to work with, it helps to pass an array to custom classes. The `UIAlertView addButtonWithTitle:` method lets you avoid the variadic declaration (that is, the initialization call that uses a series of arguments separated by commas and that ends with a `nil` argument) to add buttons from an array, for example:

```
ModalAlertDelegate *madelegate = [[ModalAlertDelegate alloc]
    initWithRunLoop:currentLoop];
UIAlertView *alertView = [[UIAlertView alloc] initWithTitle:question
    message:nil delegate:madelegate cancelButtonTitle:cancelTitle
    otherButtonTitles:nil];
for (int i = 1; i < buttons.count; i++) [alertView
```

```
    addButtonWithTitle:[buttons objectAtIndex:i]];
[alertView show];
```

Be aware that while you can run one alert after another using this method that sometimes the calls may crowd each other. Leave enough time for the previous alert to disappear before presenting the next. Should an alert fail to show onscreen, it's probably due to this overlap issue. In such a case, use a delayed selector to call the next alert request. A tenth of a second offers plenty of time to allow the new alert to show.

Recipe 10-2 **Creating Alerts That Return Immediate Results**

```
@interface ModalAlertDelegate : NSObject <UIAlertViewDelegate>
{
    CFRunLoopRef currentLoop;
    NSUInteger index;
}
@property (readonly) NSUInteger index;
@end

@implementation ModalAlertDelegate
@synthesize index;

// Initialize with the supplied run loop
-(id) initWithRunLoop: (CFRunLoopRef)runLoop
{
    if (self = [super init]) currentLoop = runLoop;
    return self;
}

// User pressed button. Retrieve results
-(void) alertView: (UIAlertView*)aView clickedButtonAtIndex: (NSInteger)anIndex
{
    index = anIndex;
    CFRunLoopStop(currentLoop);
}
@end

@implementation ModalAlert
+(NSUInteger) queryWith: (NSString *)question
    button1: (NSString *)button1 button2: (NSString *)button2
{
    CFRunLoopRef currentLoop = CFRunLoopGetCurrent();

    // Create Alert
    ModalAlertDelegate *madelegate = [[ModalAlertDelegate alloc]
        initWithRunLoop:currentLoop];
    UIAlertView *alertView = [[UIAlertView alloc]
```

```
        initWithTitle:question message:nil delegate:madelegate
        cancelButtonTitle:button1 otherButtonTitles:button2, nil];
    [alertView show];

    // Wait for response
    CFRunLoopRun();

    // Retrieve answer
    NSUInteger answer = madelegate.index;
    [alertView release];
    [madelegate release];
    return answer;
}

// Ask a Yes-No question
+ (BOOL) ask: (NSString *) question
{
    return    ([ModalAlert queryWith:question
        button1: @"Yes" button2: @"No"] == 0);
}

// Ask a Cancel-OK question
+ (BOOL) confirm: (NSString *) statement
{
    return    [ModalAlert queryWith:statement
        button1: @"Cancel" button2: @"OK"];
}
@end
```

Get This Recipe's Code

To get the code used for this recipe, go to http://github.com/erica/iphone-3.0-cookbook-, or if you've downloaded the disk image containing all of the sample code from the book, go to the folder for Chapter 10 and open the project for this recipe.

Recipe: Soliciting Text Input from the User

Alert views provide an especially simple way to prompt your user for text. Instances take hold of the screen, focusing the user on providing an answer before moving forward with those results. As with Recipe 10-2, it helps to retrieve an answer directly without having to deal with delegate callbacks. For example, the following code snippet requests the user's name and then uses that string immediately.

```
-(void) action: (UIBarButtonItem *) item
{
    NSString *answer = [ModalAlert ask:@"What is your name?"
        withTextPrompt:@"Name"];
```

```
    [self showAlert:[NSString stringWithFormat:
        @"Nice to meet you, %@.", answer]];
}
```

To make this happen you can use the same run loop approach and the same `ModalAlert` and `ModalAlertDelegate` classes from Recipe 10-2 with a few slight alterations.

Recipe 10-3 builds an alert, adds a text field to it, and displays it. Unfortunately, the normal onscreen alert position precludes using a keyboard with that text field. The keyboard would partially block the alert. You can work around this issue by moving the alert into place to allow the keyboard to appear beneath it.

This method animates the text field above the space normally occupied by the keyboard so the keyboard will not block it. This approach uses hard-coded values for the alert center. A better approach would query the keyboard for its bounds to calculate how much to move.

```
// Move alert into place to allow keyboard to appear
- (void) moveAlert: (UIAlertView *) alertView
{
    CGContextRef context = UIGraphicsGetCurrentContext();
    [UIView beginAnimations:nil context:context];
    [UIView setAnimationCurve:UIViewAnimationCurveEaseInOut];
    [UIView setAnimationDuration:0.25f];
    if (![self isLandscape])
        alertView.center = CGPointMake(160.0f, 180.0f);
    else
        alertView.center = CGPointMake(240.0f, 90.0f);
    [UIView commitAnimations];

    [[alertView viewWithTag:TEXT_FIELD_TAG] becomeFirstResponder];
}
```

The preceding code, which is called from Recipe 10-3, animates the alert out of the way and sets the text field as first responder. Doing so calls out the keyboard, showing both the alert and keyboard at once, as shown in Figure 10-4.

> **Note**
>
> A console message regarding "wait_fences: failed to receive reply" usually indicates that a child view is rendered before its parent. You can avoid this message by removing custom views from an alert in the `alertView:clickedButtonAtIndex:` method.

Recipe 10-3 **Building a Modal Text Query Alert**

```
+(NSString *) textQueryWith: (NSString *)question
    prompt: (NSString *)prompt button1: (NSString *)button1
    button2:(NSString *) button2
{
    // Create alert
    CFRunLoopRef currentLoop = CFRunLoopGetCurrent();
```

```
    ModalAlertDelegate *madelegate = [[ModalAlertDelegate alloc]
        initWithRunLoop:currentLoop];
    UIAlertView *alertView = [[UIAlertView alloc]
        initWithTitle:question message:@"\n" delegate:madelegate
        cancelButtonTitle:button1 otherButtonTitles:button2, nil];

    // Build text field
    UITextField *tf = [[UITextField alloc]
        initWithFrame:CGRectMake(0.0f, 0.0f, 260.0f, 30.0f)];
    tf.borderStyle = UITextBorderStyleRoundedRect;
    tf.tag = TEXT_FIELD_TAG;
    tf.placeholder = prompt;
    tf.clearButtonMode = UITextFieldViewModeWhileEditing;
    tf.keyboardType = UIKeyboardTypeAlphabet;
    tf.keyboardAppearance = UIKeyboardAppearanceAlert;
    tf.autocapitalizationType = UITextAutocapitalizationTypeWords;
    tf.autocorrectionType = UITextAutocorrectionTypeNo;
    tf.contentVerticalAlignment =
        UIControlContentVerticalAlignmentCenter;

    // Show alert and wait for it to finish displaying
    [alertView show];
    while (CGRectEqualToRect(alertView.bounds, CGRectZero));

    // Find the center for the text field and add it
    CGRect bounds = alertView.bounds;
    tf.center = CGPointMake(bounds.size.width / 2.0f,
        bounds.size.height / 2.0f - 10.0f);
    [alertView addSubview:tf];
    [tf release];

    // Set the field to first responder and move it into place
    [madelegate performSelector:@selector(moveAlert)
        withObject:alertView afterDelay: 0.7f];

    // Start the run loop
    CFRunLoopRun();

    // Retrieve the user choices
    NSUInteger index = madelegate.index;
    NSString *answer = [[madelegate.text copy] autorelease];
    if (index == 0) answer = nil; // assumes cancel in position 0

    [alertView release];
    [madelegate release];
    return answer;
}
```

Figure 10-4 Using careful space management and omitting the title and body text, you can add several text entry fields to a UIAlertView at once. You probably want to limit your UIAlertViews to one or two text fields.

> **Get This Recipe's Code**
>
> To get the code used for this recipe, go to http://github.com/erica/iphone-3.0-cookbook-, or if you've downloaded the disk image containing all of the sample code from the book, go to the folder for Chapter 10 and open the project for this recipe.

Recipe: Using Variadic Arguments with Alert Views

Methods that can take a variable number of arguments are called *variadic*. They are declared using ellipses after the last parameter. Both `NSLog` and `printf` are variadic. You can supply them with a format string along with any number of arguments.

Since most alerts center on text, it's handy to build methods that create alerts using format strings. Recipe 10-4 creates the `say:` method that collects the arguments passed to it and builds a string with them. The string is then passed to an autoreleased alert view, providing a handy instant display.

The `say:` method does not parse or otherwise analyze its parameters. Instead, it grabs the first argument, uses that as the format string, and passes the remaining items to the NSString `initWithFormat:arguments:` method. This builds a string, which is then passed to a one-button alert view as its title.

Defining your own utility methods with variadic arguments lets you skip several steps where you have to build a string with a format and then call a method. With `say:` you can combine this into a single call, as follows:

```
[self say:@"I am so happy to meet you, %@", yourName];
```

> **Note**
>
> You must import `<stdarg.h>` to use the variadic argument calls shown in Recipe 10-4.

Recipe 10-4 **Using a Variadic Method for UIAlertView Creation**

```
- (void) say: (id)formatstring,...
{
    va_list arglist;
    va_start(arglist, formatstring);
    id statement = [[NSString alloc] initWithFormat:formatstring
        arguments:arglist];
    va_end(arglist);

    UIAlertView *av = [[[UIAlertView alloc] initWithTitle:statement
        message:nil delegate:self cancelButtonTitle:@"Okay"
        otherButtonTitles:nil] autorelease];
    [av show];
    [statement release];
}

-(void) action: (UIBarButtonItem *) item
{
    NSDateFormatter *formatter = [[[NSDateFormatter alloc] init]
        autorelease];
    formatter.dateFormat = @"MM/dd/YY HH:mm:ss";
    NSString *timestamp = [formatter stringFromDate:[NSDate date]];

    [self say:@"At the chime, the time will be %@", timestamp];
}
```

> **Get This Recipe's Code**
>
> To get the code used for this recipe, go to http://github.com/erica/iphone-3.0-cookbook-, or if you've downloaded the disk image containing all of the sample code from the book, go to the folder for Chapter 10 and open the project for this recipe.

Recipe: Presenting Simple Menus

When it comes to menus, `UIActionSheet` instances supply the iPhone answer. They slide choices, basically a list of buttons representing possible actions, onto the screen and wait for the user to respond. Action sheets are different from pop-ups. Pop-ups stand apart from the interface and are better used for demanding attention. Menus slide into a view and better integrate with ongoing application work. Cocoa Touch supplies two ways to present menus:

- **`showInView`**—Presenting your sheet in a view is pretty much the ideal way to use menus and is the method used here. This method slides the menu up from the exact bottom of the view (see Figure 10-5).

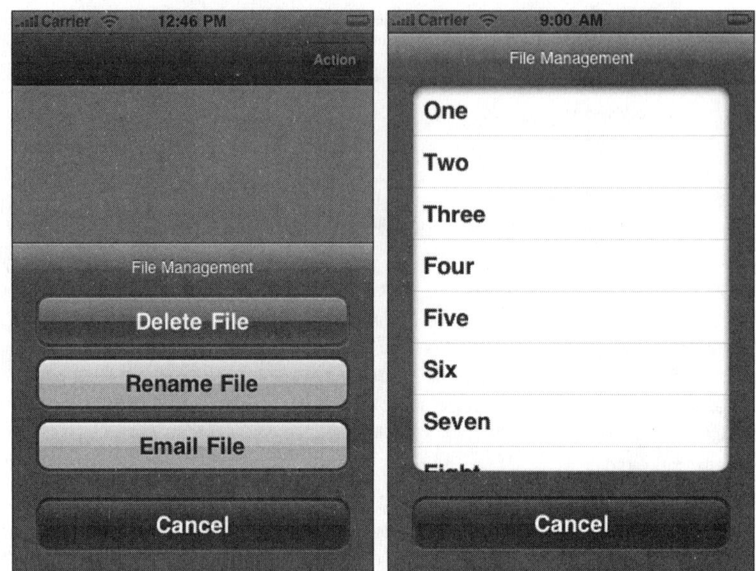

Figure 10-5 Use **`showInView:`** to create simple menu presentations. The menu slides in from the bottom of the view. Although the Delete File menu button appears gray here (left), it is red on your iPhone and indicates permanent actions with possible negative consequences to your users. Adding many menu items produces the scrolling list on the right.

- **`showFromToolBar:`** and **`showFromTabBar`**—When working with toolbars, tab bars, or any other kinds of bars that provide those horizontally grouped buttons that you see at the bottom of many applications, these methods align the menu with the top of the bar and slide it out exactly where it should be.

Recipe 10-5 shows how to initialize and present a simple `UIActionSheet` instance. Its initialization method introduces a concept missing from `UIAlertView`: the destructive button. Colored in red, a destructive button indicates an action from which there is no return, such as permanently deleting a file (see Figure 10-5). Its bright red color warns the user about the choice. Use this option sparingly.

Action sheet values are returned in button order. In the Figure 10-5 example, the Delete button is number 0 and the Cancel button is number 3. This behavior contradicts alert view values, where the Cancel button returns 0.

Scrolling Menus

As a rough rule of thumb, you can fit a maximum of about seven buttons (including Cancel) into a portrait orientation and about four buttons into landscape. Going beyond this number in iPhone OS 3.0 and later triggers the scrolling presentation shown in Figure 10-5 (right). Notice that the Cancel button is presented below the list. Its numbering remains consistent with shorter menu presentations. The Cancel button is always numbered after any previous buttons. As Figure 10-5 demonstrates, this presentation falls low on the aesthetics scale and should be avoided where possible.

> **Note**
>
> You can use the same second run loop approach shown in Recipe 10-2 to retrieve results with action sheets as you can with alert views.

Recipe 10-5 **Displaying Simple Menus**

```
- (void)actionSheet:(UIActionSheet *)actionSheet
clickedButtonAtIndex:(NSInteger)buttonIndex
{
    [actionSheet release];
    [self say:@"User Pressed Button %d\n", buttonIndex + 1];
}

-(void) action: (UIBarButtonItem *) item
{
    UIActionSheet *menu = [[UIActionSheet alloc] initWithTitle:
        @"File Management" delegate:self cancelButtonTitle:@"Cancel"
        destructiveButtonTitle:@"Delete File"
        otherButtonTitles:@"Rename File", @"Email File", nil];
    [menu showInView:self.view];
}
```

> **Get This Recipe's Code**
>
> To get the code used for this recipe, go to http://github.com/erica/iphone-3.0-cookbook-, or if you've downloaded the disk image containing all of the sample code from the book, go to the folder for Chapter 10 and open the project for this recipe.

Recipe: Displaying Text in Action Sheets

Action sheets offer many of the same text presentation features as alert views, but they do so with a much bigger canvas. Recipe 10-6 demonstrates how to display a text message using a `UIActionSheet` object. This code builds off Recipe 10-4 but adapts that method to an action sheet presentation.

Recipe 10-6 **Presenting Text in Action Sheets**

```
- (void) show: (id)formatstring,...
{
```

```
    va_list arglist;
    va_start(arglist, formatstring);
    id statement = [[NSString alloc] initWithFormat:formatstring
        arguments:arglist];
    va_end(arglist);

    UIActionSheet *actionSheet = [[[UIActionSheet alloc]
        initWithTitle:statement delegate:nil cancelButtonTitle:nil
        destructiveButtonTitle:nil otherButtonTitles:@"OK", nil]
        autorelease];
    [actionSheet showInView:self.view];
    [statement release];
}
```

Get This Recipe's Code

To get the code used for this recipe, go to http://github.com/erica/iphone-3.0-cookbook-, or if you've downloaded the disk image containing all of the sample code from the book, go to the folder for Chapter 10 and open the project for this recipe.

"Please Wait": Showing Progress to Your User

Waiting is an intrinsic part of the computing experience and will remain so for the foreseeable future. It's your job as a developer to communicate that fact to your users. Cocoa Touch provides classes that tell your user to wait for a process to complete. These progress indicators come in two forms: as a spinning wheel that persists for the duration of its presentation and as a bar that fills from left to right as your process moves forward from start to end. The classes that provide these indications are as follows:

- **`UIActivityIndicatorView`**—A progress indicator offers a spinning circle that tells your user to wait without providing specific information about its degree of completion. The iPhone activity indicator is small, but its live animation catches the user's eye and is best suited for quick disruptions in a normal application. Recipe 10-1 showed a simple alert that embedded an activity indicator.
- **`UIProgressView`**—This view presents a progress bar. The bar provides concrete feedback as to how much work has been done and how much remains while occupying a relatively small onscreen space. It presents as a thin, horizontal rectangle that fills itself from left to right as progress takes place. This classic user interface element works best for long delays, where users want to know to what degree the job has finished.

Be aware of blocking. Both of these classes must be used on your main thread, as is the rule with GUI objects. Computationally heavy code can keep views from displaying in real time. Should you need to display asynchronous feedback, use threading. The edge-detection discussed in Recipe 7-11 in Chapter 7, "Working with Images," provides a good example. It uses a `UIActivityIndicatorView` on the main thread and performs its computation on a second thread.

Using UIActivityIndicatorView

`UIActivityIndicatorView` instances offer lightweight views that display a standard rotating progress wheel, as shown previously in Figure 10-2. The keyword to keep in mind when working with these views is *small*. All activity indicators are tiny and do not look right when zoomed past their natural size.

The iPhone offers several different styles of the `UIActivityIndicatorView` class. `UIActivityIndicatorViewStyleWhite` and `UIActivityIndicatorViewStyleGray` are 20x20 pixels in size. The white version looks best against a black background, and the gray looks best against white. It's a thin, sharp style.

Take care when choosing whether to use white or gray. An all-white presentation does not show at all against a white backdrop. Unfortunately, `UIActivityIndicatorView` ➥`StyleWhiteLarge` is available only for use on dark backgrounds. It provides the largest, clearest indicator at 37x37 pixels in size.

```
UIActivityIndicatorView *aiv = [[UIActivityIndicatorView alloc]
    initWithActivityIndicatorStyle:
    UIActivityIndicatorViewStyleWhiteLarge];
```

You need not center indicators on the screen. Place them wherever they work best for you. As a clear-backed view, the indicator blends over whatever backdrop view lies behind it. The predominant color of that backdrop helps select which style of indicator to use.

For general use, just add the activity indicator as a subview to the window, view, toolbar, or navigation bar you want to overlay as shown previously in Recipe 10-1. Allocate the indicator and initialize it with a frame, preferably centered within whatever parent view you're using.

Start the indicator in action by sending `startAnimating`. To stop, call `stopAnimating`. Cocoa Touch takes care of the rest, hiding the view when not in use.

Recipe: Building a UIProgressView

Progress views enable your users to follow task progress as it happens rather than just saying "Please wait." They present bars that fill from left to right. The bars indicate the degree to which a task has finished. Progress bars work best for long waits where providing state feedback enables your users to retain the feel of control.

To create a progress view, allocate it and set its frame. To use the bar, issue `setProgress:`. This takes one argument, a floating-point number that ranges between 0.0 (no progress) and 1.0 (finished). Progress view bars come in two styles: basic white or light gray. The `setStyle:` method chooses the kind you prefer, either `UIProgressViewStyleDefault` or `UIProgressViewStyleBar`.

Unlike the other kinds of progress indicators, it's completely up to you to show and hide the progress bar's view. There's no `setVisible:` method. Adding progress bars to action sheets simplifies both bringing them onto the screen and dismissing them. Another advantage is that when alert sheets display, the rest of the screen dims. This forces a modal presentation as your task progresses. Users cannot interact with the GUI until you dismiss the alert. Recipe 10-7 shows a `UIActionSheet/UIProgressView` sample that produces the display shown in Figure 10-6. Several line feeds in the action sheet's title keep the progress bar from obscuring the title text.

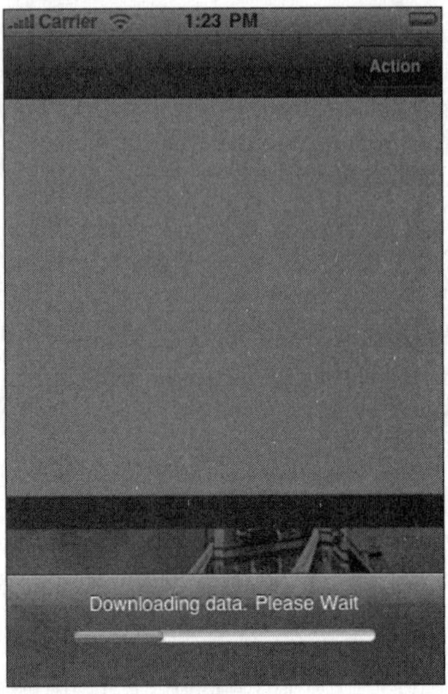

Figure 10-6 Use `UIProgressView` instances to track progress over an extended delay. Adding them to a `UIActionSheet` simplifies their presentation and dismissal.

Recipe 10-7 **Presenting Progress on an Action Sheet**

```
@interface TestBedViewController : UIViewController <UIActionSheetDelegate>
{
    float amountDone;
    UIProgressView *progressView;
    UIActionSheet *actionSheet;
}
@property (retain) UIActionSheet *actionSheet;
@end

@implementation TestBedViewController
@synthesize actionSheet;

// This callback fakes progress via setProgress:
- (void) incrementBar: (id) timer
{
```

```
    amountDone += 1.0f;
    [progressView setProgress: (amountDone / 20.0)];
    if (amountDone > 20.0)
    {
        [self.actionSheet dismissWithClickedButtonIndex:0
            animated:YES];
        self.actionSheet = nil;
        [timer invalidate];
    }
}

// Load the progress bar onto an action sheet backing
-(void) action: (UIBarButtonItem *) item
{
    amountDone = 0.0f;
    self.actionSheet = [[[UIActionSheet alloc]
        initWithTitle:@"Downloading data. Please Wait\n\n\n"
        delegate:nil cancelButtonTitle:nil destructiveButtonTitle: nil
        otherButtonTitles: nil] autorelease];
    progressView = [[UIProgressView alloc]
        initWithFrame:CGRectMake(0.0f, 40.0f, 220.0f, 90.0f)];
    [progressView setProgressViewStyle: UIProgressViewStyleDefault];
    [actionSheet addSubview:progressView];
    [progressView release];

    // Create the demonstration updates
    [progressView setProgress:(amountDone = 0.0f)];
    [NSTimer scheduledTimerWithTimeInterval: 0.5 target: self
        selector:@selector(incrementBar) userInfo: nil repeats: YES];
    [actionSheet showInView:self.view];
    progressView.center = CGPointMake(actionSheet.center.x,
        progressView.center.y);
}
@end
```

Get This Recipe's Code

To get the code used for this recipe, go to http://github.com/erica/iphone-3.0-cookbook-, or if you've downloaded the disk image containing all of the sample code from the book, go to the folder for Chapter 10 and open the project for this recipe.

Recipe: Building Custom Overlays

Although `UIAlertView` and `UIActionSheet` provide excellent modal progress indicators, you can also roll your own completely from scratch. Recipe 10-8 uses a simple tinted `UIView` overlay with a `UIActivityIndicatorView` to present the modal "in-progress" feedback shown in Figure 10-7.

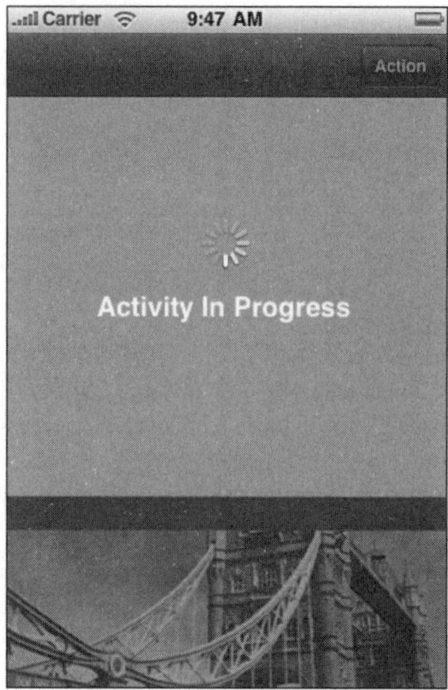

Figure 10-7 Custom views provide handy modal alerts without using prebuilt Apple classes.

This view was laid out in Interface Builder and connected to a custom class property called `overlay`. The view occupies the entire screen size so no simulated screen elements were enabled. Using the entire screen lets the overlay fit over the navigation bar. That's because the overlay view must be added to the application window and not, as you might think, to the main UIViewController's view. That view only occupies the space under the navigation bar, allowing access to any buttons and other control items in the bar.

To restrict any user touches with the screen, the overlay sets its `userInteraction` ➥`Enabled` property to `YES`. This catches any touch events, preventing them from reaching the normal GUI below the alert, creating a modal presentation where interaction cannot continue until the alert has finished.

This example uses a portrait-only presentation. As the view does not belong to a view controller, it cannot and will not update itself during iPhone orientation changes. If you need to work with a landscape/portrait aware system, you can catch that value before showing the overlay as demonstrated in the upcoming Recipe 10-10.

Recipe 10-8 **Presenting and Hiding a Custom Alert Overlay**

```
- (void) finish
{
    [(UIActivityIndicatorView *)[self.overlay viewWithTag:202]
        stopAnimating];
    [self.overlay removeFromSuperview];
```

```
}

- (void) action: (id) sender
{
    // Add the subview
    [self.view.window addSubview:self.overlay];

    // Start the activity indicator
    [(UIActivityIndicatorView *)[self.overlay viewWithTag:202]
         startAnimating];

    // Call the finish method, on delay
    [self performSelector:@selector(finish) withObject:nil
        afterDelay:3.0f];
}
```

Get This Recipe's Code

To get the code used for this recipe, go to http://github.com/erica/iphone-3.0-cookbook-, or if you've downloaded the disk image containing all of the sample code from the book, go to the folder for Chapter 10 and open the project for this recipe.

Recipe: Tappable Overlays

Use custom overlays to present information as well as to establish modal sequences. Recipe 10-9 creates a custom class called `TappableOverlay`. When tapped, this view removes itself from the screen. This behavior makes it particularly suitable for showing information in a way normally reserved for the `UIAlertView` class.

To use this class, create a view instance in Interface Builder. Add as many subviews and design elements as needed. Use File > Read Class Files to import the TappableOverlay.h header file. Then change the view class from `UIView` to `TappableOverlay` using the Identity Inspector (Command-4) and save the project.

To present the view, add it to the window just as Recipe 10-8 did.

```
- (void) action: (id) sender
{
    // Add the overlay
    [self.view.window addSubview:self.overlay];
}
```

No further programming is needed. The view waits for a user tap and when one is received, it removes itself from the window.

Figure 10-8 shows a simple example of this kind of overlay; it displays "Tap to Continue." It's easy to see how you can extend this concept to show any kind of pertinent information, creating a custom alternative to the `UIAlertView` class. As with Recipe 10-8, this example does not use any orientation awareness.

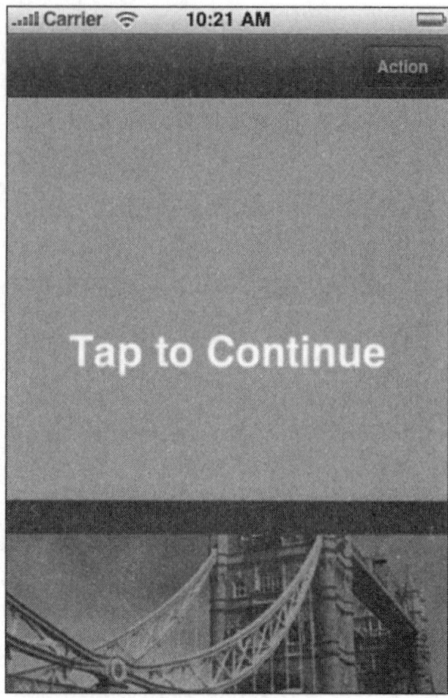

Figure 10-8 This simple overlay dismisses itself on receiving a user touch.

Recipe 10-9 **Building a Custom Dismissible Alert View That Responds to User Taps**

```
@interface TappableOverlay : UIView
@end
@implementation TappableOverlay
- (void)touchesEnded:(NSSet *)touches withEvent:(UIEvent *)event
{
    // Remove this view when it is touched
    [self removeFromSuperview];
}
@end
```

> **Get This Recipe's Code**
> To get the code used for this recipe, go to http://github.com/erica/iphone-3.0-cookbook-, or if you've downloaded the disk image containing all of the sample code from the book, go to the folder for Chapter 10 and open the project for this recipe.

Recipe: Orientable Scroll-Down Alerts

You can extend the modal concepts introduced in Recipe 10-8 to create a noninteractive overlay that acts as a backdrop for a scroll-down alert. In Recipe 10-10, that overlay hosts a view with an embedded button as shown in Figure 10-9. This view is presented and dismissed via a pair of simple `UIView` animation blocks; the OKAY button triggers the `dismiss:` method that scrolls the view offscreen.

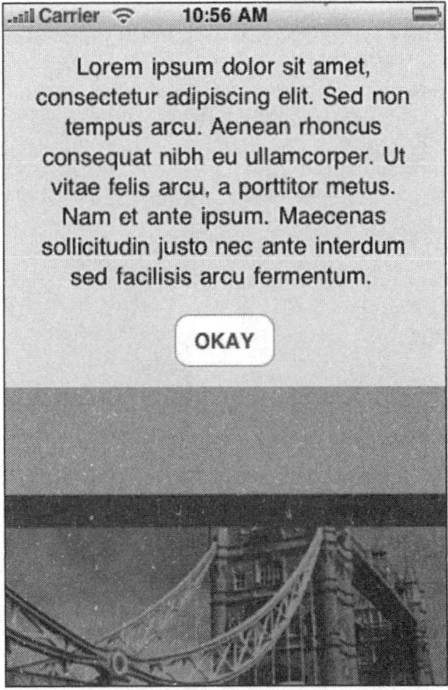

Figure 10-9 This modally presented message scrolls down into view and is dismissed by tapping the OKAY button.

The message view was created in Interface Builder as a standard `UIView`. It's added to the overlay as a subview in the `viewDidLoad` method. Rather than adding and removing the overlay from the main window, as Recipe 10-8 did, this recipe uses the overlay's `alpha` property to hide and show itself.

Unlike the previous two recipes, this recipe does pay attention to screen orientation. It adapts its size and presentation to match the current iPhone orientation. It accomplishes this in two ways. First, it applies an affine transform to the overlay when the orientation changes. Second, it adjusts the overlay and message view frames before presentation, matching the shape of the current window.

Although this example scrolls in from the top of the screen, it's trivial to adapt the math to have it scroll in from the sides (use the x origin rather than the y origin) or bottom (add 320 or 480 to the view height). Alternatively, you might center the view and animate its size so that it pops rather than slides into view.

Recipe 10-10 **Creating an Orientable Scroll-Down Overlay**

```
- (void) dismiss: (id) sender
{
```

```
    // Animate the message view away
    [UIView beginAnimations:nil context:NULL];
    [UIView setAnimationDuration:0.3f];
    [UIView setAnimationCurve:UIViewAnimationCurveLinear];
    mvframe.origin = CGPointMake(0.0f, -300.0f);
    self.messageView.frame = mvframe;
    [UIView commitAnimations];

    // Hide the overlay
    [self.overlay performSelector:@selector(setAlpha) withObject:nil
        afterDelay:0.3f];
}

- (void) action: (id) sender
{
    // Adjust the overlay sizes based on the screen orientation
    self.overlay.frame = self.view.window.frame;
    mvframe.size.width = UIDeviceOrientationIsPortrait([[UIDevice
        currentDevice] orientation]) ? 320.0f : 480.0f;
    mvframe.origin = CGPointMake(0.0f, -mvframe.size.height);
    self.messageView.frame = mvframe;

    // Show the overlay
    if (!self.overlay.superview)
        [self.view.window addSubview:self.overlay];
    self.overlay.alpha = 1.0f;

    // Animate the message view into place
    [UIView beginAnimations:nil context:NULL];
    [UIView setAnimationDuration:0.3f];
    [UIView setAnimationCurve:UIViewAnimationCurveLinear];
    mvframe.origin = CGPointMake(0.0f, 20.0f);
    self.messageView.frame = mvframe;
    [UIView commitAnimations];
}

- (void) viewDidLoad
{
    self.navigationItem.rightBarButtonItem = BARBUTTON(@"Action",
        @selector(action));

    // Initialize the overlay and message view
    self.overlay.alpha = 0.0f;
    [self.overlay addSubview:self.messageView];
    mvframe = messageView.frame;
    mvframe.origin = CGPointMake(0.0f, -300.0f);
    self.messageView.frame = mvframe;
```

```
}

- (BOOL)shouldAutorotateToInterfaceOrientation:
    (UIInterfaceOrientation)interfaceOrientation
{
    // Apply overlay transforms based on the orientation
    if (interfaceOrientation ==
        UIInterfaceOrientationPortraitUpsideDown)
        self.overlay.transform = CGAffineTransformMakeRotation(M_PI);
    else if (interfaceOrientation ==
        UIInterfaceOrientationLandscapeLeft)
        self.overlay.transform = CGAffineTransformMakeRotation(-M_PI /
            2.0f);
    else if (interfaceOrientation ==
        UIInterfaceOrientationLandscapeRight)
        self.overlay.transform = CGAffineTransformMakeRotation(M_PI /
            2.0f);
    else
        self.overlay.transform = CGAffineTransformIdentity;
    return YES;
}
```

> **Get This Recipe's Code**
>
> To get the code used for this recipe, go to http://github.com/erica/iphone-3.0-cookbook-, or if you've downloaded the disk image containing all of the sample code from the book, go to the folder for Chapter 10 and open the project for this recipe.

Recipe: Using the Network Activity Indicator

When your application accesses the Internet from behind the scenes, it's polite to let your user know what's going on. Rather than create a full-screen alert, Cocoa Touch provides a simple application property that controls a spinning network activity indicator in the status bar. Figure 10-10 shows this indicator in action, to the right of the WiFi indicator and to the left of the current time display.

Figure 10-10 The network activity indicator is controlled by a `UIApplication` property.

Recipe 10-11 demonstrates how to access this property, doing little more than toggling the indicator on or off. In real-world use, you'll likely perform your network activities on a secondary thread. Make sure you perform this property change on the main thread so the GUI can properly update itself.

Recipe 10-11 **Accessing the Status Bar's Network Activity Indicator**

```
- (void) action: (id) sender
{
    // Toggle the network activity indicator
    UIApplication *app = [UIApplication sharedApplication];
    app.networkActivityIndicatorVisible =
        !app.networkActivityIndicatorVisible;
}
```

Get This Recipe's Code

To get the code used for this recipe, go to http://github.com/erica/iphone-3.0-cookbook-, or if you've downloaded the disk image containing all of the sample code from the book, go to the folder for Chapter 10 and open the project for this recipe.

Recipe: Badging Applications

If you've used the iPhone or iPod touch for any time, you've likely seen the small, red badges that appear over applications on the home screen. These might indicate the number of missed phone calls or unread e-mails that have accumulated since the user last opened Phone or Mail.

To set an application badge from within the program itself, set the `applicationIcon` ➥`BadgeNumber` property to an integer. To hide badges, set `applicationIconBadgeNumber` to 0 (the number zero). Recipe 10-12 demonstrates how to read and set an application badge. It matches the value of its segmented control to the most recently used badge number. When users change the segmented control setting, it updates the badge accordingly. Figure 10-11 shows this in action, displaying the interface within the application and the badge number it generates.

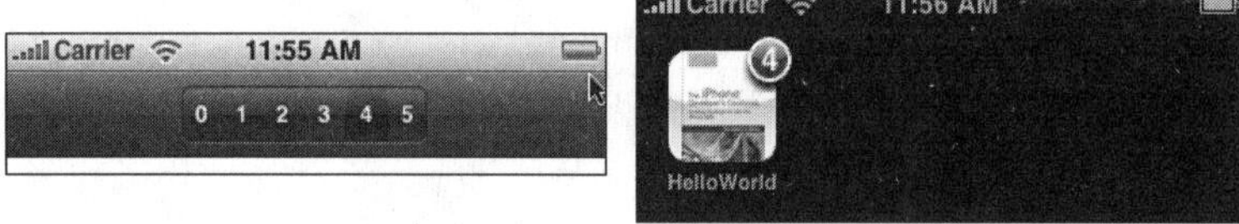

Figure 10-11 The segmented control in Recipe 10-12 updates the application badge number.

Recipe 10-12 **Reading and Updating Application Badges**

```
@implementation TestBedViewController
- (void) updateBadge: (UISegmentedControl *) seg
{
    // Set the badge number to the selected segment index
    [UIApplication sharedApplication].applicationIconBadgeNumber =
        seg.selectedSegmentIndex;
```

```
}

- (void) viewDidLoad
{
    // Create the segment control for selecting the badge number
    UISegmentedControl *seg = [[UISegmentedControl alloc]
        initWithItems:[@"0 1 2 3 4 5" componentsSeparatedByString:
        @" "]];
    seg.segmentedControlStyle = UISegmentedControlStyleBar;
    seg.selectedSegmentIndex = MIN([UIApplication
        sharedApplication].applicationIconBadgeNumber, 5);
    [seg addTarget:self action:@selector(updateBadge)
        forControlEvents:UIControlEventValueChanged];
    self.navigationItem.titleView = seg;
    [seg release];
}
@end
```

Get This Recipe's Code

To get the code used for this recipe, go to http://github.com/erica/iphone-3.0-cookbook-, or if you've downloaded the disk image containing all of the sample code from the book, go to the folder for Chapter 10 and open the project for this recipe.

Recipe: Simple Audio Alerts

Audio alerts "speak" directly to your users. They produce instant feedback—assuming users are not hearing impaired. Fortunately, Apple built basic sound playback into the Cocoa Touch SDK through System Audio services. This works very much like system audio on a Macintosh.

The alternatives include using Audio Queue calls or AVAudioPlayer. Audio Queue playback is expensive to program and involves much more complexity than simple alert sounds need. In contrast, you can load and play system audio with just a few lines of code. AVAudioPlayer also has its drawbacks. It interferes with iPod audio. In contrast, System Audio can perform a sound without interrupting any music that's currently playing, although that may admittedly not be the result you're looking for, as alerts can get lost in the music.

Alert sounds work best when kept short, preferably 30 seconds or shorter according to Apple. System Audio plays PCM and IMA audio only. That means limiting your sounds to AIFF, WAV, and CAF formats.

System Sounds

To build a system sound, call `AudioServicesCreateSystemSoundID` with a file URL pointing to the sound file. This call returns an initialized system sound object, which you can then play at will. Just call `AudioServicesPlaySystemSound` with the sound object. That single call does all the work.

```
AudioServicesPlaySystemSound(mySound);
```

The default implementation of system sounds allows them to be controlled by the Sound Effects preference in Settings. When effects are disabled, the sound will not play. To override this preference and always play the sound, you can set a property flag as such.

```
// Identify it as a non UI Sound
AudioServicesCreateSystemSoundID(baseURL, &mysound);
AudioServicesPropertyID flag = 0;  // 0 means always play
AudioServicesSetProperty(kAudioServicesPropertyIsUISound,
    sizeof(SystemSoundID), &mysound,
    sizeof(AudioServicesPropertyID), &flag);
```

When iPod audio is playing, the system sound generally plays back at the same volume, so users may miss your alert. Consider using vibration in addition to or in place of music. You can check the current playback state by testing as follows. Make sure you include `<MediaPlayer/MediaPlayer.h>` and link to the MediaPlayer framework.

```
if ([MPMusicPlayerController iPodMusicPlayer].playbackState ==
     MPMusicPlaybackStatePlaying)
```

Add an optional system sound completion callback to notify your program when a sound finishes playing by calling `AudioServicesAddSystemSoundCompletion.` Unless you use short sounds that are chained one after another, this is a step you can generally skip.

Clean up your sounds by calling `AudioServicesDisposeSystemSoundID` with the sound in question. This frees the sound object and all its associated resources.

> **Note**
>
> To use these system sound services, make sure to include `AudioToolbox/AudioServices.h` in your code and link to the Audio Toolbox framework.

Vibration

As with audio sounds, vibration immediately grabs a user's attention. What's more, vibration works for nearly all users, including those who are hearing or visually impaired. Using the same System Audio services, you can vibrate as well as play a sound. All you need is the following one-line call to accomplish it, as used in Recipe 10-13:

```
AudioServicesPlaySystemSound (kSystemSoundID_Vibrate);
```

You cannot vary the vibration parameters. Each call produces a short one- to two-second buzz. On platforms without vibration support (like the iPod touch), this call does nothing—but will not produce an error.

Alerts

Audio Services provides a vibration/sound mashup called an alert sound, which is invoked as follows.

```
AudioServicesPlayAlertSound(mySound);
```

This call, which is also demonstrated in Recipe 10-13, plays the requested sound and, possibly, vibrates or plays a second alert. On iPhones, when the user has set Settings > Sound > Ring > Vibrate to ON, it vibrates the phone. Second generation and later iPod touch units play the sound sans vibration (which is unavailable on those units) through the onboard speaker. First generation iPod touches play a short alert melody in place of the sound on the device speaker while playing the requested audio through to the headphones.

Delays

The first time you play back a system sound on the iPhone, you may encounter delays. You may want to play a silent sound on application initialization to avoid a delay on subsequent playback.

> **Note**
>
> When testing on iPhones, make sure you have not enabled the silent ringer switch on the left side of the unit. This oversight has tripped up many iPhone developers. If your alert sounds must always play, consider using the `AVAudioPlayer` class, which is discussed in Chapter 15, "Audio, Video, and MediaKit."

Recipe 10-13 **Playing Sounds, Alerts, and Vibrations Using Audio Services**

```
@implementation TestBedViewController
- (void) playSound
{
    if ([MPMusicPlayerController iPodMusicPlayer].playbackState ==
        MPMusicPlaybackStatePlaying)
        AudioServicesPlayAlertSound(mysound);
    else
        AudioServicesPlaySystemSound(mysound);
}

- (void) vibrate
{
    AudioServicesPlaySystemSound (kSystemSoundID_Vibrate);
}

- (void) viewDidLoad
{
    // create the sound
    NSString *sndpath = [[NSBundle mainBundle]
        pathForResource:@"basicsound" ofType:@"wav"];
    CFURLRef baseURL = (CFURLRef)[NSURL fileURLWithPath:sndpath];

    // Identify it as not a UI Sound
    AudioServicesCreateSystemSoundID(baseURL, &mysound);
    AudioServicesPropertyID flag = 0;  // 0 means always play
    AudioServicesSetProperty(kAudioServicesPropertyIsUISound,
```

```
        sizeof(SystemSoundID), &mysound,
        sizeof(AudioServicesPropertyID), &flag);

    self.navigationItem.rightBarButtonItem = BARBUTTON(@"Sound",
        @selector(playSound));
    self.navigationItem.leftBarButtonItem = BARBUTTON(@"Vibrate",
        @selector(vibrate));
}

-(void) dealloc
{
    // Clean up
    if (mysound) AudioServicesDisposeSystemSoundID(mysound);
    [super dealloc];
}
@end
```

Get This Recipe's Code

To get the code used for this recipe, go to http://github.com/erica/iphone-3.0-cookbook-, or if you've downloaded the disk image containing all of the sample code from the book, go to the folder for Chapter 10 and open the project for this recipe.

One More Thing: Showing the Volume Alert

The iPhone offers a built-in alert that you can display to allow users to adjust the system volume. Figure 10-12 shows this alert, which consists of a slider and a Done button. Invoke this alert by issuing the following Media Player function.

```
- (void) action
{
    // Show the Media Player volume settings alert
    MPVolumeSettingsAlertShow();
}
```

Test whether this alert is visible by issuing `MPVolumeSettingsAlertIsVisible()`.This returns a Boolean value reflecting whether the alert is already onscreen. Hide the alert with `MPVolumeSettingsAlertHide()`, which dismisses the alert regardless of whether the user taps Done. For these functions to work, you must link to the MediaPlayer framework and import the media player headers.

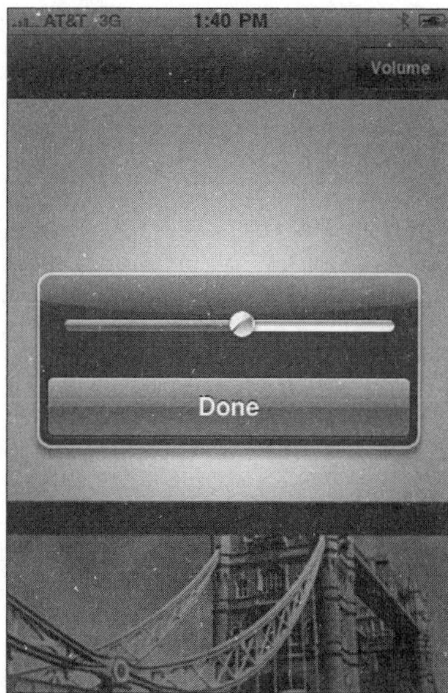

Figure 10-12 The Media Player class's utility volume alert panel.

Summary

This chapter introduced ways to interact directly with your user. You learned how to build alerts—visual, auditory, and tactile—that grab your user's attention and can request immediate feedback. Use these examples to enhance the interactive appeal of your programs and leverage some unique iPhone-only features. Here are a few thoughts to carry away from this chapter:

- Whenever any task will take a noticeable amount of time, be courteous to your user and display some kind of progress feedback. The iPhone offers many ways to do this, from heads-up displays to status bar indicators and beyond. You may need to divert the non-GUI elements of your task to new thread to avoid blocking.
- Alerts take users into the moment. They're designed to elicit responses while communicating information. And, as you saw in this chapter, they're almost insanely customizable. It's possible to build entire applications around the simple `UIAlertView`.
- Don't be afraid of the run loop. A modal response from an alert or action sheet lets you poll users for immediate choices without being dependent on asynchronous callbacks.

- If blue colored system-supplied features do not match your application design needs, skip them. You can easily build your own alerts and menus using `UIView` instances and animation.
- Audio feedback including beeps and vibration can enhance your programs and make your interaction richer. Using system sound calls means that your sounds play nicely with iPod functionality and won't ruin the ongoing listening experience. At the same time, don't be obnoxious. Use alert sounds sparingly and meaningfully to avoid annoying your users.

11

Creating and Managing Table Views

Tables provide a scrolling list-based interaction class that works particularly well on a small, cramped device. Many if not most apps that ship natively with the iPhone and iPod touch center on tables, including Contacts, Settings, iPod, YouTube, Stocks, and Weather. The iPhone's limited screen size makes tables, with their scrolling and individual item selection, an ideal way to deliver information and content in simple, easy-to-manipulate form. In this chapter, you discover how iPhone tables work, what kinds of tables are available to you as a developer, and how you can use table features in your own programs.

Introducing UITableView and UITableViewController

The standard iPhone table consists of a simple scrolling list of individual cells, providing a manipulatable data index. Users may scroll or flick their way up and down until they find an item they want to interact with. Then, they can work with that item independently of other rows. On the iPhone, tables are ubiquitous. Nearly every standard software package uses them, and they form the core of many third-party applications, too. In this section, you discover how tables function and what elements you need to bring together to create your own.

The iPhone SDK supports several kinds of tables, many of which are implemented as flavors of the `UITableView` class. In addition to the standard scrolling list of cells, which provides the most generic table implementation, you can create several specialized tables. These include the kind of tables you see in the Preferences application, with their blue-gray background and rounded cell edges; tables with sections and an index like the ones used in the Contacts application; and related classes of wheeled tables, like those used to set appointment dates and alarms. No matter what type of table you use, they all work in the same general way. They contain cells provided from a data source and respond to user interactions by calling well-defined delegate methods.

The UITableViewController class derives from the UIViewController class. Like its parent class, it helps you build onscreen presentations with minimal programming and maximum convenience. The UITableViewController class greatly simplifies the process of creating a UITableView, reducing or eliminating the repetitive steps required for working directly with table instances. UITableViewController handles the fussy details for the table view layout and provides table-specific convenience by adding a local tableView instance variable and automatic table protocol support for delegates and data sources.

Creating the Table

To implement tables, you must define three key elements: how the table is laid out, the kinds of things that are used to fill the table, and how the table reacts to user interaction. Specify these elements by adding descriptions and methods to your application. You create the visual layout when building your views, you define a data source that feeds table cells on demand, and you implement delegate methods that respond to user interactions such as row-selection changes.

Laying Out the View

UITableViews instances are, as the name suggests, views. They present interactive tables on the iPhone screen. The UITableView class inherits from the UIScrollView class. This inheritance provides the up and down scrolling capabilities used by the table. Like other views, UITableView instances define their boundaries through frames, and they can be children or parents of other views. To create a table view, you allocate it, initialize it with a frame just like any other view, and then add all the bookkeeping details by assigning data source and delegate objects.

UITableViewControllers take care of the layout work for you. The UITableViewController class creates a standard UIViewController and populates it with a single UITableView, setting its frame to allow for any navigation bars or toolbars. You may access that table view via the tableView instance variable.

One important note: When subclassing UITableViewController, if you define a loadView method, be sure to call its superclass's implementation—that is:

```
- (void) loadView
{
    [super loadView];
    ...the rest of your method...
}
```

Doing this ensures that the table view is properly set up, while letting you add custom features in the subclass such as navigation item buttons. If you create your UITableViewController using Interface Builder, you do not have to add any special calls to loadView.

Assigning a Data Source

`UITableView` instances rely on an external source to feed either new or existing table cells on demand. This external source is called a *data source* and refers to the object whose responsibility it is to return a cell to a table's query.

Data sources provide table cells based on an index path. Index paths, objects of the `NSIndexPath` class, describe the path through a data tree to a particular node, namely their section and their row. Although many simple tables only use one section, tables can use sections to split data into logical groups. A `UITableView` instance uses index paths to specify a section and the row within that section.

It's the data source's job to connect that path to a concrete `UITableViewCell` instance and return that cell on demand. You can create an index path by supplying the section and row:

```
myIndexPath = [NSIndexPath indexPathForRow:5 inSection:0];
```

Recover those values by using the `row` and `section` properties of the index path object.

The iPhone SDK provides a built-in mechanism for reusing table cells. When cells scroll off the table and out of view, the table can cache them into a reuse queue. You can tag cells for reuse and then pop them off that queue as needed. This saves memory and provides a fast, efficient way to feed cells when users scroll quickly through long lists onscreen. Recipe 11-8 looks at cell reuse in more detail.

You're not limited to single cell types either. The following snippet chooses which of two kinds of cells to request from the reusable cell queue. Default cells provide a single label; subtitle cells add a second. The identifier is arbitrary, as defined by the developer.

```
UITableViewCell *cell;
UITableViewCellStyle style;
NSString *identifier;

if (item.notes)
{
    style = UITableViewCellStyleSubtitle;
    identifier = @"notescell";
}
else
{
    style = UITableViewCellStyleDefault;
    identifier = @"basecell";
}

cell = [aTableView dequeueReusableCellWithIdentifier:identifier];
if (!cell)
    cell = [[[UITableViewCell alloc] initWithStyle:style
        reuseIdentifier:identifier] autorelease];
```

Use the table's `dataSource` property to assign an object to a table as its data source. That object must implement the `UITableViewDataSource` protocol. Most typically, the `UITableViewController` that owns the table view acts as the data source for that view. When working with `UITableViewController` subclasses, you need not declare the protocol as the parent class implicitly supports that protocol and automatically assigns the controller as the data source.

After assigning a data source, load your table up with its cells by implementing the `tableView:cellForRowAtIndexPath:` method. On calling the table's `reloadData` method, the table starts querying its data source to load the actual onscreen cells into your table. You can also call `reloadData` at any time to force the table to reload its contents.

Assigning a Delegate

Like many other Cocoa Touch interaction objects, `UITableView` instances use delegates to respond to user interactions and implement a meaningful response. Your table's delegate can respond to events like the table scrolling or row selection changes. Delegation tells the table to hand off responsibility for reacting to these interactions to the object you specify, typically the `UITableViewController` object that owns the table view.

If you're working directly with a `UITableView`, use the standard `setDelegate:` method to set your table's delegate. The delegate must implement the `UITableViewDelegate` protocol. When classes implement a delegate protocol, you add a declaration within the class header file. See Chapter 3, "Objective-C Boot Camp," for an explanation of declaring protocols.

When working with `UITableViewController`, omit the `setDelegate:` method and protocol assignment. That class automatically handles this. A full set of delegate methods is listed in the Apple SDK documentation, and the most basic ones are discussed in this chapter.

> **Note**
>
> `UITableView` instances provide notifications in addition to delegate method calls. Notifications enable different threads of your application to communicate with each other by broadcasting updates via the default `NSNotificationCenter`. You can subscribe your application to these notifications using standard `NSNotificationCenter` observers to find out when the table states change. With the 3.0 SDK, the only official table notification is `UITableViewSelectionDidChangeNotification`.

Recipe: Implementing a Very Basic Table

The `UITableViewController` class embeds a `UITableView` into a `UIViewController` object that manages its table view. This view is accessed via the `tableView` property. These controllers automatically set the data source and delegate methods for the table view to itself. So it's really a plug-and-play situation. For a really basic table, all you need to bring to the table are some data and a few data source functions that feed cells and report the number of rows and sections.

Populating a Table

Pretty much any array of strings can be used to set up and populate a table. Recipe 11-1 leverages the `UIFont` class's capability to list available system fonts, that is, a handy list of strings. A call to `[UIFont familyNames]` returns an array populated with those font names. This recipe creates a basic table based on those font names.

Figure 11-1 shows the interface produced by this code, as run on the iPhone simulator. Be aware that running this application on the simulator produces an artificially long set of fonts. That's because the list is based on the available fonts from the Macintosh running the SDK rather than the fonts on the iPhone itself.

Figure 11-1 It's easy to fill a `UITableView` with cells based on any array of strings. This table presents the font family list from the `UIFont` class. When tapped, the chosen item updates the font on the navigation bar at the top.

Data Source Methods

To display a table, every table data source must implement three core methods. These methods define how the table is structured and provide contents for the table:

- **`numberOfSectionsInTableView`**—Tables can display their data in sections or as a single list. For simple tables, return 1. This indicates that the entire table should be presented as one single list. For sectioned lists, return a value of 2 or higher.

- **`tableView:numberOfRowsInSection`**—This method returns the number of rows for each section. When working with simple lists, return the number of rows for the entire table here. For more complex lists, you'll want to provide a way to report back per section. Section ordering starts with 0.
- **`tableView: cellForRowAtIndexPath:`**—This method returns a cell to the calling table. Use the index path's `row` and `section` properties to determine which cell to provide and make sure to take advantage of reusable cells where possible to minimize memory overhead.

Reusing Cells

One of the ways the iPhone conserves memory is by reusing cells. You can assign an identifier string to each cell. This specifies what kind of cell it is, and when that cell scrolls off-screen allows that cell to be recovered for reuse. Use different IDs for different kinds of cells. For simple tables, a single identifier does the job. In the case of Recipe 11-1, it is `@"BaseCell"`. The strings are arbitrary. Define them the way you want, but when using multiple cell types keep the names meaningful. The discussion for Recipe 11-8, which follows later in this chapter, explores cell reuse.

Before allocating a new cell, always check whether a reusable cell is available. If your table returns `nil` from a request to `dequeueReusableCellWithIdentifier:`, you need to allocate a new cell.

If the method returns a cell, update that cell with the information that's meaningful for the current row and section indices. You do not need to add cells to the reuse queue. Cocoa Touch handles all those details for you.

Font Table Sample

Recipe 11-1 demonstrates how to build a simple list-based table. It creates a table and fills that table with all available font families. When tapped, the view controller assigns that font to the label in the navigation bar at the top of the screen and prints a list of available fonts for that family out to the debugger console. This behavior is defined in the `tableView:didSelectRowAtIndexPath:` delegate method, which is called when a user taps a row.

Using the `UITableViewController` as a delegate is a good choice because the table's user interactions affect its views. If you'd rather use another delegate, call `setDelegate:` with that object to override the standard `UITableViewController` settings.

Apple made several big changes in table view cells between the 2.x and 3.x SDKs. Prior to 3.0, you could set a cell's `text` and `image` properties directly. Starting with the 3.0 SDK, Apple introduced the `textLabel`, `detailLabel`, and `imageView` properties. Each property now points to an actual UI object (two `UILabels` and a `UIImageView`), offering direct access to each object.

Note

Tables enable you to set the color for the selected cell by choosing between a blue or gray overlay. Set the `selectionStyle` property to either `UITableViewCellSelection➥StyleBlue` or `UITableViewCellSelectionStyleGray`. If you'd rather not show a selection, use `UITableViewCellSelectionStyleNone`. The cell can still be selected, but the overlay color will not display.

Recipe 11-1 **Building a Basic Table**

```
#define MAINLABEL    ((UILabel *)self.navigationItem.titleView)

@interface TableListViewController : UITableViewController
@end

@implementation TableListViewController

- (NSInteger)numberOfSectionsInTableView:(UITableView *)aTableView
{
    // One section in this simple table
    return 1;
}

- (NSInteger)tableView:(UITableView *)aTableView
    numberOfRowsInSection:(NSInteger)section
{
    // Number of rows in use
    return [UIFont familyNames].count;
}

- (UITableViewCell *)tableView:(UITableView *)tView
    cellForRowAtIndexPath:(NSIndexPath *)indexPath
{
    // Attempt to dequeue a cell. If this is not possible, create one
    UITableViewCellStyle style =  UITableViewCellStyleDefault;
    UITableViewCell *cell = [tView
        dequeueReusableCellWithIdentifier:@"BaseCell"];
    if (!cell)
        cell = [[[UITableViewCell alloc] initWithStyle:style
            reuseIdentifier:@"BaseCell"] autorelease];

    // Set the cell text
    cell.textLabel.text = [[UIFont familyNames]
        objectAtIndex:indexPath.row];
    return cell;
}

- (void)tableView:(UITableView *)tableView
```

```
    didSelectRowAtIndexPath:(NSIndexPath *)indexPath
{
    // React to cell selection by updating the title view text
    NSString *font = [[UIFont familyNames]
        objectAtIndex:indexPath.row];
    [MAINLABEL setText:font];
    [MAINLABEL setFont:[UIFont fontWithName:font size:18.0f]];
}

- (void) loadView
{
    // Add a custom label to the navigation bar's title view
    [super loadView];
    self.navigationItem.titleView = [[[UILabel alloc]
        initWithFrame:CGRectMake(0.0f, 0.0f, 200.0f, 30.0f)]
        autorelease];
    [MAINLABEL setBackgroundColor:[UIColor clearColor]];
    [MAINLABEL setTextColor:[UIColor whiteColor]];
    [MAINLABEL setTextAlignment:UITextAlignmentCenter];
}
@end
```

Get This Recipe's Code

To get the code used for this recipe, go to http://github.com/erica/iphone-3.0-cookbook-, or if you've downloaded the disk image containing all of the sample code from the book, go to the folder for Chapter 11 and open the project for this recipe.

Recipe: Changing a Table's Background Color

To use a color for your table's background other than white, use the table view's `backgroundColor` property, as demonstrated in Recipe 11-2. Individual cells inherit this color, producing a table whose components all show that color. Make sure that you choose a cell text color that compliments any table background color. For a dark purple background, as defined and used in this recipe, a strong white contrasts nicely.

Unfortunately, you cannot change individual cell backgrounds directly. That is to say, you can, by setting the cell's `backgroundColor` property, but nearly all the color change will happen behind label views. The labels block the cell's background, obscuring it from view. You will see few, if any, changes to the cell. Set the table style to `UITableViewStyleGrouped` for the most (i.e., "not much") background visibility.

Recipe 11-2 **Changing the Background Color for a Table**

```
- (void)applicationDidFinishLaunching:(UIApplication *)application
{
    // Create Table View Controller and set its background color
```

```
    TableListViewController *tlvc = [[TableListViewController alloc]
        init];
    tlvc.tableView.backgroundColor = COOKBOOK_PURPLE_COLOR;

    // Initialize Navigation Controller
    UINavigationController *nav = [[UINavigationController alloc]
        initWithRootViewController:tlvc];
    nav.navigationBar.tintColor = COOKBOOK_PURPLE_COLOR;

    // Create main window
    UIWindow *window = [[UIWindow alloc] initWithFrame:[[UIScreen
        mainScreen] bounds]];
    [window addSubview:nav.view];
    [window makeKeyAndVisible];
}
```

Get This Recipe's Code

To get the code used for this recipe, go to http://github.com/erica/iphone-3.0-cookbook-, or if you've downloaded the disk image containing all of the sample code from the book, go to the folder for Chapter 11 and open the project for this recipe.

Updating the Background Color to Reflect the Degree of Scrolling

Because `UITableViews` are a subclass of the `UIScrollView` class, you can adapt your table background color to the degree that a user has scrolled down the table. For example, you might lighten or darken the background color. Use the percentage of distance as a multiplication factor for the color components used to tint the background.

In their default state, all `UITableViewController` instances are automatically set as `UIScrollView` delegates. No further work is needed before adding the following `UIScrollViewDelegate` method to your `UITableViewController` implementation. The following code calculates background color saturation from the current table offset.

```
- (void) scrollViewDidScroll: (UIScrollView *) sv
{
    float percent =  sv.contentOffset.y / sv.contentSize.height;
    percent = 0.5 + (MAX(MIN(1.0f, percent), 0.0f) / 2.0f);
    self.tableView.backgroundColor = [UIColor

        colorWithRed:percent * 0.20392 green:percent * 0.19607
        blue:percent * 0.61176 alpha: 1.0f];
}
```

Here are a few things to note about background color updates. First, if you don't enable bouncing (i.e., allowing the table to bounce past the content edges and then move back), decrease the divisor by the height of the table. Second, make sure you set your initial colors when setting up your table. Otherwise, the color will "jump" the first time the user touches the table. Finally, although this approach is not computationally overwhelming, it does require constant screen updates and should be avoided for processor-heavy applications.

Recipe: Creating a Table Image Backsplash

Recipe 11-3 expands the background color idea presented in Recipe 11-2 to create a table view with an image backdrop. Instead of coloring the background to a solid hue, this recipe uses a clear color with an alpha level of 0. By adding the backdrop to the application window before adding the table view, the image bleeds through the table, as shown in Figure 11-2.

Figure 11-2 Combine a clear table background color with a backsplash to create a table that scrolls over an image.

The table scrolls over the image, which remains static behind it. Keep the imagery relevant (for example, a corporate logo) and desaturated or otherwise lightened enough that it will not interfere with the table's text presentation. Use a text color that contrasts well with the background image.

Recipe 11-3 **Scrolling a Table over a Static Image**

```
- (void)applicationDidFinishLaunching:(UIApplication *)application
{
```

```
    // Create Table View Controller with a clear background
    TableListViewController *tlvc = [[TableListViewController alloc]
        init];
    tlvc.tableView.backgroundColor = [UIColor clearColor];

    // Initialize Navigation Controller
    UINavigationController *nav = [[UINavigationController alloc]
        initWithRootViewController:tlvc];
    nav.navigationBar.tintColor = COOKBOOK_PURPLE_COLOR;

    // Load in the backsplash image into a view
    UIImageView *iv = [[[UIImageView alloc] initWithImage:[UIImage
        imageNamed:@"Backsplash.png"]] autorelease];

    // Create main window
    UIWindow *window = [[UIWindow alloc] initWithFrame:[[UIScreen
        mainScreen] bounds]];
    [window addSubview:iv];
    [window addSubview:nav.view];
    [window makeKeyAndVisible];
}
```

Get This Recipe's Code

To get the code used for this recipe, go to http://github.com/erica/iphone-3.0-cookbook-, or if you've downloaded the disk image containing all of the sample code from the book, go to the folder for Chapter 11 and open the project for this recipe.

Recipe: Exploring Cell Types

The iPhone offers four kinds of base table view cells. These types, which are shown in Figure 11-3, provide basic utilitarian cell implementations. Each of these cell styles is new to the 3.0 SDK (although the default style was used in 2.x, it has a new style name constant) and represents a new way of creating and interacting with table cells.

Before 3.0, you assigned a cell's text directly. Now cells provide both a `textLabel` and a `detailTextLabel` property, which offer access to the labels themselves. With direct label access, you can set each label's text traits as desired. Here is a round-up of the four new styles:

- **`UITableViewCellStyleDefault`**—This cell offers a single left-aligned text label and an optional image. When images are used, the label is pushed to the right, decreasing the amount of space available for text. You can access and modify the `detailTextLabel`, but it is not shown onscreen.
- **`UITableViewCellStyleSubtitle`**—This cell, which is used in the iPod application, pushes the standard text label up a bit to make way for the smaller detail label beneath it. The detail label displays in gray. Like the default cell, the subtitle cell offers an optional image.

- **UITableViewCellStyleValue1**—This cell style, seen in the Settings application, offers a large black primary label on the left side of the cell and a slightly smaller, blue subtitle detail label to its right. This cell does not support images.
- **UITableViewCellStyleValue2**—The Phone/Contacts application uses this kind of cell, which consists of a small blue primary label on the left and a small black subtitle detail label to its right. The small width of the primary label means that most text will be cut off by an ellipsis. This cell does not support images.

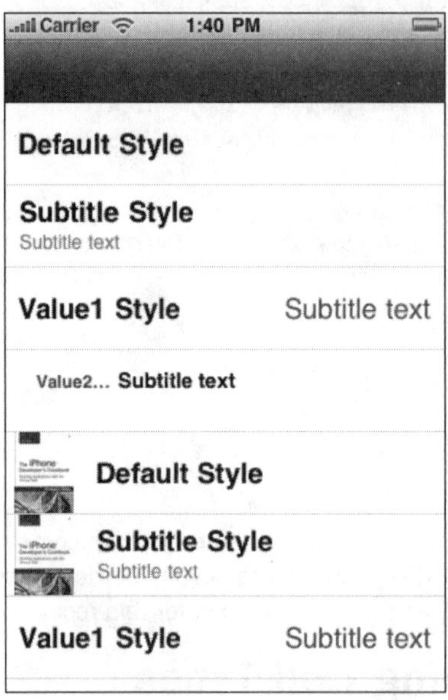

Figure 11-3 Cocoa Touch provides four standard cell types, some of which support optional images.

Recipe 11-4 shows the code that created the cells of Figure 11-3. It labels each cell with the type in use and uses that same text as the reuse identifier. Images are added to all cells past the first four, demonstrating that only the default and subtitle presentations support image display.

Recipe 11-4 Creating Various Table Cell Styles

```
- (UITableViewCell *)tableView:(UITableView *)tView
    cellForRowAtIndexPath:(NSIndexPath *)indexPath
{
    UITableViewCellStyle style;
    NSString *cellType;

    // Choose the cell style and tag
    switch (indexPath.row % 4)
```

```
    {
        case 0:
            style = UITableViewCellStyleDefault;
            cellType = @"Default Style";
            break;
        case 1:
            style = UITableViewCellStyleSubtitle;
            cellType = @"Subtitle Style";
            break;
        case 2:
            style = UITableViewCellStyleValue1;
            cellType = @"Value1 Style";
            break;
        case 3:
            style =  UITableViewCellStyleValue2;
            cellType =  @"Value2 Style";
            break;
    }

    // Dequeue a cell if possible, if not, create one.
    UITableViewCell *cell = [tView
        dequeueReusableCellWithIdentifier:cellType];
    if (!cell)
        cell = [[[UITableViewCell alloc] initWithStyle:style
        reuseIdentifier:cellType] autorelease];

    // Add images to all cells after the first four
    if (indexPath.row > 3)
        cell.imageView.image = [UIImage imageNamed:@"icon.png"];

    // Set the cell text.
    cell.textLabel.text = cellType;
    cell.detailTextLabel.text = @"Subtitle text";
    return cell;
}
```

Get This Recipe's Code

To get the code used for this recipe, go to http://github.com/erica/iphone-3.0-cookbook-, or if you've downloaded the disk image containing all of the sample code from the book, go to the folder for Chapter 11 and open the project for this recipe.

Recipe: Building Custom Cells in Interface Builder

Interface Builder makes it easy to create custom `UITableViewCell` instances without subclassing. You can build your cells directly in IB and load them in your code, which is exactly what Recipe 11-5 does. The big problem about using IB is that your custom elements are going to get covered by any cell content, as demonstrated by Figure 11-4. You may be aiming for the layout in the left image, but you usually end up with the layout in the right.

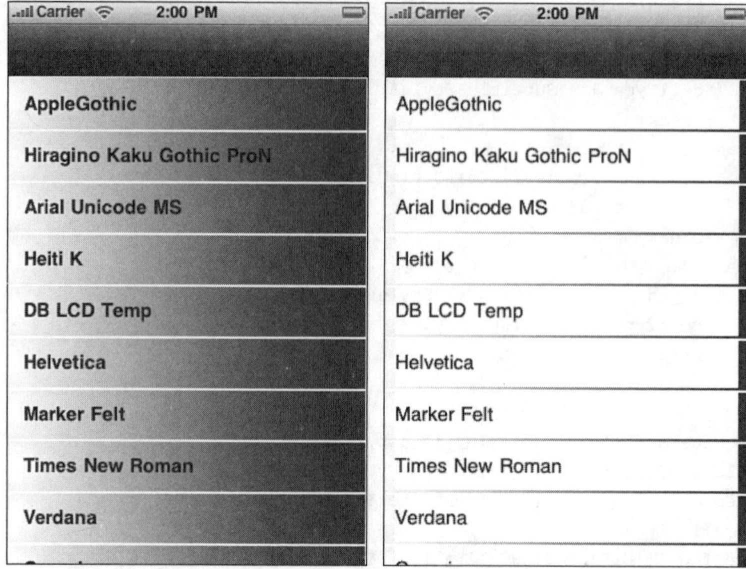

Figure 11-4 When working with cells created in Interface Builder, custom art, like that shown on the left, gets covered over by built-in cell content as shown on the right.

That's because assigning a cell's label's properties cause the cell to create that label view (plus any other necessary supporting views for that label) after the Interface Builder cell has been loaded. Those extra views are placed on top of the cell, hiding your custom art or any other IB elements you've placed into the cell.

You might consider iterating through a cell's subviews, setting their background color to clear, but Apple frowns on view spelunking. There's a simple, SDK-friendly way to work around this. Figure 11-5 (top) shows a basic `UITableViewCell` in Interface Builder, and Figure 11-5 (middle) shows that same cell overlaid with the custom art from this recipe. This is the content that the cell needs to present without being covered over like Figure 11-4.

The trick to preserving the cell art is to avoid using the cell's built-in `label` and `detailLabel` properties. Instead, add a custom label (as shown in Figure 11-5, bottom) and use that label instead of the built-in ones. The label view is tagged (in this case with 101) and recovered from the cell by using that tagging. You can set the tag in Interface Builder's attributes inspector. The following macro uses that tag to access the custom label.

```
#define TEXTLABEL ((UILabel *)[cell viewWithTag:101])
```

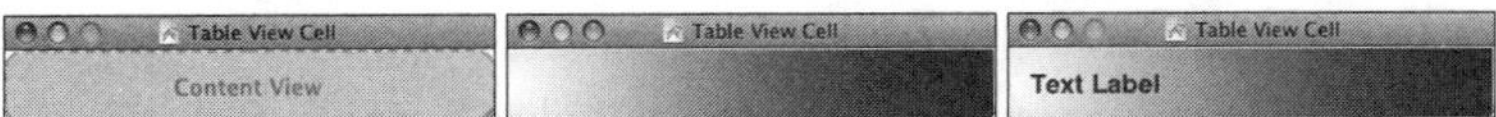

Figure 11-5 The top image shows a default cell created in Interface Builder without any content. The middle image shows that same cell after adding custom art to the cell. Adding a custom text label (bottom image) helps create a properly labeled cell like the one shown in Figure 11-4 (left).

When you need to use more than one label, for example for a subtitle, add another in Interface Builder and tag it with a different number.

Tables built with this approach are fully compliant with all table features. As Figure 11-6 shows, you can use standard editing with custom cells, and they will update, indent, and otherwise behave like any other table cells. If the label and image provided don't fit your purpose, build your own views and add them as cell subviews.

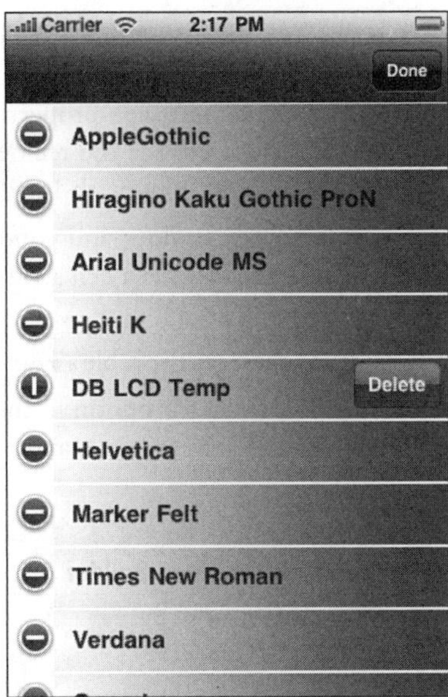

Figure 11-6 Cells built with custom labels in Interface Builder remain able to work with all standard editing tasks including shifting to accommodate the display of delete and delete confirmation buttons.

Tips for Creating Custom Cells

When building custom table view cells in Interface Builder, keep the following tips in mind:

- Create the new xib by choosing File > New File > User Interface > Empty XIB in Xcode. Name the file meaningfully, for example, BaseCell.xib, and save it.
- Open the empty xib file in Interface Builder and drag a `UITableViewCell` into your project window.
- Customize the cell contents by adding art and other interface items. Be aware that text-editing based classes such as `UITextField` and `UITextView` do not work well in table view cells unless you take special care.
- When adding custom items, try to clear enough space (about 40 pixels) on the right side of the cell to allow the cell to shift right when entering edit mode. Otherwise, those items will be cut off.
- Set the reuse identifier (e.g., "BaseCell"), in the cell's attributes inspector (Command-1). The identifier field lies near the top of the inspector.
- You can set the cell's image and selected image using the inspector, but in real life, these are usually generated based on live data. You'll probably want to handle any image setting (via the `image` and `selectedImage` properties) in code. Make sure that the images you send are properly sized. See the recipes about creating thumbnail versions of images in Chapter 7, "Working with Images."
- You cannot pick a cell style in Interface Builder, and you cannot change a cell style once you've loaded the nib. If you need to use a cell style other than the default, build your cell in code.
- Use any cell height you need and then set the table's `rowHeight` property to match.
- Although Interface Builder offers a separator option in the cell's attributes inspector, you'll want to use the table view's `separatorStyle` and `separatorColor` properties instead.

Recipe 11-5 **Using Custom Cells Built in Interface Builder**

```
- (UITableViewCell *)tableView:(UITableView *)tView
    cellForRowAtIndexPath:(NSIndexPath *)indexPath
{
    // Attempt to dequeue a cell. If that's not possible, load it.
    UITableViewCell *cell = [tView
        dequeueReusableCellWithIdentifier:@"BaseCell"];
    if (!cell)
        cell = [[[NSBundle mainBundle] loadNibNamed:@"BaseCell"
            owner:self options:nil] lastObject];

    // Set the cell text
    [TEXTLABEL setText:
        [[UIFont familyNames] objectAtIndex:indexPath.row]];
```

```
    return cell;
}
```

Get This Recipe's Code

To get the code used for this recipe, go to http://github.com/erica/iphone-3.0-cookbook-, or if you've downloaded the disk image containing all of the sample code from the book, go to the folder for Chapter 11 and open the project for this recipe.

Adding in Custom Selection Traits

When users select cells, Cocoa Touch provides you several ways to emphasize the cell's selection. Customize a cell's selection behavior by updating any of three traits. You can change the image it shows, the color of its font, and the cell's background. These are set via the `selectedImage`, `selectedTextColor`, and `selectedBackgroundView` properties.

The selected image replaces any image you have added to a cell (via the `image` property, as shown in Recipe 11-4) when the user selects the cell. The selected version should use the same size as the original so the cell layout remains stable. For example, you might want to replace an "empty" image, that is, a spaceholder, with an arrow, chevron, or finger pointing into the cell that has been selected.

The selected text color property is officially deprecated despite the fact that it is still used in Interface Builder. The Apple documents suggest using the new `textLabel` property but do not provide an easy way to hook into that object for selection/deselection updates. Until Apple addresses the issue, you can use the workaround shown in the following snippet, which avoids compile-time deprecation warnings:

```
cell.selectedBackgroundView = [[[UIImageView alloc]
    initWithImage:[UIImage imageNamed:@"cellart.png"]] autorelease];

// This is deprecated but it still works and is used in IB
[cell performSelector:@selector(setSelectedTextColor)
    withObject:COOKBOOK_PURPLE_COLOR];
```

The `selectedBackgroundView` property works exactly as you'd want the regular `backgroundView` property to work but does not (refer to Figure 11-4). When a cell is selected, the selected background appears behind the text, providing a perfect blend between art and text.

Recipe: Alternating Cell Colors

Although blue and white cell alternation is a common and highly requested table feature, Apple did not include that option in its iPhone SDK. The custom cell techniques shown previously in Recipe 11-5 let you import a cell designed in Interface Builder. Recipe 11-6 builds the alternating white/blue cell structure shown in Figure 11-7 by working with not one but two custom cell xibs.

Figure 11-7 Use custom cells to create alternating blue and white cells.

A simple even/odd check (`row % 2`) specifies whether to load a blue or white cell. Because this table uses just one section, it simplifies the math considerably. Blue/white alternating cells work best for nongrouped, nonsectioned tables both visually and programmatically.

Notice how this recipe uses cell identifiers to reuse already loaded cells as needed. The xibs use the same identifiers as their filenames, considerably simplifying this code. New blue or white cells are not created if existing ones can be consumed from the reuse queue.

Be aware that although this cell style works with edits, both deletion and reordering, you'll want to reload the table after each user change to keep the blue/white/blue/white ordering. As the user drags an item into place, it will retain its original coloring, possibly causing a visual discontinuity until the edit finishes. For reordering, issue that reload command using a delayed selector of at least a quarter to half a second.

Recipe 11-6 Building a Table with Alternately Colored Cells

```
- (UITableViewCell *)tableView:(UITableView *)tView
    cellForRowAtIndexPath:(NSIndexPath *)indexPath
{
    // Choose the cell kind
    NSString *identifier = (indexPath.row % 2) ?
        @"WhiteCell" : @"BlueCell";
```

```
    // Attempt to dequeue. Load if that's not possible.
    UITableViewCell *cell = [tView dequeueReusableCellWithIdentifier:
        identifier];
    if (!cell)
        cell = [[[NSBundle mainBundle] loadNibNamed:identifier
            owner:self options:nil] lastObject];

    // Set the cell text
    [(UILabel *)[cell viewWithTag:101] setText:
        [[UIFont familyNames] objectAtIndex:indexPath.row]];
    return cell;
}
```

Get This Recipe's Code

To get the code used for this recipe, go to http://github.com/erica/iphone-3.0-cookbook-, or if you've downloaded the disk image containing all of the sample code from the book, go to the folder for Chapter 11 and open the project for this recipe.

Recipe: Building a Custom Cell with Built-In Controls

When using Interface Builder to design a custom cell, you're not limited to background art and labels. It's easy enough to add buttons or other controls that act in cell-native ways. Recipe 11-7 manages the cells shown in Figure 11-8. These cells include a main text label, which is used to display a font name; a subtitle label, which presents a standard phrase using that font; and a family button that displays a list of all members of a given font family via an alert.

Rather than use a custom `UITableViewCell` as Recipe 11-6 did, Recipe 11-7 creates a subclass. `CustomCell` introduces three outlets. These include the button and the two labels. And it adds an action, `buttonPress:`, which is called for touch-up-inside events. The connections between the `IBOutlets`, `IBAction`, and their targets are all made directly in Interface Builder.

To make this recipe work, you must create a `UITableViewCell` instance. Import the class header for `CustomCell` (select File > Read Class Files) and then use the Identity Inspector (Tools > Identity Inspector, Command-4) to change that instance's class from `UITableViewCell` to `CustomCell`. Once that's done, you can wire up the outlets and button callback connections using Interface Builder's drag-to-connect features.

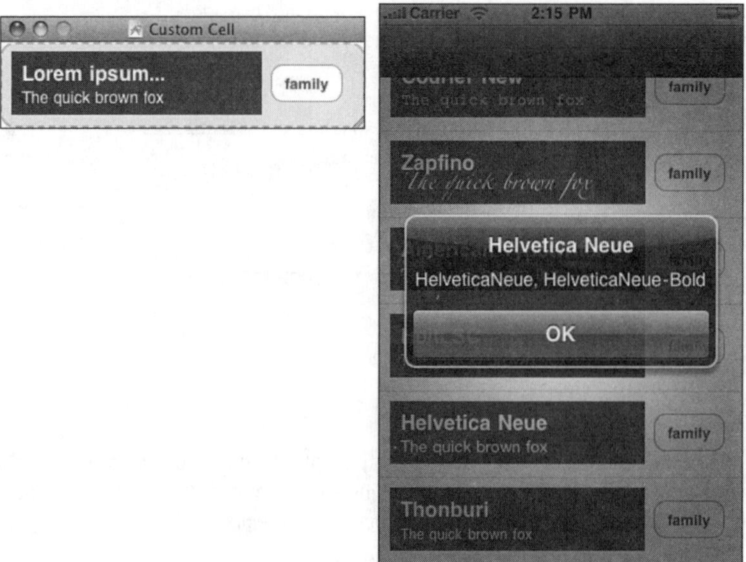

Figure 11-8 The button added in Interface Builder for this custom cell (top) launches an alert with a list of font families (bottom). Each button is tied to its own cell and works whether or not the cell is selected.

Recipe 11-7 **Creating an Embedded Cell Control Callback**

```
@interface CustomCell : UITableViewCell {
    IBOutlet UIButton *button;
    IBOutlet UILabel *primaryLabel;
    IBOutlet UILabel  *secondaryLabel;
}

@property (assign) UIButton *button;
@property (assign) UILabel *primaryLabel;
@property (assign) UILabel *secondaryLabel;

- (IBAction) buttonPress: (UIButton *) aButton;
@end

@implementation CustomCell
@synthesize button;
@synthesize primaryLabel;
@synthesize secondaryLabel;

- (IBAction) buttonPress: (UIButton *) aButton
```

```
{
    NSString *fontName = self.primaryLabel.text;
    NSArray *fonts = [UIFont fontNamesForFamilyName:fontName];
    UIAlertView *av = [[[UIAlertView alloc] initWithTitle:fontName
        message:[fonts componentsJoinedByString:@", "] delegate:nil
        cancelButtonTitle:@"OK" otherButtonTitles:nil] autorelease];
    [av show];
}
@end
```

Get This Recipe's Code

To get the code used for this recipe, go to http://github.com/erica/iphone-3.0-cookbook-, or if you've downloaded the disk image containing all of the sample code from the book, go to the folder for Chapter 11 and open the project for this recipe.

Recipe: Remembering Control State for Custom Cells

Cells have no "memory" to speak of. They do not know how an application last used them. They are views and nothing more. That means if you reuse cells without tying those cells to some sort of data model, you can end up with unexpected and unintentional results. This is a natural consequence of the Model-View-Controller design paradigm.

Consider the following scenario. Say you created a series of cells each of which owned a toggle switch. Users can interact with that switch and change its value. A cell that scrolls offscreen, landing on the reuse queue, could therefore show an already-toggled state for a table element that user hasn't yet touched.

Figure 11-9 demonstrates this problem. The cell used for Item A was reused for Item L, presenting an OFF setting, even though the user has never interacted with Item L. It's the cell that retains the setting, not the logical item. Don't depend on cells to retain state that way.

To fix this problem, check your cell state against a stored model. This keeps the view consistent with your application semantics. Recipe 11-8 uses a custom dictionary to associate cell state with the cell item. There are other ways to approach this problem, but this simple example provides a taste of the model/view balance needed by a data source whose views present state information.

Since the state is stored in the table view controller, each cell needs to be able to "call home" so to speak when its switch updates its state. The custom `tableViewController` property that is set here provides that back link, and the `customSwitch` property accesses the current user-set state.

Figure 11-9 The cell used to present Item A (left) is reused to present Item L (right) while retaining its previous switch setting.

Recipe 11-8 Using Stored State to Refresh a Reused Table Cell

```
- (UITableViewCell *)tableView:(UITableView *)tView
    cellForRowAtIndexPath:(NSIndexPath *)indexPath
{
    // Dequeue a cell if possible
    CustomCell *cell = (CustomCell *)[tView
        dequeueReusableCellWithIdentifier:@"BaseCell"];
    if (!cell)
        cell = [[[NSBundle mainBundle] loadNibNamed:@"BaseCell"
            owner:self options:nil] lastObject];

    // Determine the key and state based on the row
    NSString *key = [ALPHA objectAtIndex:indexPath.row];
    cell.customLabel.text = key;
    cell.tableViewController = self;
    if (self.switchStates)
    {
        NSNumber *state;
        if (state = [self.switchStates objectForKey:key])
            cell.customSwitch.on = [state boolValue];
        else
        {
            cell.customSwitch.on = YES;
```

```
            [self.switchStates setObject:[NSNumber numberWithBool:YES]
                forKey:key];
        }
    }

    return (UITableViewCell *)cell;
}

- (void) updateSwitch:(UISwitch *) aSwitch forItem: (NSString *) anItem
{
    // The switch sends this callback when its value changes
    if (self.switchStates)
        [self.switchStates setObject:[NSNumber
            numberWithBool:aSwitch.on] forKey: anItem];
}
```

Get This Recipe's Code

To get the code used for this recipe, go to http://github.com/erica/iphone-3.0-cookbook-, or if you've downloaded the disk image containing all of the sample code from the book, go to the folder for Chapter 11 and open the project for this recipe.

Visualizing Cell Reuse

Recipe 11-8 helps fix problems with cell/model discrepancies. The following code snippet visualizes exactly how your cells are getting reused. This implementation tags each new cell on creation, letting you track how each cell is used and reused in the lifetime of a very large table. In this case, the table is about a million items long. I encourage you to test this snippet out (a full version is included in the sample code for this book) and energetically scroll through the list in both directions. You'll see that with a jerky enough interaction style you can really mix up your cell ordering. You'll also discover that even for a million item table, you'll max out at about 11 table cells total.

```
@implementation TableListViewController
- (NSInteger)numberOfSectionsInTableView:(UITableView *)aTableView
{
    return 1;
}

- (NSInteger)tableView:(UITableView *)aTableView
    numberOfRowsInSection:(NSInteger)section
{
    return 999999; // lots
}

- (UITableViewCell *)tableView:(UITableView *)tView
    cellForRowAtIndexPath:(NSIndexPath *)indexPath
```

```
{
    UITableViewCellStyle style =  UITableViewCellStyleDefault;
    UITableViewCell *cell = [tView
        dequeueReusableCellWithIdentifier:@"BaseCell"];

    // Create a new cell with a unique number whenever
    // a cell cannot be dequeued
    if (!cell)
    {
        cell = [[[UITableViewCell alloc] initWithStyle:style
            reuseIdentifier:@"BaseCell"] autorelease];
        cell.textLabel.text = [NSString stringWithFormat:
            @"Cell %d", ++count];
    }
    return cell;
}
@end
```

Each cell implements the `prepareForReuse` method, which is invoked before a cell can be returned from the table view's dequeue request. You can subclass `UITableViewCell` and override this method to reset content before reusing a cell.

Recipe: Creating Checked Table Cells

Accessory views expand normal `UITableViewCell` functionality. The most common accessories are the Delete buttons and drag bars for reordering, but you can also add check marks to create interactive one-of-n or n-of-n selections. With these kinds of selections, you can ask your users to pick what they want to have for dinner or choose which items they want to update. This kind of radio button/check box behavior provides a richness of table interaction. Recipe 11-9 demonstrates how to create this kind of table.

Figure 11-10 shows checks in an interface, a standard `UITableView` with accessorized cells. Check marks appear next to selected items. When tapped, the checks toggle on or off. Like Recipe 11-8, this recipe uses a shared dictionary to track which logical items are checked, avoiding inconsistency issues that arise from cell reuse.

Checked items use the `UITableViewCellAccessoryCheckmark` accessory type. Unchecked items use the `UITableViewCellAccessoryNone` variation. You set these by assigning the cell's `accessoryType` property.

Note that it's the cell that's being checked here, not the logical item associated with the cell (although that logical item's value is updated in the shared `stateDictionary`). Reused cells remain checked or unchecked at next use so you must always set the accessory to match the state dictionary when dequeuing a cell. Recipe 11-8 discussed preserving cell state.

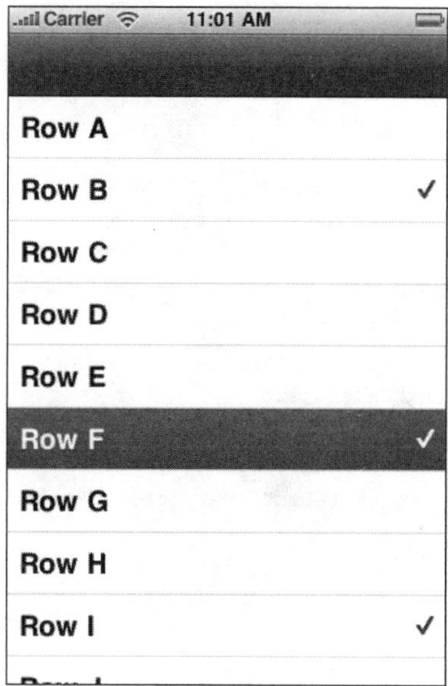

Figure 11-10 Check mark accessories offer a convenient way of making one-of-n or n-of-n selections from a list.

Recipe 11-9 **Using Accessory Check Marks with Cells**

```
- (UITableViewCell *)tableView:(UITableView *)tView
    cellForRowAtIndexPath:(NSIndexPath *)indexPath
{
    // Retrieve or create a cell
    UITableViewCellStyle style =  UITableViewCellStyleDefault;
    UITableViewCell *cell = [tView
        dequeueReusableCellWithIdentifier:@"BaseCell"];
    if (!cell) cell = [[[UITableViewCell alloc] initWithStyle:style
        reuseIdentifier:@"BaseCell"] autorelease];

    // Set cell label
    NSString *key = [@"Row " stringByAppendingString:[ALPHA
        objectAtIndex:indexPath.row]];
    cell.textLabel.text = key;

    // Set cell checkmark
    NSNumber *checked = [self.stateDictionary objectForKey:key];
    if (!checked) [self.stateDictionary setObject:(checked = [NSNumber
        numberWithBool:NO]) forKey:key];
    cell.accessoryType = checked.boolValue ?
```

```
        UITableViewCellAccessoryCheckmark :
        UITableViewCellAccessoryNone;
    return cell;
}

- (void)tableView:(UITableView *)tableView
    didSelectRowAtIndexPath:(NSIndexPath *)indexPath
{
    // Recover the cell and key
    UITableViewCell *cell = [self.tableView
        cellForRowAtIndexPath:indexPath];
    NSString *key = cell.textLabel.text;

    // Created an inverted value and store it
    BOOL isChecked = !([[self.stateDictionary objectForKey:key]
        boolValue]);
    NSNumber *checked = [NSNumber numberWithBool:isChecked];
    [self.stateDictionary setObject:checked forKey:key];

    // Update the cell accessory checkmark
    cell.accessoryType = isChecked ? UITableViewCellAccessoryCheckmark
        : UITableViewCellAccessoryNone;
}
```

Get This Recipe's Code

To get the code used for this recipe, go to http://github.com/erica/iphone-3.0-cookbook-, or if you've downloaded the disk image containing all of the sample code from the book, go to the folder for Chapter 11 and open the project for this recipe.

Recipe: Removing Selection Highlights from Cells

There are times when working with tables that you need to avoid retaining a cell state. This happens when you want users to be able to interact with the table and touch cells, but you don't want to maintain that selected state after the user has finished the interaction. Cocoa Touch offers two approaches for tables that need to deny persistent cell selection.

For the first approach you can set a cell's `selectionStyle` property to `UITableViewCellSelectionStyleNone`. This disables the blue or gray overlays that display on the selected cell, like the one shown in Figure 11-10 for Row F. The cell is still selected but will not highlight on selection in any way. If selecting your cell produces some kind of side effect other than presenting information, this is not the best way to approach things. Instead, consider the following.

The second approach allows the cell to highlight but removes that highlight after the interaction completes. You do that by telling the table to deselect the cell in question. In Recipe 11-10, each user selection triggers a delayed deselection (the custom `deselect:` method defined in the recipe) after a half a second. This method calls the table view's `deselectRowAtIndexPath:animated:` method, which fades away the current selection. Using this approach offers both the highlight that confirms a user action and the state-free display that hides any current selection from the user.

Recipe 11-10 **Deselecting a Table Row**

```
// Perform the deselection
- (void) deselect: (id) sender
{
    [self.tableView deselectRowAtIndexPath:[self.tableView
        indexPathForSelectedRow] animated:YES];
}

// Respond to user selection
- (void)tableView:(UITableView *)tableView
    didSelectRowAtIndexPath:(NSIndexPath *)newIndexPath
{
    printf("User selected row %d\n", [newIndexPath row] + 1);
    [self performSelector:@selector(deselect) withObject:nil
        afterDelay:0.5f];
}
```

> **Get This Recipe's Code**
>
> To get the code used for this recipe, go to http://github.com/erica/iphone-3.0-cookbook-, or if you've downloaded the disk image containing all of the sample code from the book, go to the folder for Chapter 11 and open the project for this recipe.

Recipe: Working with Disclosure Accessories

Disclosures refer to those small, blue or gray, right-facing chevrons found on the right of table cells. Disclosures help you to link from a cell to a view that supports that cell. In the Contacts list and Calendar applications, these chevrons connect to screens that help you to customize contact information and set appointments. Figure 11-11 shows a table view example where each cell displays a disclosure control, showing the two available types.

The blue and gray chevrons have two roles. The blue `UITableViewCellAccessoryDetailDisclosureButton` versions are actual buttons. They respond to touches and are supposed to indicate that the button leads to a full interactive detail view. The gray `UITableViewCellAccessoryDisclosureIndicator` does not track touches and should lead your users to a further options view, specifically options about that choice.

You see these two accessories in play in the Settings application. In the Wi-Fi Networks screen, the detail disclosures lead to specific details about each WiFi network: its IP address, subnet mask, router, DNS and so forth. The disclosure indicator for "Other" enables you to add a new network by scrolling up a screen for entering network information. A new network then appears with its own detail disclosure.

You also find disclosure indicators whenever one screen leads to a related submenu. When working with submenus, stick to the simple gray chevron. The rule of thumb is this: Submenus use gray chevrons, and object customization uses blue ones. Respond to cell selection for gray chevrons and to accessory button taps for blue chevrons.

Recipe 11-11 demonstrates how to use disclosure buttons (the blue accessories) in your applications. This code sets the `accessoryType` for each cell to `UITableViewCellAccessoryDetailDisclosureButton`. Importantly, it also sets `editingAccessoryType` to `UITableViewCellAccessoryNone`. When your delete or reorder controls appear, your disclosure chevron will hide, enabling your users full control over their edits without accidentally popping over to a new view.

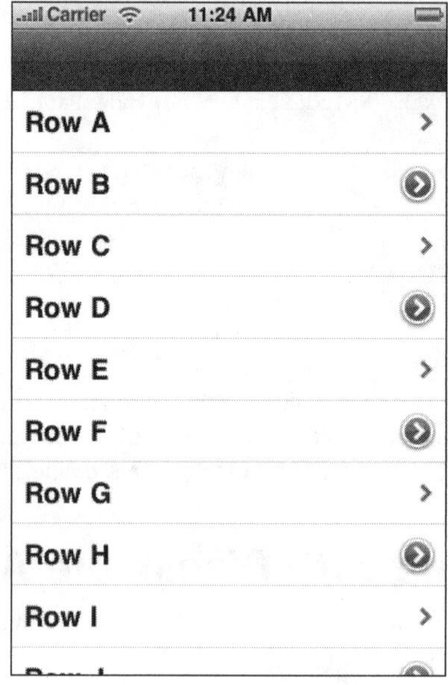

Figure 11-11 The right-pointing chevrons indicate disclosure controls, allowing you to link individual table items to another view.

To handle user taps on the disclosure, the `tableView:accessoryButtonTappedForRow➥WithIndexPath:` method enables you to determine the row that was tapped and implement some appropriate response. This sample merely pushes a new `UIViewController` that displays a stock image. In real life, you'd move to a view that explains more about the selected item and enables you to choose from additional options.

Gray disclosures use a different approach. As these accessories are not buttons, they respond to cell selection rather than the accessory button tap. Add your logic to `tableView:didSelectRowAtIndexPath:` to push the disclosure view onto your navigation stack or by presenting a modal view controller.

Recipe 11-11 **Working with Disclosure Buttons to Push New "Detail" Views**

```
- (UITableViewCell *)tableView:(UITableView *)tView
    cellForRowAtIndexPath:(NSIndexPath *)indexPath
{
    // Retrieve or create a cell
    UITableViewCellStyle style =  UITableViewCellStyleDefault;
    UITableViewCell *cell = [tView
        dequeueReusableCellWithIdentifier:@"BaseCell"];
    if (!cell) cell = [[[UITableViewCell alloc] initWithStyle:style
        reuseIdentifier:@"BaseCell"] autorelease];

    // Set cell label
    NSString *key = [@"Row " stringByAppendingString:[ALPHA
        objectAtIndex:indexPath.row]];
    cell.textLabel.text = key;

    cell.accessoryType =
        UITableViewCellAccessoryDetailDisclosureButton;
    cell.editingAccessoryType = UITableViewCellAccessoryNone;

    return cell;
}

// Respond to accessory button taps
-(void)tableView:(UITableView *)tableView
    accessoryButtonTappedForRowWithIndexPath:(NSIndexPath *)indexPath
{
    [[self navigationController] pushViewController:[ImageController
        newController] animated:YES];
}
```

Get This Recipe's Code

To get the code used for this recipe, go to http://github.com/erica/iphone-3.0-cookbook-, or if you've downloaded the disk image containing all of the sample code from the book, go to the folder for Chapter 11 and open the project for this recipe.

Recipe: Deleting Cells

In day-to-day use, every iPhone user quickly becomes familiar with the small, red circles that let them delete cells from tables. Many users also pick up on basic swipe-to-delete functionality. Interactive deletion represents one of the iPhone's best-designed features. Recipe 11-12 introduces a table that responds meaningfully to cell deletion. In this sample, users may create new cells by tapping an Add button and may remove cells either by swiping or entering edit mode and using the red remove controls (see Figure 11-12).

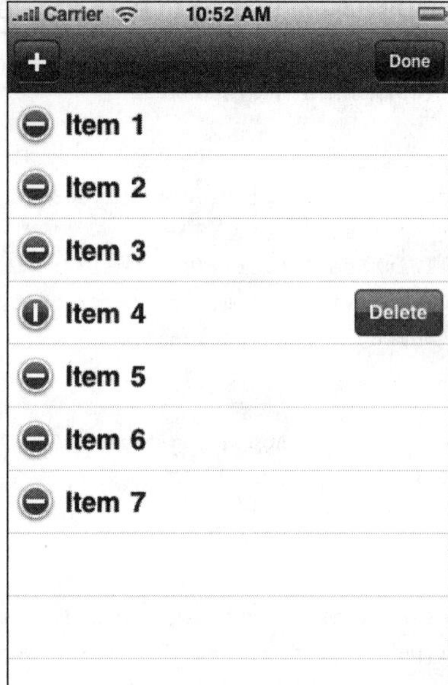

Figure 11-12 Red remove controls allow your users to interactively delete items from a table.

Displaying Remove Controls

The 3.0 SDK makes it especially easy to implement remove controls used in your program. When you want to edit cells, call `[self.tableView setEditing:YES animated:YES]`. This call updates the table's `editing` property and displays the remove controls shown in Figure 11-12.

Whenever possible, add animations to your iPhone user interfaces to lead your users from one state to the next, so they're prepared for the mode changes that happen onscreen. In the uncommon case you have some reason you'd rather not animate the change, you can pass `NO` instead of `YES`.

Recipe 11-12 uses a single method called `enterEditMode`. When a user taps the navigation bar's Edit button, the application calls this method. It removes the current item selection, calls the `setBarButtonItems` method that swaps out the title from Edit to Done, and enables the table's editing property.

Dismissing Remove Controls

When users complete their edits and want to return to normal table display, proceed in reverse. Dismiss the controls (`[self.tableView setEditing:NO animated:YES]`) and update the navigation bar button items back to their original state. Recipe 11-12 checks whether any items remain, hiding the Edit button if none do.

Handling Delete Requests

On row deletion, the table communicates with your application by issuing a `tableView:commitEditingStyle:forRowAtIndexPath:` callback. A table delete removes an item from the visual table but does not alter the underlying data. Unless you manage the item removal from your data source, the "deleted" item will reappear on the next table refresh. This method offers the place for you to update your data source and respond to the row deletion that the user just performed.

Here is where you actually delete the item from the data structure that supplies the data source methods (in this recipe, through an `NSMutableArray` of item titles) and handle any real-world action such as deleting files that occur as a consequence. In this sample code, the cell goes away, but there's no real-world consequence for the deletion. The sample is not based on a real-life model. Instead, the title list just loses that particular numbered cell title.

Notice that both adding and deleting items are handled by the same method, `updateItemAtIndexPath:withString:`. This may seem like an odd way to handle requests, as it involves an extra method and extra steps. This approach provides a foundation for undo support, which is discussed in Recipe 11-14. Using the `NSUndoManager` with a single update method provides unified undo and redo support for these two operations.

Swiping Cells

Swiping provides a clean method for removing items from your `UITableView` instances. You don't have to do anything to enable swipes. The table takes care of everything, so long as you provide the commit editing style method.

To swipe, users drag swiftly from the left to the right side of the cell. The rectangular delete confirmation appears to the right of the cell, but the cells do **not** display the round remove controls on the left.

After users swipe and confirm, the `tableView:commitEditingStyle:`
`➥forRowAtIndexPath:` method handles data updates just as if the deletion had occurred in edit mode.

Adding Cells

Recipe 11-12 introduces an add button using the system bar button item that displays as a plus sign. (See the top-left corner of Figure 11-12.) This button lets users add new table cells. To accomplish this, an `addItem:` method appends a new cell title at the end of the `items` array and then tells the table to update the data source using `reloadData`. This lets the normal table mechanism check the data and re-create the table view using the updated data source.

Recipe 11-12 **Deleting Cells On-the-Fly**

```
@implementation TableListViewController
@synthesize count;
@synthesize items;
```

```
- (NSInteger)numberOfSectionsInTableView:(UITableView *)aTableView
{
    return 1;
}

- (NSInteger)tableView:(UITableView *)aTableView
    numberOfRowsInSection:(NSInteger)section
{
    return self.items.count;
}

- (void) setBarButtonItems
{
    // Always display the add (+) button
    self.navigationItem.leftBarButtonItem =
        SYSBARBUTTON(UIBarButtonSystemItemAdd, @selector(addItem));

    // When editing, display the done button
    // When not editing, only display edit when items exist
    if (self.tableView.isEditing)
        self.navigationItem.rightBarButtonItem =
            SYSBARBUTTON(UIBarButtonSystemItemDone,
            @selector(leaveEditMode));
    else
        self.navigationItem.rightBarButtonItem = self.items.count ?
            SYSBARBUTTON(UIBarButtonSystemItemEdit,
            @selector(enterEditMode)) : nil;
}

- (UITableViewCell *)tableView:(UITableView *)tView
    cellForRowAtIndexPath:(NSIndexPath *)indexPath
{
    // Return a dequeued cell or create a new one
    UITableViewCellStyle style =  UITableViewCellStyleDefault;
    UITableViewCell *cell = [tView
        dequeueReusableCellWithIdentifier:@"BaseCell"];
    if (!cell)
        cell = [[[UITableViewCell alloc] initWithStyle:style
            reuseIdentifier:@"BaseCell"] autorelease];
    cell.textLabel.text = [items objectAtIndex:indexPath.row];
    return cell;
}

- (void) updateItemAtIndexPath: (NSIndexPath *) indexPath
    withString: (NSString *) string
{
    // You cannot insert a nil item. Passing nil is a delete request.
```

```
    if (!string)
        [self.items removeObjectAtIndex:indexPath.row];
    else
        [self.items insertObject:string atIndex:indexPath.row];

    [self.tableView reloadData];
    [self setBarButtonItems];
}

- (void) addItem: (id) sender
{
    // add a new item
    NSIndexPath *newPath = [NSIndexPath
        indexPathForRow:self.items.count inSection:0];
    NSString *newTitle = [NSString stringWithFormat:@"Item %d",
        count++];
    [self updateItemAtIndexPath:newPath withString:newTitle];
}

- (void)tableView:(UITableView *)aTableView
   commitEditingStyle:(UITableViewCellEditingStyle)editingStyle
   forRowAtIndexPath:(NSIndexPath *)indexPath
{
    // delete item
    [self updateItemAtIndexPath:indexPath withString:nil];
}


-(void)enterEditMode
{
    [self.tableView deselectRowAtIndexPath:[self.tableView
        indexPathForSelectedRow] animated:YES];
    [self.tableView setEditing:YES animated:YES];
    [self setBarButtonItems];
}

-(void)leaveEditMode
{
    [self.tableView setEditing:NO animated:YES];
    [self setBarButtonItems];
}

- (void) loadView
{
    [super loadView];
    count = 1;
```

```
    self.items = [NSMutableArray array];
    [self setBarButtonItems];
}
@end
```

Get This Recipe's Code

To get the code used for this recipe, go to http://github.com/erica/iphone-3.0-cookbook-, or if you've downloaded the disk image containing all of the sample code from the book, go to the folder for Chapter 11 and open the project for this recipe.

Recipe: Reordering Cells

You empower your users when you allow them to directly reorder the cells of a table. Figure 11-13 shows a table displaying the reorder control's stacked gray lines. Users can apply this interaction to sort to-do items by priority or choose which songs should go first in a playlist. The iPhone ships with built-in table reordering support that's easy to add to your applications. Recipe 11-13 shows how. Just add a single table delegate method.

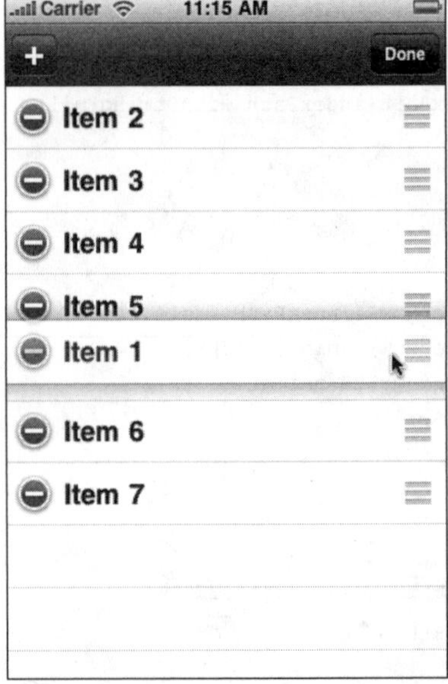

Figure 11-13 Reorder controls appear at the right of each cell during edit mode. They appear as three stacked gray lines. This screen shot shows Item 1 being dragged into place below Item 5.

It's important that your internal data model match the changes your user makes to the view. Implement the `tableView:moveRowAtIndexPath:toIndexPath` method to synchronize your data source with the onscreen changes, as you do when committing edits for cell deletion. This data source method provides the opportunity to update your data source. For this example, move the object corresponding to the cell's title to an updated location in the `items` mutable array.

To enable cell reordering, you must include this method in some form. When this method is not found, the table does not show the reorder handles when entering edit mode.

Recipe 11-13 **Reordering Table Cells**

```
-(void) tableView: (UITableView *) tableView
    moveRowAtIndexPath: (NSIndexPath *) oldPath
    toIndexPath:(NSIndexPath *) newPath
{
    // Change the data order in response to a user interaction
    NSString *title = [[self.items objectAtIndex:oldPath.row] retain];
    [self.items removeObjectAtIndex:oldPath.row];
    [self.items insertObject:title atIndex:newPath.row];
    [title release];

    [self setBarButtonItems];
}
```

Get This Recipe's Code

To get the code used for this recipe, go to http://github.com/erica/iphone-3.0-cookbook-, or if you've downloaded the disk image containing all of the sample code from the book, go to the folder for Chapter 11 and open the project for this recipe.

Recipe: Adding Undo Support to a Table

As introduced in Chapter 8, "Gestures and Touches," the `NSUndoManager` class provides undo and redo support for Cocoa Touch objects. Working with tables uses the same basic approach. You start by creating and initializing an undo manager for the table view controller.

```
self.undoManager = [[[NSUndoManager alloc] init] autorelease];
[self.undoManager setLevelsOfUndo:999];
```

Use common sense when setting the levels of undo. Recall that each undo retains the objects that are supplied as arguments. If you're working with small strings, as in this example, feel free to use a very high number. The memory overhead is minimal. When working with larger objects, limit your levels further. Three or ten undo levels, or some other small number, may be plenty for your needs.

Supporting Shake-to-Edit

If you plan to support shake-to-edit undo, declare that in your application delegate or in your view controller.

```
[[UIApplication sharedApplication]
    setApplicationSupportsShakeToEdit:YES];
```

You will also have to provide a way for your controller to assume first responder status whenever it appears onscreen. The following methods support this behavior.

```
- (BOOL)canBecomeFirstResponder {
    return YES;
}

// Become first responder whenever the view appears
- (void)viewDidAppear:(BOOL)animated {
    [super viewDidAppear:animated];
    [self becomeFirstResponder];
}

// Resign first responder whenever the view disappears
- (void)viewWillDisappear:(BOOL)animated {
    [super viewWillDisappear:animated];
    [self resignFirstResponder];
}
```

Should you use shake-to-edit with tables? Recall that each use requires the user to remember that the feature exists, which many users are not trained to use. Then, they must shake the phone, wait for an alert to appear, and select an item. That's a lot of effort, and when dealing with multiple undos or redos at a time, possibly a deal killer. Displaying Undo and Redo buttons onscreen, as Recipe 11-14 does, can minimize user dissatisfaction and provide an obvious way to move forward and back through an edit history.

Adding Undo and Redo Buttons

Cocoa touch provides two system bar button items for Undo and Redo support. The following code adapts the `setBarButtonItems` method from Recipe 11-12 and adds a custom toolbar to the navigation bar. The Undo and Redo buttons only show when the undo manager can support those actions. The bar is padded with flexible spacers at each end, and a fixed space item takes the place of each button when the undo/redo actions are not available.

```
- (void) setBarButtonItems
{
    // Add an "Add" button
    self.navigationItem.leftBarButtonItem =
        SYSBARBUTTON(UIBarButtonSystemItemAdd, @selector(addItem));
```

```
// Show either "Edit" or "Done"
if (self.tableView.isEditing)
    self.navigationItem.rightBarButtonItem =
        SYSBARBUTTON(UIBarButtonSystemItemDone,
        @selector(leaveEditMode));
else
    self.navigationItem.rightBarButtonItem = self.items.count ?
        SYSBARBUTTON(UIBarButtonSystemItemEdit,
        @selector(enterEditMode)) : nil;

// Create a new bar item array
NSMutableArray *barItems = [NSMutableArray array];
UIBarButtonItem *spacer =
    SYSBARBUTTON(UIBarButtonSystemItemFixedSpace, nil);
spacer.width = 64;

// Add spacer
[barItems
    addObject:SYSBARBUTTON(UIBarButtonSystemItemFlexibleSpace,
    nil)];

// Add Undo button if the undo manager can undo
if ([self.undoManager canUndo])
    [barItems addObject:SYSBARBUTTON(UIBarButtonSystemItemUndo,
        @selector(undo))];
else
    [barItems addObject:spacer];

// Add spacer
[barItems
    addObject:SYSBARBUTTON(UIBarButtonSystemItemFlexibleSpace,
    nil)];

// Add Redo button if the undo manager can redo
if ([self.undoManager canRedo])
    [barItems addObject:SYSBARBUTTON(UIBarButtonSystemItemRedo,
    @selector(redo))];
else
    [barItems addObject:spacer];

// Add spacer
[barItems
    addObject:SYSBARBUTTON(UIBarButtonSystemItemFlexibleSpace,
    nil)];
```

```
    // Create the toolbar
    UIToolbar *tb = [[[UIToolbar alloc] initWithFrame:
        CGRectMake(0.0f, 0.0f, 200.0f, 48.0f)] autorelease];
    tb.barStyle = UIBarStyleBlack;
    tb.tintColor = COOKBOOK_PURPLE_COLOR;
    [tb setItems:barItems animated:YES];
    self.navigationItem.titleView = tb;
}
```

Performing Undo and Redo

The actual undo and redo commands are trivial. The core work for providing table-based undo support resides in preparing the undo manager, and not, as you see, in executing the commands. Chapter 19, "A Taste of Core Data," offers another, simpler approach to undo/redo management.

```
- (void) undo: (id) sender
{
    // Undo the first item in the undo stack
    [self.undoManager undo];
    [self setBarButtonItems];
}

- (void) redo: (id) sender
{
    // Redo the first item in the redo stack
    [self.undoManager redo];
    [self setBarButtonItems];
}
```

Preparing Table Undo Operations

Recipe 11-14 shows the four critical methods that provide undo support for table operations. These include the methods that handle add and delete operations and the unified item update method that they call, plus the method that handles reorder operations.

As mentioned earlier in this chapter, the utility of providing a secondary method for add and delete lets those operations work together for undo support. Here, the item update method prepares the undo invocation for adding an item that is about to be deleted or for deleting an item that's about to be added. This combination creates a single focal point for the undo manager to work with.

The reordering method that moves rows into new paths offers an even easier solution. It swaps the old and new index paths and uses that invocation for the undo manager. There are two caveats about the move operations you need to be aware of.

First, you must check for no-move reordering. The check for `oldPath.row == newPath.row` ensures that these moves-that-aren't-really-moves will not be pushed onto the undo stack. When working with normal (non-undo) reordering, this is a step you can ignore because these "non-swaps" provide no effect on the responsiveness of the user interface. When working with undo stacks, they introduce trouble. Users do not know why the undo operation they just requested did not work even though the application did perform an "undo," by swapping an item with itself. Avoid the confusion and don't add these items to the undo stack.

Second, table views cannot be reloaded until after a move operation completes. Because the user is responsible for interacting with the cells and pulling them into a new position, you don't normally need to reload the table from the move method. In fact, doing so usually produces an infinite loop and an inevitable application crash.

When you work with the undo manager, the table still needs some way to update itself to match the updated model. You need to reload that table so the cells reflect the data after the undo operation. Adding a delayed selector, as used in this recipe, lets the move method complete before calling the reload. Doing this lets interactive table reordering complete without crashing and provides a vital way for the table to update after undo and redo calls.

Recipe 11-14 **Preparing Undo Items for Table Operations**

```
- (void) updateItemAtIndexPath: (NSIndexPath *) indexPath
    withString: (NSString *) string
{
    // Swap string to nil or vice versa for undo
    NSString *undoString = string ? nil : [self.items
        objectAtIndex:indexPath.row];
    [[self.undoManager prepareWithInvocationTarget:self]
        updateItemAtIndexPath:indexPath withString:undoString];

    // You cannot insert a nil item. Passing nil is a delete request.
    if (!string)
        [self.items removeObjectAtIndex:indexPath.row];
    else
        [self.items insertObject:string atIndex:indexPath.row];

    [self.tableView reloadData];
    [self setBarButtonItems];
}

- (void) addItem: (id) sender
{
    // Add a new item based on the current count
    NSIndexPath *newPath = [NSIndexPath
        indexPathForRow:self.items.count inSection:0];
    NSString *newTitle = [NSString stringWithFormat:@"Item %d",
        count++];
    [self updateItemAtIndexPath:newPath withString:newTitle];
}

- (void)tableView:(UITableView *)aTableView
    commitEditingStyle:(UITableViewCellEditingStyle)editingStyle
    forRowAtIndexPath:(NSIndexPath *)indexPath
```

```
{
    // Delete item
    [self updateItemAtIndexPath:indexPath withString:nil];
}

-(void) tableView: (UITableView *) tableView
    moveRowAtIndexPath: (NSIndexPath *) oldPath
    toIndexPath:(NSIndexPath *) newPath
{
    // Catch any self-moves and ignore
    if (oldPath.row == newPath.row) return;

    // prepare an undo for the row swap
    [[self.undoManager prepareWithInvocationTarget:self]
        tableView:self.tableView moveRowAtIndexPath:newPath
        toIndexPath:oldPath];

    // Perform the swap
    NSString *item = [[self.items objectAtIndex:oldPath.row] retain];
    [self.items removeObjectAtIndex:oldPath.row];
    [self.items insertObject:item atIndex:newPath.row];
    [item release];

    // Update the bar button items and reload the data
    [self setBarButtonItems];
    [self.tableView performSelector:@selector(reloadData)
        withObject:nil afterDelay:0.25f];
}
```

Get This Recipe's Code

To get the code used for this recipe, go to http://github.com/erica/iphone-3.0-cookbook-, or if you've downloaded the disk image containing all of the sample code from the book, go to the folder for Chapter 11 and open the project for this recipe.

Recipe: Sorting Tables

A table is its data source in every meaningful sense. When you sort the information that powers a table and then reload its data, you end up with a sorted table. Recipe 11-15 introduces a table view controller method that applies sorting on demand.

The three sorts used in this recipe are ascending alphabetically, descending alphabetically, and by string length. To provide the latter two requires an extension of the `NSString` class. This simple class category adds a reversed comparison and a string length comparison.

Recipe 11-15 shows only a part of the implementation, demonstrating how the data model responds to the different sort types. As the user taps the segmented control, the `items` array replaces itself with a version using the selected sort. See Chapter 19 for Core Data approaches that use sorting while fetching results from a persistent data store.

Recipe 11-15 **Sorting a UITableView**

```
@implementation NSString (sortingExtension)
- (NSComparisonResult) reverseCompare: (NSString *) aString
{
    // Invert a normal case insensitive comparison
    return -1 * [self caseInsensitiveCompare:aString];
}

- (NSComparisonResult) lengthCompare: (NSString *) aString
{
    // Return an ordering based on string length
    if (self.length == aString.length) return NSOrderedSame;
    if (self.length > aString.length) return NSOrderedDescending;
    return NSOrderedAscending;
}
@end

@implementation TableListViewController
- (void) updateSort: (UISegmentedControl *) seg
{
    // Apply the currently selected sort to the table items
    if (seg.selectedSegmentIndex == 0)
        self.items = [self.items sortedArrayUsingSelector:
            @selector(caseInsensitiveCompare)];
    else if (seg.selectedSegmentIndex == 1)
        self.items = [self.items sortedArrayUsingSelector:
            @selector(reverseCompare)];
    else if (seg.selectedSegmentIndex == 2)
        self.items = [self.items sortedArrayUsingSelector:
             @selector(lengthCompare)];

    [self.tableView reloadData];
}
@end
```

Get This Recipe's Code

To get the code used for this recipe, go to http://github.com/erica/iphone-3.0-cookbook-, or if you've downloaded the disk image containing all of the sample code from the book, go to the folder for Chapter 11 and open the project for this recipe.

Recipe: Searching Through a Table

New to the 3.0 SDK, built-in search allow users to filter a table's contents in real time. This searching uses two important classes, the previously existing `UISearchBar` class and the new `UISearchDisplayController` class. Together, these mimic the kind of search behavior offered in the Contacts application, where a search bar can be found at the head of the table.

To find the search bar, you must scroll all the way to the top of the table, as shown in Figure 11-14 (left). The search bar does not initially appear in the navigation bar. Once users tap in the search box, the view shifts and the search bar moves up to the navigation bar area, as shown in Figure 11-14 (right). It remains there until the user taps Cancel, returning the user to the unfiltered table display.

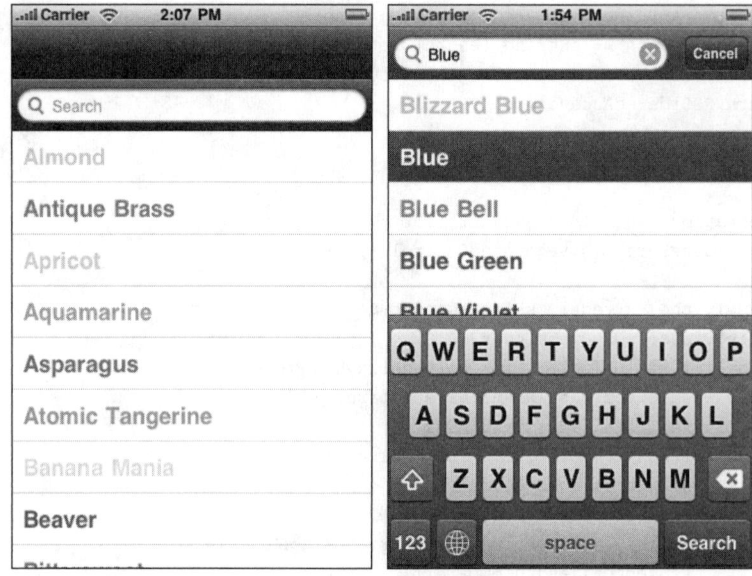

Figure 11-14 The user must scroll to the top of the table to initiate a search. The Search bar appears as the first item in the table in its header view. (Left) Once the user taps within the search bar and makes it active, the search bar jumps into the navigation bar and presents a filtered list of items based on the search criteria (Right).

Building the Search Display Controller

Search display controllers help manage the display of data owned by another controller, in this case a standard `UITableViewController`. The search display controller presents a subset of that data, usually by filtering that data source through a predicate.

Initialize a search display controller by providing it with a search bar and a contents controller. As you can see here, the search display controller uses a standard search bar, which is created programmatically in the following snippet. Pass the main `UITableViewController` instance you're defining these items within as the contents controller.

Set up the search bar's text trait features as you would normally do but do not set a delegate. The search bar works with the search display controller without explicit delegation on your part.

When setting up the search display controller, make sure you set both its search results data source and delegate as shown here. These point back to the primary table view controller subclass, which is where you'll adjust your normal data source and delegate methods to comply with the searchable table.

```
// Create a search bar
self.searchBar = [[[UISearchBar alloc] initWithFrame:
    CGRectMake(0.0f, 0.0f, 320.0f, 44.0f)] autorelease];
self.searchBar.tintColor = COOKBOOK_PURPLE_COLOR;
self.searchBar.autocorrectionType = UITextAutocorrectionTypeNo;
self.searchBar.autocapitalizationType =
    UITextAutocapitalizationTypeNone;
self.searchBar.keyboardType = UIKeyboardTypeAlphabet;
self.tableView.tableHeaderView = self.searchBar;

// Create the search display controller
self.searchDC = [[[UISearchDisplayController alloc]
    initWithSearchBar:self.searchBar contentsController:self]
    autorelease];
self.searchDC.searchResultsDataSource = self;
self.searchDC.searchResultsDelegate = self;
```

Building the Searchable Data Source Methods

The number of items displayed in the table changes as users search. You must report the correct number of rows for each. To detect whether the table view controller or the search display controller is currently in charge, compare the table view parameter against the built-in `tableView` property. If it is the same, you're dealing with the normal table view. If it differs, that means the search display controller is in charge and is using its own table view. Adjust the row count accordingly.

```
- (NSInteger)tableView:(UITableView *)aTableView
    numberOfRowsInSection:(NSInteger)section
{
    // Return the cell count for the normal table
    if (aTableView == self.tableView)
        return self.crayonColors.allKeys.count;
```

```
    // Return the cell count for the search table
    NSPredicate *predicate = [NSPredicate predicateWithFormat:
        @"SELF contains[cd] %@", self.searchBar.text];
    self.filteredArray = [self.crayonColors.allKeys
        filteredArrayUsingPredicate:predicate];
    return self.filteredArray.count;
}
```

Use a predicate to report the count of items that match the text in the search box. Predicates provide an extremely simple way to filter an array and return only those items that match a search string. The predicate used here performs a case insensitive `contains` match. Each string that contains the text in the search field returns a positive match, allowing that string to remain part of the filtered array. Alternatively, you might want to use `beginswith` to avoid matching items that do not start with that text.

Predicates go well beyond the simple string matching shown here. You can use them with all kinds of complex objects including Core Data objects to provide sophisticated filtering for your table displays.

Filtering goes beyond row count reporting. You need to filter source data to populate and return cell instances. The following method again checks the current table view to return cells that match either the default keys or the filtered set.

```
- (UITableViewCell *)tableView:(UITableView *)aTableView
    cellForRowAtIndexPath:(NSIndexPath *)indexPath
{
    // Dequeue or create a cell
    UITableViewCellStyle style =  UITableViewCellStyleDefault;
    UITableViewCell *cell = [aTableView
        dequeueReusableCellWithIdentifier:@"BaseCell"];
    if (!cell) cell = [[[UITableViewCell alloc] initWithStyle:style
        reuseIdentifier:@"BaseCell"] autorelease];

    // Retrieve the crayon and its color
    NSArray *keyCollection = (aTableView == self.tableView) ?
        DEFAULTKEYS : FILTEREDKEYS;
    NSString *crayon = [keyCollection objectAtIndex:indexPath.row];
    cell.textLabel.text = crayon;
    if (![crayon hasPrefix:@"White"])
        cell.textLabel.textColor = [self.crayonColors
            objectForKey:crayon];
    else
        cell.textLabel.textColor = [UIColor blackColor];
    return cell;
}
```

Delegate Methods

Search awareness is not limited to data sources. As Recipe 11-16 shows, determining the context of a user tap is critical for providing the correct response in delegate methods. As with the previous data source methods, this delegate method compares the table view parameter sent with the callback to the built-in parameter. Based on this result, it chooses how to act, which in this case involves coloring both the search bar and the navigation bar with the currently selected color.

Recipe 11-16 **Comparing Table Views to Produce the Correct Responses to User Input**

```
// Respond to user selections by updating tint colors
- (void)tableView:(UITableView *)aTableView
    didSelectRowAtIndexPath:(NSIndexPath *)indexPath
{
    NSArray *keyCollection = (aTableView == self.tableView) ?
        DEFAULTKEYS : FILTEREDKEYS;
    NSString *crayon = [keyCollection objectAtIndex:indexPath.row];
    self.navigationController.navigationBar.tintColor =
        [self.crayonColors objectForKey:crayon];
    self.searchBar.tintColor = [self.crayonColors objectForKey:crayon];
}
```

> **Get This Recipe's Code**
>
> To get the code used for this recipe, go to http://github.com/erica/iphone-3.0-cookbook-, or if you've downloaded the disk image containing all of the sample code from the book, go to the folder for Chapter 11 and open the project for this recipe.

Recipe: Working with Sections

Many iPhone applications use sections as well as rows. Sections provide another level of structure to lists, grouping items together into logical units. The most commonly used section scheme is the alphabet, although you are certainly not limited to organizing your data this way. You can use any section scheme that makes sense for your application.

Figure 11-15 shows a table that uses sections to display grouped names. Each section presents a separate header (i.e., "Crayon names starting with..."), and an index on the right offers quick access to each of the sections. Notice that there are no sections listed for K, Q, X, and Z in that index. This recipe eliminates empty sections from the index.

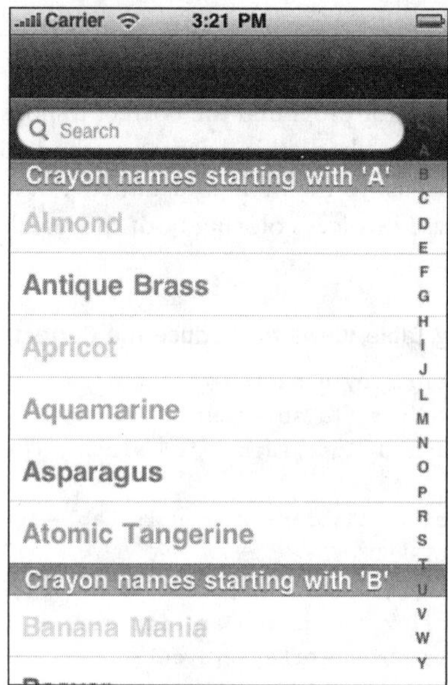

Figure 11-15 Sectioned tables let you present both headers and an index to better find information as quickly as possible.

Creating a Section-Based Data Structure

When working with groups and sections, think two dimensionally. Section arrays let you store and access the members of data in a section-by-section structure. Implement this approach by creating an array of arrays. The section array stores one array for each section, which in turn contains the titles for each cell. This snippet creates the section arrays and then populates them by looking at the location of each item's first letter within the alphabet.

```
// Create the section array
self.sectionArray = [NSMutableArray array];
for (int i = 0; i < 26; i++) [self.sectionArray
    addObject:[NSMutableArray array]];

// Populate the arrays by starting character
for (NSString *string in rawCrayons)
{
    NSUInteger firstLetter = [ALPHA rangeOfString:[string
        substringToIndex:1]].location;
    if (firstLetter != NSNotFound) [[self.sectionArray
        objectAtIndex:firstLetter] addObject:CRAYON_NAME(string)];
}
```

To work, this particular implementation relies on two things: first, that the words are already sorted—each subsection adds the words in the order they're found in the array; and second, that the sections match the words. Entries that start with punctuation or numbers won't work with this loop. You can trivially add an "other" section to take care of these cases, which this (simple) sample omits.

Although, as mentioned, alphabetic sections are useful and probably the most common grouping, you can use any kind of grouping structure you like. For example, you might group people by departments, gems by grades, or appointments by date. No matter what kind of grouping you choose, an array of arrays provides the table view data source that best matches sectioned tables.

Counting Sections and Rows

Sectioned tables require customizing two key data source methods:

- **`numberOfSectionsInTableView`**—This method specifies how many sections appear in your table, establishing the number of groups to display. When using a section array, as recommended here, return the number of items in the section array—that is, `self.sectionArray.count`. If the number of items is known in advance (26 in this case), you can hard code that amount.
- **`tableView:numberOfRowsInSection`**—This method is called with a section number. Specify how many rows appear in that section. With the recommended data structure, just return the count of items at the nth subarray: `[[self.sectionArray objectAtIndex: sectionNumber] count]`.

Notice that these methods extend the searchable table introduced in Recipe 11-16. As Figure 11-14 shows, sectioned tables and their indices are compatible with searching. The small search icon at the top of the index brings users back to the search bar at the top of the table. In this example, the search results are flat—that is, not sectioned—which is why the number of sections result returns 1 instead of 26.

```
- (NSInteger)numberOfSectionsInTableView:(UITableView *)aTableView
{
    // Section count for the normal table
    if (aTableView == self.tableView) return 26;

    // Section count for the search table
    return 1;
}

- (NSInteger)tableView:(UITableView *)aTableView
    numberOfRowsInSection:(NSInteger)section
{
    // Cell count for the normal table
    if (aTableView == self.tableView) return [[self.sectionArray
        objectAtIndex:section] count];
```

```
    // Cell count for the search table
    NSPredicate *predicate = [NSPredicate predicateWithFormat:@"SELF
        contains[cd] %@", self.searchBar.text];
    self.filteredArray = [self.crayonColors.allKeys
        filteredArrayUsingPredicate:predicate];
    return self.filteredArray.count;
}
```

Returning Cells

Sectioned tables use both row and section information to find cell data. Earlier recipes in this chapter used a flat array with a row number index. Tables with sections must use the entire index path to locate both the section and row index for the data populating a cell.

```
- (UITableViewCell *)tableView:(UITableView *)aTableView
    cellForRowAtIndexPath:(NSIndexPath *)indexPath
{
    // Dequeue or create a cell
    UITableViewCellStyle style =  UITableViewCellStyleDefault;
    UITableViewCell *cell = [aTableView
        dequeueReusableCellWithIdentifier:@"BaseCell"];
    if (!cell) cell = [[[UITableViewCell alloc] initWithStyle:style
        reuseIdentifier:@"BaseCell"] autorelease];

    NSString *crayon;

    // Retrieve the crayon and its color
    if (aTableView == self.tableView)
        crayon = [[self.sectionArray objectAtIndex:indexPath.section]
            objectAtIndex:indexPath.row];
    else
        crayon = [FILTEREDKEYS objectAtIndex:indexPath.row];

    // Set the cell text and color it
    cell.textLabel.text = crayon;
    if (![crayon hasPrefix:@"White"])
        cell.textLabel.textColor = [self.crayonColors
            objectForKey:crayon];
    else
        cell.textLabel.textColor = [UIColor blackColor];
    return cell;
}
```

Creating Header Titles

It takes very little work to add section headers to your grouped table. The optional `tableView:titleForHeaderInSection:` method supplies the titles for each section. It's passed an integer. In return, you supply a title. If your table does not contain any items in a given section or when you're only working with one section (i.e., for the search table), return `nil`.

```
- (NSString *)tableView:(UITableView *)aTableView
    titleForHeaderInSection:(NSInteger)section
{
    // Normal Table
    if (aTableView == self.tableView)
    {
        // Empty Sections
        if ([[self.sectionArray objectAtIndex:section] count] == 0)
            return nil;

        // Populated Sections
        return [NSString stringWithFormat:
            @"Crayon names starting with '%@'",
            [[ALPHA substringFromIndex:section] substringToIndex:1]];
    }
    else
        // Search Table
        return nil;
}
```

Creating a Section Index

Tables that implement `sectionIndexTitlesForTableView:` present the kind of index view that appears on the right of Figure 11-14. This method is called when the table view is created, and the array that is returned determines what items are displayed onscreen. Return `nil` to skip an index, as is done here for the search table. Apple recommends only adding section indices to plain table views, that is, table views created using the default plain style of `UITableViewStylePlain`. See Figure 11-15 for an (mildly unfortunate) example of a grouped table with a section index.

```
- (NSArray *)sectionIndexTitlesForTableView:(UITableView *)aTableView
{
    if (aTableView == self.tableView)  // Regular table
    {
        NSMutableArray *indices = [NSMutableArray
            arrayWithObject:UITableViewIndexSearch];
        for (int i = 0; i < 26; i++)
            if ([[self.sectionArray objectAtIndex:i] count])
                [indices addObject:[[ALPHA substringFromIndex:i]
                    substringToIndex:1]];
        return indices;
    }
    else return nil; // Search table
}
```

The first item added to this index is the `UITableViewIndexSearch` constant. This adds the small magnifying glass icon that indicates that the table supports searches and provides a quick jump to the beginning of the list.

Although this example uses single-letter titles, you are certainly not limited to those items. You can use words or, if you're willing to work out the Unicode equivalents, pictures including emoji items (available to iPhone users in Japan) that are part of the iPhone character library.

```
[indices addObject:@"\ue057"];
```

Handling Section Mismatches

Indices move users along the table based on the user touch offset. As mentioned earlier in this section, this particular table does not display sections for K, Q, X, and Z. These missing letters can cause a mismatch between a user selection and the results displayed by the table.

To remedy this, implement the optional `tableView:sectionForSectionIndexTitle:` method. This method's role is to connect a section index title (i.e., the one returned by the `sectionIndexTitlesForTableView:` method) with a section number. This overrides any order mismatches and provides an exact one-to-one match between a user index selection and the section displayed.

```
- (NSInteger)tableView:(UITableView *)tableView
    sectionForSectionIndexTitle:(NSString *)title
    atIndex:(NSInteger)index
{
    if (title == UITableViewIndexSearch)
    {
        // Handle the jump to the search bar
        [self.tableView scrollRectToVisible:self.searchBar.frame
            animated:NO];
        return -1;
    }

    // Return the section for a letter
    return [ALPHA rangeOfString:title].location;
}
```

The `scrollRectToVisible:animated:` call used here manually moves the search bar into place when a user taps on the magnifying glass. Otherwise, users would have to scroll back from section 0, which is the section associated with the letter A.

Delegation with Sections

As with data source methods, the trick to implementing delegate methods in a data source table involves using the index path `section` and `row` properties. These properties provide the double access needed to find the correct section array and then the item within that array for this example. Recipe 11-17 shows how to update the search and navigation bars by recovering the color associated with a user tap on a section-based table.

Recipe 11-17 **Responding to User Touches in a Section-Based Table**

```
// Respond to user selections by updating tint colors
- (void)tableView:(UITableView *)aTableView
    didSelectRowAtIndexPath:(NSIndexPath *)indexPath
{
    // Determine which crayon was selected
    NSString *crayon;
    if (aTableView == self.tableView)
        crayon = [[self.sectionArray objectAtIndex:indexPath.section]
            objectAtIndex:indexPath.row];
    else
        crayon = [FILTEREDKEYS objectAtIndex:indexPath.row];

    // Update the tint color for the navigation and search bars
    self.navigationController.navigationBar.tintColor =
        [self.crayonColors objectForKey:crayon];
    self.searchBar.tintColor = [self.crayonColors objectForKey:crayon];
}
```

Get This Recipe's Code

To get the code used for this recipe, go to http://github.com/erica/iphone-3.0-cookbook-, or if you've downloaded the disk image containing all of the sample code from the book, go to the folder for Chapter 11 and open the project for this recipe.

Recipe: Creating Grouped Tables

On the iPhone, tables come in two formats: grouped tables and plain table lists. You've already seen the latter demonstrated. The recipes earlier in this chapter focused on creating them. The Settings application on the iPhone offers grouped lists in action. These lists display on a blue-gray background, and each subsection appears within a slightly rounded rectangle. Figure 11-15 shows the grouped list built by Recipe 11-18.

To change styles, requires nothing more than initializing the table view controller with a different style. You can do this explicitly when creating a new instance, that is:

```
myTableViewController = [[UITableViewController alloc]
    initWithStyle:UITableViewStyleGrouped];
```

Or you can use the approach of Recipe 11-18. By overriding the `init` method, you ensure that new instances of this subclass produce a grouped style table.

Recipe 11-18 **Overriding the Table View Controller's init Method to Create a Grouped Style**

```
- (TableListViewController *) init
{
    // Set the grouped style
    self = [super initWithStyle:UITableViewStyleGrouped];
    return self;
}
```

Apple recommends against using a section index like the one shown in Figure 11-16 (right). The index crosses over the right side of the grouped cell, creating an unnecessarily cluttered presentation.

> **Get This Recipe's Code**
>
> To get the code used for this recipe, go to http://github.com/erica/iphone-3.0-cookbook-, or if you've downloaded the disk image containing all of the sample code from the book, go to the folder for Chapter 11 and open the project for this recipe.

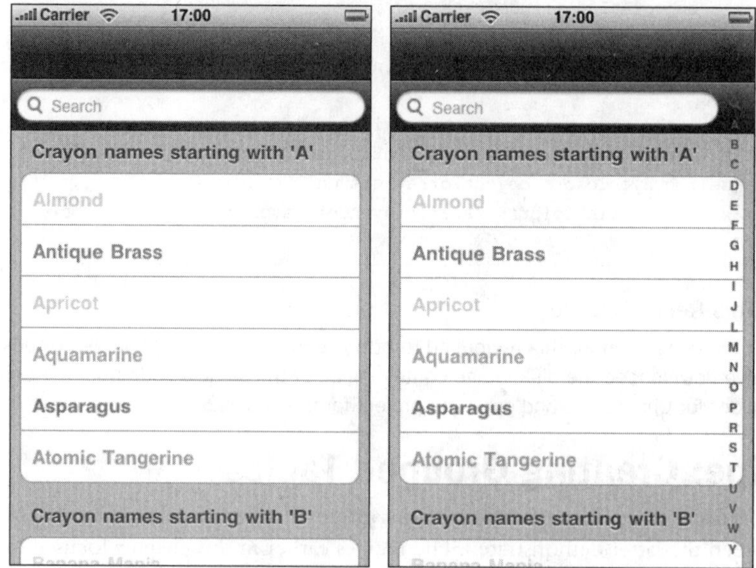

Figure 11-16 Grouped tables provide an alternate table presentation to standard table lists (left). Apple recommends against using a section index with grouped tables. As you can see, the index cuts across the cell boundaries (right).

Recipe: Customizing Headers and Footers

Sectioned table views are extremely customizable. You've read about using the `tableHeaderView` property to accommodate a `UISearchBar` search field. This, and the related `tableFooterView` property can be assigned to any type of view, each with its own subviews. So you might add in labels, text fields, buttons, and other controls to extend the table's features.

Headers and footers do not stop with the full table. Each section offers a customizable header and footer view as well. You can alter heights or swap elements out for custom views. In Figure 11-17, the left image uses a larger than normal height, and is created by implementing the optional `tableView:heightForHeaderInSection:` method. The right-hand image represents the use of custom views. The solid-colored header view, with its label and button subviews, is loaded from a xib file and returned via the optional `tableView:viewForHeaderInSection:` method. Corresponding methods exist for footers as well as headers.

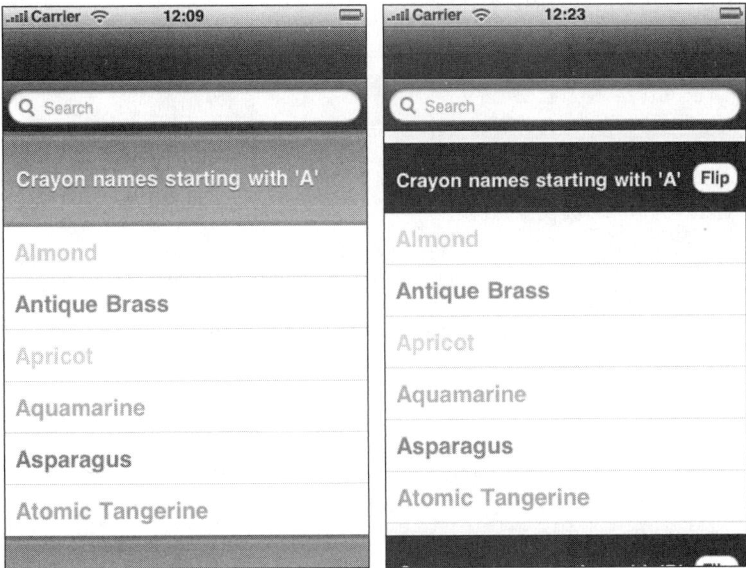

Figure 11-17 Table view delegate methods allow you to set the height and view of section headers and footers.

Recipe 11-19 shows these methods in use. The custom header is set at 70 pixels high and is loaded from a xib file. Its label is set and the button connected to a simple flip animation callback. This provides a trivial demonstration of a feature that is intrinsically much more powerful and more extensible than this simple example can express.

Recipe 11-19 Providing Custom Section Header Views

```
// Report the height for each section header
- (CGFloat)tableView:(UITableView *)tableView
    heightForHeaderInSection:(NSInteger)section
{
    return 70.0f;
}

// The button is just for demonstration purposes
// It calls this flip animation
- (void) flip: (UIButton *) button
{
    [UIView beginAnimations:nil context:nil];
    [UIView setAnimationCurve:UIViewAnimationCurveEaseInOut];
```

```
    [UIView setAnimationDuration:1.0];
    [UIView setAnimationTransition:
        UIViewAnimationTransitionFlipFromRight forView:self.view
        cache:YES];
    [UIView commitAnimations];
}

// Return the title for each section
- (NSString *)tableView:(UITableView *)aTableView
    titleForHeaderInSection:(NSInteger)section
{
    if (aTableView == self.tableView)
    {
        if ([[self.sectionArray objectAtIndex:section] count] == 0)
            return nil;
        return [NSString stringWithFormat:@"Crayon names starting with
            '%@'", [[ALPHA substringFromIndex:section]
            substringToIndex:1]];
    }
    else return nil;
}

- (UIView *)tableView:(UITableView *)tableView
    viewForHeaderInSection:(NSInteger)section
{
    // The nib contains a single object, the header view
    UIView *hView = [[[NSBundle mainBundle] loadNibNamed:@"HeaderView"
        owner:self options:nil] lastObject];

    UILabel *label = (UILabel *)[hView viewWithTag:101];
    label.text = [self tableView:self.tableView
        titleForHeaderInSection:section];

    UIButton *button = (UIButton *)[hView viewWithTag:102];
    [button addTarget:self action:@selector(flip)
        forControlEvents:UIControlEventTouchUpInside];

    return hView;
}
```

Get This Recipe's Code

To get the code used for this recipe, go to http://github.com/erica/iphone-3.0-cookbook-, or if you've downloaded the disk image containing all of the sample code from the book, go to the folder for Chapter 11 and open the project for this recipe.

Recipe: Creating a Group Table with Many Cell Types and Heights

If alphabetic section list tables are the M. C. Eschers of the iPhone table world, with each section block precisely fitting into the negative spaces provided by other sections in the list, then freeform group tables are the Marc Chagalls. Every bit is drawn as a freeform handcrafted work of art.

It's relatively easy to create all the tables you've seen so far in this chapter once you've mastered the knack. Perfecting the group table (usually called *preferences table* by iPhone devotees because that's the kind of table used in the Settings application) remains an illusion. Building group tables is all about the collage. They're all about handcrafting a look, piece by piece.

Tools like Interface Builder allow you to create any number of custom table cells, each with its own contents and height. It's up to you to programmatically put all that material together and create a table out of them. You're responsible for delivering the right kind of cells and for reporting the individual heights for each cell style, and in real-world implementations, responding to cell interaction with a meaningful result.

When you've got the basics under control, the preferences table becomes a project you can mold and shape. Figure 11-18 shows a simple preferences table that consists of two groups: a series of switches and a block with text (and a subtitle cell that's currently offscreen). Recipe 11-20 demonstrates the work that goes into providing even such a little creation.

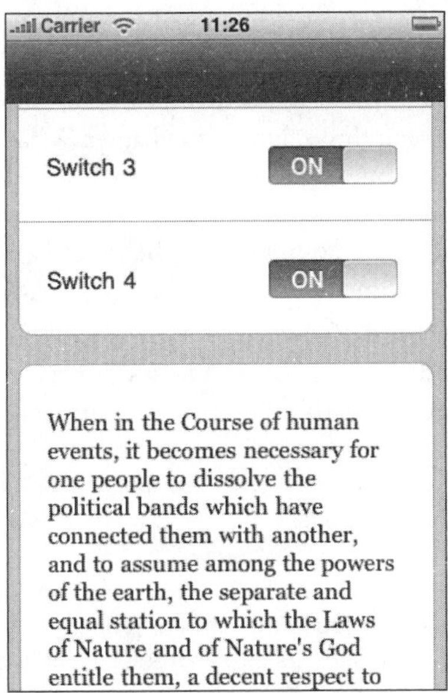

Figure 11-18 Preferences tables must be laid out by hand, with each row and group specified through your data source methods.

Unfortunately, adding new items or updating old ones requires a lot of fine detail work. That work isn't centralized in any way. You must review each of the data source methods and update with your new or refined items.

Creating Grouped Preferences Tables

There's nothing special involved in terms of laying out a new `UITableViewController` for a preferences table. You allocate it. You initialize it with the grouped table style. That's pretty much the end of it. It's the data source and delegate methods that provide the challenge. Here are the methods you'll need to define:

- **`numberOfSectionsInTableView:`**—All preferences tables contain groups of items. Each group is visually contained in a rounded rectangle. Return the number of groups you'll be defining as an integer.
- **`tableView: titleForHeaderInSection:`**—Add the titles for each section into this optional method. Return an `NSString` with the requested section name. Recipe 11-20 does not use titles.
- **`tableView: numberOfRowsInSection:`**—Each section may contain any number of cells. Have this method return an integer indicating the number of rows (that is, cells) for that group.
- **`tableView: heightForRowAtIndexPath:`**—Tables that use flexible row heights cost more in terms of computational intensity. If you need to use variable heights (Recipe 11-20 does so), implement this optional method to specify what those heights will be. Return the value by section and by row.
- **`tableView: cellForRowAtIndexPath:`**—This is the standard cell-for-row method you've seen throughout this chapter. What sets it apart is its implementation. Instead of using one kind of cell, Recipe 11-20 builds different kinds of reusable cells (with different reuse tags) for each cell type. As this recipe shows, things become much more complicated when using several cell types. Make sure you manage your reuse queue carefully. This recipe provides a trivial cell set, but real-world examples can grow more complicated.
- **`tableView: didSelectRowAtIndexPath:`**—You provide case-by-case reactions to cell selection in this optional delegate method depending on the cell type selected.

> **Note**
>
> The open-source llamasettings project at Google Code (http://llamasettings.googlecode.com) automatically produces grouped tables from property lists meant for iPhone settings bundles. It allows you to bring settings into your application without forcing your user to leave the app. The project can be freely added to commercial iPhone SDK applications without licensing fees.

Recipe 11-20 **Building a Multiheight Complex Grouped Table**

```
- (NSInteger)numberOfSectionsInTableView:
    (UITableView *)aTableView
{
    // Example table uses two sections
    return 2;
}

- (NSInteger)tableView:(UITableView *)aTableView
    numberOfRowsInSection:(NSInteger)section
{
    // First section has 4 cells, the second has 2
    if (section == 0) return 4;
    else if (section == 1) return 2;
    return 0;
}

- (UITableViewCell *)tableView:(UITableView *)tView
    cellForRowAtIndexPath:(NSIndexPath *)indexPath
{
    UITableViewCell *cell;

    if (indexPath.section == 0)
    {
        // Load a simple cell with a switch and label
        cell = [tView dequeueReusableCellWithIdentifier:@"SwitchCell"];
        if (!cell)
            cell = [[[NSBundle mainBundle] loadNibNamed:@"switchcell"
                owner:self options:nil] lastObject];
        [(UILabel *)[cell viewWithTag:101] setText:[NSString
            stringWithFormat:@"Switch %d\n", indexPath.row + 1]];
    }
    else if (indexPath.section == 1)
    {
        // First item is a big blog of text
        if (indexPath.row == 0)
        {
            cell = [tView dequeueReusableCellWithIdentifier:
                @"LibertyCell"];
            if (!cell)
                cell = [[[NSBundle mainBundle] loadNibNamed:
                @"libertycell" owner:self options:nil] lastObject];
        }
        // Second item is a standard subtitle cell
        else if (indexPath.row == 1)
        {
            cell = [[[UITableViewCell alloc]
                initWithStyle:UITableViewCellStyleSubtitle
```

```
                reuseIdentifier:@"SubtitleCell"] autorelease];
            cell.textLabel.text = @"Hello World";
            cell.detailTextLabel.text = @"Subtitle World";
        }
    }

    return cell;
}

// Reporting heights for each row can be computationally
// expensive and produce a performance hit
- (CGFloat)tableView:(UITableView *)tableView
    heightForRowAtIndexPath:(NSIndexPath *)indexPath
{
    // Determine the cell height based on section and row
    if (indexPath.section == 0) return 80.0f;
    if (indexPath.section == 1)
    {
        if (indexPath.row == 0) return 340.0f;
        if (indexPath.row == 1) return 40.0f;
    }

    return 0.0f;
}
```

Get This Recipe's Code

To get the code used for this recipe, go to http://github.com/erica/iphone-3.0-cookbook-, or if you've downloaded the disk image containing all of the sample code from the book, go to the folder for Chapter 11 and open the project for this recipe.

Recipe: Building a Multiwheel Table

Sometimes you'd like your users to pick from long lists or from several lists at once. That's where `UIPickerView` instances really excel. `UIPickerView` objects produce tables offering individually scrolling "wheels," as shown in Figure 11-19. Users interact with one or more wheels to build their selection.

These tables, although superficially similar to standard `UITableView` instances, use distinct data and delegate protocols.

- **There is no `UIPickerViewController` class**—`UIPickerView` instances act as subviews to other views. They are not intended to be the central focus of an application view. You can build a `UIPickerView` instance onto another view like the action sheet shown in Figure 11-18.
- **Picker views use numbers not objects**—Components, that is to say the wheels, are indexed by numbers and not by `NSIndexPath` instances. It's a slightly more informal class than the `UITableView`.

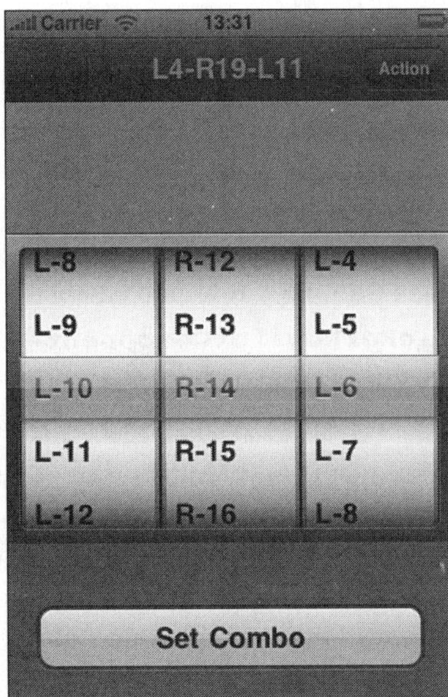

Figure 11-19 UIPickerView instances enable users to select from independently scrolling wheels.

- **The view height for pickers is static**—You can't resize pickers the way you would a standard `UITableView` just by manipulating its frame. Portrait pickers are 320-by-216 pixels in size; landscape pickers are 480-by-162. Any other frame sizes look distorted or clipped. These are the same dimensions used by the standard iPhone keyboard.

  You can supply either titles or views via the data source. Picker views can handle both approaches.

Creating the UIPickerView

Use any frame size for your `UIPickerView` as long as your height is 216 pixels and your width is 320 pixels (portrait), or your height is 162 pixels and your width is 480 pixels (landscape). That being said, you can float the table wherever you need it on the screen.

When creating the picker, remember two key points. First, you want to enable the selection indicator. That is the blue bar that floats over the selected items. So set `showsSelectionIndicator` to `YES`. If you add the picker in Interface Builder, this is already set as the default.

Second, don't forget to assign the delegate and data source. Without this support, you cannot add data to the view, define its features, or respond to selection changes. Your primary view controller should implement the `UIPickerViewDelegate` and `UIPickerViewDataSource` protocols.

Implement three key data source methods for your `UIPickerView` to make it function properly at a minimum level. These methods are as follows:

- **`numberOfComponentsInPickerView`**—Return an integer, the number of columns.
- **`pickerView: numberOfRowsInComponent:`**—Return an integer, the maximum number of rows per wheel. These numbers do not need to be identical. You can have one wheel with many rows and another with very few.
- **`pickerView:titleForRow:forComponent`**—This method specifies the text used to label a row on a given component. Return an `NSString`. (Returning a view instead of a string is covered in the next section.)

In addition to these data source methods, you might want to supply one further delegate method. This method responds to user interactions via wheel selection:

- **`pickerView:didSelectRow:inComponent`**—Add any application-specific behavior to this method. If needed, you can query the `pickerView` to return the `selectedRowInComponent:` for any of the wheels in your view.

Recipe 11-21 creates the basic picker wheel shown in Figure 11-18. It presents a "lock" picker, allowing users to enter a combination. Embedding the picker onto a `UIAlertSheet` instance allows the picker to slide in and out of view.

Recipe 11-21 Using a UIPickerView for Multicolumn Selection

```
@interface TestBedViewController : UIViewController <UIPickerViewDelegate,
➥UIPickerViewDataSource, UIActionSheetDelegate>
@end

@implementation TestBedViewController
- (NSInteger)numberOfComponentsInPickerView:(UIPickerView *)pickerView
{
    // Picker has three wheels
    return 3;
}

- (NSInteger)pickerView:(UIPickerView *)pickerView
    numberOfRowsInComponent:(NSInteger)component
{
    // Each wheel has 20 rows
    return 20;
}

- (NSString *)pickerView:(UIPickerView *)pickerView
    titleForRow:(NSInteger)row forComponent:(NSInteger)component
{
    // Each cell has a number and either R (for Right) or L (for Left)
    return [NSString stringWithFormat:@"%@-%d",
```

```
        component == 1 ? @"R" : @"L", row];
}

- (void)actionSheet:(UIActionSheet *)actionSheet
    clickedButtonAtIndex:(NSInteger)buttonIndex
{
    // Show the current combination
    UIPickerView *pickerView = (UIPickerView *)[actionSheet
        viewWithTag:101];
    self.title = [NSString stringWithFormat:@"L%d-R%d-L%d",
        [pickerView selectedRowInComponent:0],
        [pickerView selectedRowInComponent:1],
        [pickerView selectedRowInComponent:2]];
    [actionSheet release];
}

- (void) action: (id) sender
{
    // Create enough space to place the picker
    NSString *title = UIDeviceOrientationIsLandscape([UIDevice
        currentDevice].orientation) ?
        @"\n\n\n\n\n\n\n\n\n" :
        @"\n\n\n\n\n\n\n\n\n\n\n\n" ;

    // Build the action sheet and present it
    UIActionSheet *actionSheet = [[UIActionSheet alloc]
        initWithTitle:title delegate:self
        cancelButtonTitle:nil
        destructiveButtonTitle:nil
        otherButtonTitles:@"Set Combo", nil];
    [actionSheet showInView:self.view];

    // Once the sheet has been presented, add the picker subview
    UIPickerView *pickerView = [[[UIPickerView alloc] init]
        autorelease];
    pickerView.tag = 101;
    pickerView.delegate = self;
    pickerView.dataSource = self;
    pickerView.showsSelectionIndicator = YES;

    [actionSheet addSubview:pickerView];
}

- (BOOL)shouldAutorotateToInterfaceOrientation:
    (UIInterfaceOrientation)interfaceOrientation
{
    // Allow landscape and portrait presentations
```

```
    return YES;
}

- (void) viewDidLoad
{
    self.navigationItem.rightBarButtonItem = BARBUTTON(@"Action",
        @selector(action));
}
@end
```

Get This Recipe's Code

To get the code used for this recipe, go to http://github.com/erica/iphone-3.0-cookbook-, or if you've downloaded the disk image containing all of the sample code from the book, go to the folder for Chapter 11 and open the project for this recipe.

Recipe: Using a View-Based Picker

Picker views work just as well with views as they do with titles. Figure 11-20 shows a picker view that displays card suits. These images are returned by the `pickerView:` ➥`viewForRow:forComponent:reusingView:` data source method. You can use any kind of view you like, including labels, sliders, buttons, and so forth. The example in Recipe 11-22 uses a simple `UIImageView`, setting its image to one of the four suits.

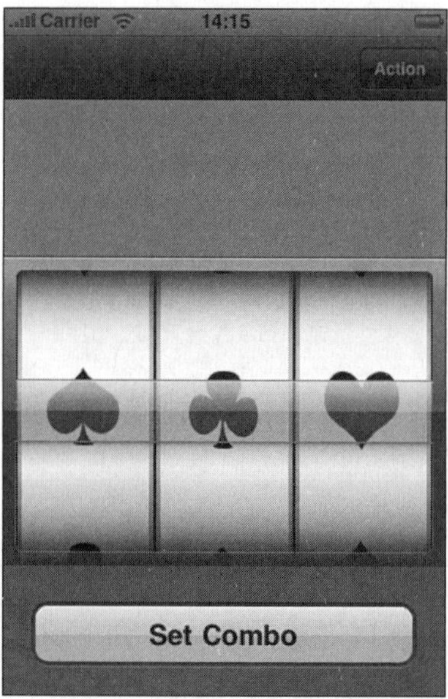

Figure 11-20 This **`UIPickerView`** presents a series of card suit images, allowing users to pick a combination of three items.

Picker views use a basic view reuse scheme, caching the views supplied to it for possible reuse. When the final parameter for this callback method is not `nil`, you can reuse that view by updating its settings or contents. Recipe 11-22 checks for the view and, only when it is not found, allocates a new image view.

The height need not match the actual view. Implement `pickerView:rowHeightFor➥Component:` to set the row height used by each component. Recipe 11-22 uses a row height of 120 pixels, providing plenty of room for each image and laying the groundwork for the illusion that the picker could be continuous rather than having a start and ending point as Recipe 11-21 did.

Notice the high number of components, namely one million. The reason for this high number lies in a desire to emulate real cylinders. Normally, picker views have a first element and a last, and that's where they end. This recipe takes another approach, asking "what if the components were actual cylinders, so the last element was connected to the first?"

To emulate this, the picker uses a far higher number of components than any user will ever be able to access. It initializes the picker to the middle of that number by calling `selectRow:inComponent:Animated:`. Each component "row" is derived by the modulo of the actual reported row and the number of individual elements to display, in this case `% 4`. While the code knows that the picker actually has a million rows per wheel, the user experience offers a cylindrical wheel of just four rows.

Recipe 11-22 **Creating the Illusion of a Repeating Cylinder**

```
- (NSInteger)pickerView: (UIPickerView *)pickerView
    numberOfRowsInComponent: (NSInteger) component
{
    // Return an insanely high number for the rows per wheel
    return 1000000;
}

- (CGFloat)pickerView: (UIPickerView *)pickerView
    rowHeightForComponent: (NSInteger) component
{
    // Produce a row height to match the art
    return 120.0f;
}

- (UIView *)pickerView: (UIPickerView *)pickerView
    viewForRow: (NSInteger) row forComponent: (NSInteger) component
    reusingView: (UIView *) view
{
    // Create a new view where needed, adding the art
    UIImageView *imageView;
    imageView = view ? (UIImageView *) view : [[UIImageView alloc]
        initWithFrame:CGRectMake(0.0f, 0.0f, 60.0f, 60.0f)];
    NSArray *names = [NSArray arrayWithObjects:@"club.png",
        @"diamond.png", @"heart.png", @"spade.png", nil];
```

```
    imageView.image = [UIImage imageNamed:
        [names objectAtIndex:(row % 4)]];
    return imageView;
}

- (void)actionSheet:(UIActionSheet *)actionSheet
    clickedButtonAtIndex:(NSInteger)buttonIndex
{
    // Set the title to match the current wheel selections
    UIPickerView *pickerView = (UIPickerView *)[actionSheet
        viewWithTag:101];
    NSArray *names = [NSArray arrayWithObjects:
        @"C", @"D", @"H", @"S", nil];
    self.title = [NSString stringWithFormat:@"%@•%
        [names objectAtIndex:([pickerView
        selectedRowInComponent:0] % 4)],
        [names objectAtIndex:([pickerView
        selectedRowInComponent:1] % 4)],
        [names objectAtIndex:([pickerView
        selectedRowInComponent:2] % 4)]];
    [actionSheet release];
}

- (void) action: (id) sender
{
    // Create enough space for the picker
    NSString *title = UIDeviceOrientationIsLandscape([UIDevice
        currentDevice].orientation) ?
        @"\n\n\n\n\n\n\n\n\n" :
        @"\n\n\n\n\n\n\n\n\n\n\n\n" ;

    // Build and present the action sheet
    UIActionSheet *actionSheet = [[UIActionSheet alloc]
        initWithTitle:title delegate:self
        cancelButtonTitle:nil destructiveButtonTitle:nil
        otherButtonTitles:@"Set Combo", nil];
    [actionSheet showInView:self.view];

    // Add the picker view once the sheet is displayed
    UIPickerView *pickerView = [[[UIPickerView alloc] init]
        autorelease];
    pickerView.tag = 101;
    pickerView.delegate = self;
    pickerView.dataSource = self;
    pickerView.showsSelectionIndicator = YES;

    [actionSheet addSubview:pickerView];
```

```
    // Pick a random item in the middle of the table
    [pickerView selectRow:50000 + (random() % 4) inComponent:0
        animated:YES];
    [pickerView selectRow:50000 + (random() % 4) inComponent:1
        animated:YES];
    [pickerView selectRow:50000 + (random() % 4) inComponent:2
        animated:YES];
}
```

Get This Recipe's Code

To get the code used for this recipe, go to http://github.com/erica/iphone-3.0-cookbook-, or if you've downloaded the disk image containing all of the sample code from the book, go to the folder for Chapter 11 and open the project for this recipe.

Recipe: Using the UIDatePicker

When you want to ask your user to enter date information, Apple supplies a tidy subclass of `UIPickerView` to handle several kinds of time entry. Figure 11-21 shows the four built-in styles of `UIDatePickers` that you can choose from. These include selecting a time, selecting a date, selecting a combination of the two, and a countdown timer. Recipe 11-23 demonstrates all of these styles.

Creating the Date Picker

Lay out a date picker exactly as you would a `UIPickerView`. The geometry is identical. After that, things get much, much easier. You need not set a delegate or define data source methods. You do not have to declare any protocols. Just assign a date picker mode. Choose from `UIDatePickerModeTime`, `UIDatePickerModeDate`, `UIDatePickerModeDateAndTime`, and `UIDatePickerModeCountDownTimer`.

Optionally, add a target for when the selection changes (`UIControlEventValueChanged`) and create the callback method for the target-action pair.

Here are a few properties you'll want to take advantage of in the `UIDatePicker` class:

- **`date`**—Set the `date` property to initialize the picker or to retrieve the information set by the user as he or she manipulates the wheels.
- **`maximumDate`** and **`minimumDate`**—These properties set the bounds for date and time picking. Assign each one a standard `NSDate`. With these, you can constrain your user to pick a date from next year rather than just enter a date and then check whether it falls within an accepted time frame.
- **`minuteInterval`**—Sometimes you want to use 5-, 10-, 15-, or 30-minute intervals on your selections, such as for applications used to set appointments. Use the `minuteInterval` property to specify that value. Whatever number you pass, it has to be evenly divisible into 60.
- **`countDownDuration`**—Use this property to set the maximum available value for a countdown timer. You can go as high as 23 hours and 59 minutes (that is, 86,399 seconds).

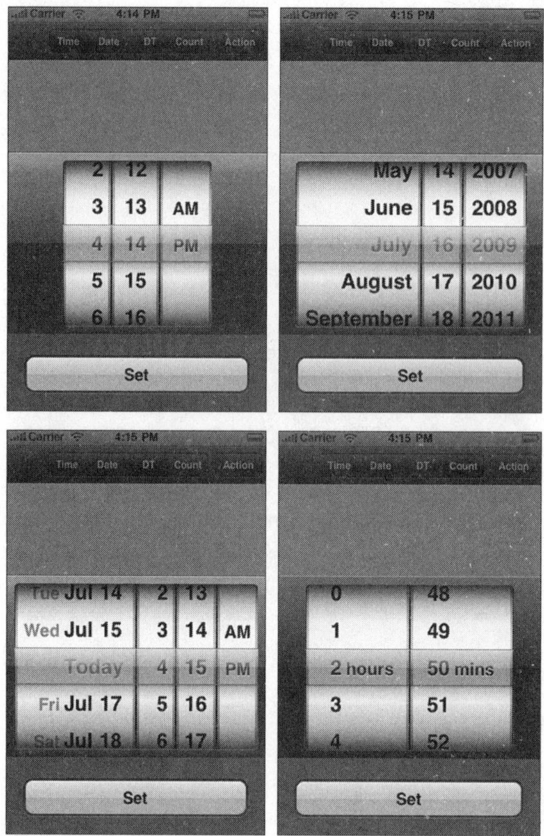

Figure 11-21 The iPhone offers four stock date picker models. Use the **datePickerMode** property to select the picker you want to use in your application.

Recipe 11-23 Using the UIDatePicker to Select Dates and Times

```
@implementation TestBedViewController
- (void)actionSheet:(UIActionSheet *)actionSheet
    clickedButtonAtIndex:(NSInteger)buttonIndex
{
    // Recover the picker
    UIDatePicker *datePicker = (UIDatePicker *)[actionSheet
        viewWithTag:101];

    // Set the date format based on the selected segment
    NSDateFormatter *formatter = [[[NSDateFormatter alloc] init]
        autorelease];
    switch ([(UISegmentedControl *)self.navigationItem.titleView
        selectedSegmentIndex])
```

```
    {
        case 0: // time picker
            formatter.dateFormat = @"h:mm a";
            break;
        case 1: // date picker
            formatter.dateFormat = @"dd MMMM yyyy";
            break;
        case 2: // date-time picker
            formatter.dateFormat = @"MM/dd/YY h:mm a";
            break;
        case 3: // countdown picker
            formatter.dateFormat = @"HH:mm";
            break;
        default:
            break;
    }

    // Create a timestamp and display it
    NSString *timestamp = [formatter stringFromDate:datePicker.date];
    [(UILabel *)[self.view viewWithTag:103] setText:timestamp];
    [actionSheet release];
}

- (void) action: (id) sender
{
    // Allow space for either a portrait or landscape presentation
    NSString *title = UIDeviceOrientationIsLandscape(
        [UIDevice currentDevice].orientation) ?
        @"\n\n\n\n\n\n\n\n\n" : @"\n\n\n\n\n\n\n\n\n\n\n\n" ;

    // Build the action sheet and present it
    UIActionSheet *actionSheet = [[UIActionSheet alloc]
        initWithTitle:title delegate:self
        cancelButtonTitle:nil destructiveButtonTitle:nil
        otherButtonTitles:@"Set", nil];
    [actionSheet showInView:self.view];

    // Create and add the date picker
    UIDatePicker *datePicker = [[[UIDatePicker alloc] init]
        autorelease];
    datePicker.tag = 101;
    datePicker.datePickerMode =
        [(UISegmentedControl *)self.navigationItem.titleView
        selectedSegmentIndex];
    [actionSheet addSubview:datePicker];

}
```

```
- (void) viewDidLoad
{
    self.navigationItem.rightBarButtonItem = BARBUTTON(@"Action",
        @selector(action));

    // Create a segmented control to choose the date style
    UISegmentedControl *seg = [[[UISegmentedControl alloc]
        initWithItems:[@"Time Date DT Count"
        componentsSeparatedByString:@" "]] autorelease];
    seg.segmentedControlStyle = UISegmentedControlStyleBar;
    seg.selectedSegmentIndex = 0;
    self.navigationItem.titleView = seg;
}
@end
```

Get This Recipe's Code

To get the code used for this recipe, go to http://github.com/erica/iphone-3.0-cookbook-, or if you've downloaded the disk image containing all of the sample code from the book, go to the folder for Chapter 11 and open the project for this recipe.

One More Thing: Formatting Dates

Although the `NSDateFormatter` class has evolved a great deal from its early days and now offers highly customizable elements that can be localized for various calendars and cultures, it helps to have a quick reference on hand for the most common date and time formats. Table 11-1 provides that reference, listing the most commonly used default codes. These codes are like the ones used in Recipe 11-23 to format the results from the date picker's `date` property for the midscreen label. Listing 11-1 uses the formats from Table 11-1 to create an `NSString` utility that converts a string into a date using a format of Month-Date-Year, for example, @"05-22-1934".

Table 11-1 **Default Format Codes for the NSDateFormatter Class**

Type	Code	Notes
Day of month	d	1 to 31, no leading zeros
	dd	01 to 31, uses leading zeros
Month	M L	1 to 12, numeric month value, no leading zeros
	MM LL	01 to 12, numeric month value, leading zeros
	MMM LLL	Jan to Dec, three letter month abbreviation

Table 11-1 **Continued**

Type	Code	Notes
	MMMM LLLL	January to December, full month name
Year	y u	e.g., 2009, four-digit year
	yy	e.g., 09, two-digit year
Hour	h K	1 to 12, no leading zeros
	hh KK	01 to 12, leading zeros
	H k	0 to 23, 24-hour clock, no leading zeros
	HH kk	00 to 23, 24-hour clock, leading zeros
Minutes	m	0 to 59, no leading zeros
	mm	00 to 59, leading zeros
Seconds	s	0 to 59, no leading zeros
	ss	0 to 59, leading zeros
AM/PM	a	
Day of Week	ccc EEE	Sun through Sat, three letter abbreviations
	cccc EEEE	Sunday through Saturday, full names
	c e	0-7 Ordinal day of week
	cc ee	00-07 Ordinal day of week
Week of Month	F	1-5, no leading zeros
	FF	01-05, leading zeros
Day of Year	D	1-366, no leading zeros
	DD	01-366, one leading zero
	DDD	001-366, two leading zeros
Week of Year	w	1-52, no leading zeros
	ww	01-51, one leading zero
Millisecond of Day	A	0- 86399999, no padding

Table 11-1 **Continued**

Type	Code	Notes
Astronomical Julian Day Number	g	Number of days since 1 January 4713 BCE
Era	G	BC, AD—Christian year notation
	GGGG	Before Christ, Anno Domini—Christian year notation
Quarter	q Q	1-4, quarter of year
	qq QQ	01-04, 1 leading zero
	qqq QQQ	Q1, Q2, Q3, Q4
	qqqq QQQQ	1st quarter, 2nd quarter, 3rd quarter, 4th quarter
Time Zone	v	2-letter time zone, e.g., MT
	V z	3-letter time zone, e.g., MDT
	vv VV zzzz	RFC 822 Time zone offset from Greenwich Mean Time, e.g., GMT-06:00
	vvvv	Time zone name, e.g., Mountain Time
	VVVV	Time zone location, e.g., United States (Denver)
	zzzz	Full time zone name, e.g., Mountain Daylight Time
	Z	GMT offset, e.g., -0600
Other characters	: - /	Colon, hyphen, slash

Listing 11-1 **Using Date Formats to Convert a String to a Date**

```
@implementation (NSString-DateUtility)
- (NSDate *) date
{
    // Return a date from a string
    NSDateFormatter *formatter =
```

```
        [[[NSDateFormatter alloc] init] autorelease];
    formatter.dateFormat = @"MM-dd-yyyy";
    NSDate *date = [formatter dateFromString:aString];
    return date;
}
@end
```

Summary

This chapter introduced iPhone tables from the simple to the complex. You saw all the basic iPhone table features, from simple tables to edits to reordering and undo. You also learned about a variety of advanced elements, from custom xib-based cells, to indexed alphabetic listings, to picker views. The skills covered in this chapter enable you to build a wealth of table-based applications for the iPhone and iPod touch. Here are some key points to take away from this chapter:

- When it comes to understanding tables, make sure you know the difference between data sources and delegate methods. Data sources fill up your tables with meaningful cells. Delegate methods respond to user interactions.
- `UITableViewControllers` simplify applications built around a central `UITableView`. Do not hesitate to use `UITableView` instances directly, however, if your application requires it. Just make sure to explicitly support the `UITableViewDelegate` and `UITableViewDataSource` protocols.
- Index controls provide a great way to navigate quickly through large ordered lists. Take advantage of their power when working with tables that would otherwise become unnavigable. Stylistically, it's best to avoid index controls when working with grouped tables.
- Date pickers are highly specialized and very good at what they do: soliciting your users for dates and times. Picker views provide a less-specialized solution but require more work on your end to bring them to life.
- This chapter introduced the `NSPredicate` class. This class provides flexible and powerful solutions that extend well beyond tables and are explored further in Chapter 18, "Connecting to the Address Book," and Chapter 19, "A Taste of Core Data."
- As complicated and annoying as preferences tables are to program, they are a highly requested feature when it comes to iPhone programming. They allow you to combine many kinds of interactive input on a good-looking and easy-to-use scrolling page. When you've conquered all the fussy aspects, they become a powerful tool in your programming arsenal.

12

Making Connections with GameKit and Bonjour

This chapter introduces GameKit, the simplest way to connect two iPhone devices. GameKit is Apple's new ad hoc networking solution for peer-to-peer connectivity. It's built on a technology called Bonjour that offers simple, no-configuration communications between devices. With GameKit and Bonjour, you can build games and utilities that move information back and forth between iPhones or between an iPhone and a desktop system. In this chapter, you discover how to use GameKit to build connected applications. You expand GameKit communications to create a cooperative drawing system that transmits both user touches and a selected color. You see how to add GameKit Voice to your applications for walkie-talkie-style voice chats. And you learn some basic Bonjour programming that goes beyond GameKit limitations, allowing you to expand your iPhone communications to the desktop.

Recipe: Creating Basic GameKit Services

GameKit provides peer-to-peer connectivity between iPhone and iPod touch devices. New to the 3.0 SDK, this framework helps you create interconnected applications that exchange live data in real time.

In its default implementation, GameKit works by creating and managing an ad hoc Bluetooth network that lets devices find each other, establish a connection, and transmit data through that connection. Starting with the iPhone 3.1 firmware, GameKit also allows you to find, connect, and transmit to devices on the same WiFi network. Using Bluetooth is a fast and reliable approach to interdevice communications. Unfortunately, Bluetooth communication using GameKit is not supported for first generation iPhones and iPod touches. GameKit offers an online (WiFi- or Internet-based) mode as well as the Bluetooth mode, but at the time of writing this book it's basically a "bring your own technology to the table" option.

Although, as the name suggests, you can build games with GameKit, you can do far more. You can create applications to support collaborative layout, picture sharing, chats, and more. So long as the same application exists on both devices, you can establish

GameKit communications either with (3.1 firmware or later) or without a shared WiFi network.

GameKit Bluetooth Limitations

All you need is proximity. GameKit's Bluetooth-based applications are limited to about 10 meters, or 30 feet. So think of your audience including people riding together on a train or in a car, in a convention hall's meeting room, or working in the same office. Within that range, your application can easily establish a peer-to-peer connection.

GameKit offers excellent performance for short, tight blips of information. Apple recommends that GameKit transmissions be limited to 1,000 bytes and under. Although GameKit can handle larger blobs, up to 95 Kilobytes at a time, it's not meant for use as general device-to-device data transfer. Try to send too much data at once and you will receive transmission errors.

If you must transfer large files, you need to break those files into manageable chunks. Make sure you use standard handshaking and packet checksumming techniques to ensure the reliability of your data.

Device Limitations

GameKit's Bluetooth networking is not for every iPhone and iPod touch. It works with the 3G iPhone and later models and with the second generation iPod touch and later models. You cannot deploy a GameKit Bluetooth application to first generation iPhones and iPod touch units. Plus, GameKit Bluetooth is only partially supported on the Simulator. That is, you can discover nearby devices, but you cannot actually connect to them.

As of the 3.1 SDK, Apple added support for the `peer-peer` key in the Info.plist `UIRequiredDeviceCapabilities` entry. This key indicates that your application requires peer-to-peer connectivity over Bluetooth. For firmware earlier than 3.1, you can specify required device features like `telephony` and `microphone`, but there's no key available to describe a Bluetooth networking prerequisite.

Make it very clear in your marketing materials which devices you do and do not support, especially if your application centers on nearby iPhone connectivity. Users cannot use GameKit Bluetooth features on noncompliant devices. When attempting to do so, they'll receive a message like the one shown in Figure 12-1, which displays a Bluetooth logo and says, "Not supported on this iPhone" (or iPod).

This is why you should strongly consider offering an "online mode" fallback. The same interface that moves you to the Bluetooth-powered "nearby mode" provides a unified GUI allowing users to access other networking options. Recipe 12-8 demonstrates this second connection layer toward the end of this chapter.

Sessions

GameKit's peer-to-peer connections are built using Bonjour networking. Bonjour, which is Apple's trade name for zero configuration networking, allows devices to advertise and discover network services. Built into Mac OS X since version 10.2, Bonjour offers these features without calling attention to itself. For example, Bonjour powers the features that

Figure 12-1 GameKit features are not universally available to all iPhone and iPod touch devices. The first generation iPhone and iPod touch units do not support GameKit Bluetooth connections. Avoid this error by specifying the `peer-peer` device requirement in your application's Info.plist file.

let users find shared music for iTunes or connect to wireless printers without requiring custom configuration. These services automatically appear when they become available and disappear when they're not. It's a powerful OS feature.

GameKit provides that same Bonjour power without having to build the often complicated Bonjour callbacks for registering and detecting services. With GameKit, you request a connection using a "peer picker" controller and then manage a "session" once the connection has been established.

GameKit's session objects provide a single focus point for data transfer management. Each session uses a unique name, which you choose, to advertise itself. When an application looks for another device to connect to, it uses this name to identify compatible services.

If you use a Bonjour browsing service to look for that name, you'll fail. Apple encodes the service name. For example, a service called "MacBTClient Sample" becomes the "_11d7n7p5tob54j._udp." Bonjour service. GameKit automatically transforms the name you supply so it knows how to find matching services.

Unfortunately, there's no Mac OS X or Windows API available to let you build services from a desktop system that would let you hook into GameKit. Apple's name encryption more or less guarantees that standard Bonjour communications will not work with iPhone-based GameKit applications.

You read about bypassing this limitation later in this chapter by working directly with Bonjour.

Servers, Clients, Peers

GameKit offers three session modes; applications can act as servers, clients, and peers. Servers advertise a service and initialize a session, allowing clients to search for and connect to them. This is the kind of behavior that a smart printer uses, letting clients find and use its capabilities. It's handy for devices that provide a fixed functionality but it's not the best choice for most iPhone applications, especially games.

Peers work as both servers and clients. They advertise and search simultaneously. Once a peer selects a service, its client/server role is hidden both from the user and from the developer. This makes the peer approach very easy to develop for iPhones. You don't have to build separate client and server applications. One peer-based application does all the work.

The Peer Connection Process

The peer picking process is handled by a class called `GKPeerPickerController`. It provides a built-in series of interactive alert dialogs that automate the task of advertising device availability and selecting a peer. Using this class is not mandatory. You can bypass it and create a custom class to search for and connect to peers. For simple connections, however, the `GKPeerPickerController` class offers a ready-to-use interface that sidesteps the need for detecting and negotiating with peers.

To use the peer picker, you allocate it, set a delegate (which must implement the `GKPeerPickerControllerDelegate` protocol), and show it. For targets earlier than the 3.1 SDK, avoid using autorelease with the picker. Instead, wait for a delegate callback and release it there, ensuring that you will not run into unexplained application crashes when the dismissal animation fails. This issue was fixed in the 3.1 firmware. With 3.1 or later, you can choose to release in the callback (3.0 compatible) or use autorelease (3.1-or-later compatible).

As mentioned, GameKit supports two kinds of connections: nearby (via Bluetooth) and online (via the Internet and WiFi). The code in this chapter's first few recipes exclusively uses a nearby connection; an online recipe appears toward the end of this chapter. The Internet-style approach is less friendly and minimally documented at the time of writing this book. In contrast, the nearby Bluetooth style is friendly, easy-to-use, and ready for inclusion in your applications.

Displaying the Peer Picker

The following code allocates and shows a new peer picker controller, setting its connection style to Nearby. This skips an optional interaction step (discussed later in this chapter) where a user selects between Online and Nearby modes. When presented, it shows the interface in Figure 12-2. You do not have to use a peer picker to establish GameKit sessions. The iPhone SDK now lets you create your own custom interfaces to work with the underlying GameKit connections. A sample that demonstrates how to do so has been added to the sample code that accompanies this chapter.

```
// Create and present a new peer picker
GKPeerPickerController *picker = [[[GKPeerPickerController alloc]
    init];
picker.delegate = self;
picker.connectionTypesMask = GKPeerPickerConnectionTypeNearby;
[picker show];
```

When your mask includes the online type as well (`GKPeerPickerConnectionTypeOnline`), the picker first asks the user which kind of connection to use before moving on to either the nearby connection interface of Figure 12-2 or to a custom online interface that you must build yourself.

Figure 12-2 This is the first screen presented to the user for peer-to-peer Bluetooth connections.

Pressing Cancel

Users may cancel out of the peer picker alert. When they do so, the delegate receives a `peerPickerControllerDidCancel:` callback. If you display a "connect" button in your application, make sure to restore it at this point so the user can try again.

Creating the Session Object

As the picker delegate, you must supply a session object on request. Sessions, which provide an abstract class that creates and manages a data socket between devices, belong to the `GKSession` class and must be initialized with a session identifier. This is the unique string used to create the Bonjour service and link together two iPhone devices (peers) both advertising the same service. By setting the display name to `nil`, the session uses the built-in device name.

```
- (GKSession *)peerPickerController:(GKPeerPickerController *)picker
      sessionForConnectionType:(GKPeerPickerConnectionType)type
{
    // Create a new session if one does not already exist
    if (!self.session) {
        self.session = [[[GKSession alloc] initWithSessionID:
            (self.sessionID ? self.sessionID : @"Sample Session")
            displayName:nil sessionMode:GKSessionModePeer]
            autorelease];
        self.session.delegate = self;
    }
    return self.session;
}
```

Although this is an optional method, you'll usually want to implement it so you can set your session ID and mode. Upon detecting another iPhone or iPod with the same advertised service ID, the peer picker displays the peer as a compatible match, as shown in Figure 12-3.

Waiting for the peer picker list can take a few seconds or up to a few minutes. During development, you usually need to allow your Bonjour network stack to clear out any previous sessions when you iterate on the code. That's what typically causes the longer delays. Apple recommends always debugging from a clean restart. If debugging delays get frustrating enough, make sure to reboot.

In normal use, connection delays usually hover around 45 seconds at a maximum. Warn your users to be patient. In Figure 12-3, Binky is the device name for a second iPhone running the same application. When the user taps the name Binky, this iPhone automatically goes into client mode, and Binky goes into server mode.

Client and Server Modes

When a device changes into client mode, it stops advertising its service. The Choose an iPhone or iPod Touch dialog shown previously in Figure 12-3 changes on the server unit. The client's peer name dims to dark gray and the words "is not available" appear underneath. A few seconds later (and this can actually run up to a minute, so again warn your users about delays), both units update their peer picker display.

Figure 12-4 shows the server and client peer pickers during this process. The client waits as the server receives the connection request (left). On the server, the host user must

Figure 12-3 The peer picker lists all devices that can act as peers.

accept or decline the connection (middle). Should they decline, an updated peer picker notifies the client (right). If they accept, both delegates receive a new callback.

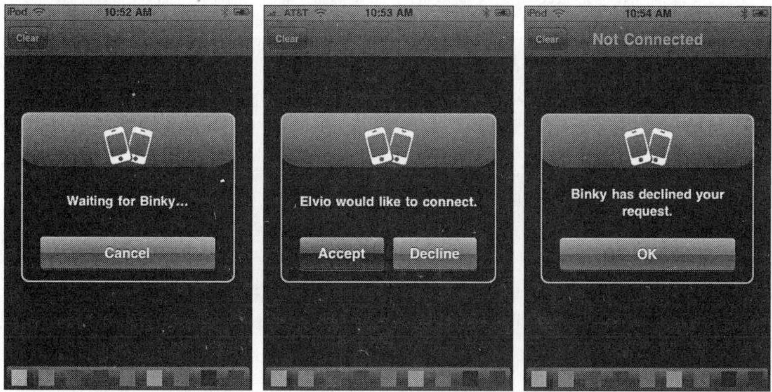

Figure 12-4 Upon choosing a partner, the client goes into wait mode (left) as the server decides whether to accept or decline the connection (middle). Should the server decline, the client receives a notice to that effect (right).

The delegate callback lets the new peers dismiss the peer picker and to set their data received handler. Make sure to release the picker at this time.

```
- (void)peerPickerController:(GKPeerPickerController *)picker
    didConnectPeer:(NSString *)peerID
    toSession: (GKSession *) session
{
    // Dismiss and release the picker, then set the data handler
    [picker dismiss];
    [picker release];
    [self.session setDataReceiveHandler:self withContext:nil];
}
```

Sending and Receiving Data

The data handler (in this case, `self`) must implement the `receiveData:fromPeer:` ➥`inSession:context:` method. The data sent to this method uses an `NSData` object; there are no hooks or handles for partial data receipt and processing. As the data arrives as a single chunk, keep your data bursts short (under 1,000 bytes) and to the point for highly interactive applications.

```
- (void) receiveData:(NSData *)data fromPeer:(NSString *)peer
    inSession: (GKSession *)session context:(void *)context
{
    // handle data here
}
```

Send data via the session object. You can send in reliable mode or unreliable mode. Reliable mode uses error checking and retrying until the data is properly sent. All items are guaranteed to arrive in the order they are sent, using TCP transmission. With unreliable mode, data is sent once using UDP transmission, with no retry, Data may arrive out of order. Use reliable mode (`GKSendDataReliable`) when you must guarantee correct delivery and unreliable mode for short bursts of data that must arrive nearly instantaneously.

```
- (void) sendDataToPeers: (NSData *) data
{
    // Send the data, checking for success or failure
    NSError *error;
    BOOL didSend = [self.session sendDataToAllPeers:data
        withDataMode:GKSendDataReliable error:&error];
    if (!didSend)
        NSLog(@"Error sending data to peers: %@",
            [error localizedDescription]);
}
```

As a rule, the one error you'll encounter here results from queuing too much data in reliable mode. This produces a "buffer full" error.

State Changes

The following session delegate callback lets you know when a peer's state has changed. The two states you want to look for are connected, that is, when the connection finally happens after the peer picker has been dismissed, and disconnected, when the other user quits the application, manually disconnects, or moves out of range.

```
- (void)session:(GKSession *)session peer:(NSString *)peerID
    didChangeState:(GKPeerConnectionState)state
{
    /* STATES:
      GKPeerStateAvailable, = 0,
      GKPeerStateUnavailable, = 1,
      GKPeerStateConnected, = 2,
      GKPeerStateDisconnected, = 3,
      GKPeerStateConnecting = 4 */

    if (state == GKPeerStateConnected)
    {
        // handle connected state
    }

    if (state == GKPeerStateDisconnected)
    {
        // handle disconnection
    }
}
```

To force a session to disconnect, use the `disconnectFromAllPeers` method.

```
- (void) disconnect
{
    // Disconnect and then reset the session property
    [self.session disconnectFromAllPeers];
    self.session = nil;
}
```

Creating a GameKit Helper

Recipe 12-1 bundles the entire peer process into a simplified helper class. This class hides most of the GameKit details connection and data transfer details, while providing a demonstration of how to use these features. More importantly, it breaks down how you might look at the GameKit process, with its two key details: connection and data.

Connecting

Any GameKit client you write must respond appropriately to the current connection state. You need to be able to establish that connection and respond when it goes live or when it drops. This class provides both **connect** and **disconnect** requests. For the most part, monitoring connections involves toggling a state Boolean (**isConnected**) and updating any buttons that control a connect/disconnect toggle.

To simplify these updates, the class allows you to assign a view controller (via the **viewController** property) and automatically updates the right-hand navigation item button. The button starts off as Connect, and when tapped disappears until the user cancels or a connection is fully established. After connecting, the button updates to Disconnect and provides a callback to the helper's disconnect method.

Handling Data

By providing the connection state details for you, you can use this **GameKitHelper** class to create simple GameKit-enabled applications. The data handling, however, remains in your hands. Consider the following snippet. It shows the entire implementation for a chat application view controller, demonstrating the data transfer methods for this app.

```
@implementation TestBedViewController
- (void)textViewDidChange:(UITextView *)textView
{
    // Perform updates only when connected
    if (![GameKitHelper sharedInstance].isConnected) return;

    NSString *text = sendView.text;

    // Check for empty text. If so, send special clear request
    if (!text || (text.length == 0)) text = @"xyzzyclear";
    NSData *textData = [text dataUsingEncoding:NSUTF8StringEncoding];
    [GameKitHelper sendData:textData];
}

-(void) receivedData: (NSData *) data
{
    NSString *text = [[[NSString alloc] initWithData:data
        encoding:NSUTF8StringEncoding] autorelease];

    // Check for clear request when updating text
    receiveView.text = [text isEqualToString:@"xyzzyclear"] ?
        @"" : text;
}

- (void) clear
{
    // Handle a clear request
    sendView.text = @"";
}

- (void) viewDidLoad
```

```
{
    self.navigationItem.leftBarButtonItem = BARBUTTON(@"Clear",
        @selector(clear));

    // Initialize the helper
    [GameKitHelper sharedInstance].sessionID = @"Typing Together";
    [GameKitHelper sharedInstance].dataDelegate = self;
    [GameKitHelper assignViewController:self];

    // Present the keyboard
    [sendView becomeFirstResponder];
}
@end
```

As you can see, this application monitors a "send" text view, and when it changes (as the user types), sends the contents of that view through GameKit to a peer. At the same time, it waits for data, and when it receives it, updates the received text view to show what the peered user has typed. A Clear button erases the "send" view text.

This application demonstrates the second half of the GameKit problem, handling data. Recipe 12-1's helper class creates a data delegate protocol, which is subscribed to by this text chat view controller. Data is passed along through the custom `receivedData:` delegate method, allowing the received text view to update with text typed on the peer device.

Similarly, the text view delegate method `textViewDidChange:` passes on responsibility for transmitting the actual text to the `GameKitHelper` class, calling the `sendData:` method to convey the data to connected peers.

> **Note**
>
> Recipe 12-1 does not address the issue of out-of-order packet receipt. See Apple's GKTank sample code for an example of network packet handling. Apple's code looks for the last packet time and the packet ID to ensure that packets are handled in the proper sequence.

The Helper Class

Recipe 12-1 contains the implementation for the `GameKitHelper` class. The associated sample code for this recipe shows the class in action, creating the text chat application discussed previously. This class was designed for reuse and can easily be decoupled from the text chat and repurposed, as you see in the next recipe.

Recipe 12-1 **GameKitHelper Class**

```
@implementation GameKitHelper
@synthesize dataDelegate;
@synthesize viewController;
@synthesize sessionID;
@synthesize session;
@synthesize isConnected;
```

```
// Macro helps check and then send selectors for data
// delegate callbacks
#define DO_DATA_CALLBACK(X, Y) if (self.dataDelegate && \
    [self.dataDelegate respondsToSelector:@selector(X)]) \
    [self.dataDelegate performSelector:@selector(X) withObject:Y];

#pragma mark Shared Instance

static GameKitHelper *sharedInstance = nil;
+ (GameKitHelper *) sharedInstance
{
    if(!sharedInstance) sharedInstance = [[self alloc] init];
    return sharedInstance;
}

#pragma mark Data Sharing

// Send data to all connected peers
- (void) sendDataToPeers: (NSData *) data
{
    NSError *error;
    BOOL didSend = [self.session sendDataToAllPeers: data
        withDataMode:GKSendDataReliable error:&error];
    if (!didSend)
        DO_DATA_CALLBACK(sentData:,
        (didSend ? nil : [error localizedDescription]));
}

// Redirect data receipt to the data delegate
- (void) receiveData:(NSData *)data fromPeer:(NSString *)peer
    inSession: (GKSession *)session context:(void *)context
{
    DO_DATA_CALLBACK(receivedData:, data);
}

#pragma mark Connections

// Start a new connection by presenting a peer picker
- (void) startConnection
{
    if (!self.isConnected)
    {
        GKPeerPickerController *picker = [[GKPeerPickerController
            alloc] init];
        picker.delegate = self;
        picker.connectionTypesMask = GKPeerPickerConnectionTypeNearby;
```

```
        [picker show];
        if (self.viewController)
            self.viewController.navigationItem.rightBarButtonItem =
                nil;
    }
}

// Dismiss the peer picker on cancel
- (void) peerPickerControllerDidCancel:
    (GKPeerPickerController *)picker
{
    [picker release];
    if (self.viewController)
        self.viewController.navigationItem.rightBarButtonItem =
            BARBUTTON(@"Connect", @selector(startConnection));
}

// Upon a successful connection, set up the data handler
- (void)peerPickerController:(GKPeerPickerController *)picker
    didConnectPeer:(NSString *)peerID
    toSession: (GKSession *) session
{
    [picker dismiss];
    [picker release];
    isConnected = YES;
    [self.session setDataReceiveHandler:self withContext:nil];
    DO_DATA_CALLBACK(connectionEstablished, nil);
}

// Provide the session information including id and mode
- (GKSession *)peerPickerController:(GKPeerPickerController *)picker
    sessionForConnectionType:(GKPeerPickerConnectionType)type
{
    if (!self.session) {
        self.session = [[GKSession alloc] initWithSessionID:
            (self.sessionID ? self.sessionID : @"Sample Session")
            displayName:nil sessionMode:GKSessionModePeer];
        self.session.delegate = self;
    }
    return self.session;
}

#pragma mark Session Handling

// Disconnect the current session
- (void) disconnect
{
```

```
    [self.session disconnectFromAllPeers];
    self.session = nil;
}

// Detect when the other peer has changed its state
- (void)session:(GKSession *)session peer:(NSString *)peerID
    didChangeState:(GKPeerConnectionState)state
{
     if (state == GKPeerStateConnected)
     {
         if (self.viewController)
             self.viewController.navigationItem.rightBarButtonItem =
                 BARBUTTON(@"Disconnect", @selector(disconnect));
     }

     if (state == GKPeerStateDisconnected)
     {
         self.isConnected = NO;
         showAlert(@"Lost connection with peer. You are no longer \
            connected to another device.");
         [self disconnect];
         if (self.viewController)
             self.viewController.navigationItem.rightBarButtonItem =
                 BARBUTTON(@"Connect", @selector(startConnection));
     }
}

// Utility method for setting up the view controller
- (void) assignViewController: (UIViewController *) aViewController
{
    self.viewController = aViewController;
    self.viewController.navigationItem.rightBarButtonItem =
        BARBUTTON(@"Connect", @selector(startConnection));
}

#pragma mark Class utility methods

// These class methods redirect to instance methods.
// They're here for convenience only
+ (void) connect
{
    [[self sharedInstance] startConnection];
}

+ (void) disconnect
{
    [[self sharedInstance] disconnect];
```

```
}

+ (void) sendData: (NSData *) data
{
    [[self sharedInstance] sendDataToPeers:data];
}

+ (void) assignViewController: (UIViewController *) aViewController
{
    [[self sharedInstance] assignViewController:aViewController];
}
@end
```

> **Get This Recipe's Code**
>
> To get the code used for this recipe, go to http://github.com/erica/iphone-3.0-cookbook-, or if you've downloaded the disk image containing all of the sample code from the book, go to the folder for Chapter 12 and open the project for this recipe.

Recipe: Peeking Behind the Scenes

At the time of writing, GameKit logs its status information as it runs, mostly by `NSLog` calls introduced by Apple's engineers. You can track this information at the debug console, or you can use the following trick to redirect it to a file (the messages will not output to the console) and then display it in-application with a text view. Recipe 12-2 uses a standard C `freopen()` call to redirect `stderr` data, which is what `NSLog()` produces, to a file. It then sets up an `NSTimer` instance to monitor that file, and when the file contents change, it updates the text view with that output. You can use this redirection approach with GameKit or with any other application that produces console output of some kind.

Take note of the way this recipe updates the content offset for the text view. It ensures that the text at the bottom of the view is always displayed after an update. It does this by setting the offset to one page height shorter than the full content size.

Recipe 12-2 **Monitoring GameKit**

```
@implementation TestBedViewController
@synthesize textView;
- (void) listenForStderr: (NSTimer *) timer;
{
    // Monitor the stderr output for new information
    NSString *contents = [NSString
        stringWithContentsOfFile:STDERR_OUT];
    contents = [contents stringByReplacingOccurrencesOfString:@"\n"
        withString:@"\n\n"];
    if ([contents isEqualToString:self.textView.text]) return;
    [self.textView setText:contents];
    self.textView.contentOffset = CGPointMake(0.0f,
```

```
        MAX(self.textView.contentSize.height -
        self.textView.frame.size.height, 0.0f));
}

- (void) viewDidLoad
{
    // Establish the GameKit session
    [GameKitHelper sharedInstance].sessionID = @"Peeking at GameKit";
    [GameKitHelper assignViewController:self];

    // Redirect stderr output to file
    freopen([STDERR_OUT fileSystemRepresentation], "w", stderr);
    [NSTimer scheduledTimerWithTimeInterval:1.0f target:self
        selector:@selector(listenForStderr) userInfo:nil repeats:YES];
}
@end
```

Get This Recipe's Code

To get the code used for this recipe, go to http://github.com/erica/iphone-3.0-cookbook-, or if you've downloaded the disk image containing all of the sample code from the book, go to the folder for Chapter 12 and open the project for this recipe.

Recipe: Sending Complex Data Through GameKit

Sending simple strings back and forth through GameKit a la Recipe 12-1 gets you only so far. Soon, you'll need to move forward to more complex objects and data. Property lists offer a good way to transmit custom objects. That's because property lists are easily serialized to and from `NSData` objects.

Property lists provide a helpful abstract data type. A property list object can point to data (`NSData`), strings (`NSString`), arrays (`NSArray`), dictionaries (`NSDictionary`), dates (`NSDate`), and numbers (`NSNumber`). When working with collection objects (i.e., arrays and dictionaries) all members and keys must be property list objects as well, that is, data, strings, numbers, and dates as well as embedded arrays and dictionaries.

While that seems limiting, you can transform most structures and objects to and from strings. For example, you can use the built-in `NSStringFromCGPoint()` or `NSStringFromClass()` functions, or you can create your own. The following pair of methods extend the `UIColor` class, providing functionality needed to send color information across a GameKit connection as strings.

```
@implementation UIColor (utilities)
- (NSString *) stringFromColor
{
    // Recover the color space and store RGB or monochrome color
    const CGFloat *c = CGColorGetComponents(self.CGColor);
    CGColorSpaceModel csm =
        CGColorSpaceGetModel(CGColorGetColorSpace(self.CGColor));
```

```
    return (csm == kCGColorSpaceModelRGB) ?
        [NSString stringWithFormat:@"%0.2f %0.2f %0.2f %0.2f",
            c[0], c[1], c[2], c[3]] :
        [NSString stringWithFormat:@"%0.2f %0.2f %0.2f %0.2f",
            c[0], c[0], c[0], c[1]];
}

+ (UIColor *) colorWithString: (NSString *) colorString
{
    // Read a color back from a string
    const CGFloat c[4];
    sscanf([colorString cStringUsingEncoding:NSUTF8StringEncoding],
        "%f %f %f %f", &c[0], &c[1], &c[2], &c[3]);
    return [UIColor colorWithRed:c[0] green:c[1] blue:c[2] alpha:c[3]];
}
@end
```

Once in property list form, you can serialize your data and send it as a single chunk. On receipt, the deserialized data is ready to use. Recipe 12-3 shows the **`transmit`** and **`receivedData:`** methods that handle this. This code comes from a sample that stores a series of drawing points (a la Recipe 8-9) along with the color used to draw them in an **`NSDictionary`** object. You can use the **`NSKeyedArchiver`** and **`NSKeyedUnarchiver`** classes as well as the **`NSPropertyListSerialization`** class shown here.

By storing both the points and colors as strings, this data can easily be converted into a form better suited for transmission via GameKit. The source code for this chapter shows these methods in action, demonstrating the full collaborative drawing tool that leverages property list transfers.

Recipe 12-3 **Serializing and Deserializing Property Lists**

```
- (void) transmit
{
    if (![GameKitHelper sharedInstance].isConnected) return;
    NSString *errorString;

    // Send a copy of the local points to the peer
    // by serializing the property list into data
    NSData *plistdata = [NSPropertyListSerialization
         dataFromPropertyList:self.points
         format:NSPropertyListXMLFormat_v1_0
         errorDescription:&errorString];
    if (plistdata)
         [GameKitHelper sendData:plistdata];
    else
         CFShow(errorString);
}
```

```
- (void) receivedData: (NSData *) thedata
{
    // Deserialize the data back into a property list
    CFStringRef errorString;
    CFPropertyListRef plist =
        CFPropertyListCreateFromXMLData(kCFAllocatorDefault,
        (CFDataRef)thedata, kCFPropertyListMutableContainers,
        &errorString);

    if (!plist)
    {
        CFShow(errorString);
        return;
    }

    // Assign the received data to foreignPoints
    self.foreignPoints = (NSArray *)plist;
}
```

Get This Recipe's Code

To get the code used for this recipe, go to http://github.com/erica/iphone-3.0-cookbook-, or if you've downloaded the disk image containing all of the sample code from the book, go to the folder for Chapter 12 and open the project for this recipe.

Recipe: GameKit Voice Chat

GameKit's In-Game Voice service lets applications create a walkie-talkie-style voice channel connecting two devices together. You can use this service with iPhones, taking advantage of their built-in speaker and microphone, or with second generation or later iPod touch units by adding an external microphone. The standard iPhone earbuds with their built-in mic work very well with iPod touches, routing the audio into the earbuds and picking up voice input through the microphone.

GameKit as Middleman

The `GameKitHelper` class introduced in Recipe 12-1 provides all the normal functionality for GameKit connections. To adapt this code for Voice Chat, you need to think of the GameKit communications as a voice chat middleman. GameKit handles the data throughput, both receipt and delivery.

The voice additions, provided by the `GKVoiceChatService` class, sit outside normal GameKit. Chat services connect into the iPhone's audio playback and recording system, so Voice Chat can listen to and play back audio. Voice Chat then sends its data through GameKit and plays back the data it receives from GameKit. Figure 12-5 shows this separation of responsibilities.

Unfortunately, you cannot use the GameKit Voice Chat service over a connection other than Bluetooth. GKVoice expects a GKSession with GKPeers in order to transmit

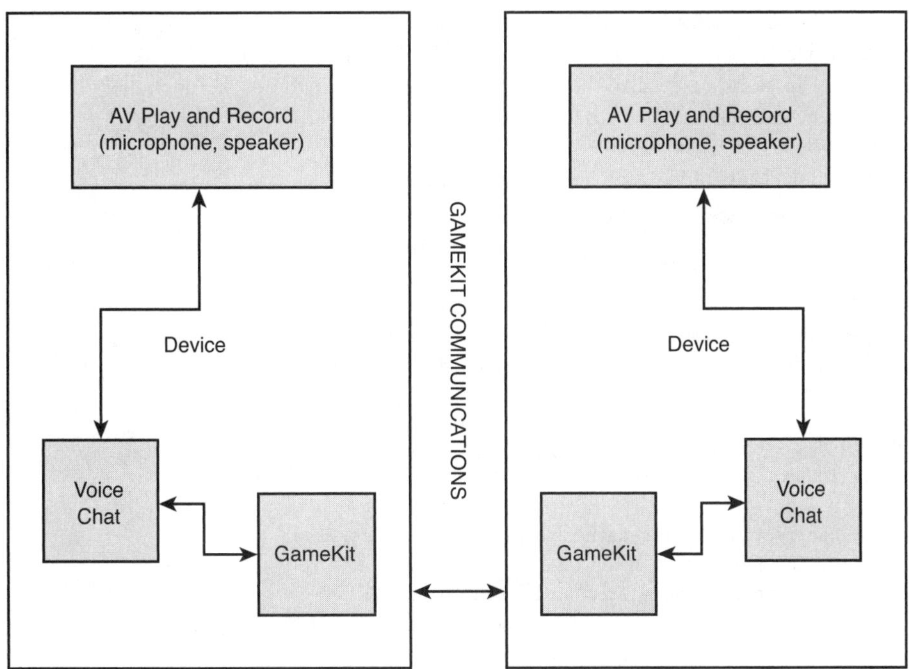

Figure 12-5 Voice Chat adds a layer outside normal GameKit communications to enable live peer-to-peer audio.

its data. If you need to use voice transmission for another connection style, you'll have to write that layer yourself.

Implementing Voice Chat

When working with voice, there's no difference in the way you get started. You display a peer picker and negotiate the connection, as you would normally do with GameKit. The difference arrives once the peer connects. You need to establish the voice chat and redirect the data to and from that service.

Upon connecting to the new peer, set up the voice chat basics. The peer connection method in Recipe 12-4 activates a play-and-record audio session, sets the default chat service client, and starts a new voice chat with that peer. By setting the `client` property, you ensure that your class receives the voice chat callbacks needed for negotiating data.

Your primary class must declare the `GKVoiceChatClient` protocol to do this. When the chat service gathers data through the microphone, it triggers the `voiceChatService:` ➥`sendData:toParticipantID:` callback. Here, you can redirect voice data to your normal GameKit session. For a voice-only connection, just send along the data. When your application handles both voice and other data, build a dictionary and tag the data with a key such as `@"voice"` or When your class receives data through the normal `receiveData:fromPeer:inSession:context:` callback, the same approaches apply.

For voice only, use `receivedData:fromParticipantID:` to send the data off to the chat service. Voice Chat allows you to mix game audio with in-game voice. For voice-data hybrid applications, deserialize the data, determine whether the packet included voice or regular data, and redirect that data to the appropriate recipient.

Recipe 12-4 **Adding In-Game Voice Chat Services**

```
- (void)voiceChatService:(GKVoiceChatService *)voiceChatService
    sendData:(NSData *)data toParticipantID:(NSString *)participantID
{
    // Send the next burst of data to peers
    [self.session sendData: data toPeers:[NSArray arrayWithObject:
        participantID] withDataMode: GKSendDataReliable error: nil];
}

- (void) receiveData:(NSData *)data fromPeer:(NSString *)peer inSession:
(GKSession *)session context:(void *)context
{
    // Redirect any voice data to the voice chat service
    [[GKVoiceChatService defaultVoiceChatService]
        receivedData:data fromParticipantID:peer];
}

- (NSString *)participantID
{
   // provide the session's participant ID for the chat
   return self.session.peerID;
}

- (void)peerPickerController:(GKPeerPickerController *)picker
    didConnectPeer:(NSString *)peerID toSession: (GKSession *) session{

    // Upon connection, close the picker and set the data handler
    [picker dismiss];
    [picker release];
    isConnected = YES;
    [self.session setDataReceiveHandler:self withContext:nil];

    // Start the audio session
    NSError *error;
    AVAudioSession *audioSession = [AVAudioSession sharedInstance];

    if (![audioSession setCategory:AVAudioSessionCategoryPlayAndRecord
        error:&error])
    {
        NSLog(@"Error setting the AV play/record category: %@", [error
        localizedDescription]);
```

```
        showAlert(@"Could not establish an Audio Connection. Sorry!");
        return;
    }

    if (![audioSession setActive: YES error: &error])
    {
        NSLog(@"Error activating the audio session: %@", [error
            localizedDescription]);
        showAlert(@"Could not establish an Audio Connection. Sorry!");
        return;
    }

    // Set the voice chat client and start voice chat
    [GKVoiceChatService defaultVoiceChatService].client = self;
    if (![[GKVoiceChatService defaultVoiceChatService]
        startVoiceChatWithParticipantID: peerID error: &error])
    {
        showAlert(@"Could not start voice chat. Sorry!");
        NSLog(@"Error starting voice chat");
    }
}
```

Get This Recipe's Code

To get the code used for this recipe, go to http://github.com/erica/iphone-3.0-cookbook-, or if you've downloaded the disk image containing all of the sample code from the book, go to the folder for Chapter 12 and open the project for this recipe.

Recipe: Using Bonjour to Create an iPhone Server

Although GameKit is built around Bonjour, sometimes you'll want to use Bonjour directly. For example, you might build an iPhone service that connects to a Macintosh-based client. (Bonjour has been ported to both Windows and Linux, but those platforms fall outside the scope of this book.)

Apple has provided bounteous quantities of Bonjour sample code, and Recipe 12-5 takes advantage of this material. The recipe uses Apple's ready-supplied `TCPServer` and `TCPConnection` classes to broadcast a Bonjour service and respond to external connections.

This code is built around the basic image-picking sample from Recipe 7-1. Instead of just selecting an image, this recipe serves that image out via a Bonjour data connection.

The handshake process starts by establishing a new `TCPServer` and setting its delegate. The `viewDidLoad` method starts the service using the current run loop and announces a `"PictureThrow"` service. When an external client connects, the `server:didOpenConnection:` callback accepts the connection and sets its `TCPConnection` delegate. The difference between the server delegate and the connection delegate is that the server is responsible for listening for new connections, and the connection is responsible for sending and receiving data.

As with GameKit, the user decides whether to accept a new connection. The `server:shouldAcceptConnectionFromAddress:` connection delegate method returns a Boolean value, allowing or denying the connection. Figure 12-6 shows the dialog displayed by Recipe 12-5 when a new connection is proposed.

Figure 12-6 Emulating GameKit, Recipe 12-5 allows the user to decide whether to accept or reject a remote connection.

After accepting the connection, the connection delegate receives a `connectionDidOpen:` callback. Here, the application finally sends the data to the client and then closes the connection with `invalidate`. This allows the client to implement a push-to-request-data button. Each press of that button initializes a new connection, and thus a new data request.

The data sent is the currently selected image. The user can update this image choice by clicking Choose Image (using a standard image picker) or Camera (to snap a photo).

As you can see, the code in this recipe is far more concerned with handling the image selection choices than the simple hooks into the Bonjour service. Just a few methods and callbacks provide a complete suite of data server connectivity.

Note

The code for Apple's classes has been included with the sample that accompanies this chapter.

Recipe 12-5 **Providing a Bonjour Service**

```
@interface TestBedViewController : UIViewController
    <UINavigationControllerDelegate, UIImagePickerControllerDelegate,
    TCPServerDelegate, TCPConnectionDelegate>
{
    UIImage *image;
    TCPServer *server;
}
@property (retain) UIImage *image;
@property (retain) TCPServer *server;
@end

@implementation TestBedViewController
@synthesize image;
@synthesize server;

- (void) baseButtons
{
    // Allow user to pick or snap an image
    self.navigationItem.leftBarButtonItem = BARBUTTON(@"Choose Image",
        @selector(pickImage));
    if ([UIImagePickerController
        isSourceTypeAvailable:UIImagePickerControllerSourceTypeCamera])
        self.navigationItem.rightBarButtonItem = BARBUTTON(@"Camera",
        @selector(snapImage));
}

- (void)imagePickerController:(UIImagePickerController *)picker
    didFinishPickingMediaWithInfo:(NSDictionary *)info
{
    // Show the selected image and dismiss the picker
    self.image = [info objectForKey:
        @"UIImagePickerControllerOriginalImage"];
    [(UIImageView *)[self.view viewWithTag:101] setImage:self.image];
    [self dismissModalViewControllerAnimated:YES];
    [picker release];
    [self baseButtons];
}

- (void) imagePickerControllerDidCancel:
    (UIImagePickerController *)picker
{
    // On cancel, dismiss the picker
    [self dismissModalViewControllerAnimated:YES];
    [picker release];
    [self baseButtons];
```

```
}

- (void) requestImageOfType: (NSString *) type
{
    // Show the picker using either the camera or photo picker
    // depending on which button the user pressed
    UIImagePickerController *ipc = [[UIImagePickerController alloc]
        init];
    ipc.sourceType = [type isEqualToString:@"Camera"] ?
        UIImagePickerControllerSourceTypeCamera :
        UIImagePickerControllerSourceTypePhotoLibrary;
    ipc.delegate = self;
    ipc.allowsImageEditing = NO;
    [self presentModalViewController:ipc animated:YES];
}

- (void) pickImage: (id) sender
{
    // Start a picking session from the photo library
    self.navigationItem.leftBarButtonItem = nil;
    self.navigationItem.rightBarButtonItem = nil;
    [self performSelector:@selector(requestImageOfType)
        withObject:@"Library" afterDelay:0.5f];
}

- (void) snapImage: (id) sender
{
    // Start a camera session
    self.navigationItem.leftBarButtonItem = nil;
    self.navigationItem.rightBarButtonItem = nil;
    [self performSelector:@selector(requestImageOfType)
        withObject:@"Camera" afterDelay:0.5f];
}

- (NSString *) hostname
{
    // Produce the host name for the iPhone
    char baseHostName[255];
    int success = gethostname(baseHostName, 255);
    if (success != 0) return nil;
    baseHostName[255] = '\0';
    return [NSString stringWithCString:baseHostName];
}

- (BOOL) server:(TCPServer*)server
    shouldAcceptConnectionFromAddress:(const struct sockaddr*)address
{
```

```
    // Allow user to deny requests. To accept all connections
    // replace this with "return YES;"
    return [ModalAlert ask:@"Accept remote connection?"];
}

- (void) connectionDidOpen:(TCPConnection*)connection
{
    // On opening the connection, send the current image
    // data to the client
    printf("Connection did open\n");
    if ([connection sendData:
        UIImageJPEGRepresentation(self.image, 0.75f)])
        printf("Data sent\n");
    [connection invalidate];
}

- (void) server:(TCPServer*)server
    didOpenConnection:(TCPServerConnection*)connection
{
    // Set the connection's delegate, to receive the open
    // callback when ready
    [connection setDelegate:self];
}

- (void) viewDidLoad
{
    // Check for a WiFi connection before proceeding
    NetReachability *nr = [[NetReachability alloc]
        initWithDefaultRoute:YES];
    if (![nr isReachable] || ([nr isReachable] && [nr isUsingCell]))
    {
        [ModalAlert performSelector:@selector(say) withObject:
            @"This application requires WiFi. Please enable WiFi in\
            Settings and run this application again." afterDelay:0.5f];
        return;
    }

    // Create a server instance, providing the Bonjour service
    self.server = [[[TCPServer alloc] initWithPort:0] autorelease];
    [self.server setDelegate:self];
    [self.server startUsingRunLoop:[NSRunLoop currentRunLoop]];
    [self.server enableBonjourWithDomain:@"local"
        applicationProtocol:@"PictureThrow" name:[self hostname]];

    // Set the default buttons and image
    [self baseButtons];
    self.image = [UIImage imageNamed:@"cover320x416.png"];
```

```
}
@end
```

Get This Recipe's Code

To get the code used for this recipe, go to http://github.com/erica/iphone-3.0-cookbook-, or if you've downloaded the disk image containing all of the sample code from the book, go to the folder for Chapter 12 and open the project for this recipe.

Recipe: Creating a Mac Client for an iPhone Bonjour Service

Apple's Bonjour sample code works with both iPhone and Macintosh applications with just a few changes needed. Notably, you need to drop any reference to the CFNetwork framework, replacing that with the AppKit framework for Mac. Recipe 12-6 provides a Macintosh client to demonstrate how to use the client side of the Bonjour sample code. This meshes with the server from Recipe 12-5.

There's nothing intrinsically specific about the roles and the platforms chosen. A Mac could just as easily provide a service and an iPhone its client. Since an iPhone/iPhone client/server pair is best implemented with GameKit, this recipe demonstrates how to cross platforms and use Bonjour for mobile desktop communication.

Because this is an iPhone book and not a Macintosh development book, Recipe 12-6 limits itself to the methods specific to the Bonjour communications. If you want to see how the rest of the application is built (and, especially, how to rectify the `UIImage` data into a properly oriented `NSImage`), please refer to the sample code that accompanies this book. Also refer to Recipe 12-8, which implements both server and client for iPhone. Figure 12-7 shows the Macintosh client application, as it was used to capture the screenshot used in Figure 12-6.

A Bonjour client begins by browsing for services. Since the service on the iPhone is provided by Bonjour and not GameKit, its name is known in advance of compilation and testing, namely `@"PictureThrow"`. This is the same name used in Recipe 12-5 by the server.

The `NSNetServiceBrowser` class provides the ability to find a given service type. Its delegate receives a `netServiceBrowser:didFindService:moreComing:` callback when a match appears. The delegate can then stop the browser and begin to resolve the service.

Resolving a service transforms a service name into an actual IP address. The same `TCPConnection` class used in Recipe 12-5 allows the Bonjour client to request data from the server. Its `connection:didReceiveData:` callback delivers that data.

Connections can close for three reasons. First, the data transferred over successfully and the host service closed it deliberately. Second, the user may have denied the connection. Third, the application might have lost its connection by quitting or moving out of range. The same `connectionDidClose:` callback must handle all three cases.

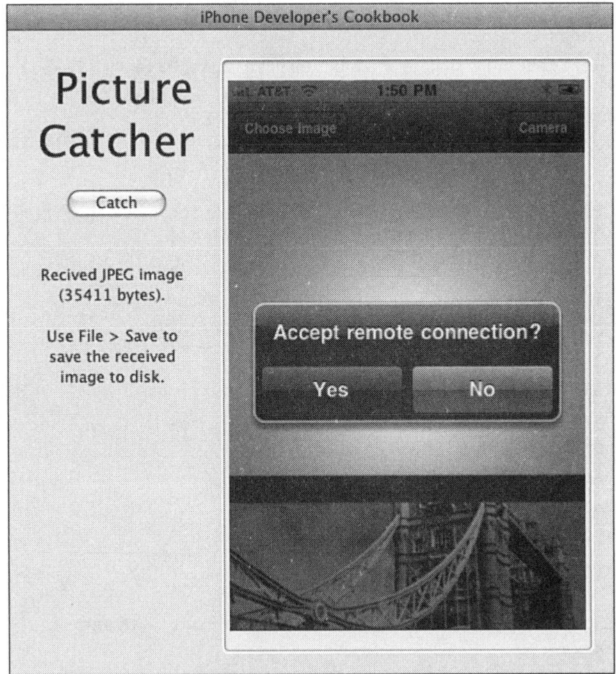

Figure 12-7 The Macintosh Bonjour client shown here was used with the iPhone Bonjour server from Recipe 12-5 to capture some of the screenshots used to illustrate this book.

In this recipe, this callback sets a Boolean value for `success`. When the connection closes, the `connectionDidClose:` callback method checks that value. If the data transfer did not succeed, the user is told that the connection was denied or lost.

Recipe 12-6 **Providing a Bonjour Client**

```
// Receive the image and update the interface
- (void) connection:(TCPConnection*)connection
    didReceiveData:(NSData*)data;
{
    // Upon receiving the image, update the image view
    success = YES;
    self.imageData = data;
    NSImage *image = [self imageFromData:data];
    [imageView setImage:image];

    // You can now save or catch another image
    [saveItem setEnabled:YES];
    [button setEnabled:YES];
    [progress stopAnimation:nil];
```

```
    // Update status
    ANNOUNCE(@"Recived JPEG image (%d bytes).\n\nUse File > Save\
       to save the received image to disk.", data.length);
}

// If there was no success, apologize and restore UI
- (void) connectionDidClose:(TCPConnection*)connection
{
    // Failed or completed connection. Check for success.
    if (success) return;
    ANNOUNCE(@"Connection denied or lost. Sorry.");

    // For a failed connection, prepare for the next catch
    self.imageData = nil;
    [saveItem setEnabled:NO];
    [imageView setImage:nil];
    [button setEnabled:YES];
    [progress stopAnimation:nil];
}

// Upon resolving address, create a connection to that address
// and request data
- (void)netServiceDidResolveAddress:(NSNetService *)netService
{
    // Gather the addresses and attempt to create a connection
    NSArray* addresses = [netService addresses];
    if (addresses && [addresses count]) {
        struct sockaddr* address = (struct sockaddr*)[[addresses
            objectAtIndex:0] bytes];
        TCPConnection *connection = [[TCPConnection alloc]
            initWithRemoteAddress:address];
        [connection setDelegate:self];
        [statusText setTitleWithMnemonic:@"Requesting data..."];
        [progress startAnimation:nil];
        [netService release];
        [connection receiveData];
    }
}

// Complain when resolve fails
- (void)netService:(NSNetService *)sender didNotResolve:
    (NSDictionary *)errorDict {
    [statusText setTitleWithMnemonic:
        @"Error resolving service. Sorry."];
}
```

```
// Upon finding a service, stop the browser and resolve
- (void)netServiceBrowser:(NSNetServiceBrowser *)netServiceBrowser
    didFindService:(NSNetService *)netService
    moreComing:(BOOL)moreServicesComing
{
    [self.browser stop];
    self.browser = nil;
    [statusText setTitleWithMnemonic:@"Resolving service."];
    [[netService retain] setDelegate:self];
    [netService resolveWithTimeout:0.0f];
}

// Begin a catch request, start the service browser, and update UI
- (IBAction) catchPlease: (id) sender
{
    success = NO;
    [self.statusText setTitleWithMnemonic:@"Scanning for service"];

    // Create a new service browser
    self.browser = [[[NSNetServiceBrowser alloc] init] autorelease];
    [self.browser setDelegate:self];
    NSString *type = [TCPConnection
        bonjourTypeFromIdentifier:@"PictureThrow"];
    [self.browser searchForServicesOfType:type inDomain:@"local"];

    // Disable and reset the interactive features while waiting
    [button setEnabled:NO];
    self.imageData = nil;
    [saveItem setEnabled:NO];
    [imageView setImage:nil];
}
```

Get This Recipe's Code

To get the code used for this recipe, go to http://github.com/erica/iphone-3.0-cookbook-, or if you've downloaded the disk image containing all of the sample code from the book, go to the folder for Chapter 12 and open the project for this recipe.

Recipe: Working Around Real-World GameKit Limitations

Although GameKit is built on Bonjour, it isn't meant to provide the same kind of general use data transfer capabilities displayed in the previous two Bonjour-only recipes. GameKit Bluetooth prefers small data packets, preferably under 1,000 bytes each. `GKSession` objects cannot send data over 95 kilobytes. When you try, the `sendDataToAllPeers:error:` method fails, returning a Boolean value of NO.

Recipe 12-7 addresses this problem by checking for data length before queuing any send requests. Short data can be shared; long data is denied. To provide a test bed, this recipe works with the iPhone's built-in pasteboard.

In the real world, you'd likely split up long data items into short bursts and send them using reliable transfer. Reliable transmission ensures that data arrives and does so in the same order that it was sent. You can implement checksumming and other standard network approaches to ensure your data arrives properly. (You might alternatively consider programming a custom Bonjour WiFi service or using Internet server connections for more intense data transfer needs.)

This recipe provides a jumping off point for testing file size elements in the GameKit world. You are welcome to expand this code to explore file decomposition and reconstruction on your own.

Using the iPhone Pasteboard

Pasteboards, also known as *clipboards*, provide a central OS feature for sharing data across applications. Users can copy data to the pasteboard in one application, switch tasks, and then paste that data into another application. Cut/copy/paste features appear in most operating systems and are new to the iPhone, having debuted in the 3.0 firmware.

The `UIPasteboard` class offers access to a shared iPhone pasteboard and its contents. As with Macs and Windows-based computers, you can use the pasteboard to share data within an application or between applications. In addition to the general shared system pasteboard, the iPhone offers both a name finding pasteboard and application-specific pasteboards to better ensure data privacy. This snippet returns the general system pasteboard, which is appropriate for most general copy/paste use.

```
UIPasteboard *pb = [UIPasteboard generalPasteboard];
```

Storing Data

Pasteboards can store one or more entries at a time. Each has an associated type, using the Uniform Type Identifier (UTI) to specify what kind of data is stored. For example, you might find `public.text` (and more specifically `public.utf8-plain-text`), `public.url`, and `public.jpeg` among common data types used on the iPhone. The dictionary that stores the type and the data is called an `item`, and you can retrieve an array of all available items via the pasteboard's `items` property.

Query a pasteboard for its available types by sending it the `pasteboardTypes` message. This returns an array of types currently stored on the pasteboard.

```
NSArray *types = [pb pasteboardTypes];
```

Pasteboards are specialized for several data types. These are colors, images, strings, and URLs. The `UIPasteboard` class provides specialized getters and setters to simplify handling these items. Because Recipe 12-7 provides a general pasting tool, only strings are demonstrated with a specialized call, that is, `setString`.

Retrieving Data

Retrieve data using `dataForPasteboardType:`. This returns the data from the first item whose type matches the one sent as the parameter. Any other matching items in the pasteboard are ignored. Should you need to retrieve all matching data, recover an `itemSetWithPasteboardTypes:` and then iterate through the set to retrieve each dictionary. Recover the data type for each item from the single dictionary key and the data from its value.

`UIPasteboard` offers two approaches for pasting to the pasteboard. Use `setValueForPasteboardType:` for Property List objects. (See the discussion earlier in this chapter about these objects.) For general data, use `setData:forPasteboardType:` as is used in this recipe. When pasteboards are changed, they issue a `UIPasteboardChanged` ➥`Notification`, which you can listen into via a default `NSNotificationCenter` observer.

Responsible Pasteboarding

Recipe 12-7 provides several checks before sending, retrieving, and copying pasteboard data. Users must confirm that they intend to share data of a given type. When receiving data, they must authorize the application to copy the data to the general system pasteboard. This approach ensures that proactive user effort must take place before performing these actions.

Recipe 12-7 **Sharing the iPhone Pasteboard over GameKit**

```
@implementation TestBedViewController

- (void) sharePasteboard
{
    // Construct a dictionary of the pasteboard type and data
    NSMutableDictionary *md = [NSMutableDictionary dictionary];
    UIPasteboard *pb = [UIPasteboard generalPasteboard];
    NSString *type = [[pb pasteboardTypes] lastObject];
    NSData *data = [pb dataForPasteboardType:type];
    [md setObject:type forKey:@"type"];
    [md setObject:data forKey:@"data"];

    // Deny any requests that are too big
    if (data.length > (95000))
    {
        [ModalAlert say:@"Too much data in pasteboard (%0.2f \
            Kilobytes). GameKit can only send up to approx 90 \
            Kilobytes at a time.", ((float) data.length) / 1000.0f];
        return;
    }
```

```
    // User must confirm share
    NSString *confirmString = [NSString stringWithFormat:
        @"Share %d bytes of type %@?", data.length, type];
    if (![ModalAlert ask:confirmString]) return;

    // Serialize and send the data
    NSString *errorString;
    NSData *plistdata = [NSPropertyListSerialization
        dataFromPropertyList:md format:NSPropertyListXMLFormat_v1_0
        errorDescription:&errorString];
    if (plistdata)
        [GameKitHelper sendData:plistdata];
    else
        CFShow(errorString);
}

- (void) sentData:(NSString *) errorString
{
    // Check to see if there was a problem sending data
    if (errorString)
    {
        [ModalAlert say:@"Error sending data: %@", errorString];
        return;
    }

    [ModalAlert say:@"Pasteboard data successfully queued for\
        transmission."];
}

// On establishing the connection, allow the user to share the pasteboard
- (void) connectionEstablished
{
    UIPasteboard *pb = [UIPasteboard generalPasteboard];
    NSArray *types = [pb pasteboardTypes];
    if (types.count == 0) return;

    self.navigationItem.leftBarButtonItem = BARBUTTON(
        @"Share Pasteboard", @selector(sharePasteboard));
}

// Hide the share option when the connection is lost
- (void) connectionLost
{
    self.navigationItem.leftBarButtonItem = nil;
}
```

```
-(void) receivedData: (NSData *) data
{
    // Deserialize the transmission
    CFStringRef errorString;
    NSDictionary *dict =
        (NSDictionary *) CFPropertyListCreateFromXMLData(
        kCFAllocatorDefault, (CFDataRef)data,
        kCFPropertyListMutableContainers, &errorString);
    if (!dict)
    {
        CFShow(errorString);
        return;
    }

    // Retrieve the type and data
    NSString *type = [dict objectForKey:@"type"];
    NSData *sentdata = [dict objectForKey:@"data"];
    if (!type || !sentdata) return;

    // Do not copy to pasteboard unless the user permits
    NSString *message = [NSString stringWithFormat:
        @"Received %d bytes of type %@. Copy to pasteboard?",
        sentdata.length, type];
    if (![ModalAlert ask:message]) return;

    // Perform the pasteboard copy
    UIPasteboard *pb = [UIPasteboard generalPasteboard];
    if ([type isEqualToString:@"public.text"])
    {
        NSString *string = [[[NSString alloc] initWithData:sentdata
            encoding:NSUTF8StringEncoding] autorelease];
        [pb setString:string];
    }
    else [pb setData:sentdata forPasteboardType:type];
}

- (void) viewDidLoad
{
    // Set up the helper
    [GameKitHelper sharedInstance].sessionID = @"Pasteboard Share";
    [GameKitHelper sharedInstance].dataDelegate = self;
    [GameKitHelper assignViewController:self];
}
@end
```

> **Get This Recipe's Code**
>
> To get the code used for this recipe, go to http://github.com/erica/iphone-3.0-cookbook-, or if you've downloaded the disk image containing all of the sample code from the book, go to the folder for Chapter 12 and open the project for this recipe.

Recipe: iPhone to iPhone Gaming Via BonjourHelper

If you're willing to forgo GameKit's Bluetooth and work with WiFi, you can duplicate many of GameKit's features on all iPhones including the older first generation units. Recipe 12-8 introduces `BonjourHelper`. It was designed to mimic `GameKitHelper` from Recipe 12-1. That recipe established its connection by setting a session identifier, a data delegate, and assigning a view controller.

```
[GameKitHelper sharedInstance].sessionID = @"Typing Together";
[GameKitHelper sharedInstance].dataDelegate = self;
[GameKitHelper assignViewController:self];
```

Substituting `BonjourHelper` for `GameKitHelper` requires very few programming changes. It uses the same initialization steps, and the data delegate receives an identical set of callbacks. You do need to omit the space in the session ID, a step that isn't needed in GameKit. GameKit encrypts its session IDs to produce a guaranteed no-space proper Bonjour identifier. `BonjourHelper`'s plain-text approach means spaces are off-limits. Limit your session ID names to simple alphanumeric text with 14 characters or fewer. Refer to RFC 2782 service types (http://www.dns-sd.org/ServiceTypes.html) for details. The `BonjourHelper` code transforms the session ID into a standard Bonjour identifier (i.e., `_typingtogether._tcp.`).

```
[BonjourHelper sharedInstance].sessionID = @"TypingTogether";
[BonjourHelper sharedInstance].dataDelegate = self;
[BonjourHelper assignViewController:self];
```

That's not to say that the functionality and implementation are identical. With `BonjourHelper`, both units must be on the same network. You lose the pretty GameKit peer connection controller sequence shown in Figures 12-2, 12-3, and 12-4. Instead, `BonjourHelper` provides a simple alert, as shown in Figure 12-8. Beyond that, `BonjourHelper` basically provides the same peer-to-peer connectivity and data flow as GameKit.

Registering Bonjour Names and Ports

You should register any Bonjour names you plan to use for commercial release with the DNS Service Discovery organization. Registration ensures that your service names and protocols will not overlap or conflict with any other vendor. A list of currently registered services is maintained at http://www.dns-sd.org/ServiceTypes.html.

These names must conform to the RFC 2782 standard. Submit your protocol name to srv_type_request@dns-sd.org. Include the up-to-14-character name of the Bonjour

Figure 12-8 The custom **BonjourHelper** class provides a simpler connection interface than GameKit.

service, a longer descriptive name, the contact information (name and e-mail address) of the person registering the service, and an information page URL. Specify the transportation protocol (i.e., _tcp or _udp) and a list of any TXT record keys used. (An example that uses and displays TXT data follows at the end of this chapter.)

It may take some time for the volunteers at the dns-sd.org site to process and respond to your query. Delays on the order of weeks are not uncommon. You may need to resubmit, so keep a copy of all your information.

If you plan to use a fixed port (most Bonjour implementations randomly pick a port at runtime to use), you'll want to submit an application for a registered port number with IANA, the Internet Assigned Numbers Authority, as well. IANA provides a central repository for port registrations and will, at some time, be merged with the dns-sd registry. IANA often takes a year or longer to finish registering new protocol port numbers.

Note

Apple maintains a list of official OS X Bonjour service types in its Technical Q&A QA1312 document, which you can find at http://developer.apple.com/mac/library/qa/qa2001/qa1312.html.

Duplex Connection

For simplicity, `BonjourHelper` works by establishing a duplex connection. Each device provides both a client and a host. This avoids any issues about trying to get two peers to negotiate with each other and assume the proper server and client roles without both of them ending up as client or server at the same time.

When resolving addresses, the helper ensures that the unit will not connect to itself. It demands a unique IP address that doesn't match the local one. If the incoming address does match, it just continues looking. The host needs no such checks; outgoing client connections are limited to foreign addresses.

When the helper has established an outgoing connection and accepted an incoming one, it stops looking for any further peers and considers itself fully connected. The helper updates the Connect/Disconnect button if a view controller has been set.

Reading Data

Unlike Recipe 12-6, Recipe 12-8 cannot use a simple read loop, that is, request data, read it, and repeat. Reading data is blocking. A read loop prevents an application from handling its server duties at the same time as its client duties.

Instead, this class uses the nonblocking `hasDataAvailable` check before asking for new data. A delayed selector adds a natural interval into the poll allowing each host time to update and prepare new data before being barraged by a new request.

Closing Connections

Connections can break in several ways. Users can quit an application, they can press the Disconnect button in the sample, or they can move out of range of the connection. `BonjourHelper` checks for disconnects exclusively from the server point of view. This simplifies its implementation, assuming that a lost client equates to a lost host and avoids the issue of multiple user notifications, i.e., "Lost connection to server" and "Lost connection to client" for both ends of the duplex connection.

> **Note**
>
> For space considerations, this listing of Recipe 12-8 omits a number of basic IP utilities, including `stringFromAddress:`, `addressFromString:address:`, and `localIPAddress`. These methods are included in the sample code that accompanies this chapter and are discussed further in Chapter 13, "Networking."

Recipe 12-8 **BonjourHelper Provides GameKit-like Connectivity over WiFi**

```
#define DO_DATA_CALLBACK(X, Y) if (sharedInstance.dataDelegate && \
    [sharedInstance.dataDelegate respondsToSelector:@selector(X)]) \
    [sharedInstance.dataDelegate performSelector:@selector(X) \
    withObject:Y];
#define BARBUTTON(TITLE, SELECTOR)      [[[UIBarButtonItem alloc] \
    initWithTitle:TITLE style:UIBarButtonItemStylePlain \
    target:[BonjourHelper class] action:SELECTOR] autorelease]
```

```
@implementation BonjourHelper
@synthesize server;
@synthesize browser;
@synthesize inConnection;
@synthesize outConnection;

@synthesize dataDelegate;
@synthesize viewController;
@synthesize sessionID;
@synthesize isConnected;
@synthesize hud;

static BonjourHelper *sharedInstance = nil;
BOOL inConnected;
BOOL outConnected;

+ (BonjourHelper *) sharedInstance
{
    if(!sharedInstance) sharedInstance = [[self alloc] init];
    return sharedInstance;
}

#pragma mark Class utilities
+ (void) assignViewController: (UIViewController *) aViewController
{
    // By assigning the optional view controller, this class
    // takes charge of the connect/disconnect button
    sharedInstance.viewController = aViewController;
    if (sharedInstance.viewController)
        sharedInstance.viewController.navigationItem.rightBarButtonItem
        = BARBUTTON(@"Connect", @selector(connect));
}

#pragma mark Handshaking

- (void) updateStatus
{
    // Must be connected to continue
    if (!(self.inConnection && self.outConnection) ||
        !(inConnected && outConnected))
    {
        self.isConnected = NO;
        return;
    }

    // Send callback, dismiss HUD, update bar button
```

```
    self.isConnected = YES;
    DO_DATA_CALLBACK(connectionEstablished, nil);
    [self.hud dismissWithClickedButtonIndex:1 animated:YES];
    if (self.viewController)
        self.viewController.navigationItem.rightBarButtonItem =
            BARBUTTON(@"Disconnect", @selector(disconnect));
}

// Upon resolving address, create a connection to that address
// and request data
- (void)netServiceDidResolveAddress:(NSNetService *)netService
{
    NSArray* addresses = [netService addresses];
    if (addresses && addresses.count)
    {
        for (int i = 0; i < addresses.count; i++)
        {
            // The IP utility implementations can be found in
            // the sample code that accompanies this chapter.
            // They are omitted here for space considerations.
            struct sockaddr* address =
                (struct sockaddr*)[[addresses objectAtIndex:i] bytes];
            NSString *addressString =
                [BonjourHelper stringFromAddress:address];
            if (!addressString) continue;

            if ([addressString hasPrefix:
                    [BonjourHelper localIPAddress]])
            {
                printf("Will not resolve with self. \
                    Continuing to browse.\n");
                continue;
            }

            printf("Found a matching external service\n");
            printf("My address: %s\n",
                [[BonjourHelper localIPAddress] UTF8String]);
            printf("Remote address: %s\n", [addressString UTF8String]);

            // Stop browsing for services
            [self.browser stop];
            [netService release];

            // Create an outbound connection to this new service
            self.outConnection = [[[TCPConnection alloc]
                initWithRemoteAddress:address] autorelease];
            [self.outConnection setDelegate:self];
            [self performSelector:@selector(checkForData)];
```

```
            [self updateStatus];
            return;
        }
    }

    [netService stop];
}

- (void)netServiceBrowser:(NSNetServiceBrowser *)netServiceBrowser
    didFindService:(NSNetService *)netService
    moreComing:(BOOL)moreServicesComing
{
    // start to resolve the service that was found
    [[netService retain] setDelegate:self];
    [netService resolveWithTimeout:0.0f];
}

+ (void) startBrowsingForServices
{
    // look for matching Bonjour services. The double-retain was
    // added for security. You can almost certainly discard it.
    sharedInstance.browser =
        [[[NSNetServiceBrowser alloc] init] retain];
    [sharedInstance.browser setDelegate:sharedInstance];
    NSString *type = [TCPConnection
        bonjourTypeFromIdentifier:sharedInstance.sessionID];
    [sharedInstance.browser searchForServicesOfType:type
        inDomain:@"local"];
}

+ (void) publish
{
    // Publish service to peers
    sharedInstance.server =
        [[[TCPServer alloc] initWithPort:0] autorelease];
    [sharedInstance.server setDelegate:sharedInstance];
    [sharedInstance.server startUsingRunLoop:
        [NSRunLoop currentRunLoop]];
    [sharedInstance.server enableBonjourWithDomain:@"local"
        applicationProtocol:sharedInstance.sessionID
        name:[self localHostname]];
}

+ (void) initConnections
{
```

```
    // Return to base unconnected state
    [sharedInstance.browser stop];
    [sharedInstance.server stop];

    sharedInstance.inConnection = nil;
    sharedInstance.outConnection = nil;
    sharedInstance.isConnected = NO;
    inConnected = NO;
    outConnected = NO;
}

- (void)alertView:(UIAlertView *)alertView
    clickedButtonAtIndex:(NSInteger)buttonIndex
{
    // Handle user request to cancel connecting
    if (buttonIndex) return;
    [BonjourHelper disconnect];
}

+ (void) connect
{
    if (sharedInstance.viewController)
        sharedInstance.viewController.navigationItem.rightBarButtonItem
            = nil;
    if (!sharedInstance.sessionID)
        sharedInstance.sessionID = @"Sample Session";

    // Create activity view with cancel button
    sharedInstance.hud = [[[UIAlertView alloc]
        initWithTitle:
        @"Searching for connection peer on your local network"
        message:@"\n\n" delegate:sharedInstance
        cancelButtonTitle:@"Cancel" otherButtonTitles:nil]
        autorelease];
    [sharedInstance.hud show];

    // Add the progress wheel
    UIActivityIndicatorView *aiv = [[[UIActivityIndicatorView alloc]
        initWithActivityIndicatorStyle:
        UIActivityIndicatorViewStyleWhiteLarge] autorelease];
    [aiv startAnimating];
    aiv.center = CGPointMake(
        sharedInstance.hud.bounds.size.width / 2.0f,
        sharedInstance.hud.bounds.size.height/2.0f);
    [sharedInstance.hud addSubview:aiv];

    // Prepare for duplex connection
    [self initConnections];
```

```
    [self startBrowsingForServices];
    [self publish];
}

+ (void) disconnect
{
    // disable current connections
    [sharedInstance.inConnection invalidate];
    [sharedInstance.outConnection invalidate];
    [self initConnections];

    // stop server
    [sharedInstance.server stop];
    [sharedInstance updateStatus];

    // reset
    [sharedInstance.hud dismissWithClickedButtonIndex:1 animated:YES];
    if (sharedInstance.viewController)
        sharedInstance.viewController.navigationItem.rightBarButtonItem
            = BARBUTTON(@"Connect", @selector(connect));
}

#pragma mark  Data Handling
- (void) checkForData
{
    // Perform a blocking receive only when data is available
    if (!self.outConnection) return;
    if ([self.outConnection hasDataAvailable])
        [self.outConnection receiveData];
    [self performSelector:@selector(checkForData)
        withObject:self afterDelay:0.1f];
}

+ (void) sendData: (NSData *) data
{
    if (!sharedInstance.outConnection) return;
    BOOL success = [sharedInstance.outConnection sendData:data];
    if (success) {
        DO_DATA_CALLBACK(sentData:, nil); }
    else {
        DO_DATA_CALLBACK(sentData:, @"Data could not be sent.");}
}

- (void) connection:(TCPConnection*)connection
    didReceiveData:(NSData*)data;
{
```

```
    // Redirect data callback
    DO_DATA_CALLBACK(receivedData:, data);
}

#pragma mark Connection Handlers

- (BOOL) server:(TCPServer*)server
    shouldAcceptConnectionFromAddress:(const struct sockaddr*)address
{
    // Accept connections only while not connected
    return !self.isConnected;
}

- (void) connectionDidFailOpening:(TCPConnection*)connection
{
    // Handled a fail open
    if (!connection) return;
    NSString *addressString = [BonjourHelper
        stringFromAddress:connection.remoteSocketAddress];
    [BonjourHelper disconnect];

    if (addressString)
        [ModalAlert say:@"Error while opening %@ connection (from %@).\
            Wait a few seconds or relaunch before trying to connect\n
            again.", (connection == self.inConnection) ? @"incoming" :
            @"outgoing", addressString];
    else
        printf("Failed to open connection from unknown address\n");
}

- (void) server:(TCPServer*)server
    didCloseConnection:(TCPServerConnection*)connection
{
    // Handle a newly closed connection
    if (!connection) return;
    NSString *addressString = [BonjourHelper
        stringFromAddress:connection.remoteSocketAddress];
    if (!addressString) return;

    BOOL wasConnected = self.isConnected;

    [BonjourHelper disconnect];
    printf("Lost connection from %s\n", [addressString UTF8String]);

    if (wasConnected)
        [ModalAlert say:@"Disconnected from peer (%@). You are no \
            longer connected to another device.", addressString];
```

```
    else
        [ModalAlert say:@"Peer was lost before full connection could \
            be established."];
}

- (void) server:(TCPServer*)server
    didOpenConnection:(TCPServerConnection*)connection
{
    // Set the connection but wait for it to fully open
    self.inConnection = connection;
    [self updateStatus];
    [connection setDelegate:self];
}

- (void) connectionDidOpen: (TCPConnection *) connection
{
    // Fully opened connection
    printf("Connection did open: %s\n", (connection ==
        self.inConnection) ? "incoming" : "outgoing");
    if (connection == self.inConnection) inConnected = YES;
    if (connection == self.outConnection) outConnected = YES;
    [self updateStatus];
}

- (void) connectionDidClose: (TCPConnection *)connection
{
    // Closed connection
    printf("Connection did close: %s\n", (connection ==
        self.inConnection) ? "incoming" : "outgoing");
    if (connection == self.inConnection) inConnected = NO;
    if (connection == self.outConnection) outConnected = NO;
    [self updateStatus];
}
@end
```

Get This Recipe's Code

To get the code used for this recipe, go to http://github.com/erica/iphone-3.0-cookbook-, or if you've downloaded the disk image containing all of the sample code from the book, go to the folder for Chapter 12 and open the project for this recipe.

Creating an "Online" GameKit Connection

In the GameKit world, "online" currently means any valid connection style other than Bluetooth. You might use a local WLAN network to connect to another device on the same network or connect through WWAN (i.e., the cellular service) or WiFi to a remote Internet-based host. GameKit takes you only so far as the dialog shown in Figure 12-9. By selecting Online, your user depends on you to create a custom connection to another device or service.

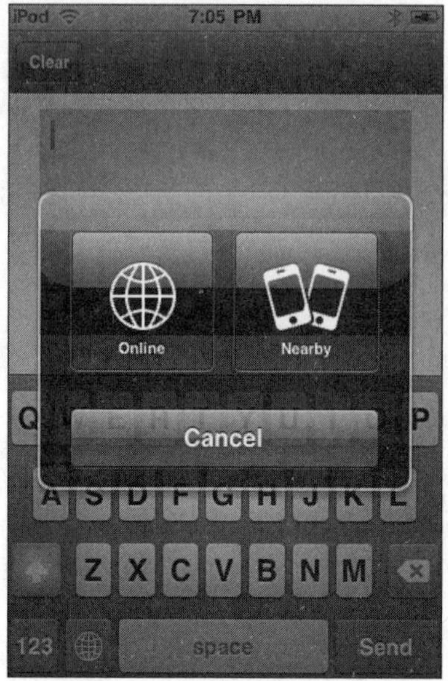

Figure 12-9 The Online GameKit connection means "bring your own networking." (Please note that the Send button shown on the keyboard here is a standard Return key. In this recipe, data is sent as it is typed.)

You create this two-item dialog by supplying the online option to the peer picker mask. In all other ways, there's no change in how you create and present a standard GameKit peer picker controller.

```
- (void) startConnection
{
    if (!self.isConnected)
    {
        GKPeerPickerController *picker = [[GKPeerPickerController
            alloc] init];
        picker.delegate = self;
        picker.connectionTypesMask = GKPeerPickerConnectionTypeNearby |
            GKPeerPickerConnectionTypeOnline;
        [picker show];
        if (self.viewController)
            self.viewController.navigationItem.rightBarButtonItem =
```

```
                nil;
    }
}
```

Catch the user selection in the `peerPickerController:didSelectConnectionType:` callback. You can assume that if the user selected Nearby that all the handshaking dialogs are taken care of for you. Should the user select Online, however, it's up to you to move things to the next step. You need to dismiss the picker and display the next stage of the connection task. Here, control passes away from the peer picker. `BonjourHelper` from Recipe 12-8 is initialized, and its connection begun. Instead of the gray peer picker dialog, `BonjourHelper`'s standard blue alert appears.

```
- (void)peerPickerController:(GKPeerPickerController *)picker
    didSelectConnectionType:(GKPeerPickerConnectionType)type
{
    if(type == GKPeerPickerConnectionTypeOnline)
    {
        [picker dismiss];
        [picker release];
        [BonjourHelper sharedInstance].sessionID = self.sessionID;
        [BonjourHelper sharedInstance].viewController =
            self.viewController;
        [BonjourHelper sharedInstance].dataDelegate =
            self.dataDelegate;
        [BonjourHelper connect];
    }
}
```

As Recipe 12-9 demonstrates, almost no changes are needed from the `BonjourHelper` side of things. The Connect button on the navigation bar must point back to GameKit's connect method, not to `BonjourHelper`'s. This ensures that users can finish a Bonjour connection and then move on to a Bluetooth one without restarting the application.

Recipe 12-9 **Updating the Macro Code to Use GameKit's Version of Connect**

```
#define GBARBUTTON(TITLE, SELECTOR) [[[UIBarButtonItem alloc] \
initWithTitle:TITLE style:UIBarButtonItemStylePlain \
target:[GameKitHelper class] action:SELECTOR] autorelease]

if (sharedInstance.viewController)
    sharedInstance.viewController.navigationItem.rightBarButtonItem =
        GBARBUTTON(@"Connect", @selector(connect));
```

Get This Recipe's Code

To get the code used for this recipe, go to http://github.com/erica/iphone-3.0-cookbook-, or if you've downloaded the disk image containing all of the sample code from the book, go to the folder for Chapter 12 and open the project for this recipe.

Additionally, you might think the Info.plist file needs a `UIRequiresPersistentWiFi` key set to the Boolean value of true. Avoid doing this. Instead, check for WiFi only when you are ready to attempt to create a WiFi connection, i.e., when the user clicks Online. GameKit Bluetooth connections don't need persistent WiFi although standard Bonjour ones do. Don't require your users to connect to a (possibly nonexistent) WiFi service when Bluetooth is sufficient for Nearby gaming.

One More Thing: Scanning for Services

The `NSNetServiceBrowser` class is not limited to a single predefined service. You can adapt the browser code to search for all available services that an iPhone can communicate with. Recipe 12-10 extends the service browsing and resolution samples used in this chapter to find all active Bonjour service providers, displaying them as a list, as shown in Figure 12-10. Tapping on a list cell moves to a service detail page.

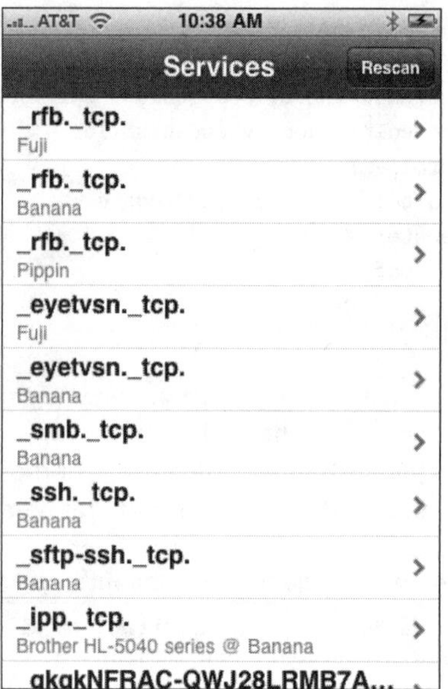

Figure 12-10 The iPhone can scan for and detect all local Bonjour services. If you are familiar with the built-in protocols, you can develop applications that communicate with those services.

This recipe works by using DNS-based service discovery by searching for `_services._dns-sd._udp`. This returns a list of records with service types. A second round of service discovery, iterating through this list, produces the actual services shown in Figure 12-10.

As each service is found, it is resolved to produce a list of service IP addresses and its TXT record data solicited (via `startMonitoring`) for further service details. When testing this recipe, try viewing the data for an attached printer service (such as the Brother HL-5040 shown in Figure 12-10) to produce a particularly detailed set of service info.

Beyond the TXT callback, which was not used in previous recipes, the methods shown in this recipe mirror their earlier uses in the chapter.

Recipe 12-10 **Bonjour Scanner**

```
- (void)netServiceDidResolveAddress:(NSNetService *)netService
{
    NSMutableDictionary *md = [self dictionaryForService:netService];
    if (!md) return;

    NSArray* addresses = [netService addresses];
    if ([addresses count] > 0)
    {
        // Iterate through each of the addresses
        NSMutableArray *naddresses = [NSMutableArray array];
        for (int i = 0; i < addresses.count; i++)
        {
            struct sockaddr* address =
                (struct sockaddr*)[[addresses objectAtIndex:i] bytes];
            NSString *addressString = [self stringFromAddress:address];
            if (!addressString) continue;
            [naddresses addObject:addressString];
        }

        [md setObject:naddresses forKey:@"addresses"];
    }

    [netService release];
}

- (void)netService:(NSNetService *)netService
    didUpdateTXTRecordData:(NSData *)data
{
    // Retrieve the TXT Record data
    NSDictionary *dict = [NSNetService
        dictionaryFromTXTRecordData:data];
    NSMutableDictionary *md = [self dictionaryForService:netService];
    if (!md) return;
    if ([[dict allKeys] count] == 0) return;
    [md setObject:[dict description] forKey:@"other"];
}
```

```
- (void) netServiceBrowser:(NSNetServiceBrowser *) netServiceBrowser
    didFindService:(NSNetService *) netService
    moreComing:(BOOL) moreServicesComing
{
    // Look for the service type items vs actual services
    if (![netService hostName] && [[netService name] hasPrefix:@"_"])
        [self.services addObject:[netService name]];
    else
    {
        // It is an actual service, so create an info dictionary
        NSMutableDictionary *md = [NSMutableDictionary dictionary];
        [md setObject:[netService type] forKey:@"type"];
        [md setObject:[netService name] forKey:@"name"];
        [md setObject:[netService domain] forKey:@"domain"];
        [netService startMonitoring];
        [[netService retain] setDelegate:self];
        [netService resolveWithTimeout:0.0f];
        [self.results addObject:md];
        [self.tableView reloadData];
    }

    if (!moreServicesComing)
    {
        // Finish scanning
        [self.browser stop];
        self.title = @"Services";

        // Iterate through any remaining services
        if ([self.services count] > 0)
        {
            NSString *type = [self.services objectAtIndex:0];
            [self.services removeObject:type];
            type = [type stringByAppendingString:@"._tcp."];
            [self.browser searchForServicesOfType:type inDomain:@""];
        }
        else
            self.navigationItem.rightBarButtonItem =
                BARBUTTON(@"Rescan", @selector(scan));
    }
}

- (void)netServiceBrowser:(NSNetServiceBrowser *)netServiceBrowser
    didNotSearch:(NSDictionary *)errorInfo
{
```

```
    // Report any search errors
    NSLog (@"Error %@", errorInfo);
}

- (void) scan: (UIBarButtonItem *) bbi
{
    // Disable interface during scan
    self.navigationItem.rightBarButtonItem = nil;
    self.title = @"Scanning...";

    // Provide a list for services yet to scan
    self.services = [NSMutableArray array];

    // Provide a list for fully scanned services
    self.results = [NSMutableArray array];

    // Start scanning. You can almost surely discard the double-retain
    self.browser = [[[NSNetServiceBrowser alloc] init] retain];
    [self.browser setDelegate:self];
    [self.browser searchForServicesOfType:
        @"_services._dns-sd._udp." inDomain:@""];
}
```

Summary

GameKit offers an exciting new player in the iPhone development arena. Its easy-to-use ad hoc Bluetooth connections make it simple for you to deliver applications that communicate outside traditional networks. In this chapter, you saw how to build those connections and produce real-time data transfers that allow games and other applications to coordinate information between separate devices. You also saw examples of iPhone and Mac-based Bonjour applications that don't rely on GameKit's proprietary connections and examples of GameKit's "bring your own technology" Online connections. Here are a few last minute thoughts on these technologies:

- Although Apple has not yet delivered GameKit for Macintosh, it's probably on their to-do list. GameKit is an exciting new technology and it's sure to grow.
- Although a full Internet-based GameKit connection fell outside the scope of this chapter, I expect to see great things from connected games developers. With proprietary networking, users will be able to connect iPhones together to play no matter where players are located, nearby and online. It's a real handheld gaming revolution from the point of view of you, the developer, and probably the user as well.

- When working with Voice Chat, remember that nearby users may produce sound loops creating feedback distortion unless they use headsets. Plus, people sitting 10 feet apart from each other can easily talk without the use of technology.
- Bonjour runs natively on Windows. Do a Google search for `mDNSResponder` for details.

13

Networking

As an Internet-connected device, the iPhone is particularly well suited to retrieving remote data and subscribing to Web-based services. Apple has lavished the platform with a solid grounding in all kinds of network computing and its supporting technologies. The iPhone SDK handles sockets, password keychains, XML processing, and more. This chapter surveys common techniques for network computing, offering recipes that simplify day-to-day tasks. You read about checking the network status, monitoring that status for changes, and testing site reachability. You also learn how to download resources asynchronously and how to respond to authentication challenges. By the time you finish this chapter, you'll have discovered how to build an FTP client, a custom iPhone-based Web browser, and more.

Recipe: Checking Your Network Status

Networked applications need a live connection to communicate with the Internet or other nearby devices. Applications should know whether that connection exists before reaching out to send or retrieve data. Checking the network status lets the application communicate with users and explain why certain functions might be disabled.

Apple has and will reject applications that do not check the network status before providing download options to the user. Apple reviewers are trained to check whether you properly notify the user, especially in the case of network errors. Always verify your network status and alert the user accordingly.

Apple also rejects applications based on "excessive data usage." If you plan to stream large quantities of data in your application, such as voice or data, you'll need to test for the current connection type. Provide lower quality data streams for users on a cell network connection and higher quality data for users with Wi-Fi connections. Apple has little tolerance for applications that place high demands on cell network data.

The iPhone can currently test for the following configuration states: some (i.e., any kind of) network connection available, Wi-Fi available, and cell service available. There are no APIs that allow the iPhone to test for Bluetooth connectivity at this time (although you can limit your application to run only on Bluetooth-enabled devices), nor can you check to see whether a user is roaming before offering data access.

The System Configuration framework offers many networking aware functions. Among these, `SCNetworkReachabilityCreateWithAddress` checks whether an IP address is reachable. Recipe 13-1 shows a simple example of this test in action.

It provides a basic detector that determines whether your device has outgoing connectivity, which it defines as having both access and a live connection. This method, based on Apple sample code, returns `YES` when the network is available and `NO` otherwise. The flags used here indicate both that the network is reachable (`kSCNetworkFlagsReachable`) and that no further connection is required (`kSCNetworkFlagsConnectionRequired`). Other flags you may use are as follows:

- **`kSCNetworkReachabilityFlagsIsWWAN`**—Tests whether your user is using the carrier's network or local Wi-Fi. When available, the network can be reached via EDGE, GPRS, or another cell connection. That means you might want to use lightweight versions of your resources (for example, smaller versions of images) due to the connection's constricted bandwidth.
- **`kSCNetworkReachabilityFlagsIsDirect`**—Tells you whether the network traffic goes through a gateway or arrives directly.

To confirm that connectivity code works, it is best evaluated on an iPhone. iPhones provide both cell and Wi-Fi support allowing you to confirm that the network remains reachable when using a WWAN connection. Test out this code by toggling Wi-Fi and airplane mode off and on in the iPhone's Setting app. Be aware that there's sometimes a slight delay when checking for network reachability, so design your applications accordingly. Let the user know what your code is up to during the check.

Recipe 13-1 **Testing a Network Connection**

```
- (BOOL) connectedToNetwork
{
    // Create zero addy
    struct sockaddr_in zeroAddress;
    bzero(&zeroAddress, sizeof(zeroAddress));
    zeroAddress.sin_len = sizeof(zeroAddress);
    zeroAddress.sin_family = AF_INET;

    // Recover reachability flags
    SCNetworkReachabilityRef defaultRouteReachability =
        SCNetworkReachabilityCreateWithAddress(NULL,
        (struct sockaddr *)&zeroAddress);
    SCNetworkReachabilityFlags flags;

    BOOL didRetrieveFlags =
        SCNetworkReachabilityGetFlags(
        defaultRouteReachability, &flags);
    CFRelease(defaultRouteReachability);
```

```
    if (!didRetrieveFlags)
    {
        printf("Could not recover network flags\n");
        return NO;
    }

    BOOL isReachable = flags & kSCNetworkFlagsReachable;
    BOOL needsConnection = flags & kSCNetworkFlagsConnectionRequired;
    return (isReachable && !needsConnection) ? YES : NO;
}
```

Get This Recipe's Code

To get the code used for this recipe, go to http://github.com/erica/iphone-3.0-cookbook-, or if you've downloaded the disk image containing all of the sample code from the book, go to the folder for Chapter 13 and open the project for this recipe.

Recipe: Extending the UIDevice Class for Reachability

The `UIDevice` class provides information about the current device in use, such as its battery state, model, orientation, and so forth. Adding reachability seems like a natural extension for a class whose purpose is to report device state. Recipe 13-2 defines a `UIDevice` category called Reachability. It hides calls to the System Configuration framework and provides a simple way to check on the current network state. You can ask if the network is active, and whether it is using cell service or Wi-Fi.

Most connectivity checking solutions assume that a connected device, whose connection is not provided by WWAN cell service, has Wi-Fi connectivity. This is an assumption that may not continue to hold true should Apple open up Bluetooth services to the SDK. Recipe 13-2 uses a direct Wi-Fi checking solution developed by Matt Brown, a software developer and a fan of the first edition of this book. It applies low-level (but SDK-friendly) calls to retrieve the local Wi-Fi IP address. If one is found, the class returns a positive result for Wi-Fi.

Note that this class uses a slightly different network check than Recipe 13-1, again one inspired by Apple sample code. Use the `ignoresAdHocWiFi` Boolean to limit network checks. When enabled, the recipe won't return a success on detecting an ad hoc Wi-Fi connection.

Recipe 13-2 **Extending UIDevice for Reachability**

```
@implementation UIDevice (Reachability)
SCNetworkConnectionFlags connectionFlags;

// Matt Brown's get WiFi IP addy solution
+ (NSString *) localWiFiIPAddress
{
```

```
    BOOL success;
    struct ifaddrs * addrs;
    const struct ifaddrs * cursor;

    success = getifaddrs(&addrs) == 0;
    if (success) {
        cursor = addrs;
        while (cursor != NULL) {
            // the second test keeps from picking up
            // the loopback address
            if (cursor->ifa_addr->sa_family == AF_INET &&
               (cursor->ifa_flags & IFF_LOOPBACK) == 0)
            {
                NSString *name = [NSString stringWithUTF8String:
                    cursor->ifa_name];
                if ([name isEqualToString:@"en0"])  // Wi-Fi adapter
                    return [NSString stringWithUTF8String:
                       inet_ntoa(((struct sockaddr_in *)
                       cursor->ifa_addr)->sin_addr)];
            }
            cursor = cursor->ifa_next;
        }
        freeifaddrs(addrs);
    }
    return nil;
}

#pragma mark Checking Connections

+ (void) pingReachabilityInternal
{
    BOOL ignoresAdHocWiFi = NO; // thanks to Apple
    struct sockaddr_in ipAddress;
    bzero(&ipAddress, sizeof(ipAddress));
    ipAddress.sin_len = sizeof(ipAddress);
    ipAddress.sin_family = AF_INET;
    ipAddress.sin_addr.s_addr = htonl(
        ignoresAdHocWiFi ? INADDR_ANY : IN_LINKLOCALNETNUM);

    // Recover reachability flags
    SCNetworkReachabilityRef defaultRouteReachability =
        SCNetworkReachabilityCreateWithAddress(
        kCFAllocatorDefault, (struct sockaddr *)&ipAddress);
    BOOL didRetrieveFlags = SCNetworkReachabilityGetFlags(
        defaultRouteReachability, &connectionFlags);

    CFRelease(defaultRouteReachability);
    if (!didRetrieveFlags)
```

```
        printf("Error. Could not recover flags\n");
}

+ (BOOL) networkAvailable
{
    [self pingReachabilityInternal];
    BOOL isReachable = ((connectionFlags &
        kSCNetworkFlagsReachable) != 0);
    BOOL needsConnection = ((connectionFlags &
        kSCNetworkFlagsConnectionRequired) != 0);
    return (isReachable && !needsConnection) ? YES : NO;
}

+ (BOOL) activeWWAN
{
    if (![self networkAvailable]) return NO;
    return ((connectionFlags &
        kSCNetworkReachabilityFlagsIsWWAN) != 0);
}

+ (BOOL) activeWLAN
{
    return ([UIDevice localWiFiIPAddress] != nil);
}
@end
```

Get This Recipe's Code

To get the code used for this recipe, go to http://github.com/erica/iphone-3.0-cookbook-, or if you've downloaded the disk image containing all of the sample code from the book, go to the folder for Chapter 13 and open the project for this recipe.

Recipe: Scanning for Connectivity Changes

Connectivity state may change while an application is running. Checking once at application launch usually isn't enough for an application that depends on data connections throughout its lifetime. You may want to alert the user that a network connection was lost—or could finally be established.

Recipe 13-3 addresses this challenge by using another `UIDevice` category to monitor reachability. It provides a pair of methods that allow you to schedule and unschedule reachability watchers, observers who must be notified when the connectivity state changes. It builds a callback that messages a watcher object when that state changes. The monitor is scheduled on the current run loop and runs asynchronously. Upon detecting a change, the callback function triggers.

Recipe 13-3's callback function redirects itself to a specific delegate method, `reachabilityChanged`, which must be implemented by an object that conforms to the `ReachabilityWatcher` protocol. That watcher object can then query `UIDevice` (via the Reachability category) for the current flags and network state.

The method that schedules the watcher assigns the delegate as its parameter.

```
- (void) reachabilityChanged
{
    [self showAlert:@"Reachability has changed."];
}

- (void) viewDidLoad
{
      [UIDevice scheduleReachabilityWatcher:self];
}
```

Your application will generally receive one callback at a time for each kind of state change, that is, when the cellular data connection is established or released, or when Wi-Fi is established or lost. Your user's connectivity settings (especially remembering and logging in to known Wi-Fi networks) will affect the kind and number of callbacks you may have to handle.

Be sure to inform your user when connectivity changes as well as update your interface to mirror the current state. You might want to disable buttons or menu items that depend on network access when that access disappears. Providing an alert of some kind lets the user know why the GUI has updated.

Recipe 13-3 **Monitoring Connectivity Changes**

```
// Reachability Watcher Protocol defines callback
@protocol ReachabilityWatcher <NSObject>
- (void) reachabilityChanged;
@end

// Schedule or unscheduled watchers via this category
@interface UIDevice (ReachabilityCallback)
+ (BOOL) scheduleReachabilityWatcher: (id) watcher;
+ (void) unscheduleReachabilityWatcher;
@end

@implementation UIDevice (ReachabilityCallback)
SCNetworkConnectionFlags connectionFlags;
SCNetworkReachabilityRef reachability;

#pragma mark Checking Connections

// Update the reachability flags
+ (void) pingReachabilityInternal
{
    if (!reachability)
    {
        BOOL ignoresAdHocWiFi = NO;
        struct sockaddr_in ipAddress;
        bzero(&ipAddress, sizeof(ipAddress));
```

```
        ipAddress.sin_len = sizeof(ipAddress);
        ipAddress.sin_family = AF_INET;
        ipAddress.sin_addr.s_addr =
            htonl(ignoresAdHocWiFi ? INADDR_ANY : IN_LINKLOCALNETNUM);

        reachability = SCNetworkReachabilityCreateWithAddress(
            kCFAllocatorDefault, (struct sockaddr *)&ipAddress);
        CFRetain(reachability);
    }

    // Recover reachability flags
    BOOL didRetrieveFlags = SCNetworkReachabilityGetFlags(reachability,
        &connectionFlags);
    if (!didRetrieveFlags)
        NSLog(@"Error. Could not recover reachability flags");
}

#pragma mark Monitoring reachability
// Actual callback redirects to delegate. Info parameter is
// defined by the passed context when setting up the callback
static void ReachabilityCallback(SCNetworkReachabilityRef target,
    SCNetworkConnectionFlags flags, void* info)
{
    NSAutoreleasePool *pool = [NSAutoreleasePool new];
    [(id)info performSelector:@selector(reachabilityChanged)];
    [pool release];
}

// Schedule a watcher
+ (BOOL) scheduleReachabilityWatcher: (id) watcher
{
    // Must conform to protocol
    if (![watcher conformsToProtocol:@protocol(ReachabilityWatcher)])
    {
        NSLog(@"Watcher doesn't conform to protocol.");
        return NO;
    }

    [self pingReachabilityInternal];

    // Here's where the watcher is set for the info parameter
    SCNetworkReachabilityContext context =
        {0, watcher, NULL, NULL, NULL};

    // Set the callback
    if(SCNetworkReachabilitySetCallback(reachability,
        ReachabilityCallback, &context))
    {
```

```
        if(!SCNetworkReachabilityScheduleWithRunLoop(reachability,
            CFRunLoopGetCurrent(), kCFRunLoopCommonModes))
        {
            NSLog(@"Error Could not schedule reachability");
            SCNetworkReachabilitySetCallback(reachability, NULL, NULL);
            return NO;
        }
    }
    else
    {
        NSLog(@"Error Could not set reachability callback");
        return NO;
    }

    return YES;
}

+ (void) unscheduleReachabilityWatcher
{
    // disable callback
    SCNetworkReachabilitySetCallback(reachability, NULL, NULL);

    // remove from runloop
    if (SCNetworkReachabilityUnscheduleFromRunLoop(reachability,
        CFRunLoopGetCurrent(), kCFRunLoopCommonModes))
        NSLog(@"Unscheduled reachability");
    else
        NSLog(@"Error Could not unschedule reachability");

    CFRelease(reachability);
    reachability = nil;
}
@end
```

Get This Recipe's Code

To get the code used for this recipe, go to http://github.com/erica/iphone-3.0-cookbook-, or if you've downloaded the disk image containing all of the sample code from the book, go to the folder for Chapter 13 and open the project for this recipe.

Recipe: Recovering IP and Host Information

In the day-to-day world of iPhone network programming, certain tasks come up over and over again, particularly those dealing with recovering the local iPhone IP address information and working with address structures. Recipe 13-4 provides a handful of utilities, several based on Apple sample code, that help you manage these tasks.

As with Recipes 13-2 and 13-3, these methods are wrapped into the `UIDevice` class as a category extension. They are, again, all implemented as class methods as their utility is not tied to any particular object instance. The methods in this recipe are as follows.

- A pair of methods (`stringFromAddress:` and `addressFromString:`) helps you convert address structures to and from string representations. The `BonjourHelper` recipes in Chapter 12, "Making Connections with GameKit and Bonjour," used these methods extensively. They integrate well with the `NSNetService` class, allowing you to convert `sockaddr` structures into `NSString` instances and back.
- The `hostname` method returns the host name for the current device. This method observes a small iPhone quirk. The simulator normally appends the `.local` domain to the current host name. The iPhone does not. This routine forces the host name into Mac-style compliance. Be aware that `hostname`, as well as some of the following methods, may fail on certain releases of the iPhone simulator, particularly in Snow Leopard (versus Leopard). It continues to work properly, at the time this book was written, on the iPhone device.
- Use `getIPAddressForHost:` to look up an address for a given host name. The sample code that accompanies this chapter uses this routine to retrieve IP addresses for www.google.com and www.amazon.com. These calls are blocking, and they take a certain amount of time to return (especially for nonexistent hosts). Use them judiciously, preferably on a secondary thread or via an `NSOperationQueue`.

```
[self doLog:@"  Google IP Addy: %@", [UIDevice
    getIPAddressForHost:@"www.google.com"]];
[self doLog:@"  Amazon IP Addy: %@", [UIDevice
    getIPAddressForHost:@"www.amazon.com"]];
```

- The `localIPAddress` method looks up the host's address and returns it as a string. Like `getIPAddressForHost:`, this method uses `gethostbyname()` to convert a host name into an IP address.
- A final method, `whatismyipdotcom`, helps move past a local LAN to determine a cable, DSL, or similar IP address. It sends out a call to the whatismyip.com Web site, which returns the connection IP address. This method is run synchronously, so it blocks. You should always make sure that you are connected to the network before attempting to call this method.

Recipe 13-4 **IP and Host Utilities**

```
@implementation UIDevice (IP)

// Produce a string representation of an IP address
+ (NSString *) stringFromAddress: (const struct sockaddr *) address
{
    if(address && address->sa_family == AF_INET) {
        const struct sockaddr_in* sin = (struct sockaddr_in*) address;
```

```
        return [NSString stringWithFormat:@"%@%d", [NSString
            stringWithUTF8String:inet_ntoa(sin->sin_addr)],
            ntohs(sin->sin_port)];
    }

    return nil;
}

// Produce an address from an NSString
+ (BOOL)addressFromString:(NSString *)IPAddress
    address:(struct sockaddr_in *)address
{
    if (!IPAddress || ![IPAddress length]) return NO;

    memset((char *) address, sizeof(struct sockaddr_in), 0);
    address->sin_family = AF_INET;
    address->sin_len = sizeof(struct sockaddr_in);

    int conversionResult = inet_aton([IPAddress UTF8String],
        &address->sin_addr);
    if (conversionResult == 0) return NO;
    return YES;
}

// Return the current host name
+ (NSString *) hostname
{
    char baseHostName[255];
    int success = gethostname(baseHostName, 255);
    if (success != 0) return nil;
    baseHostName[255] = '\0';

    #if !TARGET_IPHONE_SIMULATOR
    return [NSString stringWithFormat:@"%s.local", baseHostName];
    #else
     return [NSString stringWithFormat:@"%s", baseHostName];
    #endif
}

// Return an IP address (string form) for a given host
+ (NSString *) getIPAddressForHost: (NSString *) theHost
{
    struct hostent *host = gethostbyname([theHost UTF8String]);
    if (!host) {herror("resolv"); return NULL; }
    struct in_addr **list = (struct in_addr **)host->h_addr_list;
    NSString *addressString = [NSString
```

```
        stringWithCString:inet_ntoa(*list[0])
        encoding:NSUTF8StringEncoding];
    return addressString;
}

// Return the local IP address
+ (NSString *) localIPAddress
{
    struct hostent *host = gethostbyname([[self hostname] UTF8String]);
    if (!host) {herror("resolv"); return nil;}
    struct in_addr **list = (struct in_addr **)host->h_addr_list;
    return [NSString stringWithCString:inet_ntoa(*list[0])
        encoding:NSUTF8StringEncoding];
}

// Query http://whatismyip.com for IP address
+ (NSString *) whatismyipdotcom
{
    // This call is blocking, so use judiciously
    NSError *error;
    NSURL *ipURL = [NSURL URLWithString:
        @"http://www.whatismyip.com/automation/n09230945.asp"];
    NSString *ip = [NSString stringWithContentsOfURL:ipURL
        encoding:NSUTF8StringEncoding error:&error];
    return ip ? ip : [error localizedDescription];
}
@end
```

Get This Recipe's Code

To get the code used for this recipe, go to http://github.com/erica/iphone-3.0-cookbook-, or if you've downloaded the disk image containing all of the sample code from the book, go to the folder for Chapter 13 and open the project for this recipe.

Recipe: Checking Site Availability

After recovering a site's IP address, use the `SCNetworkReachabilityCreateWithAddress()` function to check its availability. Pass a `sockaddr` record populated with the site's IP address, and then check for the `kSCNetworkFlagsReachable` flag when the function returns. Recipe 13-5 shows the site checking the `hostAvailable:` method. It returns YES or NO.

This kind of check is synchronous and will block interaction until the method returns. Recipe 13-5 uses the `UIApplication` network activity indicator, but in real-world use, you may want to run these tests on a second thread and provide some kind of feedback during the wait. (Recipes shown later in this chapter use the `NSOperation` and

`NSOperationQueue` objects to facilitate easy threading.) During testing, this recipe took approximately 30 seconds to run all six tests, including the "notverylikely.com" test, which was included to force a lookup failure.

Recipe 13-5 **Checking Site Reachability**

```
- (BOOL) hostAvailable: (NSString *) theHost
{

    // Recover address string for host
    NSString *addressString = [self getIPAddressForHost:theHost];
    if (!addressString)
    {
        printf("Error recovering IP address from host name\n");
        return NO;
    }

    // Convert to an address
    struct sockaddr_in address;
    BOOL gotAddress = [self addressFromString:addressString
        address:&address];

    if (!gotAddress)
    {
        printf("Error recovering sockaddr address from %s\n",
            [addressString UTF8String]);
        return NO;
    }

    // Check reachability flags
    SCNetworkReachabilityRef defaultRouteReachability =
        SCNetworkReachabilityCreateWithAddress(NULL,
        (struct sockaddr *)&address);
    SCNetworkReachabilityFlags flags;

    BOOL didRetrieveFlags =
        SCNetworkReachabilityGetFlags(defaultRouteReachability,
        &flags);
    CFRelease(defaultRouteReachability);

    if (!didRetrieveFlags)
    {
        printf("Error. Could not recover flags\n");
        return NO;
    }
```

```
    BOOL isReachable = flags & kSCNetworkFlagsReachable;
    return isReachable ? YES : NO;;
}

#define CHECK(SITE) [self doLog:@"• %@ : %@", SITE, \
    [self hostAvailable:SITE] ? @"available" : @"not available"];

- (void) action: (UIBarButtonItem *) bbi
{
    [[UIApplication sharedApplication]
         setNetworkActivityIndicatorVisible:YES];
    self.log = [NSMutableString string];
    CHECK(@"www.google.com");
    CHECK(@"www.ericasadun.com");
    CHECK(@"www.notverylikely.com");
    CHECK(@"192.168.0.108");
    CHECK(@"pearson.com");
    CHECK(@"www.pearson.com");
    [[UIApplication sharedApplication]
        setNetworkActivityIndicatorVisible:NO];
```

Get This Recipe's Code

To get the code used for this recipe, go to http://github.com/erica/iphone-3.0-cookbook-, or if you've downloaded the disk image containing all of the sample code from the book, go to the folder for Chapter 13 and open the project for this recipe.

Recipe: Synchronous Downloads

Synchronous downloads allow you to request data from the Internet, wait until that data is received, and then move on to the next step in your application. For example, Recipe 7-1 from Chapter 7, "Working with Images," used synchronous downloads to initialize an image with the contents retrieved from a URL address. Here is the call that was used. Notice that this snippet is both synchronous and blocking. You will not return from this method until all the data is received.

```
+ (UIImage *) imageFromURLString: (NSString *) urlstring
{
    // This is a blocking call
    return [UIImage imageWithData:[NSData
        dataWithContentsOfURL:[NSURL URLWithString:urlstring]]];
}
```

The `NSURLConnection` class provides a more general download approach than class-specific URL initialization. It provides both synchronous and asynchronous downloads, the latter provided by a series of delegate callbacks. Recipe 13-6 focuses on the simpler, synchronous approach. It begins by creating an `NSMutableURLRequest` with the URL of choice. That request is sent synchronously using the `NSURLConnection` class.

```
NSMutableURLRequest *theRequest =
    [NSMutableURLRequest requestWithURL:url];
NSData* result = [NSURLConnection sendSynchronousRequest:
    theRequest returningResponse:&response error:&error];
```

This call blocks until the request fails (returning `nil`, and an error is produced) or the data finishes downloading.

Recipe 13-6 performs the synchronous request in a second thread. To accommodate this, the `doLog:` method, which provides updates through the download process, has been modified for thread safety. Instead of updating the text view directly, the method performs the `setText:` selector on the main (GUI-safe) thread.

```
[textView performSelectorOnMainThread:
    @selector(setText) withObject:self.log waitUntilDone:NO];
```

This example allows testing with three predefined URLs. There's one that downloads a short (3MB) movie, another using a larger (23MB) movie, and a final fake URL to test errors. The movies are sourced from the Internet Archive (archive.org), which provides a wealth of public domain data.

Some Internet providers produce a valid Web page, even when given a completely bogus URL. The data returned in the response parameter helps you determine when this happens. This parameter points to an `NSURLResponse` object. It stores information about the data returned by the URL connection. These parameters include expected content length and a suggested filename. Should the expected content length be less than zero, that's a good clue that the provider has returned data that does not match up to your expected request.

```
[self doLog:@"Response expects %d bytes",
   [response expectedContentLength]];
```

As you can see in Recipe 13-6, trying to integrate large downloads into the main application GUI gets messy and slow, even with a secondary thread. Recipe 13-7 addresses both these issues by using a more streamlined special-purpose class to handle the download.

Recipe 13-6 **Synchronous Downloads**

```
- (void) doLog: (NSString *) formatstring, ...
{
    // Logging utility method
    va_list arglist;
    if (!formatstring) return;
    va_start(arglist, formatstring);
    NSString *outstring = [[[NSString alloc]
        initWithFormat:formatstring arguments:arglist]
        autorelease];
    va_end(arglist);
    [self.log appendString:outstring];
```

```
    [self.log appendString:@"\n"];
    [textView performSelectorOnMainThread:
        @selector(setText) withObject:self.log waitUntilDone:NO];
}

// Data URL resources
#define SMALL_URL @"http://www.archive.org/download/Drive-\
    inSaveFreeTv/Drive-in—SaveFreeTv_512kb.mp4"
#define BIG_URL   @"http://www.archive.org/download/\
    BettyBoopCartoons/Betty_Boop_More_Pep_1936_512kb.mp4"
#define FAKE_URL @"http://www.idontbelievethisisvalid.com"

// Retrieve data from the net
- (void) getData: (NSNumber *) which
{
    NSAutoreleasePool * pool = [[NSAutoreleasePool alloc] init];
    self.log = [NSMutableString string];
    [self doLog:@"Download data now...\n"];
    NSDate *date = [NSDate date];

    // Determine which resource to download
    NSArray *urlArray = [NSArray arrayWithObjects:
        SMALL_URL, BIG_URL, FAKE_URL, nil];
    NSURL *url = [NSURL URLWithString:
        [urlArray objectAtIndex:[which intValue]]];

    // prepare request and start download
    NSMutableURLRequest *theRequest =
        [NSMutableURLRequest requestWithURL:url];
    NSURLResponse *response;
    NSError *error;
    NSData* result = [NSURLConnection
        sendSynchronousRequest:theRequest
        returningResponse:&response error:&error];

    // On finish, show the response parameters
    [self doLog:@"Response expects %d bytes",
        [response expectedContentLength]];
    [self doLog:@"Response suggested file name: %@",
        [response suggestedFilename]];

    // Check for errors or save data
    if (!result)
        [self doLog:@"Error downloading data: %@.",
            [error localizedDescription]];
    else if ([response expectedContentLength] < 0)
        [self doLog:@"Error with download. Carrier redirect?"];
```

```
    else
    {
        [self doLog:@"Download succeeded."];
        [self doLog:@"Read %d bytes", result.length];
        [self doLog:@"Elapsed time: %0.2f seconds.",
            -1.0f * [date timeIntervalSinceNow]];
        [result writeToFile:DEST_PATH automatically: YES];
        [self doLog:@"Data written to file."];
    }

    // Clean up after download
    [self performSelectorOnMainThread:
        @selector(finishedGettingData)
        withObject:nil waitUntilDone:NO];
    [pool release];
}

- (void) action: (UIBarButtonItem *) bbi
{
    // start download in a new thread
    NSNumber *which = [NSNumber numberWithInt:
        [(UISegmentedControl *)self.navigationItem.titleView
        selectedSegmentIndex]];
    self.navigationItem.rightBarButtonItem = nil;
    [NSThread detachNewThreadSelector:@selector(getData)
        toTarget:self withObject:which];
}
```

Get This Recipe's Code

To get the code used for this recipe, go to http://github.com/erica/iphone-3.0-cookbook-, or if you've downloaded the disk image containing all of the sample code from the book, go to the folder for Chapter 13 and open the project for this recipe.

Recipe: Asynchronous Downloads

Asynchronous downloads allow your application to download data in the background. This keeps your code from blocking while waiting for a download to finish. For example, you might use asynchronous downloads with table views, presenting placeholder images while downloading thumbnails from a service like YouTube. Recipe 13-7 looks at an asynchronous way to use `NSURLConnections`. It builds a helper class called `DownloadHelper` that hides the details involved in downloading data. It works in the following fashion. Instead of sending a synchronous request, it initializes the connection and assigns a delegate.

```
NSURLConnection *theConnection = [[NSURLConnection alloc]
    initWithRequest:theRequest delegate:sharedInstance];
```

When setting up a connection this way, the data starts to download asynchronously, but it does not yet allow the GUI to update without blocking. To accomplish that, you must schedule the connection on the current run loop. Make sure to unschedule the connection when the download finishes. A download may finish either by retrieving all the requested data or failing with an error.

```
[self.urlconnection scheduleInRunLoop:[NSRunLoop currentRunLoop]
    forMode:NSRunLoopCommonModes];
```

Delegate methods help you track download life cycle. You receive updates when new data is available, when the data has finished downloading, or if the download fails. To support these callbacks, the `DownloadHelper` class defines several key properties:

- A URL string property points to the requested resource. It's used to initialize the URL request that begins the download process (`requestWithURL:`).
- The response property keeps track of the expected content length and the filename for the downloaded object. This response is returned in the `connection:didReceiveResponse:` delegate callback.
- A data property stores the data received during the download. It's is an instance of the `NSMutableData` class. When new data arrives (`connection:didReceiveData:`), the helper appends it to the end of any existing data.
- A delegate property points to the client object. The delegate, which must implement the `DownloadHelperDelegate` protocol, is updated with optional callbacks as the download progresses. This external delegate is distinct from the internal delegate used with the `NSURLConnection` object. External callbacks occur when the download succeeds (`connection:didFinishLoading:`), fails (`connection:didFailWithError:`), when the filename becomes known (`connection:didReceiveResponse:`), and as each chunk of data arrives (`connection:didReceiveData:`). By passing a percentage with the optional `dataDownloadAtPercent:` callback, the data consumer can update a progress view to show the user how far a download has progressed.
- The `urlconnection` property stores the current `NSURLConnection` object. It is kept on hand to allow the `DownloadHelper` class's `cancel` method to halt an ongoing download, that is, `[sharedInstance.urlconnection cancel]`.

The client starts the download by assigning a `DownloadHelper` delegate (presumably itself) and requesting a download as follows. This helper class provides an extremely simple developer interface as shown here.

```
[DownloadHelper sharedInstance].delegate = self;
[DownloadHelper download:urlString];
```

Although all the `DownloadHelper` delegate methods are optional, at a minimum, the delegate should implement `didReceiveData:`, which is called with the fully downloaded data.

Note

Recipe 13-7 assumes that you are assured an expected content length from the data provider. When the server side returns a response using chunked data (i.e., `Transfer-Encoding:chunked`), the content length is not specified in the response. Recipe 13-7 does not work with chunked data as it tests for content length and fails if the expected length is unknown (i.e., `NSURLResponseUnknownLength`).

Recipe 13-7 **Download Helper**

```
@implementation DownloadHelper
@synthesize response;
@synthesize data;
@synthesize delegate;
@synthesize urlString;
@synthesize urlconnection;
@synthesize isDownloading;

- (void) start
{
    // Transform the url string to a url
    NSURL *url = [NSURL URLWithString:self.urlString];
    if (!url)
    {
        NSString *reason = [NSString stringWithFormat:
            @"Could not create URL from string %@", self.urlString];
        DELEGATE_CALLBACK(dataDownloadFailed:, reason);
        return;
    }

    // Create the request
    NSMutableURLRequest *theRequest = [NSMutableURLRequest
        requestWithURL:url];
    if (!theRequest)
    {
        NSString *reason = [NSString stringWithFormat:
            @"Could not create URL request from string %@",
            self.urlString];
        DELEGATE_CALLBACK(dataDownloadFailed:, reason);
        return;
    }

    // Create the connection
    self.urlconnection = [[NSURLConnection alloc]
        initWithRequest:theRequest delegate:self];
    if (!self.urlconnection)
    {
```

```
        NSString *reason = [NSString stringWithFormat:
            @"URL connection failed for string %@", self.urlString];
        DELEGATE_CALLBACK(dataDownloadFailed:, reason);
        return;
    }

    self.isDownloading = YES;


    // Create the new data object
    self.data = [NSMutableData data];
    self.response = nil;

    [self.urlconnection scheduleInRunLoop:
        [NSRunLoop currentRunLoop] forMode:NSRunLoopCommonModes];
}

- (void) cleanup
{
    // Clean up properties
    self.data = nil;
    self.response = nil;
    self.urlconnection = nil;
    self.urlString = nil;
    self.isDownloading = NO;
}

- (void)connection:(NSURLConnection *)connection
    didReceiveResponse:(NSURLResponse *)aResponse
{
    // store the response information
    self.response = aResponse;

    // Check for bad connection
    if ([aResponse expectedContentLength] < 0)
    {
        NSString *reason = [NSString stringWithFormat:
            @"Invalid URL [%@]", self.urlString];
        DELEGATE_CALLBACK(dataDownloadFailed:, reason);
        [connection cancel];
        [self cleanup];
        return;
    }

    if ([aResponse suggestedFilename])
        DELEGATE_CALLBACK(didReceiveFilename:,
        [aResponse suggestedFilename]);
```

```
}

- (void)connection:(NSURLConnection *)connection
    didReceiveData:(NSData *)theData
{
    // append the new data and update the delegate
    [self.data appendData:theData];

    // This assumes that you are assured an expected content length
    if (self.response)
    {
        float expectedLength = [self.response expectedContentLength];
        float currentLength = self.data.length;
        float percent = currentLength / expectedLength;
        DELEGATE_CALLBACK(dataDownloadAtPercent:, NUMBER(percent));
    }
}

- (void)connectionDidFinishLoading:(NSURLConnection *)connection
{
    // finished downloading the data, cleaning up
    self.response = nil;

    // Delegate is responsible for releasing data
    if (self.delegate)
    {
        NSData *theData = [self.data retain];
        DELEGATE_CALLBACK(didReceiveData:, theData);
    }

    [self.urlconnection unscheduleFromRunLoop:[NSRunLoop
        currentRunLoop] forMode:NSRunLoopCommonModes];
    [self cleanup];
}

- (void)connection:(NSURLConnection *)connection
    didFailWithError:(NSError *)error
{
    self.isDownloading = NO;
    NSLog(@"Error Failed connection, %@",
        [error localizedDescription]);
    DELEGATE_CALLBACK(dataDownloadFailed:, @"Failed Connection");

    [self cleanup];
}
```

```
+ (DownloadHelper *) sharedInstance
{
    if(!sharedInstance) sharedInstance = [[self alloc] init];
    return sharedInstance;
}

+ (void) download:(NSString *) aURLString
{
    // start a new download
    if (sharedInstance.isDownloading)
    {
        NSLog(@"Error Cannot start new download yet.");
        return;
    }
    sharedInstance.urlString = aURLString;
    [sharedInstance start];
}

+ (void) cancel
{
    if (sharedInstance.isDownloading)
        [sharedInstance.urlconnection cancel];
}
@end
```

Get This Recipe's Code

To get the code used for this recipe, go to http://github.com/erica/iphone-3.0-cookbook-, or if you've downloaded the disk image containing all of the sample code from the book, go to the folder for Chapter 13 and open the project for this recipe.

Recipe: Handling Authentication Challenges

Some Web sites are protected with usernames and passwords. `NSURLConnection` lets you access these sites by responding to authentication challenges. Recipe 13-8 extends `DownloadHelper` for challenges. To comply, it creates a new `NSURLCredential` object and initializes it with a username and password. It passes this object to the challenge sender, who then decides whether to accept it.

To test authentication, connect to http://ericasadun.com/Private, which was set up for use with this recipe. This test folder uses the username **PrivateAccess** and password **tuR7!mZ#eh**. Here are the calls needed to set up `DownloadHelper` to respond to an authentication challenge.

```
NSString *urlString = @"http://ericasadun.com/Private/";
[DownloadHelper sharedInstance].username = @"PrivateAccess";
[DownloadHelper sharedInstance].password = @"tuR7!mZ#eh";
```

```
[DownloadHelper sharedInstance].delegate = self;
[DownloadHelper download:urlString];
```

To test an unauthorized connection—that is, you will be refused—set the username and password to `nil` or to nonsense strings. When set to `nil`, the challenge will be sent a `nil` credential, producing an immediate failure. With nonsense strings, the challenge will fail after the sender rejects the credentials.

Recipe 13-8 **Authentication with NSURLCredential Instances**

```
- (void)connection:(NSURLConnection *)connection
    didReceiveAuthenticationChallenge:
    (NSURLAuthenticationChallenge *)challenge
{
    if (!username || !password)
    {
        [[challenge sender] useCredential:nil
            forAuthenticationChallenge:challenge];
        return;
    }
    NSURLCredential *cred = [[[NSURLCredential alloc]
        initWithUser:username password:password
        persistence:NSURLCredentialPersistenceNone] autorelease];
    [[challenge sender] useCredential:cred
        forAuthenticationChallenge:challenge];
}

- (void)connection:(NSURLConnection *)connection
    didCancelAuthenticationChallenge:
    (NSURLAuthenticationChallenge *)challenge
{
    NSLog(@"Challenge cancelled");
}
```

Get This Recipe's Code

To get the code used for this recipe, go to http://github.com/erica/iphone-3.0-cookbook-, or if you've downloaded the disk image containing all of the sample code from the book, go to the folder for Chapter 13 and open the project for this recipe.

Recipe: Using the Keychain to Store Sensitive Data

The iPhone keychain lets you store user credentials securely. "Secure" password text fields that save their data to regular files are not particularly secure. Although the text is obscured onscreen, files, including preferences files, use clear text when written to disk. You can encrypt that data yourself, but then you subject your application to a variety of export issues. With the keychain, Apple provides a built-in highly secure password service that takes care of the work for you.

Keychain Wrapper

The keychain uses the Security framework. This framework is available exclusively for the device. You cannot program for or test the keychain on the simulator. When you add the framework to your project, you must deploy to the device.

Programming the keychain is complex. Fortunately, Apple provides a simple `KeychainItemWrapper` class that handles most basic keychain work for you. To use the wrapper, you create an instance and initialize it with an identifier and access group. Create a unique identifier for each login pair you will use. This allows you to add credentials for each kind of account being used.

```
self.wrapper = [[KeychainItemWrapper alloc]
    initWithIdentifier:@"Twitter" accessGroup:nil];
```

Unless you need to use your keychain across more than one application, set the access group to `nil`. (Recipe 13-12, which follows later in this chapter, demonstrates how to use cross-application keychains.)

To write items into the keychain, use the predefined account and data keys to store the username and password as you would to update a dictionary. The wrapper automatically updates the keychain without any further work needed to confirm the storage.

```
[self.wrapper setObject:uname forKey:(id)kSecAttrAccount];
[self.wrapper setObject:pword forKey:(id)kSecValueData];
```

When you're ready to retrieve the data, use `objectForKey:`.

```
uname = [self.wrapper objectForKey:(id)kSecAttrAccount];
pword = [self.wrapper objectForKey:(id)kSecValueData];
```

Recipe 13-9 introduces a modal `SettingsViewController` class that loads a username and password into its text fields when it is presented and saves any changes when it is dismissed. It takes advantage of the keychain wrapper to do this.

Pay attention to the bar button approach used in this recipe. At first, the button shows "Back" until a text field is interacted with. Once a user starts editing, two new buttons appear: Save and Cancel. This context sensitivity presents more meaningful button choices than a simple Done button.

Keychain Persistence

Keychain data persists even after deinstalling your application. Apple's developer relations writes, "Keychain items created by any application will be persistent across uninstalls because of the mere fact that the keychain store isn't located inside of the application bundle and there is no facility by which the system can be notified of when something is uninstalled to then also uninstall all associated keychain items. It is also a policy issue between the trade-offs of losing sensitive passwords through malicious uninstalling and keeping sensitive passwords intact and potentially secured away for the user(s)."

This behavior allows you to use the keychain to maintain persistent iPhone information. You might keep track of user registration or limit demo mode usage. The persistence means that nothing short of a firmware reinstall (without a backup restore) will wipe the data.

Recipe 13-9 Accessing the iPhone Keychain Via a Modal Settings View

```
@implementation SettingsViewController
@synthesize username;
@synthesize password;
@synthesize wrapper;

- (void)textFieldDidBeginEditing:(UITextField *)textField
{
    // On edit, allow user to save or cancel
    self.navigationItem.rightBarButtonItem =
        BARBUTTON(@"Save", @selector(dismiss));
    self.navigationItem.leftBarButtonItem =
        BARBUTTON(@"Cancel", @selector(dismissCancel));
}

- (void) dismiss: (id) sender
{
    // Recover data, save it, and dismiss
    NSString *uname = [username text];
    NSString *pword = [password text];

    if (uname) [self.wrapper setObject:uname
        forKey:(id)kSecAttrAccount];
    if (pword) [self.wrapper setObject:pword
        forKey:(id)kSecValueData];
    [self.parentViewController dismissModalViewControllerAnimated:YES];
}

- (void) dismissCancel: (id) sender
{
    // Dismiss but do not save
    [self.parentViewController dismissModalViewControllerAnimated:YES];
}

- (void) viewDidLoad
{
    self.navigationItem.leftBarButtonItem =
        BARBUTTON(@"Back", @selector(dismissCancel));
```

```
    // Identifier refers to upcoming recipes that build on this example
    self.wrapper = [[KeychainItemWrapper alloc]
        initWithIdentifier:@"Twitter" accessGroup:nil];
    [self.wrapper release];

    // Retrieve any saved user name and password
    NSString *uname = [self.wrapper objectForKey:(id)kSecAttrAccount];
    NSString *pword = [self.wrapper objectForKey:(id)kSecValueData];

    if (uname) username.text = uname;
    if (pword) password.text = pword;

    username.delegate = self;
    password.delegate = self;
}

- (void) dealloc
{
    username = nil;
    password = nil;
    self.wrapper = nil;
    [super dealloc];
}
@end
```

Get This Recipe's Code

To get the code used for this recipe, go to http://github.com/erica/iphone-3.0-cookbook-, or if you've downloaded the disk image containing all of the sample code from the book, go to the folder for Chapter 13 and open the project for this recipe.

Recipe: Uploading Via POST

`NSURLRequest` instances are a lot more flexible than the recipes in this chapter so far have demonstrated. Recipe 13-10 builds a request that sends data to the Twitter social networking service. It does this by creating an HTTP-style POST request and populating it with a message.

```
[urlRequest setHTTPMethod:@"POST"];
[urlRequest setHTTPBody:
    [body dataUsingEncoding:NSUTF8StringEncoding]];
[urlRequest setValue:@"application/x-www-form-urlencoded"
    forHTTPHeaderField:@"Content-Type"];
```

The URL request allows you to set header fields, a body, and more. It basically provides an Internet-savvy class that is well suited for communicating with online services.

For this example, the username and password are sent as part of the URL, that is,

```
http://username:password@twitter.com/statuses/update.xml
```

That is not normally the case for many services (as you see in Recipe 13-11). Because of this approach, Twitter provides a good example of the simplest kind of POST-based API.

NSOperationQueue

This example uses a synchronous request to perform the upload, which can take up to a minute or so to process. To avoid blocking GUI updates, the entire submission process is embedded into an `NSOperation` subclass, `TwitterOperation`. Operations encapsulate code and data for a single task, allowing you to run that task asynchronously.

Using `NSOperation` objects lets you submit them to an asynchronous `NSOperationQueue`. Operation queues manage the execution of individual operations. Each operation is prioritized and placed into the queue, where it is executed in priority order. By submitting an operation to a queue, you can introduce GUI elements (such as an activity indicator view or progress bar) whose presentation will not be blocked by the execution of the operation.

```
TwitterOperation *operation = [[[TwitterOperation alloc] init]
   autorelease];
operation.delegate = self;
operation.theText = text;

NSOperationQueue *queue = [[[NSOperationQueue alloc] init]
     autorelease];
[queue addOperation:operation];
```

Since this operation runs asynchronously, the main view controller needs some way to know when the upload completes. During the upload, the GUI for this example is disabled and a `UIActivityIndicatorView` displayed. For this example, a delegate callback method (`doneTweeting:`) is sent from the operation. This callback lets the main GUI know when to restore itself to its normal interactive mode.

Whenever you subclass `NSOperation`, make sure to implement a `main` method. This method is called when the operation executes. When `main` returns, the operation finishes.

Recipe 13-10 **Tweeting Via POST**

```
@implementation TwitterOperation
@synthesize wrapper;
@synthesize theText;
@synthesize delegate;

#define NOTIFY_AND_LEAVE(X) {[self cleanup:X]; return;}

- (void) cleanup: (NSString *) output
{
    // Clean up after success or failure
    self.theText = nil;
    self.wrapper = nil;
```

```
    if (self.delegate && [self.delegate
        respondsToSelector:@selector(doneTweeting)])
        [self.delegate doneTweeting:output];
}

- (void) main
{
    if (!theText || ![theText length])
        NOTIFY_AND_LEAVE(@"You cannot tweet an empty message.");

    // Retrieve user credentials
    self.wrapper = [[KeychainItemWrapper alloc]
        initWithIdentifier:@"Twitter" accessGroup:nil];
    [self.wrapper release];
    NSString *uname = [self.wrapper objectForKey:(id)kSecAttrAccount];
    NSString *pword = [self.wrapper objectForKey:(id)kSecValueData];
    if (!uname || !pword || (!uname.length) || (!pword.length))
        NOTIFY_AND_LEAVE(@"Please enter your account credentials");

    // Process user credentials
    NSString *unpwraw = [NSString stringWithFormat:@"%@%@",
        uname, pword];
    NSString *unpw = ENCODE(unpwraw);
    NSString *theTweet = ENCODE(theText);
    NSString *body = [NSString stringWithFormat:
        @"source=iTweet&status=%@", theTweet];

    // Establish the Twitter API request
    NSString *baseurl = [NSString stringWithFormat:
        @"http://%@@twitter.com/statuses/update.xml", unpw];
    NSURL *url = [NSURL URLWithString:baseurl];
    NSMutableURLRequest *urlRequest =
        [NSMutableURLRequest requestWithURL:url];

    if (!urlRequest)
        NOTIFY_AND_LEAVE(@"Error creating the URL Request");

    [urlRequest setHTTPMethod: @"POST"];
    [urlRequest setHTTPBody:
        [body dataUsingEncoding:NSUTF8StringEncoding]];
    [urlRequest setValue:@"application/x-www-form-urlencoded"
        forHTTPHeaderField:@"Content-Type"];

    NSLog(@"Contacting Twitter. This can take a minute or so...");

    // Place the request and wait for a response
    NSError *error;
```

```
    NSURLResponse *response;
    NSData *tw_result = [NSURLConnection
        sendSynchronousRequest:urlRequest returningResponse:&response
        error:&error];
    NSString *tw_output = [NSString stringWithFormat:
        @"Submission error: %@", [error localizedDescription]];
    if (!tw_result) NOTIFY_AND_LEAVE(tw_output);

    // Clean up and notify the delegate
    [self cleanup:[[[NSString alloc] initWithData:tw_result
        encoding:NSUTF8StringEncoding] autorelease]];
}
@end
```

> **Get This Recipe's Code**
>
> To get the code used for this recipe, go to http://github.com/erica/iphone-3.0-cookbook-, or if you've downloaded the disk image containing all of the sample code from the book, go to the folder for Chapter 13 and open the project for this recipe.

Recipe: Uploading Data

Recipe 13-10 used a simple URL encoded form to submit data. Recipe 13-11 moves that up a notch to create a full multipart form data submission. This recipe allows you to upload images to the TwitPic.com service using your user's Twitter credentials. The TwitPic API is accessed at http://twitpic.com/api/uploadAndPost. It requires a username, password, and binary image data.

The challenge for Recipe 13-11 is to create a properly formatted body that can be used by the TwitPic service. It implements a method that generates form data from a dictionary of keys and values. For the purposes of this example, the objects in that dictionary are limited to strings and images. You can extend this approach for other data types by changing the content type string with different MIME types.

Recipe 13-11 **Uploading Images to TwitPic**

```
#define NOTIFY_AND_LEAVE(X) {[self cleanup:X]; return;}
#define DATA(X)     [X dataUsingEncoding:NSUTF8StringEncoding]

#define IMAGE_CONTENT @"Content-Disposition: form-data; name=\"%@\";\
    filename=\"image.jpg\"\r\nContent-Type: image/jpeg\r\n\r\n"
#define STRING_CONTENT @"Content-Disposition: form-data; \
    name=\"%@\"\r\n\r\n"
#define MULTIPART @"multipart/form-data; boundary=------------\
    0x0x0x0x0x0x0x0x"

@implementation TwitPicOperation
@synthesize wrapper;
```

```
@synthesize theImage;
@synthesize delegate;

- (void) cleanup: (NSString *) output
{
    self.theImage = nil;
    self.wrapper = nil;
    if (self.delegate &&
        [self.delegate respondsToSelector:@selector(doneTweeting)])
        [self.delegate doneTweeting:output];
}

- (NSData*)generateFormDataFromPostDictionary:(NSDictionary*)dict
{
    // Set the boundary
    NSString *boundary = @"------------0x0x0x0x0x0x0x0x";

    // Establish a key dictionary
    NSArray* keys = [dict allKeys];

    // Establish the output data
    NSMutableData* result = [NSMutableData data];

    for (int i = 0; i < [keys count]; i++)
    {
        // Retrieve the next key
        id value = [dict valueForKey: [keys objectAtIndex:i]];

        // Add the separator data
        [result appendData:[[NSString stringWithFormat:@"—%@\r\n",
            boundary] dataUsingEncoding:NSUTF8StringEncoding]];

        if ([value isKindOfClass:[NSData class]])
        {
            // handle image data
            NSString *formstring =
                [NSString stringWithFormat:IMAGE_CONTENT,
                [keys objectAtIndex:i]];
            [result appendData: DATA(formstring)];
            [result appendData:value];
        }
        else
        {
            // all non-image fields assumed to be strings
            NSString *formstring =
                [NSString stringWithFormat:STRING_CONTENT,
                [keys objectAtIndex:i]];
```

```
            [result appendData: DATA(formstring)];
            [result appendData:DATA(value)];
        }

        // End the part
        NSString *formstring = @"\r\n";
        [result appendData:DATA(formstring)];
    }

    // All data added, so append another boundary
    NSString *formstring =[NSString stringWithFormat:@"--%@--\r\n",
         boundary];
    [result appendData:DATA(formstring)];
    return result;
}

- (void) main
{
    if (!self.theImage)
        NOTIFY_AND_LEAVE(@"Please set image before uploading.");

    // Use Twitter credentials for TwitPic
    self.wrapper = [[KeychainItemWrapper alloc]
        initWithIdentifier:@"Twitter" accessGroup:nil];
    [self.wrapper release];

    NSString *uname = [self.wrapper objectForKey:(id)kSecAttrAccount];
    NSString *pword = [self.wrapper objectForKey:(id)kSecValueData];

    if (!uname || !pword || (!uname.length) || (!pword.length))
        NOTIFY_AND_LEAVE(@"Please enter your account credentials.");

    NSMutableDictionary* post_dict =
        [[NSMutableDictionary alloc] init];
    [post_dict setObject:uname forKey:@"username"];
    [post_dict setObject:pword forKey:@"password"];
    [post_dict setObject:@"Posted from iTweet" forKey:@"message"];
    [post_dict setObject:UIImageJPEGRepresentation(self.theImage,
        0.75f) forKey:@"media"];

    // Create the post data from the post dictionary
    NSData *postData = [self
        generateFormDataFromPostDictionary:post_dict];
    [post_dict release];

    // Establish the API request.
    NSString *baseurl = @"http://twitpic.com/api/uploadAndPost";
```

```
    NSURL *url = [NSURL URLWithString:baseurl];
    NSMutableURLRequest *urlRequest = [NSMutableURLRequest
        requestWithURL:url];
    if (!urlRequest)
        NOTIFY_AND_LEAVE(@"Error creating the URL Request");

    [urlRequest setHTTPMethod: @"POST"];
    [urlRequest setValue:MULTIPART forHTTPHeaderField:
        @"Content-Type"];
    [urlRequest setHTTPBody:postData];

    // Submit & retrieve results
    NSError *error;
    NSURLResponse *response;
    NSLog(@"Contacting TwitPic....");
    NSData* result = [NSURLConnection sendSynchronousRequest:
        urlRequest returningResponse:&response error:&error];
    if (!result)
    {
        [self cleanup:[NSString stringWithFormat:
            @"Submission error: %@", [error localizedDescription]]];
        return;
    }

    // Return results
    NSString *outstring = [[[NSString alloc] initWithData:result
        encoding:NSUTF8StringEncoding] autorelease];
    [self cleanup: outstring];
}
@end
```

> **Get This Recipe's Code**
>
> To get the code used for this recipe, go to http://github.com/erica/iphone-3.0-cookbook-, or if you've downloaded the disk image containing all of the sample code from the book, go to the folder for Chapter 13 and open the project for this recipe.

Recipe: Sharing Keychains Between Applications

Unfortunately, sharing keychains is not as simple as assigning a group name. There are several hurdles you need to pass through to work with a keychain that's valid across applications. As you can see from Recipe 13-12, there's not a lot to be done from the application end. Most of the work is done setting things up in Xcode. Here's a step-by-step walkthrough of the process:

1. Locate your Application Identifier.

a. In Xcode, open the Organizer (select Window > Organizer) and click on IPHONE DEVELOPMENT > Provisioning Profiles. Select your standard wildcard development provision, or if you're ready to distribute your application, your standard wildcard distribution provision. The application identifier ("App Identifier") appears in the profile overview.

b. This identifier should be the same for both provisions, assuming you've followed the com.yourcompany.* naming convention. A ten-character prefix should appear right before your identifier. Copy the entire identifier. For me, that identifier is Y93A4XLA79.com.sadun.*.

2. Set your keychain access group.

   In your application, update all your wrapper initializations to use the following access group. Substitute `GenericKeychainSuite` for the final asterisk in the identifier, but otherwise use the identifier you copied from the provision listing, that is, don't use Y93A4XLA79. That identifier is assigned to com.sadun, not to your company.

   The phrase `GenericKeychainSuite` is arbitrary. You can use another suite name if desired, but adapt the rest of these instructions accordingly if you do so.

3. Create a new entitlement.

   In Xcode, choose File > New File > Code Signing > Entitlements and click Next. Name the new entitlement KeychainEntitlement.plist (again, this is an arbitrary name) and click Finish. Xcode adds the new file to your active project.

4. Edit the entitlement.

   Delete the get-task-allow entry in your new property list. Then add a new item called keychain-access-groups. Use this phrase exactly. Set its type to Array. Add one item; the name is "Item 1" by default. Set the string value of this item to your access group name, for example, Y93A4XLA79.com.sadun.GenericKeychainSuite. Again, make sure you use your own company and your own provisioning identity. Save the file and close it.

5. Update the target.

   a. In the Project window, select Groups & Files > Targets > *YourApplicationName*. Click the blue Info button at the top of the Project window. Open the Build tab.

   b. When the Build Tab is displayed, scroll down to find the Code Signing > Code Signing Entitlements section. Double-click to open the entitlements editor. Type KeychainEntitlement.plist into the text field and click OK. This filename must match the actual property list you edited in the previous step.

   c. Close the target window when you are done.

After following these steps, you will have updated your project to allow you to share the same keychain across multiple applications. To test, copy your project, change the application identifier in the Info.plist file, and run it on your iPhone. The new application should have equal access to the data. When deployed, users can update credentials for popular services in one of your applications, and they'll be ready for use in all your apps.

Note

The same entitlement and access group can be used for multiple login items within the same or separate applications. Just use different identifiers for each login item.

Recipe 13-12 **Wrapper Initialization for Keychain Sharing**

```
self.wrapper = [[KeychainItemWrapper alloc]
    initWithIdentifier:@"SharedTwitter"
    accessGroup:@"Y93A4XLA79.com.sadun.GenericKeychainSuite"];
[self.wrapper release];
```

Get This Recipe's Code

To get the code used for this recipe, go to http://github.com/erica/iphone-3.0-cookbook-, or if you've downloaded the disk image containing all of the sample code from the book, go to the folder for Chapter 13 and open the project for this recipe.

Recipe: Converting XML into Trees

The `NSXMLParser` class provided in the iPhone SDK scans through XML, creating callbacks as new elements are processed and finished (i.e., using the typical logic of a SAX parser). The class is terrific for when you're downloading simple data feeds and want to scrape just a bit or two of relevant information. It's not so great when you're doing production-type work that relies on error checking, status information, and back-and-forth handshaking.

Tree data structures offer a better way to represent XML data. They allow you to create search paths through the data, so you can find just the data you're looking for. You can retrieve all "entries," search for a success value, and so forth. Trees convert text-based XML back into a multidimensional structure.

To bridge the gap between `NSXMLParser` and tree-based parse results, you can use an `NSXMLParser`-based helper class to return more standard tree-based data. This requires a simple tree node like the kind shown here. This node uses double linking to access its parent and its children allowing two-way traversal in a tree.

```
@interface TreeNode : NSObject
{
    TreeNode        *parent;
    NSMutableArray  *children;
    NSString        *key;
    NSString        *leafvalue;
}
```

```
@property (retain)     TreeNode        *parent;
@property (retain)     NSMutableArray  *children;
@property (retain)     NSString        *key;
@property (retain)     NSString        *leafvalue;
@end
```

Building a Parse Tree

Recipe 13-13 introduces the `XMLParser` class. Its job is to build a parse tree as the `NSXMLParser` class works its way through XML source. The three standard `NSXML` routines (start element, finish element, and found characters) perform a recursive depth-first descent through the tree.

The class adds new nodes when reaching new elements (`parser:didStartElement:` ➥`qualifiedName:attributes:`) and adds leaf values when encountering text (`parser:foundCharacters:`). Because XML allows siblings at the same tree depth, this code uses a stack to keep track of the current path to the tree root. Siblings always pop back to the same parent in `parser:didEndElement:`, so they are added at the proper level.

After finishing the XML scan, the `parseXMLFile:` method returns the root node.

Recipe 13-13 **The XMLParser Helper Class**

```
@implementation XMLParser
// Parser returns the tree root. You have to go down
// one node to the real results
- (TreeNode *) parse: (NSXMLParser *) parser
{
    stack = [NSMutableArray array];

    TreeNode *root = [TreeNode treeNode];
    root.parent = nil;
    root.leafvalue = nil;
    root.children = [NSMutableArray array];

    [stack addObject:root];

    [parser setDelegate:self];
    [parser parse];
    [parser release];

    // pop down to real root
    TreeNode *realroot = [[root children] lastObject];
    root.children = nil;
    root.parent = nil;
```

```
    root.leafvalue = nil;
    root.key = nil;

    realroot.parent = nil;
    return realroot;
}

// Descend to a new element
- (void)parser:(NSXMLParser *)parser
    didStartElement:(NSString *)elementName
    namespaceURI:(NSString *)namespaceURI
    qualifiedName:(NSString *)qName
    attributes:(NSDictionary *)attributeDict
{
    if (qName) elementName = qName;

    TreeNode *leaf = [TreeNode treeNode];
    leaf.parent = [stack lastObject];
    [(NSMutableArray *)[[stack lastObject] children] addObject:leaf];

    leaf.key = [NSString stringWithString:elementName];
    leaf.leafvalue = nil;
    leaf.children = [NSMutableArray array];

    [stack addObject:leaf];
}

// Pop after finishing element
- (void)parser:(NSXMLParser *)parser
    didEndElement:(NSString *)elementName
    namespaceURI:(NSString *)namespaceURI
    qualifiedName:(NSString *)qName
{
    [stack removeLastObject];
}

// Reached a leaf
- (void)parser:(NSXMLParser *)parser foundCharacters:(NSString *)string
{
    if (![[stack lastObject] leafvalue])
    {
        [[stack lastObject] setLeafvalue:[NSString
             stringWithString:string]];
        return;
    }
```

```
        [[stack lastObject] setLeafvalue:
            [NSString stringWithFormat:@"%@%
            [[stack lastObject] leafvalue], string]];
}
@end
```

> **Get This Recipe's Code**
>
> To get the code used for this recipe, go to http://github.com/erica/iphone-3.0-cookbook-, or if you've downloaded the disk image containing all of the sample code from the book, go to the folder for Chapter 13 and open the project for this recipe.

Using the Tree Results

Listing 13-1 demonstrates an XML parse-tree consumer that works with the data returned from Recipe 13-13. This example presents a series of table view controllers that drill down from the root of the tree until the leaves. Whenever leaves are encountered, their values are displayed in an alert. Subtrees lead to additional view controller screens.

This example uses the `TreeNode` class trivially. The only items of interest are the leaf values and the child nodes. The class can do far more, including returning leaves and objects that match a given key. This functionality lets you retrieve information without knowing the exact path to a child node as long as you know what the node is called, such as "entry" or "published." These two names are in fact used by Twitter's API. The `TreeNode` search facility is demonstrated further in Recipe 16-3 in Chapter 16, "Push Notifications," which uses this to retrieve individual tweets and the time they were published.

Listing 13-1 **Browsing the Parse Tree**

```
@implementation TreeBrowserController
@synthesize root;

// Each instance of this controller has a separate root, as
// descending through the tree produces new roots.
- (id) initWithRoot:(TreeNode *) newRoot
{
    if (self = [super init])
    {
        self.root = newRoot;
        if (newRoot.key) self.title = newRoot.key;
    }
    return self;
}

- (NSInteger)numberOfSectionsInTableView:(UITableView *)tableView
{
    return 1;
}
```

```
// The number of rows equals the number of children for a node
- (NSInteger)tableView:(UITableView *)tableView
    numberOfRowsInSection:(NSInteger)section
{
    return [self.root.children count];
}

// Color code the cells that can be navigated through
- (UITableViewCell *)tableView:(UITableView *)tableView
    cellForRowAtIndexPath:(NSIndexPath *)indexPath
{
    UITableViewCell *cell = [tableView
        dequeueReusableCellWithIdentifier:@"generic"];
    if (!cell) cell = [[[UITableViewCell alloc]
        initWithFrame:CGRectZero reuseIdentifier:@"generic"]
        autorelease];
    TreeNode *child = [[self.root children]
        objectAtIndex:[indexPath row]];

    // Set text
    if (child.hasLeafValue)
        cell.textLabel.text = [NSString stringWithFormat:@"%@%@",
        child.key, child.leafvalue];
    else
        cell.textLabel.text = child.key;

    // Set color
    if (child.isLeaf)
        cell.textLabel.textColor = [UIColor darkGrayColor];
    else
        cell.textLabel.textColor = [UIColor blackColor];

    return cell;
}

// On selection, either push a new controller or show the leaf value
- (void)tableView:(UITableView *)tableView
    didSelectRowAtIndexPath:(NSIndexPath *)indexPath
{
    TreeNode *child =
        [self.root.children objectAtIndex:[indexPath row]];
    if (child.isLeaf)
    {
        showAlert(@"%
        return;
    }
    TreeBrowserController *tbc = [[[TreeBrowserController alloc]
```

```
        initWithRoot:child] autorelease];
    [self.navigationController pushViewController:tbc animated:YES];
}

// These controllers are ephemeral and need dealloc
- (void) dealloc
{
    self.root = nil;
    [super dealloc];
}
@end
```

Tearing Down a Tree

The XML parser code used in this recipe builds a two-way linked object tree. Parents own their children, and children own their parents. To properly dispose of this memory when you are done using it, make sure you tear down the tree to remove these links so each node's retain count can go down to zero.

The following `TreeNode` method should be issued to the root of the tree in use, just before you release the root. Do not tear down the tree until you're ready for the entire structure to be deallocated.

```
- (void) teardown
{
    for (TreeNode *node in [[self.children copy] autorelease])
        [node teardown];
    [self.parent.children removeObject:self];
    self.parent = nil;
}
```

Recipe: Building a Simple Web-Based Server

A Web server provides one of the cleanest ways to serve data off your phone to another computer. You don't need special client software. Any browser can list and access Web-based files. Best of all, a Web server requires just a few key routines. You must establish the service, creating a loop that listens for a request (`startServer`), and then pass those requests onto a handler (`handleWebRequest:`) that responds with the requested data. Recipe 13-14 shows a `WebHelper` class that handles establishing and controlling a Web service.

The loop routine uses low-level socket programming to establish a listening port and catch client requests. When the client issues a `GET` command, the server intercepts that request and passes it to the Web request handler. The handler decomposes it, typically to find the name of the desired data file. The default version of the `WebHelper` class shown here assumes that you will add your own handler method via a category (rather than a subclass). This recipe produces a single, simple feedback page regardless of the **GET** request received. You might want to expand this class to provide file access or access to services from your application. An example file service category is included with this chapter's sample code.

Recipe 13-14 **Serving iPhone Files Through a Web Service**

```
@implementation WebHelper
@synthesize cwd;
@synthesize isServing;
@synthesize delegate;
@synthesize chosenPort;

static WebHelper *sharedInstance = nil;

+ (WebHelper *) sharedInstance
{
    if(!sharedInstance) sharedInstance = [[self alloc] init];
    return sharedInstance;
}

- (NSString *) getRequest: (int) fd
{
    // Read the request and transform to an NSString
    static char buffer[BUFSIZE+1];
    int len = read(fd, buffer, BUFSIZE);
    buffer[len] = '\0';
    return [NSString stringWithCString:buffer
        encoding:NSUTF8StringEncoding];
}

// Serve files to GET requests
- (void) handleWebRequest:(int) fd
{
    // recover request
    NSString *request = [self getRequest:fd];

    // Create a category and implement this meaningfully
    // This is just a placeholder.
    NSMutableString *outcontent = [NSMutableString string];
    [outcontent appendString:
        @"HTTP/1.0 200 OK\r\nContent-Type: text/html\r\n\r\n"];
    [outcontent appendString:
        @"<html><h3>Notice</h3>"];
    [outcontent appendString:
        @"<p>Please add a WebHelper category that responds  "];
```

```
    [outcontent appendString:
        @"to the following request:</p>"];
    [outcontent appendFormat:@"<pre>%
    write (fd, [outcontent UTF8String], [outcontent length]);
    close(fd);
}

// Listen for external requests
- (void) listenForRequests
{
    NSAutoreleasePool *pool = [[NSAutoreleasePool alloc] init];
    static struct    sockaddr_in cli_addr;
    socklen_t        length = sizeof(cli_addr);


    // Read data forever, or until the isServing property
    // is set to NO, or until encountering a socket accept error
    while (1 > 0) {
        if (!self.isServing) return;

        if ((socketfd = accept(listenfd,
            (struct sockaddr *)&cli_addr, &length)) < 0)
        {
            self.isServing = NO;
            DO_CALLBACK(serviceWasLost, nil);
            return;
        }

        // Hand off responsibility for reading the socket data
        // and replying to it
        [self handleWebRequest:socketfd];
    }

    [pool release];
}

// Begin serving data; private method called by startService
- (void) startServer
{
    static struct    sockaddr_in serv_addr;

    // Set up socket
    if((listenfd = socket(AF_INET, SOCK_STREAM,0)) < 0)
    {
        self.isServing = NO;
        DO_CALLBACK(serviceCouldNotBeEstablished, nil);
        return;
```

```
    }

    // Serve to a random port
    serv_addr.sin_family = AF_INET;
    serv_addr.sin_addr.s_addr = htonl(INADDR_ANY);
    serv_addr.sin_port = 0;

    // Bind
    if(bind(listenfd, (struct sockaddr *)&serv_addr,
        sizeof(serv_addr)) <0)
    {
        self.isServing = NO;
        DO_CALLBACK(serviceCouldNotBeEstablished, nil);
        return;
    }

    // Find out what port number was chosen.
    int namelen = sizeof(serv_addr);
    if (getsockname(listenfd, (struct sockaddr *)&serv_addr,
        (void *) &namelen) < 0)
    {
        close(listenfd);
        self.isServing = NO;
        DO_CALLBACK(serviceCouldNotBeEstablished, nil);
        return;
    }

    chosenPort = ntohs(serv_addr.sin_port);

    // Listen
    if(listen(listenfd, 64) < 0)
    {
        self.isServing = NO;
        DO_CALLBACK(serviceCouldNotBeEstablished, nil);
        return;
    }

    DO_CALLBACK(serviceWasEstablished, nil);
    [NSThread detachNewThreadSelector:
        @selector(listenForRequests) toTarget:self withObject:NULL];
}

- (void) startService
{
    if (self.isServing) return; // already listening
    [self startServer];
    self.isServing = YES;
```

```
}
@end
```

Get This Recipe's Code

To get the code used for this recipe, go to http://github.com/erica/iphone-3.0-cookbook-, or if you've downloaded the disk image containing all of the sample code from the book, go to the folder for Chapter 13 and open the project for this recipe.

One More Thing: FTPHelper

The File Transfer Protocol is especially nice to use because it's standard across so many platforms. Apple's Core Foundation FTP sample code is easy to work with, if you're willing to overlook a bit of inelegant coding. You can find the source at http://developer.apple.com/samplecode/CFFTPSample. There's little you have to do to get the upload and download functionality working. Once you have a user's name, password, and host information stored, FTP data transfer can be easily automated.

At the request of any number of readers, I have included an `FTPHelper` class with the sample code for this chapter. It is not an elegant solution by any stretch of the imagination, but it offers enough functionality to provide a jumping-off point for anyone who wants to use FTP access from an application. You probably shouldn't deploy code based on this helper to App Store without a lot of testing and tweaking, but you can learn about how FTP access basically works.

The `FTPHelper` class provides access to file upload, download, and directory lists. Here's how you set up the delegate for all three operations.

```
[FTPHelper sharedInstance].delegate = self;
[FTPHelper sharedInstance].uname = BASE_USERNAME;
[FTPHelper sharedInstance].pword = BASE_PASSWORD;
[FTPHelper sharedInstance].urlString = BASE_URL;

// Listing
[FTPHelper list:BASE_URL];

// Download
[FTPHelper download:FILE_TO_MOVE];

// Upload
[FTPHelper upload:FILE_TO_MOVE];
```

Use simple string constants for the username and password. The base URL path does not point to a specific resource. Instead, you give it a general ftp address like @"ftp://MySystem.local", @"ftp://somehost.com", or even @"ftp://somehost.com/ftp/UploadArea". Make sure you use the ftp:// prefix.

When uploading and downloading, specify the filename as a separate parameter. In the current implementation, all files move into and out from the main Documents folder in the sandbox.

Listing 13-2 shows the interface for the `FTPHelper` class and the protocol for its delegate. It provides its functionality via simple class methods.

Listing 13-2 FTPHelper

```
@protocol FTPHelperDelegate <NSObject>
@optional
// Successes
- (void) receivedListing: (NSDictionary *) listing;
- (void) downloadFinished;
- (void) dataUploadFinished: (NSNumber *) bytes;
- (void) progressAtPercent: (NSNumber *) aPercent;


// Failures
- (void) listingFailed;
- (void) dataDownloadFailed: (NSString *) reason;
- (void) dataUploadFailed: (NSString *) reason;
- (void) credentialsMissing;
@end

@interface FTPHelper : NSObject
{
    NSString *urlString;
    id <FTPHelperDelegate> delegate;
    NSString *uname;
    NSString *pword;
    NSMutableArray *fileListings;
    NSString *filePath;
}
@property (retain) NSString *urlString;
@property (retain) id delegate;
@property (retain) NSString *uname;
@property (retain) NSString *pword;
@property (retain) NSMutableArray *fileListings;
@property (retain) NSString *filePath; // valid after download

+ (FTPHelper *) sharedInstance;
+ (void) download:(NSString *) anItem;
+ (void) upload: (NSString *) anItem;
+ (void) list: (NSString *) aURLString;

+ (NSString *) textForDirectoryListing: (CFDictionaryRef) dictionary;
@end
```

Summary

This chapter introduced a wide range network supporting technologies. You saw how to check for network connectivity, work with keychains for secure authentication challenges, upload and download data via `NSURLConnection`, via FTP, and more. Here are a few thoughts to take away with you before leaving this chapter:

- Most of Apple's networking support is provided through very low-level C-based routines. If you can find a friendly Objective-C wrapper to simplify your programming work, consider using it. The only drawback occurs when you specifically need tight networking control at the most basic level of your application.
- There was not space in this chapter to discuss more detailed authentication schemes for data APIs. If you need access to OAuth, for example, search for existing Cocoa implementations. A number are available in open source repositories, and they are easily ported to Cocoa Touch. If you need to work with simpler data checksum, digest, and encoding routines, point your browser to http://www.cocoadev.com/index.pl?NSDataCategory. This extremely handy `NSData` category offers md5, sha1, and base32 solutions, among others.
- Many data services provide simple to use APIs such as Twitter and TwitPic. These APIs are often more limited than the fully authorized developer APIs, which typically require developer credentials and advanced authorization. At the same time, they often offer simple solutions to the tasks you actually need to perform, especially if you're not writing a full client specific to a given service.
- Sharing keychains across applications is tied to the provision that signed them. You can share user login items between your own applications but not with other developers. Make sure you take care when creating and using keychain entitlement files to follow every step of the process. This avoids a lot of frustration when trying to produce a successful compilation.
- Even when Apple provides Objective-C wrappers, as they do with `NSXMLParser`, it's not always the class you wanted or hoped for. Adapting classes is a big part of the iPhone programming experience. This chapter introduced many custom classes that simplify access to core Cocoa Touch objects.

14

Device Capabilities

Each iPhone device represents a meld of unique, shared, momentary, and persistent properties. These properties include the device's current physical orientation, its model name, its battery state, and its access to onboard hardware. This chapter looks at the device from its build configuration to its active onboard sensors. It provides recipes that return a variety of information items about the unit in use. You read about testing for hardware prerequisites at runtime and specifying those prerequisites in the application's Info.plist file. You discover how to solicit sensor feedback and subscribe to notifications to create callbacks when those sensor states change. This chapter covers the hardware, file system, and sensors available on the iPhone device and helps you programmatically take advantage of those features.

Recipe: Accessing Core Device Information

The `UIDevice` class enables you to recover key device-specific values, including the iPhone or iPod touch model being used, the device name, and the OS name and version. As Recipe 14-1 shows, it's a one-stop solution for pulling out certain system details. Each method is an instance method, which is called using the `UIDevice` singleton, via `[UIDevice currentDevice]`.

The information you can retrieve from `UIDevice` includes these items:

- **System name**—This returns the name of the operating system currently in use. For current generations of iPhones, there is only one OS that runs on the platform: iPhone OS.
- **System version**—This value lists the firmware version currently installed on the unit, for example, 2.2.1, 3.0, 3.1, and so on.
- **Unique identifier**—The iPhone unique identifier provides a hexadecimal number that is guaranteed to be unique for each iPhone or iPod touch. According to Apple, the iPhone produces this identifier by applying an internal hash to several hardware specifiers, including the device serial number. The iPhone's unique identifier is used to register devices at the iPhone portal for provisioning, including Ad Hoc distribution.

- **Model**—The iPhone model returns a string that describes its platform, namely iPhone and iPod touch. Should the iPhone OS be extended to new devices, additional strings will describe those models.
- **Name**—This string presents the iPhone name assigned by the user in iTunes such as "Joe's iPhone" or "Binky." This name is also used to create the local host name for the device. See Chapter 13, "Networking," for more details about host name retrieval.

Recipe 14-1 **Using the UIDevice Class**

```
- (void) action: (UIBarButtonItem *) bbi
{
    [self doLog:@"System Name: %@",
        [[UIDevice currentDevice] systemName]];
    [self doLog:@"System Version: %@",
        [[UIDevice currentDevice] systemVersion]];
    [self doLog:@"Unique ID: %@",
        [[UIDevice currentDevice] uniqueIdentifier]];
    [self doLog:@"Model %@", [[UIDevice currentDevice] model]];
    [self doLog:@"Name %@", [[UIDevice currentDevice] name]];
}
```

Get This Recipe's Code

To get the code used for this recipe, go to http://github.com/erica/iphone-3.0-cookbook-, or if you've downloaded the disk image containing all of the sample code from the book, go to the folder for Chapter 14 and open the project for this recipe.

Adding Device Capability Restrictions

When you submit 3.0 applications to iTunes, you no longer specify which platforms your application is compatible with. Instead, you tell iTunes what device features your application needs.

Each iPhone and iPod touch provides a unique feature set. Some devices offer cameras and GPS capabilities. Others don't. Some support OpenGL ES 2.0. Others are limited to OpenGL ES 1.1. Starting in firmware 3.0, you can specify what features are needed to run your application on a device.

When you include the `UIRequiredDeviceCapabilities` key in your Info.plist file, iTunes limits application installation to devices that offer the required capabilities. Provide this list as an array of strings, whose possible values are detailed in Table 14-1. Only include those features that your application requires. If your application can provide workarounds, do not add the restriction.

Table 14-1 **Required Device Capabilities**

Key	Use
telephony	Application requires the Phone application or uses tel:// URLs.
sms	Application requires Messages application or uses sms:// URLs.
still-camera	Application uses camera mode for the image picker controller.
auto-focus-camera	Application requires extra focus capabilities for macro photography or especially sharp images for in-image data detection.
video-camera	Application uses video mode for the image picker controller.
wifi	Application requires local 802.11-based network access.
accelerometer	Application requires accelerometer-specific feedback beyond simple `UIViewController` orientation events.
location-services	Application uses Core Location.
gps	Application uses Core Location and requires the additional accuracy of GPS positioning.
magnetometer	Application uses Core Location and requires heading-related events, i.e., the direction of travel. (The magnetometer is the built-in compass.)
microphone	Application uses either built-in microphones or (approved) accessories that provide a microphone.
opengles-1	Application uses OpenGL ES 1.1.
opengles-2	Application uses OpenGL ES 2.0.
armv6	Application is compiled *only* for the armv6 instruction set (3.1 or later).
armv7	Application is compiled *only* for the armv7 instruction set (3.1 or later).
peer-peer	Application uses GameKit peer-to-peer connectivity over Bluetooth (3.1 or later).

For example, consider an application that offers an option for taking pictures when run on a camera-ready device. If the application otherwise works on iPod touch units, do not include the still-camera restriction. Instead, use check for camera capability from within the application and present the camera option when appropriate. Adding a still-camera restriction eliminates all first, second, and third generation iPod owners from your potential customer pool.

Adding Device Requirements

To add device requirements to the Info.plist file open it in the Xcode editor. Select the last row (usually Application Requires iPhone Environment) and press Return. A new item appears, already set for editing. Enter "Req", and Xcode auto completes to "Required device capabilities". This is the "human readable" form of the

`UIRequiredDeviceCapabilities` key. You can view the normal key name by right-clicking (Ctrl-clicking) any item in the key list and choosing Show Raw Keys/Values.

Xcode automatically sets the item type to an array and adds a new Item 1. Edit the value to your first required capability. To add more items, select any item and press Return. Xcode inserts a new key-value pair. Figure 14-1 shows the editor in action.

Key	Value
▼ Information Property List	(12 items)
Localization native development re	English
Bundle display name	${PRODUCT_NAME}
Executable file	${EXECUTABLE_NAME}
Icon file	
Bundle identifier	com.sadun.${PRODUCT_NAME:rfc1034identifier}
InfoDictionary version	6.0
Bundle name	${PRODUCT_NAME}
Bundle OS Type code	APPL
Bundle creator OS Type code	????
Bundle version	1.0
Application requires iPhone enviror	☑
▼ Required device capabilities	(2 items)
Item 1	wifi
Item 2	telephony

Figure 14-1 Adding required device capabilities to the Info.plist file in Xcode.

Recipe: Recovering Additional Device Information

Both `sysctl()` and `sysctlbyname()` allow you to retrieve system information. These standard UNIX functions query the operating system about hardware and OS details. You can get a sense of the kind of scope on offer by glancing at the /usr/include/sys/sysctl.h include file on the Macintosh. There you find an exhaustive list of constants that can be used as parameters to these functions.

These constants allow you to check for core information like the system's CPU frequency, the amount of available memory, and more. Recipe 14-2 demonstrates this. It introduces a `UIDevice` category that gathers system information and returns it via a series of method calls.

You might wonder why this category includes a platform method, when the standard `UIDevice` class returns device models on demand. The answer lies in distinguishing different types of iPhones and iPod touch units.

An iPhone 3GS's model is simply "iPhone," as is the model of an iPhone 3G and the original iPhone. In contrast, this recipe returns a platform value of "iPhone2,1" for the 3GS. This allows you to programmatically differentiate the unit from a first generation iPhone ("iPhone1,1") or iPhone 3G ("iPhone1,2").

Each model offers distinct built-in capabilities. Knowing exactly which iPhone you're dealing with helps you determine whether that unit supports features like accessibility, GPS, and magnetometers.

Recipe 14-2 **Accessing Device Information Through sysctl() and sysctlbyname()**

```
@implementation UIDevice (Hardware)
+ (NSString *) getSysInfoByName:(char *)typeSpecifier
{
    // Recover sysctl information by name
    size_t size;
    sysctlbyname(typeSpecifier, NULL, &size, NULL, 0);
    char *answer = malloc(size);
    sysctlbyname(typeSpecifier, answer, &size, NULL, 0);
    NSString *results = [NSString stringWithCString:answer
        encoding: NSUTF8StringEncoding];
    free(answer);
    return results;
}

- (NSString *) platform
{
    return [UIDevice getSysInfoByName:"hw.machine"];
}

+ (NSUInteger) getSysInfo: (uint) typeSpecifier
{
    size_t size = sizeof(int);
    int results;
    int mib[2] = {CTL_HW, typeSpecifier};
    sysctl(mib, 2, &results, &size, NULL, 0);
    return (NSUInteger) results;
}

- (NSUInteger) cpuFrequency
{
    return [UIDevice getSysInfo:HW_CPU_FREQ];
}

- (NSUInteger) busFrequency
{
    return [UIDevice getSysInfo:HW_BUS_FREQ];
}

- (NSUInteger) totalMemory
{
    return [UIDevice getSysInfo:HW_PHYSMEM];
}

- (NSUInteger) userMemory
{
```

```
    return [UIDevice getSysInfo:HW_USERMEM];
}

- (NSUInteger) maxSocketBufferSize
{
    return [UIDevice getSysInfo:KIPC_MAXSOCKBUF];
}
@end
```

Get This Recipe's Code

To get the code used for this recipe, go to http://github.com/erica/iphone-3.0-cookbook-, or if you've downloaded the disk image containing all of the sample code from the book, go to the folder for Chapter 14 and open the project for this recipe.

Recipe: Monitoring the iPhone Battery State

The 3.0 and later API allows you to keep track of the iPhone's battery level and charge state. The level is a floating-point value that ranges between 1.0 (fully charged) and 0.0 (fully discharged). It provides an approximate discharge level that you can use to query before performing operations that put unusual strain on the device.

For example, you might want to caution your user about performing a large series of convolutions and suggest that the user plug in to a power source. You retrieve the battery level via this `UIDevice` call. The value returned is produced in 5% increments.

```
NSLog(@"Battery level: %0.2f%",
    [[UIDevice currentDevice] batteryLevel] * 100);
```

The iPhone charge state has four possible values. The unit can be charging (i.e., connected to a power source), full, unplugged, and a catchall "unknown." Recover the state using the `UIDevice batteryState` property.

```
NSArray *stateArray = [NSArray arrayWithObjects:
    @"Battery state is unknown",
    @"Battery is not plugged into a charging source",
    @"Battery is charging",
    @"Battery state is full", nil];

 NSLog(@"Battery state: %@",
    [stateArray objectAtIndex:
    [[UIDevice currentDevice] batteryState]]);
```

Don't think of these choices as persistent states. Instead, think of them as momentary reflections of what is actually happening to the device. They are not flags. They are not or'ed together to form a general battery description. Instead, these values reflect the most recent state change.

Recipe 14-3 monitors state changes. When it detects that the battery state has changed, only then does it check to see what that state change indicated. In this way, you can catch momentary events, such as when the battery finally recharges fully, when the user has plugged in to a power source to recharge, and when the user disconnects from that power source.

To start monitoring, set the `batteryMonitoringEnabled` property to `YES`. During monitoring, the `UIDevice` class produces notifications when the battery state or level changes. Recipe 14-3 subscribes to both notifications. Please note that you can also check these values directly, without waiting for notifications. Apple provides no guarantees about the frequency of level change updates, but as you can tell by testing this recipe, they arrive in a fairly regular fashion.

Recipe 14-3 **Monitoring the iPhone Battery**

```
- (void) checkBattery: (id) sender
{
    NSArray *stateArray = [NSArray arrayWithObjects:
        @"Battery state is Unknown",
        @"Battery is unplugged",
        @"Battery is charging",
        @"Battery state is full", nil];

    NSLog(@"Battery level: %0.2f%",
        [[UIDevice currentDevice] batteryLevel] * 100);
    NSLog(@"Battery state: %@", [stateArray
        objectAtIndex:[[UIDevice currentDevice] batteryState]]);
}

- (void) viewDidLoad
{
    // Enable battery monitoring
    [[UIDevice currentDevice] setBatteryMonitoringEnabled:YES];

    // Add observers for battery state and level changes
    [[NSNotificationCenter defaultCenter] addObserver:self
        selector:@selector(checkBattery)
        name:UIDeviceBatteryStateDidChangeNotification
        object:nil];
    [[NSNotificationCenter defaultCenter] addObserver:self
        selector:@selector(checkBattery)
        name:UIDeviceBatteryLevelDidChangeNotification
        object:nil];
}
```

Get This Recipe's Code

To get the code used for this recipe, go to http://github.com/erica/iphone-3.0-cookbook-, or if you've downloaded the disk image containing all of the sample code from the book, go to the folder for Chapter 14 and open the project for this recipe.

Recipe: Enabling and Disabling the Proximity Sensor

Unless you have some pressing reason to hold an iPhone against body parts (or vice versa), enabling the proximity sensor accomplishes little. When enabled, it has one primary task. It detects whether there's a large object right in front of it. If so, it switches the screen off and sends off a general notification. Move the blocking object away and the screen switches back on. This prevents you from pressing buttons or dialing the phone with your ear when you are on a call. Some poorly designed protective cases keep the iPhone's proximity sensors from working properly.

The Google Mobile application on App Store used this feature to start a voice recording session. When you held the phone up to your head it would record your query, sending it off to be interpreted when moved away from your head. The developers didn't mind that the screen blanked as the voice recording interface did not depend on a visual GUI to operate.

Recipe 14-4 demonstrates how to work with proximity sensing on the iPhone. It uses the `UIDevice` class to toggle proximity monitoring and subscribes to `UIDeviceProximity` ➥`StateDidChangeNotification` to catch state changes. The two states are on and off. When the `UIDevice proximityState` property returns `YES`, the proximity sensor has been activated.

> **Note**
>
> Prior to the 3.0 firmware, proximity used to be controlled by the `UIApplication` class. This approach is now deprecated. Also be aware that `setProximityState:` is documented, but the method is actually nonexistent. Proximity state is a read-only property.

Recipe 14-4 **Enabling Proximity Sensing**

```
- (void) toggle: (id) sender
{
    // Determine the current proximity monitoring and toggle it
    BOOL isIt = [UIDevice currentDevice].proximityMonitoringEnabled;
    [UIDevice currentDevice].proximityMonitoringEnabled = !isIt;
    NSString *title = isIt ? @"Enable" : @"Disable";
    self.navigationItem.rightBarButtonItem =
        BARBUTTON(title, @selector(toggle));

    NSLog(@"You have %@ the Proximity sensor.",
        isIt ? @"disabled" : @"enabled");
}

- (void) stateChange: (NSNotificationCenter *) notification
{
    // Log the notifications
    NSLog(@"The proximity sensor %@",
        [UIDevice currentDevice].proximityState ?
```

```
        @"will now blank the screen" :
        @"will now restore the screen");
}

- (void) viewDidLoad
{
    self.navigationItem.rightBarButtonItem =
        BARBUTTON(@"Enable", @selector(toggle));

    // Add proximity state observer
    [[NSNotificationCenter defaultCenter]
        addObserver:self selector:@selector(stateChange)
        name:@"UIDeviceProximityStateDidChangeNotification"
        object:nil];
}
```

Get This Recipe's Code

To get the code used for this recipe, go to http://github.com/erica/iphone-3.0-cookbook-, or if you've downloaded the disk image containing all of the sample code from the book, go to the folder for Chapter 14 and open the project for this recipe.

Recipe: Using Acceleration to Locate "Up"

The iPhone provides three onboard sensors that measure acceleration along the iPhone's perpendicular axis; that is, left/right (X), up/down (Y), and front/back (Z). These values indicate the forces affecting the iPhone, from both gravity and user movement. You can get some really neat force feedback by swinging the iPhone around your head (centripetal force) or dropping it from a tall building (freefall). Unfortunately, you might not be able to recover that data after your iPhone becomes an expensive bit of scrap metal.

To subscribe an object to iPhone accelerometer updates, set it as delegate. The object set as the delegate must implement the `UIAccelerometerDelegate` protocol.

```
[[UIAccelerometer sharedAccelerometer] setDelegate:self]
```

Once assigned, your delegate receives `accelerometer:didAccelerate:` messages, which you can track and respond to. Normally, you assign the delegate as your primary view controller, but you can also do so with a custom helper class.

The `UIAcceleration` object sent to the delegate method returns floating-point values for the X, Y, and Z axes. Each value ranges from -1.0 to 1.0.

```
float x = [acceleration x];
float y = [acceleration y];
float z = [acceleration z];
```

Recipe 14-5 uses these values to help determine the "up" direction. It calculates the arctangent between the X and Y acceleration vectors, returning the up-offset angle. As new acceleration messages are received, the recipe rotates a `UIImageView` with its picture of an arrow, which you can see in Figure 14-2, to point up. The real-time response to user actions ensures that the arrow continues pointing upward, no matter how the user reorients the phone.

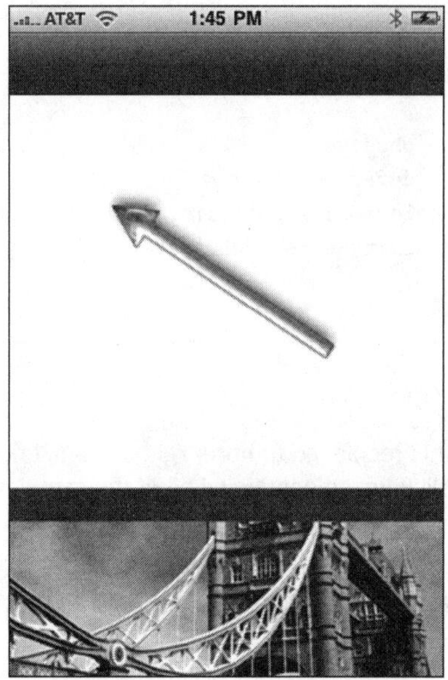

Figure 14-2 A little math recovers the "up" direction by performing an arctan function using the x and y force vectors. In this sample, the arrow always points up, no matter how the user reorients the iPhone.

Recipe 14-5 **Catching Acceleration Events**

```
- (void)accelerometer:(UIAccelerometer *)accelerometer
    didAccelerate:(UIAcceleration *)acceleration
{
    // Determine up from the x and y acceleration components
    float xx = -[acceleration x];
    float yy = [acceleration y];
    float angle = atan2(yy, xx);
    [self.arrow setTransform:
        CGAffineTransformMakeRotation(angle)];
}
```

```
- (void) viewDidLoad
{
    // Init the delegate to start catching accelerometer events
    [[UIAccelerometer sharedAccelerometer] setDelegate:self];
}
```

Get This Recipe's Code

To get the code used for this recipe, go to http://github.com/erica/iphone-3.0-cookbook-, or if you've downloaded the disk image containing all of the sample code from the book, go to the folder for Chapter 14 and open the project for this recipe.

Recipe: Using Acceleration to Move Onscreen Objects

With a bit of clever programming, the iPhone's onboard accelerometer can make objects "move" around the screen, responding in real time to the way the user tilts the phone. Recipe 14-6 builds an animated butterfly that users can slide across the screen.

The secret to making this work lies in adding what I call a "physics timer" to the program. Instead of responding directly to changes in acceleration, the way Recipe 14-5 did, the accelerometer callback does nothing more than measure the current forces. It's up to the timer routine to apply those forces to the butterfly over time by changing its frame.

- As long as the direction of force remains the same, the butterfly accelerates. Its velocity increases, scaled according to the degree of acceleration force in the X or Y direction.
- The `tick` routine, called by the timer, moves the butterfly by adding the velocity vector to the butterfly's origin.
- The butterfly's range is bounded. So when it hits an edge, it stops moving in that direction. This keeps the butterfly onscreen at all times. The slightly odd nested if structure in the `tick` method checks for boundary conditions. For example, if the butterfly hits a vertical edge, it can still move horizontally.

Recipe 14-6 **Sliding an Onscreen Object Based on Accelerometer Feedback**

```
- (void)accelerometer:(UIAccelerometer *)accelerometer
    didAccelerate:(UIAcceleration *)acceleration
{
    // extract the acceleration components
    float xx = -[acceleration x];
    float yy = [acceleration y];

    // Has the direction changed?
    float accelDirX = SIGN(xvelocity) * -1.0f;
    float newDirX = SIGN(xx);
    float accelDirY = SIGN(yvelocity) * -1.0f;
    float newDirY = SIGN(yy);
```

```
    // Accelerate. To increase viscosity lower the additive value
    if (accelDirX == newDirX)
        xaccel = (abs(xaccel) + 0.85f) * SIGN(xaccel);
    if (accelDirY == newDirY)
        yaccel = (abs(yaccel) + 0.85f) * SIGN(yaccel);

    // Apply acceleration changes to the current velocity
    xvelocity = -xaccel * xx;
    yvelocity = -yaccel * yy;
}

- (CGRect) offsetButterflyBy: (float) dx and: (float) dy
{
    CGRect rect = [self.butterfly frame];
    rect.origin.x += dx;
    rect.origin.y += dy;
    return rect;
}

- (void) tick
{
    // Move the butterfly according to the current velocity vector
    CGRect rect;

    // free movement
    if (CGRectContainsRect(self.view.bounds,
        rect = [self offsetButterflyBy:xvelocity and:yvelocity]));

    // vertical edge
    else if (CGRectContainsRect(self.view.bounds,
        rect = [self offsetButterflyBy:xvelocity and:0.0f]));

    // horizontal edge
    else if (CGRectContainsRect(self.view.bounds,
        rect = [self offsetButterflyBy:0.0f and:yvelocity]));

    // corner
    else return;

    [butterfly setFrame:rect];
}

- (void) initButterfly
{
    // Load the animation cells
    NSMutableArray *bflies = [NSMutableArray array];
```

```
    for (int i = 1; i <= 17; i++)
        [bflies addObject:[UIImage imageNamed:
            [NSString stringWithFormat:@"bf_%d.png", i]]];

    // Create the butterfly, begin the animation
    self.butterfly = [[[UIImageView alloc] initWithFrame:
        CGRectMake(0.0f, 0.0f, 150.0f, 76.5f)] autorelease];
    [self.butterfly setAnimationImages:bflies];
    self.butterfly.animationDuration = 0.75f;
    [self.butterfly startAnimating];
    self.butterfly.center = CGPointMake(160.0f, 100.0f);
    [self.view addSubview:butterfly];

    // Set the butterfly's initial speed and acceleration
    xaccel = 2.0f;
    yaccel = 2.0f;
    xvelocity = 0.0f;
    yvelocity = 0.0f;

    // Activate the accelerometer
    [[UIAccelerometer sharedAccelerometer] setDelegate:self];

    // Start the physics timer
    [NSTimer scheduledTimerWithTimeInterval: 0.03f
        target: self selector: @selector(tick)
        userInfo: nil repeats: YES];
}
```

Get This Recipe's Code

To get the code used for this recipe, go to http://github.com/erica/iphone-3.0-cookbook, or if you've downloaded the disk image containing all of the sample code from the book, go to the folder for Chapter 14 and open the project for this recipe.

Recipe: Detecting Device Orientation

The iPhone orientation refers to the way that a user is holding the device. Query the device orientation at any time by retrieving `[UIDevice currentDevice].orientation`. This property returns a device orientation number. This number is equal to one of the following orientation states.

```
typedef enum {
   UIDeviceOrientationUnknown,
   UIDeviceOrientationPortrait,
   UIDeviceOrientationPortraitUpsideDown,
   UIDeviceOrientationLandscapeLeft,
   UIDeviceOrientationLandscapeRight,
   UIDeviceOrientationFaceUp,
```

```
    UIDeviceOrientationFaceDown
} UIDeviceOrientation;
```

The portrait and landscape orientations are self-explanatory. The face up/face down orientations refer to an iPhone sitting on a flat surface, with the face facing up or down. These orientations are computed by the SDK using the onboard accelerometer and math calculus that is similar to the one presented in the previous recipe.

Usually, the most important thing to know about the current orientation is whether it is portrait or landscape. To help determine this, Apple offers two built-in helper macros. You pass an orientation to these macros, which are shown in the following code snippet. Each macro returns a Boolean value, `YES` or `NO`, respectively indicating portrait or landscape compliance, as shown here.

```
- (BOOL) shouldAutorotateToInterfaceOrientation:
    (UIInterfaceOrientation) anOrientation
{
    printf("Is Portrait?: %s\n",
        UIDeviceOrientationIsPortrait(anOrientation)
        ? "Yes" : "No");
    printf("Is Landscape?: %s\n",
        UIDeviceOrientationIsLandscape(anOrientation)
        ? "Yes" : "No");
    return YES;
}
```

When you want to determine the orientation outside the "should autorotate" callback for the view controller, the code becomes a little tedious and repetitious. Recipe 14-7 creates an Orientation category for the `UIDevice` class, providing `isLandscape` and `isPortrait` properties. In addition, the recipe creates an `orientationString` property that returns a text-based description of the current orientation.

> **Note**
>
> At the time of writing, the iPhone does not report a proper orientation when first launched. It updates the orientation only after the iPhone has been moved into a new position. An application launched in portrait orientation will not read as "portrait" until the user moves the device out of and then back into the proper orientation. This bug exists on the simulator as well as on the iPhone device and is easily tested with Recipe 14-7. For a workaround, consider using the angular orientation recovered from Recipe 14-5. This bug does not affect proper interface display via the `UIViewController` class.

Recipe 14-7 **A UIDevice Orientation Category**

```
@implementation UIDevice (Orientation)
- (BOOL) isLandscape
{
    return (self.orientation == UIDeviceOrientationLandscapeLeft)
        || (self.orientation == UIDeviceOrientationLandscapeRight);
}
```

```
- (BOOL) isPortrait
{
    return (self.orientation == UIDeviceOrientationPortrait)
        || (self.orientation == UIDeviceOrientationPortraitUpsideDown);
}

- (NSString *) orientationString
{
    switch ([[UIDevice currentDevice] orientation])
    {
        case UIDeviceOrientationUnknown: return @"Unknown";
        case UIDeviceOrientationPortrait: return @"Portrait";
        case UIDeviceOrientationPortraitUpsideDown:
            return @"Portrait Upside Down";
        case UIDeviceOrientationLandscapeLeft:
            return @"Landscape Left";
        case UIDeviceOrientationLandscapeRight:
            return @"Landscape Right";
        case UIDeviceOrientationFaceUp: return @"Face Up";
        case UIDeviceOrientationFaceDown: return @"Face Down";
        default: break;
    }
    return nil;
}
@end
```

Get This Recipe's Code

To get the code used for this recipe, go to http://github.com/erica/iphone-3.0-cookbook-, or if you've downloaded the disk image containing all of the sample code from the book, go to the folder for Chapter 14 and open the project for this recipe.

Recipe: Detecting Shakes Using Motion Events

When the iPhone detects a motion event, it passes that event to the current first responder, the primary object in the responder chain. Responders are objects that can handle events. All views and windows are responders and so is the application object.

The responder chain provides a hierarchy of objects, all of which can respond to events. When an object toward the start of the chain receives an event, that event does not get passed further down. The object handles it. If it cannot, that event can move on to the next responder.

Objects often become first responder by declaring themselves to be so, via `becomeFirstResponder`. In this snippet, a `UIViewController` ensures that it becomes first responder whenever its view appears onscreen. Upon disappearing, it resigns the first responder position.

```
- (BOOL)canBecomeFirstResponder {
    return YES;
}

// Become first responder whenever the view appears
- (void)viewDidAppear:(BOOL)animated {
    [super viewDidAppear:animated];
    [self becomeFirstResponder];
}

// Resign first responder whenever the view disappears
- (void)viewWillDisappear:(BOOL)animated {
    [super viewWillDisappear:animated];
    [self resignFirstResponder];
}
```

First responders receive all touch and motion events. The motion callbacks mirror the touch ones discussed in Chapter 8, "Gestures and Touches." They are

- **`motionBegan:withEvent:`**—This callback indicates the start of a motion event. At the time of writing this book, there was only one kind of motion event recognized: a shake. This may not hold true for the future, so you might want to check the motion type in your code.
- **`motionEnded:withEvent:`**—The first responder receives this callback at the end of the motion event.
- **`motionCancelled:withEvent:`**—As with touches, motions can be cancelled by incoming phone calls and other system events. Apple recommends that you implement all three motion event callbacks (and, similarly, all four touch event callbacks) in production code.

Recipe 14-8 shows a pair of motion callback examples. If you test this out on a device, you'll notice several things. First, the began- and ended-events happen almost simultaneously from a user perspective. Playing sounds for both types is overkill. Second, there is a bias toward side-to-side shake detection. The iPhone is better at detecting side-to-side shakes than front-to-back or up-down versions. Finally, Apple's motion implementation uses a slight lockout approach. You cannot generate a new motion event until a second or so after the previous one was processed. This is the same lockout used by Shake to Shuffle and Shake to Undo events.

Recipe 14-8 **Catching Motion Events in the First Responder**

```
- (void)motionBegan:(UIEventSubtype)motion
    withEvent:(UIEvent *)event {
    // Play a sound whenever a shake motion starts
    if (motion != UIEventSubtypeMotionShake) return;
    [self playSound:startSound];
}
```

```
- (void)motionEnded:(UIEventSubtype)motion withEvent:(UIEvent *)event
{
    // Play a sound whenever a shake motion ends
     if (motion != UIEventSubtypeMotionShake) return;
    [self playSound:endSound];
}
```

Get This Recipe's Code

To get the code used for this recipe, go to http://github.com/erica/iphone-3.0-cookbook-, or if you've downloaded the disk image containing all of the sample code from the book, go to the folder for Chapter 14 and open the project for this recipe.

Recipe: Detecting Shakes Directly from the Accelerometer

Recipe 14-9 mimics the Apple motion detection system while avoiding the need for the event consumer to be the first responder. It's built on two key parameters: a sensitivity level that provides a threshold that must be met before a shake is acknowledged and a lockout time that limits how often a new shake can be generated.

This `AccelerometerHelper` class stores a triplet of acceleration values. Each value represents a force vector in 3D space. Each successive pair of that triplet can be analyzed to determine the angle between the two vectors. In this example, the angles between the first two items and the second two help determine when a shake happens. This code looks for a pair whose second angle exceeds the first angle. If the angular movement has increased enough between the two (i.e., an acceleration of angular velocity, basically a "jerk"), a shake is detected.

The helper generates no delegate callbacks until a second hurdle is passed. A lockout prevents any new callbacks until a certain amount of time expires. This is implemented by storing a trigger time for the last shake event. All shakes that occur before the lockout time expires are ignored. New shakes can be generated after.

Apple's built-in shake detection is calculated with more complex accelerometer data analysis. It analyzes and looks for oscillation in approximately eight to ten consecutive data points, according to a technical expert informed on this topic. Recipe 14-9 provides a less complicated approach, demonstrating how to work with raw acceleration data to provide a computed result from those values.

Recipe 14-9 **Detecting Shakes with the Accelerometer Helper**

```
@implementation AccelerometerHelper
- (id) init
{
    if (!(self = [super init])) return self;

    self.triggerTime = [NSDate date];
```

```
    // Current force vector
    cx = UNDEFINED_VALUE;
    cy = UNDEFINED_VALUE;
    cz = UNDEFINED_VALUE;

    // Last force vector
    lx = UNDEFINED_VALUE;
    ly = UNDEFINED_VALUE;
    lz = UNDEFINED_VALUE;

    // Previous force vector
    px = UNDEFINED_VALUE;
    py = UNDEFINED_VALUE;
    pz = UNDEFINED_VALUE;

    self.sensitivity = 0.5f;
    self.lockout = 0.5f;

    // Start the accelerometer going
    [[UIAccelerometer sharedAccelerometer] setDelegate:self];

    return self;
}

- (void) setX: (float) aValue
{
    px = lx;
    lx = cx;
    cx = aValue;
}

- (void) setY: (float) aValue
{
    py = ly;
    ly = cy;
    cy = aValue;
}

- (void) setZ: (float) aValue
{
    pz = lz;
    lz = cz;
    cz = aValue;
}
```

```
- (float) dAngle
{
    if (cx == UNDEFINED_VALUE) return UNDEFINED_VALUE;
    if (lx == UNDEFINED_VALUE) return UNDEFINED_VALUE;
    if (px == UNDEFINED_VALUE) return UNDEFINED_VALUE;

    // Calculate the dot product of the first pair
    float dot1 = cx * lx + cy * ly + cz * lz;
    float a = ABS(sqrt(cx * cx + cy * cy + cz * cz));
    float b = ABS(sqrt(lx * lx + ly * ly + lz * lz));
    dot1 /= (a * b);

    // Calculate the dot product of the second pair
    float dot2 = lx * px + ly * py + lz * pz;
    a = ABS(sqrt(px * px + py * py + pz * pz));
    dot2 /= a * b;

    // Return the difference between the vector angles
    return acos(dot2) - acos(dot1);
}

- (BOOL) checkTrigger
{
    if (lx == UNDEFINED_VALUE) return NO;

    // Check to see if the new data can be triggered
    if ([[NSDate date] timeIntervalSinceDate:self.triggerTime]
        < self.lockout) return NO;

    // Get the current angular change
    float change = [self dAngle];

    // If we have not yet gathered two samples, return NO
    if (change == UNDEFINED_VALUE) return NO;

    // Does the dot product exceed the trigger?
    if (change > self.sensitivity)
    {
        self.triggerTime = [NSDate date];
        return YES;
    }
    else return NO;
}

- (void)accelerometer:(UIAccelerometer *)accelerometer
    didAccelerate:(UIAcceleration *)acceleration
{
    // Adapt values for a standard coordinate system
```

```
    [self setX:-[acceleration x]];
    [self setY:[acceleration y]];
    [self setZ:[acceleration z]];

    // All accelerometer events
    if (self.delegate &&
        [self.delegate respondsToSelector:@selector(ping)])
        [self.delegate performSelector:@selector(ping)];

    // All shake events
    if ([self checkTrigger] && self.delegate &&
        [self.delegate respondsToSelector:@selector(shake)])
    {
        [self.delegate performSelector:@selector(shake)];
    }
}

@end
```

Get This Recipe's Code

To get the code used for this recipe, go to http://github.com/erica/iphone-3.0-cookbook-, or if you've downloaded the disk image containing all of the sample code from the book, go to the folder for Chapter 14 and open the project for this recipe.

One More Thing: Checking for Available Disk Space

The `NSFileManager` class allows you to determine both how much space is free on the iPhone, plus how much space is provided on the device as a whole. Listing 14-1 demonstrates how to check for these values and show the results using a friendly comma-formatted string. The values returned represent the free space in bytes.

Listing 14-1 **Recovering File System Size and File System Free Size**

```
- (NSString *) commasForNumber: (long long) num
{
    // Produce a properly formatted number string
    // Alternatively use NSNumberFormatter
    if (num < 1000) return [NSString stringWithFormat:@"%d", num];
    return    [[self commasForNumber:num/1000]
        stringByAppendingFormat:@",%03d", (num % 1000)];
}

- (void) action: (UIBarButtonItem *) bbi
{
    NSFileManager *fm = [NSFileManager defaultManager];
```

```
    NSDictionary *fattributes =
        [fm fileSystemAttributesAtPath:NSHomeDirectory()];
    NSLog(@"System space: %@",
        [self commasForNumber:[[fattributes
        objectForKey:NSFileSystemSize] longLongValue]]);
    NSLog(@"System free space: %@",
        [self commasForNumber:[[fattributes
        objectForKey:NSFileSystemFreeSize] longLongValue]]);
}
```

Summary

This chapter introduced core ways to interact with an iPhone device. You saw how to recover device info, check the battery state, and subscribe to proximity events. You discovered the accelerometer and saw it in use through several examples, from the simple "finding up" to the more complex shake detection algorithm. You learned how to differentiate the iPod touch from the iPhone and determine which model you're working with. Here are a few parting thoughts about the recipes you just encountered:

- The iPhone's accelerometer provides a novel way to complement its touch-based interface. Use acceleration data to expand user interactions beyond the "touch here" basics and to introduce tilt-aware feedback.
- Low-level calls can be SDK friendly. They don't depend on Apple APIs that may change based on the current firmware release. UNIX system calls may seem daunting, but many are fully supported by the iPhone.
- Remember device limitations. You may want to check for free disk space before performing file-intensive work and for battery charge before running the CPU at full steam.
- When submitting to iTunes, remember that 3.0 and later applications no longer specify which device to use. Instead, use your Info.plist file to determine which device capabilities are required. iTunes uses this list of required capabilities to determine whether an application can be downloaded to a given device and run properly on that device.

15

Audio, Video, and MediaKit

The iPhone is a media master; its built-in iPod features expertly handle both audio and video. The iPhone SDK exposes that functionality to developers. A rich suite of classes simplifies media handling via playback, search, and recording. This chapter introduces recipes that use those classes, presenting media to your users and letting your users interact with that media. You see how to build audio and video viewers as well as audio and video recorders. You discover how to browse the iPod library and how to choose what items to play. The recipes you're about to encounter provide step-by-step demonstrations showing how to add these media-rich features to your own apps.

Recipe: Playing Audio with AVAudioPlayer

As its name suggests, the `AVAudioPlayer` class plays back audio data. It provides a simple-to-use class that offers numerous features, several of which are highlighted in Figure 15-1. With this class, you can load audio, play it, pause it, stop it, monitor average and peak levels, adjust the playback volume, and set and detect the current playback time. All these features are available with little associated development cost. As you are about to see, the `AVAudioPlayer` class provides a solid API.

Initializing an Audio Player

The audio playback features provided by `AVAudioPlayer` take little effort to implement in your code. Apple has provided an uncomplicated class that's streamlined for loading and playing files.

To begin, create your player and initialize it, either with data or with the contents of a local URL. This snippet uses a file URL to point to an audio file. It reports any error involved in creating and setting up the player. You can also initialize a player with data that's already stored in memory using `initWithData:error:`. That's handy for when you've already read data into memory (such as during an audio chat) rather than reading from a file stored on the device.

```
self.player = [[AVAudioPlayer alloc] initWithContentsOfURL:
    [NSURL fileURLWithPath:self.path] error:&error];
```

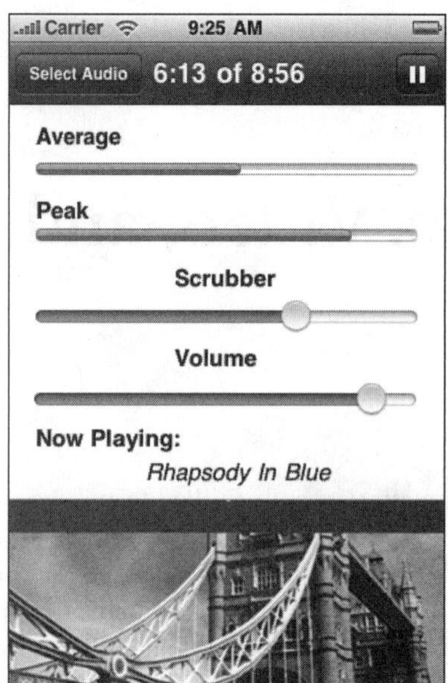

Figure 15-1 The features highlighted in this screenshot were built with a single class, `AVAudioPlayer`. This class provides time monitoring (in the title bar center), sound levels (average and peak), scrubbing and volume sliders, and play/pause control (at the right of the title bar).

```
if (!self.player)
{
      NSLog(@"Error %@", [error localizedDescription]);
      return;
}
```

Once you've initialized the player, prepare it for playback. Calling `prepareToPlay` ensures that when you are ready to `play` the audio, that playback starts as quickly as possible. The call preloads the player's buffers and initializes the audio playback hardware.

```
[self.player prepareToPlay];
```

Pause playback at any time by calling `pause`. Pausing does not affect the player's `currentTime` property. You can resume playback from that point by calling `play` again.

Halt playback entirely with `stop`. Stopping playback undoes the buffered setup you initially established with `prepareToPlay`. It does not, however, set the current time back to 0.0; you can pick up from where you left off by calling `play` again, just as you would with `pause`. You may experience starting delays as the player reloads its buffers.

Monitoring Audio Levels

When you intend to monitor audio levels, start by setting the `meteringEnabled` property. Enabling metering lets you check levels as you play back or record audio.

```
self.player.meteringEnabled = YES;
```

The `AVAudioPlayer` class provides feedback for average and peak power, which you can retrieve on a per-channel basis. Query the player for the number of available channels (via the `numberOfChannels` property) and then request each power level by supplying a channel index. A mono signal uses channel 0, as does the left channel for a stereo recording.

In addition to enabling metering as a whole, you need to call `updateMeters` each time you want to test your levels; this AV player method updates the current meter levels. Once you've done so, use the `peakPowerForChannel:` and `averagePowerForChannel:` methods to read those levels. Recipe 15-7, later in this chapter, shows the details of what's likely going on under the hood in the player when it requests those power levels. You can see that code request the meter levels and then extract either the peak or average power. The `AVAudioPlayer` class hides those details, simplifying access to these values.

The `AVAudioPlayer` measures power in Decibels, which is supplied in floating-point format. Decibels use a logarithmic scale to measure sound intensity. Power values range from 0 dB at the highest to some negative value representing less-than-maximum power. The lower the number (and they are all negative), the weaker the signal will be.

```
int channels = self.player.numberOfChannels;
[self.player updateMeters];
for (int i = 0; i < channels; i++)
{
    // Log the peak and average power
    NSLog(@"%d %0.2f %0.2f",
        [self.player peakPowerForChannel:i],
        [self.player averagePowerForChannel:i];
}
```

To query the audio player gain (i.e., its "volume"), use the `volume` property. This property also returns a floating-point number, here between 0.0 and 1.0, and applies specifically to the player volume rather than the system audio volume. You can set this property as well as read it. This snippet can be used with a target-action pair to update the volume when the user manipulates an onscreen volume slider.

```
- (void) setVolume: (id) sender
{
    // Set the audio player gain to the current slider value
    if (self.player) self.player.volume = volumeSlider.value;
}
```

Playback Progress and Scrubbing

Two properties, `currentTime` and `duration`, monitor the playback progress of your audio. To find the current playback percentage, divide the current time by the total audio duration.

```
progress = self.player.currentTime / self.player.duration;
```

When you want to scrub your audio, that is, let your user select the current playback position within the audio track, make sure to pause playback. The `AVAudioPlayer` class is not built to provide audio-based scrubbing hints. Instead, wait until the scrubbing finishes to begin playback at the new location.

Make sure to implement at least two target-action pairs if you base your scrubber on a standard `UISlider`. For the first target-action item, mask `UIControlEventTouchDown` with `UIControlEventValueChanged`. These event types allow you to catch the start of a user scrub and whenever the value changes. Respond to these events by pausing the audio player and provide some visual feedback for the newly selected time.

```
- (void) scrub: (id) sender
{
    // Pause the player
    [self.player pause];

    // Calculate the new current time
    self.player.currentTime = scrubber.value * self.player.duration;

    // Update the title with the current time
    self.title = [NSString stringWithFormat:@"%@ of %@",
        [self formatTime:self.player.currentTime],
        [self formatTime:self.player.duration]];
}
```

For the second target-action pair, this mask of three values—`UIControlEventTouchUp` ➥`Inside | UIControlEventTouchUpOutside | UIControlEventCancel`—allows you to catch release events and touch interruptions. Upon release, you want to start playing at the new time set by the user's scrubbing.

```
- (void) scrubbingDone: (id) sender
{
    // resume playback here
}
```

Catching the End of Playback

Detect the end of playback by setting the player's delegate and catching the `audioPlayerDidFinishPlaying:successfully:` delegate callback. That method is a great place to clean up any details like reverting the pause button back to a play button. Apple provides several system bar button items specifically for media playback. They are

- `UIBarButtonSystemItemPlay`
- `UIBarButtonSystemItemPause`
- `UIBarButtonSystemItemRewind`
- `UIBarButtonSystemItemFastForward`

The rewind and fast forward buttons provide the double-arrowed icons that are normally used to move playback to a previous or next item in a playback queue. You could also use them to revert to the start of a track or progress to its end. Unfortunately, the Stop system item is an X, used for stopping an ongoing load operation and not the standard filled square used on many consumer devices for stopping playback or a recording.

Recipe 15-1 puts all these pieces together to create the unified interface you saw in Figure 15-1. Here, the user can select audio, start playing it back, pause it, adjust its volume, scrub, and so forth.

The XMAX approach you see here is a bit of a hack. It uses an arbitrary maximum value to estimate the dynamic range of the input levels. Unlike direct Audio Queue calls (that return a float value between 0.0 and 1.0), the decibel levels here have to be approximated to set a progress view value for live feedback. Feel free to adjust the XMAX values to best fit your tests during development.

Recipe 15-1 **Playing Back Audio with AVAudioPlayer**

```
- (void) updateMeters
{
    // Retrieve the meter data and update the on-screen display
    [self.player updateMeters];
    float avg = [self.player averagePowerForChannel:0];
    float peak = [self.player peakPowerForChannel:0];
    meter1.progress = (XMAX + avg) / XMAX;
    meter2.progress = (XMAX + peak) / XMAX;

    // Show current progress and update the scrubber
    self.title = [NSString stringWithFormat:@"%@ of %@",
        [self formatTime:self.player.currentTime],
        [self formatTime:self.player.duration]];
    scrubber.value = (self.player.currentTime / self.player.duration);
}

- (void) pause: (id) sender
{
    // Pause playback, update the play/pause button
    if (self.player) [self.player pause];
    self.navigationItem.rightBarButtonItem =
        SYSBARBUTTON(UIBarButtonSystemItemPlay, self,
        @selector(play));
```

```
    // Disable meters, invalidate the monitor timer
    meter1.progress = 0.0f;
    meter2.progress = 0.0f;
    [timer invalidate];

    // Disable the volume slider
    volumeSlider.enabled = NO;

    // Disable the scrubber
    scrubber.enabled = NO;
}

- (void) play: (id) sender
{
    // Start or resume playback
    if (self.player) [self.player play];

    // Update and enable the volume slider
    volumeSlider.value = self.player.volume;
    volumeSlider.enabled = YES;

    // Update the play/pause button
    self.navigationItem.rightBarButtonItem =
        SYSBARBUTTON(UIBarButtonSystemItemPause, self,
        @selector(pause));

    // Start monitoring the levels
    timer = [NSTimer scheduledTimerWithTimeInterval:0.1f
        target:self selector:@selector(updateMeters)
        userInfo:nil repeats:YES];

    // Enable the scrubber during playback
    scrubber.enabled = YES;
}

- (void) setVolume: (id) sender
{
    // Respond to user changes to the user volume
    if (self.player) self.player.volume = volumeSlider.value;
}

- (void) scrubbingDone: (id) sender
{
    // Start playing at the scrubbed location
    [self play:nil];
}
```

```
- (void) scrub: (id) sender
{
    // Pause the player
    [self.player pause];

    // Calculate the new current time
    self.player.currentTime = scrubber.value * self.player.duration;

    // Update the title, nav bar
    self.title = [NSString stringWithFormat:
        @"%@ of %@", [self formatTime:self.player.currentTime],
        [self formatTime:self.player.duration]];
    self.navigationItem.rightBarButtonItem =
        SYSBARBUTTON(UIBarButtonSystemItemPlay, self,
        @selector(play));
}

- (BOOL) prepAudio
{
    // Check that audio file exists
    NSError *error;
    if (![[NSFileManager defaultManager]
        fileExistsAtPath:self.path]) return NO;

    // Initialize the player
    self.player = [[AVAudioPlayer alloc] initWithContentsOfURL:
        [NSURL fileURLWithPath:self.path] error:&error];
    if (!self.player)
    {
        NSLog(@"Error %@", [error localizedDescription]);
        return NO;
    }

    // Prepare the player, meters, etc
    [self.player prepareToPlay];
    self.player.meteringEnabled = YES;
    meter1.progress = 0.0f;
    meter2.progress = 0.0f;
    self.player.delegate = self;
    scrubber.enabled = NO;

    // Set the play/pause button
    self.navigationItem.rightBarButtonItem =
        SYSBARBUTTON(UIBarButtonSystemItemPlay, self,
        @selector(play));
```

```
    return YES;
}

- (void)audioPlayerDidFinishPlaying:(AVAudioPlayer *)player
successfully:(BOOL)flag
{
    // At the end of play, stop the GUI
    self.navigationItem.rightBarButtonItem = nil;
    scrubber.value = 0.0f;
    scrubber.enabled = NO;
    volumeSlider.enabled = NO;

    // Prepare for a re-play
    [self prepAudio];
}
```

Get This Recipe's Code

To get the code used for this recipe, go to http://github.com/erica/iphone-3.0-cookbook-, or if you've downloaded the disk image containing all of the sample code from the book, go to the folder for Chapter 15 and open the project for this recipe.

Recipe: Looping Audio

Loops help present ambient background audio. You can use a loop to play an audio snippet several times or play it continuously. Recipe 15-2 demonstrates an audio loop that plays only during the presentation of a particular video controller, providing an aural backdrop for that controller.

You set the number of times an audio plays before the playback ends. A high number (like 999999) essentially provides for an unlimited number of loops. For example, a 4-second loop would take more than 1,000 hours to play back fully with a loop number that high.

```
// Prepare the player and set the loops
[self.player prepareToPlay];
[self.player setNumberOfLoops:999999];
```

Recipe 15-2 uses looped audio for its primary view controller. Whenever its view is onscreen the loop plays in the background. Hopefully you choose a loop that's unobtrusive, that sets the mood for your application, and that smoothly transitions from the end of playback to the beginning.

This recipe uses a fading effect to introduce and hide the audio. It fades the loop into hearing when the view appears and fades it out when the view disappears. It accomplishes this with a simple approach. A loop iterates through volume levels, from 0.0 to 1.0 on appearing, and 1.0 down to 0.0 on disappearing. A call to `NSThread`'s built-in sleep functionality adds the time delays (a tenth of a second between each volume change) without affecting the audio playback.

Recipe 15-2 **Creating Ambient Audio Through Looping**

```
@implementation TestBedViewController
@synthesize player;

- (BOOL) prepAudio
{
    // Check for audio file
    NSError *error;
    NSString *path = [[NSBundle mainBundle]
        pathForResource:@"loop" ofType:@"mp3"];
    if (![[NSFileManager defaultManager] fileExistsAtPath:path])
        return NO;

    // Initialize the player
    self.player = [[AVAudioPlayer alloc] initWithContentsOfURL:
        [NSURL fileURLWithPath:path] error:&error];
    if (!self.player)
    {
        NSLog(@"Error %@", [error localizedDescription]);
        return NO;
    }

    // Prepare the player and set the loops to, basically, unlimited
    [self.player prepareToPlay];
    [self.player setNumberOfLoops:999999];

    return YES;
}

- (void) viewDidAppear: (BOOL) animated
{
    // Start playing at no-volume
    self.player.volume = 0.0f;
    [self.player play];

    // Fade in the audio over a second
    for (int i = 1; i <= 10; i++)
    {
        self.player.volume = i / 10.0f;
        [NSThread sleepUntilDate:
            [NSDate dateWithTimeIntervalSinceNow:0.1f]];
    }
```

```
    // Add the push button
    self.navigationItem.rightBarButtonItem =
        BARBUTTON(@"Push", @selector(push));
}

- (void) viewWillDisappear: (BOOL) animated
{
    // Fade out the audio over a second
    for (int i = 9; i >= 0; i--)
    {
        self.player.volume = i / 10.0f;
        [NSThread sleepUntilDate:
            [NSDate dateWithTimeIntervalSinceNow:0.1f]];
    }

    [self.player pause];
}

- (void) push
{
    // Create a simple new view controller
    UIViewController *vc = [[UIViewController alloc] init];
    vc.view.backgroundColor = [UIColor whiteColor];
    vc.title = @"No Sounds";

    // Disable the now-pressed right-button
    self.navigationItem.rightBarButtonItem = nil;

    // push the new view controller
    [self.navigationController
        pushViewController:[vc autorelease] animated:YES];
}

- (void) viewDidLoad
{
    self.navigationItem.rightBarButtonItem =
        BARBUTTON(@"Push", @selector(push));
    self.title = @"Looped Sounds";
    [self prepAudio];
}
@end
```

Get This Recipe's Code

To get the code used for this recipe, go to http://github.com/erica/iphone-3.0-cookbook-, or if you've downloaded the disk image containing all of the sample code from the book, go to the folder for Chapter 15 and open the project for this recipe.

Recipe: Handling Audio Interruptions

When users receive phone calls during audio playback, that audio fades away. The standard answer/decline screen appears. As this happens, `AVAudioPlayer` delegates receive the `audioPlayerBeginInterruption:` callback that is shown in Recipe 15-3. The audio session deactivates, and the player pauses. You cannot restart playback until the interruption ends.

Should the user accept the call, the application terminates, and the application delegate receives an `applicationWillResignActive:` callback. When the call ends, the application relaunches (with an `applicationDidBecomeActive:` callback). If the user declines the call or if the call ends without an answer, the delegate is instead sent `audioPlayerEnd` ➥`Interruption:`. You can resume playback from this method.

If it is vital that playback resumes after accepting a call, and the application needs to relaunch, you can save the current time as shown in Recipe 15-3. The `viewDidLoad` method in this recipe checks for a stored interruption value in the user defaults. When it finds one, it uses this to set the current time for resuming playback.

This approach takes into account the fact that the application relaunches rather than resumes after the call finishes. You do not receive the end interruption callback when the user accepts a call.

Recipe 15-3 **Storing the Interruption Time for Later Pickup**

```
- (void)audioPlayerBeginInterruption:(AVAudioPlayer *)player
{
    // Perform any interruption handling here
    printf("Interruption Detected\n");
    [[NSUserDefaults standardUserDefaults]
        setFloat:[self.player currentTime]
        forKey:@"Interruption"];
}

- (void)audioPlayerEndInterruption:(AVAudioPlayer *)player
{
    // Resume playback at the end of the interruption
    printf("Interruption ended\n");
    [self.player play];

    // Remove the interruption key. It won't be needed
    [[NSUserDefaults standardUserDefaults]
            removeObjectForKey:@"Interruption"];
}

- (void) viewDidLoad
{
    [self prepAudio];
```

```
    // Check for previous interruption
    if ([[NSUserDefaults standardUserDefaults]
        objectForKey:@"Interruption"])
    {
        self.player.currentTime =
            [[NSUserDefaults standardUserDefaults]
            floatForKey:@"Interruption"];
        [[NSUserDefaults standardUserDefaults]
            removeObjectForKey:@"Interruption"];
    }

    // Start playback
    [self.player play];
}
```

> **Get This Recipe's Code**
>
> To get the code used for this recipe, go to http://github.com/erica/iphone-3.0-cookbook-, or if you've downloaded the disk image containing all of the sample code from the book, go to the folder for Chapter 15 and open the project for this recipe.

Recipe: Audio That Ignores Sleep

Locking an iPhone by pressing the sleep/wake button causes an iPhone or iPod to experience the same interruption events that occur with phone calls. When the unit locks, the `AVAudioPlayer` issues an interruption callback. The audio fades away and stops playback. On unlock, the `audioPlayerEndInterruption:` callback triggers and the audio playback continues from where it left off. Try testing Recipe 15-3 by locking and unlocking an iPhone to see this behavior in action.

When you need your audio to continue playing regardless of whether a user locks a phone, respond by updating the current audio session. Audio sessions set the context for an application's audio, providing direct control over the playback hardware.

To keep playing audio, you need to use a session style that doesn't respond to autolock. For example, you might use a play and record session:

```
if (![[AVAudioSession sharedInstance]
    setCategory:AVAudioSessionCategoryPlayAndRecord error:&error])
{
    // Error establishing the play & record session
    NSLog(@"Error %@", [error localizedDescription]);
    return NO;
}
```

Add this snippet to your code before you allocate a new player and sure enough, your audio will ignore lock events. You can tap the sleep/wake button, causing your iPhone screen to go black. The audio will continue to play.

There's a problem though. When you use a play and record session, the iPhone automatically lowers the volume on speaker output. This is by design. Lowering the playback volume avoids feedback loops when a user records audio at the same time as playing audio back. That's great for two-way voice chat but bad news for general playback when you need a full range of audio levels.

Recipe 15-4 presents a workaround that preserves the audio dynamic range while ignoring lock events. It calls a low-level C-language audio session function to set the session category. The "media" playback category it uses is not available as a standard `AVAudioSession` constant. That is why you need this alternative approach. Like play and record, a media session ignores sleep/wake button events and continues playback, but unlike play and record, it provides full volume playback.

When initializing the audio session in this manner, you supply a callback function rather than a method. Recipe 15-4 demonstrates this by implementing `interruption➥ListenerCallback()`, a basic skeleton. Since all interruptions are already caught in the delegate code from Recipe 15-3, this function simply adds a couple of print statements. You may omit those if you want.

When phone calls arrive, the delegate callbacks from Recipe 15-3 handle the interruption and possible relaunch of the application. However, the application never responds to lock/unlock events. You can see this in action by running the sample code and testing for the five primary interruption configurations: call answered, call declined, call ignored, lock, and unlock. By changing the audio session type, those callbacks are no longer generated and the audio remains unaffected by the sleep/wake button.

Recipe 15-4 **Creating Full-Volume Lock-Resistant Audio Playback**

```
void interruptionListenerCallback (void *userData,
    UInt32  interruptionState)
{
    if (interruptionState == kAudioSessionBeginInterruption)
        printf("(ilc) Interruption Detected\n");
    else if (interruptionState == kAudioSessionEndInterruption)
        printf("(ilc) Interruption ended\n");
}

- (BOOL) prepAudio
{
    NSError *error;
    NSString *path = [[NSBundle mainBundle]
        pathForResource:@"MeetMeInSt.Louis1904" ofType:@"mp3"];
    if (![[NSFileManager defaultManager] fileExistsAtPath:path])
        return NO;

    /* Not this: Audio ends up too low!
    if (![[AVAudioSession sharedInstance]
        setCategory:AVAudioSessionCategoryPlayAndRecord error:&error])
```

```
    {
        NSLog(@"Error %@", [error localizedDescription]);
        return NO;
    }
     */


    // Catch interruptions via callback
    AudioSessionInitialize(NULL, NULL,
        interruptionListenerCallback, self);
    AudioSessionSetActive(true);
    UInt32 sessionCategory = kAudioSessionCategory_MediaPlayback;
    AudioSessionSetProperty( kAudioSessionProperty_AudioCategory,
        sizeof(sessionCategory), &sessionCategory);


    // Initialize the player
    self.player = [[AVAudioPlayer alloc] initWithContentsOfURL:
        [NSURL fileURLWithPath:path] error:&error];
    self.player.volume = 1.0f;
    self.player.delegate = self;
    if (!self.player)
    {
        NSLog(@"Error %@", [error localizedDescription]);
        return NO;
    }

    [self.player prepareToPlay];

    return YES;
}
```

Get This Recipe's Code

To get the code used for this recipe, go to http://github.com/erica/iphone-3.0-cookbook-, or if you've downloaded the disk image containing all of the sample code from the book, go to the folder for Chapter 15 and open the project for this recipe.

Recipe: Recording Audio

The `AVAudioRecorder` class simplifies audio recording in your applications. It provides the same API friendliness as `AVAudioPlayer`, along with similar feedback properties. Together, these two classes leverage development for many standard application audio tasks.

Start your recordings by establishing an `AVAudioSession`. Use a play and record session if you intend to switch between recording and playback in the same application. Use a simple record session (via `AVAudioSessionCategoryRecord`) otherwise. Once you have a session, you can check its `inputIsAvailable` property. This property indicates that the current device has access to a microphone.

```
- (BOOL) startAudioSession
{
    // Prepare the audio session
    NSError *error;
    self.session = [AVAudioSession sharedInstance];

    if (![self.session
        setCategory:AVAudioSessionCategoryPlayAndRecord
        error:&error])
    {
        NSLog(@"Error %@", [error localizedDescription]);
        return NO;
    }

    // Activate the session
    if (![self.session setActive:YES error:&error])
    {
        NSLog(@"Error %@", [error localizedDescription]);
        return NO;
    }

    return self.session.inputIsAvailable;
}
```

Recipe 15-5 demonstrates the next step after creating the session. It sets up the recorder and provides methods for pausing, resuming, and stopping the recording.

To start recording, it creates a settings dictionary and populates it with keys and values that describe how the recording should be sampled. This example uses mono Linear PCM sampled 8000 times a second, a fairly low sample rate. Here are a few points about customizing formats. Unfortunately, Apple does not offer a best practice guide for audio settings at this time.

- Set `AVNumberOfChannelsKey` to 1 for mono audio, 2 for stereo.
- Audio formats (`AVFormatIDKey`) that work well on the iPhone include `kAudioFormatLinearPCM` (very large files) and `kAudioFormatAppleIMA4` (compact files).
- Standard `AVSampleRateKey` sampling rates include 8000, 11025, 22050, and 44100.
- For the linear PCM-only bit depth (`AVLinearPCMBitDepthKey`), use either 16 or 32 bits.

The code allocates a new AV and initializes it with both a file URL and the settings dictionary. Once created, this code sets the recorder's delegate and enables metering. Metering for `AVAudioRecorder` instances works like metering for AVAudioPlayer instances, as was demonstrated in Recipe 15-3. You must update the meter before requesting average and peak power levels.

This method uses the same XMAX approach to create an approximate dynamic range for the feedback meters that was shown in Recipe 15-1. Feel free to adjust XMAX to best match the actual dynamic range for your application.

```
- (void) updateMeters
{
    // Show the current power levels
    [self.recorder updateMeters];
    float avg = [self.recorder averagePowerForChannel:0];
    float peak = [self.recorder peakPowerForChannel:0];
    meter1.progress = (XMAX + avg) / XMAX;
    meter2.progress = (XMAX + peak) / XMAX;

    // Update the current recording time
    self.title = [NSString stringWithFormat:@"%
        [self formatTime:self.recorder.currentTime]];
}
```

This code also tracks the recording's `currentTime`. When you pause a recording, the current time stays still until you resume. Basically, the current time indicates the recording duration to date.

When you're ready to proceed with the recording, use `prepareToRecord` and then start the recording with `record`. Issue `pause` to take a break in recording; resume again with another call to `record`. The recording picks up where it left off. To finish a recording, use `stop`. This produces a callback to `audioRecorderDidFinishRecording:successfully:`. That's where you can clean up your interface and finalize any recording details.

Recipe 15-5 **Audio Recording with AVAudioRecorder**

```
- (void) stopRecording
{
    // This causes the didFinishRecording delegate method to fire
    [self.recorder stop];
}

- (void) continueRecording
{
    // Resume from a paused recording
    [self.recorder record];
    self.navigationItem.rightBarButtonItem =
        BARBUTTON(@"Done", @selector(stopRecording));
    self.navigationItem.leftBarButtonItem =
        SYSBARBUTTON(UIBarButtonSystemItemPause, self,
        @selector(pauseRecording));
}
```

```
- (void) pauseRecording
{
    // Pause an ongoing recording
    [self.recorder pause];
    self.navigationItem.leftBarButtonItem =
        BARBUTTON(@"Continue", @selector(continueRecording));
    self.navigationItem.rightBarButtonItem = nil;
}

- (BOOL) record
{
    NSError *error;

    // Recording settings
    NSMutableDictionary *settings = [NSMutableDictionary dictionary];
    [settings setValue:
        [NSNumber numberWithInt:kAudioFormatLinearPCM]
        forKey:AVFormatIDKey];
    [settings setValue:
        [NSNumber numberWithFloat:8000.0]
        forKey:AVSampleRateKey];
    [settings setValue:
        [NSNumber numberWithInt: 1]
        forKey:AVNumberOfChannelsKey]; // mono
    [settings setValue:
        [NSNumber numberWithInt:16]
        forKey:AVLinearPCMBitDepthKey];
    [settings setValue:
        [NSNumber numberWithBool:NO]
        forKey:AVLinearPCMIsBigEndianKey];
    [settings setValue:
        [NSNumber numberWithBool:NO]
        forKey:AVLinearPCMIsFloatKey];

    // File URL
    NSURL *url = [NSURL fileURLWithPath:FILEPATH];

    // Create recorder
    self.recorder = [[AVAudioRecorder alloc]
        initWithURL:url settings:settings error:&error];
    if (!self.recorder)
    {
        NSLog(@"Error %@", [error localizedDescription]);
        return NO;
    }
```

```
    // Initialize degate, metering, etc.
    self.recorder.delegate = self;
    self.recorder.meteringEnabled = YES;
    meter1.progress = 0.0f;
    meter2.progress = 0.0f;
    self.title = @

    if (![self.recorder prepareToRecord])
    {
        NSLog(@"Error Prepare to record failed");
        [ModalAlert say:@"Error while preparing recording"];
        return NO;
    }

    if (![self.recorder record])
    {
        NSLog(@"Error Record failed");
        [ModalAlert say:@"Error while attempting to record audio"];
        return NO;
    }

    // Set a timer to monitor levels, current time
    timer = [NSTimer scheduledTimerWithTimeInterval:0.1f
        target:self selector:@selector(updateMeters)
        userInfo:nil repeats:YES];

    // Update the navigation bar
    self.navigationItem.rightBarButtonItem =
        BARBUTTON(@"Done", @selector(stopRecording));
    self.navigationItem.leftBarButtonItem =
        SYSBARBUTTON(UIBarButtonSystemItemPause, self,
        @selector(pauseRecording));

    return YES;
}
```

Get This Recipe's Code

To get the code used for this recipe, go to http://github.com/erica/iphone-3.0-cookbook-, or if you've downloaded the disk image containing all of the sample code from the book, go to the folder for Chapter 15 and open the project for this recipe.

Recipe: Recording Audio with Audio Queues

In addition to the `AVAudioPlayer` class, Audio Queues can handle recording and playing tasks in your applications. Audio Queues were needed for recording before the `AVAudioRecorder` class debuted. Using queues directly helps demonstrate what's going on under the hood of the `AVAudioRecorder` class.

Recipe 15-6 records audio at the Audio Queue level, providing a taste of the C-style functions and callbacks used. This code is heavily based on Apple sample code and specifically showcases functionality that is hidden behind the `AVAudioRecorder` wrapper.

The settings used in Recipe 15-6's `setupAudioFormat:` method have been tested and work reliably on the iPhone. It's easy, however, to mess up these parameters when trying to customize your audio quality. If you don't have the parameters set up just right, the queue may fail with little feedback. Google provides copious settings examples.

> **Note**
>
> Interested in learning more about other approaches for iPhone audio? iPhone developer Ben Britten has posted a nice introduction to OpenAL audio on the iPhone at http://benbritten.com/blog/2008/11/06/openal-sound-on-the-iphone/. OpenAL offers a multidimensional, positional audio API.

Recipe 15-6 **Recording with Audio Queues: The Recorder.m Implementation**

```
// Write out current packets as the input buffer is filled
static void HandleInputBuffer (void *aqData,
    AudioQueueRef inAQ, AudioQueueBufferRef inBuffer,
    const AudioTimeStamp *inStartTime,
    UInt32 inNumPackets,
    const AudioStreamPacketDescription *inPacketDesc)
{
    RecordState *pAqData = (RecordState *) aqData;

    if (inNumPackets == 0 &&
        pAqData->dataFormat.mBytesPerPacket != 0)
        inNumPackets = inBuffer->mAudioDataByteSize /
            pAqData->dataFormat.mBytesPerPacket;

    if (AudioFileWritePackets(pAqData->audioFile, NO,
        inBuffer->mAudioDataByteSize, inPacketDesc,
        pAqData->currentPacket, &inNumPackets,
        inBuffer->mAudioData) == noErr)
    {
        pAqData->currentPacket += inNumPackets;
        if (pAqData->recording == 0) return;
        AudioQueueEnqueueBuffer (pAqData->queue, inBuffer,
            0, NULL);
    }
}
```

```
@implementation Recorder

// Set up the recording format as low quality mono AIFF
- (void)setupAudioFormat:(AudioStreamBasicDescription*)format
{
    format->mSampleRate = 8000.0;
    format->mFormatID = kAudioFormatLinearPCM;
    format->mFormatFlags = kLinearPCMFormatFlagIsBigEndian |
        kLinearPCMFormatFlagIsSignedInteger |
        kLinearPCMFormatFlagIsPacked;

    format->mChannelsPerFrame = 1; // mono
    format->mBitsPerChannel = 16;
    format->mFramesPerPacket = 1;
    format->mBytesPerPacket = 2;
    format->mBytesPerFrame = 2;
    format->mReserved = 0;
}

// Begin recording
- (BOOL) startRecording: (NSString *) filePath
{
    // Many of these calls mirror the process for AVAudioRecorder

    // Set up the audio format and the url to record to
    [self setupAudioFormat:&recordState.dataFormat];
    CFURLRef fileURL =  CFURLCreateFromFileSystemRepresentation(
        NULL, (const UInt8 *) [filePath UTF8String],
        [filePath length], NO);
    recordState.currentPacket = 0;

    // Initialize the queue with the format choices
    OSStatus status;
    status = AudioQueueNewInput(&recordState.dataFormat,
        HandleInputBuffer, &recordState,
        CFRunLoopGetCurrent(),kCFRunLoopCommonModes, 0,
        &recordState.queue);
    if (status) {
        printf("Could not establish new queue\n");
        return NO;
    }

    // Create the output file
    status = AudioFileCreateWithURL(fileURL,
        kAudioFileAIFFType, &recordState.dataFormat,
        kAudioFileFlags_EraseFile, &recordState.audioFile);
```

```
    if (status)
    {
        printf("Could not create file to record audio\n");
        return NO;
    }

    // Set up the buffers
    DeriveBufferSize(recordState.queue, recordState.dataFormat,
        0.5, &recordState.bufferByteSize);
    for(int i = 0; i < NUM_BUFFERS; i++)
    {
        status = AudioQueueAllocateBuffer(recordState.queue,
            recordState.bufferByteSize, &recordState.buffers[i]);
        if (status) {
            printf("Error allocating buffer %d\n", i);
            return NO;
        }
        status = AudioQueueEnqueueBuffer(recordState.queue,
            recordState.buffers[i], 0, NULL);
        if (status) {
            printf("Error enqueuing buffer %d\n", i);
            return NO;
        }
    }

    // Enable metering
    UInt32 enableMetering = YES;
    status = AudioQueueSetProperty(recordState.queue,
        kAudioQueueProperty_EnableLevelMetering,
        &enableMetering,sizeof(enableMetering));
    if (status)
    {
        printf("Could not enable metering\n");
        return NO;
    }

    // Start the recording
    status = AudioQueueStart(recordState.queue, NULL);
    if (status)
    {
        printf("Could not start Audio Queue\n");
        return NO;
    }

    recordState.currentPacket = 0;
    recordState.recording = YES;
    return YES;
}
```

```
// Return the average power level
- (float) averagePower
{
    AudioQueueLevelMeterState state[1];
    UInt32  statesize = sizeof(state);
    OSStatus status;
    status = AudioQueueGetProperty(recordState.queue,
        kAudioQueueProperty_CurrentLevelMeter, &state, &statesize);
    if (status)
    {
        printf("Error retrieving meter data\n");
        return 0.0f;
    }
    return state[0].mAveragePower;
}

// Return the peak power level
- (float) peakPower
{
    AudioQueueLevelMeterState state[1];
    UInt32  statesize = sizeof(state);
    OSStatus status;
    status = AudioQueueGetProperty(recordState.queue,
        kAudioQueueProperty_CurrentLevelMeter, &state, &statesize);
    if (status)
    {
        printf("Error retrieving meter data\n");
        return 0.0f;
    }
    return state[0].mPeakPower;
}


// There's generally about a one-second delay before the
// buffers fully empty
- (void) reallyStopRecording
{
    AudioQueueFlush(recordState.queue);
    AudioQueueStop(recordState.queue, NO);
    recordState.recording = NO;

    for(int i = 0; i < NUM_BUFFERS; i++)
    {
        AudioQueueFreeBuffer(recordState.queue,
            recordState.buffers[i]);
    }
```

```
    AudioQueueDispose(recordState.queue, YES);
    AudioFileClose(recordState.audioFile);
}

// Stop the recording after waiting just a second
- (void) stopRecording
{
    [self performSelector:@selector(reallyStopRecording)
        withObject:NULL afterDelay:1.0f];
}

// Pause after allowing buffers to catch up
- (void) reallyPauseRecording
{
    if (!recordState.queue) {printf("Nothing to pause\n"); return;}
    OSStatus status = AudioQueuePause(recordState.queue);
    if (status) {printf("Error pausing audio queue\n"); return;}
}

// Pause the recording after waiting a half second
- (void) pause
{
    [self performSelector:@selector(reallyPauseRecording)
        withObject:NULL afterDelay:0.5f];
}

// Resume recording from a paused queue
- (BOOL) resume
{
    if (!recordState.queue)
    {
        printf("Nothing to resume\n");
        return NO;
    }

    OSStatus status = AudioQueueStart(recordState.queue, NULL);
    if (status)
    {
        printf("Error restarting audio queue\n");
        return NO;
    }

    return YES;
}
```

```
// Return the current recording duration
- (float) currentTime
{
    AudioTimeStamp outTimeStamp;
    OSStatus status = AudioQueueGetCurrentTime (
        recordState.queue, NULL, &outTimeStamp, NULL);
    if (status)
    {
        printf("Error: Could not retrieve current time\n");
        return 0.0f;
    }

    // 8000 samples per second
    return outTimeStamp.mSampleTime / 8000.0f;
}

// Return whether the recording is active
- (BOOL) isRecording
{
    return recordState.recording;
}
@end
```

Get This Recipe's Code

To get the code used for this recipe, go to http://github.com/erica/iphone-3.0-cookbook-, or if you've downloaded the disk image containing all of the sample code from the book, go to the folder for Chapter 15 and open the project for this recipe.

Recipe: Playing Video with the Media Player

The `MPMoviePlayerController` class simplifies video display in your applications. This class, which is part of the MediaPlayer framework, plays by its own rules. You do not push it onto a navigation stack. You do not invoke it modally. Instead, you create it and tell it to play. It takes control of the screen, offering the controls shown in Figure 15-2.

To regain control, subscribe your application to the `MPMoviePlayerPlaybackDid➥FinishNotification` notification. This notification is sent under two circumstances: when playback naturally ends, or when the user taps Done. Using the class couldn't be simpler. Allocate a new instance of the `MPMoviePlayer` class, initialize it with a URL, and tell it to `play`. Release the player when the playback ends.

Recipe 15-7 includes two methods. One starts playback; the other cleans up when playback ends. This exact code can be used to play back either video or audio. Just provide a source URL pointing to a supported file type. Supported file types include MOV, MP4, MPV, M4V, and 3GP, as well as MP3, AIFF, and M4A, among others.

This code uses an off-phone resource via an external URL. Be aware that such connections can be slow (and possibly nonexistent) so prepare for possible lags during

Figure 15-2 The full-screen media player interface offers extensive user control over video playback. This is the same video interface used in the iPod and YouTube applications. (This screenshot is from a public domain Betty Boop cartoon, courtesy of the Internet Archive at archive.org.)

playback. Local file URLs (as shown previously in Recipe 15-1) produce more reliable playback for video and audio resources.

Unfortunately, the `MPMoviePlayer` object offers limited API control. If you need to loop a movie, you can restart playback after catching the finish notification, as shown here.

```
-(void)myMovieFinishedCallback:(NSNotification*)aNotification
{
    MPMoviePlayerController* theMovie=[aNotification object];
    [theMovie play];
}
```

This causes a visual hiccup between the time the movie first ends and then starts up again. You want to take this into account, perhaps overlaying your main GUI with a black view. Users may need to tap the play button again. While you can limit user interaction with the movie by setting the player's `movieControlMode` to a no-interaction or volume-only mode, these modes hide the play button from the user.

Note

Recipe 13-7 demonstrated how to fully (and asynchronously) download a file from a remote server before playing back that movie.

Recipe 15-7 **Playing Back Videos Using the MPMoviePlayer**

```
// Offsite resource Betty Boop Cinderella @Archive.org
#define PATHSTRING \
    @"http://www.archive.org/download/bb_poor_cinderella/\
    bb_poor_cinderella_512kb.mp4"
```

```
@interface TestBedViewController : UIViewController
@end

@implementation TestBedViewController
-(void)myMovieFinishedCallback:(NSNotification*)aNotification
{
    // Clean up after the movie finishes
    MPMoviePlayerController* theMovie=[aNotification object];
    [[NSNotificationCenter defaultCenter] removeObserver:self
        name:MPMoviePlayerPlaybackDidFinishNotification
        object:theMovie];
    [theMovie release];
    self.navigationItem.rightBarButtonItem =
        BARBUTTON(@"Play", @selector(play));
    self.title = nil;
}

- (void) play: (UIBarButtonItem *) bbi
{
    // Hide the play button and present the player
    self.navigationItem.rightBarButtonItem = nil;
    self.title = @"Contacting Server";
    MPMoviePlayerController* theMovie=[[MPMoviePlayerController alloc]
        initWithContentURL:[NSURL URLWithString:PATHSTRING]];
    [[NSNotificationCenter defaultCenter] addObserver:self
        selector:@selector(myMovieFinishedCallback)
        name:MPMoviePlayerPlaybackDidFinishNotification
        object:theMovie];
    [theMovie play];
}
```

Get This Recipe's Code

To get the code used for this recipe, go to http://github.com/erica/iphone-3.0-cookbook-, or if you've downloaded the disk image containing all of the sample code from the book, go to the folder for Chapter 15 and open the project for this recipe.

Recipe: Recording Video

Before you can record video, you must detect whether the device supports camera-based video recording. Checking for an onboard camera, such as those in the first generation and 3G iPhones, is not sufficient. Only the 3GS and newer units provide video recording capabilities. Perform two checks: first, that a camera is available, and second, that the available capture types includes video. The following method performs those checks.

```
- (BOOL) videoRecordingAvailable
{
    // The source type must be available
    if (![UIImagePickerController isSourceTypeAvailable:
        UIImagePickerControllerSourceTypeCamera])
    return NO;

    // And the media type must include the movie type
    NSArray *mediaTypes = [UIImagePickerController
        availableMediaTypesForSourceType:
        UIImagePickerControllerSourceTypeCamera]

    return  [mediaTypes containsObject:@"public.movie"];
}
```

Note that this method searches for a `public.movie` media type using a constant string. At some point in the future of the iPhone SDK, you should be able to use the `kUTTypeMovie` constant instead. These types are defined in the MobileCoreServices public framework in UTCoreTypes.h.

As Recipe 15-8 demonstrates, recording video proves to be similar to capturing still images with the onboard camera. You allocate and initialize a new image picker, set its delegate, select whether to allow editing, and present it.

Unlike still image capture, you must set three key properties. First, select a video quality. Recipe 15-8 uses a medium quality, but you can also choose high or low. Second, specify a maximum video duration in seconds. Recipe 15-8 allows the user to record up to 30 seconds of video. (The maximum can range up to 10 minutes using the video image picker.) Finally, set the media type array for the picker to a one-object list using the movie media type. You can include `public.image` to provide the user with the option to switch between still and video capture, as highlighted in Figure 15-3.

By setting the `allowsEditing` property to `YES`, you permit users to use the built-in video editor to trim their clips before saving or otherwise working with that data. Whether you allow editing or not, when the user finishes the video capture, the standard image picker callbacks inform the delegate.

With video, you retrieve a URL instead of the actual data. As Recipe 15-8 demonstrates, you should check whether that video is compatible with the built-in album before attempting to save. If it is, you may save it using the `UISaveVideoAtPath` `➥ToSavedPhotosAlbum()` function. Examples of incompatible clips include MPEG-4 videos downloaded from the Internet Archive (http://archive.org) that you might want to add to your photo album. These files are not album compatible.

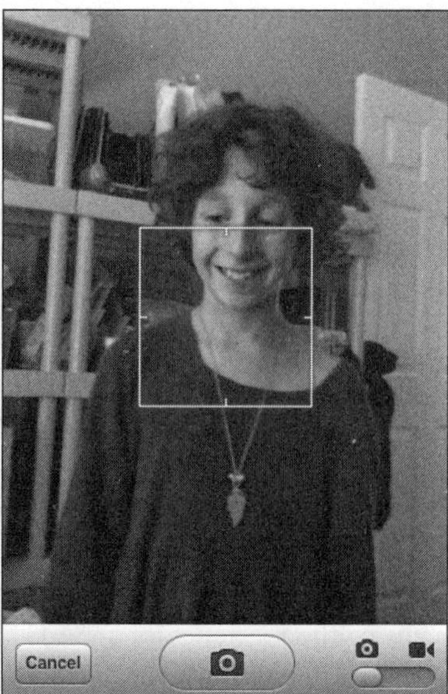

Figure 15-3 Developers may specify one or more media types for the image picker controller. The screenshot on the left demonstrates a video-only capture. The right screenshot shows a picker that supports both image and video capture.

Recipe 15-8 **Using UIImagePickerController to Record Video**

```
- (void)video:(NSString *)videoPath
    didFinishSavingWithError:(NSError *)error
    contextInfo:(void *)contextInfo
{
    // Check for save errors
    if (!error)
        self.title = @"Saved!";
    else
        CFShow([error localizedDescription]);
}

- (void) imagePickerControllerDidCancel:
    (UIImagePickerController *) picker
{
    // User pressed cancel so dismiss the picker
    [self dismissModalViewControllerAnimated:YES];
    [picker release];
}

- (void)imagePickerController:(UIImagePickerController *)picker
    didFinishPickingMediaWithInfo:(NSDictionary *)info
```

```
{
    // Recover video URL
    NSURL *url = [info objectForKey:UIImagePickerControllerMediaURL];

    // Check if video is compatible with album
    BOOL compatible =
        UIVideoAtPathIsCompatibleWithSavedPhotosAlbum([url path]);

    // Save
    if (compatible)
        UISaveVideoAtPathToSavedPhotosAlbum([url path], self,
            @selector(videodidFinishSavingWithError:contextInfo:),
            NULL);

    [self dismissModalViewControllerAnimated:YES];
    [picker release];
}

- (void) recordVideo: (id) sender
{
   // Present the video recorder
    UIImagePickerController *ipc =
        [[UIImagePickerController alloc] init];
    ipc.sourceType =  UIImagePickerControllerSourceTypeCamera;
    ipc.delegate = self;
    ipc.allowsEditing = YES;
    ipc.videoQuality = UIImagePickerControllerQualityTypeMedium;
    ipc.videoMaximumDuration = 30.0f; // 30 seconds
    ipc.mediaTypes = [NSArray arrayWithObject:@"public.movie"];
    [self presentModalViewController:ipc animated:YES];
}
```

Get This Recipe's Code

To get the code used for this recipe, go to http://github.com/erica/iphone-3.0-cookbook-, or if you've downloaded the disk image containing all of the sample code from the book, go to the folder for Chapter 15 and open the project for this recipe.

Recipe: Picking and Editing Video

The `mediaTypes` property used in Recipe 15-8 affects media selection as well as media capture. To request a picker that presents video assets only, create a photo library picker and use a media array that consists of a single `public.movie` string. The following method creates a video-only picker.

```
- (void) pickVideo: (id) sender
{
    // Present a video-only picker
    UIImagePickerController *ipc =
        [[UIImagePickerController alloc] init];
```

```
    ipc.sourceType =  UIImagePickerControllerSourceTypePhotoLibrary;
    ipc.delegate = self;
    ipc.allowsEditing = NO;
    ipc.videoQuality = UIImagePickerControllerQualityTypeMedium;
    ipc.videoMaximumDuration = 30.0f; // 30 seconds
    ipc.mediaTypes = [NSArray arrayWithObject:@"public.movie"];
    [self presentModalViewController:ipc animated:YES];
}
```

To edit an already-existing video, start by checking that the video asset can be modified as shown in Recipe 15-9. Call the `UIVideoEditorController` class method `canEditVideoAtPath:`. This returns a Boolean value that indicates whether the video is compatible with the editor controller.

If it is, you can allocate a new editor, set its `delegate` and `videoPath` properties, and present it. The editor uses a set of delegate callbacks that are similar to but not identical to the ones used by the `UIImagePickerController` class. Callbacks include methods for success, failure, and user cancellation.

When a user has finished editing the video, the controller saves that video to a temporary path and calls `videoEditorController:didSaveEditedVideoToPath:`. That path resides in the application sandbox's tmp folder. If you do nothing with the data, it will be deleted the next time the iPhone reboots. You can, however, save that data either locally into the sandbox's Documents folder or into the shared iPhone photo album. To do so, follow the example shown in Recipe 15-8. Regardless of which callback is sent, it's up to you to dismiss the editor and release it.

Recipe 15-9 **Using the Video Editor Controller**

```
- (void)videoEditorController:(UIVideoEditorController *)editor
    didSaveEditedVideoToPath:(NSString *)editedVideoPath
{
    CFShow(editedVideoPath);

    // Can do save here. The data has *not* yet
    // been saved to the photo album

    [self dismissModalViewControllerAnimated:YES];
    [editor release];
}

- (void)videoEditorControllerDidCancel:
    (UIVideoEditorController *)editor
{
    // Hide the picker as the user has canceled
    [self dismissModalViewControllerAnimated:YES];
    [editor release];
}

- (void)videoEditorController:(UIVideoEditorController *)editor
```

```
    didFailWithError:(NSError *)error
{
    // Respond to an editor failure
    [self dismissModalViewControllerAnimated:YES];
    [editor release];

    NSLog(@"Fail! %@", [error localizedDescription]);
}

- (void) doEdit
{
    // Make sure that editing is possible
    if (![UIVideoEditorController canEditVideoAtPath:self.vpath])
    {
        self.title = @"Cannot Edit Video";
        printf("Cannot edit vid at path\n");
        return;
    }

    // If so, present the editor
    UIVideoEditorController *vec =
        [[UIVideoEditorController alloc] init];
    vec.videoPath = self.vpath;
    vec.delegate = self;
    [self presentModalViewController:vec animated:YES];
}
```

Get This Recipe's Code

To get the code used for this recipe, go to http://github.com/erica/iphone-3.0-cookbook-, or if you've downloaded the disk image containing all of the sample code from the book, go to the folder for Chapter 15 and open the project for this recipe.

Recipe: Picking Audio with the MPMediaPickerController

The `MPMediaPickerController` class provides an audio equivalent for the image-picking facilities of the `UIImagePickerController` class. It allows users to choose an item or items from their music library including music, podcasts, and audio books. The standard iPod-style interface allows users to browse via playlists, artists, songs, albums, and more.

To use this class, allocate a new picker and initialize it with the kinds of media to be used. You can choose from `MPMediaTypeMusic`, `MPMediaTypePodcast`, `MPMediaTypeAudioBook`, `MPMediaTypeAnyAudio`, and `MPMediaTypeAny`. These are flags and can be or'ed together to form a mask.

```
MPMediaPickerController *mpc = [[MPMediaPickerController alloc]
    initWithMediaTypes:MPMediaTypeAny];
mpc.delegate = self;
```

```
mpc.prompt = @"Please select an item";
mpc.allowsPickingMultipleItems = NO;
[self presentModalViewController:mpc animated:YES];
```

Next, set a delegate and optionally set a prompt. The prompt is text that appears at the top of the media picker, as shown in Figure 15-4. When you choose to allow multiple item selection, the Cancel button on the standard picker is replaced by the label Done. Normally, the dialog ends when a user taps a track. With multiple selection, users can keep picking items until they press the Done button. Selected items are updated to use gray labels.

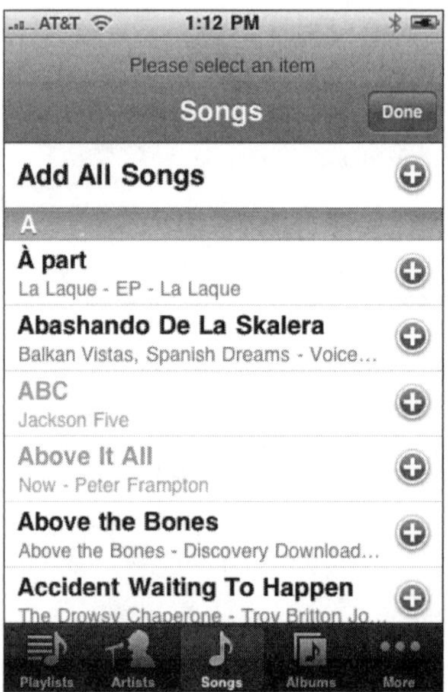

Figure 15-4 In this multiple selection media picker, already selected items appear in gray (see ABC and Above It All). Users tap Done when finished. In the normal selection picker, the Done button is replaced by Cancel, allowing users to leave without selecting an item. An optional prompt field (here, Please Select an Item) appears above the normal picker elements.

The `mediaPicker:didPickMediaItems:` delegate callback handles the completion of a user selection. The `MPMediaItemCollection` instance that is passed as a parameter can be enumerated by accessing its `items`. Each item is a member of the `MPMediaItem` class and can be queried for its properties, as shown in Recipe 15-10. Recipe 15-10 uses a media picker to select multiple music tracks. It logs the items the user selected by artist and title.

Table 15-1 lists the available properties for media items, the type they return and whether they can be used to construct a media property predicate. Building queries and using predicates is discussed in Recipe 15-11.

Table 15-1 **Media Item Properties**

Properties	Type	Filterable
General Media Item		
`MPMediaItemPropertyPersistentID`	`uint64_t`	Yes
`MPMediaItemPropertyMediaType`	`NSNumber` `Integer`	Yes
`MPMediaItemPropertyTitle`	`NSString`	Yes
`MPMediaItemPropertyAlbumTitle`	`NSString`	Yes
`MPMediaItemPropertyArtist`	`NSString`	Yes
`MPMediaItemPropertyAlbumArtist`	`NSString`	Yes
`MPMediaItemPropertyGenre`	`NSString`	Yes
`MPMediaItemPropertyComposer`	`NSString`	Yes
`MPMediaItemPropertyPlayback` `Duration`	`NSNumber` `NSTimeInterval`	
`MPMediaItemPropertyAlbumTrack` `Number`	`NSNumber` `Integer`	
`MPMediaItemPropertyAlbumTrackCount`	`NSNumber` `Integer`	
`MPMediaItemPropertyDiscNumber`	`NSNumber` `integer`	
`MPMediaItemPropertyDiscCount`	`NSNumber` `integer`	
`MPMediaItemPropertyArtwork`	`MPMediaItemArtwork`	
`MPMediaItemPropertyLyrics`	`NSString`	
`MPMediaItemPropertyIsCompilation`	`NSNumber` `Boolean`	Yes
Podcast Item		
`MPMediaItemPropertyPodcastTitle`	`NSString`	
User Defined		
`MPMediaItemPropertyPlayCount`	NSNumber `Integer`	
`MPMediaItemPropertySkipCount`	`NSNumber` `Integer`	

Table 15-1 **Continued**

Properties	Type	Filterable
MPMediaItemPropertyRating	NSNumber Integer between 0 and 5	
MPMediaItemPropertyLastPlayedDate	NSDate	

Recipe 15-10 **Selecting Music Items from the iPod Library**

```
@implementation TestBedViewController
- (void)mediaPicker: (MPMediaPickerController *)mediaPicker
    didPickMediaItems:(MPMediaItemCollection *)mediaItemCollection
{
    // Show the selected items
    for (MPMediaItem *item in [mediaItemCollection items])
        NSLog(@"[%@] %@",
            [item valueForProperty:MPMediaItemPropertyArtist],
            [item valueForProperty:MPMediaItemPropertyTitle]);

    [self dismissModalViewControllerAnimated:YES];
    [mediaPicker release];
}

- (void)mediaPickerDidCancel:(MPMediaPickerController *)mediaPicker
{
    // Respond to user cancel
    [self dismissModalViewControllerAnimated:YES];
    [mediaPicker release];
}

- (void) action: (UIBarButtonItem *) bbi
{
    // Present the picker, allowing multiple selections
    MPMediaPickerController *mpc = [[MPMediaPickerController alloc]
        initWithMediaTypes:MPMediaTypeMusic];
    mpc.delegate = self;
    mpc.prompt = @"Please select an item";
    mpc.allowsPickingMultipleItems = YES;
    [self presentModalViewController:mpc animated:YES];
}

- (void) viewDidLoad
{
    self.navigationItem.rightBarButtonItem =
```

```
        BARBUTTON(@"Action", @selector(action));
}
@end
```

Get This Recipe's Code

To get the code used for this recipe, go to http://github.com/erica/iphone-3.0-cookbook-, or if you've downloaded the disk image containing all of the sample code from the book, go to the folder for Chapter 15 and open the project for this recipe.

Creating a Media Query

Media Queries allow you to filter your iPod library contents, limiting the scope of your search. Table 15-2 lists the nine class methods that **MPMediaQuery** provides for predefined searches. Each query type controls the grouping of the data returned. Each collection is organized as tracks by album, or by artist, or by audio book, and so on.

Table 15-2 **Query Types**

Class Method	Global?	Filter	Group Type
albumsQuery	No	MPMediaTypeMusic	MPMediaGrouping ➥Album
artistsQuery	No	MPMediaTypeMusic	MPMediaGrouping ➥Artist
audiobooksQuery	No	MPMediaTypeAudioBook	MPMediaGrouping ➥Title
compilations ➥Query	No	MPMediaTypeAny | MPMediaItemPropertyIs ➥Compilation	MPMediaGroupingAlbum
composersQuery	Yes	MPMediaTypeAny	MPMediaGrouping ➥Composer
genresQuery	Yes	MPMediaTypeAny	MPMediaGroupingGenre
playlistsQuery	Yes	MPMediaTypeAny	MPMediaGrouping ➥Playlist
podcastsQuery	No	MPMediaTypePodcast	MPMediaGrouping ➥PodcastTitle
songsQuery	No	MPMediaTypeMusic	MPMediaGroupingTitle

This approach reflects the way that iTunes works on the desktop. In iTunes, you select a column to organize your results, but you search by entering text into the application's Search field.

Building a Query

Count the number of albums in your library using an album query. This snippet creates that query and then retrieves an array, each item of which represents a single album. These album items are collections of individual media items. A collection may contain a single track or many.

```
MPMediaQuery *query = [MPMediaQuery albumsQuery];
NSArray *collections = query.collections;
NSLog(@"You have %d albums in your library\n", collections.count);
```

Many iPhone users have extensive media collections often containing hundreds or thousands of albums, let alone individual tracks. A simple query like this one may take several seconds to run and return a data structure that represents the entire library.

A search using a different query type allows returns collections organized by that type. You can use a similar approach to recover the number of artists, songs, composers, and so on.

Using Predicates

A media property predicate efficiently filters the items returned by a query. For example, you might want to find only those songs whose title matches the phrase "road." The following snippet creates a new songs query and adds a filter predicate to search for that phrase. The predicate is constructed with a value (the search phrase), a property (searching the song title), and a comparison type (in this case "contains"). Use `MPMediaPredicate➥ComparisonEqualTo` for exact matches and `MPMediaPredicateComparisonContains` for substring matching.

```
MPMediaQuery *query = [MPMediaQuery songsQuery];

// Construct a title comparison predicate
MPMediaPropertyPredicate *mpp = [MPMediaPropertyPredicate
    predicateWithValue:@"road"
    forProperty:MPMediaItemPropertyTitle
    comparisonType:MPMediaPredicateComparisonContains];
[query addFilterPredicate:mpp];

// Recover the collections
NSArray *collections = query.collections;
NSLog(@"You have %d matching tracks in your library\n",
    collections.count);
```

```
// Iterate through each item, logging the song and artist
for (MPMediaItemCollection *collection in collections)
{
      for (MPMediaItem *item in [collection items])
      {
            NSString *song = [item valueForProperty:
                MPMediaItemPropertyTitle];
            NSString *artist = [item valueForProperty:
                MPMediaItemPropertyArtist];
            NSLog(@"%@, %@", song, artist);
      }
}
```

Note

If you'd rather use regular predicates with your media collections than media property predicates, I have created an MPMediaItem properties category (http://github.com/erica/MPMediaItem-Properties). This category allows you to apply standard NSPredicate queries against collections, such as those returned by a multiple-item selection picker.

Handling Speed Issues

The preceding snippet runs slowly. Recovering property values takes far more time than you might expect, up to a second each on a large library on a modern iPhone 3GS or third generation iPod touch, the fastest available iPhone devices at the time this book was written. There's no apparent reason for why a property query should take much time at all or why these property retrievals might be choked or affected by library size.

Delays make it hard to use these kinds of queries to provide a data source for a table view. Recipe 15-11 shows this problem in action. It builds a list of song titles from a user search. Even using a cache to avoid recovering already-used cell titles, the recipe demonstrates that creating your own pickers is impractical for now due to speed issues.

Unless Apple greatly speeds up data recovery, you're better off using the built-in `MPMediaPickerController` class to retrieve individual `MPMediaItems`.

Recipe 15-11 **Demonstrating the Choke Time for Media Queries**

```
- (void)searchBarSearchButtonClicked: (UISearchBar *) searchBar
{
    // Hide keyboard
    [searchBar resignFirstResponder];

    // Reset the title cache
    self.titleCache = [NSMutableDictionary dictionary];

    // Create a new query
    MPMediaQuery *query = [MPMediaQuery songsQuery];
    MPMediaPropertyPredicate *mpp = [MPMediaPropertyPredicate
        predicateWithValue:searchBar.text
```

```
        forProperty:MPMediaItemPropertyTitle
        comparisonType:MPMediaPredicateComparisonContains];
    [query addFilterPredicate:mpp];

    // Retrieve the results and reload the table data
    self.songCollections = query.collections;
    [self.tableView reloadData];
}

- (NSInteger)numberOfSectionsInTableView:(UITableView *)aTableView
{
    // Combine all data into a single section
    return 1;
}

- (NSInteger)tableView:(UITableView *)aTableView
    numberOfRowsInSection:(NSInteger)section
{
    // The number of rows is set by the matching collections
    return [self.songCollections count];
}

- (UITableViewCell *)tableView:(UITableView *)tView
    cellForRowAtIndexPath:(NSIndexPath *)indexPath
{
    // To give a sense of the timing
    printf("Retrieving cell %d\n", indexPath.row);

    UITableViewCellStyle style =  UITableViewCellStyleDefault;
    UITableViewCell *cell = [tView
        dequeueReusableCellWithIdentifier:@"BaseCell"];
    if (!cell) cell = [[[UITableViewCell alloc] initWithStyle:style
        reuseIdentifier:@"BaseCell"] autorelease];

    // Retrieve the item
    MPMediaItem *item = [[[self.songCollections
        objectAtIndex:indexPath.row] items] lastObject];
    NSString *label = [item valueForProperty:MPMediaItemPropertyTitle];
    cell.textLabel.text = label;
    return cell;
}

- (void) viewDidLoad
{
    self.navigationController.navigationBar.tintColor =
        COOKBOOK_PURPLE_COLOR;
```

```
    // Set up the search bar
    UISearchBar *sb = [[[UISearchBar alloc]
        initWithFrame:CGRectMake(0.0f, 0.0f, 320.0f, 44.0f)]
        autorelease];
    sb.autocapitalizationType = UITextAutocapitalizationTypeNone;
    sb.autocorrectionType = UITextAutocorrectionTypeNo;
    sb.backgroundColor = [UIColor clearColor];
    sb.tintColor = COOKBOOK_PURPLE_COLOR;
    self.navigationItem.titleView = sb;
    sb.delegate = self;

    self.titleCache = [NSMutableDictionary dictionary];
}
```

Get This Recipe's Code

To get the code used for this recipe, go to http://github.com/erica/iphone-3.0-cookbook-, or if you've downloaded the disk image containing all of the sample code from the book, go to the folder for Chapter 15 and open the project for this recipe.

Recipe: Using the MPMusicPlayerController

Cocoa Touch includes a simple-to-use music player class that works seamlessly with media collections. Despite what its name implies, the `MPMusicPlayerController` class is not a view controller. It provides no onscreen elements for playing back music. Instead, it offers an abstract controller that handles playing and pausing music.

It publishes optional notifications when its playback state changes. The class offers two shared instances, the `iPodMusicPlayer` and an `applicationMusicPlayer`. Always use the former. It provides reliable state change feedback, which you will want to catch programmatically.

Initialize the player controller by calling `setQueueWithItemCollection:` with an `MPMediaItemCollection`.

```
[[MPMusicPlayerController iPodMusicPlayer]
    setQueueWithItemCollection:self.songs];
```

Alternatively, you can load a queue with a media query. For example, you might set a `playlistsQuery` matching a specific playlist phrase, or an artist query to search for songs by a given artist. Use `setQueueWithQuery:` to generate a queue from an `MPMediaQuery` instance.

If you want to shuffle playback, assign a value to the controller's `shuffleMode` property. Choose from `MPMusicShuffleModeDefault`, which respects the user's current setting, `MPMusicShuffleModeOff` (no shuffle), `MPMusicShuffleModeSongs` (song-by-song shuffle), and `MPMusicShuffleModeAlbums` (album-by-album shuffle). A similar set of options exists for the music's `repeatMode`.

Once you set the item collection, you can play, pause, skip to the next item in the queue, go back to a previous item, and so forth. To rewind without moving back to a previous item, issue `skipToBeginning`. You can also seek within the currently playing item, moving the playback point forward or backward.

Recipe 15-12 offers a simple media player that shows the currently playing song (along with its artwork, if available). When run, the user selects a group of items using an `MPMediaPickerController`. This item collection is returned and assigned to the player, which begins playing back the group.

A pair of observers use the default notification center to watch for two key changes: when the current item changes and when the playback state changes. To catch these changes, you must manually request notifications. This allows you to update the interface with new "now playing" information when the playback item changes.

```
[[MPMusicPlayerController iPodMusicPlayer]
    beginGeneratingPlaybackNotifications];
```

You may undo this request by issuing `endGeneratingPlaybackNotifications`, or you can simply allow the program to tear down all observers when the application naturally terminates. Please note that because this recipe uses iPod music player, playback continues after leaving the application unless you specifically stop it. Playback is not affected by the application teardown.

```
- (void) applicationWillTerminate: (UIApplication *) application
{
    // Stop player when the application quits
    [[MPMusicPlayerController iPodMusicPlayer] stop];
}
```

In addition to demonstrating playback control, Recipe 15-12 shows how to display album art during playback. It uses the same kind of `MPItem` property retrieval used in previous recipes. In this case, it queries for `MPMediaItemPropertyArtwork`, and if artwork is found it uses the `MPMediaItemArtwork` class to convert that artwork to an image of a given size.

Recipe 15-12 **Simple Media Playback with the iPod Music Player**

```
#define PLAYER [MPMusicPlayerController iPodMusicPlayer]

#pragma mark PLAYBACK
- (void) pause
{
    // Pause playback
    [PLAYER pause];
    toolbar.items = [self playItems];
}

- (void) play
{
    // Restart play
    [PLAYER play];
    toolbar.items = [self pauseItems];
}
```

```
- (void) fastforward
{
    // Skip to the next item
    [PLAYER skipToNextItem];
}

- (void) rewind
{
    // Skip to the previous item
    [PLAYER skipToPreviousItem];
}


#pragma mark STATE CHANGES
- (void) playbackItemChanged: (NSNotification *) notification
{
    // Update title and artwork
    self.title = [PLAYER.nowPlayingItem
        valueForProperty:MPMediaItemPropertyTitle];
    MPMediaItemArtwork *artwork = [PLAYER.nowPlayingItem
        valueForProperty: MPMediaItemPropertyArtwork];
    imageView.image = [artwork imageWithSize:[imageView frame].size];
}

- (void) playbackStateChanged: (NSNotification *) notification
{
    // On stop, clear title, toolbar, artwork
    if (PLAYER.playbackState == MPMusicPlaybackStateStopped)
    {
        self.title = nil;
        toolbar.items = nil;
        imageView.image = nil;
    }
}

#pragma mark MEDIA PICKING
- (void)mediaPicker: (MPMediaPickerController *)mediaPicker
    didPickMediaItems:(MPMediaItemCollection *)mediaItemCollection
{
    // Set the songs to the collection selected by the user
    self.songs = mediaItemCollection;

    // Update the playback queue
    [PLAYER setQueueWithItemCollection:self.songs];
```

```
    // Display the play items in the toolbar
    [toolbar setItems:[self playItems]];

    // Clean up the picker
    [self dismissModalViewControllerAnimated:YES];
    [mediaPicker release];
}

- (void)mediaPickerDidCancel:(MPMediaPickerController *)mediaPicker
{
    // User has canceled
    [self dismissModalViewControllerAnimated:YES];
    [mediaPicker release];
}

- (void) pick: (UIBarButtonItem *) bbi
{
    // Select the songs for the playback queue
    MPMediaPickerController *mpc = [[MPMediaPickerController alloc]
        initWithMediaTypes:MPMediaTypeMusic];
    mpc.delegate = self;
    mpc.prompt = @"Please select items to play";
    mpc.allowsPickingMultipleItems = YES;

    [self presentModalViewController:mpc animated:YES];
}


#pragma mark INIT VIEW
- (void) viewDidLoad
{
    self.navigationItem.rightBarButtonItem = BARBUTTON(@"Pick",
        @selector(pick));
    toolbar.tintColor = COOKBOOK_PURPLE_COLOR;

    // Stop any ongoing music
    [PLAYER stop];

    // Add observers for state and item changes
    [[NSNotificationCenter defaultCenter] addObserver:self
        selector:@selector(playbackStateChanged)
        name:MPMusicPlayerControllerPlaybackStateDidChangeNotification
        object:PLAYER];
    [[NSNotificationCenter defaultCenter] addObserver:self
        selector:@selector(playbackItemChanged)
        name:MPMusicPlayerControllerNowPlayingItemDidChangeNotification
        object:PLAYER];
```

```
    [PLAYER beginGeneratingPlaybackNotifications];
}
@end
```

> **Get This Recipe's Code**
>
> To get the code used for this recipe, go to http://github.com/erica/iphone-3.0-cookbook-, or if you've downloaded the disk image containing all of the sample code from the book, go to the folder for Chapter 15 and open the project for this recipe.

One More Thing: Additional Movie Player Properties

The `MPMoviePlayerController` class that was introduced in this chapter offers a few helpful properties not covered in earlier recipes. These properties help control the way the player is presented onscreen.

The player's `backgroundColor` controls the tinting of the backsplash that lies behind the movie. Normally the player appears in black, and the movie fades in when it finishes preloading. To connect the video more closely to your normal interface, you can set this property to `[UIColor clearColor]`. Your interface will bleed through behind the player.

Another property is the movie player's `scalingMode`, which sets how the video fits within the player's frame. By default, the player attempts to fit the video onscreen to fill at least one dimension without cropping the other. This corresponds to the `MPMovieScaling➥ModeAspectFit` constant. The two other options for scaling (in addition to none, which provides no scaling) are aspect fill and normal fill. Aspect fill (`MPMovieScaling➥ModeAspectFill`) fills the entire screen, while retaining the aspect ratio, clipping off portions that fall outside the display. Normal fill (`MPMovieScalingModeFill`) discards the aspect ratio and scales the horizontal and vertical axes independently.

When you want to control the point at which playback begins, set the `initialPlayback➥Time` property. Taking an `NSTimeInterval`, this property offsets the start of the movie playback to a point that you specify. Unfortunately, you cannot directly query the player for the current time to store a pickup point for a later playback session. Hopefully Apple will address that in future SDK releases.

Summary

This chapter introduced many ways to handle audio and video media, including playback and recording. You saw recipes that worked with high-level Objective-C classes, and those that worked with lower-level C functions. You discovered local and remote data sources and read about media pickers, controllers, and more. Here are a few thoughts to take away from this chapter:

- Apple is still in the process of building its AV media playback classes. Although many of those classes seem to be preliminary or bare bones at this time, expect these to grow as subsequent firmware debuts. The `AVAudioPlayer` did not debut until the 2.2 firmware; the `AVAudioRecorder` debuted even later. Media playback and control remains a work in progress.

- When you plan to work with video, be aware of bandwidth limitations. Local phone carriers may not appreciate you burdening their networks with excessive data transfer, and that burden may affect your ability to place your application in App Store.
- Audio Queue provides powerful low-level audio routines, but they're not for the faint of heart or for anyone who just wants a quick solution. If you need the kind of fine-grained audio control that Audio Queues bring, Apple supplies extensive documentation on achieving your goals.
- The `MPMusicPlayerController` provides a really simple way to interact with music from your onboard iTunes library. There is no way that I know of to access music data directly, so be sure to master both `AVAudioPlayer` use for local data files as well as `MPMusicPlayerController` for iTunes.

16

Push Notifications

When developers need to communicate directly with users, push notifications provide the solution. They deliver messages directly to the iPhone screen via a special Apple service. Push notifications let the iPhone display an alert, play a custom sound, or update an application badge. In this way, off-phone services connect with an iPhone-based client, letting them know about new data or updates. Unlike most other iPhone development arenas, nearly all the push story takes place off the phone. Developers must create Web-based services to manage and deploy these updates. In this chapter, you learn how push notifications work and dive into the details needed to create your own push-based system.

Introducing Push Notifications

Push notifications, also called *remote notifications*, refer to a kind of message sent to iPhones by an outside service. These push-based services work with any kind of application that normally checks for information updates. For example, a service might poll for new direct messages on Twitter or respond to sensors for in-home security systems. When new information becomes available for a client, the service pushes that update through Apple's remote notification system. The notification transmits directly to the phone, which has registered to receive those updates.

The key to push is that these messages originate from outside the device itself. They are part of a client-server paradigm that lets Web-based server components communicate with iPhone clients through an Apple-supplied service. With push, developers can send nearly instant updates to iPhones that don't rely on users launching a particular application. Instead, processing occurs on the server side of things. When push messages arrive, the iPhone client can respond by displaying a badge, playing a sound, and/or showing an alert box.

According to Apple, battery life is the single biggest reason for endorsing push notification. When many applications run at once via background processes, these processes can put an undue burden on a device battery, shortening the amount of time available before a recharge is needed. With push, applications can learn about new updates even when they're not running. This lets Apple enforce its strict one-third-party-application-at-a-time policy while at the same time allowing users to receive notifications that are tied to application state changes.

Moving application logic to a server also limits the client-side complexity. Offsite processing provides energy savings for iPhone-based applications. They can now rely on push rather than using the iPhone's local CPU resources to monitor and react to important information changes.

Push's reason for being is not only tied into local resources. It also offers a valuable solution for communicating with Web-based services that goes beyond poll-and-update applications. For example, push might allow you to hook into a recommendation service that produces restaurant suggestions even when an application isn't running or to a calendar service that sends you reminder notices about an upcoming appointment. So don't think about push solely as a battery saver. Also think about it as a conduit for Web services as well.

From social networking to monitoring RSS feeds, push lets iPhone users keep on top of asynchronous data feeds. It offers a powerful solution for connecting iPhone clients to Web-based systems of all kinds. With push, the services you write can connect to your installed iPhone base and communicate updates in a clean, functional manner.

How Push Works

Push notifications aren't just a general way to talk directly to iPhones at will. They are tied to specific applications and require several security checks. A push server can only communicate with those iPhones that are running its application, that are online, and that have opted to receive remote messages. Users have the ultimate say in push updates. They can allow or disallow that kind of communication, and a well-written application lets users opt-in and opt-out of the service at will.

The chain of communication between server and client works like this. Push providers deliver message requests through a central Apple server and via that server to their iPhone clients. In normal use, the server triggers on some event (like new mail or an upcoming appointment) and generates notification data aimed at a specific iPhone device. It sends this message request to the Apple Push Notification Service (APNS). This notification uses JSON formatting and is limited to 256 bytes each, so the information that can be pushed through on that message is quite limited. This formatting and size ensures that APNS limits bandwidth to the tightest possible configuration.

APNS offers a centralized system that negotiates communication with iPhones in the real world. It passes the message through to the designated iPhone. A handler on the iPhone decides how to process the message. As Figure 16-1 shows, push providers talk to APNS, sending their message requests, and APNS talks to phones, relaying those messages to handlers on the unit.

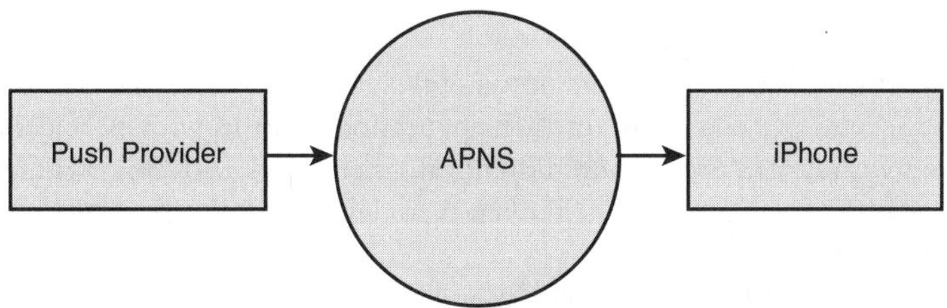

Figure 16-1 Providers send messages through Apple's centralized push notification service to communicate with an iPhone.

Multiple Provider Support

APNS was built to support multiple provider connections, allowing many services to communicate with it at once. It offers multiple gateways into the service so that each push service does not have to wait for availability before sending its message. Figure 16-2 illustrates the many-to-many relationship between providers and iPhones. APNS allows providers to connect at once through multiple gateways. Each provider can push messages to many different iPhones.

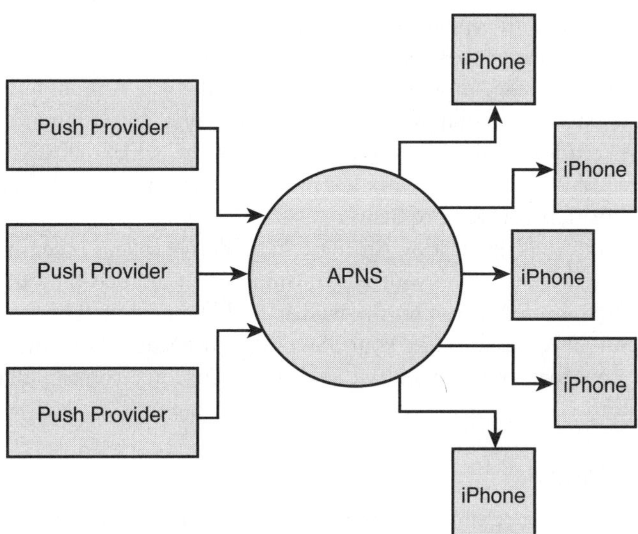

Figure 16-2 Apple's Push Notification Service offers many gateways on its provider-facing side, allowing multiple providers to connect in parallel. Each push provider may connect to any number of iPhone devices.

Security

Security is a primary component of remote notifications. The push provider must sign up for a secure sockets layer certificate for each application it works with. Services cannot communicate with APNS unless they authenticate themselves with this certificate. They must also provide a unique key called a token that identifies both the phone to message and the application to notify.

After receiving an authenticated message and device token, APNS contacts the phone in question. Each iPhone or member of the iPhone family such as the iPod touch must be online in some way to receive a notification. They can be connected to a cellular data network or to a Wi-Fi hotspot. APNS establishes a connection with the device and relays the notification request. If the device is offline and the APNS server cannot make a connection, the notification is queued for later delivery.

Upon receiving the request, the iPhone performs a number of checks. Push requests are ignored when the user disables push updates for a given application; users can do so in the Settings application on their iPhone. When updates are allowed, and only then, the iPhone determines whether the client application is currently running. If so, it sends a message directly to the running application via the application delegate. If not, it performs some kind of alert, whether displaying text, playing a sound, or updating a badge.

When an alert displays, users typically have the option to close the alert or tap View. If they choose View, the iPhone launches the application in question and sends it the notification message that it would have received while running. If the user taps Close, the notification gets ignored and the application does not launch.

This pathway, from server to APNS to iPhone to application, forms the core flow of push notifications. Each stage moves the message along the way. Although the multiple steps may sound extensive, in real life the notification arrives almost instantaneously. Once you set up your certificates, identifiers, and connections, the actual delivery of information becomes trivial. Nearly all the work lies in first setting up that chain and then in producing the information you want to deliver.

Make sure you treat all application certificates and device tokens as sensitive information. When storing these items on your server, you must ensure that they are not generally accessible. Should this information hit the wild, it could be exploited by third parties. This would likely result in Apple revoking your SSL push certificate. This would disable all remote notifications for any apps you have sold and might force you to pull the application from the store.

Push Limitations

Push notifications are not reliable. In reality, they can be fairly flaky. Apple does not guarantee the delivery of each notification or the order in which notifications arrive. Never send vital information by push. Reserve this feature for helpful notifications that update the user, but that the user can miss without consequence.

Items in the push delivery queue may be displaced by new notifications. That means that notifications may have to compete and may get lost along the way. Although Apple's feedback service reports failed deliveries (i.e., messages that cannot be properly sent through the push service, specifically to applications that have been removed from a device), you cannot retrieve information regarding bumped notifications. From the APN service point of view, a lost message was still successfully "delivered."

Provisioning Push

To start push development, you must visit Apple's iPhone Developer Program portal. This portal is located at http://developer.apple.com/iphone/manage/overview/index.action. Sign in with your iPhone developer credentials to gain access to the site. Here at the portal, you can work through the steps needed to create a new application identifier that can be associated with a push service.

There's a fair amount of detail involved. Make sure you hit every point. The following sections walk you through the process. You see how to create a new identifier, generate a certificate, and request a special provisioning profile so you can build push-enabled applications. Without a push-enabled profile, your application will not be able to receive remote notifications.

Generate a New Application Identifier

At the developer portal, click on App IDs. You'll find this option in the column on the left side of the Web page. This opens a page that allows you to create new application identifiers. Each push service is based on a single identifier, which you must create and then set to allow remote notification. You cannot use a wild-card identifier with push applications; every push-enabled app demands a unique identifier.

In the App IDs section, click Add ID; this button appears at the top-right of the Web page. Once clicked, the site opens a new Create App ID page. Enter a name that describes your new identifier, such as "My First Push Application" and a new bundle identifier.

These IDs typically use reverse domain patterns like com.*domainname.appname*, such as com.sadun.firstpushapp. The identifier must be unique and may not conflict with any other registered application identifier in Apple's system. The bundle identifier for your application (set in the Info.plist file) needs to exactly match the last part of this string. If, for example, the ID in the portal is XYZZYPLUGH.com.sadun.pushapp, then the bundle identifier of your app should be com.sadun.pushapp.

Click Submit to add the new identifier. This adds the app ID irrevocably to Apple's system, where it is now registered to you. You return to the App ID page with its list of identifiers and are now ready to establish that identifier as push compliant.

> **Note**
>
> Apple does not provide any way to remove an application identifier from the program portal once it has been created.

Generate Your SSL Certificate

On the App ID page, you can see which identifiers work with push and which do not. The Apple Push Notification column shows whether push has been enabled for each app ID. The three states for this column are

- Unavailable (gray) for IDs that are no longer available
- Available (yellow) for apps that can be used with push but that haven't yet been set up to do so
- Enabled (green) for apps that are ready for push

You'll find two dots next to each application identifier—one for Development and another for Production. These options are configured separately. Locate your new app ID, make sure the yellow Available for Development is shown, and click Configure. This option appears in the rightmost column. When clicked, the browser opens a new Configure App ID page that permits you to associate your identifier with the push notification service.

An Enable Push Notification Services check box appears about halfway down the page. Check this box to start the certificate creation process. Once checked, the two Configure buttons on the right side of the page become enabled. Click that button. A page of instructions loads, showing you how to proceed. It guides you through creating a secure certificate that will be used by your server to sign messages it sends to the APNS.

As instructed, launch the Keychain Access application. This application is located on your Macintosh in the /Applications/Utilities folder. Once launched, choose Keychain Access > Certificate Assistant > Request a Certificate From a Certificate Authority (see Figure 16-3). You need to perform this step again even if you've already created previous requests for your developer and distribution certificates. The new request adds information that uniquely identifies the SSL certificate.

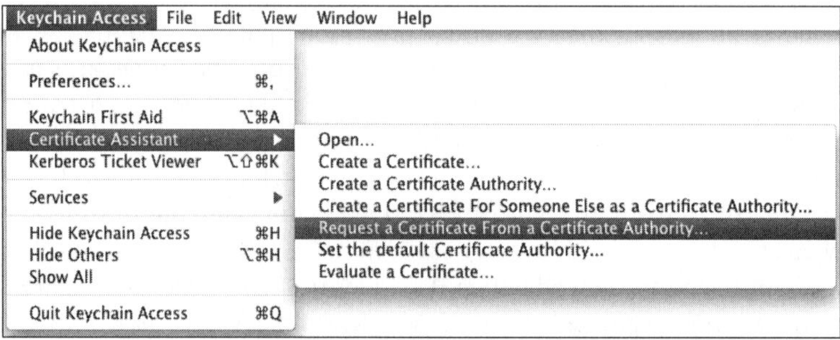

Figure 16-3 Create a new certificate request even though you've probably already done so in the past for your developer and distribution certificates.

Once the Certificate Assistant opens, enter your e-mail address and add a recognizable common name such as First Push App. This common name is important. It will come in handy for the future, so choose one that is easy to identify and that describes your project accurately. The common name lets you distinguish otherwise similar looking keychain items from each other in the OS X Keychain Access utility.

After specifying a common name, choose Saved to Disk and click Continue. The Certificate Assistant prompts you to choose a location to save to (the Desktop is handy). Click Save, wait for the certificate to be generated, and then click Done. Return to your Web browser and click Continue. You are now ready to submit the certificate-signing request.

Click Choose File and navigate to the request you just generated. Select it and click Choose. Click Generate to build your new SSL push service certificate. This can take a minute or two, so be patient and do not close the Web page. Once the certificate has been generated, click Continue. Download the new certificate by clicking Download Now. Finally, click Done. You return to the App ID page where a new, green Enabled indicator should appear next to your app ID (see Figure 16-4). Apple also e-mails you a confirmation that your certificate request was approved.

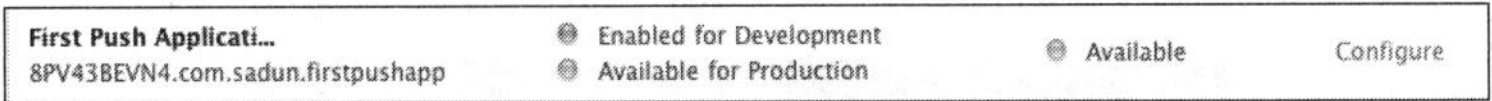

Figure 16-4 The Enabled label appears next to application identifiers that have been approved for push notification. You must create separate SSL certificates for development and for production.

> **Note**
>
> Should you ever need to download your SSL certificate again, click Configure to return to the Configure App ID page. There, you can click Download to request another copy.

If you plan to run your Push Server from your Macintosh, add the new certificate to your keychain by double-clicking the downloaded .cer file. It will be added to your login keychain and appear in your Certificates. Figure 16-5 shows that you can identify the certificate by clicking the small triangle next to it to reveal the common name you used when creating the certificate request.

Push-Specific Provisions

You cannot use wild-card provisions for push-enabled applications. Instead, you must create a single provision for just that application. This means that if you intend to create development, ad hoc, and distribution versions of your app, you must request three new mobile provision files in addition to whatever provisions you have already created for other work.

Go to the Provisioning section of the developer portal and choose whether to create a Development or Distribution profile by clicking the appropriate tab. Click Add Profile to begin creating your new provision. A Create iPhone Provisioning Profile page opens, whether for development or distribution.

- **Development Provision**—For development, enter a profile name such as "My First Push App Development." Check the certificate you will be using and choose your application identifier from the pop-up list. Select the devices you will be using and click Submit.

- **Distribution Provision**—For distribution, select App Store or Ad Hoc. Enter a name for your new provision such as "My First Push App Distribution" or "My First Push App Ad Hoc." Choose your application identifier from the pop-up list. For Ad Hoc distribution only, select the devices to include in your provision. Click Submit to finish.

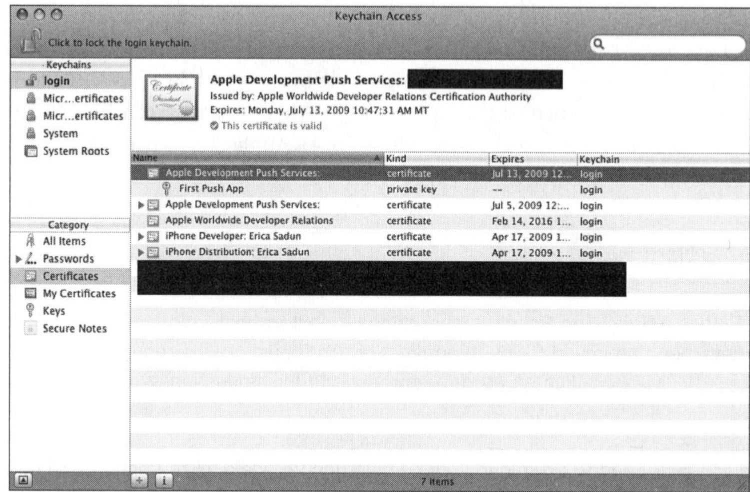

Figure 16-5 Identify which Push Service SSL certificate you are dealing with by clicking the down arrow. This reveals the common name used to generate the original certificate request.

It may take a minute or two for your profile to generate. Wait a short while and reload the page. The provision status should change from Pending to Active. Download your new provision and add it to Xcode by dragging it onto the Xcode application icon.

Registering Your Application

Signing an application with a push-compatible mobile provision is just the first step to working with push notifications. The application must request to register itself with the iPhone's remote notification system. You do this with a single `UIApplication` call, as follows. The application did finish launching delegate method provides a particularly convenient place to call this.

```
[[UIApplication sharedApplication]
   registerForRemoteNotificationTypes:types];
```

This call tells the iPhone OS that your application wants to accept push messages. The types you pass specify what kinds of alerts your application will receive. The iPhone offers three types of notifications:

- **`UIRemoteNotificationTypeBadge`**—This kind of notification adds a red badge to your application icon on SpringBoard.
- **`UIRemoteNotificationTypeSound`**—Sound notifications let you play sound files from your application bundle.
- **`UIRemoteNotificationTypeAlert`**—This style displays a text alert box in SpringBoard or any other application with a custom message using the alert notification.

Choose the types you want to use and `or` them together. They are bit flags, which combine to tell the notification registration process how you want to proceed. For example, the following flags allow alerts and badges but not sounds.

```
types = UIRemoteNotificationTypeBadge | UIRemoteNotificationTypeAlert;
```

Performing the registration updates user settings. As Figure 16-6 shows, a Notifications pane gets added to Settings if one has not already been created by another program. Your application appears as a subpane, offering user control over notification types. Switches appear only for those notifications that you registered. If your application uses just two types, then two switches appear in that pane. Figure 16-6 shows an application that has registered for all three.

To remove your application from active participation in push notifications, send `unregisterForRemoteNotifications`. This unregisters your application for all notification types and does not take any arguments.

```
[[UIApplication sharedApplication] unregisterForRemoteNotifications];
```

Retrieving the Device Token

Your application cannot receive push messages until it generates and delivers a device token to your server. It must send that device token to the offsite service that pushes the actual notifications. Recipe 16-1, which follows this section, does not implement server functionality. It provides only the client software.

A token is tied to one device. In combination with the SSL certificate, it uniquely identifies the iPhone and can be used to send messages back to the phone in question. Be aware that device tokens can change after you restore iPhone firmware.

Device tokens are created as a byproduct of registration. Upon receiving a registration request, the iPhone OS contacts the Apple Push Notification Service. It uses a secure socket layer (SSL) request. Somewhat obviously, the unit must be connected to the Internet. If it is not, the request will fail. The iPhone forwards the request to APNS and waits for it to respond with a device token.

APNS builds the device token and returns it to the iPhone OS, which in turn passes it back to the application via an application delegate callback, namely

```
application:didRegisterForRemoteNotificationsWithDeviceToken:
```

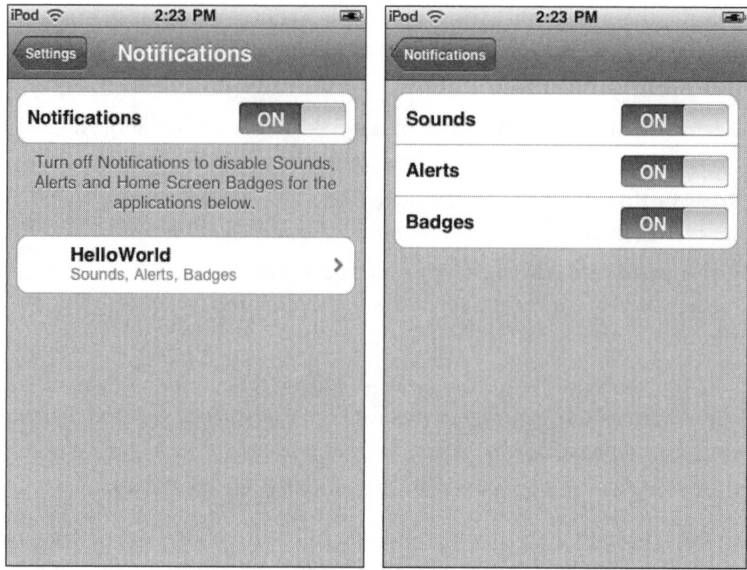

Figure 16-6 Remote notification controls appear for each application that has registered with the iPhone for push support. These controls are removed when applications unregister.

Your application must retrieve this token and pass it to the provider component of your service, where it needs to be stored securely. Anyone who gains access to a device token and the application's SSL certificate could spam messages to iPhones. You must treat this information as sensitive and protect it accordingly.

Note

At times, the token may take time to generate. Consider designing around possible delays into your application by registering at each application run. Until the token is created and uploaded to your site, you will not be able to provide remote notifications to your users.

Handling Token Request Errors

At times, APNS is unable to create a token or your device may not be able to send a request. For example, you cannot generate tokens from the simulator. A `UIApplicationDelegate` method `application: didFailToRegisterForRemote` ➥`NotificationsWithError:` lets you handle these token request errors. For the most part, you'll want to retrieve the error and display it to the user.

```
// Provide a user explanation for when the registration fails
- (void)application:(UIApplication *)application
    didFailToRegisterForRemoteNotificationsWithError:(NSError *)error
{
```

```
    UITextView *tv = (UITextView *)[[application keyWindow]
        viewWithTag:TEXTVIEWTAG];
    NSString *status = [NSString stringWithFormat:
        @"%@\nRegistration failed.\n\nError: %@", pushStatus(),
        [error localizedDescription]];
    tv.text = status;
}
```

Responding to Notifications

The iPhone uses a set chain of operations (see Figure 16-7) in responding to push notifications. When an application is running, the notification is sent directly to a `UIApplicationDelegate` method, `application: didReceiveRemoteNotification:`. The payload, which is sent in JSON format, is converted automatically into an `NSDictionary`, and the application is free to use the information in that payload however it wants. As the application is already running, no further sounds, badges, or alerts are invoked.

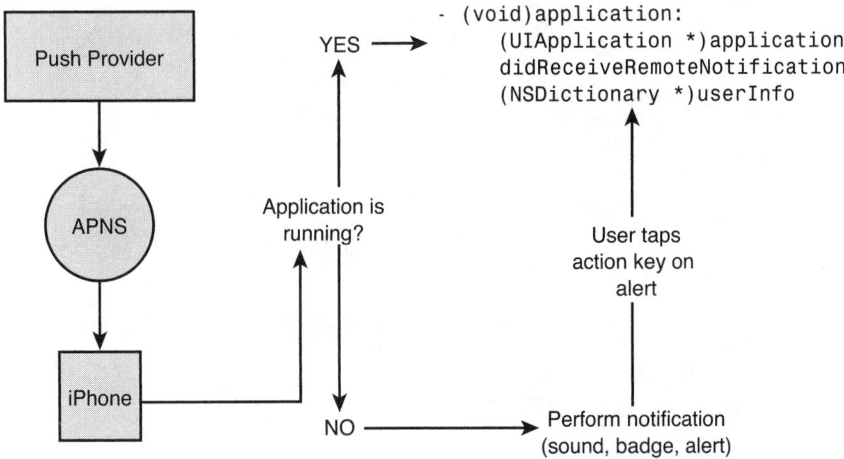

Figure 16-7 Visible and audible notification are only presented when the application is not running. Should the user click on an alert's action key (normally View), the application launches and the payload is sent as a notification to the `UIApplicationDelegate`.

```
// Handle an actual notification
- (void)application:(UIApplication *)application
    didReceiveRemoteNotification:(NSDictionary *)userInfo
{
    UITextView *tv = (UITextView *)[[application keyWindow]
```

```
        viewWithTag:TEXTVIEWTAG];
    NSString *status = [NSString stringWithFormat:
        @"Notification received:\n%@",[userInfo description]];
    tv.text = status;
    NSLog(@"%
}
```

When an application is not running, the iPhone performs all requested notifications that are allowed by registration and by user settings. These notifications may include playing a sound, badging the application, and/or displaying an alert. Playing a sound can also trigger iPhone vibration when a notification is received.

In the case of an alert, all two-buttoned alerts offer a pair of choices. The user can tap Close (the leftmost button) and close the alert or tap the alert's action key (the rightmost button) and launch the app. Upon launching, the application delegate receives the same remote notification callback that an already-running application would have seen (see Figure 16-8). Alerts appear on the lock screen when the iPhone is locked.

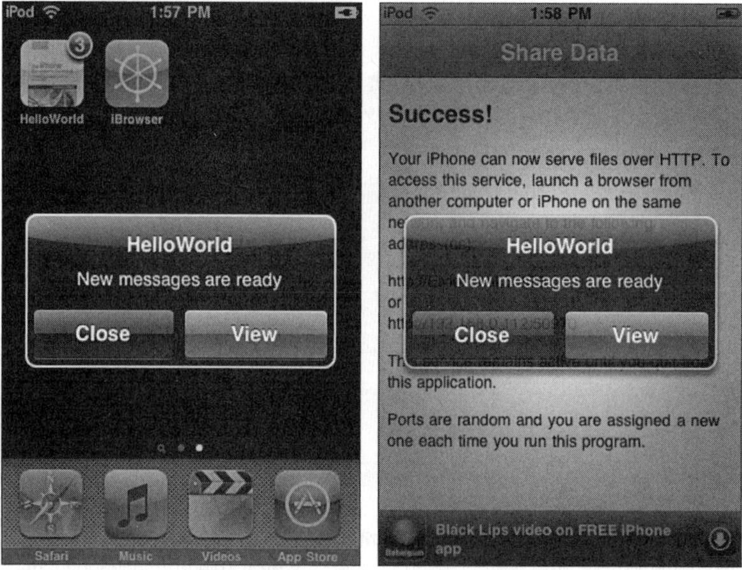

Figure 16-8 Remote alerts can appear in SpringBoard (left) or in third-party applications (right). Users may Close the alert or, by pressing the action button on the right, switch to the notifying application. In this case, that application is HelloWorld, whose name is clearly seen on the alert. The action button text is customizable.

Recipe: Push Client Skeleton

Recipe 16-1 introduces a basic client that allows users to register and unregister for push notifications. The interface (shown in Figure 16-9) uses three switches that control the services to be registered. When the application launches, it queries the app's enabled remote notification types and updates the switches to match. Thereafter, the client keeps track of registrations and unregistrations, adjusting the switches to keep sync with the reality of the settings.

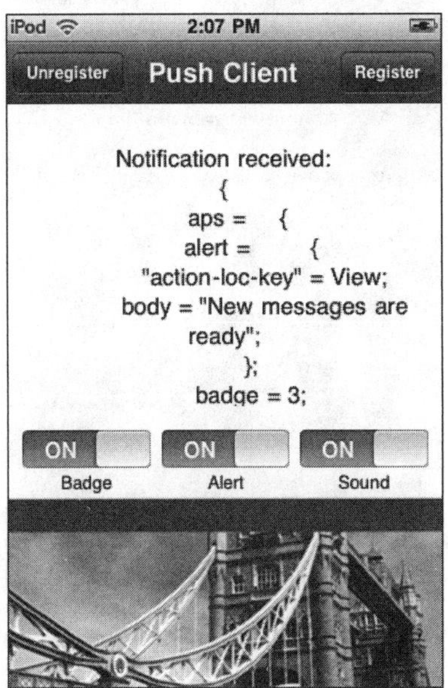

Figure 16-9 The Push Client skeleton introduced in Recipe 16-1 lets users specify which services they want to register.

Two buttons at the top left and right of the interface let users unregister and register their application. As mentioned earlier in this chapter, unregistering disables all services associated with the app. It provides a clean sweep. In contrast, registering apps requires flags to indicate which services are requested.

When requesting new services, the user is always prompted to approve. Figure 16-10 shows the dialog that appears. The user must confirm by explicitly granting the application permission. If the user does not, by tapping Don't Allow, the flags remain at their previous settings.

Unfortunately, the confirmation dialog does not generate a callback when it is dismissed, regardless of whether the user agreed or not. To catch this event, you can listen for a general notification (`UIApplicationDidBecomeActiveNotification`) that gets generated when the dialog returns control to the application. It's a hack and is not guaranteed to work in the long term, but at the time of writing, Apple has not provided any other way to know when the user responded and how the user responded. In Recipe 16-1, the `confirmationWasHidden:` method catches this notification and updates the switches to match any new registration settings.

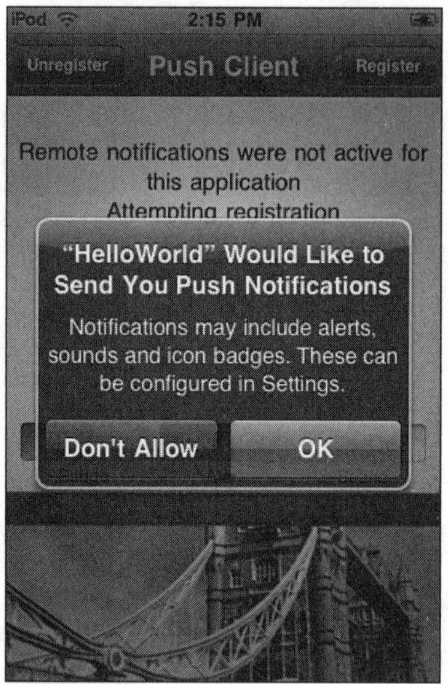

Figure 16-10 Users must explicitly grant permission for an application to receive remote notifications.

Being something of a skeletal system, this push client doesn't actually respond to push notifications beyond showing the contents of the user info payload that gets delivered. Figure 16-9 illustrates the actual payload that was sent in Figure 16-10. This display is performed in the `application: didReceiveRemoteNotification:` method in the application delegate.

> **Note**
>
> The three sound files included in the online sample project (ping1.caf, ping2.caf, and ping3.caf) let you test sound notifications with real audio.

Recipe 16-1 **Push Client Skeleton**

```
#define TEXTVIEWTAG    11

NSString *pushStatus ()
{
```

```
    return [[UIApplication sharedApplication]
        enabledRemoteNotificationTypes] ?
        @"Remote notifications were active for this application" :
        @"Remote notifications were not active for this application";
}

@implementation TestBedController

// Fetch the current switch settings
- (NSUInteger) switchSettings
{
    NSUInteger which = 0;
    if ([(UISwitch *)[self.view viewWithTag:101] isOn])
        which = which | UIRemoteNotificationTypeBadge;
    if ([(UISwitch *)[self.view viewWithTag:102] isOn])
        which = which | UIRemoteNotificationTypeAlert;
    if ([(UISwitch *)[self.view viewWithTag:103] isOn])
        which = which | UIRemoteNotificationTypeSound;
    return which;
}

// Change the switches to match reality
- (void) updateSwitches
{
    NSUInteger rntypes = [[UIApplication sharedApplication]
        enabledRemoteNotificationTypes];
    [(UISwitch *)[self.view viewWithTag:101] setOn:
        (rntypes & UIRemoteNotificationTypeBadge)];
    [(UISwitch *)[self.view viewWithTag:102] setOn:
        (rntypes & UIRemoteNotificationTypeAlert)];
    [(UISwitch *)[self.view viewWithTag:103] setOn:
        (rntypes & UIRemoteNotificationTypeSound)];
}

// Little hack work-around to catch the end when the
// confirmation dialog goes away. Apple has given this
// the thumbs up for use after I filed a technical query
- (void) confirmationWasHidden: (NSNotification *) notification
{
    [[UIApplication sharedApplication]
        registerForRemoteNotificationTypes: [self switchSettings]];
    [self updateSwitches];
}

// Register application for the services set out by the switches
- (void) doOn
{
```

```
    UITextView *tv = (UITextView *)[self.view viewWithTag:TEXTVIEWTAG];
    if (![self switchSettings])
    {
        tv.text = [NSString stringWithFormat:
            @"%@\nNothing to register. Skipping.\n\
            (Did you mean to press Unregister instead?)",
            pushStatus()];
        [self updateSwitches];
        return;
    }

    NSString *status = [NSString stringWithFormat:
        @"%@\nAttempting registration", pushStatus()];
    tv.text = status;
    [[UIApplication sharedApplication]
         registerForRemoteNotificationTypes:[self switchSettings]];
}

// Unregister application for all push notifications
- (void) doOff
{
    UITextView *tv = (UITextView *)[self.view viewWithTag:TEXTVIEWTAG];
    NSString *status = [NSString stringWithFormat:
        @"%@\nUnregistering.", pushStatus()];
    tv.text = status;

    [[UIApplication sharedApplication]
        unregisterForRemoteNotifications];
    [self updateSwitches];
}

- (void)loadView
{
    self.view = [[[NSBundle mainBundle] loadNibNamed:@"view" owner:self
        options:NULL] objectAtIndex:0];
    self.title = @"Push Client";

    self.navigationItem.rightBarButtonItem = BARBUTTON(@"Register",
        @selector(doOn));
    self.navigationItem.leftBarButtonItem = BARBUTTON(@"Unregister",
        @selector(doOff));
    [self updateSwitches];
    [[NSNotificationCenter defaultCenter] addObserver:self
        selector:@selector(confirmationWasHidden)
        name:@"UIApplicationDidBecomeActiveNotification" object:nil];
}
@end
```

```
@interface SampleAppDelegate : NSObject <UIApplicationDelegate>
@end

@implementation SampleAppDelegate
- (void) showString: (NSString *) aString
{
    UITextView *tv = (UITextView *)[[[UIApplication sharedApplication]
        keyWindow] viewWithTag:TEXTVIEWTAG];
    tv.text = aString;
}

// Retrieve the device token
- (void)application:(UIApplication *)application
        didRegisterForRemoteNotificationsWithDeviceToken:
           (NSData *)deviceToken
{
    NSUInteger rntypes = [[UIApplication sharedApplication]
       enabledRemoteNotificationTypes];
    NSString *results = [NSString stringWithFormat:
        @"Badge: %@, Alert:%@, Sound: %@",
        (rntypes & UIRemoteNotificationTypeBadge) ? @"Yes" : @"No",
        (rntypes & UIRemoteNotificationTypeAlert) ? @"Yes" : @"No",
        (rntypes & UIRemoteNotificationTypeSound) ? @"Yes" : @"No"];

    NSString *status = [NSString stringWithFormat:
        @"%@\nRegistration succeeded.\n\nDevice Token: %@\n%@",
        pushStatus(), deviceToken, results];
    [self showString:status];
    NSLog(@"deviceToken %@", deviceToken);
}

// Provide a user explanation for when the registration fails
- (void)application:(UIApplication *)application
       didFailToRegisterForRemoteNotificationsWithError:
          (NSError *)error
{
    NSString *status = [NSString stringWithFormat:
        @"%@\nRegistration failed.\n\nError: %@", pushStatus(),
        [error localizedDescription]];
    [self showString:status];
    NSLog(@"Error in registration. Error: %@", error);
}

// Handle an actual notification
- (void)application:(UIApplication *)application
        didReceiveRemoteNotification:(NSDictionary *)userInfo
```

```
{
    NSString *status = [NSString stringWithFormat:
        @"Notification received:\n%@",[userInfo description]];
    [self showString:status];
    CFShow([userInfo description]);
}

// Report the notification payload when launched by alert
- (void) launchNotification: (NSNotification *) notification
{
    [self performSelector:@selector(showString)
        withObject:[[notification userInfo] description]
        afterDelay:1.0f];
}

- (void)applicationDidFinishLaunching:(UIApplication *)application {
    UIWindow *window = [[UIWindow alloc]
        initWithFrame:[[UIScreen mainScreen] bounds]];
    UINavigationController *nav = [[UINavigationController alloc]
        initWithRootViewController:[[TestBedController alloc] init]];
    [window addSubview:nav.view];
    [window makeKeyAndVisible];

    // Listen for remote notification launches
    [[NSNotificationCenter defaultCenter] addObserver:self
        selector:@selector(launchNotification)
        name:@"UIApplicationDidFinishLaunchingNotification"
        object:nil];
}
@end
```

Get This Recipe's Code

To get the code used for this recipe, go to http://github.com/erica/iphone-3.0-cookbook-, or if you've downloaded the disk image containing all of the sample code from the book, go to the folder for Chapter 16 and open the project for this recipe.

Building Notification Payloads

Delivering push notification through APNS requires three things: your SSL certificate, a device ID, and a custom payload with the notification you want to send. The payload uses JSON formatting. You've already read about generating the certificate and producing the device identifiers, which you need to pass up to your server. Building the JSON payloads basically involves transforming a small well-defined dictionary into JSON format.

JSON (JavaScript Object Notation) is a simple data interchange format based on key-value pairs. The JSON Web site (www.json.org) offers a full syntax breakdown of the format, which allows you to represent values that are strings, numbers, and arrays. The APNS payload consists of up to 256 bytes, which must contain your complete notification information.

Notification payloads must include an `aps` dictionary. This dictionary defines the properties that produce the sound, badge, and/or alert sent to the user. In addition, you may add custom dictionaries with any data you need to send to your application so long as you stay within the 256 byte limit. Figure 16-11 shows the hierarchy for basic (nonlocalized) alerts.

```
aps
    badge : number
    sound : sound file name string
    alert : string
    alert
        body : string
        action-loc-key : string
```

Figure 16-11 The `aps` dictionary may contain one or more notification types including a badge request, a sound file, and/or an alert.

The `aps` dictionary contains one or more notification types. These include the standard types you've already read about: badges, sounds, and alerts. Badge and sound notifications each take one argument. The badge is set by a number, the sound by a string that refers to a file already inside the application bundle. If that file is not found (or the developer passes `default` as the argument), a default sound plays for any notification with a sound request. When a badge request is not included, the iPhone removes any existing badge from the application icon.

There are two ways to produce an alert. You can pass a string, which defines the message to show. This automatically produces a notification with two buttons under that message: Close and View. To customize buttons, pass a dictionary instead. Send the message text as the body and the string to use for the Action key (normally View) as `action-loc-key`. This replaces View with whatever text you specify.

To produce an alert with a single OK button, pass `null` as the argument to `action-loc-key`. This creates a special alert style with one button. Just as when a user taps Close, the OK style alert will not pass any data directly to your application. The app must poll for any updates when next opened by the user.

Localized Alerts

When working with localized applications, construct your `aps > alert` dictionary with two additional keys. Use `loc-key` to pass a key that is defined in your application's Localizable.strings file. The iPhone looks up the key and replaces it with the string found for the current localization.

At times, localization strings use arguments like `%@` and `%n$@`. Should that hold true for the localization you are using, you can pass those arguments as an array of strings via `loc-args`. As a rule, Apple recommends against using complicated localizations as they can consume a major portion of your 256-byte bandwidth.

Transforming from Dictionary to JSON

Once you've designed your dictionary, you must transform it to JSON. The JSON format is simple but precise. If you can, use an automated library to convert your dictionary to the JSON string. There are numerous solutions for this for any number of programming languages, including JavaScript, Perl, and so on. Here's a quick rundown of JSON basics. Table 16-1 offers examples of these rules in action.

Table 16-1 **JSON Payload Samples**

Sample Type	JSON
Hello message, displays with two buttons.	`{"aps":{"alert":"hello"}}`
Hello message, displays with two buttons, but built using JSON with an alert dictionary.	`{"aps":{"alert":{"body":"hello"}}}`
Hello message with one OK button.	`{"aps":{"alert":{"action-loc-key":null,"body":"hello"}}}`
Hello message with two buttons, Close and Open, the latter being a custom replacement for View.	`{"aps":{"alert":{"action-loc-key":"Open","body":"hello"}}}`
Hello message that adds an application badge of 3.	`{"aps":{"badge":3,"alert":{"body":"hello"}}}`
Play a sound without an alert.	`{"aps":{"sound":"ping2.caf","alert":{}}}`
Play sound, display badge, display alert, use a custom button.	`{"aps":{"sound":"ping2.caf","badge":2,"alert":{"action-loc-key":"Open","body":"Hello"}}}`
Add a custom payload including an array.	`{"aps":{"alert":{"body":"Hello"}},"key1":"value1","key2":["a","b","c"]}`

- The entire payload is a dictionary. Dictionaries consist of key-value pairs stored between brackets, that is, {key:value, key:value, key:value, ...}.
- Key-value pairs are separated with commas.
- Strings use double quotes; numbers do not. Reserved words include true, false, and null. Reserved words are not quoted.
- Arrays consist of a list of items between square brackets, that is, [item, item, item,...].

- The following symbols must be escaped in strings by using a backslash literal indicator: `'` `"` `\` `/`.
- You may want to remove carriage returns (`\r`) and new lines (`\n`) from your payloads when sending messages.
- Spaces are optional. Save space by omitting them between items.
- The `aps` dictionary appears within the top-level folder, so the most basic payload looks something like `{aps:{}}`.

Custom Data

So long as your payload has room left, keeping in mind your tight byte budget, you can send additional information in the form of key-value pairs. As Table 16-1 showed, these custom items can include arrays and dictionaries as well as strings, numbers, and constants. You define how to use and interpret this additional information. The entire payload dictionary is sent to your application so whatever information you pass along will be available to the `application: didReceiveRemoteNotification:` method via the user dictionary.

A dictionary containing custom key-value pairs does *not* need to provide an alert, although doing so allows your user to choose to open your application if it isn't running. If your application is already launched, the key-value pairs arrive as a part of the payload dictionary.

Receiving Data on Launch

When your client receives a notification, tapping the action key (by default, View) launches your application. Then after launching, the iPhone sends your application delegate an optional callback. The delegate recovers its notification dictionary by implementing a method named `application:didFinishLaunchingWithOptions:`. Unfortunately, this method might not work properly. So here are both the standard ways of retrieving notification information plus a work-around.

Normally, the iPhone passes the notification dictionary to the delegate method via the launch options parameter. For remote notifications, this is the official callback to retrieve data from an alert-box launch. The `didReceiveRemoteNotification:` method is not called when the iPhone receives a notification and the application is not running.

This "finished launching" method is actually designed to handle two completely different circumstances. First, it handles these notification alert launches, allowing you to recover the payload dictionary and use the data that was sent. Second, it works with application launches from `openURL:`. If your app has published a URL scheme, and that scheme is used by another application, the application delegate handles that launch with this method.

In either case, the method must return a Boolean value. As a rule, return YES if you were able to process the request or NO if you were not. This value is actually ignored in the case of remote notification launches, but you must still return a value.

At the time of writing, implementing this method does not work properly. The application will hang without displaying a GUI. Fortunately, there's an easy work-around that does not rely on the callback method. You can, instead, listen for a launch notification and catch the `userInfo` dictionary that is sent with it. This solution has the advantage of being reliable and tested. Keep an eye on Apple's developer forums (http://devforums.apple.com) to keep track of when this issue gets fixed.

Start by adding your application delegate as a listener via the default `NSNotificationCenter` in your normal `applicationDidFinishLaunching` method.

```
[[NSNotificationCenter defaultCenter] addObserver:self
    selector:@selector(launchNotification)
    name:@"UIApplicationDidFinishLaunchingNotification" object:nil];
```

Then implement the method for the selector you provided. Here, the application waits for the GUI to finish loading and then displays the user info dictionary, where the remote notification data has been stored.

```
- (void) launchNotification: (NSNotification *) notification
{
    [self performSelector:@selector(showString) withObject:
    [[notification userInfo] description] afterDelay:1.0f];
}
```

Between the notification listener and the method callback, you can reliably grab the user data from remote notifications. This work-around should remain viable regardless of when and how Apple addresses the `didFinishLaunchingWithOptions` method.

> **Note**
>
> When your user taps Close and later opens your application, the notification is not sent on launch. You must check in with your server manually to retrieve any new user information. Applications are not guaranteed to receive alerts. In addition to tapping Close, the alert may simply get lost. Always design your application so that it doesn't rely solely on receiving push notifications to update itself and its data.

Recipe: Sending Notifications

The notification process involves several steps (see Figure 16-12). First, you build your JSON payload, which you just read about in the previous section. Next, you retrieve the SSL certificate and the device token for the unit you want to send to. How you store these is left up to you, but you must remember that these are sensitive pieces of information. Open a secure connection to the APNS server. Finally, you handshake with the server, send the notification package, and close the connection.

This is the most basic way of communicating and assumes you have just one payload to send. In fact, you can establish a session and send many packets at a time; however, that is left as an exercise for the reader as is creating services in languages other than Objective-C. The Apple Developer Forums (devforums.apple.com) host ongoing discussions about push providers and offer an excellent jumping off point for finding sample code for PHP, Perl, and other languages.

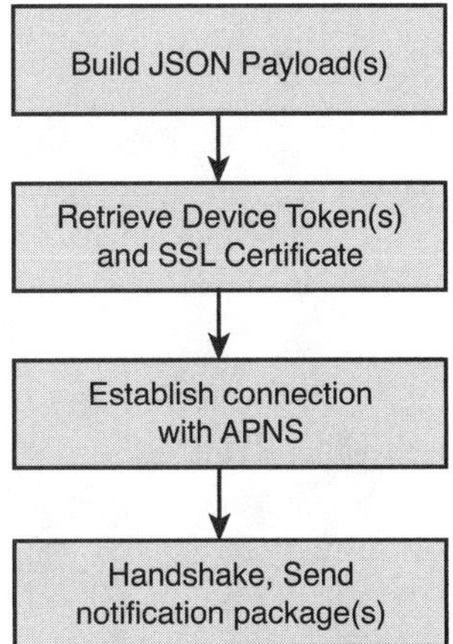

Figure 16-12 The steps for sending remote notifications.

Be aware that APNS may react badly to a rapid series of connections that are repeatedly established and torn down. If you have multiple notifications to send at once, go ahead and send them during a single session. Otherwise, APNS might confuse your push deliveries with a denial of service attack.

Recipe 16-2 demonstrates how to send a single payload to APNS, showing the steps needed to implement the fourth and final box in Figure 16-12. The recipe is built around code developed by Stefan Hafeneger and uses Apple's ioSock sample source code.

The individual server setups vary greatly depending on your security, databases, organization, and programming language. Recipe 16-2 demonstrates a minimum of what is required to implement this functionality and serves as a template for your own server implementation in whatever form this might take.

Sandbox and Production

Apple provides both sandbox (development) and production (distribution) environments for push notification. You must create separate SSL certificates for each. The sandbox helps you develop and test your application before submitting to App Store. It works with a smaller set of servers and is not meant for large-scale testing. The production system is reserved for deployed applications that have been accepted to App Store.

- The Sandbox servers are located at gateway.sandbox.push.apple.com, port 2195.
- The Production servers are located at gateway.push.apple.com, port 2195.

Recipe 16-2 **Pushing Payloads to the APNS Server**

```
// Adapted from code by Stefan Hafeneger
- (BOOL) push: (NSString *) payload
{
```

```
otSocket socket;
SSLContextRef context;
SecKeychainRef keychain;
SecIdentityRef identity;
SecCertificateRef certificate;
OSStatus result;

// Ensure device token
if (!self.deviceTokenID)
{
    printf("Error: Device Token is nil\n");
    return NO;
}

// Ensure certificate
if (!self.certificateData)
{
    printf("Error: Certificate Data is nil\n");
    return NO;
}

// Establish connection to server.
PeerSpec peer;
result = MakeServerConnection("gateway.sandbox.push.apple.com",
    2195, &socket, &peer);
if (result)
{
    printf("Error creating server connection\n");
    return NO;
}

// Create new SSL context.
result = SSLNewContext(false, &context);
if (result)
{
    printf("Error creating SSL context\n");
    return NO;
}

// Set callback functions for SSL context.
result = SSLSetIOFuncs(context, SocketRead, SocketWrite);
if (result)
{
    printf("Error setting SSL context callback functions\n");
    return NO;
}
```

```
// Set SSL context connection.
result = SSLSetConnection(context, socket);
if (result)
{
    printf("Error setting the SSL context connection\n");
    return NO;
}

// Set server domain name.
result = SSLSetPeerDomainName(context,
    "gateway.sandbox.push.apple.com", 30);
if (result)
{
    printf("Error setting the server domain name\n");
    return NO;
}

// Open keychain.
result = SecKeychainCopyDefault(&keychain);
if (result)
{
    printf("Error accessing keychain\n");
    return NO;
}

// Create certificate from data
CSSM_DATA data;
data.Data = (uint8 *)[self.certificateData bytes];
data.Length = [self.certificateData length];
result = SecCertificateCreateFromData(&data, CSSM_CERT_X_509v3,
    CSSM_CERT_ENCODING_BER, &certificate);
if (result)
{
    printf("Error creating certificate from data\n");
    return NO;
}

// Create identity.
result = SecIdentityCreateWithCertificate(keychain, certificate,
    &identity);
if (result)
{
    printf("Error creating identity from certificate\n");
    return NO;
}

// Set client certificate.
```

```
CFArrayRef certificates = CFArrayCreate(NULL,
    (const void **)&identity, 1, NULL);
result = SSLSetCertificate(context, certificates);
if (result)
{
    printf("Error setting the client certificate\n");
    return NO;
}

CFRelease(certificates);

// Perform SSL handshake.
do {result = SSLHandshake(context);}
    while(result == errSSLWouldBlock);


// Convert string into device token data.
NSMutableData *deviceToken = [NSMutableData data];
unsigned value;
NSScanner *scanner = [NSScanner
    scannerWithString:self.deviceTokenID];
while(![scanner isAtEnd]) {
    [scanner scanHexInt:&value];
    value = htonl(value);
    [deviceToken appendBytes:&value length:sizeof(value)];
}

// Create C input variables.
char *deviceTokenBinary = (char *)[deviceToken bytes];
char *payloadBinary = (char *)[payload UTF8String];
size_t payloadLength = strlen(payloadBinary);

// Prepare message
uint8_t command = 0;
char message[293];
char *pointer = message;
uint16_t networkTokenLength = htons(32);
uint16_t networkPayloadLength = htons(payloadLength);

// Compose message.
memcpy(pointer, &command, sizeof(uint8_t));
pointer += sizeof(uint8_t);
memcpy(pointer, &networkTokenLength, sizeof(uint16_t));
pointer += sizeof(uint16_t);
memcpy(pointer, deviceTokenBinary, 32);
pointer += 32;
memcpy(pointer, &networkPayloadLength, sizeof(uint16_t));
```

```
    pointer += sizeof(uint16_t);
    memcpy(pointer, payloadBinary, payloadLength);
    pointer += payloadLength;

    // Send message over SSL.
    size_t processed = 0;
    result = SSLWrite(context, &message, (pointer - message),
        &processed);
    if (result)
    {
        printf("Error sending message via SSL.\n");
        return NO;
    }
    else
    {
        printf("Message sent.\n");
        return YES;
    }
}
```

Get This Recipe's Code

To get the code used for this recipe, go to http://github.com/erica/iphone-3.0-cookbook-, or if you've downloaded the disk image containing all of the sample code from the book, go to the folder for Chapter 16 and open the project for this recipe.

Recipe: Push in Action

Once you set up a client such as the one discussed in Recipe 16-1 and routines like Recipe 16-2 that let you send notifications, it's time to think about deploying an actual service. Recipe 16-3 introduces a Twitter client that repeatedly scans a search.twitter.com RSS feed and pushes notifications whenever a new tweet is found (see Figure 16-13).

This code is built around the push routine from Recipe 16-2 and the XML parser from Recipe 13-13. This utility pulls down Twitter search data as an XML tree and finds the first tree node of the type "entry," which is how Twitter stores each tweet.

Next, it creates a string by combining the poster name (from the "name" leaf) and the post contents (from the "title" leaf). It then adds a JSON-escaped version of this string to the `aps > alert` dictionary as the message body. The alert sound and one-button style are fixed in the main `aps` payload dictionary.

The application runs in a loop with a time delay set by a command-line argument. Every n seconds (determined by the second command-line argument), it polls, parses, and checks for a new tweet, and if it finds one, pushes it out through APNS. Figure 16-13 shows this utility in action, displaying a tweet alert on the client iPhone.

Figure 16-13 Twitter provides an ideal way to test a polled RSS feed.

Recipe 16-3 **Wrapping Remote Notifications into a Simple Twitter Utility**

```
#define TWEET_FILE       [NSHomeDirectory()\
    stringByAppendingPathComponent:@".tweet"]
#define URL_STRING \
    @"http://search.twitter.com/search.atom?q=+ericasadun"
#define SHOW_TICK    NO
#define CAL_FORMAT    @%Y-%m-%dT%H:%M:%SZ"

int main (int argc, const char * argv[]) {

    if (argc < 2)
    {
        printf("Usage: %s delay-in-seconds\n", argv[0]);
        exit(-1);
    }

    NSAutoreleasePool *pool = [[NSAutoreleasePool alloc] init];

    // Fetch certificate and device information from the current
    // directory as set up with pushutil
    char wd[256];
    getwd(wd);
```

```
NSString *cwd = [NSString stringWithCString:wd];
NSArray *contents = [[NSFileManager defaultManager]
    directoryContentsAtPath:cwd];

NSArray *dfiles = [contents pathsMatchingExtensions:
    [NSArray arrayWithObject:@"devices"]];
if (![dfiles count])
{
    printf("Error retrieving device token\n");
    exit(-1);
}
NSDictionary *dict = [NSDictionary dictionaryWithContentsOfFile:
    [cwd stringByAppendingPathComponent:[dfiles lastObject]]];
if (!dict || ([[dict allKeys] count] < 1))
{
    printf("Error retrieving device token\n");
    exit(-1);
}
[APNSHelper sharedInstance].deviceTokenID = [dict objectForKey:
    [[dict allKeys] objectAtIndex:0]];

NSArray *certs = [contents pathsMatchingExtensions:
    [NSArray arrayWithObject:@"cer"]];
if ([certs count] < 1)
{
    printf("Error finding SSL certificate\n");
    exit(-1);
}
NSString *certPath = [certs lastObject];
NSData *dCert = [NSData dataWithContentsOfFile:certPath];
if (!dCert)
{
    printf("Error retrieving SSL certificate\n");
    exit(-1);
}
[APNSHelper sharedInstance].certificateData = dCert;

// Set up delay
int delay = atoi(argv[1]);
printf("Initializing with delay of %d\n", delay);

// Set up dictionaries
NSMutableDictionary *mainDict = [NSMutableDictionary dictionary];
NSMutableDictionary *payloadDict =
    [NSMutableDictionary dictionary];
NSMutableDictionary *alertDict = [NSMutableDictionary dictionary];
```

```
[mainDict setObject:payloadDict forKey:@"aps"];
[payloadDict setObject:alertDict forKey:@"alert"];
[payloadDict setObject:@"ping1.caf" forKey:@"sound"];
[alertDict setObject:[NSNull null] forKey:@"action-loc-key"];

while (1 > 0)
{

    NSAutoreleasePool *wadingpool =
        [[NSAutoreleasePool alloc] init];
    TreeNode *root = [[XMLParser sharedInstance] parseXMLFromURL:
        [NSURL URLWithString:URL_STRING]];
    TreeNode *found = [root objectForKey:@"entry"];

    if (found)
    {
        // Recover the string to tweet
        NSString *tweetString = [NSString stringWithFormat:
            @"%@-%@", [found leafForKey:@"name"],
            [found leafForKey:@"title"]];

        // Recover pubbed date
        NSString *dateString = [found leafForKey:@"published"];
        NSCalendarDate *date = [NSCalendarDate dateWithString:
            dateString calendarFormat:CAL_FORMAT];

        // Recover stored date
        NSString *prevDateString = [NSString
            stringWithContentsOfFile: TWEET_FILE
            encoding:NSUTF8StringEncoding error:nil];
        NSCalendarDate *pDate = [NSCalendarDate dateWithString:
            prevDateString calendarFormat:CAL_FORMAT];

        // Tweet only if there is either no stored date or
        // the dates are not equal
        if (!pDate || ![pDate isEqualToDate:date])
        {
            // Update with the new tweet information
            NSLog(@"\nNew tweet from %\n   \"%@\"\n\n",
               [found leafForKey:@"name"],
               [found leafForKey:@"title"]);

            // Store the tweet time
            [dateString writeToFile:TWEET_FILE atomically:YES
                encoding:NSUTF8StringEncoding error:nil];
```

```
            // push it
            [alertDict setObject:jsonescape(tweetString)
                forKey:@"body"];
            [[APNSHelper sharedInstance] push: [JSONHelper
                jsonWithDict:mainDict]];
        }
    }

    root = nil;
    found = nil;

    [wadingpool drain];

    [NSThread sleepForTimeInterval:(double) delay];
    if (SHOW_TICK) printf("tick\n");
  }

  [pool drain];
  return 0;
}
```

Get This Recipe's Code

To get the code used for this recipe, go to http://github.com/erica/iphone-3.0-cookbook-, or if you've downloaded the disk image containing all of the sample code from the book, go to the folder for Chapter 16 and open the project for this recipe.

Feedback Service

Apps don't live forever. Users add, remove, and replace applications on their iPhones all the time. From an APNS point of view, it's pointless to deliver notifications to iPhones that no longer host your application. As a push provider, it's your duty to remove inactive device tokens from your active support list. As Apple puts it, "APNS monitors providers for their diligence in checking the feedback service and refraining from sending push notifications to nonexistent applications on devices." Big Brother *is* watching.

Apple provides a simple way to manage inactive device tokens. When users uninstall apps from a device, push notifications begin to fail. Apple tracks these failures and provides reports from its APNS feedback server. The APNS feedback service lists devices that failed to receive notifications. As a provider, you need to fetch this report on a periodic basis and weed through your device tokens.

The feedback server hosts sandbox and production addresses, just like the notification server. You find these at feedback.push.apple.com (port 2196) and feedback.sandbox.push.apple.com. You contact the server with a production SSL certificate and shake hands in the same way you do to send notifications. After the handshake, read your results. The server sends data immediately without any further explicit commands on your side.

The feedback data consists of 38 bytes. This includes the time (4 bytes), the token length (2 bytes), and the token itself (32 bytes). The timestamp tells you when APNS first determined that the application no longer existed on the device. This uses a standard UNIX epoch, namely seconds since Midnight, January 1st, 1970. The device token is stored in binary format. You need to convert it to a hex representation to match it to your device tokens if you use strings to store token data. At the time of writing this book, you can ignore the length bytes. They are always 0 and 32, referring to the 32-byte length of the device token.

```
// Retrieve message from SSL.
size_t processed = 0;
char buffer[38];
do
{
    // Fetch the next item
    result = SSLRead(context, buffer, 38, &processed);
    if (result) break;

    // Recover Date from data
    char *b = buffer;
    NSTimeInterval ti = ((unsigned char)b[0] << 24) +
       ((unsigned char)b[1] << 16) +
       ((unsigned char)b[2] << 8) +
       (unsigned char)b[3];
    NSDate *date = [NSDate dateWithTimeIntervalSince1970:ti];

    // Recover Device ID
    NSMutableString *deviceID = [NSMutableString string];
    b += 6;
    for (int i = 0; i < 32; i++) [
        deviceID appendFormat:@"%02x", (unsigned char)b[i]];

    // Add dictionary to results
    [results addObject:
        [NSDictionary dictionaryWithObject:date
        forKey:deviceID]];

} while (processed > 0);
```

Note

Search your Xcode Organizer Console for “aps” to locate APNS error messages.

Designing for Push

When designing for push, keep scaling in mind. Normal computing doesn’t need to scale. When coding is done, an app runs on a device using the local CPU. Should a developer deploy an extra 10,000 copies, there’s no further investment involved other than increased technical support.

Push computing does scale. Whether you have 10,000 or 100,000 or 1,000,000 users matters. That's because developers must provide the service layer that handles the operations for every unit sold. The more users supported, the greater the costs will be. Consider that these services need to be completely reliable and that consumers will not be tolerant of extended downtimes.

Consider an application with just 10,000 users. It might service a million uses per day, assuming update checks every 15 minutes. More time-critical uses might demand checks every few minutes or even several times a minute. As the computational burden builds, so do the hosting costs. While cloud computing provides an excellent match to these kinds of needs, that kind of solution comes with a real price in development, maintenance, and day-to-day operations.

On top of reliability, add in security concerns. Many polled services require secure credentials. Those credentials must be uploaded to the service for remote use rather than being stored solely on the device. Even if the service in question does not use that kind of authentication, the device token that allows your service to contact a specific phone is sensitive in itself. Should that identifier be stolen, it could let spammers send unsolicited alerts. Any developer who enters this arena must take these possible threats seriously and provide highly secure solutions for storing and protecting information.

These concerns, when taken together, point to the fact that push notifications are serious business. Some small development houses may completely opt out of being push providers for apps that depend on new information notifications. Between infrastructure and security concerns, the work it will take to properly offer this kind of service may price itself out of reach for those developers. Third party providers like Key Lime Tie (keylimetie.com) and Urban Airship (urbanairship.com) offer ready-to-use Push infrastructure with affordable pricing plans. They handle the remote notification deployment for you.

On the other hand, many developers may employ push for occasional opt-in notifications, such as alerting users that upgrades are now available in the App Store or to send tips about using the product. How tolerant iPhone users will be of this kind of use remains to be seen.

Summary

In this chapter, you saw push notifications both from a client-building point of view and as a provider. You learned about the kinds of notifications you can send and how to create the payload that moves those notifications to the device. You discovered registering and unregistering devices and how users can opt in and out from the service. You saw how to create a provider utility that pushes new Twitter items.

Much of the push story lies outside this chapter. It's up to you to set up a server and deal with security, bandwidth, and scaling issues. The reality of deployment is that there are many platforms and languages that can be used that go beyond the Objective-C sample code shown here. Regardless, the concepts discussed and recipes shown in this chapter give you a good stepping off point. You know what the issues are and how things have to work. Now it's up to you to put them to good use.

- The big wins of notifications are their instant updates and immediate presentation. Like SMS messages, they're hard to overlook when they arrive on your iPhone. There's nothing wrong in opting out of push if your application does not demand that kind of immediacy.
- Guard your SSL certificate and device tokens. Although it's too early to say how Apple will respond to security breaches, experience suggests that it will be messy and unpleasant.
- Don't leave users without service when you have promised to provide it to them. Build a timeline into your business plan that anticipates what it will take to keep delivering notifications over time and how you will fund this. Consumers will not be tolerant of extended downtimes; your service must be completely reliable.
- Build to scale. Although your application may not initially have tens of thousands of users, you must anticipate a successful app launch as well as a modest one. Create a system that can grow along with your user base.

17

Using Core Location and MapKit

Core Location infuses the iPhone with on-demand geopositioning based on a variety of technologies and sources. MapKit adds interactive in-application mapping allowing users to view and manipulate annotated maps. With Core Location and MapKit, you can develop applications that help users meet up with friends, search for local resources, or provide location-based streams of personal information. This chapter introduces these location-aware frameworks and shows you how you can integrate them into your iPhone applications.

How Core Location Works

Location is meaningful. Cocoa Touch understands that. Where we compute is fast becoming just as important as how we compute and what we compute. The iPhone is constantly on the go, traveling along with its users, throughout the course of the day, both at home and on the road. Core Location brings the iPhone's mobility into application development.

Core Location addresses location-based programming. It enables applications to hook into location-aware Web APIs like fireeagle.com, outside.in, upcoming.org, twitter.com, and flickr.com. It helps you provide geotagged content to your user and lets your user search for local resources such as restaurant and event listings. With on-demand geolocation, mobile computing opens itself up to a wide range of Web 2.0 API libraries.

All of these features depend on one thing: location. And it's up to Core Location to tell your application where your users are. The iPhone uses several methods to locate you. These technologies depend on several providers including Skyhook Wireless (http://skyhookwireless.com, aka http://loki.com), Google Maps (http://maps.google.com/), and the U.S. Department of Defense Global Positioning System (http://tycho.usno.navy.mil/gpsinfo.html). The following sections provide a rundown of the ways an iPhone can detect and report position.

GPS Positioning

On newer-model 3G/3GS iPhones, the onboard GPS system tracks movement courtesy of a series of medium Earth orbit satellites provided by the U.S. Department of Defense. These satellites emit microwave signals, which the iPhone picks up and uses to triangulate position to a high level of accuracy. Like any GPS system, the iPhone requires a clear path between the user and the satellites, so it works best outdoors and away from trees.

GPS positioning is not currently available for the first generation iPhone or the iPod touch line. These units must fall back to other ways of tracking location, just as a 3G/3GS iPhone does when it cannot lock to a satellite signal.

SkyHook Wi-Fi Positioning

In the United States, Core Location's preferred pseudo-GPS geopositioning method calls on SkyHook Wireless. SkyHook offers extremely accurate Wi-Fi placement. When an iPhone detects nearby Wi-Fi and WiMax routers, it uses their MAC addresses to search SkyHook's databases, positioning you from that data. All iPhone models, including the touch line, are Wi-Fi enabled, allowing them to scan for those units.

SkyHook Wi-Fi data collection works like this. SkyHook sends drivers and pedestrians down city streets throughout its covered territories, which includes most U.S. metropolitan areas. These agents scan for Wi-Fi hotspots (called *access points*) and when found, they record the location using traditional GPS positioning matched to the Wi-Fi MAC address.

This works great when Wi-Fi routers stay still. This works terribly when people pack up their Wi-Fi routers and move with them to, say, Kentucky. That having been said, SkyHook data does get updated. It provides pretty accurate positioning and can usually locate you within a few hundred feet of your actual location, even though people and their routers will continue to move to Kentucky and other places. You can submit coordinate and MAC address information directly through Skyhook's volunteer location program. Visit http://www.skyhookwireless.com/howitworks/submit_ap.php for details.

Cell Tower Positioning

A less-accurate location approach involves cell tower positioning. Here, the iPhone uses its antenna to find the nearest four or five cell towers and then triangulates your position based on the cell tower signal strength. You've probably seen cell tower location in action; it's the kind that shows you about a half mile away from where you are standing—assuming you're not standing right next to an actual cell tower.

iPod touch units cannot use cell tower positioning, lacking the GPRS cell tower antennas that are iPhone standard issue. Cell tower-based location usually acts as a fallback method due to its low accuracy.

Internet Provider Positioning

SkyHook actually offers a third positioning approach, but it is one I've never seen the iPhone use. Then again, I live in a major metropolitan area; I haven't given it a very good try. This last-ditch approach uses an Internet provider location to find the nearest mapped Internet provider's central office. This is a solution of last resort. The returned data is typically up to several miles off your actual location—unless you happen to be visiting your Internet provider.

Hybridizing the Approaches

The iPhone approaches location in stages. Based on the accuracy level you request, it uses a fallback method. If it cannot accurately locate you with GPS or Wi-Fi technology, it falls back to cell tower location for iPhone users. If that doesn't work, it presumably falls back further to Internet provider location. And if that doesn't work, it finally fails.

The latest releases of the SDK provide multiple asynchronous success callbacks for each of these fallback methods. You may receive three or four results at any time. What's more, those methods keep working over time, as the iPhone's location changes. Each callback includes an accuracy measure, indicating the method used.

Knowing how the iPhone does this is important. That's because any ten attempts to grab your location on a first generation iPhone may result in maybe three or four Wi-Fi successes, the remainder falling back to cell tower hits. Although you can set your desired location accuracy to the highest possible settings, unless you listen for multiple callbacks, you might miss out on catching the best possible location.

The cost to this is time. A location request may take 10 or 15 seconds to establish itself. Working with multiple requests, averaging, and best-results repetition is best done in the background away from the GUI. When possible, avoid making your user wait for your program to finish its location queries.

> **Note**
>
> Apple requires that users authorize all location requests when Core Location is first launched. Once authorized, you may use location for the duration of the application session.

Recipe: Core Location in a Nutshell

Core Location is easy to use, as demonstrated by the following steps. They walk you through a process of setting up your program to request location data that's representative of normal use. These steps and Recipe 17-1 provide just one example of using Core Location's services, showing how you might pinpoint a user's location.

1. Add the Core Location framework to your project. Drag it into your Xcode project and add it to the Frameworks folder in the Groups & Files column. Make sure to include the CoreLocation headers in your code.

2. Allocate a location manager. Set the manager's delegate to your primary view controller or application delegate. Optionally, set its desired distance filter and accuracy.

The distance filter specifies a minimum distance in meters. The device must move at least this distance before it can register a new update. If you set the distance for 5 meters, for example, you will not receive new events until the device has moved that far.

The accuracy property specifies the degree of precision that you're requesting. To be clear, the location manager does not guarantee any actual accuracy. Setting the requested accuracy asks the manager to (attempt to) retrieve at least that level. When you do not need precision, the manager will deliver its results using whatever technology is most available.

When you do need precision, the `desiredAccuracy` property informs the manager of that need. You'll find a high level of accuracy especially important for walking and running applications. A lower accuracy level may work for driving in a car or for locating users within large geographical boundaries like cities, states, and countries.

3. Check whether the user has enabled Core Location by testing the location manager's `locationServicesEnabled` property. Users have the option to switch off Core Location from General > Location Services in the Settings application.

4. Start locating. Tell the location manager to start updating the location. Delegate callbacks let you know when the location has been found. This can take many seconds or up to a minute to occur.

5. Handle the location event delegate callbacks. You'll deal with two types of callbacks: successes that return `CLLocation` data (`locationManager:didUpdateToLocation:` `➥fromLocation:`) and failures that do not (`locationManager:didFailWithError:`). Add these delegate methods to your code to catch location updates. In Recipe 17-1, the successful location logs an information overview (`description`) that includes the current latitude and longitude results.

   Depending on your requested accuracy, you may receive three or four location callbacks based on the various location methods used and the requested accuracy, so take this nonlinearity into account.

6. Wait. Callbacks arrive asynchronously, as location data becomes available. The location information returned to your application includes positioning information along with accuracy measures that you can use to evaluate precision.

Test your Core Location applications on the device and not in the simulator. The simulator is hard coded to return the geocoordinates of Apple Headquarters in Cupertino. Deploying Recipe 17-1 to the device allows you to test results as you walk or drive around with your iPhone.

Recipe 17-1 **Using Core Location to Retrieve Latitude and Longitude**

```
@interface TestBedViewController : UIViewController <CLLocationManagerDelegate>
{
    IBOutlet UITextView *textView;
    CLLocationManager *locManager;
}
@property (retain) CLLocationManager *locManager;
@end

@implementation TestBedViewController
@synthesize locManager;

- (void)locationManager:(CLLocationManager *)manager
    didFailWithError:(NSError *)error
{
    // Respond to the (rare) location manager failure
    NSLog(@"Location manager error: %@", [error description]);
    return;
}

- (void)locationManager:(CLLocationManager *)manager
    didUpdateToLocation:(CLLocation *)newLocation
    fromLocation:(CLLocation *)oldLocation
{
    // Output a summary of the current location result
    NSLog(@"%@\n", [newLocation description]);
}

- (void) viewDidLoad
{
    // Initialize the location manager
    self.locManager = [[[CLLocationManager alloc] init] autorelease];
    if (!self.locManager.locationServicesEnabled)
    {
        NSLog(@"User has opted out of location services");
        return;
    }

    self.locManager.delegate = self;
    self.locManager.desiredAccuracy = kCLLocationAccuracyBest;

    // Set the optional distance filter
    self.locManager.distanceFilter = 5.0f; // in meters

    // Start recovering location information
    [self.locManager startUpdatingLocation];
}
```

Get This Recipe's Code

To get the code used for this recipe, go to http://github.com/erica/iphone-3.0-cookbook-, or if you've downloaded the disk image containing all of the sample code from the book, go to the folder for Chapter 17 and open the project for this recipe.

Location Properties

Each `CLLocation` instance returned by the updated location callback contains a number of properties that describe the device as it travels. Location objects can combine their various properties into a single text result, as used in Recipe 17-1, via the `description` instance method. Alternatively, you can pull out each value on a property-by-property basis. Location properties include the following:

- **`altitude`**—This property returns the currently detected altitude. It returns a floating-point number in meters above sea level. Speaking as a resident of the "Mile High City," I can assure you the accuracy of this value is minimal at best. Use these results with caution.
- **`coordinate`**—Recover the device's detected geoposition through the `coordinate` property. A coordinate is a structure with two fields, `latitude` and `longitude`, both of which store a floating-point value. Positive values for latitude lie north of the equator; negative ones south of the equator. Positive longitudes lie east of the meridian; negative longitudes west of the meridian.
- **`course`**—Use the `course` value to determine the general direction in which the device is heading. This value, which is 0 degrees for North, 90 degrees for East, 180 degrees for South, and 270 degrees for West, roughly approximates the direction of travel. For better accuracy, use headings (`CLHeading` instances) rather than courses. Headings provide access to magnetic and true North readings via the magnetometer. They are another feature of Core Location and are detailed later in this chapter.
- **`horizontalAccuracy`**—This property indicates the accuracy (i.e., the uncertainty or measurement error) of the current coordinates. Think of the coordinates that are returned as the center of a circle, and the horizontal accuracy as its radius. The true device location falls somewhere in that circle. The smaller the circle, the more accurate the location. The larger the circle, the less accurate it is. Negative accuracy values indicate a measurement failure.
- **`verticalAccuracy`**—This property offers an altitude equivalent for horizontal accuracy. It returns the accuracy related to the true value of the altitude, which may (in theory) vary between the altitude minus that amount to the altitude plus that amount. In practice, altitude readings are extremely inaccurate, and the vertical accuracy typically bears little relationship to reality.
- **`speed`**—In theory, this value returns the speed of the device in meters per second. In practice, this property is best reserved for car travel rather than walking. Recipes follow later in this chapter that demonstrate how this raw property value is used, and that derive velocity independently.

- **`timestamp`**—This property identifies the time at which the location measurement took place. It returns an `NSDate` instance set to the time when the location was determined by Core Location.

> **Note**
>
> Running a continuous location query is a power-consuming choice. Location services may result in a short battery life, as has been demonstrated by many jogging and biking applications currently released on App Store.

Recipe: Tracking Speed

The built-in `speed` property returned by each `CLLocation` instance allows you to track the device's velocity over time. Recipe 17-2 highlights its use. When the location manager callback updates the device's location, the code recovers the speed and logs it. This recipe computes the current speed in miles per hour by multiplying the meters per second value by 2.23693629.

The following `viewDidLoad` method sets the desired accuracy to the nearest 10 meters, skipping the distance filtering used by Recipe 17-1. This example is intended for use in a vehicle rather than walking. For walking, running, or biking, you want to use a higher level of accuracy and use a strategy that eliminates inaccurate readings. Recipe 17-3 shows how to do so.

Recipe 17-2 **Recovering the speed Property from a Location Instance**

```
- (void)locationManager:(CLLocationManager *)manager
    didUpdateToLocation:(CLLocation *)newLocation
    fromLocation:(CLLocation *)oldLocation
{
    // If a speed is detected, log that data in miles per hour
    if (newLocation.speed > 0.0f)
    {
        NSString *speedFeedback = [NSString stringWithFormat:
            @"Speed is %0.1f miles per hour",
            2.23693629 * newLocation.speed];
        NSLog(@"%
    }
}

- (void) viewDidLoad
{
    self.locManager = [[[CLLocationManager alloc] init] autorelease];
    if (!self.locManager.locationServicesEnabled)
    {
        NSLog(@"User has opted out of location services");
        return;
    }
```

```
    // Set the delegate and requested accuracy
    self.locManager.delegate = self;
    self.locManager.desiredAccuracy =
        kCLLocationAccuracyNearestTenMeters;

    // Start capturing location data
    [self.locManager startUpdatingLocation];
}
```

Get This Recipe's Code

To get the code used for this recipe, go to http://github.com/erica/iphone-3.0-cookbook-, or if you've downloaded the disk image containing all of the sample code from the book, go to the folder for Chapter 17 and open the project for this recipe.

Recipe: Computing Speed and Distance

When moving slowly, or at least more slowly than a car typically moves, you want make two specific code accommodations. First, increase your desired accuracy to the highest possible value. Second, ignore the built-in speed property and calculate your speed from scratch. Recipe 17-3 meets these two goals by keeping track of the last-detected most accurate location possible. For purposes of this recipe, "most accurate" is defined as within 100 meters, that is, a likely GPS position.

It uses "accurate" positions to calculate a distance by calling `CLLocation`'s `getDistanceFrom:` method. Dividing the distance by the change in time yields the device's velocity. The method discards values with lower accuracy and values where the device has not moved at least a meter in distance.

For walking and biking, this method produces a more accurate speed while still falling far short of "precise." This is best demonstrated by testing the sample code in the real world with a 3G or later GPS-enabled iPhone. Should you need to deploy a Core Location-based application with higher accuracy than these samples provide, you'll need to tweak your sample rates and feedback based on the likely real-world use for the device.

Recipe 17-3 **Deriving Location Information**

```
- (void)locationManager:(CLLocationManager *)manager
    didUpdateToLocation:(CLLocation *)newLocation
    fromLocation:(CLLocation *)oldLocation
{
    if (newLocation.horizontalAccuracy <
        kCLLocationAccuracyHundredMeters) // within 300 feet or so
    {
        // Need a baseline to compute from
        if (self.lastAccurateLocation)
        {
            // Calculate the change in time and distance
```

```
            NSTimeInterval dTime = [newLocation.timestamp
                timeIntervalSinceDate:
                    self.lastAccurateLocation.timestamp];
            float distance = [newLocation
                getDistanceFrom:lastAccurateLocation];
            if (distance < 1.0f) return;

            // Sum up the aggregate distance
            aggregateDistance += distance;

            // Report the speed and distance
            NSString *reportString = [NSString stringWithFormat:
                @"Speed: %0.1f miles per hour. %0.1f meters.",
                2.23693629 * distance / dTime, aggregateDistance];
            NSLog(@"%
        }

        // Update the last accurate location
        self.lastAccurateLocation = newLocation;
    }
}

- (void) viewDidLoad
{
    // Use the best accuracy
    self.locManager = [[[CLLocationManager alloc] init] autorelease];
    if (!self.locManager.locationServicesEnabled)
    {
        NSLog(@"User has opted out of location services");
        return;
    }

    // Initialize the location manager
    self.locManager.delegate = self;
    self.locManager.desiredAccuracy = kCLLocationAccuracyBest;
    [self.locManager startUpdatingLocation];
    aggregateDistance = 0.0f;
}
```

Get This Recipe's Code

To get the code used for this recipe, go to http://github.com/erica/iphone-3.0-cookbook-, or if you've downloaded the disk image containing all of the sample code from the book, go to the folder for Chapter 17 and open the project for this recipe.

Recipe: Keeping Track of "North" by Using Heading Values

The iPhone's onboard location manager can return a computed `course` value that indicates the current direction of travel, that is, North, South, Southeast, and so on. These values take the form of a floating-point number between 0 and 360, with 0 degrees indicating North, 90 degrees being East, and so forth. This computed value is derived from tracking a user's location over time. Newer iPhone units have a better way to determine a user's course. Recent devices provide an onboard magnetometer, which can return both magnetic North and true North values.

Not every iPhone supports headings. A magnetometer was first released on the iPhone 3GS. Test each device for this ability before subscribing to heading callbacks. If the location manager can generate heading events, the `headingAvailable` property returns `YES`. Use this result to control your `startUpdatingHeading` requests.

```
if (self.locManager.headingAvailable)
        [self.locManager startUpdatingHeading];
```

Cocoa Touch allows you to filter heading callbacks just as you do with distance ones. Set the location manager's `headingFilter` property to a minimal angular change, specified as a floating-point number. For example, if you don't want to receive feedback until the device has rotated at least 5 degrees, set the property to 5.0. All heading values use degrees, between 0.0 and 360.0. To convert a heading value to radians, divide by 180.0 and multiply it by pi.

Heading callbacks return a `CLHeading` object. You can query the heading for two properties, `magneticHeading` and `trueHeading`. The former returns the relative location of magnetic North, the latter true North. True North always points to the geographic north pole. Magnetic North corresponds to the pole of the Earth's geomagnetic field, which changes over time. The iPhone uses a computed offset (called a *declination*) to determine the difference between these two.

On an enabled iPhone, magnetic heading updates are available even if the user has switched off location updates in the Settings application. What's more, users are not prompted to give permission to use heading data. Magnetic heading information cannot compromise user privacy so it remains freely available to your applications.

You can only use the `trueHeading` property in conjunction with location detection. The iPhone requires a device's location to compute the declination needed to determine true North. Declinations vary by geoposition. The declination for Los Angeles is different from Perth's, which is different from Moscow's, and London's, and so forth. Some locations cannot use magnetometer readings at all. Certain anomalous regions like Michipicoten Island in Lake Superior and Grants, New Mexico, offer iron deposits and lava flows that interfere with normal magnetic compass use. Metallic and magnetic sources, such as your computer, car, or refrigerator, may also affect the magnetometer. Several "metal detector" applications in App Store leverage this quirk.

The `headingAccuracy` property provides an error value. This number indicates a plus or minus range that the actual heading falls within. A smaller error bar indicates a more accurate reading. A negative value represents an error in reading the heading.

You can retrieve raw magnetic values along the X, Y, and Z axes using the `x`, `y`, and `z` `CLHeading` properties. These values are measured in microteslas and normalized into a range that Apple states is -128 to 128. (The actual range is more likely to be -128 to 127 based on standard bit math.) Each axis value represents an offset from the magnetic field lines tracked by the device's built-in magnetometer.

Recipe 17-4 uses `CLHeading` data to rotate a small image view with an arrow pointer. The rotation ensures that the arrow always points North. Figure 17-1 shows the interface in action.

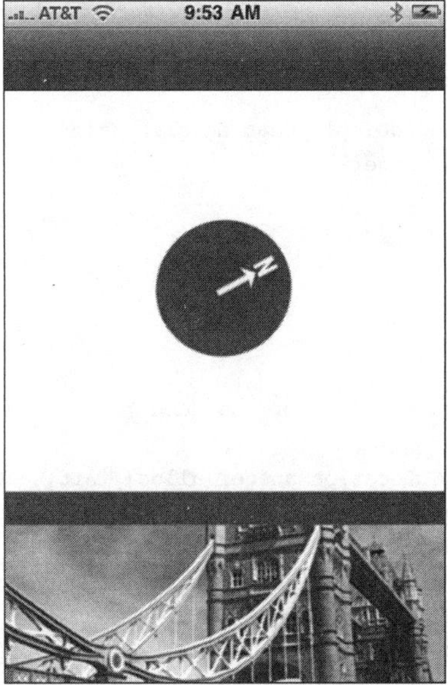

Figure 17-1 The iPhone's built-in magnetometer and the code from Recipe 17-4 ensure that this arrow always points North.

Recipe 17-4 **Detecting the Direction of North**

```
@implementation TestBedViewController
@synthesize locManager;

// Catch location errors
- (void)locationManager:(CLLocationManager *)manager
    didFailWithError:(NSError *)error
{
```

```
    NSLog(@"Location manager error: %@", [error description]);
}

// Respond to new heading
- (void)locationManager:(CLLocationManager *)manager
    didUpdateHeading:(CLHeading *)newHeading
{
    // Convert the heading into radians
    CGFloat heading = -1.0f * M_PI *
        newHeading.magneticHeading / 180.0f;

    // Rotate the North arrow accordingly
    arrow.transform = CGAffineTransformMakeRotation(heading);
}

// Allow Core Location to display the device calibration
// panel when needed
- (BOOL)locationManagerShouldDisplayHeadingCalibration:
    (CLLocationManager *)manager
{
    return YES;
}

- (void) viewDidLoad
{
    // Initialize the location manager. No need to test for
    // user opt-in/opt-out
    self.locManager = [[[CLLocationManager alloc] init] autorelease];
    self.locManager.delegate = self;
    if (self.locManager.headingAvailable)
        [self.locManager startUpdatingHeading];
    else
        arrow.alpha = 0.0f;
}
@end
```

Get This Recipe's Code

To get the code used for this recipe, go to http://github.com/erica/iphone-3.0-cookbook-, or if you've downloaded the disk image containing all of the sample code from the book, go to the folder for Chapter 17 and open the project for this recipe.

Recipe: Reverse Geocoding

The phrase *reverse geocoding* means transforming latitude and longitude information into human-recognizable address information. MapKit offers a reverse geocoder class that converts from coordinates to location descriptions by way of Google. Using this feature binds you to the Google Maps terms of service, which you can read about at http://code.google.com/apis/maps/iphone/terms.html.

Performing a reverse geocoding request requires little more than allocating a new `MKReverseGeocoder` instance, setting its coordinate and delegate and telling it to start. The delegate declares the `MKReverseGeocoderDelegate` protocol and implements the two callbacks (success and failure) shown in Recipe 17-5.

When a reverse geocoding request succeeds, the delegate callback provides an `MKPlaceMark` instance. This object includes an `addressDictionary` that contains key-value pairs describing the address. Figure 17-2 shows the contents of the address dictionary for Lollipop Lake in Denver.

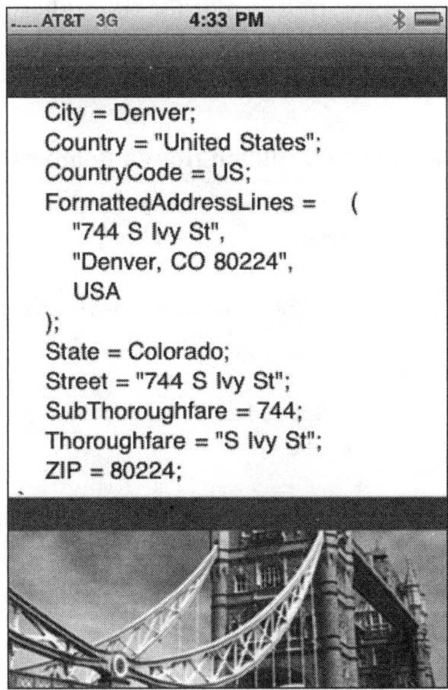

Figure 17-2 Address Dictionary contents for Lollipop Lake at Garland Park in Denver, Colorado.

The `MKPlaceMark` object also offers individual properties with the same information outside the dictionary structure. These properties include the following:

- `subThoroughfare` stores the street number, e.g., the "1600" for 1600 Pennsylvania Avenue.
- `thoroughfare` contains the street name, e.g., Pennsylvania Avenue.
- `sublocality`, when available, refers to the local neighborhood name or a landmark, e.g., White House.
- `subAdministrativeArea` is typically the local county, parish, or other administrative area.

- `locality` stores the city, e.g., Washington, D.C.
- `administrativeArea` corresponds to the state, such as Maryland or Virginia.
- `postalCode` is the zip code, e.g., 20500
- `country` is self-explanatory, storing the country name, such as the United States.
- `countryCode` provides an abbreviated country name, like "US".

These properties' names are used in capitalized form in the address dictionary. For example, the `subThoroughfare` property corresponds to the `SubThoroughfare` key. You can see this capitalization in the keys shown in Figure 17-2.

In addition to these properties, the address dictionary offers a `FormattedAddressLines` entry that stores an array of preformatted strings for the address in question. You can use these strings to display an address, for example, "1600 Pennsylvania Avenue NW", "Washington, DC 20500", "USA."

Recipe 17-5 **Recovering Address Information from a Coordinate**

```
- (void)locationManager:(CLLocationManager *)manager
    didFailWithError:(NSError *)error
{
    NSLog(@"Location manager error: %@", [error description]);
}

- (void)reverseGeocoder:(MKReverseGeocoder *)geocoder
    didFailWithError:(NSError *)error
{
    NSLog(@"Reverse geocoder error: %@", [error description]);
}

- (void)locationManager:(CLLocationManager *)manager
    didUpdateToLocation:(CLLocation *)newLocation
    fromLocation:(CLLocation *)oldLocation
{
    MKReverseGeocoder *geocoder =
        [[MKReverseGeocoder alloc]
            initWithCoordinate:newLocation.coordinate];
    geocoder.delegate = self;
    [geocoder start];
}

- (void)reverseGeocoder:(MKReverseGeocoder *)geocoder
        didFindPlacemark:(MKPlacemark *)placemark
{
    NSLog([placemark.addressDictionary description]);
    if ([geocoder retainCount]) [geocoder release];
}
```

> **Get This Recipe's Code**
>
> To get the code used for this recipe, go to http://github.com/erica/iphone-3.0-cookbook-, or if you've downloaded the disk image containing all of the sample code from the book, go to the folder for Chapter 17 and open the project for this recipe.

Recipe: Viewing a Location

The `MKMapView` class presents users with interactive maps built on the coordinates and scale you provide. Available in Interface Builder, you can easily drag a map view into your GUI and access it via an `IBOutlet`. The following code snippet sets a map's region to a detected Core Location coordinate, showing 0.1 degrees of latitude and longitude around that point. In the United States, a region with that range corresponds to the size of a relatively small city or large town, about seven by five miles. Figure 17-3 (left) shows that 0.1 degree-by-0.1 degree range on a map view.

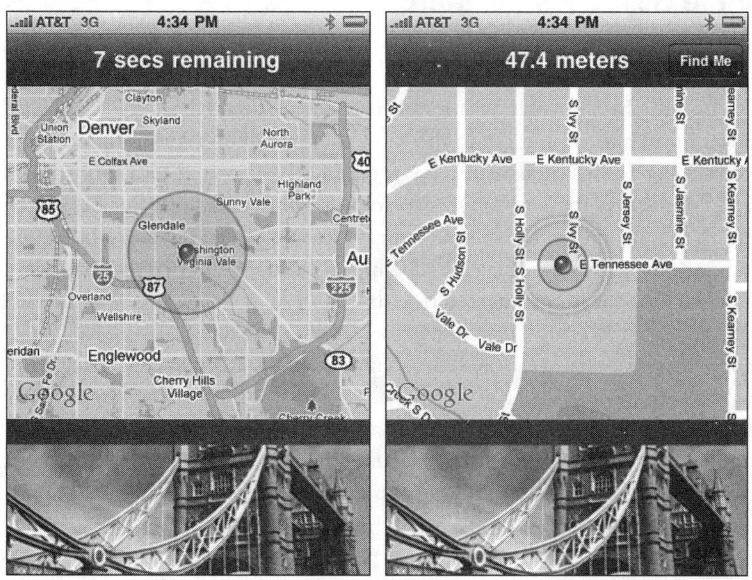

Figure 17-3 A coordinate region of a tenth of a degree latitude by a tenth of a degree longitude covers an area the size of a smallish city or large town, approximately 5 to 7 miles on a side. Shrinking that region down to 0.005 degrees on a side produces a street-level display (left). These streets lie within Denver's Garland Park/Virginia Vale neighborhood (right).

```
mapView.region = MKCoordinateRegionMake(
    self.bestLocation.coordinate, MKCoordinateSpanMake(0.1f, 0.1f));
```

Region size changes occur due to the curvature of the earth. At the equator, one degree of longitude corresponds to about 69 miles (~111 kilometers). This shrinks to zero at the poles. Latitude is not affected by position. One degree of latitude is always approximately 69 miles (~111 km).

To view map data on a neighborhood level, cut the coordinate span down to 0.01 by 0.01. For a street-by-street level, you can use a smaller span, say, 0.005 degrees latitude by 0.005 degrees longitude. Figure 17-3 (right) shows the Garland Park neighborhood at this range.

You can avoid dealing with latitude and longitude degrees and create regions by specifying distance in meters. This snippet sets the view region to a 500-by-500 meter square around the central coordinate. That roughly approximates the 0.005 by 0.005 degree lat/lon span, showing a street-by-street presentation.

```
mapView.region = MKCoordinateRegionMakeWithDistance(
    self.bestLocation.coordinate, 500.0f, 500.0f);
```

Finding the Best Location Match

Recipe 17-6 performs an on-demand location search using a timed approach. When the user taps the Find Me button, the code starts a 10-second timer. During this search, it attempts to find the best possible location. It uses the horizontal accuracy returned by each location hit to choose and retain the most accurate geoposition. When the time ends, the view controller zooms in its map view, revealing the detected location.

Recipe 17-6 displays the current user location both during and after the search. It does this by setting the `showsUserLocation` property to `YES`. When enabled, this property produces a pulsing purple pushpin that initially appears at the center of the map view at the device location. That location is detected with Core Location. Figure 17-3 shows the user pushpin at the center of both screenshots.

Whenever this property is enabled, the map view tasks Core Location with finding the device's current location. So long as this property remains set to `YES`, the map will continue to track and periodically update the user location. A pulsing circle that surrounds the pushpin indicates the most recent search accuracy. Recipe 17-7 later in this chapter takes advantage of this built-in functionality to skip the search-for-the-best-result approach used here in Recipe 17-6.

Once the location is set, the Recipe 17-6 permits the user to start interacting with the map. Enabling the `zoomEnabled` property means users can pinch, drag, and otherwise interact with and explore the displayed map. This recipe waits until the full search completes before allowing this interaction, ensuring that the user location remains centered until control returns to the user.

Upon finishing the search, the recipe stops requesting location callbacks by calling `stopUpdatingLocation`. At the same time, it permits the map view to continue tracking the user, leaving the `showsUserLocation` property set to `YES`.

After unsubscribing to updates, the view controller instance sets its location manager delegate to `nil`. This assignment prevents any outstanding callbacks from reaching the controller after the timer finishes. Otherwise, the user and the outstanding callbacks might compete for control of the screen.

Recipe 17-6 **Presenting User Location Within a Map**

```
@implementation TestBedViewController
@synthesize locManager;
@synthesize bestLocation;

- (void)locationManager:(CLLocationManager *)manager
    didFailWithError:(NSError *)error
{
    NSLog(@"Location manager error: %@", [error description]);
}

- (void)locationManager:(CLLocationManager *)manager
    didUpdateToLocation:(CLLocation *)newLocation
    fromLocation:(CLLocation *)oldLocation
{
    // Keep track of the best location found
    if (!self.bestLocation) self.bestLocation = newLocation;
    else if (newLocation.horizontalAccuracy <
        bestLocation.horizontalAccuracy)
        self.bestLocation = newLocation;

    // Show the location within a cityscape while searching
    mapView.region = MKCoordinateRegionMake(
        self.bestLocation.coordinate,
        MKCoordinateSpanMake(0.1f, 0.1f));

    // Show the user location but prevent interaction
    mapView.showsUserLocation = YES;
    mapView.zoomEnabled = NO;
}

// Search for n seconds to get the best location during that time
- (void) tick: (NSTimer *) timer
{
    if (++timespent == MAX_TIME)
    {
        // Invalidate the timer
        [timer invalidate];

        // Stop the location task
        [self.locManager stopUpdatingLocation];
        self.locManager.delegate = nil;

        // Restore the find me button
        self.navigationItem.rightBarButtonItem =
            BARBUTTON(@"Find Me", @selector(findme));
```

```
        if (!self.bestLocation)
        {
            // No location found
            self.title = @"";
            return;
        }

        // Note the final accuracy in the title bar
        self.title = [NSString stringWithFormat:@"%0.1f meters",
            self.bestLocation.horizontalAccuracy];

        // Update the map to street-level and allow user interaction
        [mapView setRegion:MKCoordinateRegionMake(
            self.bestLocation.coordinate,
            MKCoordinateSpanMake(0.005f, 0.005f)) animated:YES];
        mapView.showsUserLocation = YES;
        mapView.zoomEnabled = YES;
    }
    else
        self.title = [NSString stringWithFormat:@"%d secs remaining",
           MAX_TIME - timespent];
}

// Perform user-request for location
- (void) findme
{
    // Disable right button
    self.navigationItem.rightBarButtonItem = nil;

    // Search for the best location
    timespent = 0;
    self.bestLocation = nil;
    self.locManager.delegate = self;
    [self.locManager startUpdatingLocation];
    [NSTimer scheduledTimerWithTimeInterval:1.0f target:self
        selector:@selector(tick) userInfo:nil repeats:YES];
}

- (void) viewDidLoad
{
    self.locManager = [[[CLLocationManager alloc] init] autorelease];
    if (!self.locManager.locationServicesEnabled)
    {
        NSLog(@"User has opted out of location services");
        return;
    }
```

```
    else
    {
        // User generally allows location calls
        self.locManager.desiredAccuracy = kCLLocationAccuracyBest;
        self.navigationItem.rightBarButtonItem =
            BARBUTTON(@"Find Me", @selector(findme));
    }
}
@end
```

Get This Recipe's Code

To get the code used for this recipe, go to http://github.com/erica/iphone-3.0-cookbook-, or if you've downloaded the disk image containing all of the sample code from the book, go to the folder for Chapter 17 and open the project for this recipe.

Recipe: User Location Annotations

Recipe 17-6 provided a way to visually track a location event as it focused over time. Recipe 17-7 kicks this idea up a notch to track a device as it moves over time. Instead of sampling locations over time and picking the best result, it employs a far easier approach while achieving similar results. It hands over all responsibility for user location to the map view and its `userLocation` property.

As mentioned in the discussion for Recipe 17-6, enabling the `showsUserLocation` property automatically tasks Core Location to track the device. Recipe 17-7 leverages this capability by checking that location once a second. It updates the map view to reflect that location, keeping the map centered on the user and adding a custom annotation to the user pin to display the current coordinates.

Annotations are pop-up views that attach to locations on the map. They offer a title and a subtitle, which you can set as desired. Figure 17-4, which follows in the next section, shows a map that displays an annotation view.

The `MKUserLocation` class provides direct access to the user location pin and its associated annotation. It offers two readable and writable properties called `title` and `subtitle`. Set these properties as desired. Recipe 17-7 sets the title to "Location Coordinates" and the subtitle to a string containing the latitude and longitude.

The `MKUserLocation` class greatly simplifies annotation editing, but you are limited to working with the map view's user location property. The more general case for annotations proves more complicated. It is detailed in Recipe 17-8, which follows this section.

Recipe 17-7 **Tracking the Device Through the MapView**

```
@implementation TestBedViewController
@synthesize locManager;

// Search for n seconds to get the best location during that time
- (void) tick: (NSTimer *) timer
```

```
{
    if (mapView.userLocation)
        [mapView setRegion:
            MKCoordinateRegionMake(
                mapView.userLocation.location.coordinate,
                MKCoordinateSpanMake(0.005f, 0.005f)) animated:NO];
    mapView.userLocation.title = @"Location Coordinates";
    mapView.userLocation.subtitle = [NSString stringWithFormat:
        @"%f, %f",
        mapView.userLocation.location.coordinate.latitude,
        mapView.userLocation.location.coordinate.longitude];
}

// Perform user-request for location
- (void) findme
{
    self.navigationItem.rightBarButtonItem = nil;
    [self.locManager startUpdatingLocation];
    [NSTimer scheduledTimerWithTimeInterval:1.0f target:self
        selector:@selector(tick) userInfo:nil repeats:YES];
}

- (void) viewDidLoad
{
    self.locManager = [[[CLLocationManager alloc] init] autorelease];
    if (!self.locManager.locationServicesEnabled)
    {
        NSLog(@"User has opted out of location services");
        return;
    }
    else
    {
        // User generally allows location calls
        self.locManager.desiredAccuracy = kCLLocationAccuracyBest;
        self.navigationItem.rightBarButtonItem =
            BARBUTTON(@"Find Me", @selector(findme));
        mapView.showsUserLocation = YES;
        mapView.zoomEnabled = NO;
    }
}
@end
```

Figure 17-4 This annotated map view was created using data from MapKit and the outside.in Web site.

> **Get This Recipe's Code**
>
> To get the code used for this recipe, go to http://github.com/erica/iphone-3.0-cookbook-, or if you've downloaded the disk image containing all of the sample code from the book, go to the folder for Chapter 17 and open the project for this recipe.

Recipe: Creating Map Annotations

Cocoa Touch does not provide a map annotation class. This is surprising since annotations play such an important role in most map-based applications. Instead, Cocoa Touch defines an `MKAnnotation` protocol. You must design your own classes that conform to this protocol, which demands a `coordinate` property and `title` and `subtitle` instance methods. Listing 17-1 demonstrates how to do this. It builds a simple `MapAnnotation` class, providing the coordinate, title, and subtitle features demanded by the protocol.

Listing 17-1 **Building a Map Annotation Object**

```
@interface MapAnnotation : NSObject <MKAnnotation>
{
    CLLocationCoordinate2D coordinate;
    NSString *title;
    NSString *subtitle;
}
@property (nonatomic, readonly) CLLocationCoordinate2D coordinate;
@property (nonatomic, retain) NSString *title;
```

```
@property (nonatomic, retain) NSString *subtitle;
@end
@implementation MapAnnotation
@synthesize coordinate;
@synthesize title;
@synthesize subtitle;

// Initialize with a coordinate
- (id) initWithCoordinate: (CLLocationCoordinate2D) aCoordinate
{
    if (self = [super init]) coordinate = aCoordinate;
    return self;
}

-(void) dealloc
{
    self.title = nil;
    self.subtitle = nil;
    [super dealloc];
}
@end
```

Creating, Adding, and Removing Annotations

To use annotations, you must create them and add them to a map view. You can do so by adding a single annotation at a time:

```
anAnnotation = [[[MapAnnotation alloc]
    initWithCoordinate:coord] autorelease];
[mapView addAnnotation:anAnnotation];
```

Alternatively, you can build an array of annotations and add them all at once:

```
[annotations addObject:annotation];
[mapView addAnnotations:annotations];
```

Delete annotations from a map by performing `removeAnnotation:` to remove just one annotation or `removeAnnotations:` to remove all items in an array.

If you need to return a map view to a no-annotations state, remove all its existing annotations. This snippet recovers the array of existing annotations via the `annotations` property. It then removes these from the map.

```
[mapView removeAnnotations:mapView.annotations];
```

Annotation Views

Annotation objects are not views. The `MapAnnotation` class laid out in Listing 17-1 does not create any onscreen elements. It is an abstract class that describes an annotation. It's the map view's job to convert that annotation description into an actual onscreen view.

Those views belong to the `MKAnnotationView` class. You can retrieve the annotation view for an existing annotation by querying the map. Supply the annotation and request the matching view.

```
annotationView = [mapView viewForAnnotation:annotation];
```

Nearly all annotation views you'll work with belong to an `MKAnnotationview` subclass, namely `MKPinAnnotationView`. These are the pins that you can drop onto maps. When tapped, they display a callout view. Figure 17-4 shows a map view with ten annotations, one of which has been tapped. Its callout shows information for the 5280 Magazine headquarters along with an information URL and an accessory button that links to that URL.

Customizing Annotation Views

After adding annotations, via `addAnnotation:` or `addAnnotations:`, the map view starts building the annotation views that correspond to those annotations. When it finishes, its delegate, which must declare the `MKMapViewDelegate` protocol, receives a callback. The delegate is notified with `mapView:didAddAnnotationViews:` once the views are built and added to the map. This callback provides your application with an opportunity to customize those annotation views.

An array of annotation views is passed as the second parameter to that callback. You can iterate through this array to set features like the view's `image` or to customize its accessory buttons. Listing 17-2 shows how you might prepare each of these annotation views for use based on their annotations.

Listing 17-2 **Preparing Annotation Views for Use**

```
- (void)mapView:(MKMapView *)mapView
    didAddAnnotationViews:(NSArray *)views
{
    for (MKPinAnnotationView *mkaview in views)
    {
        if ([mkaview.annotation.title
            isEqualToString:@"Current Location"])
        {
            // Current location is purple, no button
            mkaview.pinColor = MKPinAnnotationColorPurple;
            mkaview.rightCalloutAccessoryView = nil;
            continue;
        }

        // Other annotations are red, with a button
        mkaview.pinColor = MKPinAnnotationColorRed;
        UIButton *button = [UIButton buttonWithType:
            UIButtonTypeDetailDisclosure];
        mkaview.rightCalloutAccessoryView = button;
    }
}
```

This example uses the annotation title to choose a pin color and whether to display a button. You are not limited to the built-in annotation protocol, which was minimally satisfied with the class defined in Listing 17-1. Design your annotation class with any instance variables and methods you like for more control over how you query the annotations to prepare your annotation views.

Each annotation view provides direct access to its annotation via its `annotation` property. Use that annotation data to build the exact view you need. Here are some of the annotation view properties you'll want to customize in your MapKit applications.

Each `MKPinAnnotationView` uses a color. You set this color via the `pinColor` property. MapKit provides three color choices: red (`MKPinAnnotationColorRed`), green (`MKPinAnnotationColorGreen`), and purple (`MKPinAnnotationColorPurple`). According to Apple's human interface guidelines, red pins indicate destination points, places that the user may want to explore or navigate to. Green pins are starting points, places from which the user can begin a journey. Purple pins are user-specified. When you encourage users to add new data into the map, use purple to indicate that the user has defined them. As you saw in previous recipes, a map view-defined purple pin also indicates the current user location.

Each annotation view offers two slots, on the left and right of the callout bubble. The `rightCalloutAccessoryView` and `leftCalloutAccessoryView` properties allow you to add buttons or any other custom subview to your callout. Figure 17-4 shows a callout that uses a right-side detail disclosure button. This button was built in Listing 17-2. You are not limited to buttons, however. You might add image views or other standard Cocoa Touch views as needed.

The `canShowCallout` property controls whether tapping a button produces a callout view. Enabled by default, you can set this property to `NO` if you do not want user taps to open callouts.

You can offset the callouts (normally they appear directly above the pin in question) by changing the `calloutOffset` property to a new `CGPoint`. You can also change the position for the annotation view itself by adjusting its `centerOffset` property. With pin annotations, the view's art is set by default, but you can create custom annotation art by assigning a `UIImage` to the view's `image` property. Combine custom art with the center offset to produce the exact map look you want.

Responding to Annotation Button Taps

MapKit simplifies button tap management. Whenever you set a callout accessory view property to a control, MapKit takes over the control callback. You do not need to add a target and action. MapKit handles that for you. All you have to do is implement the `mapView:annotationView:calloutAccessoryControlTapped:` delegate callback, as demonstrated in Recipe 17-8.

Recipe 17-8 uses the outside.in Web service (http://outside.in) to locate noteworthy places near any given coordinate. It derives the coordinate of interest from user interactions with the map view. Whenever the user adjusts the map, the map view delegate receives a `mapView:regionDidChangeAnimated:` callback. The callback pulls the coordinate of the map center via its `centerCoordinate` property. It submits this coordinate to outside.in and retrieves an XML list of places.

The recipe iterates through these places, adding an annotation for each. The XML data supplies the title for each place and an outside.in URL, used as a subtitle. This information is used in the accessory control callback. When the user taps the button, the callback method opens the subtitle URL, providing a hot link between the callout view and a Safari page with location details.

Recipe 17-8 **Creating an Annotated, Interactive Map**

```
@implementation TestBedViewController
@synthesize locManager;
@synthesize current;

- (void)locationManager:(CLLocationManager *)manager
    didFailWithError:(NSError *)error
{
    NSLog(@"Location manager error: %@", [error description]);
}

// Update map when the user interacts with it
- (void)mapView:(MKMapView *)aMapView
    regionDidChangeAnimated:(BOOL)animated
{
    // Gather annotations
    MapAnnotation *annotation;
    NSMutableArray *annotations = [NSMutableArray array];
    self.title = @"Searching...";

    // Add a current location annotation
    if (self.current)
    {
        annotation = [[[MapAnnotation alloc]
            initWithCoordinate:self.current.coordinate] autorelease];
        annotation.title = CURRENT_STRING;
        [annotations addObject:annotation];
    }

    // Clean up the map
    [mapView removeAnnotations:mapView.annotations];

    // Fetch all the new locations from outside.in
    [self performSelector:@selector(setTitle)
        withObject:@"Contacting Outside.in..." afterDelay:0.1f];
    NSString *urlstring = [NSString stringWithFormat:
        @"http://api.outside.in/radar.xml?lat=%f&lng=%f",
        mapView.centerCoordinate.latitude,
```

```
        mapView.centerCoordinate.longitude];
    NSData *data = [NSData dataWithContentsOfURL:
        [NSURL URLWithString:urlstring]];
    printf("Received %d bytes of data from outside.in\n", data.length);

    // Check to see if we got valid data
    NSString *xml = [[[NSString alloc] initWithData:data
        encoding:NSUTF8StringEncoding] autorelease];
    if ([xml rangeOfString:@"places"].location == NSNotFound)
    {
        // Clean up and return
        [mapView addAnnotations:annotations];
        return;
    }

    // If so, parse the data and find the place information
    TreeNode *root = [[XMLParser sharedInstance]
        parseXMLFromData:data];

    // Add an annotation for each "place", using the coordinates,
    // name and URL
    for (TreeNode *node in [root objectsForKey:@"place"])
    {
        // Extract the coordinates
        NSArray *coords = [[node leafForKey:@"georsspoint"]
            componentsSeparatedByString:@" "];
        if (coords.count < 2) continue;
        CLLocationCoordinate2D coord;
        coord.latitude = [[coords objectAtIndex:0] floatValue];
        coord.longitude = [[coords objectAtIndex:1] floatValue];

        // Create the annotation
        annotation = [[[MapAnnotation alloc]
            initWithCoordinate:coord] autorelease];
        annotation.title = [node leafForKey:@"name"];
        annotation.subtitle = [node leafForKey:@"url"];

        // Add it
        [annotations addObject:annotation];
    }

    // Clean up the root
    [root teardown];

    // Add the annotations
    [mapView addAnnotations:annotations];
}
```

```
- (void)locationManager:(CLLocationManager *)manager
    didUpdateToLocation:(CLLocation *)newLocation
    fromLocation:(CLLocation *)oldLocation
{
    // Disable further location for the moment
    self.locManager.delegate = nil;
    [self.locManager stopUpdatingLocation];

    // Set the current location
    self.current = newLocation;

    // Set the map to that location and allow user interaction
    mapView.region = MKCoordinateRegionMake(newLocation.coordinate,
        MKCoordinateSpanMake(0.02f, 0.02f));
    mapView.zoomEnabled = YES;

    // Restore find me button
    self.navigationItem.rightBarButtonItem =
        BARBUTTON(@"Find Me", @selector(findme));
}

// Perform user-request for location
- (void) findme
{
    // Disable right button
    self.navigationItem.rightBarButtonItem = nil;
    self.title = @"Searching for location...";

    // Search for location
    self.locManager.delegate = self;
    [self.locManager startUpdatingLocation];
}

- (void)mapView:(MKMapView *)mapView
    annotationView:(MKAnnotationView *)view
    calloutAccessoryControlTapped:(UIControl *)control
{
    MapAnnotation *annotation = view.annotation;
    [[UIApplication sharedApplication] openURL:
        [NSURL URLWithString:annotation.subtitle]];
}

- (void)mapView:(MKMapView *)mapView
    didAddAnnotationViews:(NSArray *)views
```

```
{
    // Initialize each view
    for (MKPinAnnotationView *mkaview in views)
    {
        // The current location does not get a button
        if ([mkaview.annotation.title
            isEqualToString:CURRENT_STRING])
        {
            mkaview.pinColor = MKPinAnnotationColorPurple;
            mkaview.rightCalloutAccessoryView = nil;
            continue;
        }

        // All other locations are red with a button
        mkaview.pinColor = MKPinAnnotationColorRed;
        UIButton *button = [UIButton buttonWithType:
            UIButtonTypeDetailDisclosure];
        mkaview.rightCalloutAccessoryView = button;
    }
}

- (void) viewDidLoad
{
    self.locManager = [[[CLLocationManager alloc] init] autorelease];
    if (!self.locManager.locationServicesEnabled)
    {
        NSLog(@"User has opted out of location services");
        return;
    }
    else // User allows location calls via settings
    {
        self.locManager.desiredAccuracy = kCLLocationAccuracyBest;
        self.navigationItem.rightBarButtonItem =
            BARBUTTON(@"Find Me", @selector(findme));
        mapView.delegate = self;
    }
}
@end
```

Get This Recipe's Code

To get the code used for this recipe, go to http://github.com/erica/iphone-3.0-cookbook-, or if you've downloaded the disk image containing all of the sample code from the book, go to the folder for Chapter 17 and open the project for this recipe.

One More Thing: Geocoding

Geocoding means to turn a normal street address into a latitude and longitude. For example, you might start with "1600 Pennsylvania Avenue NW, Washington D.C." and end up with 38.879971, -76.982887, the latitude and longitude of the United States White House.

As you can see, this is the opposite process of reverse geocoding, which starts with a coordinate and returns a human-readable address. Geocoding starts with the human-readable version and returns a coordinate.

Unfortunately, Apple did not build normal geocoding into MapKit. Fortunately, there are other external providers for this service, including Yahoo, MapQuest, and Virtual Earth. Yahoo's Geocoding API (http://developer.yahoo.com/maps/rest/V1/geocode.html) offers on-demand geocoding using a simple REST API.

To use it, you must sign up for a developer API key. Your requests will not work without that key, and you will be subject to Yahoo's terms and conditions. A rate limit applies, and Yahoo reserves the right to charge fees at some point in the future for its services. You need a separate API key for each application you build. Requesting that key is simple and requires little more than describing the application, offering a Web site link, and signing in with your Yahoo credentials.

To use the API, you submit your app ID, and the street and city you want located. The more information you provide, the more specific your geocoded result will be. This snippet creates a RESTful URL for the Big Chicken in Marietta, Georgia. The Yahoo service responds with a short XML result, providing the latitude and longitude information for that location.

```
NSMutableString *urlstring = [NSMutableString string];
[urlstring appendFormat:
    @"http://local.yahooapis.com/MapsService/V1/geocode?appid=%@",
    API_KEY];
[urlstring appendFormat:
    @"&street=12+Cobb+Parkway&city=Marietta&zip=30062"]
```

Recipe 17-9 uses the Yahoo API to find several points of interest within the United States. It uses those geocoded coordinates to create custom annotations, presenting the interface shown in Figure 17-5. This recipe relies on an annotation object that has been expanded somewhat from the one used for Recipe 17-8. Its annotation stores a URL string for the disclosure button and an image URL string to help create the image shown at the left of the disclosure.

As the recipe shows, addresses, Web sites, and image URLs have been hard coded into the example. You could easily expand this to a more general API service that offers local sites of interest.

Recipe 17-9 **Reverse Geocoding Locations for Use with MapKit**

```
- (void) findme
{
    NSString *whichLocation = [LOCATIONS objectAtIndex:whichItem];
```

```
    // Geocode the location
    [self performSelector:@selector(setTitle)
        withObject:whichLocation afterDelay:0.1f];

    // Create the REST URL
    NSMutableString *urlstring = [NSMutableString string];
    [urlstring appendFormat:
        @"http://local.yahooapis.com/MapsService/V1/geocode?appid=%@",
        API_KEY];

    NSString *locationURLString;
    NSString *picstring;
    // All images courtesy of Wikipedia (http://en.wikipedia.org)
    // and under either Creative Commons Attribution or Public Domain
    switch (whichItem)
    {
        case 0:
            // White House
            [urlstring appendFormat:
                @"&street=Pennsylvania+Avenue&city=@Washington+DC"];
            locationURLString =
                @"http://en.wikipedia.org/wiki/White_house";
            picstring = @"http://upload.wikimedia.org/\
                wikipedia/commons/a/af/WhiteHouseSouthFacade.JPG";
            break;
        case 1:
            // Big Chicken of Marietta
            [urlstring appendFormat:
                @"&street=12+Cobb+Parkway&city=Marietta&zip=30062"];
            locationURLString =
                @"http://en.wikipedia.org/wiki/Big_Chicken";
            picstring = @"http://upload.wikimedia.org/wikipedia/\
                commons/e/ed/Thebigchicken.jpg";
            break;
        case 2:
            // LA Zoo
            [urlstring appendFormat:
                @"&street=5333+Zoo+Drive&city=Los+Angeles&zip=90027"];
            locationURLString =
                @"http://en.wikipedia.org/wiki/LA_Zoo";
            picstring = @"http://upload.wikimedia.org/\
                wikipedia/en/c/c9/LAzoo.jpg";
            break;
        case 3:
            // Big Hot Dog
            [urlstring appendFormat:
                @"&street=10+Old+Stagecoach+Road&city=Baily&state=CO"];
```

```
        locationURLString =
            @"http://en.wikipedia.org/wiki/\
            Coney_Island_Hot_Dog_Stand";
        picstring = @"http://upload.wikimedia.org/wikipedia/\
            commons/e/ea/Coney_Island_2007.JPG";
        break;
    case 4:
        // Randy's Donuts
        [urlstring appendFormat:
            @"&street=4805+West+Manchester+Avenue\
            &city=Inglewood&zip=90301"];
        locationURLString =
            @"http://en.wikipedia.org/wiki/Randy%27s_Donuts";
        picstring = @"http://upload.wikimedia.org/\
            wikipedia/commons/1/1d/2008-0914-RandysDonuts.jpg";
    default:
        break;
}

// Retrieve the geocoded result
NSData *data = [NSData dataWithContentsOfURL:
    [NSURL URLWithString:urlstring]];
printf("Received %d bytes of data from Yahoo\n", data.length);

// Recover the coordinate
TreeNode *root = [[XMLParser sharedInstance]
    parseXMLFromData:data];
CLLocationCoordinate2D coord;
coord.latitude = [[root leafForKey:@"Latitude"] floatValue];
coord.longitude = [[root leafForKey:@"Longitude"] floatValue];

// Set up the map view
mapView.region =
    MKCoordinateRegionMakeWithDistance(coord, 10000, 10000);
mapView.zoomEnabled = YES;

// Create the annotation if it is not in the dictionary
// This annotation implementation has been extended from
// Recipe 17-8 to include a picture and a url
if (![annotationDict objectForKey:whichLocation])
{
    MapAnnotation *annotation = [[[MapAnnotation alloc]
        initWithCoordinate:coord] autorelease];
    annotation.title = whichLocation;
    annotation.urlstring = locationURLString;
    annotation.picstring = picstring;
```

```
        annotation.subtitle = [NSString stringWithFormat:
            @"%f, %f", coord.latitude, coord.longitude];
        [annotationDict setObject:annotation forKey:whichLocation];

        // Reload the annotations including the new one
        [mapView removeAnnotations:mapView.annotations];
        [mapView addAnnotations:[annotationDict allValues]];
    }

    whichItem = (whichItem + 1) % [LOCATIONS count];
    self.navigationItem.rightBarButtonItem =
        BARBUTTON(whichLocation, @selector(findme));
}
```

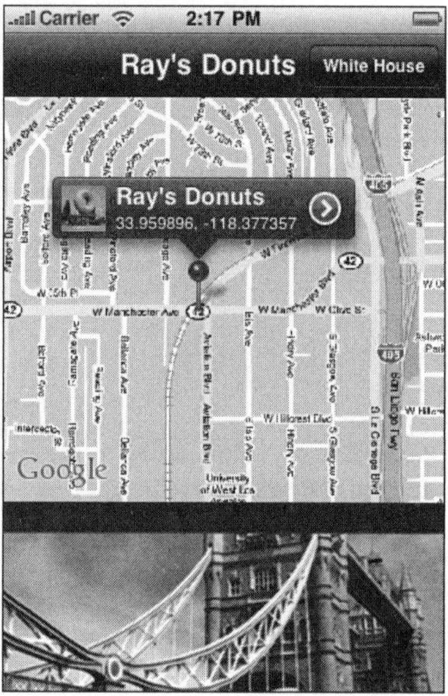

Figure 17-5 Reverse geocoding a street address lets MapKit display an annotation at the proper map location.

Get This Recipe's Code

To get the code used for this recipe, go to http://github.com/erica/iphone-3.0-cookbook-, or if you've downloaded the disk image containing all of the sample code from the book, go to the folder for Chapter 17 and open the project for this recipe.

Summary

Core Location and MapKit go hand in hand, offering ways to locate a device's geoposition and present related location information in a coherent map-based presentation. In this chapter, you discovered how to use Core Location to obtain real-time latitude and longitude coordinates and how to reverse geocode those coordinates into real address information. You read about working with speed and course headings both in their native and computed forms. You learned how to set up a map, adjust its region, and add a user location and custom annotations. Here are a few final thoughts for you before you navigate away from this chapter:

- Know your audience and how they will be using your application before deciding how you will approach your location needs. Some Core Location features work better for driving, others for walking and biking.
- Test, test, test, test, test, test. Core Location applications must be exhaustively tested and tuned in the field as well as at Xcode for best results in App Store.
- "Oh, didn't I see you at -104.28393 west today?" Addresses are a lot more meaningful to most people than coordinates. Use reverse geocoding to produce human-readable information.
- Zip codes are especially API-friendly. Even if you do not plan to use a map presentation in your application, zip codes are ready for traditional GUI integration. A reverse-geocoded zip code can help retrieve nearby retail information such as addresses and phone numbers as well as information about nearby parks and attractions.
- Well-designed annotation views help bring meaningful interactivity into a map view. Don't be afraid to use buttons, images, and other custom elements that expand a map's utility.

18

Connecting to the Address Book

In addition to standard user interface controls and media components that you'd see on any computer, the iPhone SDK provides a number of tightly focused developer solutions specific to iPhone and iPod touch delivery. The most useful of these include Address Book access, allowing you to programmatically access and manage the contacts database. This chapter introduces the Address Book and demonstrates how to use its frameworks in your applications. You read about accessing information on a contact-by-contact basis, how to modify and update contact information, and how to use predicates to find just the contact you're interested in. This chapter also covers the GUI classes that provide interactive solutions for picking, viewing, and modifying contacts. By the time you've read through this chapter, you'll have discovered the address book from the bottom up.

Recipe: Working with the Address Book

The iPhone SDK provides not one but two address book frameworks. These are AddressBook.framework and AddressBookUI.framework. As their names suggest, they occupy distinct niches in the iPhone SDK. AddressBook provides low-level C-based structures and routines for accessing contact information from the iPhone's onboard SQLite databases. AddressBookUI offers high-level Objective-C based `UIViewController` browser objects to present to users. Both frameworks are small. They provide just a few classes and data types.

On the iPhone, contact data resides in the home Library folder. On the Macintosh-based iPhone simulator, you can freely access these files in ~/Library/Application Support/iPhone Simulator/User/Library/AddressBook. The two files, AddressBook.sqlitedb and AddressBookImages.sqlitedb use standard SQLite to store contact information and, in the latter file, optional contact images. On the iPhone, the same files live in /var/mobile/Library/AddressBook, that is, out of the application sandbox. You must use the two Address Book frameworks to query or modify the user's contact information rather than accessing these files directly.

Address Book UI

The AddressBookUI framework provides several precooked view controllers that interact with the onboard contacts database. These interfaces include a general people picker, a contact viewer, and a contact editor. You set a delegate and then push these controllers onto your navigation stack or display them modally, as shown in the recipes in this chapter.

Like the image picker and video camera controllers you saw in Chapter 7, "Working with Images," and Chapter 15, "Audio, Video, and MediaKit," the AddressBookUI controllers are not very flexible. Apple intends you to use them as provided, with little or no customization from the developer. What's more, they require a certain degree of low-level programming prowess. As you see in this chapter, these classes interact with the underlying Address Book in circuitous ways.

Address Book

In the C-based AddressBook framework, the `ABRecordRef` type provides a core contact structure. This record stores all information for each contact, including name, e-mail, phone numbers, and so forth. Every record corresponds to a complete address book contact. Query the address book for the number of objects currently stored in its database. Despite the name, the `ABAdressbookCreate()` function does not create a new address book; it creates a reference to the system address book.

```
+ (int) contactsCount
{
    ABAddressBookRef addressBook = ABAddressBookCreate();
    return ABAddressBookGetPersonCount(addressBook);
}
```

Recover individual records by calling the `ABAddressBookCopyArrayOfAllPeople()` function. The following method retrieves those records as an array and then adds each record into an `ABContact` object. `ABContact` is a custom Objective-C wrapper developed for this book. Objective-C wrappers provide easy integration between the C-based address book calls and normal Cocoa Touch development and memory management. The full source for this, and a couple of other wrapper classes, can be found in the sample code for this chapter.

```
+ (NSArray *) contacts
{
    ABAddressBookRef addressBook = ABAddressBookCreate();
    NSArray *thePeople = (NSArray *)
        ABAddressBookCopyArrayOfAllPeople(addressBook);
    NSMutableArray *array = [NSMutableArray
        arrayWithCapacity:thePeople.count];
    for (id person in thePeople)
        [array addObject:[ABContact
            contactWithRecord:(ABRecordRef)person]];
    [thePeople release];
```

```
    return array;
}
```

The ABContact class hides an internal ABRecordRef, the CF type that corresponds to each contact record. The remaining portion of the wrapper involves nothing more than generating properties and methods that allow you to reach into the ABRecordRef to set and access its subrecords.

```
@interface ABContact : NSObject
{
      ABRecordRef record;
}
@end
```

Nearly all ABRecordRef functions use the ABPerson prefix. This prefix corresponds to the ABPerson class that is available on the Macintosh but not on the iPhone. So while the function calls are ABPerson-centric, all the data affected by these calls are actually ABRecordRef instances. The reason for this becomes clearer when you notice that the same ABRecordRef structure is used in the AddressBook framework to represent both people (individual contacts, whether people or businesses) and groups (collections of contacts, such as work colleagues and personal friends). The SDK provides ABGroup functions as well as ABPerson ones. You read about groups later in this section.

Retrieving and Setting ABRecord Strings

Each ABRecord stores a number of simple string values that represent, along with other items, a person's name, title, job, and organization. Retrieve these items by copying field values from the record. The following method uses a property constant (ABPropertyID) that identifies the requested field in the record. The method copies this value, casts it to a string, and returns that content.

```
- (NSString *) getRecordString:(ABPropertyID) anID
{
    return [(NSString *) ABRecordCopyValue(record, anID) autorelease];
}

// Sample uses
- (NSString *) firstname
    {return [self getRecordString:kABPersonFirstNameProperty];}
- (NSString *) lastname
    {return [self getRecordString:kABPersonLastNameProperty];}
```

The 13 string-based fields you can recover in this fashion are as follows. These identifiers are defined as constant integers in the ABPerson.h header file. They identify fields in an ABRecordRef that store a single string for each property.

- kABPersonFirstNameProperty
- kABPersonLastNameProperty

- kABPersonMiddleNameProperty
- kABPersonPrefixProperty
- kABPersonSuffixProperty
- kABPersonNicknameProperty
- kABPersonFirstNamePhoneticProperty
- kABPersonLastNamePhoneticProperty
- kABPersonMiddleNamePhoneticProperty
- kABPersonOrganizationProperty
- kABPersonJobTitleProperty
- kABPersonDepartmentProperty
- kABPersonNoteProperty

Setting string-based properties proves to be just as simple as retrieving them. Cast the string you want to set to a `CFStringRef`. Use `ABRecordSetValue()` to store the data back into the record. Take note that these calls do not update the address book. They only change the data within the record. If you want to store a user's contact information, you have to write that information back to the address book. A solution for doing so follows later in this section.

```
- (BOOL) setString: (NSString *) aString
    forProperty:(ABPropertyID) anID
{
    CFErrorRef error;
    BOOL success = ABRecordSetValue(record, anID,
        (CFStringRef) aString, &error);
    if (!success) NSLog(@"Error %@",
        [(NSError *)error localizedDescription]);
    return success;
}

// Examples of use
- (void) setFirstname: (NSString *) aString
    {[self setString: aString forProperty:
        kABPersonFirstNameProperty];}

- (void) setLastname: (NSString *) aString
    {[self setString: aString forProperty: kABPersonLastNameProperty];}
```

Simple Date Properties

In addition to the string properties you just saw, the address book stores three key dates: an optional birthday, the date the record was created, and the date the record was last modified. These items use the following property constants.

- kABPersonBirthdayProperty
- kABPersonCreationDateProperty
- kABPersonModificationDateProperty

Access these items exactly as you would with strings but cast to and from `NSDate` instances instead of `NSString` instances. Although you can, theoretically, modify the latter two properties, you're best allowing the address book to handle them.

```
// Return a date-time field from a record
- (NSDate *) getRecordDate:(ABPropertyID) anID
{
    return [(NSDate *) ABRecordCopyValue(record, anID) autorelease];
}

// Get the contact's birthday
- (NSDate *) birthday
    {return [self getRecordDate:kABPersonBirthdayProperty];}

// Set a date-time field in a record
- (BOOL) setDate: (NSDate *) aDate forProperty:(ABPropertyID) anID
{
    CFErrorRef error;
    BOOL success = ABRecordSetValue(record, anID,
        (CFDateRef) aDate, &error);
    if (!success) NSLog(@"Error %@",
        [(NSError *)error localizedDescription]);
    return success;
}

// Set the contact's birthday
- (void) setBirthday: (NSDate *) aDate
    {[self setDate: aDate forProperty: kABPersonBirthdayProperty];}
```

Getting and Setting Multivalue Record Properties

Each person may have multiple e-mail addresses, phone numbers, and important dates (beyond the birthday singleton) associated with his or her contact. `ABPerson` uses a *multivalue* structure to store lists of these items. Each multivalue item is basically an array. You can recover each array from the record via its property identifier. Instead of returning a string, the record returns a `CFArrayRef`.

The multivalue property identifiers you may work with are as follows:

- kABPersonEmailProperty
- kABPersonPhoneProperty
- kABPersonURLProperty

- kABPersonDateProperty
- kABPersonAddressProperty
- kABPersonInstantMessageProperty

The first three of these items (e-mail, phone, and URL) store *multistrings*—that is, arrays of strings. Their associated type is the `kABMultiStringPropertyType`. Each multivalue type plays an important role in storing data back to the record. The type is used to allocate memory and determine the size for each field within the record.

The next item, the date property, stores an array of dates using `kABMultiDateTimePropertyType`. Both the address and instant message properties consist of arrays of dictionaries and use `kABMultiDictionaryPropertyType`.

Note

"Related names" represents another multistring property but one that does not actually get used on the iPhone Contacts application at this time. It uses the `kABPersonRelatedNames➥Property` constant and stores names and their relationships, for example, Mary Ball Washington might be stored in George Washington's contact using the `kABPersonMother➥Label`. See ABPerson.h for a full list of relation constants.

It's straightforward to retrieve an array of values for any of these properties. Just copy the property out of the record (using `ABRecordCopyValue()`) and then break it down into its component array. The address book provides a function that copies the array from the property into a standard `CFArrayRef`.

```
- (NSArray *) arrayForProperty: (ABPropertyID) anID
{
    CFTypeRef theProperty = ABRecordCopyValue(record, anID);
    NSArray *items =
        (NSArray *)ABMultiValueCopyArrayOfAllValues(theProperty);
    CFRelease(theProperty);
    return [items autorelease];
}
```

Although you might think you've retrieved all the information with those two calls, you have not. Value retrieval alone is not sufficient for working with multivalued items. Each element stored in a multivalue array uses a label as well as a value. Figure 18-1 shows part of an address book contact page. Grouped items use labels to differentiate the role for each e-mail, phone number, and so forth. This contact has three phone numbers and three e-mail address, each of which displays a label indicating the value's role.

You must copy the labels from the property as well as the values to retrieve all the information stored for each multivalue property. The following method copies each label by its index and adds it to a labels array. Together, the labels and the values comprise a complete multivalue collection.

```
- (NSArray *) labelsForProperty: (ABPropertyID) anID
{
```

```
    CFTypeRef theProperty = ABRecordCopyValue(record, anID);
    NSMutableArray *labels = [NSMutableArray array];
    for (int i = 0; i < ABMultiValueGetCount(theProperty); i++)
    {
        NSString *label =
            (NSString *)ABMultiValueCopyLabelAtIndex(theProperty, i);
        [labels addObject:label];
        [label release];
    }
    CFRelease(theProperty);
    return labels;
}
```

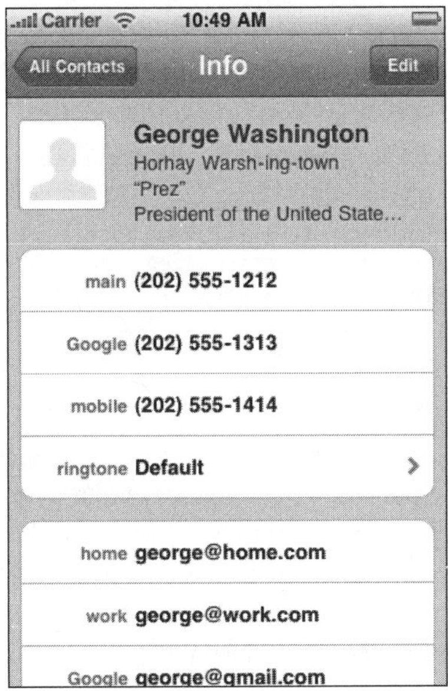

Figure 18-1 Multivalue items consist of both a label (e.g., main, Google, and mobile for these phone numbers, or home, work, and Google for these e-mail addresses) and a value.

Saving into multivalue objects works the same way but in reverse. To store multivalued items into a record, you must transform your Cocoa Touch objects into a form the record can work with. The following method expects an array of dictionaries. Each dictionary must contain two keys: value and label. The objects for these keys correspond to the value and label retrieved from the original multivalued property. This code iterates through that array of dictionaries and adds each value and label to the mutable multivalue object.

```
- (ABMutableMultiValueRef) createMultiValueFromArray:
    (NSArray *) anArray withType: (ABPropertyType) aType
```

```
{
    ABMutableMultiValueRef multi = ABMultiValueCreateMutable(aType);
    for (NSDictionary *dict in anArray)
        ABMultiValueAddValueAndLabel(multi,
            (CFTypeRef) [dict objectForKey:@"value"],
            (CFTypeRef) [dict objectForKey:@"label"], NULL);
    return multi;
}
```

Notice how this method creates the multivalue object using an `ABPropertyType` supplied as the method parameter. This is where the various kinds of multistring types come into play.

For example, you can populate an e-mail property with strings and labels using `kABMultiStringPropertyType`. This method calls the one that creates a multivalue object, providing both value-label dictionaries and the multiproperty type to use. Once that multivalue item is created, it is passed to another method to be set.

```
- (void) setEmailDictionaries: (NSArray *) dictionaries
{
    ABMutableMultiValueRef multi = [self
        createMultiValueFromArray:dictionaries
        withType:kABMultiStringPropertyType];
    [self setMulti:multi forProperty:kABPersonEmailProperty];
    CFRelease(multi);
}
```

Assigning a multivalue object to a record is simple. Use the standard `ABRecordSetValue()` call. The following method performs the assignment of a multivalued object to a property within a record. There is essentially no difference between this call and the calls that set a single date or string property. All the work is done in creating the multivalue item in the first place.

```
- (BOOL) setMulti: (ABMutableMultiValueRef) multi
    forProperty: (ABPropertyID) anID
{
    CFErrorRef error;
    BOOL success = ABRecordSetValue(record, anID, multi, &error);
    if (!success)
        NSLog(@"Error %@",
            [(NSError *)error localizedDescription]);
    return success;
}
```

Addresses and Instant Message Properties

Both address and instant message (SMS) properties use dictionaries rather than strings or dates. This adds an extra step to the creation of a multivalue array. You must populate a set of dictionaries and then add them to an array along with their labels. Figure 18-2 illustrates this additional layer. As this figure shows, e-mail multivalue items consist of an array of label-value pairs, where each value is a single string. In contrast, addresses use a separate dictionary, which is bundled into the value item.

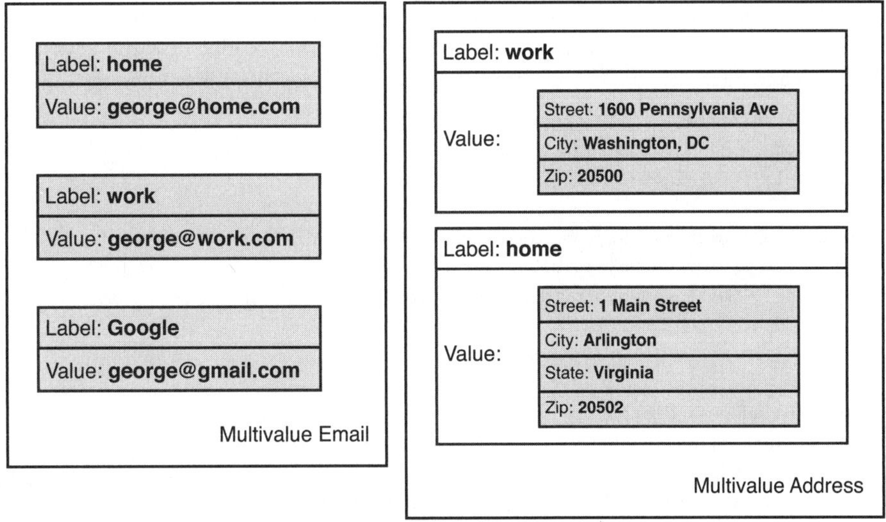

Figure 18-2 Unlike multivalue e-mail, which stores a single string for each value, multivalue addresses contain an entire address dictionary.

Here's an example that demonstrates the steps involved in creating a two-address multivalue item. This code builds the dictionaries and then adds them, along with their labels, to a base array. The array created by this code corresponds to the multivalue address object shown on the right side of Figure 18-2.

```
// Create the array that will store all the address
// value-label dictionaries
NSMutableArray *addresses = [NSMutableArray array];

// Create White House Address and add it to the array
NSDictionary *wh_addy = [ABContact
    addressWithStreet:@"1600 Pennsylvania Avenue"
    withCity:@"Washington, DC" withState:nil
    withZip:@"20500" withCountry:nil withCode:nil];
[addresses addObject:[ABContact dictionaryWithValue:wh_addy
    andLabel:kABWorkLabel]];

// Create a home address and add it to the array
NSDictionary *home_addy = [ABContact
    addressWithStreet:@"1 Main Street" withCity:@"Arlington"
    withState:@"Virginia" withZip:@"20502"
```

```
    withCountry:nil withCode:nil];
[addresses addObject:[ABContact dictionaryWithValue:home_addy
    andLabel:kABHomeLabel]];
```

This code relies on convenience methods to create both the address dictionaries and the value/label dictionaries used for the multivalue array. The following methods produce the label/value dictionaries, and the address and SMS dictionaries. Notice how the keys for the address and SMS dictionaries are predefined, using address book key constants.

```
// Create a value/label dictionary
+ (NSDictionary *) dictionaryWithValue: (id) value
    andLabel: (CFStringRef) label
{
    NSMutableDictionary *dict = [NSMutableDictionary dictionary];
    if (value) [dict setObject:value forKey:@"value"];
    if (label) [dict setObject:(NSString *)label forKey:@"label"];
    return dict;
}

// Create an address dictionary
+ (NSDictionary *) addressWithStreet: (NSString *) street
    withCity: (NSString *) city
    withState:(NSString *) state withZip: (NSString *) zip
    withCountry: (NSString *) country withCode: (NSString *) code
{
    NSMutableDictionary *md = [NSMutableDictionary dictionary];
    if (street) [md setObject:street
        forKey:(NSString *) kABPersonAddressStreetKey];
    if (city) [md setObject:city
        forKey:(NSString *) kABPersonAddressCityKey];
    if (state) [md setObject:state
        forKey:(NSString *) kABPersonAddressStateKey];
    if (zip) [md setObject:zip
        forKey:(NSString *) kABPersonAddressZIPKey];
    if (country) [md setObject:country
        forKey:(NSString *) kABPersonAddressCountryKey];
    if (code) [md setObject:code
        forKey:(NSString *) kABPersonAddressCountryCodeKey];
    return md;
}

// Create an sms dictionary
+ (NSDictionary *) smsWithService: (CFStringRef)
    service andUser: (NSString *) userName
{
    NSMutableDictionary *sms = [NSMutableDictionary dictionary];
    if (service) [sms setObject:(NSString *) service
```

```
        forKey:(NSString *) kABPersonInstantMessageServiceKey];
    if (userName) [sms setObject:userName
        forKey:(NSString *) kABPersonInstantMessageUsernameKey];
    return sms;
}
```

Working with Address Book Images

Each record in the address book may be associated with an optional image. You can copy image data to and from each record. The `ABPersonHasImageData()` function indicates whether data is available for a given record. Use this to test whether you can retrieve image data.

Image data is stored as `CFData`, which is toll-free bridged with `NSData`. As the `UIImage` class fully supports converting images into data and creating images from data, you just need to cast that data as needed. Use the `UIImagePNGRepresentation()` function to transform a `UIImage` instance into an `NSData` representation. Use `imageWithData:` to create a new image from `NSData`.

```
// Return an image from a Contact's record
- (UIImage *) image
{
    if (!ABPersonHasImageData(record)) return nil;
    CFDataRef imageData = ABPersonCopyImageData(record);
    UIImage *image = [UIImage imageWithData:(NSData *) imageData];
    CFRelease(imageData);
    return image;
}

// Set the record's image
- (void) setImage: (UIImage *) image
{
    CFErrorRef error;
    BOOL success;

    if (image == nil) // remove
    {
        if (!ABPersonHasImageData(record)) return;
        success = ABPersonRemoveImageData(record, &error);
        if (!success) NSLog(@"Error %@",
            [(NSError *)error localizedDescription]);
        return;
    }

    NSData *data = UIImagePNGRepresentation(image);
    success = ABPersonSetImageData(record, (CFDataRef)data, &error);
    if (!success) NSLog(@"Error %@",
```

```
        [(NSError *)error localizedDescription]);
}
```

Creating, Adding, and Deleting Records

The `ABPersonCreate()` function returns a new `ABRecordRef` instance. This record exists outside the address book and represents a freestanding data structure. To date, all the methods you've seen in this chapter have modified individual records, but none so far has actually saved a record to the address book. Keep that in mind as you look at this convenience method that returns a newly initialized contact.

```
+ (id) contact
{
    ABRecordRef person = ABPersonCreate();
    id contact = [ABContact contactWithRecord:person];
    CFRelease(person);
    return contact;
}
```

To write new information to the address book takes two steps. You must add the record and then save the address book. New iPhone developers often forget the second step, leading to an address book that appears to resist changes. This method adds a new contact to the address book, first by adding the record and then by saving the changes.

```
+ (NSString *) addContact: (ABContact *) aContact
{
    ABAddressBookRef addressBook = ABAddressBookCreate();
    CFErrorRef error;
    BOOL success = ABAddressBookAddRecord(addressBook,
        aContact.record, &error);
    if (!success) return [(NSError *)error localizedDescription];
    success = ABAddressBookSave(addressBook, &error);
    return success ? nil : [(NSError *)error localizedDescription];
}
```

You cannot overwrite new contact information to a contact that already exists in the address book. If you create a new "George Washington" record and attempt to save it to an address book that already has a "George Washington" record, you'll fail. That's because the new record does not have the same record identifier as the original. The mismatch between the two records causes the error. Here is how you query a record for its unique identifier.

```
- (ABRecordID) recordID {return ABRecordGetRecordID(record);}
```

You can update contact information only by reading out the existing record, modifying it, and saving it (this approach is used in Recipe 18-7), or by removing the record and then adding back a new version.

Removing a record from the address book requires a save step, just like adding a record. Once removed, the record still exists as an object, but it no longer is stored in the address book database. Here's how you can remove a record from the address book.

```
- (NSString *) removeSelfFromAddressBook
{
    ABAddressBookRef addressBook = ABAddressBookCreate();
    CFErrorRef error;
    BOOL success = ABAddressBookRemoveRecord(addressBook,
        self.record, &error);
    if (!success) return [(NSError *)error localizedDescription];
    success = ABAddressBookSave(addressBook, &error);
    return success ? nil : [(NSError *)error localizedDescription];
}
```

Searching for Contacts

The default address book framework allows you to perform a prefix search across records. This function returns an array of records whose composite names (typically first name appended by last name, but localizable to countries where that pattern is reversed) match the supplied string.

```
NSArray *array = (NSArray *)ABAddressBookCopyPeopleWithName(
    addressBook, CFSTR("Eri"));
```

> **Note**
>
> Address Book routines are written using C-based Core Foundation libraries. Many classes live in both the Cocoa Touch Foundation and Core Foundation worlds. For example, an `NSArray*` pointer corresponds to Core Foundation `CFArrayRef`. These classes are "toll free bridged." They provide identical structure and functionality, and you can cast one to the other without penalty. The snippet shown above casts the array reference returned by the Core Foundation `ABAddressBookCopyPeopleWithName()` into an `NSArray` pointer for easier Objective-C wrapping.

It's far easier to combine a set of properties, like those provided in the custom `ABContact` class, with `NSPredicate` instances. The following code matches a string against a contact's first name, middle name, last name, and nickname. The predicate uses property names to define how it matches or rejects contacts. It does this using a case and diacritical insensitive match (`[cd]`) that compares against all points within each string (`contains`), not just the start (`begins with`).

```
+ (NSArray *) contactsMatchingName: (NSString *) fname
{
    NSPredicate *pred;
    NSArray *contacts = [ABContactsHelper contacts];
    pred = [NSPredicate predicateWithFormat:
        @"firstname contains[cd] %@ OR lastname contains[cd] %@ OR\
```

```
        nickname contains[cd] %@ OR middlename contains[cd] %@",
        fname, fname, fname, fname];
    return [contacts filteredArrayUsingPredicate:pred];
}
```

> **Note**
>
> Apple's Predicate Programming Guide offers a comprehensive introduction to predicate basics. It demonstrates how to create predicates and use them in your application.

Working with Groups

Groups allow you to collect contacts into related sets such as work, home, and other natural groupings. Each group is nothing more than another `ABRecord` but with a few special properties. Groups don't store names, addresses, and phone numbers. Instead, they store a reference to other contact records.

Are you unfamiliar with groups on the iPhone? That's because Apple's iPhone Contact application doesn't provide a way to create them. The only way to add groups of contacts to your iPhone is via the SDK or by synchronizing an address book from your Macintosh.

You can count the number of groups in the current address book by retrieving the group records, as shown in this method. There's no direct way to query the number of groups as there is with the number of person contacts. The following methods are part of an `ABGroup` wrapper class that provides an Objective-C wrapper for address book groups like `ABContact` wraps address book contacts.

```
+ (int) numberOfGroups
{
    ABAddressBookRef addressBook = ABAddressBookCreate();
    NSArray *groups =
        (NSArray *)ABAddressBookCopyArrayOfAllGroups(addressBook);
    int ncount = groups.count;
    [groups release];
    return ncount;
}
```

Create groups using the `ABGroupCreate()` function. This function returns an `ABRecordRef` in the same way that `ABPersonCreate()` does. The difference lies in the record type. For groups, this property is set to `kABGroupType` instead of `kABPersonType`.

```
+ (id) group
{
    ABRecordRef grouprec = ABGroupCreate();
    id group = [ABGroup groupWithRecord:grouprec];
    CFRelease(grouprec);
    return group;
}
```

Add and remove members of a group by calling `ABGroupAddMember()` and `ABGroupRemoveMember()`. These calls affect records only and are not stored until you save the address book.

```
- (BOOL) addMember: (ABContact *) contact
    withError: (NSError **) error
{
    return ABGroupAddMember(self.record, contact.record,
        (CFErrorRef *) error);
}

- (BOOL) removeMember: (ABContact *) contact
    withError: (NSError **) error
{
    return ABGroupRemoveMember(self.record, contact.record,
        (CFErrorRef *) error);
}
```

Each member of a group is a person, or using this chapter's `ABContact` terminology, a contact. This method scans through a group's members and returns an array of `ABContact` instances, each initialized with the `ABRecordRef` for a group member.

```
- (NSArray *) members
{
    NSArray *contacts =
        (NSArray *)ABGroupCopyArrayOfAllMembers(self.record);
    NSMutableArray *array =
        [NSMutableArray arrayWithCapacity:contacts.count];
    for (id contact in contacts)
        [array addObject:
            [ABContact contactWithRecord:(ABRecordRef)contact]];
    [contacts release];
    return array;
}
```

Every group has a name. It is the primary group property that you can set and retrieve. It uses the `kABGroupNamePropert` identifier, and it otherwise works just like the contacts properties.

```
- (NSString *) getRecordString:(ABPropertyID) anID
{
    return [(NSString *) ABRecordCopyValue(record, anID) autorelease];
}

- (NSString *) name
{
    NSString *string = [self getRecordString:kABGroupNameProperty];
    return [string autorelease];
}
```

```
- (void) setName: (NSString *) aString
{
    CFErrorRef error;
    BOOL success = ABRecordSetValue(record,
        kABGroupNameProperty, (CFStringRef) aString, &error);
    if (!success)
        NSLog(@"Error %@", [(NSError *)error localizedDescription]);
}
```

ABContact, ABGroup, and ABContactsHelper

The sample code that accompanies this section includes source for three wrapper classes. The snippets shown throughout this discussion highlight the techniques used in these classes. Due to the length and overall redundancy of the classes, a single recipe listing (normally Recipe 18-1) has been omitted from this section. The examples you've already seen together comprise this section's "recipe." The sample code joins these techniques together into a group of Address Book wrappers. So Recipe 18-1 can be found in the sample code for this chapter.

The custom `ABContact` class is somewhat based on the Mac-only `ABPerson` class. It provides a more Cocoa Touch interface with built-in Objective-C 2.0 properties than the C-style property queries that Apple's `ABPerson` uses. All the contact-specific methods you've seen to date in this section derive from this class.

A second class called `ABGroup` wraps all the group functionality for `ABRecordRef` instances. It offers Objective-C access to group creation and management. Use this class to build new classes, and add and remove members.

The final class, `ABContactsHelper` provides address book-specific methods. Use this class to search through the address book, retrieve arrays of records, and so forth. Although I have included a few basic searches across names and phone numbers, you can easily expand this class, which is hosted at http://github.com/erica, for more complex queries.

Recipe: Searching the Address Book

Predicate-based searches are both fast and effective. Recipe 18-2 shows predicate-based queries in action. It presents a search table (like the one introduced in Recipe 11-16) that displays a scrolling table of contacts. This table responds to user search bar queries with live updates.

Because search tables have two data sources, this recipe uses two arrays. A contacts array stores the entire address book contacts list. A second, filtered array is built each time the user updates the search bar, using the `contactsMatchingName:` method you just read about in the preceding section.

When a user taps a row, this recipe displays an `ABPersonViewController` instance. This class offers a view that displays the details for a given record, similar to Figure 18-1. To use this view controller, you allocate and initialize it and set its `displayedPerson` property. As you'd expect, this property stores an `ABRecordRef`.

Person view controllers offer a limited delegate. By setting the `personViewDelegate` property, you can subscribe to the `personViewController:shouldPerformDefault ➥ActionForPerson:` method. This method triggers when users select certain items in the view, including phone numbers, e-mail addresses, URLs, and addresses. Return `YES` to perform the default action (dialing, e-mailing, etc.) or `NO` to skip. Recipe 18-2 uses this callback to display the value for the selected item in the debug console. Although you can interact with other display elements like the contact note and ringtone, these items do not produce callbacks.

To extend this recipe to allow editing, set the person view controller's `allowsEditing` property to `YES`. This provides the edit button that appears at the top right of the display. When tapped, the edit button triggers the same editing features in the person view that you normally see in the Contacts application.

Recipe 18-2 **Selecting and Displaying Contacts with Search**

```
- (NSInteger)tableView:(UITableView *)aTableView
    numberOfRowsInSection:(NSInteger)section
{
    // Normal table
    if (aTableView == self.tableView)
        return self.contacts.count;

    // Search table
    self.filteredArray = [ABContactsHelper
        contactsMatchingName:self.searchBar.text];
    return self.filteredArray.count;
}

- (UITableViewCell *)tableView:(UITableView *)aTableView
    cellForRowAtIndexPath:(NSIndexPath *)indexPath
{
    // Dequeue or create a cell
    UITableViewCellStyle style =  UITableViewCellStyleSubtitle;
    UITableViewCell *cell = [aTableView
        dequeueReusableCellWithIdentifier:@"BaseCell"];
    if (!cell) cell = [[[UITableViewCell alloc] initWithStyle:style
        reuseIdentifier:@"BaseCell"] autorelease];

    // Retrieve the contact information and set the cell text
    NSArray *collection = (aTableView == self.tableView) ?
        self.contacts : self.filteredArray;
    ABContact *contact = [collection objectAtIndex:indexPath.row];
    cell.textLabel.text = contact.contactName;
    cell.detailTextLabel.text = contact.phonenumbers;
```

```
    return cell;
}

- (BOOL)personViewController:
    (ABPersonViewController *)personViewController
    shouldPerformDefaultActionForPerson:(ABRecordRef)person
    property:(ABPropertyID)property
    identifier:(ABMultiValueIdentifier)identifierForValue
{
    // Reveal the item that was selected
    if ([ABContact propertyIsMultivalue:property])
    {
        NSArray *array = [ABContact arrayForProperty:property
            inRecord:person];
        CFShow([array objectAtIndex:identifierForValue]);
    }
    else
    {
        id object = [ABContact objectForProperty:property
            inRecord:person];
        CFShow([object description]);
    }
    return YES;
}

- (void)tableView:(UITableView *)aTableView
    didSelectRowAtIndexPath:(NSIndexPath *)indexPath
{
    // Respond to row selection by displaying the person view
    ABPersonViewController *pvc =
        [[[ABPersonViewController alloc] init] autorelease];
    NSArray *collection = (aTableView == self.tableView) ?
        self.contacts : self.filteredArray;
    ABContact *contact = [collection objectAtIndex:indexPath.row];
    pvc.displayedPerson = contact.record;
    pvc.personViewDelegate = self;
    // pvc.allowsEditing = YES; // optional editing
    [[self navigationController] pushViewController:pvc animated:YES];
}
```

Get This Recipe's Code

To get the code used for this recipe, go to http://github.com/erica/iphone-3.0-cookbook-, or if you've downloaded the disk image containing all of the sample code from the book, go to the folder for Chapter 18 and open the project for this recipe.

Recipe: Accessing Image Data

Recipe 18-3 expands on Recipe 18-2 by adding contact image thumbnails to each table cell. It does this by creating a new 45-by-45 pixel image. When image data is available, that image is rendered onto the thumbnail. When it is not, the thumbnail is left blank. Upon being drawn, the image is assigned to the cell's `imageView`. Please note that the `imageView` property was introduced in the 3.0 SDK. For deployment to pre-3.0 firmware, you may use the cell's `image` property, which is now deprecated.

Figure 18-3 shows the interface for this recipe. In this screenshot, a search is in progress (matching against the letter "e"). The records that match the search each display their image thumbnail.

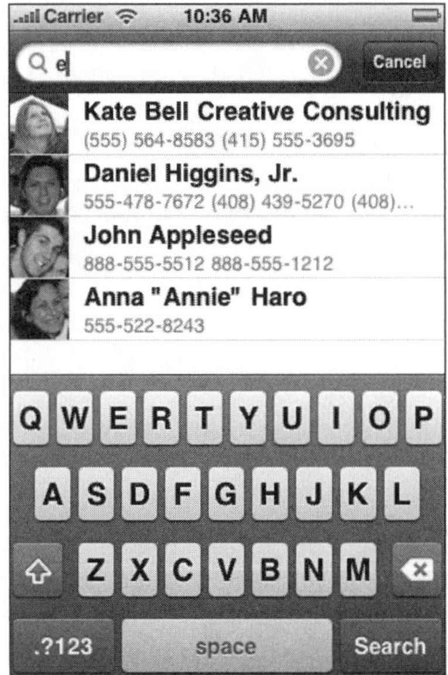

Figure 18-3 You can easily retrieve and display the image data associated with address book contacts.

Notice how simple it is to create and use thumbnails in this recipe. It takes just a few lines of code to build a new image context, draw into it (for contacts with images), and save it out to a `UIImage` instance.

Recipe 18-3 **Displaying Address Book Images in Table Cells**

```
- (UITableViewCell *)tableView:(UITableView *)aTableView
    cellForRowAtIndexPath:(NSIndexPath *)indexPath
{
```

```
    // Dequeue or create a cell
    UITableViewCellStyle style =  UITableViewCellStyleSubtitle;
    UITableViewCell *cell = [aTableView
        dequeueReusableCellWithIdentifier:@"BaseCell"];
    if (!cell) cell = [[[UITableViewCell alloc] initWithStyle:style
        reuseIdentifier:@"BaseCell"] autorelease];

    // Recover the contact
    NSArray *collection = (aTableView == self.tableView) ?
        self.contacts : self.filteredArray;
    ABContact *contact = [collection objectAtIndex:indexPath.row];
    cell.textLabel.text = contact.contactName;
    cell.detailTextLabel.text = contact.phonenumbers;

    // Draw the image into a thumbnail
    UIGraphicsBeginImageContext(CGSizeMake(45.0f, 45.0f));
    if (contact.image)
        [contact.image drawInRect:
            CGRectMake(0.0f, 0.0f, 45.0f, 45.0f)];
    UIImage *img = UIGraphicsGetImageFromCurrentImageContext();
    UIGraphicsEndImageContext();

    // Set the image for the cell
    cell.imageView.image = img;

    return cell;
}
```

Get This Recipe's Code

To get the code used for this recipe, go to http://github.com/erica/iphone-3.0-cookbook-, or if you've downloaded the disk image containing all of the sample code from the book, go to the folder for Chapter 18 and open the project for this recipe.

Recipe: Picking People

The AddressBookUI framework offers a handy people picker controller. Browsing your entire Contacts list is just as easily accomplished as displaying an individual contact screen. Use the `ABPeoplePickerNavigationController` class to present an interactive browser, as shown in Figure 18-4.

Allocate and display the controller before presenting it modally. Make sure to set the `peoplePickerDelegate` property, which allows you to catch user interactions with the view.

```
- (void) action: (UIBarButtonItem *) bbi
{
    ABPeoplePickerNavigationController *ppnc =
        [[ABPeoplePickerNavigationController alloc] init];
```

```
    ppnc.peoplePickerDelegate = self;
    [self presentModalViewController:ppnc animated:YES];
}
```

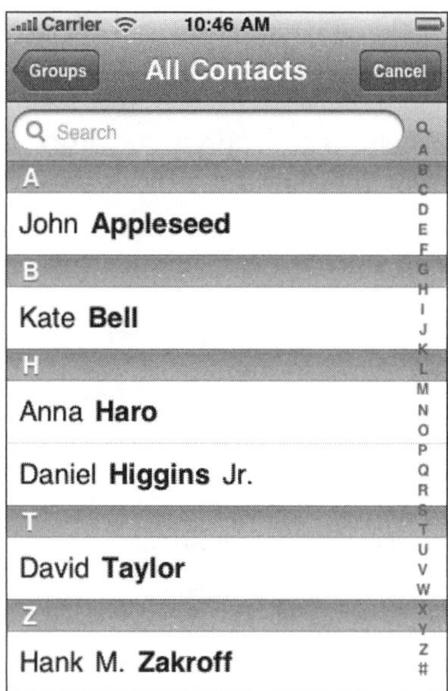

Figure 18-4 The iPhone people picker navigation control enables users to search through the contacts database and select a person or organization.

When you declare the `ABPeoplePickerNavigationControllerDelegate` protocol, your class must implement the following three methods. These methods respond to users when they tap a contact, or any of a contact's properties, or when the user taps Cancel:

- **`peoplePickerNavigationController:shouldContinueAfter`** **`➥SelectingPerson:`**—When users tap a contact, you have two choices. You can accept the person as the final selection and dismiss the modal view controller (as is done here in Recipe 18-4), or you can navigate to the individual display. To pick just the person, this method returns `NO`. To continue to the individual screen, return `YES`. The second argument contains the selected person, in case you want to stop after selecting any `ABPerson` record.
- **`peoplePickerNavigationController:shouldContinueAfter`** **`➥SelectingPerson:property:identifier:`**—This method does not get called until the user has progressed to an individual contact display screen. Then, it's up to you whether to return control to your program (return `NO`) or to continue (return `YES`). You can determine which property has been tapped and to recover its value using the code from Recipe 18-2. Although this method should be optional, it is not at the time of writing this book.

- **`peoplePickerNavigationControllerDidCancel:`**—When a user taps Cancel, you still want a chance to dismiss the modal view. This method catches the cancel event, allowing you to use it to perform the dismissal.

Recipe 18-4 presents the simplest possible people picking example. It presents the picker and waits for a user to select a contact. When the user does so, it dismisses the picker and changes the view controller title (in the navigation bar) to show the composite name of the selected person. Returning `NO` from the primary callback means the property callback will never be called. You must still include it in your code as all three methods are required.

Recipe 18-4 Picking People

```
// Respond to the selection of a contact by a user
- (BOOL)peoplePickerNavigationController:
    (ABPeoplePickerNavigationController *)peoplePicker
    shouldContinueAfterSelectingPerson:(ABRecordRef)person
{
    self.title = [[ABContact contactWithRecord:person] compositeName];
    [self dismissModalViewControllerAnimated:YES];
    [peoplePicker release];
    return NO; // do not continue further
}

// Required method that is never called in the people-only-picking
- (BOOL)peoplePickerNavigationController:
    (ABPeoplePickerNavigationController *)peoplePicker
    shouldContinueAfterSelectingPerson:(ABRecordRef)person
    property:(ABPropertyID)property
    identifier:(ABMultiValueIdentifier)identifier
{
    [self dismissModalViewControllerAnimated:YES];
    [peoplePicker release];
    return NO;
}

// Handle a user cancel
- (void)peoplePickerNavigationControllerDidCancel:
    (ABPeoplePickerNavigationController *)peoplePicker
{
    [self dismissModalViewControllerAnimated:YES];
    [peoplePicker release];
}

// Present the picker
- (void) action: (UIBarButtonItem *) bbi
```

```
{
    ABPeoplePickerNavigationController *ppnc =
        [[ABPeoplePickerNavigationController alloc] init];
    ppnc.peoplePickerDelegate = self;
    [self presentModalViewController:ppnc animated:YES];
}
```

Recipe: Limiting Contact Picker Properties

When you need users to pick a certain kind of property, such as an e-mail address, you won't want to present users with a person's street address or fax number. Limit the picker's displayed properties to show just those items you want the users to select from. Figure 18-5's picker has been limited to e-mail selection.

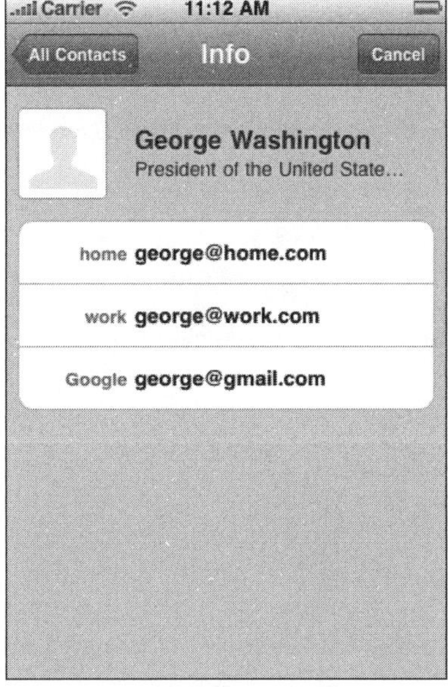

Figure 18-5 The people picker's displayed properties allows you to choose which properties to present to users, in this case e-mail only.

To make this happen, choose the displayed properties by submitting an array of property types to the controller. Set the picker's `displayedProperties` property. Recipe 18-5 offers two picking options, one for e-mail, the other for phone numbers. Although these examples use a single property for the properties array, you can choose to display any number of properties.

Recipe 18-5 **Choosing Display Properties**

```
// Ensure that users can access the detail screen
- (BOOL)peoplePickerNavigationController:
    (ABPeoplePickerNavigationController *)peoplePicker
    shouldContinueAfterSelectingPerson:(ABRecordRef)person
{
    return YES;
}

// Display the selected property
- (BOOL)peoplePickerNavigationController:
    (ABPeoplePickerNavigationController *)peoplePicker
    shouldContinueAfterSelectingPerson:(ABRecordRef)person
    property:(ABPropertyID)property
    identifier:(ABMultiValueIdentifier)identifier
{
    // We are guaranteed to only be working with e-mail or phone
    [self dismissModalViewControllerAnimated:YES];
    NSArray *array = [ABContact arrayForProperty:property
        inRecord:person];
    self.title = (NSString *)[array objectAtIndex:identifier];
    [peoplePicker release];
    return NO;
}

// Handle user cancels
- (void)peoplePickerNavigationControllerDidCancel:
    (ABPeoplePickerNavigationController *)peoplePicker
{
    [self dismissModalViewControllerAnimated:YES];
    [peoplePicker release];
}

// Select an e-mail address
- (void) email
{
    ABPeoplePickerNavigationController *ppnc =
        [[ABPeoplePickerNavigationController alloc] init];
    ppnc.peoplePickerDelegate = self;
    [ppnc setDisplayedProperties:[NSArray
        arrayWithObject:NUMBER(kABPersonEmailProperty)]];
    [self presentModalViewController:ppnc animated:YES];
}

// Select a phone number
- (void) phone: (UIBarButtonItem *) bbi
```

```
{
    ABPeoplePickerNavigationController *ppnc =
        [[ABPeoplePickerNavigationController alloc] init];
    ppnc.peoplePickerDelegate = self;
    [ppnc setDisplayedProperties:[NSArray
        arrayWithObject:NUMBER(kABPersonPhoneProperty)]];
    [self presentModalViewController:ppnc animated:YES];
}
```

Get This Recipe's Code

To get the code used for this recipe, go to http://github.com/erica/iphone-3.0-cookbook-, or if you've downloaded the disk image containing all of the sample code from the book, go to the folder for Chapter 18 and open the project for this recipe.

Recipe: Adding New Contacts

Allow your users to create new contacts with the `ABNewPersonViewController` class. This view controller offers an editing screen that simplifies the interactive creation of a new address book entry. After allocating and initializing the view controller, start by creating a new contact and assigning it to the `displayedPerson` property. If you want, you can prefill the contact's record with properties first. Recipe 18-7, which follows this one, uses prefilling to modify already-existing contacts.

Next, assign the `newPersonViewDelegate` and declare the `ABNewPersonView➥ControllerDelegate` protocol. Delegates receive one callback, `newPersonView➥Controller:didCompleteWithNewPerson:`. This callback is sent for both selection and cancel events. Check the `person` parameter to determine which case applies, as shown in Recipe 18-6.

If the user taps Done after editing the new contact, save the contact data to the address book. If you're doing this manually rather than using the `ABContactsHelper` helper class, make sure you both add the record and save the address book.

When a contact already exists with the same credentials, you need to handle the situation in some fashion. This recipe removes the existing contact to replace it with the new one, but you can also throw up an alert and ask the user how to proceed. The user might choose to keep the original or the replacement, or if you want, you can try to merge the two records somehow.

Recipe 18-6 **Using the New Person View Controller**

```
- (void)newPersonViewController:
    (ABNewPersonViewController *)newPersonViewController
    didCompleteWithNewPerson:(ABRecordRef)person
{
    if (person)
    {
        ABContact *contact = [ABContact contactWithRecord:person];
```

```
        self.title = [NSString stringWithFormat:
            @"Added %@", contact.compositeName];
        if (![ABContactsHelper addContact:contact withError:nil])
        {
            // May already exist so remove and add again to
            // replace existing with new
            [contact removeSelfFromAddressBook:nil];
            [ABContactsHelper addContact:contact withError:nil];
        }
    }
    else
        self.title = @"Cancelled";

    [self.navigationController popViewControllerAnimated:YES];
}

- (void) add
{
    // Create a new view controller
    ABNewPersonViewController *npvc =
        [[[ABNewPersonViewController alloc] init] autorelease];

    // Create a new contact
    ABContact *contact = [ABContact contact];
    npvc.displayedPerson = contact.record;

    // Set delegate
    npvc.newPersonViewDelegate = self;

    [self.navigationController pushViewController:npvc animated:YES];
}
```

Get This Recipe's Code

To get the code used for this recipe, go to http://github.com/erica/iphone-3.0-cookbook-, or if you've downloaded the disk image containing all of the sample code from the book, go to the folder for Chapter 18 and open the project for this recipe.

Recipe: Modifying Existing Contacts

Recipe 18-7 uses the `ABNewPersonViewController` class's ability to prefill a form to modify existing contacts. The modify method starts by presenting a people picker controller. Once a user selects a contact, the application responds by using that contact information to populate the new person controller, which is then pushed onto the navigation stack.

As with Recipe 18-6, the code differentiates between cancel and done. This recipe, however, does not try to replace an existing contact. Instead, it simply adds the contact back into place. The contact's record ID is established by the people picker, and that same record ID allows the new changes to overwrite the old.

Recipe 18-7 **Selecting and Modifying an Address Book Contact**

```
#pragma mark NEW PERSON DELEGATE METHODS
- (void)newPersonViewController:
    (ABNewPersonViewController *)newPersonViewController
    didCompleteWithNewPerson:(ABRecordRef)person
{
    if (person)
    {
        // Save the edited contact
        ABContact *contact = [ABContact contactWithRecord:person];
        self.title = [NSString stringWithFormat:
            @"Updated %@", contact.compositeName];
        [ABContactsHelper addContact:contact withError:nil];
    }
    else
        self.title = @"Cancelled";

    [self.navigationController popViewControllerAnimated:YES];
}

#pragma mark PEOPLE PICKER DELEGATE METHODS
- (BOOL)peoplePickerNavigationController:
    (ABPeoplePickerNavigationController *)peoplePicker
    shouldContinueAfterSelectingPerson:(ABRecordRef)person
{
    [self dismissModalViewControllerAnimated:YES];
    [peoplePicker release];
    ABContact *contact = [ABContact contactWithRecord:person];

    // Handle the modification request by pre-filling the
    // new person view controller
    ABNewPersonViewController *npvc =
        [[ABNewPersonViewController alloc] init];
    npvc.displayedPerson = contact.record;
    npvc.newPersonViewDelegate = self;
    [self.navigationController pushViewController:npvc
        animated:YES];
    return NO;
}

- (BOOL)peoplePickerNavigationController:
    (ABPeoplePickerNavigationController *)peoplePicker
    shouldContinueAfterSelectingPerson:(ABRecordRef)person
```

```
    property:(ABPropertyID)property
    identifier:(ABMultiValueIdentifier)identifier
{
    // Required method that is never called in the people-only-picking
    [self dismissModalViewControllerAnimated:YES];
    [peoplePicker release];
    return NO;
}

- (void)peoplePickerNavigationControllerDidCancel:
    (ABPeoplePickerNavigationController *)peoplePicker
{
    // Handle a cancel by dismissing the controller
    [self dismissModalViewControllerAnimated:YES];
    [peoplePicker release];
}

#pragma mark Base GUI
- (void) modify
{
    // Call out a new picker controller
    ABPeoplePickerNavigationController *ppnc =
        [[ABPeoplePickerNavigationController alloc] init];
    ppnc.peoplePickerDelegate = self;
    [self presentModalViewController:ppnc animated:YES];
}
```

Get This Recipe's Code

To get the code used for this recipe, go to http://github.com/erica/iphone-3.0-cookbook-, or if you've downloaded the disk image containing all of the sample code from the book, go to the folder for Chapter 18 and open the project for this recipe.

Recipe: The ABUnknownPersonViewController

What happens when you have some information like an e-mail address or a phone number, but you don't have a contact to associate with it yet? The `ABUnknownPersonView` ➥`Controller` allows you to add that information to a new or existing contact. This class exists to associate known properties with unknown contacts. It works like this.

You allocate and initialize the view controller and then create and prefill a record. Recipe 18-8 defines a record with a single e-mail address. You can add more items if you want, and each will be displayed in the view controller. Figure 18-6 (left) shows this recipe's controller with its single e-mail. Assign the prefilled record to the `displayedPerson` property.

The Create New Contact and Add to Existing Contact buttons are controlled by the `allowsAddingToAddressBook` property. When a user taps on the new contact button, a

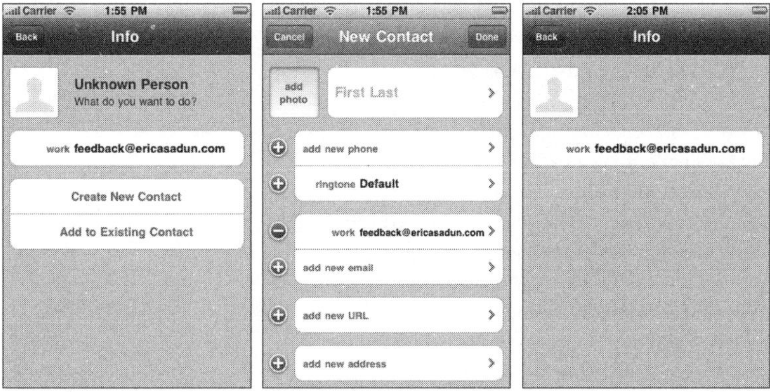

Figure 18-6 (Left) The Unknown Person Controller allows you to display properties and add them to a new or existing contact. (Middle) The properties you set prefill the new contact form when the user taps Create New Contact. (Right) When you disable the address book features and enable actions, you create a sheet that offers one-tap access to phone numbers, e-mail addresses, URLs, and so forth.

form appears (see Figure 18-6, middle) that is prefilled with the properties from that record. If you disable this adding property, the buttons do not appear (see Figure 18-6, right). When you set the `allowsAction` property to `YES`, users can still tap on these elements to connect to an e-mail address, to phone numbers, and so forth. This provides a handy way to present a list of interactive contact information and URLs with an already-defined view controller.

The `alternateName` and `message` properties provide the text that fills the name and organization fields in Figure 18-6 (left). Although you can populate these fields with data via the record, the alternate options do not transfer to contacts. Therefore they provide a nice way to prompt the user without side effects.

Set the `unknownPersonViewDelegate` property and declare the `ABUnknownPersonView` ➥`ControllerDelegate` protocol to receive the `unknownPersonViewController:did` ➥`ResolveToPerson:` method. Called when the user taps Done, this method allows you to recover the record that the data was saved to. It also provides a place where you can pop the view controller and release it, knowing that the user has finished interaction with the dialog.

Recipe 18-8 **Adding Existing Properties to Contacts**

```
- (void)unknownPersonViewController:
    (ABUnknownPersonViewController *)unknownPersonView
    didResolveToPerson:(ABRecordRef)person
{
    [self.navigationController popViewControllerAnimated:YES];
    [unknownPersonView release];
```

```
}

- (void) action: (UIBarButtonItem *) bbi
{

    // Create the controller
    ABUnknownPersonViewController *upvc =
        [[ABUnknownPersonViewController alloc] init];
    upvc.unknownPersonViewDelegate = self;

    // Create and prefill record
    ABContact *contact = [ABContact contact];
    NSArray *emails = [NSArray arrayWithObject:
        [ABContact dictionaryWithValue:@"feedback@ericasadun.com"
        andLabel:kABWorkLabel]];
    contact.emailDictionaries = emails;
    upvc.displayedPerson = contact.record;

    // Actions make calls, send text, email, etc. Set to NO to disallow
    upvc.allowsActions = NO;

    // YES means can add these properties to a new or existing contact
    upvc.allowsAddingToAddressBook = YES;

    // Default value to show in place of name
    upvc.alternateName = @"Unknown Person";

    // Optional text to display below alternate name
    upvc.message = @"What do you want to do?";


    [self.navigationController pushViewController:upvc animated:YES];
}
```

Get This Recipe's Code

To get the code used for this recipe, go to http://github.com/erica/iphone-3.0-cookbook-, or if you've downloaded the disk image containing all of the sample code from the book, go to the folder for Chapter 18 and open the project for this recipe.

One More Thing: Adding Random Contact Art

The Monster ID project consists of a collection of body part art that can be compiled together to form random pictures. It was developed by Andreas Gohr, and was inspired by a Web post by Don Park and the combinatoric critters. Built up by adding predrawn arms, legs, a body, and so forth, the resulting composite image produces a full creature.

The `randomImage` method in Recipe 18-9 builds a monster image from its components. This art can be assigned directly to an address book contact or can be used as the seed for a new contact using the unknown person controller. Either way, you can use an `ABContact` instance and assign an image using its `image` property. If you're not using the controller, don't forget to save the address book after updating a record's image.

Recipe 18-9 uses the unknown person controller approach. When the user taps an action button, it requests a Monster ID image and presents the controller, which is shown in Figure 18-7. The image appears in the Info page, and the standard create/add buttons allow users to add the generated art to a new or existing contact. Users can tap Back to return without adding the image. A new monster generates each time the sheet appears.

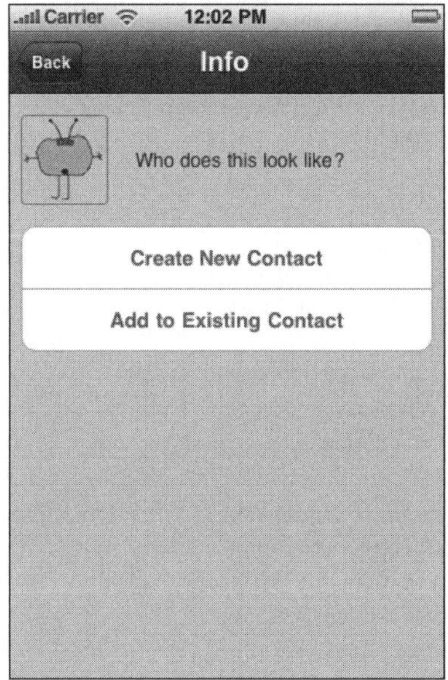

Figure 18-7 You can add images to contacts with the unknown person controller as well as e-mail addresses, phone numbers, and other text-based data.

Recipe 18-9 **Combining Random Art with the Unknown Person Controller**

```
// Graphics from: http://www.splitbrain.org/go/monsterid
- (UIImage *) randomImage
{
    // Build a random image based on the monster id art

    CGRect rect = CGRectMake(0.0f, 0.0f, 120.0f, 120.0f);
    UIGraphicsBeginImageContext(CGSizeMake(120.0f, 120.0f));
```

```
    UIImage *part;
    part = [UIImage imageNamed:IMAGEFILE(@"oldarms_%d.png", 5)];
    [part drawInRect:rect];
    part = [UIImage imageNamed:IMAGEFILE(@"oldlegs_%d.png", 5)];
    [part drawInRect:rect];
    part = [UIImage imageNamed:IMAGEFILE(@"oldbody_%d.png", 15)];
    [part drawInRect:rect];
    part = [UIImage imageNamed:IMAGEFILE(@"oldmouth_%d.png", 10)];
    [part drawInRect:rect];
    part = [UIImage imageNamed:IMAGEFILE(@"oldeyes_%d.png", 15)];
    [part drawInRect:rect];
    part = [UIImage imageNamed:IMAGEFILE(@"oldhair_%d.png", 5)];
    [part drawInRect:rect];

    UIImage *image = UIGraphicsGetImageFromCurrentImageContext();
    UIGraphicsEndImageContext();

    return image;
}

- (void) action: (UIBarButtonItem *) bbi
{
    // Build an empty contact with a random image
    ABContact *contact = [ABContact contact];
    contact.image = [self randomImage];

    // Present unknown person controller
    ABUnknownPersonViewController *upvc =
        [[ABUnknownPersonViewController alloc] init];
    upvc.unknownPersonViewDelegate = self;
    upvc.allowsAddingToAddressBook = YES;
    upvc.message = @"Who does this look like?";
    upvc.displayedPerson = contact.record;

    [self.navigationController pushViewController:upvc animated:YES];
}

- (void) viewDidLoad
{
    srandom(time(0)); // randomize
    self.navigationItem.rightBarButtonItem =
        BARBUTTON(@"Action", @selector(action));
}
```

Get This Recipe's Code

To get the code used for this recipe, go to http://github.com/erica/iphone-3.0-cookbook-, or if you've downloaded the disk image containing all of the sample code from the book, go to the folder for Chapter 18 and open the project for this recipe.

Summary

This chapter introduced Address Book core functionality for both the AddressBook and AddressBookUI frameworks. Here are a few parting thoughts about the frameworks you just encountered:

- Although useful, the low-level Address Book functions can prove frustrating to work with directly. The various helper classes that accompany this chapter may help make your life a little easier.
- Accessing and modifying an address book image works like any other field. Supply image data instead of strings, dates, or multivalue arrays. Don't hesitate to use image data in your contacts applications.
- The view controllers provided by the AddressBookUI framework work seamlessly with the underlying AddressBook routines. There's no need to roll your own GUIs for most common address book interaction tasks.
- The unknown person controller provides a really great way to store specific information (such as a company's e-mail address, an important Web site, etc.) into a contact while allowing user discretion for where (or whether) to place that information.

19

A Taste of Core Data

Beginning with the 3.0 SDK, Apple has finally brought Core Data to the iPhone. The Core Data framework provides persistent data solutions. It offers managed data stores that can be queried and updated from your application. With Core Data, you gain a Cocoa Touch-based object interface that brings relational data management out from SQL queries and into the Objective-C world of iPhone development. This chapter introduces Core Data. It provides just enough recipes to give you a taste of the technology, offering a jumping off point for further Core Data learning. By the time you finish reading through this chapter, you'll have seen Core Data in action. You'll gain an overview of the technology and have worked through several common Core Data scenarios. This chapter cannot provide a full review of Core Data—there are stand-alone books for that—but it does offer a jumping off point for anyone who wants to integrate this technology into their iPhone applications.

Introducing Core Data

Core Data simplifies the way your applications create and use managed objects. Until the 3.0 SDK, all data management and SQL access were left to fairly low-level libraries. It wasn't pretty, and it wasn't easy to use. Now Core Data has joined the Cocoa Touch framework family, bringing easy data management to the iPhone. Core Data provides a flexible object management infrastructure. It offers tools for working with persistent data stores, generating solutions for the complete object life cycle.

Core Data lives in the Model portion of the Model-View-Controller paradigm. Core Data understands that application-specific data must be defined and controlled outside the application's GUI. Because of that, the application delegate, view controller instances, and custom model classes provide the most natural homes for Core Data functionality. Where you place the ownership depends on how you'll use the data.

As a rule, your application delegate usually owns any shared database that gets used throughout the application. Simpler applications may get by with a single view controller that manages the same data access. The key lies in understanding that the owner controls all data access—reading, writing, and updating. Any part of your application that works with Core Data must coordinate with that owner.

While it's agreed that the data model portion of the application exists separately from its interface, Apple understands that data does not exist in a vacuum. The 3.0 SDK integrates seamlessly with `UITableView` instances. Cocoa Touch's fetched-results controller class was designed and built with tables in mind. It offers useful properties and methods that support table integration. You see this integration in action via recipes later in this chapter.

Creating and Editing Model Files

Model files define how Core Data objects are structured. Each project that links against the Core Data framework includes one or more model files. These .xcdatamodel files define the objects, their attributes, and their relationships.

Each object may own any number of properties, which are called attributes. Attribute types include strings, dates, numbers, and data. Each object can also have relationships, which are links between one object and another. These relationships can be single, using a one-to-one relationship, or they can be multiple, using a one-to-many relationship. In addition, those relationships can be one-way, or they can be reciprocal, providing an inverse relationship.

You define your model in Xcode by laying out a new data model file. Create these Xcode model files by selecting File > New File > iPhone OS > Resource > Data Model > Next. Enter a name for your new file, click Next, and click Finish. Xcode adds the new model file to your project.

Double-click the .xcdatamodel file to open it in an editor window, as shown in Figure 19-1. Add new object entities (basically "classes") in the top-left list; define attributes and relationships in the top middle (essentially "instance variables"). The top right offers a context-sensitive inspector. An object graph appears below, offering a grid-based visual presentation of the entities you have defined.

Tap the + button at the bottom-left of the Entity list at the top-left of the window to add a new entity (a class definition that acts as an object skeleton) to your model. By default all new entities are instantiated at runtime as instances of the `NSManagedObject` class. Edit the word "Entity" to give your new object a name, for example, Person.

With the entity selected, you can add attributes. Each attribute has a name and is typed, just as you'd define an instance variable. Relationships are pointers to other objects. You can define a single pointer for a one-to-one relation (the single manager for a department) or a set for a one-to-many relation (all the members of a department).

Take note of the inspector at the top-right. Here, you can edit an object's name, set its type, define its default value, and more.

The graph at the bottom of the editor shows the entities you have defined. It provides arrows that represent the relationships between the various kinds of entities in your project. In this model, every person belongs to a department. Each department has a manager (a one-to-one relationship) and any number of members (a one-to-many relationship).

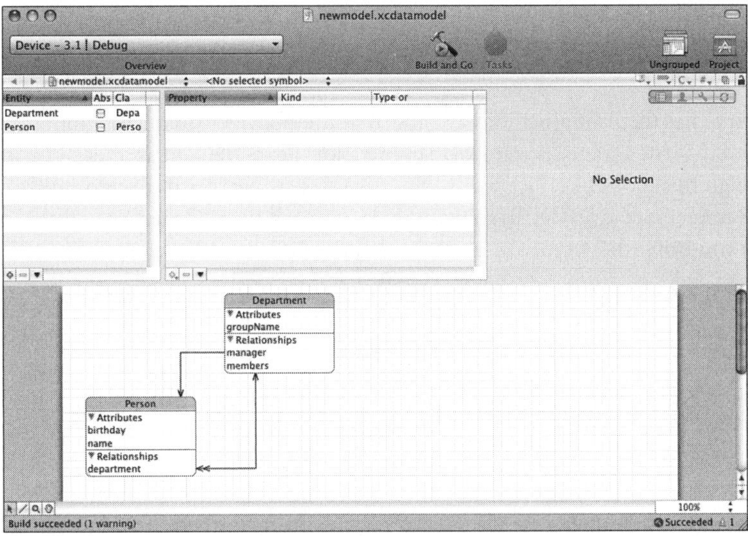

Figure 19-1 The model editor allows you to build object definitions for your Core Data applications.

Generating Header Files

Once you have laid out and saved your model, you can generate header files for each entity. These header files are not required, but they allow you to use dot notation in your applications, which saves you from having to use `valueForKey:` calls to retrieve managed object attributes.

Select an entity, and choose File > New File > iPhone OS > Cocoa Touch Class > Managed Object Class > Next > Next > Finish. Xcode generates a pair of .h/.m files for the entity and adds it to your project. For example, here is the Department header for the project shown in Figure 19-1.

```
#import <CoreData/CoreData.h>


@interface Department :  NSManagedObject
{
}

@property (nonatomic, retain) NSString * groupName;
@property (nonatomic, retain) NSManagedObject * manager;
@property (nonatomic, retain) NSSet* members;
@end

@interface Department (CoreDataGeneratedAccessors)
- (void)addMembersObject:(NSManagedObject *)value;
- (void)removeMembersObject:(NSManagedObject *)value;
```

```
- (void)addMembers:(NSSet *)value;
- (void)removeMembers:(NSSet *)value;
@end
```

You can see that the group name is a string, that the manager points to another managed object, and that the members one-to-many relationship is defined as a set.

Although this looks like a standard Objective-C class header file, importantly there are no actual implementation details that you have to work with. Core Data takes care of those for you using the `@dynamic` compiler keywords.

```
@implementation Department


@dynamic groupName;
@dynamic manager;
@dynamic members;


@end
```

The main reason for generating Core Data files lies in their ability to add new behavior and transient attributes, that is, attributes not saved in the persistent store. For example, you might create a `fullName` attribute returning a name built from a person's `firstName` and `lastName`. Plus, there's nothing to stop you from using a managed object class like any other class, that is, using and manipulating all kinds of data. You can bundle any kind of Objective-C behavior into a managed object instance by editing its implementation file. You can add instance and class methods as needed.

Creating a Core Data Context

After designing the managed object model, it's time to build code that accesses a data file. To work with Core Data you need to programmatically create a managed object context. A context performs all the access and update functions needed to coordinate your model with a file.

The following method initializes the context for an application. This work is all done for you when you use a prebuilt Core Data template; this method shows how to do the same work by hand. It starts by reading in all the model files from the application bundle and merging them into a central model. It then initializes a persistent store coordinator. This coordinator provides low-level file access using the central model. You supply a URL that points to the file you want to use to store the model's data. Finally, this method initializes a new context using the coordinator and stores it as a retained instance variable.

```
- (void) initCoreData
{
    NSError *error;

    // Path to sqlite file.
    NSString *path = [NSHomeDirectory()
```

```
        stringByAppendingString:@"/Documents/cdintro_00.sqlite"];
    NSURL *url = [NSURL fileURLWithPath:path];

    // Init the model
    NSManagedObjectModel *managedObjectModel =
        [NSManagedObjectModel mergedModelFromBundles:nil];

    // Establish the persistent store coordinator
    NSPersistentStoreCoordinator *persistentStoreCoordinator =
        [[NSPersistentStoreCoordinator alloc]
            initWithManagedObjectModel:managedObjectModel];

    if (![persistentStoreCoordinator
        addPersistentStoreWithType:NSSQLiteStoreType
        configuration:nil URL:url options:nil error:&error])
            NSLog(@"Error %@", [error localizedDescription]);
    else
    {
        // Create the context and assign the coordinator
        self.context =
            [[[NSManagedObjectContext alloc] init] autorelease];
        [self.context
            setPersistentStoreCoordinator:persistentStoreCoordinator];
    }
    [persistentStoreCoordinator release];
}
```

It's important to maintain a context instance that you can refer to, whether from a view controller (for a simple Core Data application) or from your application delegate (the typical location for more complex applications). The context is used for all read, search, and update operations in your application.

Adding Objects

Create new objects by inserting entities into your managed context. The following snippet builds three new items, a department and two people. After inserting the object, which returns the new instance, you set the managed object's properties (its attributes and relationships) by assignment. Each person belongs to a department. Each department has a set of members and one manager. This code reflects the design built in Figure 19-1. You do not have to explicitly set the department's members. The inverse relationship takes care of that for you, adding the members into the department when you set the person's department attribute.

```
- (void) addObjects
{
    // Add a new department
    Department *department = (Department *)[NSEntityDescription
```

```
        insertNewObjectForEntityForName:@"Department"
        inManagedObjectContext:self.context];
    department.groupName = @"Office of Personnel Management";

    // Add a person
    Person *person1 = (Person *)[NSEntityDescription
        insertNewObjectForEntityForName:@"Person"
        inManagedObjectContext:self.context];
    person1.name = @"John Smith";
    person1.birthday = [self dateFromString:@"12-1-1901"];
    person1.department = department;

    // Add another person
    Person *person2 = (Person *)[NSEntityDescription
        insertNewObjectForEntityForName:@"Person"
        inManagedObjectContext:self.context];
    person2.name = @"Jane Doe";
    person2.birthday = [self dateFromString:@"4-13-1922"];
    person2.department = department;

    // Set the department relationships
    department.manager = person1;


    // Save out to the persistent store
    NSError *error;
    if (![self.context save:&error])
        NSLog(@"Error %@", [error localizedDescription]);
}
```

No changes to the persistent store file take effect until you save. A save operation brings the database file up to date with the model stored in memory. The single save request in this code tells the context to synchronize its state with the persistent store, writing out all changes to the database file.

If you run this code in the simulator, you can easily inspect the .sqlite file that's created. Navigate to the simulator folder (~/Library/Application Support/iPhone Simulator/User/Applications) and into the folder for the application itself. Stored in the Documents folder (depending on the URL used to create the persistent store), a .sqlite file contains the database representation that you've created.

Use the command-line sqlite3 utility to inspect the contents by performing a .dump operation. Here you see the two SQL table definitions (department and manager) that store the information for each object plus the insert commands used to store the instances built in your code.

```
% sqlite3 cdintro_00.sqlite
SQLite version 3.4.0
Enter ".help" for instructions
```

```
sqlite> .dump
BEGIN TRANSACTION;
CREATE TABLE ZDEPARTMENT ( Z_PK INTEGER PRIMARY KEY, Z_ENT INTEGER, Z_OPT INTEGER,
ZMANAGER INTEGER, ZGROUPNAME VARCHAR );
INSERT INTO "ZDEPARTMENT" VALUES(1,1,1,1,'Office of Personnel Management');
CREATE TABLE ZPERSON ( Z_PK INTEGER PRIMARY KEY, Z_ENT INTEGER, Z_OPT INTEGER,
ZDEPARTMENT INTEGER, ZBIRTHDAY TIMESTAMP, ZNAME VARCHAR );
INSERT INTO "ZPERSON" VALUES(1,2,1,1,-3126877200,'John Smith');
INSERT INTO "ZPERSON" VALUES(2,2,1,1,-2484234000,'Jane Doe');
CREATE TABLE Z_PRIMARYKEY (Z_ENT INTEGER PRIMARY KEY, Z_NAME VARCHAR, Z_SUPER
INTEGER, Z_MAX INTEGER);
INSERT INTO "Z_PRIMARYKEY" VALUES(1,'Department',0,1);
INSERT INTO "Z_PRIMARYKEY" VALUES(2,'Person',0,2);
CREATE TABLE Z_METADATA (Z_VERSION INTEGER PRIMARY KEY, Z_UUID VARCHAR(255),
Z_PLIST BLOB);
INSERT INTO "Z_METADATA" VALUES(1,'A4ADDA90-5C26-4E01-8E68-
1C4BB7A910B1',X'62706C6973743030D60102030405060708090A0B105F10204E5353746F72654D6F
64656C56657273696F6E48617368657356657273696F6E5F101E4E5353746F72654D6F64656C566572
73696F6E4964656E746966696572735B4E5353746F7265547970655F101D4E535065727369737465E
63654672616D65776F726B56657273696F6E5F10194E5353746F72654D6F64656C56657273696F6E48
61736865735F10125F4E534175746F56616375756D4C6576656C1003A05653514C69746510F1D20C0D
0E0F5A4465706172746D656E745650657273736F6E4F10203B34C3D1DAC08316B2656664A26C9EAC82FE
04E4C34FC75A3E0981E678F3909B4F1020DE27A38E814A2A5F72418573563732F83CBC1CACAADF39FA
559420B155E5A97351320008001500380059006500850A0100B600B800B900C000C200C700D200D900
FC011F0000000000000201000000000000001100000000000000000000000000000121');
CREATE INDEX ZDEPARTMENT_ZMANAGER_INDEX ON ZDEPARTMENT (ZMANAGER);
CREATE INDEX ZPERSON_ZDEPARTMENT_INDEX ON ZPERSON (ZDEPARTMENT);
COMMIT;
sqlite>
```

Querying the Data Base

Retrieve objects from the database by performing fetch requests. A fetch request describes your search criteria. It's passed through and used to initialize a results object that contains a pointer to the managed objects that meet those criteria. The results controller executes the fetch before passing back the array of managed object results.

The following `fetchObjects` method creates a new request, setting its entity type to Person. This search looks for `Person` objects in the shared managed store. Each request must contain at least one sort descriptor. For this example, the search returns a list of `Person` records sorted in ascending order by their name field. Although you can produce more complicated queries, this example shows the simplest "please return all managed items of a given type" request.

```
- (void) fetchObjects
{
    // Create a basic fetch request
    NSFetchRequest *fetchRequest = [[NSFetchRequest alloc] init];
    [fetchRequest setEntity:[NSEntityDescription
        entityForName:@"Person" inManagedObjectContext:self.context]];
```

```
    // Add a sort descriptor. Mandatory.
    NSSortDescriptor *sortDescriptor = [[NSSortDescriptor alloc]
        initWithKey:@"name" ascending:YES selector:nil];
    NSArray *descriptors = [NSArray arrayWithObject:sortDescriptor];
    [fetchRequest setSortDescriptors:descriptors];
    [sortDescriptor release];

    // Init the fetched results controller
    NSError *error;
    self.fetchedResultsController = [[NSFetchedResultsController alloc]
        initWithFetchRequest:fetchRequest
        managedObjectContext:self.context
        sectionNameKeyPath:nil cacheName:@"Root"];
    if (![self.fetchedResultsController performFetch:&error])
        NSLog(@"Error %@", [error localizedDescription]);

    [self.fetchedResultsController release];
    [fetchRequest release];
}

- (void) action: (UIBarButtonItem *) bbi
{
    [self fetchObjects];
    for (Person *person in
        self.fetchedResultsController.fetchedObjects)
        NSLog(@"%@ : %@", person.name, person.department.groupName);
}
```

The fetch request is used to initialize an `NSFetchedResultsController` object. This class manages the results returned from a Core Data fetch. The results controller is kept on hand via a retained class property (`self.fetchedResultsController`). Fetch results provide concrete access to the data model objects. After fetching the data, this `action:` method lists out each person by name and department. It uses the results' `fetchedObjects` property to do so.

Detecting Changes

Fetched results might be used as a table data source or to fill out an object settings form, or for any other purpose you might think of. Whether you're retrieving just one object or many, the fetched results controller offers you direct access to those managed objects on request.

So how do you make sure that your fetched data remains current? After adding new objects or otherwise changing the data store, you want to fetch a fresh set of results. Subscribe to the results controller's `controllerDidChangeContent:` callback. This method notifies your class when changes affect your fetched objects. To subscribe, declare the

`NSFetchedResultsControllerDelegate` protocol and assign the controller's delegate as follows. After setting the results' delegate, you receive a callback each time the data store updates.

```
self.fetchedResultsController.delegate = self.
```

Removing Objects

Removing objects, especially those that use relationships in addition to simple properties, can prove harder than you might first expect. Consider the following code. It goes through each person in the fetched object results and deletes them before saving the context. This method fails as it tries to save the context to file.

```
- (void) removeObjects
{
    NSError *error = nil;
    for (Person *person in
        self.fetchedResultsController.fetchedObjects)
        [self.context deleteObject:person];

    if (![self.context save:&error])
        NSLog(@"Error %@ (%@)", [error localizedDescription]);
    [self fetchObjects];
}
```

That's because Core Data ensures internal consistency before writing data out, throwing an error if it cannot. The managed model from Figure 19-1 uses several cross-references. Each person may belong to a department, which stores a list of its members and its manager. These references must be cleared before the object can safely be removed from the persistent store. If not, objects may point to deleted items, a situation that can lead to bad references.

The following is another version of the same method, one that saves without errors. This updated version removes all references from the department object. It checks whether a person is a manager, removing that connection if it exists. It also filters the person out of its department members using a predicate to return an updated set. Once these connections are removed, the context will save out properly.

```
- (void) removeObjects
{
    NSError *error = nil;

    if (!self.fetchedResultsController.fetchedObjects.count)
    {
        NSLog(@"No one to delete");
        return;
    }
```

```
    // Remove each person
    for (Person *person in
        self.fetchedResultsController.fetchedObjects)
    {
        // Remove person as manager if necessary
        if (person.department.manager == person)
            person.department.manager = nil;

        // Remove person from department
        NSPredicate *pred = [NSPredicate predicateWithFormat:
            @"SELF != %@", person];
        if (person.department.members)
            person.department.members = [person.department.members
                filteredSetUsingPredicate:pred];

        // Delete the person object
        [self.context deleteObject:person];
    }

    // Save
    if (![self.context save:&error])
        NSLog(@"Error %@", [error localizedDescription]);
}
```

In addition to this kind of manual disconnection, you can set Core Data delete rules in the data model editor. Delete rules control how an object responds to an attempted delete. You can `Deny` delete requests, ensuring that a relationship has no connection before allowing object deletion. `Nullify` resets inverse relationships before deleting an object. `Cascade` deletes an object plus all its relationships; for example, you could delete an entire department (including its members) all at once with a cascade. `No Action` provides that the objects pointed to by a relationship remain unaffected, even if those objects point back to the item about to be deleted.

In the sample code that accompanies this chapter, the introductory project (essentially Recipe 0 for this chapter) nullifies its connections. The department/members relationship represents an inverse relationship. By using `Nullify`, the default delete rule, you do not need to remove the member from the department list before deleting a person.

On the other hand, the department's manager relationship is not reciprocal. As there is no inverse relationship, you cannot delete objects without resetting that manager. Taking these delete rules into account, the remove objects method for this example can be shortened to the following.

```
- (void) removeObjects
{
    NSError *error = nil;

    // Remove all people (if they exist)
```

```
    [self fetchObjects];
    if (!self.fetchedResultsController.fetchedObjects.count)
    {
        NSLog(@"No one to delete");
        return;
    }

    // Remove each person
    for (Person *person in
        self.fetchedResultsController.fetchedObjects)
    {
        // Remove person as manager if necessary
        if (person.department.manager == person)
            person.department.manager = nil;

        // Delete the person object
        [self.context deleteObject:person];
    }

    // Save
    if (![self.context save:&error])
        NSLog(@"Error %@", [error localizedDescription]);
}
```

Xcode issues warnings when it detects nonreciprocal relationships. Avoid these unbalanced relationships to simplify your code and provide better internal consistency. If you cannot avoid nonreciprocal items, you need to take them into account when you create your delete methods, as was done here.

Recipe: Using Core Data for a Table Data Source

Core Data on the iPhone works closely with table views. The `NSFetchedResults` ➥`Controller` class includes features that simplify the integration of Core Data objects with table data sources. As you can see in the following list, many of the fetched results class's properties and methods are designed for table support.

- **Index path access**—The fetched results class offers object-index path integration in two directions. You can recover objects from a fetched object array using index paths by calling `objectAtIndexPath:`. You can query for the index path associated with a fetched object by calling `indexPathForObject:`. These two methods work with both sectioned tables and those tables that are flat—that is, that only use a single section for all their data.
- **Section key path**—The `sectionNameKeyPath` property links a managed object attribute to section names. This property helps determine which section each managed object belongs to. You can set this property directly at any time or you initialize it when you set up your fetched results controller.

Recipe 19-1 uses an attribute named `section` to distinguish sections, although you can use any attribute name for this key path. For this example, this attribute uses the first character of each object name to assign a managed object to a section. Set the key path to `nil` to produce a flat table without sections.

- **Section groups**—Recover section subgroups with the `sections` property. This property returns an array of sections, each of which stores the managed objects whose section attribute maps to the same letter.

  Each returned section implements the `NSFetchedResultsSectionInfo` protocol. This protocol ensures that sections can report their `objects` and `numberOfObjects`, their `name`, and an `indexTitle`, that is, the title that appears on the quick reference index optionally shown above and at the right of the table.

- **Index titles**—The `sectionIndexTitles` property generates a list of section titles from the sections within the fetched data. For Recipe 19-1, that array includes single letter titles. The default implementation uses the value of each section key to return a list of all known sections.

  Two further instance methods, `sectionIndexTitleForSectionName:` and `sectionForSectionIndexTitle:atIndex:`, provide section title lookup features. The first returns a title for a section name. The second looks up a section via its title. Override these to use section titles that do not match the data stored in the section name key.

As these properties and methods reveal, fetched results instances are both table aware and table ready for use. Recipe 19-1 uses these features to duplicate the indexed color name table first introduced in Chapter 11, "Creating and Managing Table Views." The code in this recipe recovers data from the fetched results using index paths, as shown in the method that produces a cell for a given row and the method that tints the navigation bar with the color from the selected row.

Each method used for creating and managing sections is tiny. The built-in Core Data access features reduce these methods to one or two lines each. That's because all the work in creating and accessing the sections is handed over directly to Core Data. The call that initializes each fetched data request specifies what data attribute to use for the sections. Core Data then takes over and does the rest of the work.

```
self.fetchedResultsController = [[NSFetchedResultsController alloc]
    initWithFetchRequest:fetchRequest
    managedObjectContext:self.context
    sectionNameKeyPath:@"section" cacheName:@"Root"];
```

Caching reduces overhead associated with producing data that's structured with sections and indices. Multiple fetch requests are ignored when the data has not changed, minimizing the cost associated with fetch requests over the lifetime of an application. The name used for the cache is completely arbitrary. Either use `nil` to prevent caching or supply a name in the form of an `NSString`. The snippet above uses `"Root"`, but there's no reason you can't use another string.

Recipe 19-1 Building a Sectioned Table with Core Data

```
- (UITableViewCell *)tableView:(UITableView *)tableView
    cellForRowAtIndexPath:(NSIndexPath *)indexPath
{
    // Retrieve or create a cell
    UITableViewCell *cell =
        [tableView dequeueReusableCellWithIdentifier:@"basic cell"];
    if (!cell) cell = [[[UITableViewCell alloc]
        initWithStyle:UITableViewCellStyleDefault
        reuseIdentifier:@"basic cell"] autorelease];

    // Recover object from fetched results
    NSManagedObject *managedObject =
        [self.fetchedResultsController objectAtIndexPath:indexPath];
    cell.textLabel.text = [managedObject valueForKey:@"name"];
    UIColor *color =
        [self getColor:[managedObject valueForKey:@"color"]];
    cell.textLabel.textColor =
        ([[managedObject valueForKey:@"color"] hasPrefix:@"FFFFFF"]) ?
            [UIColor blackColor] : color;

    return cell;
}

- (void)tableView:(UITableView *)tableView
    didSelectRowAtIndexPath:(NSIndexPath *)indexPath
{
    // When a row is selected, color the navigation bar accordingly
    NSManagedObject *managedObject =
        [self.fetchedResultsController objectAtIndexPath:indexPath];
    UIColor *color =
        [self getColor:[managedObject valueForKey:@"color"]];
    self.navigationController.navigationBar.tintColor = color;
}

#pragma mark Sections
- (NSInteger)numberOfSectionsInTableView:(UITableView *)tableView
{
    // Use the fetched results section count
    return [[self.fetchedResultsController sections] count];
}
```

```
- (NSInteger)tableView:(UITableView *)tableView
    numberOfRowsInSection:(NSInteger)section
{
    // Return the count for each section
    return [[[self.fetchedResultsController sections]
        objectAtIndex:section] numberOfObjects];
}

- (NSArray *)sectionIndexTitlesForTableView:(UITableView *)aTableView
{
    // Return the array of section index titles
    return self.fetchedResultsController.sectionIndexTitles;
}

- (NSString *)tableView:(UITableView *)aTableView
    titleForHeaderInSection:(NSInteger)section
{
    // Return the title for a given section
    NSArray *titles = [self.fetchedResultsController
        sectionIndexTitles];
    if (titles.count <= section) return @"Error";
    return [titles objectAtIndex:section];
}

- (NSInteger)tableView:(UITableView *)tableView
    sectionForSectionIndexTitle:(NSString *)title
    atIndex:(NSInteger)index
{
    // Query the titles for the section associated with an index title
    return [self.fetchedResultsController.sectionIndexTitles
        indexOfObject:title];
}
```

Get This Recipe's Code

To get the code used for this recipe, go to http://github.com/erica/iphone-3.0-cookbook-, or if you've downloaded the disk image containing all of the sample code from the book, go to the folder for Chapter 19 and open the project for this recipe.

Recipe: Search Tables and Core Data

Core Data stores are designed to work efficiently with `NSPredicates`. Predicates allow you to create fetch requests that select only those managed objects that match the predicate's rule or rules. Adding a predicate to a fetch request limits the fetched results to matching objects.

Recipe 19-2 adapts the search table from Recipe 11-16 to build a Core Data-based solution. This recipe uses a search bar to select data from the persistent store, displaying the results in a table's search sheet. Figure 19-2 shows a search in progress.

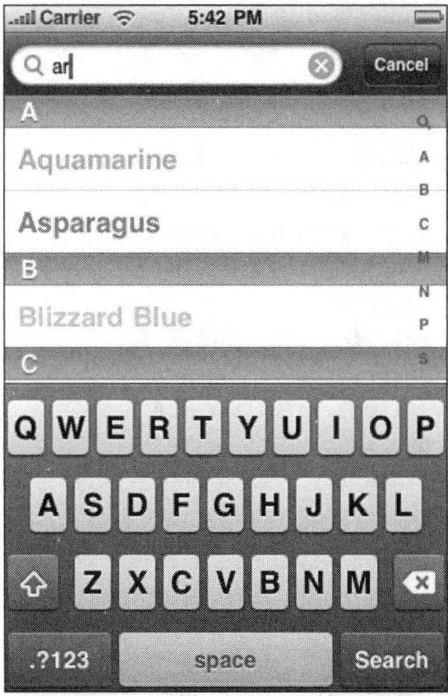

Figure 19-2 To power this search table with Core Data, the fetched results must update each time the text in the search box changes.

As the text in the search bar at the top of the table changes, the search bar's delegate receives a `searchBar:textDidChange:` callback. In turn, that method performs a new fetch. Recipe 11-16 shows that fetch method, which builds a restrictive predicate.

The recipe's `performFetch` method creates that simple predicate based on the text in the search bar. It sets the request's `predicate` property to limit matches to names that contain the text, using a case insensitive match. `contains` matches text anywhere in a string. The `[cd]` after `contains` refers to case and diacritic insensitive matching. Diacritics are small marks that accompany a letter, such as the dots of an umlaut or the tilde above a Spanish n.

For more complex queries, assign a compound predicate. Compound predicates allow you to combine simple predicates together using standard logical operations like AND, OR, and NOT. Use the `NSCompoundPredicate` class to build a compound predicate out of a series of component predicates, or include the AND, OR, and NOT notation directly in `NSPredicate` text, as was done in Chapter 18, "Connecting to the Address Book."

None of the methods from Recipe 19-1 need updating for use with Recipe 19-2's `performFetch` method. All the cell and section methods are tied to the `results` object and its properties, simplifying implementation even when adding these search table features.

Recipe 19-2 **Using Fetch Requests with Predicates**

```
- (void) performFetch
{
    // Init a fetch request
    NSFetchRequest *fetchRequest = [[NSFetchRequest alloc] init];
    NSEntityDescription *entity = [NSEntityDescription
        entityForName:@"Crayon" inManagedObjectContext:self.context];
    [fetchRequest setEntity:entity];

    // Apply an ascending sort for the color items
    NSSortDescriptor *sortDescriptor =
        [[NSSortDescriptor alloc] initWithKey:@"name"
        ascending:YES selector:nil];
    NSArray *descriptors = [NSArray arrayWithObject:sortDescriptor];
    [fetchRequest setSortDescriptors:descriptors];

    // Recover query
    NSString *query = self.searchBar.text;
    if (query && query.length) fetchRequest.predicate =
        [NSPredicate predicateWithFormat:@"name contains[cd] %@",
        query];

    // Init the fetched results controller
    NSError *error;
    self.fetchedResultsController =
        [[NSFetchedResultsController alloc]
            initWithFetchRequest:fetchRequest
            managedObjectContext:self.context
            sectionNameKeyPath:@"section" cacheName:@"Root"];
    self.fetchedResultsController.delegate = self;
    [self.fetchedResultsController release];
    if (![[self fetchedResultsController] performFetch:&error])
        NSLog(@"Error %@", [error localizedDescription]);

    [fetchRequest release];
    [sortDescriptor release];
}
```

Get This Recipe's Code

To get the code used for this recipe, go to http://github.com/erica/iphone-3.0-cookbook-, or if you've downloaded the disk image containing all of the sample code from the book, go to the folder for Chapter 19 and open the project for this recipe.

Recipe: Integrating Core Data Tables with Live Data Edits

Recipe 19-3 demonstrates how to move basic table editing tasks into the Core Data world. Its code is based on the basic edits of Recipe 11-12. There are, however, real changes that must be made to provide its Core Data solution. These changes include the following adaptations.

- **Adding and deleting items are restricted to the data source**—Methods that commit an editing style (i.e., perform deletes) and that add new cells do not directly address the table view. In the original recipe, each method reloaded the table view data after adds and deletes. Recipe 19-3 saves data to the managed context but does *not* call `reloadData`.
- **Data updates trigger table reloads**—The actual `reloadData` call triggers when the fetched results delegate receives a `controllerDidChangeContent:` callback. This method gets sent when the fetched results object recognizes that the stored data has updated. That happens after data changes have been saved via the managed object context.
- **The table forbids reordering**—Recipe 19-3's `tableView:canMoveRowAtIndexPath:` method hard codes its result to `NO`. When working with sorted fetched data sources, users may not reorder that data. This method reflects that reality.

Together, these changes allow your table to work with add and delete edits, as well as content edits. Although content edits are not addressed in this recipe, they involve a similar fetch update approach when users modify attributes used by sort descriptors.

The actual add and delete code follows the approach detailed at the start of this chapter. Objects are added by inserting a new entity description. Their attributes are set and the context saved. Objects are deleted from the context, and again the context is saved. These updates trigger the content changed callbacks for the fetched results delegate.

As this recipe shows, the Core Data interaction simplifies the integration between the data model and the user interface. And that's due in large part to Apple's thoughtful class designs that handle the managed object responsibilities. Recipe 19-3 highlights this design, showcasing the code parsimony that results from using Core Data.

Recipe 19-3 **Adapting Table Edits to Core Data**

```
-(void)enterEditMode
{
    // Start editing
    [self.tableView deselectRowAtIndexPath:
        [self.tableView indexPathForSelectedRow] animated:YES];
    [self.tableView setEditing:YES animated:YES];
    [self setBarButtonItems];
}
```

```
-(void)leaveEditMode
{
    // Finish editing
    [self.tableView setEditing:NO animated:YES];
    [self setBarButtonItems];
}

- (BOOL)tableView:(UITableView *)tableView
    canMoveRowAtIndexPath:(NSIndexPath *)indexPath
{
    return NO; // no reordering allowed
}

- (void)tableView:(UITableView *)tableView
    commitEditingStyle:(UITableViewCellEditingStyle)editingStyle
    forRowAtIndexPath:(NSIndexPath *)indexPath
{
    // Delete request
    if (editingStyle == UITableViewCellEditingStyleDelete)
    {
        NSError *error = nil;
        [self.context deleteObject:[fetchedResultsController
            objectAtIndexPath:indexPath]];
        if (![self.context save:&error])
            NSLog(@"Error %@", [error localizedDescription]);
    }

    // Update buttons after delete action
    [self setBarButtonItems];

    // Update sections
    [self performFetch];
}


- (void) add
{
    // Request a string to use as the action item
    NSString *todoAction =
        [ModalAlert ask:@"What Item?" withTextPrompt:@"To Do Item"];
    if (!todoAction || todoAction.length == 0) return;

    // Build a new item and set its action field
    ToDoItem *item = (ToDoItem *)[NSEntityDescription
        insertNewObjectForEntityForName:@"ToDoItem"
        inManagedObjectContext:self.context];
    item.action = todoAction;
```

```
    item.sectionName =
        [[todoAction substringToIndex:1] uppercaseString];

    // Save the new item
    NSError *error;
    if (![self.context save:&error])
       NSLog(@"Error %@", [error localizedDescription]);

    // Update buttons after add
    [self setBarButtonItems];

    // Update sections
    [self performFetch];
}

- (void)controllerDidChangeContent:
    (NSFetchedResultsController *)controller
{
    // Update table when the contents have changed
    [self.tableView reloadData];
}
```

Get This Recipe's Code

To get the code used for this recipe, go to http://github.com/erica/iphone-3.0-cookbook-, or if you've downloaded the disk image containing all of the sample code from the book, go to the folder for Chapter 19 and open the project for this recipe.

Recipe: Implementing Undo-Redo Support with Core Data

Core Data simplifies table undo-redo support to an astonishing degree. It provides automatic support for these operations with little programming effort. Here are the steps you need to take to add undo-redo to your table based application.

1. Add an undo manager to the managed object context. After establishing a managed object context (typically in your application delegate), set its undo manager to a newly allocated instance.

   ```
   self.context.undoManager =
       [[[NSUndoManager alloc] init] autorelease];
   ```

2. Assign that undo manager in your view controller. Set your view controller's undo manager to point to the undo manager used by the managed object context.

   ```
   self.context = [(TestBedAppDelegate *)
       [[UIApplication sharedApplication] delegate] context];
   self.undoManager = self.context.undoManager;
   ```

3. Optionally, provide shake-to-edit support. If you want your application to respond to device shakes by offering an undo-redo menu, add the following line to your application delegate.

```
application.applicationSupportsShakeToEdit = YES;
```

4. Ensure that your view controller becomes the first responder when it is onscreen. Provide the following suite of methods. These methods allow the view responder to become first responder whenever it appears. The view controller resigns that first responder status when it moves offscreen.

```
- (BOOL)canBecomeFirstResponder {
    return YES;
}

- (void)viewDidAppear:(BOOL)animated {
    [super viewDidAppear:animated];
    [self becomeFirstResponder];
}

- (void)viewWillDisappear:(BOOL)animated {
    [super viewWillDisappear:animated];
    [self resignFirstResponder];
}
```

The preceding steps provide all the setup needed to use undo management in your table. Recipe 19-4 integrates that undo management into the actual delete and add methods for the table. To make this happen, it brackets the core data access with an undo grouping. The `beginUndoGrouping` and `endUndoGrouping` calls appear before and after the context updates and saves with changes. An action name describes the operation that just took place.

These three calls (begin, undo, and setting the action name) comprise all the work needed to ensure that Core Data can reverse its operations. For this minimal effort, your application gains a fully realized undo management system, courtesy of Core Data. Be aware that any undo/redo data will not survive quitting your application. This works just as you'd expect with manual undo/redo support.

Recipe 19-4 **Expanding Cell Management for Undo/Redo Support**

```
- (void)tableView:(UITableView *)tableView
    commitEditingStyle:(UITableViewCellEditingStyle)editingStyle
    forRowAtIndexPath:(NSIndexPath *)indexPath
{
    [self.context.undoManager beginUndoGrouping];

    // Delete request
    if (editingStyle == UITableViewCellEditingStyleDelete)
```

```
    {
        NSError *error = nil;
        [self.context deleteObject:
            [fetchedResultsController objectAtIndexPath:indexPath]];
        if (![self.context save:&error])
            NSLog(@"Error %@", [error localizedDescription]);
    }

    [self.context.undoManager endUndoGrouping];
    [self.context.undoManager setActionName:@"Delete"];

    // Update buttons after delete action
    [self setBarButtonItems];

    // Update sections
    [self performFetch];
}


- (void) add
{
    // Request a string to use as the action item
    NSString *todoAction = [ModalAlert ask:@"What Item?"
        withTextPrompt:@"To Do Item"];
    if (!todoAction || todoAction.length == 0) return;

    [self.context.undoManager beginUndoGrouping];

    // Build a new item and set its action field
    ToDoItem *item = (ToDoItem *)[NSEntityDescription
        insertNewObjectForEntityForName:@"ToDoItem"
        inManagedObjectContext:self.context];
    item.action = todoAction;

    // Index by the first character of the action
    item.sectionName =
        [[todoAction substringToIndex:1] uppercaseString];

    // Save the new item
    NSError *error;
    if (![self.context save:&error])
        NSLog(@"Error %@", [error localizedDescription]);

    [self.context.undoManager endUndoGrouping];
    [self.context.undoManager setActionName:@"Add"];
```

```
    // Update buttons after add
    [self setBarButtonItems];

    // Update sections
    [self performFetch];
}
```

Get This Recipe's Code

To get the code used for this recipe, go to http://github.com/erica/iphone-3.0-cookbook-, or if you've downloaded the disk image containing all of the sample code from the book, go to the folder for Chapter 19 and open the project for this recipe.

Summary

This chapter offered just a taste of Core Data's capabilities. These recipes showed you how to design and implement basic Core Data applications. They used Core Data features to work with its managed object models. You read about defining a model and implementing fetch requests. You saw how to add objects, delete them, modify them, and save them. You learned about predicates and undo operations, and discovered how to integrate Core Data with table views. After reading through this chapter, here are a few final thoughts to take away with you:

- Xcode issues a standard compiler warning when it encounters relationships that are not reciprocal. Nonreciprocal relationships add an extra layer of work, preventing you from taking advantage of simple delete rules like `Nullify`. Avoid these relationships when possible.
- When moving data from a pre-3.0 store into a new SQLite database, be sure to use some sort of flag in your user defaults. Check whether you've already performed a data upgrade or not. You want to migrate user data once when the application is upgraded but not thereafter.
- Predicates are one of my favorite 3.0 SDK features. Spend some time learning how to construct them and use them with all kinds of objects like arrays and sets, not just with Core Data.
- Core Data's capabilities go way beyond the basic recipes you've seen in this chapter. Check out Tim Isted's Core Data for iPhone, available from Pearson Education/Addison-Wesley for an in-depth exploration of Core Data and its features.

20

StoreKit: In-App Purchasing

New to the 3.0 SDK, StoreKit offers in-app purchasing that integrates into your software. With StoreKit, end users can use their iTunes credentials to buy features, subscriptions, or consumable assets from within an application after initially purchasing and installing the application from App Store. This chapter introduces StoreKit and shows you how to use the StoreKit API to create purchasing options for users. In this chapter, you read about getting started with StoreKit. You learn how set up products at iTunes Connect and localize their descriptions. You see what it takes to create test users and how to work your way through various development/deployment hurdles. This chapter teaches you how to solicit purchase requests from users and how to hand over those requests to the store for payment. By the time you finish this chapter, you'll have learned about the entire StoreKit picture, from product creation to sales.

Getting Started with StoreKit

When your application demands a more complex purchase model than buy-once use-always, consider StoreKit. StoreKit offers developers a way to sell additional products from within an application. It offers iTunes payments to create additional revenue streams. There are many reasons to use StoreKit. You might support a subscription model, provide extra game levels on demand, or introduce other unlockable features via this new 3.0 framework.

That isn't to say that users download new code. All StoreKit-based applications ship with their features already built in. For example, StoreKit purchases might let users access parts of your application that you initially set as off limits. They can also download or unlock new data sets, or authorize access to subscription-based Web feeds. StoreKit provides the way users can pay to access these features, letting them go live after purchase.

It's important to note that you cannot use in-app purchasing to sell "hard" assets (such as T-shirts) nor intermediate currency (such as store credit for a Web site) at this time. And, yes, real gambling is forbidden as well. Any goods sold via in-app purchase must be able to be delivered digitally to your application.

With StoreKit, you choose the items you want to sell and you set their price. StoreKit and iTunes take care of the details. They provide the infrastructure that brings that storefront into your application through a series of API calls and delegate callbacks.

Unfortunately, StoreKit presents a paradox, which is this: You cannot fully develop and test your in-application purchasing until you have already submitted your application to iTunes. And you cannot fully submit your application to iTunes knowing that you're not done developing it. So what's a developer to do? How do you properly develop for StoreKit?

There is, fortunately, a solution. This solution is shown in Figure 20-1. To work around the StoreKit paradox, you upload a somewhat-working but not fully functional application skeleton to iTunes Connect. You do this with the full understanding that you'll be rejecting your binary and replacing it at some point in the future.

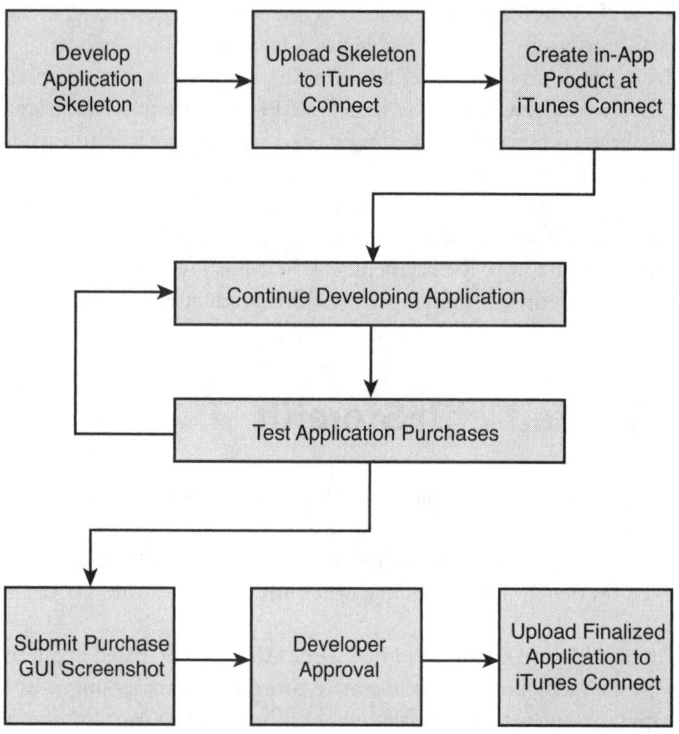

Figure 20-1 The StoreKit development process.

The reason you have to upload that skeleton is that you need an application in active review to begin developing StoreKit applications and products. You cannot create new in-application purchases at iTunes Connect, and you cannot test those purchases with the sandbox version of StoreKit without a "live" application. For purposes of StoreKit, this means you need an application either in review or already accepted at App Store.

> **Note**
>
> When submitting your skeleton application for testing, roll back your availability date in the iTunes Connect Pricing tab. This prevents your "not ready for prime time" app from inadvertently appearing for sale on App Store until you're ready. Reset that date once you're ready to go live.
>
> Until October 2009, StoreKit applications could not be free. Before then, you needed to choose at least Tier 1 (corresponding to US$0.99) or higher when pricing your application. StoreKit and iTunes Connect no longer limit in-application purchasing to paid applications.

Once you've submitted your application and created at least one in-application purchase item, you can begin to fully develop and test your application and its purchases. Use the sandbox version of StoreKit along with test user accounts to buy new items without charging a real credit card. The sandbox StoreKit lets you test your application features before, during, and after payment.

When you have finished development, and are ready to submit a final version to App Store, you complete the StoreKit development process at iTunes Connect. You must upload a screenshot showing the GUI for your application purchase, you must explicitly approve each in-app purchase item, and you must reject your skeleton and upload a fully working version of your application.

The following sections one walk you through this process. You read about each of these steps in greater detail and learn how to add StoreKit to your application.

Creating Test Accounts

Test accounts play a key role in the StoreKit development scenario. Create one or more new user accounts before you begin developing new StoreKit-enabled applications. These accounts allow you to log in to iTunes to test your application payments without charging real money.

Here's how you add a new user. Log in to iTunes Connect, and choose Manage Users > In App Purchase Test User. Click Add New User. iTunes Connect presents the form shown in Figure 20-2. When filling out this form, keep the following points in mind.

- Each e-mail address must be unique, but it doesn't have to be real. So long as the address does not conflict with any other one in the system, you'll be fine. As you might guess, other developers have already taken the easy to type addresses like abc.com, abcd.com, and so on.
- Names do not have to be real. Birthdates do not have to be real. I use a basic alphabetical naming system. My users are "a Sadun," "b Sadun," "c Sadun," and so forth. Everyone was born on January 1st.
- Passwords must be at least six characters long. If you plan on typing the password in repeatedly, stick to lowercase letters. If you use uppercase, you'll have to handle the

Caps key on the iPhone. If you use numbers, you'll have to switch between keyboard styles. A single easy-to-remember disposable password can be used for all your test accounts.

- The secret question/answer fields are meaningless in this context, but they cannot be left empty. You cannot enter the same string for both fields, and each field must be at least six characters long. Consider using a question/answer pair like "aaaaaa" and "bbbbbb" to simplify account creation.
- Selecting an iTunes Store is required. This store sets the region for your testing. If you plan to use multiple language support for various stores, make sure you create a test account in each affected region.
- You can delete user accounts and add new ones on the fly. If you run out of users who haven't yet purchased any items, just create new users as needed.
- You do not want to sign into your "account" in the Settings application. If you try to do so, the iPhone will force you to consent to its standard user agreement and will then try to extract a valid credit card from you. Use Settings to log out of an account but avoid it for logging in to one.

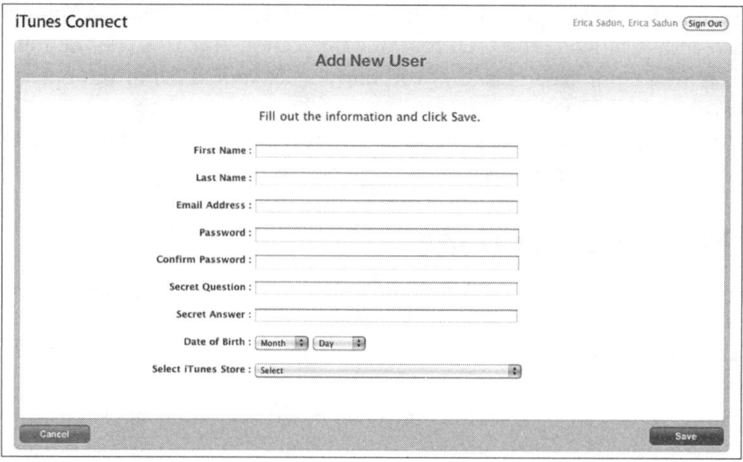

Figure 20-2 Add new test users in iTunes Connect by filling out this form.

Creating New In-App Purchase Items

Each in-application purchase item must be registered at iTunes Connect. To create a new purchase, log in and navigate to Manage Your In App Purchases. Click Create New and choose an application from the list shown. That list reflects all apps, whether already in App Store or currently in review. Select the application by clicking on its icon.

After selecting an application, iTunes Connect prompts you to create a new in-app purchase, as shown in Figure 20-3. This figure shows the two top sections from that screen (pricing and details). A third, review, section appears below this, and you can scroll down to see it.

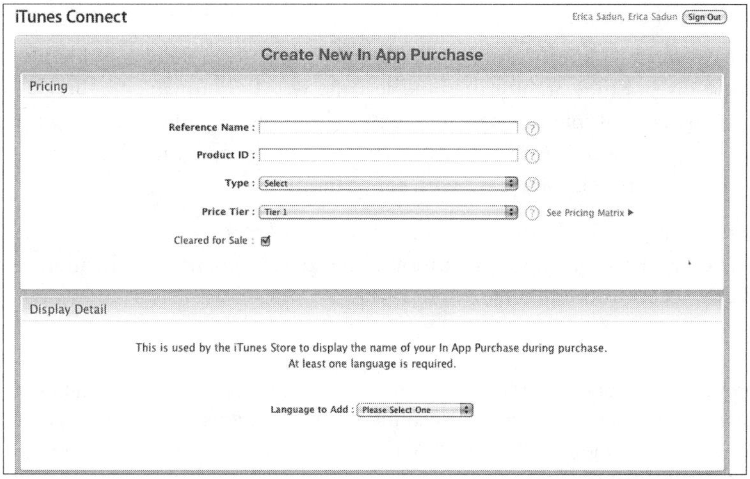

Figure 20-3 Create new purchase items in iTunes Connect by filling out this form.

Filling Out the Pricing Section

The pricing section specifies how a purchase is identified and priced. You must enter a reference name and a product identifier. The reference name is arbitrary. It is used to provide a name for iTunes Connect's search results and in the application's Top In-App Purchase section in App Store. So enter a meaningful name (e.g., "Unlock Level 3 Purchase") that helps you and others know what the item is and how it is used in your application.

The product ID is a unique identifier, similar to the application identifier used for your app. As a rule, I use my application ID and append a purchase name to that such as `com.sadun.scanner.optionalDisclosure`. You need this identifier to query the store and retrieve details about this purchase. The same rules apply to the product ID as to application IDs. You cannot use an identifier more than once. You cannot "remove" it from App Store. Once registered, it's registered forever.

Next, select a purchase type. You may choose any of the following three types. Once you select a type and save the new purchase item, you cannot go back and change it. That type is irrevocably tied to the product ID. If you make a mistake, you must create a new item with a new product ID.

- **Non-consumable**—Users purchase this item once. Thereafter, they can redownload this purchase for free, as many times as they want. Use this option for features that users can unlock like extra game levels.

- **Subscription**—Users purchase this item over and over during the lifetime of the application. You can check whether an account has already purchased an item, but you cannot redownload the item without paying again. Use subscriptions to provide paid access to controlled data for a period of time like for-pay newspaper articles and medical database searches.
- **Consumable**—Consumables work like subscriptions in that each download must be paid for, but they are not used in the same way. Consumables are items that can be purchased multiple times, such as extra hit points or additional CPU time on a primary server. Consumable items can be used up ("consumed") without an associated time period like you have with subscriptions.

Leave the final item in the Pricing section (Cleared for Sale) checked. The Cleared for Sale check box ensures that your applications, both development and distribution, have programmatic access to the purchase item.

> **Note**
>
> You can change the pricing tier and Cleared for Sale check box at any time during review. You must submit new changes for review once the purchased items have been approved. You cannot edit the identifier or reuse an existing identifier, nor can you change the type of product after creating the purchase item.

Adding Item Details

Each purchasable item must be able to describe itself to your application. The item has to report its price, which was set in the Pricing section, and offer both a display name (the name of the product that is being purchased) and description (an explanation to the user that describes what the purchase is and does). These latter two elements are localized to specific languages. At the time of writing this book, those languages are

- English (also Australian English, Canadian English, UK English)
- Dutch
- French (also Canadian French)
- German
- Italian
- Japanese
- Spanish (also Mexican Spanish)
- Simplified Chinese

You can create data for any or all these languages so long as you define at least one. You cannot submit a new purchase item without creating one or more name/description pairs. For most developers who are targeting the U.S. store, a single English entry should cover your needs.

If your application is sold world wide, you'll likely want to mirror the existing localizations you use with your app descriptions and in-app features. If your iTunes store marketing material provides a Japanese localization, for example, and your application offers a Japanese language version, you'll want to create a Japanese-localized in-app purchase description as well. If you do not, you can still use in-app purchases but the language will default to whatever localizations you have provided.

> **Note**
>
> Always use native speakers to localize, edit, and proof text.

When entering this data, keep some points in mind. Your application is the consumer for this information. The text you type in iTunes Connect helps create the purchase GUI that your application presents to the user. The user's language settings select the localization. If you plan to use a simple alert sheet with a Buy/Cancel choice, keep your wording tight. Limit your verbosity. If you will use a more complex view, consider that as well.

No matter how you will create your GUI, remember that your description has to convey the action of purchasing as well as a description of the item being purchased—for example, "When purchased, this option unlocks this application's detail screens. These screens reveal even more data about the scanned MDNS services." A shorter description like "Extra detail screens" or "Unlock more details" doesn't explain to users how the purchase works and what they can expect to receive.

> **Note**
>
> You can edit item display details at any time during review at iTunes Connect. You must submit new changes for review once the purchased items have been approved.

Submitting a Purchase GUI Screenshot

The For Review section appears at the bottom of the item sheet. You do not use this section until you have finished developing and debugging your application. When you have done so, upload a screenshot into the provided field. The screenshot must show the in-app purchase in action, demonstrating the custom GUI you built.

Figure 20-4 displays the kind of screenshot you might submit. Valid pictures must be 320x480, 480x320, 320x460, or 480x300 pixels in size. (These latter two sizes use screenshots with the 20-pixel status bar removed.) The screenshot highlights how you have developed the purchase feature. Submit an image highlighting the purchase.

Developer Approval

After you have finished your sandbox testing and are confident that the application and the in-app purchasing are ready for Apple to review, you must personally approve the application. Go to iTunes Connect > Manage In-App Purchases and select any purchase item. Click the green Approve button.

You are prompted to select how you want to submit, as shown in Figure 20-5. Choose Submit With Binary to submit the purchase item with your next binary upload. Choose Submit Now for review with an already-approved 3.x or later application. The first option

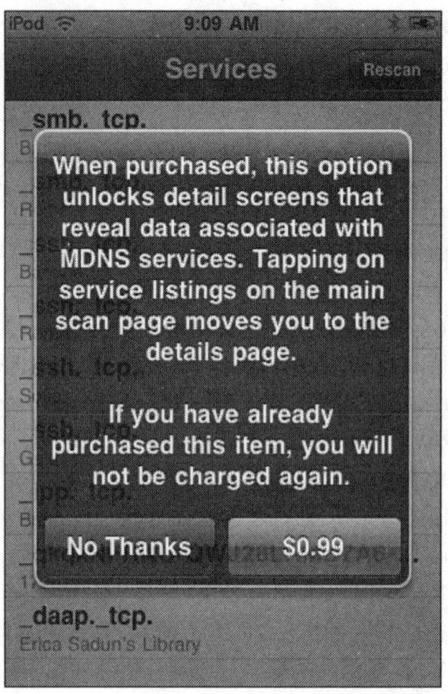

Figure 20-4 You must submit a screen shot showing your in-application purchase GUI to Apple when you are ready to have that purchase reviewed.

is meant for applications that have just now added an in-application purchase feature. The second option allows you to add new purchases to an existing, tested product.

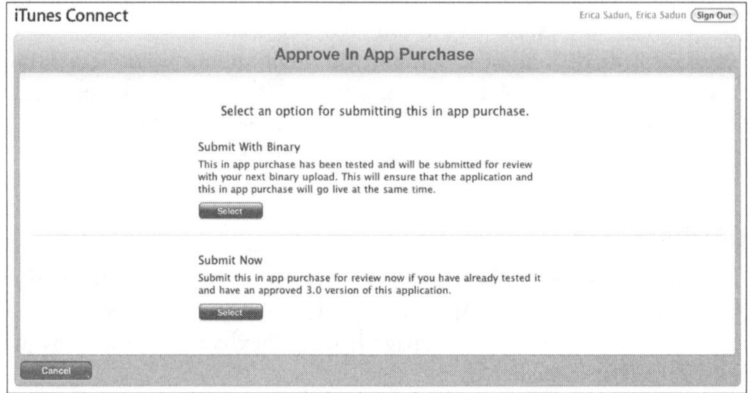

Figure 20-5 Choose the way you want Apple to review an in-application purchase choice.

Submitting the Application

Once you approve the application, it's ready to enter the review queue. If you chose the first option, make sure you follow up by submitting a new copy of your binary. Otherwise, the purchase item and the application will not be reviewed together.

To submit the new binary, reject the current version. Upon doing so, you no longer are able to test your application with the sandbox purchase server. You must have an application that's in review or accepted to use these services. Go ahead and upload the new fully working version.

Upon reuploading a binary, iTunes Connect prompts you to submit in-app purchases. Figure 20-6 illustrates this. Check the in-app items you want to use and save your changes. The purchase item and the application will be reviewed together, solving the "which came first" paradox.

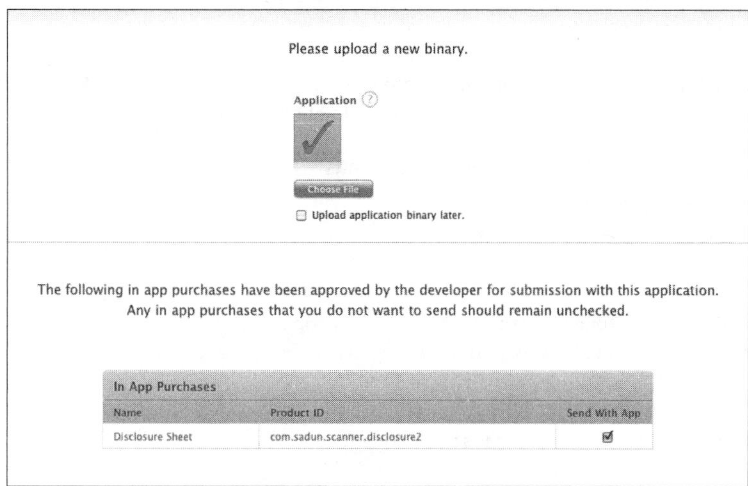

Figure 20-6 Choose the in-app purchases you want to have reviewed when you resubmit your self-rejected binary.

Building a GUI

Apple's StoreKit framework does not provide a built-in GUI for soliciting user purchases. You must create your own, like the one shown previously in Figure 20-4. You retrieve localized prices and descriptions from the App Store by creating `SKProductsRequest` instances. This class asks the store for that information based on the set of identifiers you provide. Each identifier must be registered at iTunes Connect as an in-app purchase item.

Allocate a new products request instance and initialize it with that set. You can add identifiers for items you've already established as well as items you're planning on adding in the future. Since each identifier is basically a string, you could create a loop that builds identifiers according to some naming scheme (e.g., com.sadun.app.item1, com.sadun.app.item2, etc.) to provide for future growth. This snippet searches for a single item.

```
// Create the product request and start it
SKProductsRequest *preq = [[SKProductsRequest alloc]
    initWithProductIdentifiers:[NSSet setWithObject:PRODUCT_ID]];
preq.delegate = self;
[preq start];
```

When using a products request, your delegate must declare and implement the `SKProductsRequestDelegate` protocol. This consists of three simple callbacks. Listing 20-1 shows these callback methods for a simple application. When a response is received, this code looks for a product (only one was requested, per the code snippet right before this paragraph) and retrieves its localized price and description.

It then builds a simple alert using the description as the alert text and two buttons (the price and "No Thanks"). This alert functions as a basic purchase GUI.

> **Note**
>
> StoreKit will not work if you are not connected to the network in some way. Refer to Chapter 14, "Device Capabilities," to find recipes that help check for network access.

Listing 20-1 **Products Request Callback Methods**

```
- (void)request:(SKRequest *)request
    didFailWithError:(NSError *)error
{
    [self doLog:
        @"Error: Could not contact App Store properly, %@",
        [error localizedDescription]];
}

- (void)requestDidFinish:(SKRequest *)request
{
    // Release the request
    [request release];
    [self doLog:@"Request finished."];
}

- (void)productsRequest:(SKProductsRequest *)request
    didReceiveResponse:(SKProductsResponse *)response
{
    // Find a product
    SKProduct *product = [[response products] lastObject];
    if (!product)
    {
        [self doLog:@"Error Could not find matching products"];
        return;
    }
```

```
    // Retrieve the localized price
    NSNumberFormatter *numberFormatter =
        [[NSNumberFormatter alloc] init];
    [numberFormatter
        setFormatterBehavior:NSNumberFormatterBehavior10_4];
    [numberFormatter setNumberStyle:NSNumberFormatterCurrencyStyle];
    [numberFormatter setLocale:product.priceLocale];
    NSString *formattedString = [numberFormatter
        stringFromNumber:product.price];
    [numberFormatter release];

    // Show the information
    [self doLog:product.localizedTitle];
    [self doLog:product.localizedDescription];
    [self doLog:@"Price %@", formattedString];

    // Create the GUI
    NSArray *buttons = [NSArray arrayWithObject: formattedString];
    if ([ModalAlert ask:describeString withCancel:@"No Thanks"
        withButtons:buttons])
    {
         // Carry out the purchase
    }
}
```

Purchasing Items

To purchase items from your application, start by adding a transaction observer. The best place to do this is in your application delegate's finished-launching method. Use your primary model class as the observer and make sure that class declares and implements the `SKPaymentTransactionObserver` protocol.

```
[[SKPaymentQueue defaultQueue] addTransactionObserver:mainClass];
```

With an observer in place, you can use the GUI from Listing 20-1 to begin the actual purchase.

```
if ([ModalAlert ask:describeString
    withCancel:@"No Thanks" withButtons:buttons])
{
    // Purchase the item
    SKPayment *payment = [SKPayment
          paymentWithProductIdentifier:PRODUCT_ID];
    [[SKPaymentQueue defaultQueue] addPayment:payment];
}
```

```
else
{
    // restore the GUI to provide a buy/purchase button
    // or otherwise to a ready-to-buy state
}
```

StoreKit prompts the user to confirm the in-app purchase, as shown in Figure 20-7, and then takes over the purchase process. Users may need to log in to an account before they can proceed.

Figure 20-7 Users must confirm the purchase after moving past your user interface into the actual App Store/StoreKit purchasing system.

Signing Out of Your iTunes Account for Testing

To use the test accounts you set up in iTunes Connect, be sure to sign out of your current, real account. Launch the Settings application, choose the Store preferences, and click Sign Out.

As mentioned earlier in this chapter, *do not* attempt to sign in again with your test account credentials. Just quit out of Settings and return to your application. After clicking Buy, you are prompted to sign in to iTunes. At that prompt, choose Use Existing Account and enter your account details.

Note

You cannot use the simulator to test StoreKit. All testing must be performed on an actual iPhone or iPod touch.

Regaining Programmatic Control After a Purchase

The payments transaction observer receives callbacks based on the success or failure of the payment process. Listing 20-2 shows a skeleton for responding to both finished and unfinished payments. After the user finishes the purchase process, the transaction will have succeeded or failed. On success, perform whatever action the user has paid for, whether by downloading data or unlocking features.

Listing 20-2 **Responding to Payments**

```
- (void)paymentQueue:(SKPaymentQueue *)queue
    removedTransactions:(NSArray *)transactions
{
}

- (void) completedPurchaseTransaction:
    (SKPaymentTransaction *) transaction
{
    // PERFORM THE SUCCESS ACTION THAT UNLOCKS THE FEATURE HERE

    // Finish transaction
    [[SKPaymentQueue defaultQueue] finishTransaction: transaction];
    [ModalAlert say:@"Thank you for your purchase."];
}

- (void) handleFailedTransaction: (SKPaymentTransaction *) transaction
{
    if (transaction.error.code != SKErrorPaymentCancelled)
        [ModalAlert say:@"Transaction Error. Please try again later."];
    [[SKPaymentQueue defaultQueue] finishTransaction: transaction];
}

- (void)paymentQueue:(SKPaymentQueue *)queue
    updatedTransactions:(NSArray *)transactions
{
    for (SKPaymentTransaction *transaction in transactions) {
        switch (transaction.transactionState) {
            case SKPaymentTransactionStatePurchased:
            case SKPaymentTransactionStateRestored:
                [self completedPurchaseTransaction:transaction];
                break;
            case SKPaymentTransactionStateFailed:
                [self handleFailedTransaction:transaction];
```

```
                break;
            case SKPaymentTransactionStatePurchasing:
                [self repurchase];
                break;
            default: break;
        }
    }
}
```

Registering Purchases

You can use any of a number of approaches to register purchases. You can synchronize with a Web server, create local files, set user defaults, or add keychain entries. The solution you choose is left up to you. Just don't lose track of purchases. Once a user buys an unlockable feature, subscription, or data, you must guarantee that your application supplies the promised element or elements.

It's easiest to unlock features through user preferences. This snippet creates a new default, indicating that the user has purchased a disclosure feature. Upon completing the purchase, the code updates the user defaults database and hides the "buy" button from the interface.

```
// Update user defaults
[[NSUserDefaults standardUserDefaults] setBool:YES
    forKey:@"Supports Disclosure"];
[[NSUserDefaults standardUserDefaults] synchronize];

// Hide "buy" button
self.navigationItem.leftBarButtonItem = nil;
```

The application can check for this preference each time it launches.

For the most part, users cannot hack their way into your application to update preferences settings by hand. The application is sandboxed (other applications cannot access your files), and the data cannot be edited from the Macintosh backup system. It is possible in jailbroken systems, if you use just a simple preference like this. For anyone worried about piracy, consider a more secure approach.

If you have any concerns, consider using some sort of verifiable authentication key rather than a standard Boolean value. Alternatively, use the system keychain (see Chapter 13, "Networking"). The keychain provides a secure data store that cannot easily be manipulated from the jailbroken iPhone command line.

A simple example of storing the purchase on the keychain would be a routine like this.

```
-(void) unlockMaxGameLevels
{
    KeychainItemWrapper *wrapper = [[KeychainItemWrapper alloc]
        initWithIdentifier:@"CustomGameApp" accessGroup:nil];
    [wrapper setObject:@"MaxUnlocked" forKey:(id)kSecValueData];
```

```
    [wrapper release];
}
```

Using the keychain provides the additional benefit that the data stored here will survive an application being deleted and then later reinstalled.

When you use an offsite server to register and authenticate purchases, make sure to echo those settings on the device. Users must be able to use their applications regardless of whether they have network access. A local setting (e.g., "Service enabled until 6 June 2011") lets the application run and provide proper feedback, even when a subscribed service is inaccessible.

Several start-ups like Urban Airship (urbanairship.com) and Key Lime Tie's iLime service (ilime.com) now offer support for in-app purchase data delivery. They provide servers that allow you to offload content from your application, handle its delivery to your customers, and allow you to keep that content up to date as needed.

Restoring Purchases

Purchase may be restored on a device where an application was uninstalled and then reinstalled, or where an application was installed on a second device associated with the same iTunes account. If a customer's iTunes account has multiple devices, like a family with five iPhones and iPods, a purchase by any of the devices allows all the devices to download that purchase with no additional charge.

StoreKit allows you to restore purchases, which is particularly important for consumable and subscription items where you do not want to allow the user to repurchase an already-valid item. In the case of a nonconsumable item, the user can repurchase without cost ad infinitum. For these nonconsumable items, you can simply submit your purchase request. The App Store interface will present a window informing the user that they have already purchased this item, and that they can download it again for free.

To restore purchases associated with an iTunes account, call `restoreCompletedTransactions`. This works just like adding a payment and involves the same callbacks. To catch a repurchase separately from a purchase, check for `SKPaymentTransactionStateRestored` as the payment transaction state, as in Listing 20-2.

```
- (void) repurchase
{
    // Repurchase an already purchased item
    [[SKPaymentQueue defaultQueue] restoreCompletedTransactions];
}
```

That's because purchase events provide not one but two possible successful outcomes. The first is a completed purchase. The user has bought the item and the payment has finished processing. The second is the restored purchase described here. Make sure your payment queue handler looks for both states.

There's a loophole here. Consider providing a consumable purchase item such as a credit to send a FAX. Should the user uninstall the application and then reinstall, any repurchase functionality may restore an asset that has already been used. Applications with consumable products must be designed with more thought for the security infrastructure and demand server-side accounting that keeps track of user credits and consumed assets.

Go ahead and restore purchases but ensure that those purchases properly coordinate with your server database. As you'll read about shortly in the section that follows this one, Apple provides a unique identifier for each purchase by way of a purchase receipt. A repurchased item retains that original identifier, allowing you to distinguish between new purchases and restored ones.

Purchasing Multiple Items

Users can purchase more than one copy of consumable items and subscriptions. Set the `quantity` property for a payment to request a multiple purchase. This snippet adds a payment request for three copies of a product, perhaps adding three months to a subscription, 3,000 hit points to a character, or so forth.

```
SKMutablePayment *payment = [SKMutablePayment
    paymentWithProductIdentifier:PRODUCT_ID];
payment.quantity = 3;
[[SKPaymentQueue defaultQueue] addPayment:payment];
```

Handling Delays in Registering Purchases

If your purchase connects with a server and you cannot complete the purchase registration process, *do not finalize the transaction*. Do not call `finishTransaction:` until you are guaranteed that all establishment work has been done for your customer.

Should you fail to set up your user with his or her newly purchased items before the application is quit, that's okay. The transaction remains in the purchase queue until the next time the application launches. You are given another opportunity to try to finish your work.

Validating Receipts

A successful purchase transaction contains a receipt. This receipt, which is sent in raw `NSData` format, corresponds to an encoded JSON string. It contains a signature and purchase information. Here is a sample receipt, from one of my purchases.


```
{
      "signature" =
"AbtAgJQlIPicxP/g4ubwT/noCER4jE+LuGNfxfy++DsiEUrdOYNcf6GqljT+/qDlLCvSZUnWGG7YrACLD
FQRREftjNDmkgekbErdP8uI9IAN0sH6vkHx5sc/2p9hHRbG6AY/CDDj1lg+esLRe8HYGxCBaHlIMa+o/ZK
tHr3Rl+jUMIIDUzCCAjugAwIBAgIIZRSRTdlYBLUwDQYJKoZIhvcNAQEFBQAwfzELMAkGA1UEBhMCVVMxE
zARBgNVBAoMCkFwcGxlIEluYy4xJjAkBgNVBAsMHUFwcGxlIENlcnRpZmljYXRpb24gQXV0aG9yaXR5MTM
wMQYDVQQDDCpBcHBsZSBpVHVuZXMgU3RvcmUgQ2VydGlmaWNhdGlvbiBBdXRob3JpdHkwHhcNMDkwNjE1M
jIwNTU2WhcNMTQwNjE0MjIwNTU2WjBkMSMwIQYDVQQDDBpQdXJjaGFzZVJlY2VpcHRDZXJ0aWZpY2F0ZTE
bMBkGA1UECwwSQXBwbGUgaVR1bmVzIFN0b3JlMRMwEQYDVQQKDApBcHBsZSBJbmMuMQswCQYDVQQGEwJVU
zCBnzANBgkqhkiG9w0BAQEFAAOBjQAwgYkCgYEAytGMXZy3gitJ2JMKFojSDynC/9yYezyn9HBX+u3/3Vc
```

```
pWE2XhcgGKYqNBA1+AewOzrKO774OsokTu4qymEx10ph8UTmsZewB0ESMHBEjF7FN6/HccsQUYC3WagrHn
Tl2HG2Ih0OAm/ZhpWzj0HS4m813LpIyo00sewMvMNL2hkcCAwEAAaNyMHAwDAYDVR0TAQH/BAIwADAfBgN
VHSMEGDAWgBQ2HejinYLSARi1MmsO10MLkVhDOjAOBgNVHQ8BAf8EBAMCB4AwHQYDVR0OBBYEFKmDg/IZS
MU+ElcIFMzNo36ZXyTlMBAGCiqGSIb3Y2QGBQEEAgUAMA0GCSqGSIb3DQEBBQUAA4IBAQARpJs+O2Y3gL8
gHdASkrfZHFpwINd1VcB5VF5LkVpnFz63zylA/3cGIDG91b/d5NIwZjkVt4Bgvd62o/mCbzCsWiNfSKTJV
FK1D78BDQoSO2oHTuQuz1BR7xzNHxQZ90zUS6ZX9SC8N3g3A1jEtAyDhZNB+CRBBXLwZdnBUeBsT9QLpjv
TnekZcGTnU08zfCjGF3eBJEu9eP6WgexK1xMSp72kEOmYbn6yTi3D4YrcYx4Q3n/57VBP2en8qXWeP5oHD
sLTGzLRsWdoB3VxJLrF2ivL8JS8zqC0qyac452pN6xunRuzyyfpaqzQL12BzFEe44xna2byektSbtquA5L
NAAAAAA==";
       "purchase-info" =
"ewoJIml0ZW0taWQiID0gIjMzMDI5MjgwNiI7Cgkib3JpZ2luYWwtdHJhbnNhY3Rpb24taWQiID0gIjEwM
DAwMDAwMDAwNTIyOTMiOwoJInB1cmNoYXNlLWRhdGUiID0gIjIwMDktMDktMDQgMTU6MzU6MjYgRXRjL0d
NVCI7CgkicHJvZHVjdC1pZCIgPSAiY29tLnNhZHVuLnNjYW5uZXIuZGlzY2xvc3VyZTIiOwoJInRyYW5zY
WN0aW9uLWlkIiA9ICIxMDAwMDAwMDAwMDUyMjkzIjsKCSJxdWFudGl0eSIgPSAiMSI7Cgkib3JpZ2luYWw
tcHVyY2hhc2UtZGF0ZSIgPSAiMjAwOS0wOS0wNCAxNTozNToyNiBFdGMvR01UIjsKCSJiaWQiID0gImNvb
S5zYWR1bi5TY2FubmVyIjsKCSJidnJzIiA9ICIxLjAiOwp9";
       "pod" = "100";
       "signing-status" = "0";
}
```


Apple strongly recommends that you validate all receipts with their servers to prevent hacking and ensure that your customers actually purchased the items they are requesting. Listing 20-3 shows how.

You must POST a request to one of Apple's two servers. The URL you use depends on the deployment of the application. Use buy.itunes.apple.com for production software and sandbox.itunes.apple.com for development.

The request body consists of a JSON dictionary. The dictionary is composed of one key ("receipt-data") and one value (a Base64-encoded version of the transaction receipt data. I normally use the CocoaDev NSData Base 64 extension (from http://www.cocoadev.com/index.pl?BaseSixtyFour) to convert `NSData` objects into Base64-encoded strings. CocoaDev provides many great resources for Mac and iPhone developers.

A valid receipt returns a JSON dictionary similar to the following. The receipt includes the transaction identifier, a product ID for the item purchased, the bundle ID for the host application, and a purchase date. Most importantly, it returns a status.


```
{"receipt":{"item_id":"330292806",
    "original_transaction_id":"1000000000052438", "bvrs":"1.0",
    "product_id":"com.sadun.scanner.disclosure2",
    "purchase_date":"2009-09-04 19:23:15 Etc/GMT", "quantity":"1",
    "bid":"com.sadun.Scanner",
    "original_purchase_date":"2009-09-04 19:23:15 Etc/GMT",
    "transaction_id":"1000000000052438"}, "status":0}
```


A valid receipt always has a 0 status. Any number other than 0 indicates that the receipt is invalid.

Simply checking for the status may not be sufficient for validation. It's not too difficult to set up a proxy server to intercept calls to the validation server and return JSON {"status":0} to all requests. What's more, the receipt data that is sent along with the validation request can be easily deserialized into exactly the same data shown in the "receipt" portion of the JSON dictionary shown above. For that reason, you should always use receipt validation cautiously and as part of the overall purchase process, where it's less likely that proxy servers can override communications with Apple.

Listing 20-3 **Checking a Receipt**

```
// Produce a JSON request
NSString *json = [NSString stringWithFormat:
    @"receipt-data\":\"%@\"}",
    [transaction.transactionReceipt base64Encoding]];

// Choose a server to verify the receipt
NSString *urlsting = SANDBOX ?
    @"https://sandbox.itunes.apple.com/verifyReceipt" :
    @"https://buy.itunes.apple.com/verifyReceipt";

// Create a url request
NSMutableURLRequest *urlRequest = [NSMutableURLRequest
    requestWithURL:[NSURL URLWithString: urlsting]];
if (!urlRequest) NOTIFY_AND_LEAVE(@"Error creating the URL Request");

// Use POST and set the body to the encoded JSON
[urlRequest setHTTPMethod: @"POST"];
[urlRequest setHTTPBody:[json dataUsingEncoding:NSUTF8StringEncoding]];

// Submit the request and recover the response
NSError *error;
NSURLResponse *response;
NSData *result = [NSURLConnection sendSynchronousRequest:urlRequest
returningResponse:&response error:&error];

// A valid JSON string with a receipt dictionary should be received
NSString *resultString = [[NSString alloc] initWithData:result
encoding:NSUTF8StringEncoding];
CFShow(resultString);
[resultString release];
```

Summary

The StoreKit framework offers a great new way to monetize your applications. As you read in this chapter, you can set up your own storefront to sell services and features from your application. Here are a few final thoughts:

- Although the entire setup and testing process may seem a little "Which came first? The chicken or the egg?" it is demonstrably possible to develop and deploy a StoreKit-based application with a minimum of headaches.
- Remember to reject and then resubmit your binaries after adding new purchasable items. You want to ensure that both the application and the items are ready for Apple to review.
- Avoid finalizing transactions until your new-purchase setup is completely, utterly, 100% done, even if that means waiting for an application relaunch. At the same time, inform the user that the purchase process is experiencing unexpected delays.
- Your methods can only request product information from in-app items that are registered to the currently running application. You cannot share requests across apps.
- Don't forget to set up the purchase observer! More heads have been banged against desks and hair pulled out over that one step than any other StoreKit issue.

21

Accessibility and Other iPhone OS Services

Applications interact with standard iPhone services in a variety of ways. This chapter introduces several approaches. Applications can define their interfaces to the iPhone's VoiceOver accessibility handler, creating descriptions of their GUI elements. Developers can create bundles to work with the built-in Settings applications so that users can access applications' defaults using that interface. Applications can also declare public URL schemes allowing other iPhone applications to contact them and request services that they themselves offer. This chapter explores these application service interactions. It shows you how to implement these features in your applications. You see how to build these service bridges through code, through Interface Builder, and through supporting files.

Adding VoiceOver Accessibility to Your Apps

Accessibility enhancements open up the iPhone to users with disabilities. iPhone OS features allow users to magnify (or "zoom") displays, invert colors, and more. As a developer, accessibility enhancement centers on VoiceOver, a way that visually impaired users can "listen" to their GUI. VoiceOver converts an application's visual presentation into an audio description.

Don't confuse VoiceOver with Voice Control. The former is a method for presenting an audio description of a user interface and is highly gesture-based. The latter refers to Apple's proprietary voice recognition technology for hands-free interaction.

This section offers a brief overview of VoiceOver accessibility. You read about adding accessibility labels and hints to your applications and testing those features in the simulator and on the iPhone. Accessibility is available and can be tested on third generation or later devices, including the iPhone 3GS and the third generation iPod touch.

Accessibility in Interface Builder

Use the Identity Inspector > Accessibility pane in Interface Builder (see Figure 21-1) to add labels and hints to the `UIKit` elements in your interface. Enter strings in either or both of the two fields provided. As you do so, know that these fields and the text they contain play different roles in the bigger accessibility picture. Labels identify views; hints describe them. In addition to these fields, you'll find a general accessibility Enabled check box and a number of Traits check boxes.

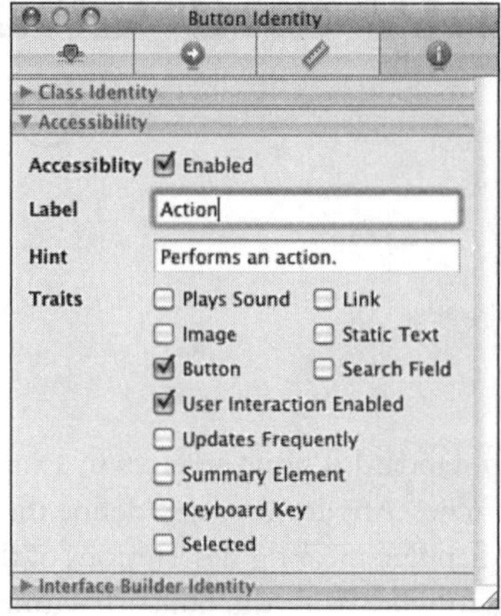

Figure 21-1 Interface Builder's Identity Inspector lets you specify object accessibility information.

Labels

A good label tells the user what an item is, often with a single word. Label an accessible GUI the same way you'd label a button with text. "Edit," "Delete," and "Add" all describe what objects do. They're excellent button text and accessibility label text.

But accessibility isn't just about buttons. "Feedback," "User Photo," and "User Name" might describe the contents and function of a text view, an image view, and a text label. If an object plays a visual role in your interface, it should play an auditory role in VoiceOver. Here are a few tips for designing your labels:

- **Do not add the view type into the label**—For example, don't use "Delete button," "Feedback text view," or "User name text field." VoiceOver adds this information automatically, so "Delete button" in the identity pane becomes "Delete button button" in the actual VoiceOver playback.
- **Capitalize the label but don't add a period**—VoiceOver uses your capitalization to properly inflect the label when it speaks. Adding a period typically causes VoiceOver to end the label with a downward tone, which does not blend well into the object-type that follows. "Delete. button" sounds wrong. "Delete button" does not.
- **Aggregate information**—When working with complex views that function as a single unit, build all the information in that view into a single descriptive label and attach it to that parent view. For example, in a table view cell with several subviews

but without individual controls, you might aggregate all the text information into a single label that describes the entire cell.

- **Label only at the lowest interaction level**—When users need to interact with subviews, label at that level. Parent views, whose children are accessible, do not need labels.
- **Localize**—Localizing your accessibility strings opens them up to the widest audience of users.

Hints

Hints tell users what to expect from interaction. In particular, they describe any nonobvious results. For example, consider an interface where tapping on a name, for example, John Smith attempts to call that person by telephone. The name itself offers no information about the interaction outcome. So offer a hint telling the user about it—for example, "Places a phone call to this person," or even better, "Places a phone call to John Smith." Here are tips for building better hints.

- **Use sentence form**—Start with a capital letter and end with a period. Do this even though each hint has a missing subject. This format ensures that VoiceOver speaks the hint with proper inflection.
- **Use verbs that describe what the element does, not what the user does**—*"[This text label]* Places a phone call to this person." provides the right context for the user. "*[You will]* Place a phone call to this person." does not.
- **Do not say the name or type of the GUI element**—Avoid hints that refer to the UI item being manipulated. Skip the GUI name (its label, such as "Delete") and type (its class, such as "button"). VoiceOver adds that information where needed, preventing any overly redundant playback such as "Delete button *[label]* button *[VoiceOver description]* button *[hint]* removes item from screen." Use "Removes item from screen." instead.
- **Avoid the action**—Do not describe the action that the user takes. Do not say "Swiping places a phone call to this person" or "Tapping places a phone call to this person." VoiceOver uses its own set of gestures to activate GUI elements. Never refer to gestures directly.
- **Be verbose**—"Place call" does not describe the outcome as well as "Place a call to this person," or, even better, "Place a call to John Smith." A short but thorough explanation better helps the user than one that is so terse that the user has to guess about details. Avoid hints that require the user to listen again before proceeding.
- **Localize**—As with labels, localizing your accessibility hints works with the widest user base.

Enabling Accessibility

The Enabled check box controls whether a UIKit view works with VoiceOver. As a rule, keep this item checked unless the view is a container whose subviews need to be accessible. Enable only those items at the most direct level of interaction or presentation. Views that organize other views don't play a meaningful role in the voice presentation. Exclude them.

Table view cells offer a good example of accessibility containers, that is, objects that contain other objects. The rules for table view cells are as follows:

- A table view cell without embedded controls should be accessible.
- A table view cell with embedded controls should not be. Its child controls should be.

Outside Interface Builder, nonaccessible containers are responsible for reporting how many accessible children they contain and which child views those are. See Apple's Accessibility Programming Guide for iPhone for further details about programming containers for accessibility. Custom container views need to declare and implement the `UIAccessibilityContainer` protocol.

Traits

Traits characterize UIKit item behaviors. VoiceOver uses these traits while describing interfaces. As Figure 21-1 shows, there are 12 possible traits you can assign to views. Select the traits that apply to the selected view, keeping in mind that you can always update these choices programmatically.

Apple's accessibility documents request that you only check one of the following four mutually exclusive items at any time: Button, Link, Static Text, or Search Field. If a button works as a link as well, choose either the button trait or the link trait but not both. You choose which best characterizes how that button is used. At the same time, a button might show an image and play a sound when tapped, and you can freely add those traits.

Working with Accessibility from Code

Every UIKit view conforms to the `UIAccessibility` protocol, offering properties that let you set labels and hints, along with the other accessibility features shown in Figure 21-1. You can set those properties in Interface Builder or use them directly in code. Listing 21-1 sets the `accessibilityHint` property to update a button's hint as a user types a username into a related text field. As the text in that field changes, the button's hint updates to reflect that value.

Listing 21-1 **Programmatically Updating Accessibility Information**

```
- (BOOL)textField:(UITextField *)textField
    shouldChangeCharactersInRange:(NSRange)range
    replacementString:(NSString *)string
{
    // Catch the change to the user name field and update
    // the accessibility hint to mirror that
```

```
    NSString *username = textField.text;
    if (username && username.length > 1)
        callbutton.accessibilityHint = [NSString
        stringWithFormat:@"Places a call to %@", username];
    else
        callbutton.accessibilityHint =
            @"Places a call to the person named in the text field.";
    return YES;
}
```

Testing with the Simulator

The iPhone simulator's Accessibility Inspector is designed for testing accessible applications before deploying them to the iPhone. The simulator's inspector simulates VoiceOver interaction with your application, providing immediate visual feedback via a floating pane (there is no actual voice produced) without having to use the VoiceOver gesture interface directly. As you cannot replicate many VoiceOver gestures with the simulator (such as triple-swipes and sequential hold-then-tap gestures), the inspector focuses on describing interface items rather than responding to VoiceOver gestures.

Enable this feature by opening Settings > General > Accessibility. Switch the Accessibility Inspector to On. The inspector, shown in Figure 21-2 immediately appears. It lists the current settings for the currently selected accessible element.

Know how to enable and disable the inspector: The circled X in the top-left corner of the inspector controls that behavior. Click it once to shrink the inspector to a disabled single line. Click again to restore the inspector to active mode. For the most part, keep the inspector disabled until you actually need to inspect a GUI item.

Like VoiceOver, the inspector interferes with normal application gestures. It will slow down your work, so use it sparingly, normally when you are ready to test. You want to launch your application with the inspector disabled but available. Navigate to the screen you want to work with and then enable the inspector.

The application shown in Figure 21-1 uses the code from Listing 21-1. The Call button's accessibility hint updates as the text in the field changes. Activating the inspector allows you to view the current hint as you update the text field, ensuring that the button hint properly matches the label text.

Testing Accessibility on the iPhone

Testing on the iPhone is a critical part of accessibility development. The iPhone allows you to work with the actual VoiceOver utility rather than a window-based inspector. You hear what your users will hear and are able to test your GUI with your fingers and ears rather than with your eyes.

Like the Simulator, the iPhone provides a way to enable and disable VoiceOver on the fly. Although you can enable VoiceOver in Settings and then test your application with VoiceOver running, you'll find that it's far easier to use a special toggle. The toggle lets you avoid the hassle of navigating out of Settings and over to your application using VoiceOver gestures. You can switch VoiceOver off, use normal iPhone interactions to get your application started, and then switch VoiceOver back on when you're ready to test.

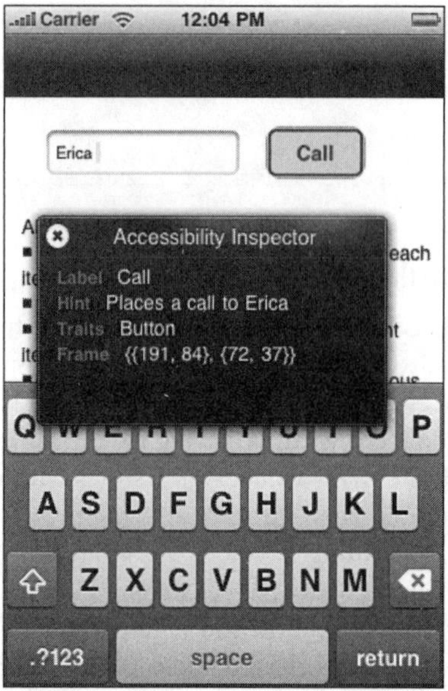

Figure 21-2 The iPhone simulator's Accessibility Inspector highlights the currently selected GUI feature, revealing its label, hint, and other accessibility properties.

Here are the steps you need to take to enable that toggle.

1. Go to the Accessibility settings pane. Navigate to Settings > General > Accessibility.
2. Locate the Triple-click Home choice. The Triple-click Home button provides a user-settable shortcut for accessibility choices. Tap on Triple-click Home to open the Home pane.
3. Choose Toggle VoiceOver. Select Toggle VoiceOver to set it as your triple-click action. Once selected (a check appears to its right), you can enable and disable VoiceOver by triple-clicking the physical Home button at the bottom of your iPhone. A spoken prompt confirms the current VoiceOver setting.

This VoiceOver toggle offers you the ability to skip many of the laborious details involved in navigating to your application using triple-fingered drags, and multistage button clicks. At the same time, you should be conversant with VoiceOver gestures and interactions. Table 21-1 offers a summary of VoiceOver gestures that you need to know for testing your application.

Table 21-1 **Common VoiceOver Gestures for Applications as of iPhone OS 3.1**

Task	VoiceOver Equivalent
Toggle VoiceOver	Triple-click the physical Home button.
Toggle ScreenCurtain	Triple-tap the screen, three times (i.e., a triple-tap with three fingers).
Toggle VoiceOver speech	Toggle the VoiceOver speech entirely (not just for a single description) by triple-tapping the screen twice (i.e., a double-tap with three fingers). Neither of these options disables VoiceOver.
Stop speaking the current item	Double-tap the screen twice (i.e., double-tap with two fingers). Double-tap again to resume the description. In the home screen, when VoiceOver is not active, this gesture stops and resumes audio playback.
Tapping buttons	Method 1: Tap and hold the button with one finger. Tap the screen with another finger. Method 2: Tap the button to select it. Double-tap the screen to activate the button.
Scrolling a text view	Method 1: Tap and hold the text view with one finger. Tap with a second finger to scroll to the top or bottom of the text scroller. Method 2: Tap the text view to select it. Double-tap the screen to scroll to the top or bottom of the text scroller.
Adjusting the text insertion point	With an editable text view or field selected, adjust the insertion point by flicking up or down with a single finger. The point may move by characters or by word depending on how you have set up your preferences.
Accessing the spoken text menu	Tap and hold one finger in the text view. Flick up and down with another finger to choose between character movement, word movement, and edit mode, which uses the last-chosen movement option. (This gesture, properly known as the "rotor," is supposed to be performed as a twisted two-finger drag. The approach used here worked more consistently in testing.)
Selecting text	Set the insertion point and enter edit mode (see above). Tap and hold one finger in the text view. Drag left or drag right.

Table 21-1 **Continued**

Task	VoiceOver Equivalent
Typing text	Enter text edit mode by selecting a text field or text view and then double-tap the screen. The keyboard appears onscreen. Typing method 1: Tap and hold a keyboard button with your left pointer finger. Tap somewhere else on the screen with your right pointer finger. This is the best way to use the delete key repeatedly. Typing method 2: Tap on a key to select it. Double-tap the screen to type that key.
Moving sliders	Select the slider and then flick up or down with a single finger to adjust the slider value.
Scroll a list	Flick three fingers up or down.
Paging through the home page iPhone application launcher	Flick three fingers left or right.
Select and speak an item	Tap the item.
Spell out the selected item one character or word at a time	Flick a single finger up or down. This uses the settings from the spoken text menu.
Speak the next or previous item	Flick a single finger left or right.
Read the entire screen	Double-flick upwards. This doesn't work as consistently as it could. So alternatively use the following approach: Flick left repeatedly to the first item in the screen. Then two-fingered stroke down. You can read the screen starting from the currently selected item using the double-fingered stroke down gesture.
Unlock iPhone	Select the Unlock slider. Double-tap the screen.

Take special note of ScreenCurtain, which allows you to blank your iPhone display, offering a true test of your application as an audio-based interface. Try the iPhone calculator application with ScreenCurtain enabled to gain a true sense of the challenge of using an iPhone application without sight.

Recipe: Adding Custom Settings Bundles

The iPhone uses the `NSUserDefaults` class to access and manage application preferences. With it, you can store information that your application needs to preserve between successive runs. For example, you might save a current player name, a list of high scores, or the last-used view configuration. User defaults programmatically assign values to a persistent database associated with your application. These defaults are stored in your application sandbox's Library folder, in a property list file named with your application identifier.

Treat user defaults as a mutable dictionary. Set and retrieve objects using keys, just as you would with that dictionary. Defaults entries are limited to standard property list types—that is, `NSString`, `NSNumber`, `NSDate`, `NSData`, `NSArray`, and `NSDictionary`. When you need to store information that does not fall into one of these classes, consider using another file (such as one that resides in your sandbox's Library or Documents folders) or serialize your object into `NSData` and store that data in defaults.

The `synchronize` method forces the defaults database to update to the latest changes made in memory. Synchronizing assures you that the file-based defaults data is up-to-date, an important factor if your application gets interrupted for some reason. The following snippet demonstrates setting, synchronizing, and retrieving data from the user defaults system, per Recipe 8-5.

```
[[NSUserDefaults standardUserDefaults]
    setObject:colors forKey:@"colors"];
[[NSUserDefaults standardUserDefaults]
    setObject:locs forKey:@"locs"];

[[NSUserDefaults standardUserDefaults] synchronize];

NSLog(@"%@", [[NSUserDefaults] objectForKey@"lastViewTag"]);
```

The Settings App

iPhone applications can add custom preferences into the main Settings app (see Figure 21-3). These preferences access the same application-specific user defaults that you work with programmatically. The difference is that Settings provides a friendly GUI for your users. Any changes your users make to these screens update and synchronize with standard user defaults.

Custom settings are listed after system settings, but otherwise look and act like the ones that Apple preloaded into your system. As the screenshots in Figure 21-3 show, custom preferences provide a variety of data interaction styles, including text fields, switches, and sliders.

Because these settings create standard `NSUserDefaults` entries, you can easily query and modify any of these settings from code. For example, Recipe 21-1 defines a field called "Name" (see Figure 21-3, right screenshot, first item in the top Group). This text field stores its value to the `@"name_preference"` key. You can see whether the user has entered a value for this key from your application.

```
NSLog(@"% objectForKey:@"name_preference"];
```

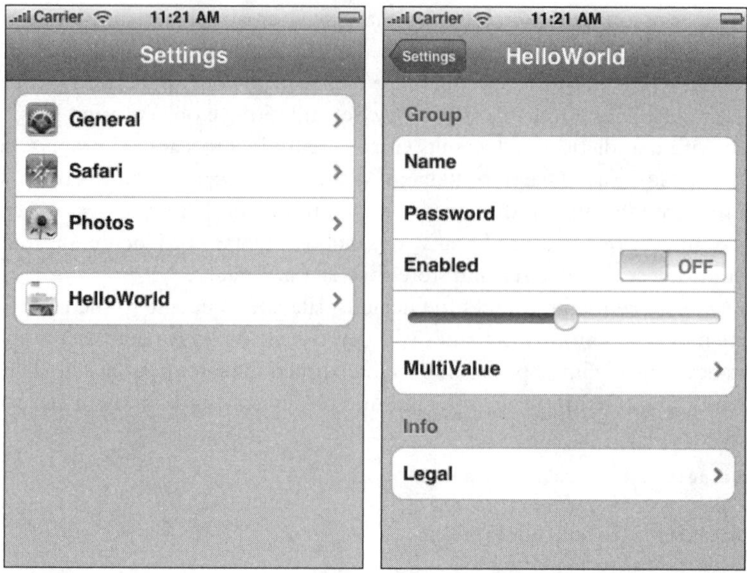

Figure 21-3 (Left) Custom settings bundles for third-party applications appear on the Settings screen after the built-in settings. On the iPhone, you may have to scroll down a bit to find them. (Right) Developer-defined preferences elements can include text fields (both regular and secure), switches, sliders, multivalue choices, group titles, and child panes.

Avoid Sensitive Information

Use settings to store nonsensitive account preferences such as usernames and option toggles. Although passwords are visually obscured with dots, they're stored in clear text in your application sandbox. When working with sensitive information, use your iPhone's secure keychain instead. Settings bundles do not offer keychain integration at this time. Keychain recipes appear in Chapter 13, "Networking."

Settings Schema

A copy of the settings schema resides in your Developer folder at /Developer/Platforms/iPhoneOS.platform/Developer/Library/Xcode/Plug-ins/iPhoneSettingsPlistStructDefs.xcodeplugin. Xcode uses this file to check its property list syntax. In the file, you can see all the definitions and the required and optional attributes used to specify custom preferences. If Apple should ever expand or change its definitions, you'll be able to find those changes in this file.

Defining a Settings Bundle

Each settings pane corresponds to one property list file. Recipe 21-1 shows the source for the pane in Figure 21-3 (right). It demonstrates each SDK settings type and provides a sample definition. Types include text fields (strings), sliders (floating-point numbers), switches (Boolean values), and multiple selection (one-of-n choices). In addition, you can group items and link to child panes.

To add new settings, build a dictionary and add it to the `PreferencesSpecifiers` array. Each individual preference dictionary needs, at a minimum, a type and a title. Some settings, like the `PSGroupSpecifier` group item, require nothing more to work. Others, such as text fields, use quite a few properties. You want to specify capitalization and auto-correction behaviors as well as the keyboard type and whether the password security feature obscures text, as you can see in Recipe 21-1.

To add a settings bundle to your program, follow these steps. Alternatively, you can create a new settings bundle by choosing File > New File > iPhone OS > Resource > Settings Bundle.

1. Create each of the property lists, one for each screen. The primary plist must be named Root.plist.

2. Create a new folder and add your property lists.

3. Rename the folder to Settings.bundle. OS X warns you about the name; go ahead and confirm the rename. The folder transforms into a bundle. (To view the contents of your new bundle, right-click [Control-click] and choose Show Package Contents from the contextual pop-up.)

4. Drag the bundle into the Groups & File column of your Xcode project (see Figure 21-4).

5. Create a 29x29 version of your main application icon file (typically icon.png) and add it to your project with the name Icon-Settings.png. This art is used by the Settings application to label your bundle along with the application name. You can see this in Figure 21-3 (left). The small icon to the left of HelloWorld uses this special icon.

When you next run your program, the settings bundle installs and makes itself available to the Settings application. Should your source have any syntax errors, you find a blank screen rather than the settings you expect. It helps to build your settings in stages to avoid this.

Xcode offers a limited interactive syntactically aware editing window. Open the property list and then choose View, Property List Type, iPhone Settings plist. You may find it easier to edit by hand in TextEdit or the stand-alone Property List Editor if you're comfortable with lower-level tools.

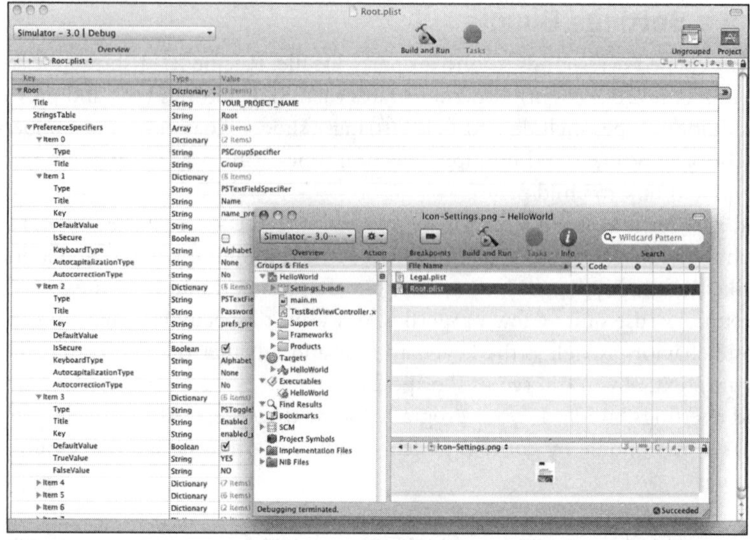

Figure 21-4 Add the Settings.bundle into your project's Groups & Files list. Double-click the property lists to edit them further in Xcode.

> **Note**
>
> In Recipe 21-1, the `File` property uses no extension; the .plist extension is understood.

Recipe 21-1 **Creating a Custom Settings Pane**

```
<?xml version="1.0" encoding="UTF-8"?>
<!DOCTYPE plist PUBLIC "-//Apple//DTD PLIST 1.0//EN"
"http://www.apple.com/DTDs/PropertyList-1.0.dtd">
<plist version="1.0">
<dict>
    <key>Title</key>
    <string>YOUR_PROJECT_NAME</string>
    <key>StringsTable</key>
    <string>Root</string>
    <key>PreferenceSpecifiers</key>
    <array>
        <dict>
            <key>Type</key>
            <string>PSGroupSpecifier</string>
            <key>Title</key>
            <string>Group</string>
        </dict>
        <dict>
            <key>Type</key>
            <string>PSTextFieldSpecifier</string>
            <key>Title</key>
```

```
        <string>Name</string>
        <key>Key</key>
        <string>name_preference</string>
        <key>DefaultValue</key>
        <string></string>
        <key>IsSecure</key>
        <false/>
        <key>KeyboardType</key>
        <string>Alphabet</string>
        <key>AutocapitalizationType</key>
        <string>None</string>
        <key>AutocorrectionType</key>
        <string>No</string>
    </dict>
    <dict>
        <key>Type</key>
        <string>PSTextFieldSpecifier</string>
        <key>Title</key>
        <string>Password</string>
        <key>Key</key>
        <string>prefs_preference</string>
        <key>DefaultValue</key>
        <string></string>
        <key>IsSecure</key>
        <true/>
        <key>KeyboardType</key>
        <string>Alphabet</string>
        <key>AutocapitalizationType</key>
        <string>None</string>
        <key>AutocorrectionType</key>
        <string>No</string>
    </dict>
    <dict>
        <key>Type</key>
        <string>PSToggleSwitchSpecifier</string>
        <key>Title</key>
        <string>Enabled</string>
        <key>Key</key>
        <string>enabled_preference</string>
        <key>DefaultValue</key>
        <true/>
        <key>TrueValue</key>
        <string>YES</string>
        <key>FalseValue</key>
        <string>NO</string>
    </dict>
    <dict>
```

```
        <key>Type</key>
        <string>PSSliderSpecifier</string>
        <key>Key</key>
        <string>slider_preference</string>
        <key>DefaultValue</key>
        <real>0.5</real>
        <key>MinimumValue</key>
        <integer>0</integer>
        <key>MaximumValue</key>
        <integer>1</integer>
        <key>MinimumValueImage</key>
        <string></string>
        <key>MaximumValueImage</key>
        <string></string>
    </dict>
    <dict>
        <key>Type</key>
        <string>PSMultiValueSpecifier</string>
        <key>Key</key>
        <string>multi_preference</string>
        <key>DefaultValue</key>
        <string>One</string>
        <key>Title</key>
        <string>MultiValue</string>
        <key>Titles</key>
        <array>
            <string>one</string>
            <string>two</string>
            <string>three</string>
            <string>four</string>
        </array>
        <key>Values</key>
        <array>
            <string>one</string>
            <string>two</string>
            <string>three</string>
            <string>four</string>
        </array>
    </dict>

    <dict>
        <key>Type</key>
        <string>PSGroupSpecifier</string>
        <key>Title</key>
        <string>Info</string>
    </dict>
    <dict>
```

```
            <key>Type</key>
            <string>PSChildPaneSpecifier</string>
            <key>Title</key>
            <string>Legal</string>
            <key>File</key>
            <string>Legal</string>
        </dict>
    </array>
</dict>
</plist>
```

Get This Recipe's Code

To get the code used for this recipe, go to http://github.com/erica/iphone-3.0-cookbook-, or if you've downloaded the disk image containing all of the sample code from the book, go to the folder for Chapter 21 and open the project for this recipe.

Settings and Users

Although settings bundles offer a well-defined resource for developers to centralize their user-defined defaults, real-world experience suggests they're a feature you may not actually want to use. Few iPhone users are aware of third-party settings outside their applications. Even fewer actually use those settings on a regular basis. Most users want to stay within the bounds of an application for all app-related tasks, including settings.

Because of this, many (if not most) App Store developers have moved away from settings bundles and brought their settings directly into the application. Adding settings views allows users to find and set preferences easily. Unfortunately, creating those screens is labor intensive and fussy.

There is, fortunately, a middle ground between relying solely on settings bundles and building your own views. The Llama Settings project at Google Code (http://code.google.com/p/llamasettings/) offers a set of classes that read property lists (including from your settings bundles), allowing you to display settings screens within your application without much extra work or overhead. The project was developed and is maintained by Scott Lawrence.

Open sourced, the Llama Settings classes provide similar kinds of display and interactive elements including group titles, sliders, and switches. In addition, the project adds support for color selectors, URL launchers, and more. Although these items are not supported in Apple's Settings app, you can use them within your program by defining standard property lists without further programming.

Checking User Defaults

You may solicit and set defaults via settings bundles, application-based views, code-level access, or a hybrid of these approaches. When using those settings, be aware that certain items may not yet exist. If a user hasn't opened your settings bundle, the default settings you specified in the bundle's property lists may not have ever been set. For most objects, you can test for this via `objectForKey:`. This method returns `nil` for nonexistent keys.

Here's one reason a `nil` value may play a role in your programming. One default that you'll always want to set through code is a "last version" key. This key records the application version that was most recently run. You'll want to check for this default whenever your application launches.

If that default is `nil`, the application is a new install. You may want to prepare files and perform other setup tasks at first run. After that setup, set a value for the key, one that indicates the currently deployed app version. (And don't forget to `synchronize` after setting that key.)

It doesn't end with a check for `nil`, though. You'll always know when the user has just upgraded from a previous version by checking that setting. When the last run version differs from your current version, you have the opportunity to perform any updates that bring your user into data compliance for the most recent release.

Recipe: Creating URL-Based Services

Apple's built-in applications offer a variety of services that can be accessed via URL calls. You can ask Safari to open Web pages, Maps to show a map, or use the mailto: style URL to start composing a letter in Mail. A URL scheme refers to the first part of the URL that appears before the colon, such as http or ftp.

These services work because the iPhone knows how to match URL schemes with applications. A URL that starts with http: opens in Mobile Safari. The mailto: URL always links to Mail. What you may not know is that you can define your own URL schemes and implement them in your applications. Not all standard schemes are supported on the iPhone. The ftp scheme is not available for use.

Custom schemes allow applications to launch whenever Mobile Safari (or another application) opens a URL of that type. For example, should your application register xyz, any xyz:// links go directly to your application for handling, where they're passed to the optional application: `handleOpenURL:` method. The applications launch whether you've defined a handler method or not. If all you want to do is run an application, adding the scheme and opening the URL enables cross-application launching.

Handlers extend launching to allow applications to do something with the URL that's been passed to it. They might open a specific data file, retrieve a particular name, display a certain image, or otherwise process information included in the call.

Using URL Schemes

The advantages of scheme-based launching are many. Take the Iconfactory's Twitterrific, for example. Developer Craig Hockenberry introduced a custom service that lets users and third-party developers launch his application and open a prefilled, ready-to-post tweet.

This lets developers add Twitter support to their applications without any programming needed. Since Twitterrific already stores sensitive username and password information, all that you have to supply is the body text. When invoked, control passes to

Twitterrific, which takes over and allows users to finish tweeting. When done, users quit Twitterrific and may return to the original application if desired.

These kinds of services work best when they provide some kind of performance boost or data leverage. In the case of Twitterrific, it's not about tweeting. It takes very little code to tweet. (See Chapter 13.) At the same time, doing so requires you to take on either the responsibility of securely storing user credentials or forcing users to enter those credentials on each use. The Twitterrific service lets you bypass those issues and expand the way your application works.

Service Downsides

It's not all good news on the services front; there's definitely a downside to third-party services. Once your application depends on a service, you basically force your users to download a second application. And that application may not always be the one they want to use. Consider the loyal Echofon (formerly TwitterFon) user who might not have Twitterrific installed on his or her phone. If you demand Twitterrific, you may meet resistance.

Any features that depend on third-party services must always be optional. Consider if, for example, Echofon were to introduce its own tweeting URL scheme. If your application offered service-based tweeting, you should in response make your application robust and flexible enough to allow users to choose their preferred client.

Another downside is this: iPhone applications cannot tell what schemes are available. There's no way to poll for on-offer services. Apple provides no public registry that you can scan through to see what's out there. Using services is basically a matter of trust.

That being said, you can test whether a URL service is available. If the `UIApplication`'s `canOpenURL:` method returns `YES`, you are guaranteed that `openURL:` will be able to launch another application to open that URL. You are not guaranteed that the URL is valid, only that its scheme is registered properly to an existing application.

```
if ([[UIApplication sharedApplication] canOpenURL:aURL])
    [[UIApplication sharedApplication] openURL:aURL];
```

Cross-Promotion

There is another important business-oriented aspect to scheme-based launching, namely cross-promotion. Defining URL schema allows your application to test whether other applications exist from your company's lineup. If the application cannot handle the URL (i.e., `canOpenURL:` returns `NO`), you can provide links to App Store, encouraging users to download other applications from your company.

Registering Schemes: Declaring the URL

It takes two steps to add services to your application. First, declare your URL scheme in your Info.plist. Second, add a handler to your application delegate. Here are the steps you take to do this.

To declare your URL scheme, you need to specify information for the iPhone's Launch Services. Add a `CFBundleURLTypes` entry into your Info.plist. This consists of an array of dictionaries that describe the URL types the application can open and handle. Each dictionary contains two keys: a `CFBundleURLName` and an array of `CFBundleURLSchemes`.

The URL name is an abstract name (also known as its "kind"). You can use any string. On the Mac, this provides the visible description shown in Finder. On the iPhone, it's just a way of keeping your schemes straight.

The Schemes array is a list of prefixes that belong to the abstract name. You can add one scheme or many. The following declares just one. You may want to prefix your name with an x. Although the iPhone is not part of any standards organization, the x prefix indicates that this is an unregistered name.

```
<key>CFBundleURLTypes</key>
<array>
    <dict>
        <key>CFBundleURLName</key>
        <string>com.sadun.demonstration</string>
        <key>CFBundleURLSchemes</key>
        <array>
            <string>x-sadun-services</string>
        </array>
    </dict>
</array>
```

iPhone developer Emanuele Vulcano has started an informal registry over at the CocoaDev Web site (http://cocoadev.com/index.pl?ChooseYourOwniPhone URLScheme). iPhone Developers can share their schemes in a central listing, so that you can discover services you want to use and promote services that you offer. The registry lists services, their URL schemes, and describes how these services can be used by other developers.

Registering Schemes: Adding the Handler Method

The second part of implementing URL handling means providing an application delegate method called `application:handleOpenURL:`.

```
- (BOOL)application:(UIApplication *)application
    handleOpenURL:(NSURL *)url {}
```

When implemented by your app delegate, this method lets you respond to an `openURL:` call made by another application. Your method must return a Boolean value, either `YES` to indicate that the URL handling succeeded or `NO` when it fails. Here's the basic skeleton of the function:

```
- (BOOL)application:(UIApplication *)application
    handleOpenURL:(NSURL *)url
{
    // Recover the string
    if (!url) return NO;
    NSString *URLString = [url absoluteString];
```

```
    // YOUR WORK HERE
    return YES;
}
```

With iPhone URL schemes, the colon is mandatory, but you need not use forward slashes after. For example, mailto:foo@bar.com is a valid URL. You need not use mailto://foo@bar.com.

To parse out your calling string, you want to remove the initial URL scheme up to the colon.

```
NSRange colon = [URLString rangeOfString:@""];
NSString *request = [URLString substringFromIndex:
    (colon.location + 1)];
```

It's up to your handler to deal with whatever request has been forwarded. You define the protocol and you implement how that is recovered. Consider the following sample request protocol:

```
x-sadun-services:command?param1=p1&param2=p2&param3=p3&...
```

This protocol assumes that a command will be followed by a question mark, followed by a set of parameter pairs. Each pair uses the equal symbol and provides a plain-text parameter name and a URI-encoded text-based parameter value.

Your code handles all request parsing. Could providing URL scheme support open an attack vector from third parties? No. The reality is that the danger is minimal or non-existent. You can choose to handle the request, ignore the request, and so forth. `NSStrings` present little danger to your application.

Returning Control to a Calling Application

With careful programming, you can allow the calling application to regain control after handling a URL request. An application might send back requested material along with a status indication of whether the operation was a success. It depends on how you define and implement your protocol. Here's a sample of a paste request from an application that supports interapplication copy and paste.

```
x-sadun-services:paste?scheme=iping&data=hello+world&\
clipboard=test1&password=foobar&expire=1500
```

This example URL shows a request to paste "Hello World" into a clipboard named test1. It's a secured clipboard whose data will expire after 1,500 seconds (25 minutes). What's notable here is the "scheme" parameter. It tells this service who to respond to. After performing the paste, the service opens a new URL with the results, using that scheme to call home.

On most iPhones and iPod touch units, the entire trip has a latency of about 4.5 to 5 seconds. You can try this for yourself. The sample code for this recipe contains two applications. One (iPong) is a copy/paste server, another (iPing) is a test client. The client keeps track of time from when it first sends out its request to when it receives the response

URL. Once you have installed the server, you can mess with the client to test out all kinds of scenarios to test the service and its protocol.

A minor vulnerability is exposed here. Should the calling client lie or provide the wrong scheme parameter, control may be transferred to a third application. If the scheme does not refer to a real application, the request will simply hang. On the other hand, allowing the service to return to the originating application is a huge win. It keeps the user from having to quit and relaunch that first application and is a feature more applications should offer once they have finished handling a request, be it sending e-mail or posting a tweet.

Implementing Custom Schemes

When the iPhone installs an application, its Info.plist list tells the iPhone OS to associate that application with any schemes you've defined. Thereafter, whenever the OS encounters a matching scheme, the proper application launches to handle the URL. Recipe 21-2 shows a sample method skeleton that handles the opening of that URL.

This recipe demonstrates how to recover the URL scheme and break it down into parameters, and how to return to a calling application. The actual sample code for iPong contains all these components but uses a more complicated handler than the method shown in Recipe 21-2.

> **Note**
>
> Use the following native URL strings for opening videos in YouTube: http://www.youtube.com/watch?v=VIDEO_IDENTIFIER, or http://www.youtube.com/v/VIDEO_IDENTIFIER. The iPhone does not use a YouTube-specific schema.

Recipe 21-2 **Responding to URL Scheme Requests**

```
- (BOOL)application:(UIApplication *)application
    handleOpenURL:(NSURL *)url
{
    // Recover the string
    if (!url) return YES;
    NSString *URLString = [url absoluteString];

    // Recover the colon location
    NSRange colon = [URLString rangeOfString:@""];
    if (colon.location == NSNotFound) return YES;

    // Extract command and parameter dictionary
    NSString *action = [URLString substringFromIndex:
        (colon.location + 1)];
    NSMutableDictionary *paramDict = [NSMutableDictionary dictionary];
    NSRange r = [action rangeOfString:@"?"];
    if (r.location != NSNotFound)
    {
```

```
        NSString *paramString = [action substringFromIndex:
            (r.location + 1)];
        NSArray *parameters = [paramString
            componentsSeparatedByString:@"&"];
        action = [action substringToIndex:r.location];

        for (NSString *eachParam in parameters)
        {
            NSArray *pair = [eachParam
                componentsSeparatedByString:@"="];
            if ([pair count] != 2) continue;
            NSString *key = [[pair objectAtIndex:0] lowercaseString];
            NSString *value = [pair objectAtIndex:1];
            [paramDict setValue:value forKey:key];
        }
    }

    // Perform any actual work here using those parameters

    // pong back with a result
    NSString *scheme = [paramDict objectFoKey:@"scheme"];
    if (!scheme) return YES;

    NSString *urlString = [NSString stringWithFormat:
        @:pasteservice?status=Success", scheme];
    NSURL *outurl = [NSURL urlWithString:urlString];
    if ([application canOpenURL:outurl]
        [application openURL:outurl];

    return YES;
}
```

Get This Recipe's Code

To get the code used for this recipe, go to http://github.com/erica/iphone-3.0-cookbook-, or if you've downloaded the disk image containing all of the sample code from the book, go to the folder for Chapter 21 and open the project for this recipe.

Summary

When an iPhone application opens itself to iPhone OS services, it becomes an active participant in a wider ecosystem. Accessibility, settings, and URL schemes all demonstrate how an application can fit into the iPhone OS beyond the immediate functionality provided by the application itself. Here are a few thoughts to take away with you as you finish this chapter:

- VoiceOver and the iPhone's accessibility features as a whole are still very, very new. Expect them to develop further as the platform matures. This is a feature that will continue to change as Apple grows the iPhone's disabled audience.
- Including accessibility labels and hints creates new audiences for your application, just like language localizations do. Adding these takes relatively little work to achieve and offers excellent payoffs to your users.
- Although most users do not use third-party preferences in the Settings apps, some do. Consider offering your settings both inside and outside your application.
- Expand your application's user base by exposing helpful functionality to other applications. URL schemes let you create a demand by other application developers that can trickle down into end-user sales for your product. A great set of services that's easy to use can be marketed to other developers through custom URL schemes.

A

Info.plist Keys

Table A-1 lists many of the Info.plist keys available for the iPhone and describes their use. The raw key name is listed first. The English localized string appears just below, where available. This latter item is the string that Xcode shows you in the Info.plist editor when you have not chosen Show Raw Keys/Values from the editor's contextual pop-up menu.

Table A-1 **Common Info.plist Keys**

Key	Type	Use
`CFBundleDisplayName` Bundle display name.	String	App bundle's display name. This name can be localized with InfoPlist.strings. Xcode initially sets this value to the name used to create your Xcode project.
`CFBundleName` Bundle name.	String	The application's short display name, normally the same as `CFBundleDisplayName`.
`CFBundleDevelopmentRegion` Localization native development region.	String	Native region for the bundle's author. Sets a default value for the native localization.
`CFBundleAllowMixedLocalizations` Localized resources can be mixed.	Boolean	Allows frameworks to retrieve localized resources.

Table A-1 **Continued**

Key	Type	Use
`CFBundleExecutable` Executable file.	String	(Required key) Name of the executable file in the .app bundle. The name of this property is automatically added to your property list. It is initially based on the `${EXECUTABLE_NAME}` set in your Xcode project, typically the same name as your project.
`CFBundleIconFile` Icon file.	String	Name of the icon file for the application. Normally icon.png, but you can use another name. Xcode does not add a default value. App Store requires this value to be properly set.
`CFBundleIdentifier` Bundle identifier.	String	(Required key) The unique identifier for your application. See Chapter 1, "Introducing the iPhone SDK," and Chapter 2, "Building Your First Project," for information about choosing and registering application identifiers.
`CFBundleInfoDictionary` ➥`Version` InfoDictionary version.	String	(Required key) Normally set to 6.0. This value defines the current version of the property list structure. Xcode automatically adds this value to your Info.plist. Leave it as set.
`CFBundleLocalizations` Localizations.	Array	A list of strings that specify all supported localizations, e.g., `en`, `fr`, `ja`, etc. Each entry in this property's array is a string that identifies a language name and can include regional localizations like en-us and en-uk.
`CFBundleVersionString` Bundle version.	String	Version-number string for the application. Required by App Store to be unique for each application update build.
`CFBundleShortVersionString` Bundle version string, short.	String	Although supported on the iPhone, this key is meant for Mac apps that use a three-number version system of release numbers, revision numbers, and maintenance release numbers.
`CFBundleURLTypes` URL types.	Array	Array of dictionaries describing the URL schemes supported by the application. See Chapter 21, "Accessibility and Other iPhone OS Services," for details on constructing this array.

Table A-1 **Continued**

Key	Type	Use
`LSRequiresIPhoneOS` Application requires iPhone environment.	Boolean	Indicates that the application is meant to run only on iPhone OS.
`NSMainNibFile` Main nib file base name.	String	Specifies the primary xib/nib file used by the application.
`UIInterfaceOrientation` Initial interface orientation.	String	Specify the initial interface orientation to use when the application launches. Values may be set to `UIInterfaceOrientationPortrait` (Portrait, Default), `UIInterfaceOrientation` `➥PortraitUpsideDown` (Portrait), `UIInterfaceOrientationLandscapeLeft` (Landscape), or `UIInterfaceOrientation` `➥LandscapeRight` (Landscape).
`UIPrerenderedIcon` Icon already includes gloss and bevel effects.	Boolean	Determines whether the iPhone applies a shine and gloss effect to the application icon (`NO`) or uses the icon as is (`YES`).
`UIRequiresPersistentWiFi` Application uses Wi-Fi.	Boolean	When enabled, tells the iPhone OS that the application needs a Wi-Fi connection to run. If a Wi-Fi connection is not found, the user is prompted at launch to connect to a Wi-Fi network. When set to `NO`, the iPhone OS closes any active Wi-Fi connection after 30 minutes. When set to `YES`, this does not happen, allowing persistent use of the Wi-Fi connection.
`UIStatusBarHidden` Status bar is initially hidden.	Boolean	Set to true to hide the status bar on launch.
`UIStatusBarStyle` Status bar style.	String	Chooses an initial status bar style using the standard constants. Defaults to a gray status bar. Values may be set to `UIStatus` `➥BarStyleDefault` (Gray style (default)), `UIStatusBarStyleBlackTranslucent` (Transparent black style [alpha of 0.5]), or `UIStatusBarStyleBlackOpaque` (Opaque black style).

Table A-1 **Continued**

Key	Type	Use
`UIRequiredDeviceCapabilities` Required device capabilities.	Array	Capabilities required on device for the application to run, such as a camera. As of the 3.1 iPhone OS, legal values include `wifi`, `accelerometer`, `location-services`, `gps`, `magnetometer`, `microphone`, `opengles-1`, `opengles-2`, `armv6`, `armv7`, and `peer-peer`. This information helps App Store and iTunes know which device-related features are required by an application in order to function properly. See Chapter 14, "Device Capabilities," for details on using this option.
`UISupportedExternalAccessory` ➥`Protocols` Supported external accessory protocols.	Array	Defines the accessory protocols supported by the application for communicating with third-party hardware.
`UIViewEdgeAntialiasing` Renders with edge antialiasing.	Boolean	Indicates whether Core Animation layers antialias data that's not pixel-aligned. The default is `NO` and setting it to `YES` reduces performance while increasing rendering quality. When enabled, it provides sophisticated rendering with a noticeable performance impact.
`UIViewGroupOpacity` Renders with group opacity.	Boolean	Indicates whether Core Animation sublayers inherit the opacity of their superlayer. Defaults to `NO`.

Symbols

A

B

C

D

G

H

J–K

L

M

N

O

Q–R

S

T

U

W

X–Y–Z

SAMS

Essential Resources for Apple Developers

Cocoa® Programming for Mac® OS X, Third Edition

Aaron Hillegass | ISBN-13: 978-0-321-50361-9

The bestselling introduction to Cocoa—now revised!

Once again updated to cover the latest Mac programming technologies and still enthusiastically recommended by experienced Mac OS X developers.

Core Animation

Marcus Zarra / Matt Long
ISBN-13: 978-0-321-61775-0

The definitive, full-color, task-based reference to Core Animation.

iPhone® for Programmers: An App-Driven Approach

Deitel and Associates
ISBN-13: 978-0-13-705842-6

The professional programmer's DEITEL® guide to iPhone app development using iPhone SDK 3.x, Xcode, Objective-C, and Cocoa.

informIT For more information and to read sample material, please visit informit.com/learnmac.

Titles are also available at safari.informit.com.

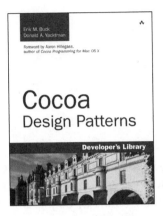

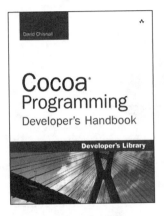

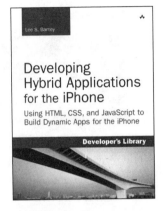